BARRY ORDNANCE SURVEY SHEET ST 06/16

Scale 1:25 000

1000 Metres 0 Kilometres 1 2

1000 Yards 0 Miles 1

With many thanks for your support to date!
Malcolm Cook

5/8 £4.50

BARRY

THE CENTENARY BOOK

BARRY

THE CENTENARY BOOK

Edited by

DONALD MOORE

THE BARRY CENTENARY BOOK COMMITTEE LIMITED

BARRY

First Published 1984
by the Barry Centenary Book Committee Limited
22 Redbrink Crescent
Barry Island, South Glamorgan

Printed by Qualitex Printing Limited, Cardiff
Set in Baskerville I

ISBN 0 9509 7380 7

CONTENTS

CONTENTS

continued

BARRY CENTENARY BOOK COMMITTEE LIMITED

Chairman G. Beaudette

Secretary K. F. Beaudette, B.A.

Treasurer R. W. Thomas, B.A., Dip.Arch., A.R.I.B.A.

Members

M. J. B. Cook, B.A.
G. Dowdell, B.A., Dip.G.S.
B. Daly
J. Daly
M. Griffiths, M.A., D.Phil.
B. C. Luxton, B.A.
D. Moore, R.D., B.A., M.Ed., F.S.A.
I. W. Prothero, B.A.
S. Prosser
P. Stead, B.A.
H. J. Thomas, M.A., F.S.A.
G. R. Tyley

EDITOR'S FOREWORD

The passage of a hundred years is a compelling inducement to commemorate any event which has produced a dramatic change in human activities in some part of the world, and that is why this book has come into being. On 14th August, 1884, the Royal Assent was given to the Barry Dock and Railways Bill, and on 14th November the Rt. Hon. The Lord Windsor cut the first sod to mark the beginning of the constructional work. This integrated scheme for a new dock and railway meant the birth of the modern town of Barry. Some would say that a more significant date was when the first ship entered the completed dock on 18th July, 1889. However, by then the nucleus of the new town was in existence, and in any case the promoters of the present volume were far too impatient to wait until the second date. Now, thanks to the generous financial support of the Barry Town Council, they have been enabled to launch the publication in November 1984.

The size of this *Centenary Book* and its obvious depth of scholarship shows how far local historical research has gone since 1921, when Thomas Ewbank, the Headmaster of Cadoxton Boys' School, published a small and slender volume of 150 pages, entitled *The Geography and History of Barry.* His aim was 'to create in the minds of our young people a justifiable pride in their native town and stimulate them in their efforts to become worthy citizens and emulators of their predecessors'. This high purpose was a reflection of the spirit of his time, a point emphasised in more than one chapter of this present volume.

Other writers, such as R. J. Rimell, Stan Awbery, and D. S. Barrie have published studies of various aspects of the town's history. That indefatigable editor and publisher, Stewart Williams, has brought before the public numerous articles on the town and its hinterland, and Brian C. Luxton produced in 1975 a concise account of Barry in *South Glamorgan: A County History.* This *Centenary Book,* however, is the first attempt at a comprehensive and standard work. The amount of new knowledge brought to light by the present authors has been immense, and the editor knows well how much has had to be omitted from the volume.

Although the present town is a creation of the last hundred years, the story begins with the formation of the rocks of the locality and of those to the north where coal was found, for this fuel was the prime cause of the building of the dock, the railway and the town.

An astonishing advance in prehistoric studies is evident in Chapter II, thanks to the assiduous efforts of amateur and professional archaeologists in the locality and to the progress of archaeological studies generally. Thomas

Ewbank had devoted two pages to geology and prehistory, and referred to the 'half-clad, short-legged Iberians' as sometime inhabitants, but the picture today is much more complex. Barry town has never been remarkable for its visible antiquities, though a few miles distant can be seen the Neolithic burial chambers at Dyffryn and the Iron-Age fortifications at the Bulwarks (Porthkerry), and on the island of Sully. Now the foundations of a mysterious Roman building at the Knap are on view for all to see, and the ruins of Barry Castle and St. Barruc's Chapel have been made presentable. A few ancient churches are still in existence and many 'recent' buildings begin to acquire a historic status.

The reader will find the chapters diverse in approach and content, not simply because the contributors are different, but because the evidence to which they have had recourse is different in nature. The first chapter depends on the study of the material world of the rocks and fossils, the second is based on objects left by early man. The third, dealing with the Middle Ages, relies partly on physical remains in the form of sites and artefacts, but also draws upon early documents; it is possible to produce, with carefully controlled imagination, reconstruction pictures to show how medieval buildings might have looked in their hey-day. The two articles on the 'early modern period', Chapters IV and V, have been based on documents and early maps, and again the story has a distinctive emphasis; now we begin to see named people emerging in the pages of history. Much of the story concerns the ordinary business of farming life, but sometimes an unusual event or situation stands out. The records have never before been studied to this intensity for the area.

The book falls into two main sections. The first relates the story of a short stretch of the Glamorgan coast and the growth of a few rural villages enjoying important links by sea with other parts of Wales and with England. The second half of the book tells of the transformation wrought by the arrival of large-scale commerce and transport systems and by the building of a bustling town. Chapter VI, on the Port and Railways, begins this second episode and four more chapters are needed to tell of the growth of the town, its early optimism and its sober maturity.

In a distant village of Montgomeryshire there stands a statue of a 'local boy-made-good', David Davies of Llandinam. There is a similar statue in Barry Docks, just in front of the prestigious Dock Offices (now unhappily damaged by fire in the centenary year). David Davies holds a huge plan of the docks which he is credited with constructing in order to export coal more expeditiously from his collieries in the north of Glamorgan. Doubt may be cast on the role traditionally attributed to David Davies, but not on the enormous success of his docks and the subsequent prosperity of the dynasty which he founded. It was an epoch marked by energy, achievement and pride—work for many, wealth for some, and a municipality among the most progressive of its day. The exciting story of early growth is told in Chapter VII, relying to a great extent on reports in contemporary local newspapers. How the town gained its physical appearance is described in Chapter VIII, on architecture and planning; there still remain some distinguished buildings and a solid stock of houses, but many opportunities have been lost in the town's recent development. The last two chapters present a social history of recent years. Much of this period will be familiar to Barrians alive today, either from their own experience or from the tales told by their parents and grandparents. The ambition and pride which characterised the early ethos of the town was perpetuated in succeeding generations, even institutionalised in school songs. That of the 'County School' summarised the theme of this book (though we may flinch at the obtrusive alliteration!):

To our town where mighty Severn opens to the ocean blue
Come the ships from every quarter, bringing treasures old and new.
Rear the walls of rising Barry, spread her squares and stretch her streets,
Port to be, where outbound sailor sailor coming homeward greets.

It continued with a refrain that called for high moral qualities:

Boys of Barry, this your watchword: be ye faithful, trustful, true.
Welcome ever light of duty, bravely bear and nobly do.

Personal ambition was commended as well as civic pride. This is seen in the song of Romilly elementary school (named after Lord Romilly, a local landowner):

Higher, higher will we climb up the mount of glory
That our names may live through time in our country's story.

In 1939, against all the trends of the time, the town achieved Borough status by means of a Royal Charter of Incorporation with a handsome coat of arms and a motto: '*Cadernid, Cyfiawnder, Cynnydd*' ('Strength, Justice, Progress'). The festal song, specially composed to celebrate the Charter declared a feeling of pride in the town, a pledge to 'guard her noble state' and a recognition of the reason for the town's existence—coal. The original words were written by the well-known Welsh poet, J. M. Edwards, who then resided in Barry, and they began:

Cydganwn heddiw gyda llawen lef
Ar ddydd o ŵyl i'n hyfryd fro a'n tref.

There were two English translations—one by Major Edgar Jones, Headmaster of the Boys' County School, and another by his successor, E. T. Griffiths.

These quotations give an insight into the tremendous confidence which the inhabitants used to feel in their town and its future. But the last article of this book raises a more sober, even sombre thought—what of the future, as seen from 1984? The export of coal has now ceased and industries set up to compensate have not always fulfilled expectations.

The Centenary Book has come into being by the devoted efforts of many people, most of them natives of the town. The idea was first mooted in 1974, and five years later, after much discussion among enthusiasts, a Book Committee was formed. It had to raise funds in order to constitute itself as a limited company and it is grateful to all those supporters who made advance payments towards the cost of their copies, confident that the book would eventually appear. This procedure proved an important preliminary.

Maps form an indispensable basis for the study of local history, and the contributors have made special efforts to present their findings in this way. To show the whole area as it now appears there could be no better map than the Ordnance Survey Pathfinder map, 1:25,000 scale, and the Committee is most grateful to the Survey for permission to reproduce a substantial portion of its mapping as endpapers in this volume.

The spelling of local place-names has presented some difficulties. They may be of Welsh, Scandinavian, English or Norman origin, and elements may be mixed in the same word. Spelling has varied over the centuries, and sometimes an old form will convey the period atmosphere better. The general policy has been to use the most common local form and to give other forms afterwards in brackets, if thought helpful. This means that place-names of Welsh origin may not always appear in the most up-to-date orthography.

The contributors have pursued extensive researches at their own expense; indeed, the degree of voluntary effort elicited by this project has been extraordinary. The members of the Book Committee, the contributors of articles and the specialist advisers have their roll of honour on other pages. To all of them the warmest thanks must be given.

But all this effort would have been in vain were it not for the munificent gesture of the Barry Town Council in December 1983 which enabled publication to go forward. The Committee gratefully acknowledges a substantial grant, as well as a loan against expected revenue from sales. In this way the price of the volume can be kept within reach of more purchasers. It has been agreed that any profit which might eventually accrue should be devoted to furthering the study of local history in the schools of the area.

DONALD MOORE

THE CONTRIBUTORS

GERALD BEAUDETTE

Born and bred in Barry, educated at schools in Barry and Cardiff. After four years with the Glamorgan Constabulary, returned to full-time education at Coleg Harlech in North Wales; then trained as a teacher at Barry College of Education. Has been a primary teacher with the Local Education Authority since 1975. Has long-standing interest in archaeology and local history; was an early member of the Barry and Vale Archaeological Group and participated in many local excavations. Has also dug at Wharram Percy in Yorkshire and for the Winchester Excavations Committee. Serves on the committees of the Barry Preservation Society and Civic Trust and the Glamorgan-Gwent Archaeological Trust Ltd.; is local secretary of the National Union of Teachers and Chairman of the Barry Centenary Book Committee Ltd.

KATHERINE F. BEAUDETTE, B.A.

Born and educated in Massachusetts, U.S.A.; took degree at Smith College. Came to U.K. *via* archaeology and to Barry *via* marriage. Having spent four seasons digging for the Winchester Excavations Committee, she settled in Barry in 1970. Worked for two years in a university bookshop and subsequently in a medical research library. Her interest in local history led to involvement with the Barry Preservation Society and Civic Trust, which she served for ten years, first as secretary and then as chairman. Is currently Treasurer of the South Wales Record Society and Secretary to the Barry Centenary Book Committee Ltd.

GARETH DOWDELL, B.A., Dip.G.S.

A native of Barry, educated at local schools and Coleg Harlech, graduated in archaeology at University of Southampton. Was Archaeological Officer for Poole and south-east Dorset for three years, and returned to South Wales to become first Director of the Glamorgan-Gwent Archaeological Trust Limited, on its formation in 1975. Now lives at Swansea, where Trust headquarters is situated. Responsible for supervising a broad programme of rescue excavations in south-east Wales.

MATTHEW GRIFFITHS, M.A., D.Phil.

Brought up in Barry, son of a local headmaster; educated at Barry Boys' Comprehensive School and Jesus College, Oxford. Took first-class honours degree in Modern History in 1974 and was awarded doctorate in 1979 for thesis on an Oxfordshire community in the Middle Ages. Was Fellow of the University of Wales at University College Cardiff, 1979-81. Since 1982 has been Investigator for the Royal Commission on Ancient and Historical Monuments in Wales. Author of various articles in historical journals; active in affairs of local history societies. Has family links with early days of Barry Docks and Railways.

IORWERTH W. PROTHERO, B.A.

Born in Barry, son of a blacksmith who turned coal-trimmer. Educated at local schools and University College Cardiff, where he took a degree in English and History. Became teacher, at first in South Wales, but spent most of career in or near London. After war-time service in Royal Artillery and Royal Army Education Corps, he taught at London and Kent grammar schools. His last post was Liberal Studies Tutor at Kent College of Technology. After retirement, has been part-time tutor at Coleg y Fro, Rhoose. Has been rugby coach, referee and journalist, and is keenly interested in the Welsh language.

PETER STEAD, B.A.

A native of Barry, educated at Barry Boys' Grammar School and University College of Swansea, specialising in recent social and political history, as well as history of films. Author of *Coleg Harlech: the first fifty years.* Regular broadcaster on Radio Wales. Widely travelled, making frequent visits to America, where he is Visiting Lecturer and Scholar-in-residence at Wellseley College, Massachusetts. Was last Labour candidate to stand for the old Barry parliamentary constituency in 1979.

HOWARD J. THOMAS, M.A., F.S.A.

A native of Barry, educated at Romilly Schools, Coleg Harlech and St. John's College, Cambridge. Active in Glamorgan local history and archaeology since 1954; has directed excavations for Barry and Vale Archaeological Group on medieval village sites at Barry, Porthkerry and Highlight. In 1977 directed (with G. Dowdell) emergency excavations at Barry Old Village. From 1968 has been employed as Investigator for Royal Commission on Ancient and Historical Monuments in Wales, based on Aberystwyth. A trustee of the Glamorgan-Gwent Archaeological Trust. Has contributed many articles and notes on local history and archaeology to local and national journals.

BRIAN C. LUXTON, B.A.

Born in Cadoxton, educated at Cadoxton Boys' Secondary Modern School, Barry Boys' Grammar School and University College Cardiff. Graduated in History in 1963, and now teaches that subject at Barry Boys' Comprehensive School. Has compiled two volumes entitled *Old Barry in Photographs,* published by Stewart Williams (1977, 1978), as well as articles on the same topic, published earlier. Is People's Warden at Cadoxton parish church and author of a history of that church (1970). Has written on Hezekiah Jones, the Red Priest of Colcot, and William Jenkins, the Wizard of Cadoxton; has researched the history of trade-unionism.

DONALD MOORE, R.D., B.A., M.Ed., F.S.A.

A native of Barry, educated at Romilly Schools, Barry County School for Boys, University College of Wales, Aberystwyth, and Oxford University. War service in Army and Royal Navy, and later career in Royal Naval Reserve; retired as Commander, R.N.R., in 1977. After period as Tutor for Adult Education in Shropshire, joined Museum Schools Service of National Museum of Wales, which he left as Senior Officer in 1977. Subsequently Keeper of Pictures and Maps at National Library of Wales until 1984. Author of numerous articles and books in English and Welsh on art history, archaeology and museums. Active in many societies.

RICHARD WYN THOMAS, B.A., Dip.Arch., R.I.B.A.

Has spent most of his life in Barry and has strong family links with the coalmining industry and the Barry Railway Company. Educated at Taunton School, he studied Architecture at the University of Wales Institute of Science and Technology, gaining a Diploma in Architecture in 1970. Was elected to membership of the Royal Institute of British Architects in 1972, and awarded a B.A. degree of the Open University in 1979. Received a post-graduate award from the Crowther Fund in 1980 for research on 19th- and 20th-century architecture. Founder-member and current Chairman of Barry Preservation Society and Civic Trust. Treasurer of the Barry Centenary Book Committee Ltd.

BARRY CENTENARY BOOK COMMITTEE LIMITED

BARRY:
THE HISTORY RESOURCE PACK

The resource pack described in *Barry: The Centenary Book* is primarily designed for use by teachers in the classrooms of schools and colleges, as an independent teaching medium. However, it is also envisaged that a wider audience would be attracted as well to such a pack: libraries, local history groups, teaching and resource centres. The flexible nature of the material will make it appropriate for use across all age groups.

The resource pack has always been considered an integral part of the centenary history. Used on its own or in conjunction with the centenary book which it supplements, it should be a unique contribution to the study and teaching of local and environmental history.

The history resource pack is being prepared by Malcolm J. B. Cook, B.A., the Humanities Adviser for South Glamorgan Education Authority. A native of Barry, he received his degree in History from the University of Wales, Cardiff. He taught in Lewis School, Pengam, Cathays High School and Llanedeyrn High School before coming to his present post. He is Chairman of the Association of History Teachers in Wales and a member of the Welsh History Resources Unit.

The History Resource Pack will be available during 1985. If you are interested in acquiring this pack and would like to receive further details and an order form closer to the date of publication, please complete and detach the form below and return it to:

History Resource Pack
The Barry Centenary Book Committee Ltd.
c/o 22 Redbrink Crescent
Barry Island
South Glamorgan CF6 8TT

Please send me further details of Barry: The History Resource Pack.

____________________ Name (individual or organization)

____

____________________ Address

____

____

Postcode

ACKNOWLEDGEMENTS

Many individuals and institutions have helped in the production of this book, and the Committee here records its grateful thanks.

The contributors have received scholarly assistance in their studies from many quarters, and they have made their acknowledgements at the end of their chapters. But there are certain institutions which deserve special thanks: the National Library of Wales, the National Museum of Wales (including the Welsh Industrial and Maritime Museum), the Royal Commission on Ancient and Historical Monuments (Wales), The Glamorgan Record Office, the Glamorgan-Gwent Archaeological Trust, the Cardiff Central Reference Library of the County of South Glamorgan, the House of Lords Record Office, the Public Record Office, Associated British Ports and British Rail. Much help and advice was received in the early stages from the specialist readers, whose names are listed below.

The contributors are grateful to those specialists in graphic design and photography who have prepared maps, drawings and photographs for the chapters, especially to the following: DAVID CROUCH, B.A., Ph.D., BERNARD DALY, JIM DALY, CHARLES W. FARROW, N.D.D., A.T.D., SIMON PROSSER, GARETH R. TYLEY. Thanks are also due to DIANE BROOK, M.A. and MATTHEW GRIFFITHS for their work on the Index, and to ROSE BROWN for her assistance with typing.

Various individuals have generously put their personal collections of photographs and memorabilia at the disposal of the Committee, and they are acknowledged beside the illustrations concerned, as are the commercial and other sources, when known. Facilities for taking photographs were kindly afforded by the Sully Hospital authorities, the Headmistress of Bryn Hafren Comprehensive School for Girls and Associated British Ports.

The Committee records its warmest appreciation of the advice and help received from the staff of Qualitex Printing Limited in the production of this volume.

Finally, it must be said that the publication and the launch of the book for the Centenary celebrations of Barry have been made possible through the generous financial assistance of the Barry Town Council.

SPECIALIST READERS

STANLEY HALL COX, Senior Lecturer, The Welsh School of Architecture, Cardiff.

PROF. GWYNEDD PIERCE, M.A., F.R.Hist.S., Professor of the History of Wales and Head of Department, University College Cardiff.

DR. H. N. SAVORY, M.A., D.Phil., F.S.A., formerly Chairman, Glamorgan-Gwent Archaeological Trust.

DR. D. B. SMITH, M.A., Department of the History of Wales, University College Cardiff.

JACK SPURGEON, B.A., F.S.A., Senior Investigator, Royal Commission on Ancient and Historical Monuments (Wales), Aberystwyth.

ALUN J. THOMAS, B.Sc., Schools Service Officer in Geology, National Museum of Wales, Cardiff.

LISTS OF ILLUSTRATIONS, MAPS & TABLES

FIGURES

Acknowledgements to the source of illustrations and figures appear on the page concerned.

TABLES

LIST OF ADVANCE SUBSCRIBERS

Mr D. L. Atkins, Rhoose.
Mr B. L. Baldwin, Southampton.
Mr G. Beaudette, Barry Island.
Mr H. E. Beaudette, Barry Island.
Mrs K. F. Beaudette, Barry Island.
Mrs P. L. Beaudette, Barry Island.
Mr G. C. Boon, Penarth.
Sir Hugo Boothby, Bart., Fonmon.
Mr H. G. Boudier, Penarth.
The Rev. R. L. Brown, Tongwynlais.
Ms A. Bucknell, London.
Mr G. Cule, Barry.
Mr E. J. Davies, Llantwit Major.
Mr S. D. Davies, Barry.
Mr M. G. Davies, Yelverton.
Miss M. Donovan, Barry.
Mrs D. Edmunds, Bath.
Mr D. G. Evans, Barry.
Mr A. Weston-Evans, J.P., Cardiff.
Mr C. Griffiths, Bargoed.
Mrs N. I. Hanstead, Upminster.
Mr E. Hughes, Barry.
Mr J. V. Hughes, Port Talbot.
Mr W. J. Hughes, Barry.
Mr N. G. Israel, Talbot Green.
N. E. and S. E. Jones, Barry.
Pete and Sally Lennox, Barry.
Mr T. H. Martin, Barry.
Ms V. M. Metcalf, Swansea.
National Museum of Wales, Cardiff.
Mr B. Powney, Dinas Powys.
Mrs P. J. Roberts, Barry.
Mr R. Shardelow, Barry.
Mr A. J. Thomas, Barry.
Mrs E. Thomas, Dinas Powys.
Mr J. F. Thomas, Barry.
Mr J. Varley, Llanblethian.
Mrs A. M. Vevers, Barry Island.
Mr H. Walters, Glanamman.
Mrs B. Watson, Barry.
Mr B. L. Williams, Barry.

BARRY: A HISTORY RESOURCE PACK FOR SCHOOLS

THE PRODUCTION of this volume has created an opportunity to provide schools with a great deal of material not hitherto at their disposal when studying the locality. Naturally, the book itself will be of value, but much information has been gathered which could not be included in it, and this, too, could be of service in the classroom. There are new maps and plans, reproductions of old maps, documents and ephemera which could be studied individually in various contexts. In leading pupils towards the study of a particular aspect of the town's history, the teacher may find, for example, that medieval Barry will serve as a guide to medieval society in some other parts of Wales. The economic and social consequences of the opening of Barry Docks may encourage 'then-and-now' comparisons. Tomorrow's citizens should be aware of the town's political development earlier in this century.

It is intended to reproduce the material in various forms, but especially as slides, and full teaching notes will be supplied. All this will offer a new dimension in which both teacher and pupil may view Barry. The wealth of material which has now emerged merits study and discussion, examination and appreciation. The student cannot fail to be the richer from a closer acquaintance with it.

MALCOLM J. B. COOK

LIST OF ABBREVIATIONS

A.D.	*Anno Domini*
Arch. Camb.	*Archaeologia Cambrensis*
b.	born
BBCS	*Bulletin of the Board of Celtic Studies*
B.C.	Before Christ
b.c.	radio-carbon date
BP	British Petroleum
B.R.	Barry Railway
Beds.	Bedfordshire
c.	*circa* (about)
CNST	*Cardiff Naturalists' Society Transactions*
coll.	collection
d.	died
E.	East
ed.	editor
fig.	figure
GGAT	Glamorgan-Gwent Archaeological Trust Limited
GRO	Glamorgan Record Office
G.W.R.	Great Western Railway
ibid.	in the same source
m.	married
M.P.	Member of Parliament
MS(S)	Manuscript(s)
N.	North
NLW	National Library of Wales
NMW	National Museum of Wales
op. cit.	work already cited
PRO	Public Record Office
RCAM or RCAHM	Royal Commission on Ancient (and Historical) Monuments
ref.	reference
RO	Record Office
S.	South
St.	Saint
Trans.	*Transactions*
W.	West

CHAPTER I

The Foundations of Barry Rocks and Landscape

G. BEAUDETTE and K. F. BEAUDETTE

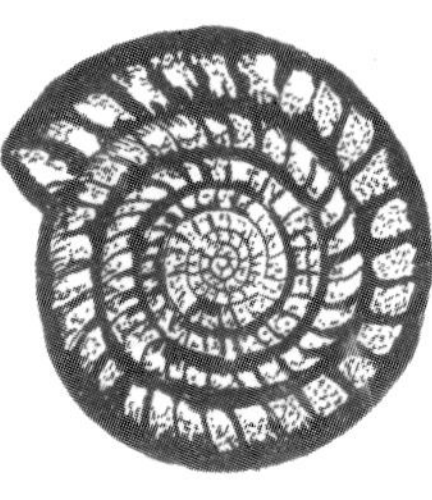

Ammonite from the Lias Limestone.
Simon Prosser.

UNTIL a hundred years ago the area now covered by the town of Barry was relatively undisturbed by the activities of man. Admittedly there was human activity in every period of history; people came and went, and some settled, as is clear from the tangible remains of their presence. But not until the late Victorian period did the great transformation take place which created the scene that we inherit today.

Two incidental effects were brought about by all this development: first a popular misconception that before the advent of modern Barry, there was nothing but an empty landscape waiting to be developed. That belief has now been effectively disproved. Secondly, and more importantly for any discussion of the geology of the area, the development has obscured and even removed much of the visible geology which had shaped the landscape and which, in the most basic sense, determined all that came after. The passing of millions of years, the quiet laying-down of sands, the ebbing and flowing of countless tides, the elevation of the shore, the dramatic uplift of layers of rock—all this record has been blown up and dug out for the building of the docks, the port and the railways—or simply built over.

There is a record to be seen and read—in two sources. First there is the work of the geologists who studied the area before its transformation, and any study must take into account their literature. Even the Ordnance Survey geological map is based on an original survey done in the 19th century, revised in 1878 and 1902, and thereafter simply reprinted. Secondly, and more fortunately, in the cliffs and on the shores the rocks are there to be seen, touched and studied. For the latter reason much of the following discussion will refer to the coastline and to Barry Island as accessible reference points to the visible geology.

Fig. 1. THE GEOLOGICAL TIME-SCALE

ERAS	PERIODS & SYSTEMS	DERIVATION OF NAMES
CAENOZOIC *Kainos* or *Cenos* = recent *Zoe* = life	QUATERNARY	
	Recent	
	Pleistocene	*pleiston* = most
	TERTIARY	
	Pliocene	*pleion* = more
	Miocene	*meion* = less
	Oligocene	*oligos* = few
	Eocene	*eos* = dawn
	Palaeocene	*palaios* = old
		(Pleistocene to Palaeocene:) *cene* from *kainos* = recent
MESOZOIC *Mesos* = middle	CRETACEOUS	*creta* = chalk
	JURASSIC	*Jura* Mountains
	TRIASSIC	*Threefold* division in Germany
PALAEOZOIC *Palaios* = ancient (Ancient life)	UPPER PALAEOZOIC PERMIAN	*Permia*, ancient kingdom between Urals and Volga
	CARBONIFEROUS	*Coal* (carbon-bearing)
	DEVONIAN	*Devon* (marine sediments)
	LOWER PALAEOZOIC SILURIAN	*Silures,* Celtic tribe of south-east Wales
	ORDOVICIAN	*Ordovices,* Celtic tribe of North Wales
	CAMBRIAN	*Cambria*, Latin name for Wales
	PRECAMBRIAN	
	UNDATED INTERVAL	
	ORIGIN OF THE EARTH	

MILLION YEARS AGO	DISTINCTIVE LIFE FORMS
	Modern man
to present	Stone-Age man
2 to 2	Mammals, especially elephants, widespread
5 to 12	Flowering plants; ancestral dogs and bears
0 to 25	Ancestral pigs and apes
0 to 40 0 to 60	Ancestral horses, cattle and elephants
35 to 70	Extinction of dinosaurs and ammonites Mammals and flowering plants emerging
80 to 135	Dinosaurs and ammonites abundant; birds and mammals appear
25 to 180	Flying reptiles and amphibians; first corals of modern types
70 to 225	Rise of reptiles and amphibians Conifers and beetles appear
50 to 270	Coal forests First reptiles and winged insects
00 to 350	First amphibians and ammonites; earliest trees and spiders; fishes
40 to 400	First spore-bearing land plants Earliest known coral reef
00 to 440	First fish-like vertebrates Trilobites and graptolites abundant
00 to 500	Trilobites, graptolites, brachiopods, molluscs, crinoids, radiolaria, foraminifera
,800 to 600	Primitive invertebrates, sponges, worms, algae, bacteria Primitive algae and bacteria (few at first)
,600 to 3,800	
,600 million years ago	

From these foundations it is possible to build a picture of that landscape which man entered, and which continued to alter independently even as he started to make his mark on it. Thereafter through the action of wind, water and man, as well as of deeper movements in the earth's crust, change went on inexorably and is continuing today.

Basic principles

The geologist James Hutton was formulating a novel concept in 1795, when he stated:

> 'The ruins of an older world are visible in the structure of our planet, and the strata which now compose our continents have been once beneath the sea and were formed out of the waste of pre-existing continents.'[1]

To talk about the geology of Barry is to enter a world in which the ordinary perception of time and events does not apply. Every geological essay must begin with an appreciation of the immensity of time in which geological events took place and the vast scale on which they occurred. These events have produced the landscape which we see in our own lifetime.

There are two aspects of geological time: the 'years ago' label attached to certain periods or events, tens of millions and hundreds of millions of years which have passed in the formation of our landscape—these figures strain the imagination but at the same time fascinate and intrigue it. It seems not to matter to people that they cannot comprehend what 100 million years means; they still want to know how long ago.

Secondly, and more importantly for the geologist as well as for the layman wishing to appreciate the panorama of events, is the sequential time when deposits of material were laid down one after another: land and sea rose and fell in turn and new strata were laid upon old.

Leaving aside the specific instances of disturbance to these strata caused by upheavals of the earth's crust, bending and folding, erosion and denudation, one must state a general principle: the oldest rocks are the lowest. Through the agencies of wind and water, uplift and submergence, older rocks may appear at the surface when the newer have been worn away or folded to a lower level, but the principle still obtains, those that were deposited first are the oldest.

That seems an obvious statement but until it was made and accepted, a scientific study of the history of the earth, and all the discoveries that have proceeded from it, could not take place. Now the basic sequence of events has been established and to it has been attached a scale of 'years ago' which is not absolute, for further studies may render the dating more precise. The Geological Time Scale provided in Figure 1 will serve as a guide through the periods of the geological story.

The second point to emphasise at the outset of a local study is the scale of geological events. Barry has a geological past which is on view. The record of the rocks visible on a coastal walk from the Bendricks to Porthkerry is a fascinating display. The distant events seen here did not happen only in Barry. This simple statement makes for a clearer understanding of the forces at work. Geological processes cannot be studied within present-day social and political boundaries. There are local peculiarities in every geological record, but for most of the time under discussion, the configurations of land and sea that we recognize as the north-west corner of Europe will not apply. Not until late in our story will land masses even remotely familiar emerge from what has gone before. Much of the following discussion will be, of necessity, a general geological history of this area, confined where possible to South Wales and the Bristol Channel. There will be specific references to Barry and Barry Island, where there is accessible evidence for these events.

It remains to mention the nature of the geological processes themselves. We may speak of the passage of time and of happenings in a remote past as if they are finished once and for all. This is a mistake. Geology is a continuous process; some of its agents are occasionally seen in their more spectacular forms, such as volcanic eruptions and earthquakes. Other, more subtle processes go on around us in the form of erosion by sea, river and rain, or denudation by wind. We shall see later that the final configuration of the land, including the formation of some prominent features of our landscape, has happened in the relatively recent past; and what we consider to be a stable feature of our surroundings, the relative position of land and sea, is recent and has altered since man appeared in the area. F. J. North commented thus on this relativity:

> "The land in which *he* [our early man] lived differed considerably in the details of its appearance and outline from the land *we* know, and we are not entitled to discuss the conditions of prehistoric times in terms of present day geography.'[2]

Our scenery and coastline are the temporary result of an on-going struggle between the processes of construction and destruction. We occupy but a split second in the time-span of this evolution. We see now not an end-product, but only a resting stage. All will alter—either gradually or suddenly—and the story will go on without us.

Basic themes

Two major factors are important to the town. The influence of coal was immense and is dealt with in a later chapter. It is curious that geological events which gradually took place over 200 million years ago resulted in the explosive development of the town, whose period of glory lasted well under 100 years. And although the story of the Coal Measures has been told many times in other places, it would seem churlish not to restate it here in view of the black rock's impact on Barry.

The other factor is the Bristol Channel itself. The story of its evolution is fascinating and worth pursuing as a separate study.[3] But here it will run as an additional thread in the backcloth of our story.

Fig. 2a. CONJECTURAL MAPS TO ILLUSTRATE THE EVOLUTION OF THE BRISTOL CHANNEL

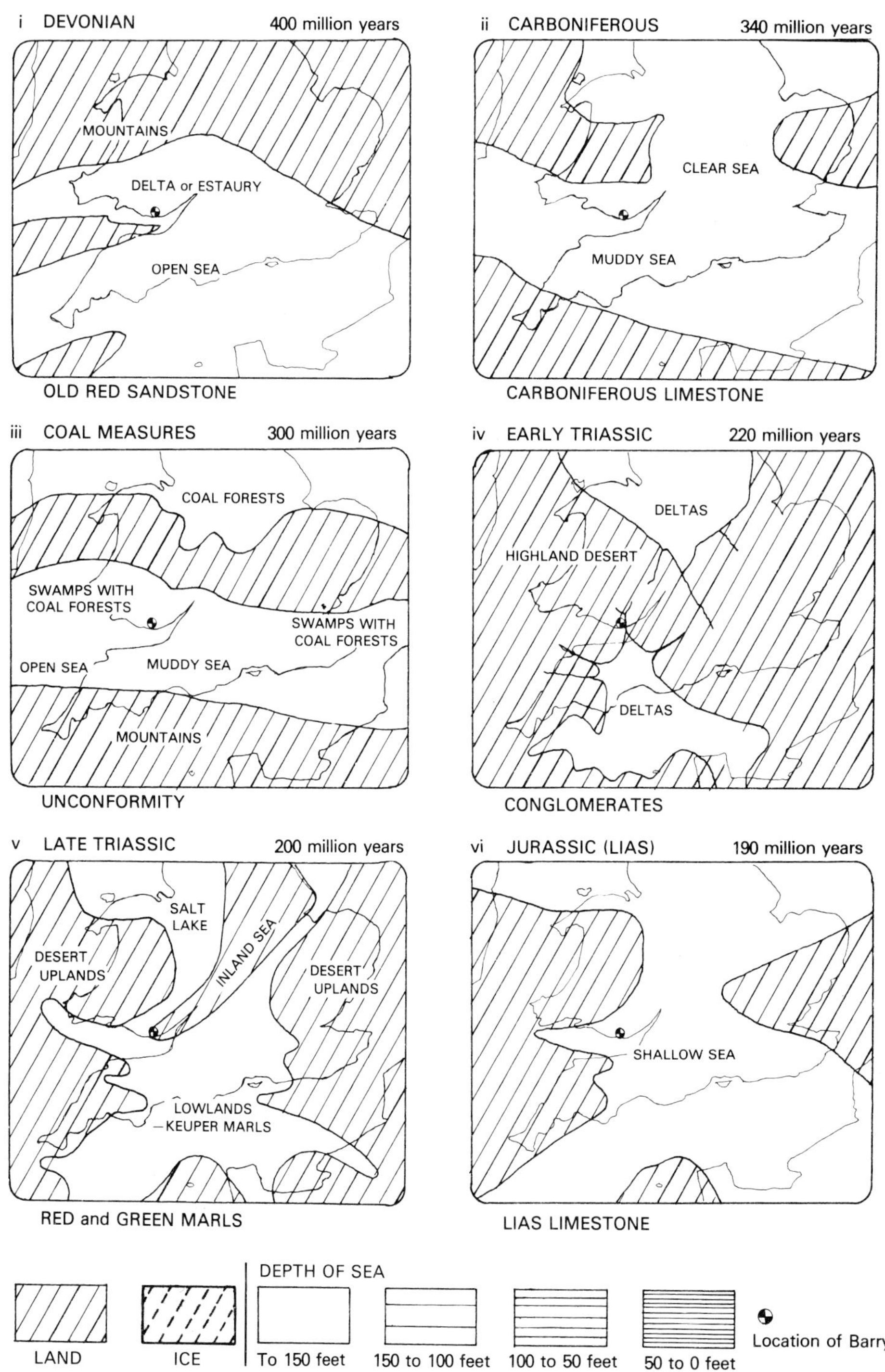

Fig. 2a. CONJECTURAL MAPS TO ILLUSTRATE THE EVOLUTION OF THE BRISTOL CHANNEL (cont.)

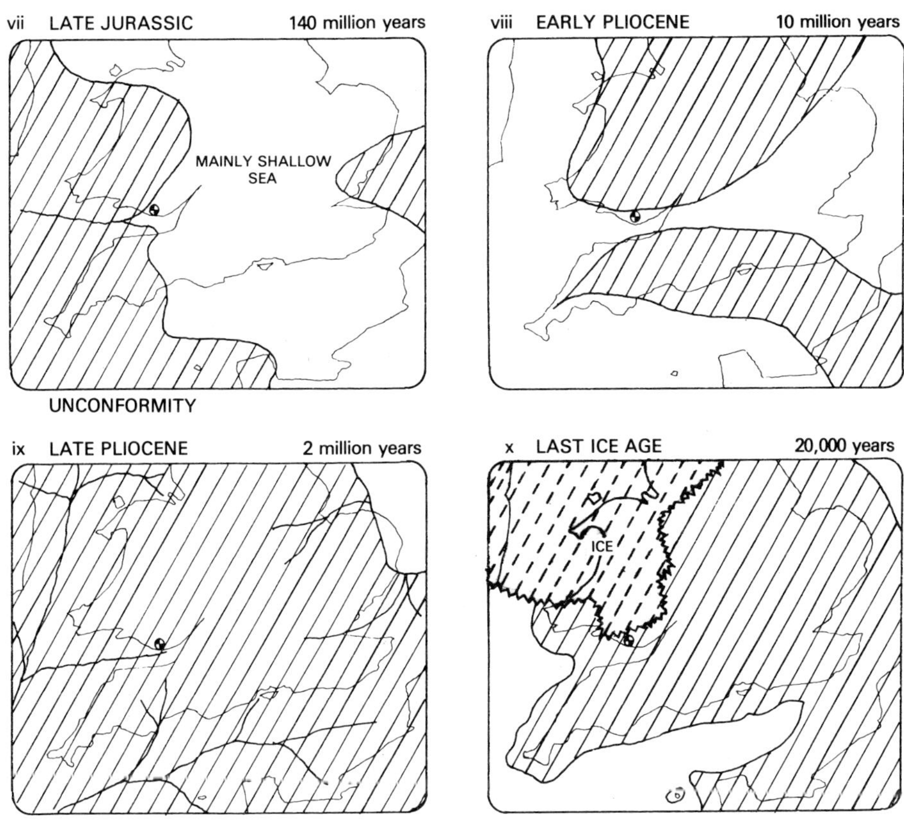

Fig. 2b. THE BRISTOL CHANNEL SOUTH AND WEST OF BARRY

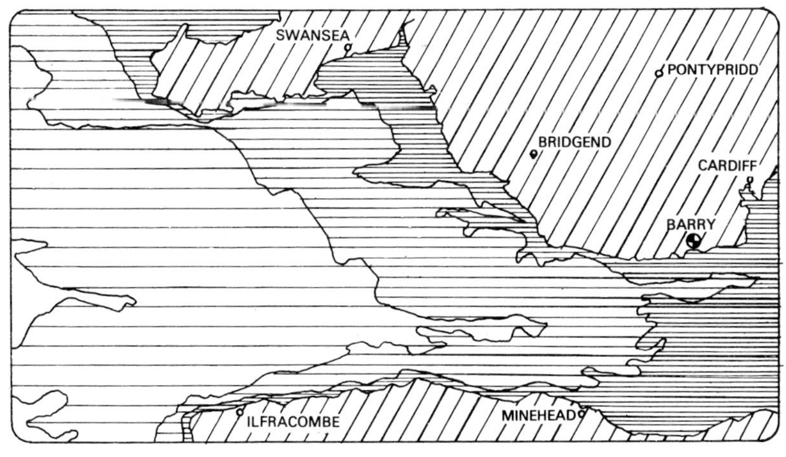

All maps by G.B. after F. J. North.

Ground rules

All the rocks to be studied in the South Wales area are sedimentary: they are composed of material derived from land and deposited by the agencies of wind and water over a period of time in varying circumstances. The derivation of these sediments, their method of deposition and the conditions in which they were laid down can all be read from the rocks which they created; these rocks in turn can tell an amazingly complete story of what a time-traveller, arriving every million years or so, would have witnessed on this part of the earth's surface.

Fossils are the remains of living creatures or plants and they may have been deposited in salt or fresh water; the rocks themselves may indicate muddy or clear water, sand deposited in shallow water, or pebbles left along the shore, in estuaries or deep seas. From their position can be gauged, sometimes to within feet, the uplift and subsidence of the land, the extent of the influx and retreat of the sea. The land conditions that prevailed while these sediments were being laid down or worn away—desert, semi-arid or lush vegetation, marsh and swamp—can also be postulated. Even where the rocks no longer remain, the negative evidence can tell a story. As vast sections of the geological time-scale are missing in this area, negative evidence helps to fill a considerable gap.

The sequence of rocks

The oldest rocks which can be studied anywhere on the earth's surface are the Precambrian. They were formed under a variety of conditions, land and marine, with some volcanic activity and mountain building. The lower date for the Precambrian rocks has receded considerably, the oldest rock yet dated being 3.6 thousand million years old. Less than twenty years ago it could be stated that Precambrian rocks contained no fossil remains;[4] but the oldest traces of life, three thousand million years old, have been detected in these rocks, including the fossils of primitive invertebrates, sponges, worms, algae and bacteria. With few exceptions, they are too deeply buried to be studied, are visible nowhere in our area and only infrequently crop out in West Wales (Late Precambrian).[5] This oldest, longest and least studied geological era represents a time span several times longer than all that has happened since.

The Palaeozoic Era followed the Precambrian and lasted for nearly 400 million years. The word palaeozoic means literally 'old life' and refers to the fossil remains in these rocks which represent life types completely different from those of the present. This era is divided into Lower and Upper, or older and newer sections, differentiated by the character of the sediments. Those belonging to the Lower Period are entirely marine in character, while the Upper Palaeozoic sediments were deposited in fresh water.

Geological eras are divided into periods, and the Lower Palaeozoic is represented in Wales by three periods. Indeed Wales has given the names by which these periods are known, as they are well-exposed in Wales and were first studied here. As with the Precambrian, the Cambrian rocks are too deeply buried in South Wales to be studied, if they are present at all. The Ordovician Period is also not represented locally, though strata in central and south-west Wales show that they are marine in character. However, this period is of interest because for the first time it is possible to detect in the geological record a structural feature which relates in position and trend to the Bristol Channel of today.[6] It is by no means a direct ancestor of the present Channel, but it is an indication which can be clearly followed through subsequent periods that there is here a predisposition in the earth's crust which will result in the evolution of the Bristol Channel. At this point, at least 400 million years ago, there was a peninsula of land extending westward from an eastern land mass, which was not related to what later became the British Isles.[7]

The only Lower Palaeozoic rocks found in South Glamorgan are limited outcrops from the Silurian Period, which have been studied near Cardiff. However, they give a clue to the conditions prevailing at the time. Our occasional visitor would have seen part of this area submerged beneath a shallow, muddy sea with areas of low-lying land. By this time a western land mass has appeared, from which the forerunner of the Bristol Channel now extends as a peninsula.

With the end of the Silurian Period, general marine conditions ceased to prevail, and the Upper Palaeozoic began with the Devonian Period. As a result of the Caledonian earth movements, there was great uplift over northern Europe, resulting in the emergence of a continental land mass which extended north-east to Scandinavia and westward to an unknown extent, the sea now located to the south of Devon and Cornwall. Although the earth movements were not severe in South Wales, they were sufficient to raise previously submerged land, leaving behind lagoons and the estuaries of large shifting rivers. Into these were deposited vast quantities of material derived from the newly-formed mountains to the north. These deposits resulted in the formation of what is known as the Old Red Sandstone Series. Once again it is interesting to note that the Old Red Sandstone does not appear south of the Bristol Channel area, which could at this time have been occupied by a barrier of some sort, perhaps a ridge, island or peninsula extending from the west, or simply a sandbank.[8]

The Old Red Sandstones are not comprised exclusively of sandstone, but include marls and conglomerates. It was perhaps the composite nature of this strata which led to some confusion over the only local identification of these rocks. The Cardiff antiquary John Storrie, surveying Barry Island in 1884 prior to the commencement of the building of the docks, identified an outcrop of Old Red Sandstone. As he appears to be the only person to have done so, his comments are worth quoting in full:

> 'The strata near Barry Dock entrance has been somewhat misunderstood, the principal mistake being as to the beds lying immediately to the north of the Mark Rock and extending to the fault which crosses the channel about two hundred yards north of Redbrink Point from Cold Knap to near Warren Tump. The survey officers were perfectly correct in indicating a line of Mountain Limestone running nearly parallel with, and about one hundred yards south of the fault, but they gave no indication of the beds south of the ridge, or rather they misled by indicating them as Triassic conglomerate. I will be able to show that they are really an anticlinal of Old Red Sandstone age, and this really forms the key to the whole place, and at once reduces what seems to be a very broken piece of ground to clear and definite order.'[9]

Fig. 3.

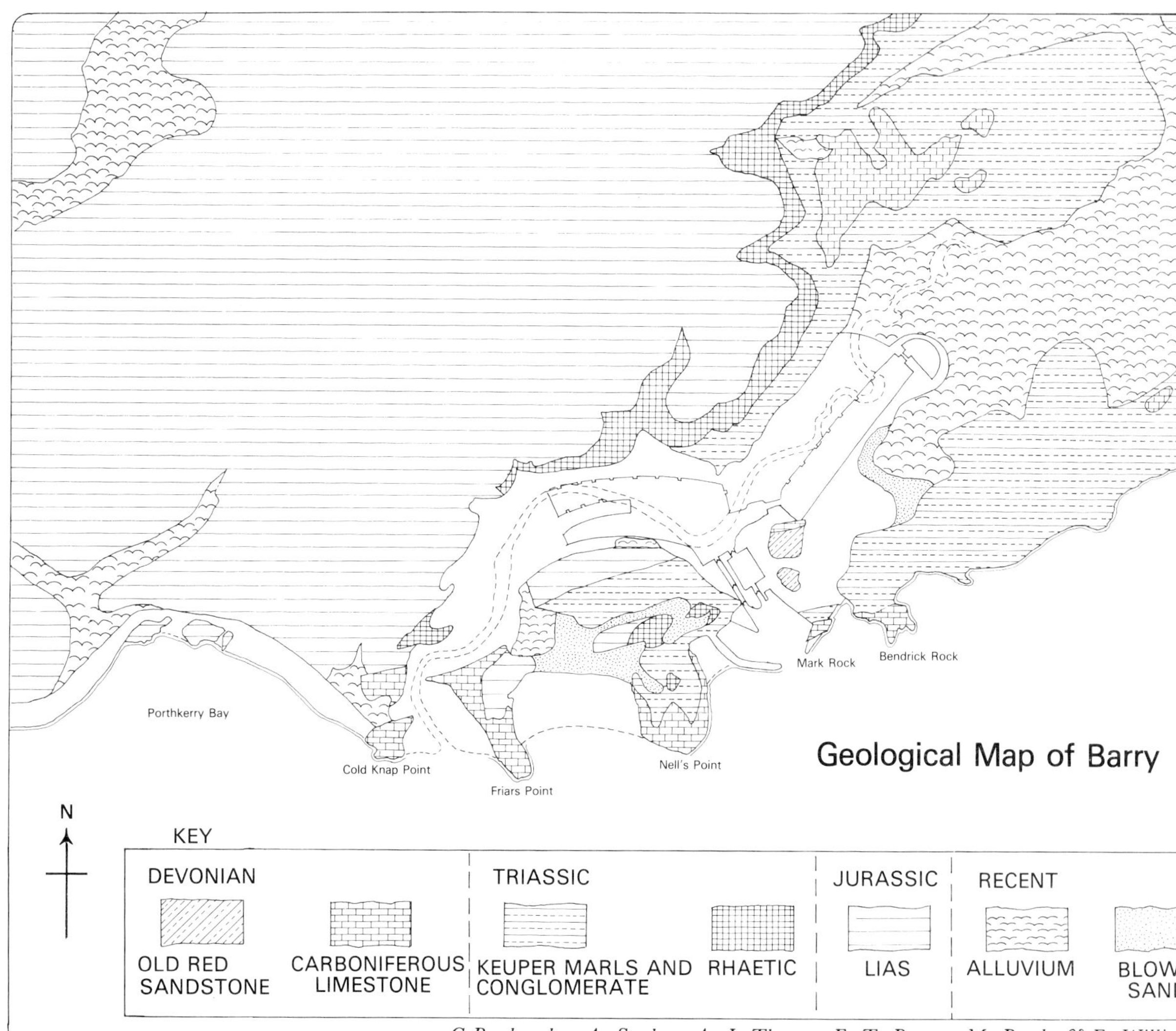

G.B., based on A. Strahan, A. J. Thomas, F. T. Banner, M. Brooks & E. Willia

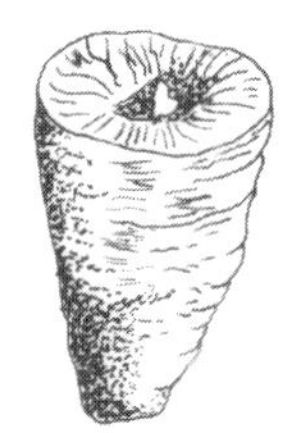

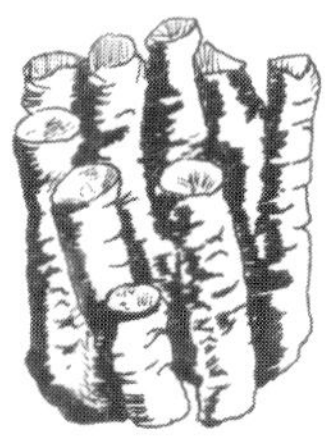

Corals.

Brachiopods.

Fig. 4.
Representative fossils of the Carboniferous Limestone.
Simon Prosser.

Storrie was a learned and observant man whose methodology in his own field was in advance of his day. His interests were wide and his standards high. Though not now widely known, in his own time he was highly regarded. By 1912 his identification of the Old Red Sandstone at Barry had been accepted and is still accepted today.[10]

The absence of marine fossils in these rocks suggests that this area was occupied by a large lake in a shallow basin separated from the sea by a narrow barrier along the line of the present Bristol Channel. This basin slowly sank at a rate which allowed the water level to remain constant as the deposited material flowed in. Under these conditions it is entirely possible that a low barrier of sandbanks was formed, but as the Devonian Period was between 350 and 400 million years ago, any number or combination of circumstances could have applied. What is clear is the striking difference between the deposits to the north and the south of whatever barrier there was. There were possibly occasional penetrations by the sea into this lake, altering the salinity of the water. There is no indication of a rich invertebrate life, though there are fossils of primitive vertebrates, fish. The shells are those of animals restricted to fresh or brackish water, and the first examples of woody-tissue plants appear.

The scarcity of fossils and the reddish colour of the deposits suggest land conditions of extreme aridity in which there was no decaying organic material to reduce the iron compounds in the soil, which remained in their ferric state and gave their characteristic colour to the soil. So although the Old Red Sandstone Series is not widely enough represented in the Vale of Glamorgan area to exert any influence on the subsequent scenery and topography, we do have a clear picture of the conditions which prevailed when the deposits were being laid down.

At the end of the Devonian Period the British area as a whole subsided beneath the sea. This alteration from land to marine conditions seems to have taken place without any great disturbance, although the slow subsidence was neither continuous nor uniform. The invading sea extended from the west of Ireland eastward across Europe to Russia, with an island from Central Wales west to Ireland, known as St. George's Land. This was a vast, shallow, warm sea undisturbed by deposits of mud and sand, in whose clear waters there thrived corals, molluscs, brachiopods and crinoids whose fossils formed the Carboniferous Limestones.

The rocks of the Carboniferous Period can be divided into two groups, the lower group being characterized by the Carboniferous Limestones and the upper group by the Millstone Grit and the Coal Measures.

The thickness of the Carboniferous Limestone deposits, not less than 3,000 feet (916 metres), indicates millions of years of accumulation. The basin of the shallow sea in which these sediments were laid down subsided gently at a rate that kept pace with the rate of deposition. That this rate was not constant, or the conditions of deposition uniform is shown by the variations in the limestones, which can be divided into five zones, the changes recorded by the fauna found in them.[11]

Present outcrops of Carboniferous Limestone, for reasons given later, are confined to Gower, the south-east border of the coalfield and the Vale of Glamorgan, the latter being of particular interest to this study. These are most spectacularly visible on Barry Island, but a sizeable outcrop occurs at Cadoxton, where the limestone has been extensively quarried and can be seen in the hillsides. Flat and Steep Holm are entirely of Carboniferous Limestone.

The absence of land-derived sediment in the seas of the Carboniferous Limestone Period suggests a land surface of low relief, few hills and arid conditions in which few rivers carried any material to the sea. This period of quiet subsidence and deposition came to an end at the close of Carboniferous Limestone times with a period of rapid upheaval in which the land was thrown into high relief. The slopes of streams increased and consequently, their velocity. The mud, sand and pebbles they now carried produced the rocks known as the Millstone Grit, which are completely different in the character of the rocks and in the forms of the deposits from the preceding limestone. The sediments are land-derived, presumably from a land mass to the north.[12] The beds vary widely in their lateral extent and are graded from north to south, showing increasing fineness of grain as they progress southwards from the contemporary shoreline.

The Millstone Grit marks the transition from the Lower to the Upper Carboniferous rocks. The period of uplift ended and was replaced again by one of slow, intermittent subsidence—slow, because although the deposits which comprise the shales and sandstones of the Coal Measures are thick, their upper surface seems to have remained always constant.

The great thicknesses of rock collectively known as the Coal Measures range in depth from 3,000 to 8,000 feet (915 to 2,440 metres) as they run from east to west. Within this depth the layers of coal which have assumed such great economic importance occur only as relatively thin bands. However it is the formation of this black rock, (coal is a mono-mineralic rock), that captures the imagination.

The period of subsidence that followed the deposition of the Millstone Grit gradually halted, the river gradients lessened, so that finer particles of silt and mud accumulated. In the wide, continuous zone that is now north-west Europe, many basins of deposition gradually filled up. Swampy mud flats developed, in which flourished great masses of swamp-loving vegetation. Occasionally these swamps dried out sufficiently to permit the advance of forest. This can be assumed from the rootlet beds which appear under coal seams and represent the soil in which the vegetation grew.

The species of vegetation which did grow under these conditions are all now extinct as are the main groups to which they belonged. There is no evidence to suggest that they were primarily ferns, but they were diverse flora. Some grew in drier ground, some more comfortably with their roots in water, their diversity reflecting possible changes in climate. However, like all plants, they grew up, flourished and died, depositing masses of rotting vegetation. Some lay where they fell, others floated in great rafts around lakes and channels, became waterlogged and sank.

Gradual subsidence of the land recommenced but at so slow a rate that the layer of rotting plants continued to accumulate to a great thickness, while the surface layer remained level and the material stayed waterlogged. At some point the rate of subsidence increased, the forests and swamps were drowned and the layers of vegetation sealed by deposits of sand or mud from rivers. Gradually the subsidence decreased, sediments once again filled the lakes, swamps reappeared and the full cycle repeated itself, not once, but many times, until many thousands of feet of material had been deposited. Within these cycles the swamp periods must have lasted a very long time, as the accumulation of vegetable matter must have been at least ten times as thick as the resulting coal seam, and these thicknesses would have taken a much longer time to accumulate than an equivalent thickness of sand or mud.

Although the Coal Measures of South Wales concern us here, their formation must not be seen as a local incident. Correlating coal seams and tracing individual beds is now seen as a naïve analytical tool, but the correlation between the Coal Measure marine bands, which are few in number and thin in extent, has been much refined, owing to the nature of their fossil species.[13] The picture of swamps and lagoons filled with rotting vegetation over the area of South Wales is intriguing enough; but even with local variations in the deposits, it is possible to envisage roughly uniform conditions over a vast area from Britain in the west, eastwards to Russia.[14]

The shore of the vast sea of the Lower Carboniferous and that of the beginning of the Upper phase probably coincided roughly with the northern border of the old county of Glamorgan. But during Coal Measure time, the east-west frontier along the path of the Bristol Channel reasserted itself as sediments which became fine grained sandstones and shales were deposited to the south over Devon and Cornwall.

The earth moves

With the formation of the Coal Measures we come to the end of the Carboniferous Period and, for this part of South Wales at least, to the end of the first phase in the story. For over 300 million years the processes of rock building had been carrying on, but a change was about to take place. Great pressure from the south forced the relatively horizontal beds of these older strata up against the more stable mass of rocks of Central Wales, bending and folding the strata. This earth movement was much more intensely felt in South Wales than the earlier Caledonian movement and drastically altered the lie of the land and the conditions to which it was subsequently subjected. These changes were probably influenced by an alteration in latitude due to continental drift.[15]

As a result of this movement of the earth, a chain of mountains was created to the south and south-west of Britain which caused desert conditions to be established on the northern side of the chain. As now, the moisture-bearing winds prevailed from the south-west, but encountering this chain of mountains, they deposited their moisture on the southern slopes and only dry winds passed over. This range of mountains takes its name from the ancient name of Brittany and is called the Armorican. This name has also been given to this episode of earth movement and to the predominantly east-west folds it threw up in Britain.

The strata were not all squeezed in the same direction, or in uniform, simple curves; although the east-west folds predominate in South Wales, a north-south fold separates this coalfield from that of the Forest of Dean. Only a little imagination is required to see that horizontal beds, when squeezed, will produce trough-like folds and arch-like folds, known geologically as synclines and anticlines.

The South Wales coalfield was compressed in a syncline which has had two curious effects. This downward compacting of the layers has produced rocks resistant to erosion, resulting over a period in an area of high ground, while at the same time bringing closer to the surface seams of coal that otherwise might not have been economically worked in modern times.

To the south, the area of the Vale and the Bristol Channel was folded in a series of anticlines which has again produced contradictory results. The arched rocks were strained and weakened, and were more susceptible to the forces of erosion by wind and water, producing eventually lower-lying sloping ground. More particularly it is this southern anticline that is responsible for the exposure of Carboniferous Limestone in a ridge running from Dinas Powys *via* St. Nicholas to Cowbridge and known as the Cardiff-Cowbridge anticline, while smaller anticlinal folds have allowed the exposure of Carboniferous Limestone at Barry, Cadoxton and on the islands in the Bristol Channel.

These upward folds were immediately subjected to the most severe sub-aerial denudation, made possible by the climatic changes already mentioned. The upper part of the Coal Measures was removed, as was all the coal to the south, unless some has been preserved at great depth in a fold between the Cardiff-Cowbridge anticline and the Carboniferous Limestone at Barry.[16] If coal is there, it is likely to remain so, as there is no reason to look for it at such an uneconomic depth. The severity of the erosion resulted in the removal of over 8,000 feet (2,440 metres) of rock which means that the original uplift must have been roughly equivalent.

It is not unreasonable to ask where so much eroded material could go. Unfortunately these periods, the Permian at the end of the Palaeozoic Era and the early Triassic at the start of the Mesozoic Era, are missing from the geological record in this area. The extent of the break in the stratigraphical record can be determined by the character of the flora and fauna; when deposition recommenced, the Palaeozoic life forms had all disappeared and been replaced by other kinds of organisms.[17]

Rebuilding

We come now to a gap of nearly 50 million years in the geological record. While the Permian and early Triassic strata were being laid down elsewhere, our local anticlinal area was subjected to continued erosion, possibly as a result of desert conditions. The strained folds of the higher ground were rapidly worn away, producing our low-lying area and exposing an older, uneven land surface. How uneven can be seen from the location of the first Triassic layers we have in the Vale of Glamorgan, which were formed along the shore of a steadily advancing Triassic sea. These beds consist of boulders, conglomerates (rounded pebbles) and breccias (angular pebbles and stones) banked against the sides of older hills. These deposits can now be seen at a height of some 300 feet (90 metres) in one location, but occur at a depth of at least 600 feet (180 metres) in another, giving a total difference in the level of the landscape of nearly 1,000 feet (300 metres). Whether this can be attributed to a gradual slope, a series of cliffs or one huge escarpment is not shown by the evidence.[18] At Barry Island the basement bed rests unconformably on the sloping anticlinal Carboniferous Limestone and can easily be seen in Jackson's Bay. In fact the northern end of the footpath running from Whitmore Bay around Nell's Point to Jackson's Bay has been constructed in part on a wave-cut ledge with the Carboniferous Limestone rising dramatically on the seaward side and the breccias and conglomerates clearly visible in the cliff face, virtually at knee height.

With the beginning of the deposition of the Triassic marls we have reached the point where the coast of Barry provides a spectacular display of the rocks we shall be discussing.

Just prior to the encroachment of the seas in later Triassic times, we would have seen a landscape of uneven surface with a broad east-west depression in the area of the Bristol Channel, with high ground rising to the north and south. So our Channel does not yet exist but is foreshadowed by a dry basin.

Later on in Triassic times vast inland seas and salt lakes spread over the area, owing either to subsidence or to shallow seas expanding as their basins

Plate I.
Wave-cut ledge with Carboniferous Limestone on east side of Friars Point, Barry Island.
B. Daly.

filled with sediment. In these seas were deposited the wind-blown particles that became the Keuper Marls. The shorelines of these seas at the beginning of Keuper time are clearly visible in the pebble beaches and wave-cut platforms; fine examples of these exist on Barry Island, as already mentioned.

The main mass of the Keuper Marls forms the cliffs in Jackson's Bay and around Redbrink Point, which derives its name from the chief characteristic of the sediments deposited at this time. They are predominantly Red Marls, a soft stone, interbedded with some thinner hard layers, with occasional patches of green. The Red Marls merge gradually upwards to the Tea Green Marls which are of the same character, but different in colour. These in turn merge upwards again to the Grey Marls. These striking changes in colour probably reflect changes in the climatic conditions at the time these deposits were laid down. This multicoloured layering is also clearly visible in the cliff face along the railway line between Barry Dock and Cadoxton.

It is possible, when standing on the footpath in Jackson's Bay, on the rocky surface of a beach cut by waves over 200 million years ago, to imagine that the waters of the Bristol Channel are those of an ancient, gradually encroaching sea. The cliffs behind will slowly be built up from dust deposited in that sea, and finally after millions of years have passed, we can stand once again on this ancient shoreline.

The configuration of the coastline would have seemed somehow familiar to us. Off the shore of the Triassic mainland were numerous islands, of which the main headlands at Barry were three. These were originally covered with Triassic deposits, along with Sully Island, though the Barry headlands have since been eroded, leaving the Carboniferous Limestone. Sully Island still wears its cap of Triassic layers. The shapes of the modern headlands and islands coincide closely to those of Triassic times and give a striking instance of geological history repeating itself.

Mainland conditions, however, would not have been remotely familiar. The characteristic red colour of the Keuper Marls suggests an arid climate, with near desert conditions. The seas were shallow, giving rise to the occasional ripple marks and sun-cracks which can be seen in the marls. Organic remains are scarce if not totally absent. Life in the shallow salt lakes was impossible and the land provided only a sparse growth of vegetation to support an even sparser population of reptiles. These have left the occasional

Plate II.
Keuper marls at west end of Whitmore Bay, Barry Island.
B. Daly.

Fig. 5. Reconstruction of Anchisauripus, whose footprints were found in Triassic beds near Bendrick Rock. *Simon Prosser, after G.B.*

footprint as they walked across the sticky surface of the shore. Prints of two small dinosaurs found at Sully in 1974 are now in the National Museum of Wales.[19]

The Triassic Period ended with the evaporation of the inland seas and lakes. The final series of this period, the Rhaetic, is marked by the foundering of the region and the rapid return of the sea. The sea, the first of the Mesozoic seas—Triassic waters were inland lakes—returned so rapidly, possibly as the result of a barrier breaking further to the south, that the bottom bed of the Rhaetic series is a bone bed. It consists mainly of the fossil remains of those animals, chiefly reptiles, who could not adapt to the new conditions, and most of them must have perished almost instantly.

The Rhaetic strata are dark shales and pale, thinly-bedded limestones and were laid down over a wide area, apparently completely covering the earlier, even Triassic surface, though like the Triassic strata they do not over-run the higher ground to the north.

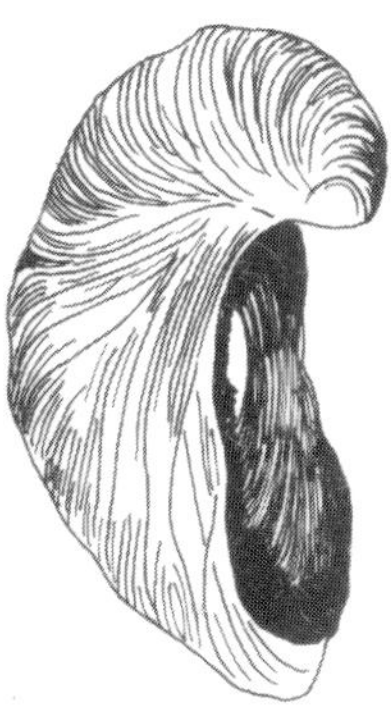

Gryphaea (Devil's toe-nail).

Nowhere is the total accumulation of this period more than 100 feet (30 metres) thick, and it is usually less; these layers consequently have little effect upon our scenery. The 'bone bed' exists on Barry Island, but its position, high on the cliff faces, makes it dangerous to examine at close quarters. The Rhaetic strata also appear thinly across the top of Redbrink Point and can be followed, with interruptions, to Whitmore Bay and Friars Point.

The Rhaetic strata are now considered to be the last of the Triassic Period, and because they indicate a return to marine conditions of deposition, they have assumed an interest out of proportion to their thickness. In Glamorgan, the black shales and limestones are laid down in the east, while further west are found the sandstones of beach deposits, indicating that the relative positions of land and sea were reversed from those of today, the so-called Bristol Channel occupying a wide gulf between the uplands to our north and Devon—but opening to the east rather than to the west.[20]

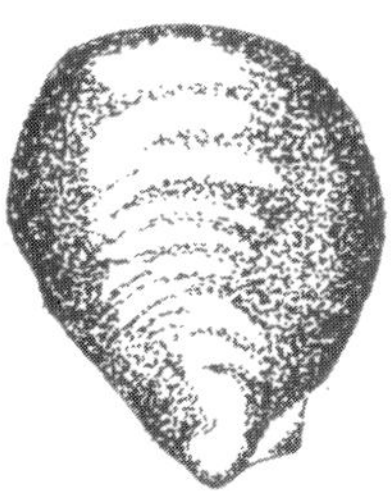

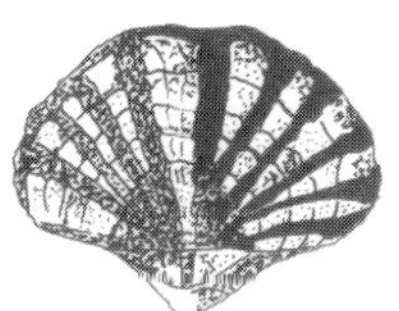

Bivalves.

The boundary between the Rhaetic and the Liassic, the first series of the Jurassic Period, is marked by the finely grained White Lias Limestone which indicates that ordinary marine life has returned after the mingling of the desert lakes with the ocean. The White Lias at Barry was buried by construction debris from the docks.

However, it is the Blue Lias, representing the lowest portion of the Lower Lias, that is the most familiar feature of our local scene. It is the stone on which Barry for the most part is built; although the alternating bands of shale and limestone are most characteristic of the vertical coastal cliffs from Barry to Southerndown, they extend widely inland. As in Keuper times, beaches were cut and shore deposits formed. The latter are worth mentioning because, though not seen in the Barry area, further west they produced a white or pale limestone known as Sutton Stone which was widely used as building stone and for the Norman fonts found in many churches in the Vale of Glamorgan.

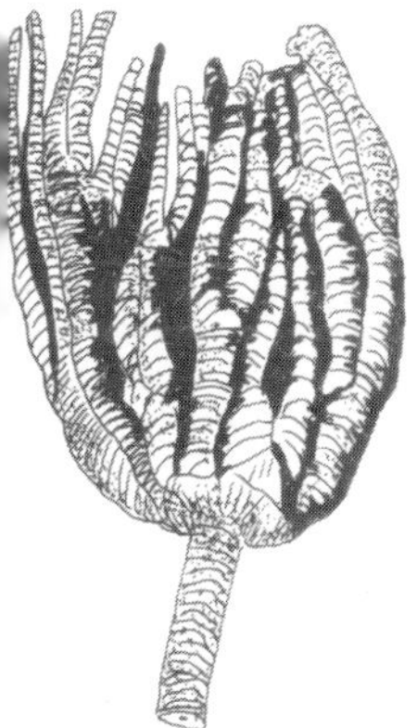

Crinoid (Sea Lily).

Fig. 6. Representative fossils of the Lias Limestone. *Simon Prosser.*

To judge from the inland positions of the wave-cut beaches and platforms of this period, the Liassic sea extended further inland with more vigorous wave action than had the Triassic waters. The shoreline was well north of the present coast, and there is evidence to suggest an offshore archipelago formed from a large Triassic island to the west of Barry. This area would have been well beneath the surface of this shallow sea.

Missing rocks

As has been mentioned, only the lower part of the Lower Lias is found in this area, and with the deposition of the Blue Lias we come to the end of 'solid geology' in Barry. The rest of the Mesozoic Era, the remaining Jurassic Period and the entire Cretaceous Period (the Chalk Epoch), as well as all of the Tertiary Era, are completely missing here. Some 150 million years of rocks, presuming they were ever deposited, have completely disappeared.

It is possible to assume the conditions of these times based on indirect evidence—there is no record of what happened, only of what might have happened.

It is likely that by the end of the Jurassic Period South Wales was part of a western land mass with a river flowing to the east over the site of the present Channel. No new deposits were being laid down and those that were exposed were being worn away. These conditions probably continued into the early Cretaceous Period followed by the great subsidence in which our western land mass was submerged by a vast, clear shallow sea, the Chalk sea—with a few islands in North and mid Wales. By the end of the Cretaceous, probably even these were submerged. If there was chalk deposition here, there remains no evidence of it.

Familiar scenes

We are gradually approaching a time when, had we stood at the top of Barry and gazed north and south, we should have recognized not the landscape of today, but a surface which at least resembled a landscape. Until now we have imagined the area of our town and surrounding countryside as an alien world of red deserts or huge lagoons filled with rotting vegetation, or vast shallow seas warm enough to allow corals to grow. There remain only two major events which will give our landscape its present shape.

Earth movements at the end of the Cretaceous were forerunners of a greater period of crustal unrest which occurred some 25 million years ago in the Miocene (Tertiary Period) and which resulted in the formation of the Alps and Himalayas. Wales was on the northern fringes of this movement, which was sufficient to fold the Mesozoic and early Tertiary layers along the pattern of the earlier folds. One local result of this Miocene folding was that the ancestral Bristol Channel now opened to the west, rather than to the east as has been previously emphasized.[21] Another result was that the Mesozoic strata in this area were subjected to extensive denudation which re-exposed the older Triassic strata. However, there is no evidence to suppose that the land mass which became the British Isles and more locally the coastline of South Glamorgan took on a recognizable shape before the late Pliocene times, nearly 10 million years later.

The period of unrest in Miocene times was followed by the relative quiet of the Pliocene. The level of the land, already lower than at present, gradually subsided beneath the surface of another encroaching sea. It was at this time that the gently rolling area of Glamorgan south of the coalfield was given its evenly-stepped skyline by the wave action of this Pliocene sea. Today this feature is not obvious from the land where the surface is broken by river valleys. But the view from the sea presents a different picture, where the valleys cannot be seen and the uniform profile of the hilltops is noticeable. In fact it is possible to detect a series of wide, level terraces at progressively higher elevations. These shelves were formed as a result of marine rather than sub-aerial denudation and were planed off by the sea during long periods when the relative positions of land and sea remained constant. These resting stages were followed by an episode of pulsing uplift when the level areas were raised out of reach of the sea, with no evidence of warping or folding. The cycle then recommenced with a wide new terrace being cut, and it continued until the sea retreated far to the west, the shoreline coinciding with the present 100-fathom contour.[22] The coastline of South Glamorgan was gradually emerging from the Pliocene sea and the Bristol Channel area now became a wide valley with a gently sloping floor.

After the period of the Miocene uplift and during the less restless Pliocene, while the marine platforms were being cut and raised, a primary river system established itself on this evenly eroded surface. Much study was devoted to the late emergence of a drainage pattern, and although some details of these early theories have since been modified, the basic conclusions remain unchallenged.[23] The river system for South Wales in general bears little relation to the older, underlying structural geology. The land surface at this time, the end of the Tertiary Period, though since eroded, was sufficiently different in character from that of earlier periods for the river system not only to establish itself, but subsequently to remain uninfluenced, for the most part, by such factors as the direction of folding, the system of faulting or the relative hardness of the older rocks.

The landscape around Barry is traversed by no major river system, but there are small rivers and streams of local interest. The behaviour of these water courses is more determined by the existence of the wave-cut platforms and their relative levels of elevation. The Weycock River flows in a valley between the ridge of the Barry Port Road and the next higher ridge of the A48 road, while the course of the Cadoxton River lies almost totally within what is thought to be the elevation of the most recent wave-cut platform.[24]

The existence of this series of terraces planed off by marine erosion suggests that the level of the land was lower than at present just prior to and at the onset of the next and final severe disturbance to the land, the invasion of ice. The Pleistocene Period and the Great Ice Age are a mere one million years past; and compared with all that has gone before, the final evolution of the details of our landscape has been rapid indeed.

At the time of maximum glaciation, almost all Britain north of the Severn and the Thames was buried beneath a massive ice sheet. In South Wales the ice gathered in the Brecon Beacons and flowed down the valleys of the coalfield. How far it extended over the coastal lowlands into the Vale of Glamorgan is not certain, but this local Welsh ice did not cross to Somerset and Devon. However, a much larger ice sheet moved down the Irish Sea and eastward along the southern edge of the Welsh ice sheet. It flowed along the depression of the Bristol Channel to east Glamorgan and possibly as far as the north coast of Devon. The direction and area of the ice can be traced by the extent of the drift, or by the material left behind by the retreating ice. The different sources of this drift can also be distinguished; some material is obviously locally derived, while there are occurrences in the Vale and as far east as Cardiff of more far-travelled material, of rock types foreign to South Wales.[25]

This picture is further complicated by the fact that there were two episodes of glaciation, separated by an interlude of more benign climatic conditions. There are consequently two series of glacial deposits, known as Older and Newer Drift. It is sometimes difficult to distinguish between the two, but the evidence suggests that the second phase of glaciation was more local in origin and less severe in extent than the first. The period of maximum glaciation probably occurred 190,000 years ago, but the ice may well not have completely retreated much more than 10,000 or 12,000 years ago.

South of the coalfield area, the drift thins out and disappears; there is no evidence of it south of a ridge that runs from Wenvoe through St. Nicholas.[26] Although the area was undoubtedly affected by the conditions prevailing during glaciation and as the ice retreated, it is unlikely that Barry itself was engulfed by the ice.

Following the retreat of the ice, congenial climatic conditions returned. The great weight of ice upon the land gradually lessened, and the vast amount of water which had been frozen was released. As a result of these two factors, the next phase in the development of the landscape is dominated by the relative rise and fall of land surfaces against a background of steadily-rising sea level, from which has emerged the modern coastline. With these changes comes the first evidence of man's presence in the area and we move from the study of geology to that of prehistory.

Barry has some of the best available evidence for the conditions of 5,000 years ago. The remains of submerged land surfaces were discovered in excavations made during the construction of East Barry Dock in 1895. The section through the strata has been studied in detail and throws light on the changing relationship between land and sea.[27] Figure 7 illustrates this series of layers. They represent a period of intermittent subsidence when land surfaces became waterlogged, with dry land occasionally re-establishing itself when the submergence ended. This oscillation terminated with the final incursion of the sea.

The lowest and therefore earliest deposit from the Barry section consists of soil with roots and land shells, and clearly represents an old land surface nearly 40 feet (33 metres) below present sea level. The peat bed above this land surface contained the remains of many logs, including much oak wood. This surface must have been at all times above high water mark, as even one

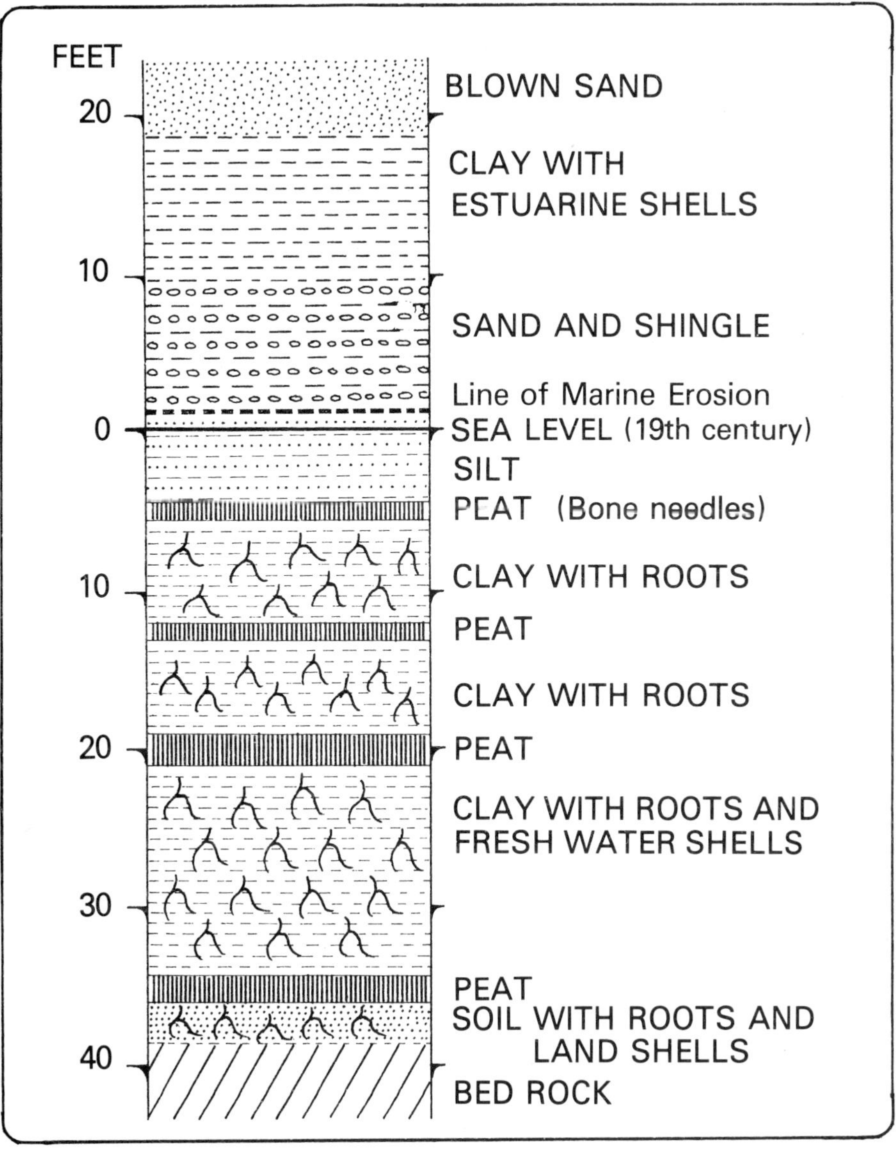

Fig. 7.
Section illustrating the sequence of deposits associated with the submerged peat beds at Barry Dock.
G.B. after J. Storrie.

penetration of salt water would have made the growth of oak impossible. Above this are nearly 30 feet (9 metres) of blue clays and silts with four distinct layers of peat. The clays and silt contain fresh water and land shells while the peats contain the remains of varied plant life. Although submergence had begun, the peats represent the re-establishment of dry-land conditions. The remains of sedges predominate in the higher peat beds, indicating that at this point the land is no longer dry enough for true forest growth.

It is in the uppermost peat bed, 4 feet (1·2 metres) below sea level, that John Storrie found two bone needles, now thought to belong to the New Stone Age (Neolithic). Man clearly is moving across the landscape before the final land configurations emerge.

This thick band is topped by a layer of sand and gravel which rests on a surface levelled by the sea, the underlying deposits being estuarine rather than marine in character. This layer obviously represents the final incursion of the sea and can be dated probably to the close of the Bronze Age. Evidence from other sources also proves that the relationship between land and sea along the Bristol Channel has not altered substantially in the past 2,000 years.[28]

It is possible to calculate from the evidence of the Barry Dock section a minimum figure for the extent of vertical adjustment that has taken place along the coast. Allowing for the depth of the deposits and the maximum height of the tides, a figure of 54 to 56 feet (16·46 to 17 metres) is not unreasonable. It is not possible to determine if or how far these old land surfaces extend beneath the sea. However it has been estimated that the total rise in sea level could be as much as 100 feet (30·48 metres).[29] This figure coincides remarkably well with the evidence of a recent survey of the approaches to Barry, which suggests a connection between the Breaksea Valley system at approximately 100 feet (30·48 metres) below present sea level and the development of the Bristol Channel.[30]

The details of the Barry Dock section and the bathymetric survey are fascinating in themselves; but more interestingly for a general survey, they provide the framework for an imaginative reconstruction of the local scene in which man began to exert his influence. A Neolithic visitor would have wandered through woods of oak, hazel, hawthorn and willow on the slopes of a wide valley through which a great river flowed to a much further western shore, probably in the region of Swansea. Perhaps he hunted the red deer, wolf and ox that shared the river valley with him. His Bronze-Age descendant would have crossed a land surface of combined marsh and woodland. The Cadoxton River would have flowed westward on its old course to emerge between Cold Knap and Friars Point; the extent of its original outfall can be surmised from the sea bed survey already mentioned.[31] Barry Island would still have been a peninsula extending westwards from Sully, not fully insulated until the end of the Bronze Age, as represented by the top layer of the Barry Dock section. And finally only one

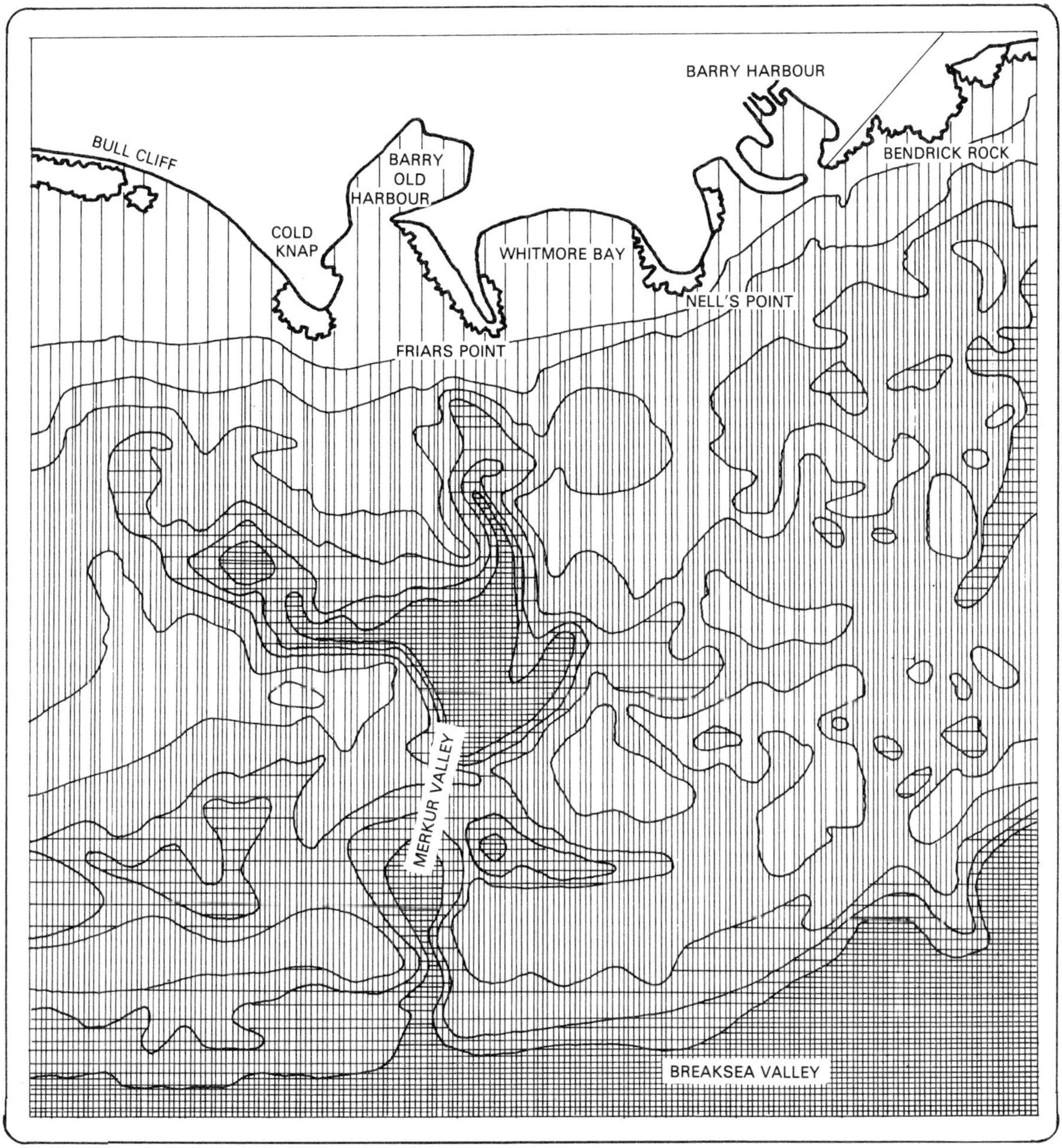

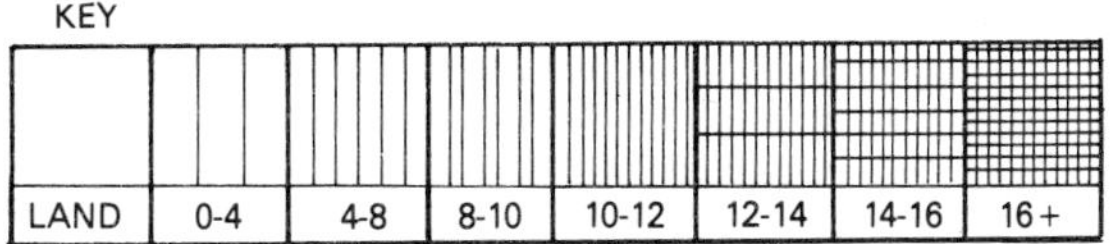

metres below sea level

Fig. 8.
Sea-bed contours in relation to coast at Barry.
C. Farrow.

hundred years or so before the arrival of the Romans, our distant ancestor would have looked out on a coastal scene we ourselves would unhesitatingly recognise.

During the Middle Stone Age (Mesolithic) occurred the severing of the land connection between the British Isles and the European continent, the submergence of a land bridge with Ireland, and the final step in the evolution of the Bristol Channel. More correctly the latter is a river valley which has been drowned—or entered by the sea. Contours which are presently submarine probably refer to, but are not identical with, the outline of the land before it was submerged, in view of the amount of material that has since been deposited. All subsequent changes in and around these islands are a matter of degree rather than kind and revolve around gains and losses of material along the shore. They are chiefly of two types: (1) alluvial mud and (2) blown sand. These changes are directly important to man and bring us well into historical times. Because of their recent origin and their accumulation on the surface, they have influenced man's activities out of all proportion to their geological importance.

The Severn and its tributaries carry vast quantities of suspended material. It has been estimated that if this material had been evenly distributed on the floor of the Bristol Channel over the past 2,000 years, it would account for a layer nearly 7 feet (2·13 metres) thick.[32] But of course it is not so deposited. Some matter is left at the mouths of the tributary rivers and along the shore where it can build up, and if sealed behind a natural or man-made barrier which moves it out of reach of the tide, it eventually becomes land more suited to man's use. However, much material remains suspended in the river (and this includes contributions from man's activities), and can remain in the area for some time, even weeks, before actually being washed out to sea. In fact the current in the Bristol Channel moves fast enough to bring matter in with the tide as well as out. Tide-flow studies have demonstrated that some material deposited by man will reappear at a location further up the Channel than that at which it was deposited. Thermal radiation data collected from satellites have confirmed this restricted deep water interchange.[33] This behaviour obviously has implications for our future on this coast.

At Barry there are several accumulations of alluvium. The most substantial is to the east and is undoubtedly related to the original course of the Cadoxton River. Another alluvial deposit at the Knap, on the site of the Marine Lake, represents a marshy estuary which has been altered in modern times. The streams which run through Porthkerry Park are responsible for a considerable deposit. Barry Brook flows down Cwm Barry to meet Nant Talwg which runs through Cwm Cidy and along the foot of Cliff Wood. It in turn is met by Whitelands Brook. The outlet for this combined stream is modern, the original having been blocked by the

Plate III.
Present configuration of coast at Barry, showing Carboniferous Limestone headlands (from centre upwards): Nell's Point, Friars Point and Cold Knap.
Copyright: West Air Photography.

formation of the pebble beach. These streams and their valleys figure in Barry's later history.

The South Wales coast provides some dramatic examples of the action of wind-blown sand, all of which has accumulated in the last 2,000 years. Two distinct layers can be identified most readily on Barry Island, the first a maximum of 18 inches (45·7 centimetres) thick which probably began to accumulate late in prehistoric times. The second deposit varies in thickness from 3 to 20 feet (1 to 6 metres), is of relatively recent origin, and was discovered by John Storrie to seal completely the remains of early medieval occupation on the Island. The distinction between these two layers and their dating is paralleled by other evidence along the coast.

There remains only one characteristic feature of Barry to discuss—the pebble beaches, which are the most recent coastal addition. They are derived from the Lias Limestone cliffs at Porthkerry and have travelled eastwards along the coast towards Barry since the 16th century. The journey of the pebbles has been closely studied and reveals that they move in a characteristic zig-zag fashion along the shore, one stone travelling eastwards towards Cold Knap as much as 100 feet (30·48 metres) in a single tide.[34] Fortunately they are also carried back which has prevented them from overtopping Cold Knap Point. Specially marked pebbles have been traced for a number of years in their progress, some of them remaining buried on the beach, protected from abrasion, for as long as eight years before re-emerging.

This eastward drift of sand and pebbles has altered the character and use of the Barry coast. In the absence of the pebbles, the beach at Glan-y-môr and the marshy estuary on the site of the Lake were put to other use by the Romans at Barry. However, further discussion of their influence belongs to a following chapter.

Conclusion

Barry's geological history is remarkable for its simplicity. So few processes have been at work in creating our landscape; elevation and subsidence, erosion and deposition by wind and water—almost alone these have been responsible. Their actions across an awesome time span have been relentless. Much of the geological record is missing; that which remains lends itself equally to complex and detailed study and to a more general understanding. The succession of coastlines, valleys and estuaries, though completely different from those of the present, cannot be regarded as unrelated, and in some instances have repeated themselves after millions of years. Each stage was influenced by what came before and in its turn influenced what came after, the evolution of the Bristol Channel through all its phases being a prime example.

We should also do well to remember that our present familiar landscape is but a temporary feature on the surface of the earth. The forces of wind and water are at work around us all the time; elevation and subsidence, sudden or slow, may recommence. All about us will alter and we shall take our place in the strata of geology.

Man has contributed almost nothing so far to this story. The passage of millions of years has been described in these introductory pages; the period since his arrival covers only thousands of years, but requires the rest of the book.

References

1 J. Hutton, *Theory of the earth with proofs and illustrations* (Edinburgh, 1795), quoted in: F. J. North, *The evolution of the Bristol Channel*, 3rd ed. (Cardiff, 1964), p. 2.
2 F. J. North, *op. cit.*, p. 4.
3 *Ibid.*
4 A. K. Wells and J. F. Kirkaldy, *Outline of historical geology*, 6th ed. (London, 1966), p. 29.
5 T. N. George, *British regional geology. South Wales*, 3rd ed. (London, 1970), p. 11.
6 F. J. North, *op. cit.*, p. 15.
7 *Ibid.*, Conjectural maps, pp. 22-24.
8 *Ibid.*, p. 17.
9 J. Storrie, *Barry Island and Ely Racecourse* (Cardiff, 1896), pp. 54-55.
10 A. Strahan and T. C. Cantrill, 'The country around Cardiff'. *Mem. Geol. Survey* 1912, part 2, p. 83, and F. T. Banner, M. Brooks and E. Williams, 'The geology of the approaches to Barry, Glamorgan', *Proc. Geol. Assoc.* 1971, 82, Fig. 3.
11 A. H. Cox and A. E. Trueman, 'The geological history of Glamorgan', in: W. M. Tattersall (ed.), *Glamorgan County History*, (Cardiff, 1936), Vol. 1, p. 35.
12 T. N. George, *op. cit.*, p. 76.
13 *Ibid.*, p. 84.
14 A. K. Wells and J. F. Kirkaldy, *op. cit.*, p. 257.
15 The theories of continental drift, plate tectonics and palaeomagnetism as mechanisms for geological events are now firmly established. See: I. G. Gass, P. J. Smith and R. C. L. Wilson (eds.), *Understanding the earth*, 2nd ed. (Open University, 1972), and R. Redfern, *The making of a continent* (London, 1983).
16 F. J. North, *op. cit.*, p. 29.
17 T. N. George, *op. cit.*, p. 111.
18 F. J. North, *op. cit.*, p. 34.
19 'Where dinosaurs walked'. National Museum of Wales, Museum Schools Service paper. A. J. Thomas, 'Triassic rocks of the Bendricks'. NMW MSS paper No. 1750.
20 F. J. North, *op. cit.*, p. 37.
21 *Ibid.*, p. 43.
22 *Ibid.*, p. 50.
23 O. T. Jones, 'Drainage system of Wales'. *Quart. J. Geol. Sci.* 1951, 107, pp. 201-225. Also T. N. George, *op. cit.*, p. 123.
24 *Ibid.*
25 *Ibid.*, p. 128.
26 A. Strahan and T. C. Cantrill, *op. cit.*, p. 77.
27 *Ibid.*, pp. 84-90, and J. Storrie, *op. cit.*, pp. 58-59.
28 F. J. North, *op. cit.*, p. 72.
29 *Ibid.*, p. 63.
30 F. T. Banner, M. Brooks, and E. Williams, *op. cit.*, p. 244.
31 *Ibid.*, Fig. 1.
32 F. J. North, *op. cit.*, p. 73.
33 *Severn Barrage Seminar*. Report of proceedings. Department of Energy, Energy Paper No. 27 (London, 1978), p. 47.
34 F. J. North, *op. cit.*, p. 83.

EXCAVATION OF
A ROMAN
MILITARY BASE

CHAPTER II

Before Barry began: Palaeolithic to Pre-Norman

GARETH DOWDELL

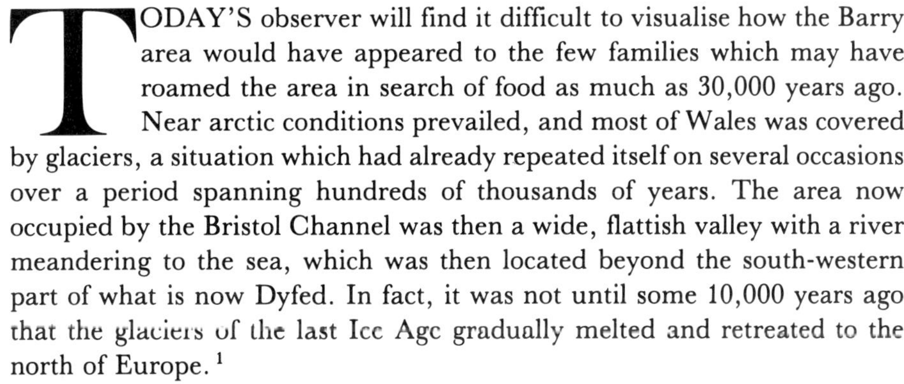

TODAY'S observer will find it difficult to visualise how the Barry area would have appeared to the few families which may have roamed the area in search of food as much as 30,000 years ago. Near arctic conditions prevailed, and most of Wales was covered by glaciers, a situation which had already repeated itself on several occasions over a period spanning hundreds of thousands of years. The area now occupied by the Bristol Channel was then a wide, flattish valley with a river meandering to the sea, which was then located beyond the south-western part of what is now Dyfed. In fact, it was not until some 10,000 years ago that the glaciers of the last Ice Age gradually melted and retreated to the north of Europe.[1]

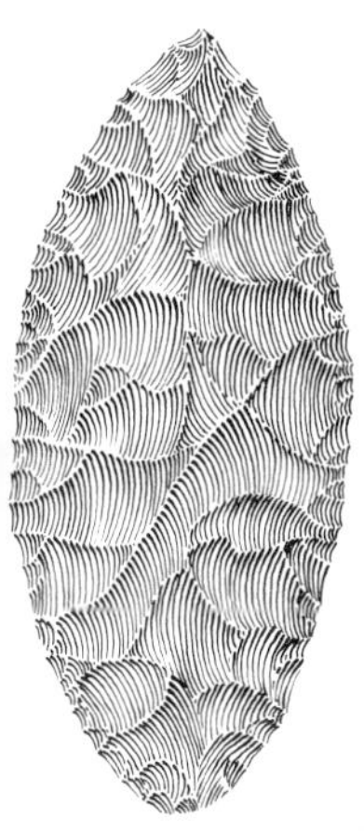

Leaf-shaped arrow-head from Friars Point, Barry Island. *J. Daly.*

Hunters of the Old Stone Age

The Gower peninsula, however, was apparently free of glaciers, and there, in a cave at Paviland, the first evidence of human habitation has been discovered. It should, however, be mentioned that a flint hand-axe, found at nearby Rhosili[2] and estimated to be between 125,000 and 75,000 years old, as well as another, possibly older, found on Pen-y-lan Hill, Cardiff,[3] must bear silent but adequate testimony to man's presence in Glamorgan long before Paviland's 'Red Lady' lived.[4]

The so-called 'Red Lady of Paviland', in fact a young man in his early twenties, was found by Dean Buckland in 1823 during one of the earliest recorded cave excavations conducted in Britain. Working within the 'Goat's Hole', Buckland uncovered parts of a human skeleton which had evidently been buried with some ceremony. The body, interred in a shallow grave, had been covered with red ochre, presumably to represent blood; hence the name given to the remains, which had become stained red. Accompanying the body were several objects, including fragments of rings and some rods

Plate IV. Excavation of Roman site at Glan-y-môr, Cold Knap, Barry, 1980. *Will Lewis.*

made from the ivory of mammoth tusk; the skull of a mammoth had been placed over the burial.[5]

The Paviland remains have been dated to about 16,500 b.c.[6] by the radio-carbon 14 method and therefore belong to a period referred to as the 'Upper Palaeolithic' or 'later Old Stone Age'. No other human remains and few man-made tools of this remote period of prehistory have been found in West or South Glamorgan.

From this scanty information a picture emerges of small groups of hunters occasionally visiting the fringes of ice-bound Wales, depending for food mainly on wild animals such as mammoth, oxen, horses and deer, with the addition of shellfish, berries, edible roots and nuts.[7] Given the climate and the attentions of various predators, such as bears, wolves and lions, life at this time must have been harsh and dangerous.

When the British Isles took shape

The encroachment of the sea to form what is now the Bristol Channel about 6,500 years ago began in what is called the 'Mesolithic' period, or 'Middle Stone Age'. During this time the British Isles became separated from the rest of Europe. The climate had improved and most of the country was covered by forests; it is probably to this period that the preserved trees and peat deposits found during the construction of Barry Docks in the last century belong.[8]

The period was characterised by tools manufactured from very small pieces of flint, now known as 'microliths'. These have been found at Friars Point, Barry Island, on the sea-eroded surface of that headland, and in plough-disturbed deposits at Coldbrook Fach[9] and Vianshill, near Wenvoe.[10]

Plate V.
Microliths from Friars Point, Barry Island. (Scale in millimetres.)
National Museum of Wales.

In contrast to the preceding period, there is now some evidence for settlement in Barry and the surrounding area. This is hardly surprising, as much of the food supply of Mesolithic man appears to have come from the sea; indeed, most of the known Welsh sites are located on the coast, including the two settlements at Burry Holms on the Gower peninsula, and Nab Head in Dyfed. At the latter site recent excavations have shown that the inhabitants were using microlithic tools and perforated hammers, and were decorating themselves with bead necklaces made of locally-obtained shale; their diet was mainly shellfish gathered from nearby beaches.

In the absence of investigation, it cannot be determined whether similar settlements existed in Barry, although the presence of microliths in the area does provide some indication of the possibility. The presence of two hearths and 'waste' flints overlying the natural rock surface at Coldbrook Fach might be argued as evidence for a settlement located beside a marshy lake in Mesolithic times, now Biglis Moors.[11] If so, it can be tentatively suggested that the settlement might have resembled the one excavated at Star Carr in Yorkshire. There archaeologists concluded that the settlement was seasonal, indicating a nomadic society, where the inhabitants hunted wild fowl and game, and fished from the lake alongside.[12]

The first farmers

From about 4,000 B.C. onward there occurred throughout the British Isles a transformation of the way that people lived, so far-reaching that it has been called the 'Neolithic Revolution'. Domesticated animals, such as goats and pigs, were gradually introduced from Europe, as well as the cultivation of cereals and legumes. A new type of stone-tool technology was developed, hence the term 'Neolithic' or 'New Stone Age'. Several fine polished axe-heads have been found in the Barry area, perhaps best exemplified by those found at St. Andrews Major, near Dinas Powys.[13] At this time pottery was first made.

Plate VI. Polished stone axe-head from St. Andrew's Major, near Dinas Powys. *National Museum of Wales.*

While many people were probably still nomadic, settlements of a more or less permanent nature began to appear. Their establishment would have coincided with the clearance of woodland for farming activities. At Coed-y-cymdda, near Wenvoe, the excavation of a hill-slope fort of Early Iron-Age date revealed on the old ground surface a number of broken flint axe-heads with other flint implements, thus demonstrating that the area was first cleared during the Neolithic period.[14] It is probable that Neolithic farmers employed the 'slash and burn' technique, *i.e.* cutting down trees and leaving them to dry before burning them.

Apart from Coed-y-cymdda, numerous scatters of flint tools and waste material have been found both in Barry, notably on the sea-eroded surface of Friars Point,[15] and in the surrounding district, especially in the Sully and Cog area. These finds suggest further land-use and settlements so far undetected. The nearest known settlement to Barry was discovered in 1952, by H. N. Savory, at Mount Pleasant, Newton Down, near Porthcawl.[16] Here, a rectangular dry-stone building, some 5·5 metres (18 feet) long and 2·5 metres (8 feet) wide was found underlying a later Bronze-Age burial cairn. It has been argued that the building probably had a gabled roof, covered with thatch, with the possibility of a protective clay bank on its south side.

No settlements of this period have been found in the Barry area, although the discovery of flint tools and bone needles during the construction of Barry Docks perhaps can be taken as evidence for their existence in the vicinity.

Fig. 9.
G. Beaudette, after R.C.A.H.M. & G.G.A.T.

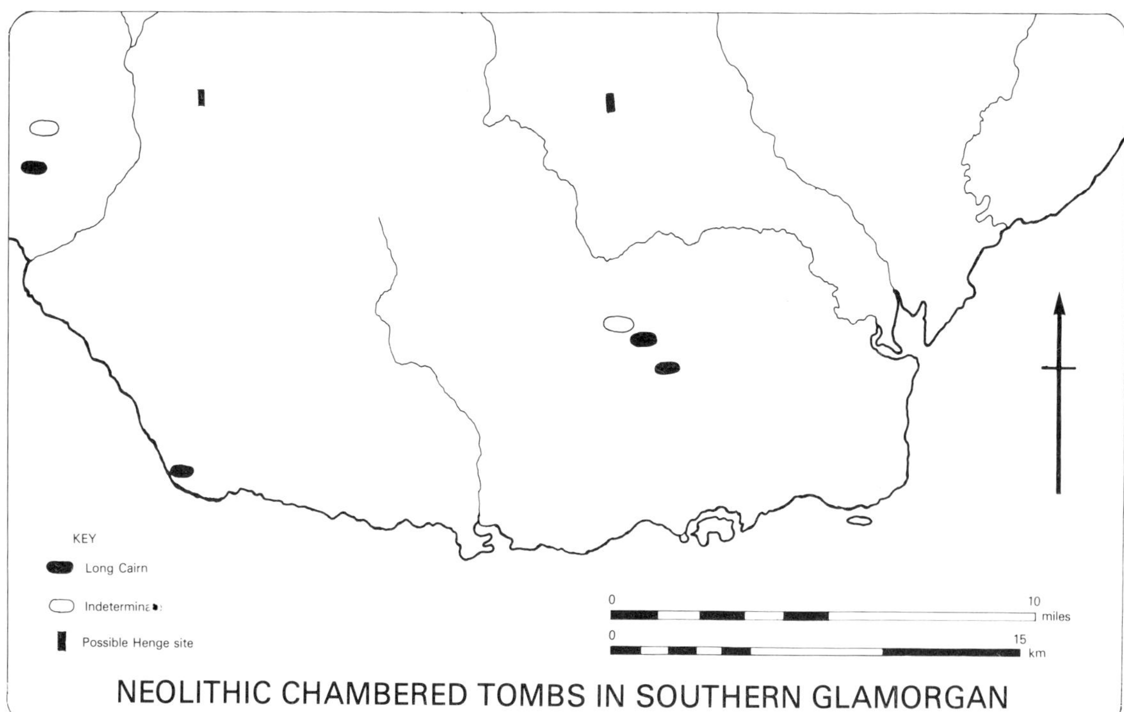

On the other hand, there exist two major monuments of a different significance, the magnificent stone-built, chambered tombs located at St. Lythan's and Tinkinswood, near Dyffryn. These tombs, probably built during the 4th millenium B.C., were communal burial places, a fact demonstrated at Tinkinswood, where the remains of at least 50 individuals were found by J. Ward during his excavations in 1914.[17]

Fig. 10. Forecourt of Tinkinswood burial chamber, as restored by excavator. *J. Daly.*

The construction of these tombs would even today be a major engineering task, for the Tinkinswood capstone is estimated to weigh about 40 tons, and a large number of persons would have been required to build such monuments. Elsewhere these people were also concerned with the construction of the first stages of other monuments on a greater scale, the world-renowned ritual complexes of Stonehenge and Avebury.

The achievement of Neolithic society in the construction of these monuments does, however, tend to overshadow equally great efforts in agriculture and its associated technology, notably spinning and weaving cloth, and in industrial processes. Stone axe-head 'factories' were established in many parts of Britain, including centres at Mynydd Rhiw and Penmaen-mawr, both in North Wales, while others are known from the Preseli Hills and on Ramsey Island. At such centres roughly-shaped axe-heads were produced from the locally-obtained hard rock and traded to distant localities where they were hand-polished to a smooth finish and ground to a sharp cutting edge.

The various finds and monuments from the Barry area reflect the presence of Neolithic man on a fair scale. Here for the first time man was making an impact upon his environment through his agricultural and constructional activities. Industries and trade developed, and possibly a priesthood and ruling class.

Archaeologists have long argued that Neolithic people, unlike those of the Iron Age, enjoyed a peaceful existence. This view has recently been challenged as a consequence of evidence from a number of excavated sites, particularly Crickley Hill in Gloucestershire, which suggests that tribal warfare may have been commonplace. However, no such evidence has emerged in the Barry area.

The first metal-workers

Some 1,000 years after the construction of the Tinkinswood burial chamber the first metal users began to settle in the British Isles. These people are known as the 'Beaker folk', from the distinctive pottery vessels deposited with the burials of their dead; the burials were individual inhumations within a round mound of earth or stones, in contrast to the collective burials of the Neolithic period in large chambered tombs.

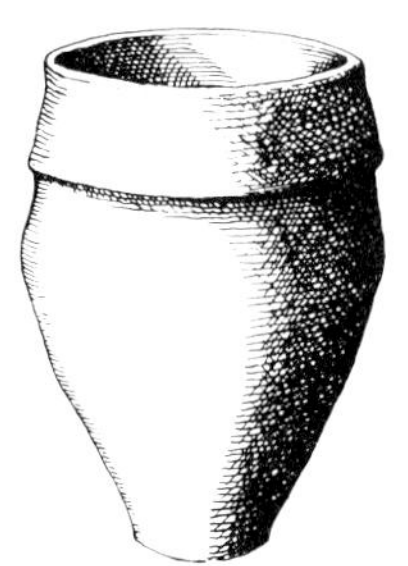

Fig. 11.
Bronze-Age urn from Friars Point, Barry Island.
J. Daly.

Later in the Bronze Age the cremation of the dead became common; the ashes were interred within a pottery urn; an example was found by J. Romilly Allen on Friars Point, Barry Island, during the last century.[18]

Within the Early Bronze Age or Beaker period, the use of metal seems to have been confined to the production of small dagger blades and a flat type of axe. These were produced in simple moulds; copper was used at first, but was later mixed with tin to give bronze. Flint continued to be used extensively for arrowheads, knives and scrapers; arrowheads are well exemplified by the magnificent 'barbed and tanged' types found during the excavation of a burial mound, or 'barrow', at Breach Farm, Llanblethian, near Cowbridge. In the immediate area of Barry flint tools and arrowheads of Bronze-Age date have been found at Biglis, Sully, Cosmeston and Friars Point, among many locations.[19]

Fig. 12.
G. Beaudette, after R.C.A.H.M. & G.G.A.T.

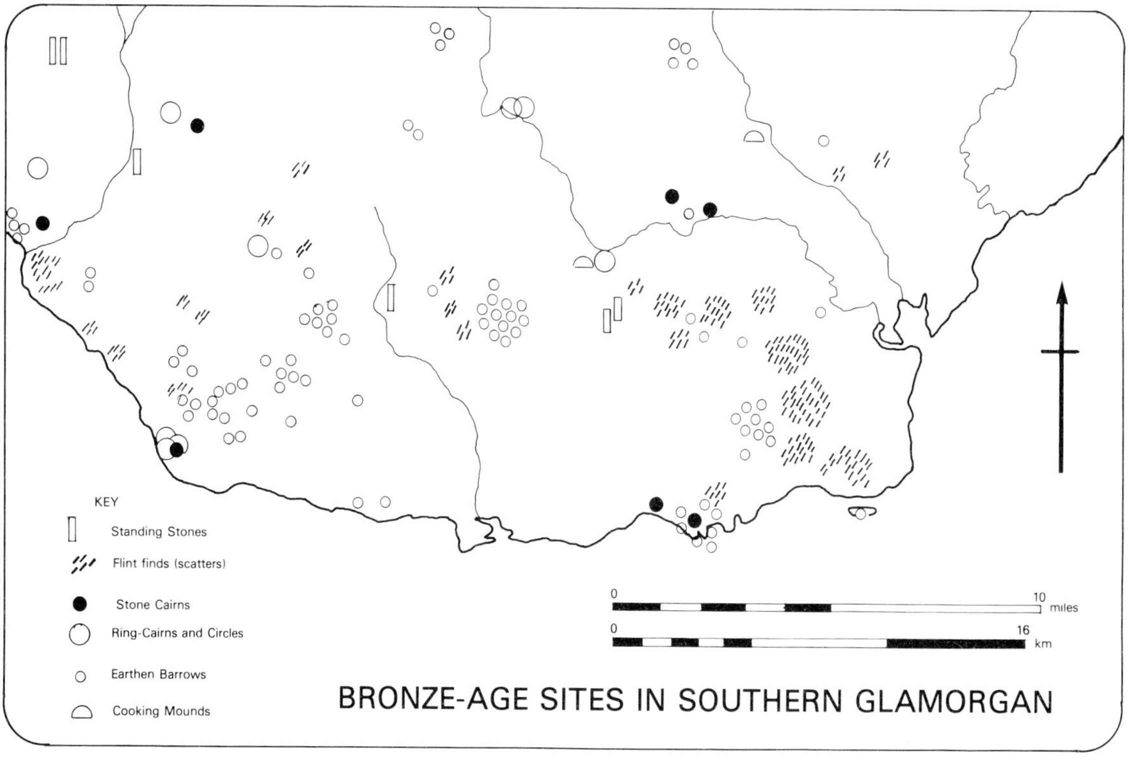

KEY
Standing Stones
Flint finds (scatters)
Stone Cairns
Ring-Cairns and Circles
Earthen Barrows
Cooking Mounds

0 10 miles
0 16 km

BRONZE-AGE SITES IN SOUTHERN GLAMORGAN

Bronze-Age barrows are known on Friars Point and Cold Knap Point, at Pencoedtre and on Sully Island, but only those on Friars Point have been the subject of archaeological excavations, poorly conducted in the 19th century by J. Romilly Allen and later re-examined by John Storrie.[20] In total, there are fourteen such burial mounds recorded in the Barry area, and of these one on Cold Knap Point has produced two cinerary urns.[21]

Plate VII.
Flint arrowheads, knives and scrapers from Friars Point, Barry Island.
(Scale in millimetres.)
National Museum of Wales.

While a wealth of objects and barrows has appeared both in Barry and its district, few settlements belonging to the period are known. On Merthyr Mawr Warren there is conclusive evidence of settlement, but only at Saint-y-nyll, near St. Brides-super-Ely has the presence of buildings been archaeologically attested.[22] Here, as at Newton Down, underlying a later barrow (of Bronze-Age date), were the remains of three buildings, designated by the excavator as Huts A, B and C. The latest and largest, Hut A, was like the other two, oval in plan, and measured about 4·6 by 3·7 metres (15 by 9 feet). It was constructed of timber uprights, presumably covered with wattle and daub (woven branches covered with a mixture of clay and animal dung).

It would seem that Hut A was still standing, although probably not in use, when the barrow was constructed. The pottery recovered from the settlement site suggests that it may have belonged to the Early Bronze Age with secondary Neolithic affinities.[23]

Although settlements have for the most part eluded the archaeologist, evidence of widespread activity during this period of Barry's past is to be adduced from many scattered flint tools, mainly recovered from ploughed fields in the present day. Bronze-Age life continued with little change, although the warmer climate, which began in the preceding period, must have increased the area available for agricultural activities. This is well demonstrated in the upland region of Mid Glamorgan and further north.[24]

As the Bronze Age progressed, a change in religious ceremony can be deduced from burial practices. A water deity is implied by the deliberate deposit of bronze objects in rivers, lakes and bogs. This must have been the case with the hoard of material belonging to the late Bronze Age and Early Iron Age found in Llyn Fawr, Mid Glamorgan. Here objects ranging from axe-heads to cauldrons and sickles had been deposited in a small lake.[25]

A new religious development is represented by the erection of large, upright standing stones, of which less than 25 survive today in the area covered by the former county of Glamorgan. The majority are found in Gower, although examples are known near Barry, at Cowbridge and St. Nicholas. While few of these have been archaeologically investigated, recent excavation at Devil's Point on Stackpole Warren in Dyfed have revealed a complex arrangement of other, smaller stones around the main monument and traces of a fairly substantial timber building in association.[26]

During the Bronze Age other changes no doubt occurred within society, leading to well-defined tribal groupings. It has recently been suggested that geographical boundaries within which individual tribes settled may be defined on the east and west sides of the Thaw valley. The apparent differences in burial practices observed within the Llanblethian barrow group, and in a burial recently examined at Welsh St. Donat's[27] are used as evidence to support this theory.[28] It may well be that the barrows of the Barry area represent a separate tribal group, their land boundary delimited perhaps by the Weycock Valley.

Hillfort builders of the Early Iron Age

The first iron-using people began to arrive in Wales from about 600 B.C. onward. The archaeological record now becomes clearer. The excavation of Iron-Age settlements in the vicinity of Barry has produced a comparative wealth of information, which, taken with similar work elsewhere, has allowed a reasonable reconstruction of everyday life before the Roman conquest of Wales. Written evidence now begins to supplement the archaeological. These iron-using people occupied most of Western Europe and Britain, sharing a common identity as Celts. References in Latin and Greek literature are an important source of information about the peoples of Britain, even though they themselves were non-literate.

Settlements of this period, whether in the neighbourhood of Barry or elsewhere in Wales, can be divided into two broad categories. The first comprises large defended enclosures, the biggest of which are called hillforts; good examples are on the headland at Dunraven, which covered about 25 acres (10·1 hectares) and, nearer Barry, the Bulwarks at Porthkerry, which was once about 10·1 acres (4·1 hectares) in extent.

Fig. 13.
G. Beaudette, after R.C.A.H.M. & G.G.A.T.

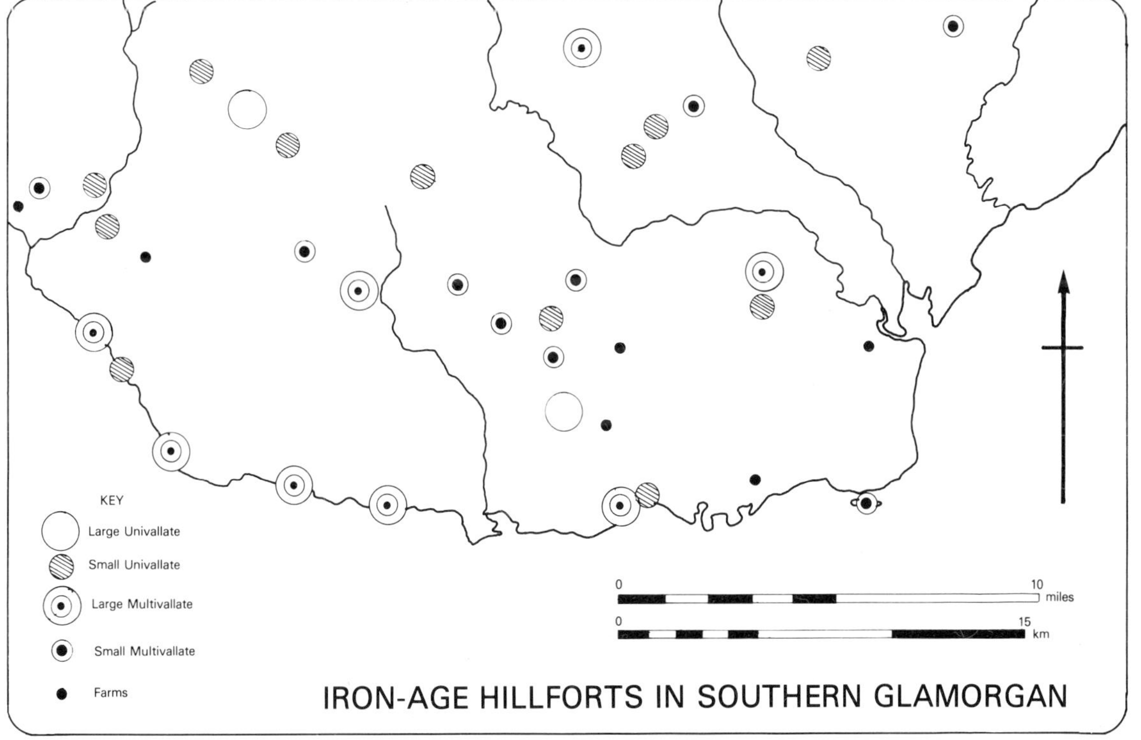

The second category encompasses small defended enclosures and undefended settlements, ranging in size from less than one acre to about four. An excellent example of the defended type has been fully excavated at Whitton, a few miles to the north of Barry.[29] The settlement found beneath the Roman villa at Llandough in 1979 may also be of this type; traces of a ditch enclosing a circular timber hut were noted, but only partly examined.[30] Undefended settlements are mostly found in lowland Glamorgan but there was one at Moulton,[31] found beneath the Roman villa, and at Biglis,[32] a site which has been fully excavated in recent years.

Owing to the lack of a thorough and extensive programme of investigation into the larger hillforts in Glamorgan it is not possible to suggest, as has been done elsewhere in Britain, that these large, defended settlements fulfilled the same function as towns.[33] Of the hillforts located near Barry selective excavations have been conducted at a site of 10·4 acres (4·2 hectares) known as Castle Ditches, near Llancarfan,[34] while at the Bulwarks, Porthkerry, some 200 square metres has been examined.[34] Consequently, in order to understand the role of the hillfort, it is necessary to turn to other sites in Wales which have been intensively excavated. One of the most interesting sites is Moel-y-gaer in Clwyd, the interior of which totalled some 3,000 square metres. The site was excavated during the 1970s and revealed among other things, traces of nearly 70 timber buildings, some round, some rectangular.[36]

If Moel-y-gaer is taken as representative, it can be suggested that the hillforts around Barry were intensively occupied, and contained many buildings; that they served as centres of refuge in times of unrest, and that they performed some administrative role. It has been suggested that Caer Dynnaf hillfort near Cowbridge, by virtue of its nearly central position within the Vale of Glamorgan, may have been a tribal capital.[37]

Whatever the role of these large, defended sites, there is less uncertainty about the smaller settlements, or farmsteads, which prospered towards the end of the first millenium B.C. and continued during and after the period of the Roman conquest. At Whitton, excavation has demonstrated that occupation began about A.D. 30, while the farmstead at Biglis commenced slightly later, as did Llandough. At each of these sites, whether defended by a simple bank and ditch or not, the structures in which the occupants resided and carried out various activities, presumably connected mainly with agriculture, were fairly large, timber-constructed, round houses with thatched roofs; the walling was of woven branches, cracks in which were smeared over with a mixture of clay and sometimes animal manure. During the Romano-British period, from the 2nd century A.D. the timber structures at Whitton and Llandough were gradually replaced by stone buildings, while at Biglis timber continued to be the chief building material throughout its occupation. From the excavations at the former two sites it has been shown that the occupants were engaged both in the raising of livestock—cattle, pigs, sheep or goats—and in the sowing of crops. The occurrence at these sites of pottery vessels, very similar both in shape and decoration to examples found on the opposite side of the Bristol Channel, known as 'Glastonbury ware', argues for either cross-channel trading, or at least cultural contacts outside the immediate area, activities which are attested in later periods and in modern times.

Other sites of this period worthy of mention which have recently come to light in Barry include a possible Early Iron-Age farmstead, perhaps dating from the 4th century B.C., found during the construction of the College of Further Education off Colcot Road.[38] At Victoria Park, Cadoxton,[39] there have been numerous finds of Iron-Age pottery in the flower beds of the park; in addition, a rock-cut ditch was observed during cable-laying work near Cadoxton School. The area overlooks and in some respects dominates the surrounding landscape, and it is tempting to suggest that some substantial settlement existed here, perhaps even a hillfort.

On the eve of the Roman conquest of Wales, the picture which emerges of life in the Barry area is of iron-using people living in large farmsteads and in hillforts sited either on cliff-tops or hills. The inhabitants of the farmsteads at Biglis, Whitton and Llandough exploited the land on a larger scale than in previous times; a situation repeated in the Romano-British period. The Severn Sea offered a highway to both Celt and Roman for communication, trade and war.

While little of note has been found in the immediate area of Barry to illustrate the artistic craftsmanship of this period it is clear from discoveries made elsewhere in Wales that a section of society had appeared to which the term 'artisan' can be correctly applied. The magnificent workmanship of the enamelled bronzes from Seven Sisters, Neath,[40] the graceful flow of the decoration of the tankard from Trawsfynydd, Gwynedd, are but a few examples of the high-quality craftsmanship achieved by these Celtic people in Wales.

The emergence of artisans implies that other sections of society in Iron-Age Wales could produce enough wealth to support their services. Julius Caesar, in his account of the Gallic wars, stated that the social orders in Celtic society were princes, warriors and slaves. Such a simplified view of a complex social structure can be understood by realising that Caesar was viewing the Celtic people when the upper classes were engaged in warfare and all others were assisting the war effort. Of great importance to Iron-Age society were the religious leaders, known as Druids, who taught through oral tradition; they venerated various gods and instilled a belief in transmigration of souls.[41]

This pattern of society cannot fully describe the situation in the Barry area. The various farmsteads around imply the presence of farmers, shepherds and herdsmen, in effect, a class to which the term 'yeoman' could in many respects apply. One positive fact about the local people is known from the evidence of classical writers; the tribe inhabiting south-east Wales was known as the Silures. They were renowned for their fierce and warlike ways, and the Romans, during their invasion, were to learn much to their cost about those qualities.[42]

The coming of the Romans

Less than thirty years ago any attempt to write a chapter concerning the Roman occupation of the Barry area would have been doomed to failure owing to the paucity of information then available. It would have been possible to make some reference to the coin hoard found on Sully Moors,[43] to discuss the villas at Ely[44] and Llantwit Major,[45] all found during the late 19th century, and perhaps make some observations on the role of the fort at Cardiff,[46] but little else could have been achieved. It was not until the late 1950s that a radical transformation occurred in our knowledge of Roman settlement in the low-lying area of Glamorgan where Barry is situated. Exactly why this part of Wales was so long considered part of the military frontier has always been a puzzle to the author. The answer may lie in the classical education and military background of many of the Roman scholars who involved themselves in the archaeology of Roman Wales. It is significant that John Storrie who first investigated these villas had no military background whatsoever. More recently, fieldwork, notably by H. J. Thomas and others, followed later by

Fig. 14. *G. Beaudette, after R.C.A.M. & G.G.A.T.*

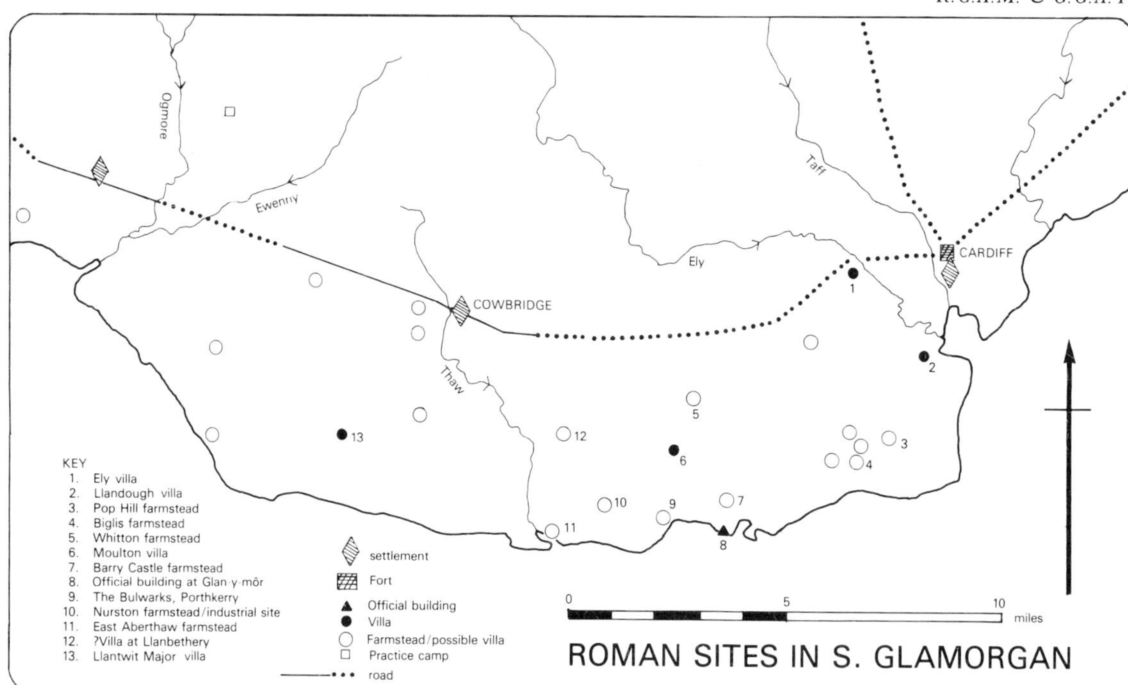

excavation, especially at Whitton[47] and Llandough[48] demonstrated that the district was as densely settled by civilian population as any other comparable area of Roman Britain. It is thus possible to recreate a fairly clear picture of settlement in the area following the Roman conquest of South Wales.

Although the Roman invasion of Britain began in A.D. 43 under the Emperor Claudius, it was not until A.D. 55-60 that the initial steps were taken, probably by the 20th Legion, towards capturing the territory of the Silures of south-east Wales. Excavations have shown that by that time a large military base had been established at Usk from which troops were able to move westward as far as Cardiff.[49] It is possible that the land-based troops may have been supported by a seaborne invasion, and while there is no evidence as yet, the excellent harbour facilities at Barry may have assisted such an operation. It was not however until the governorship of Sextus Julius Frontinus (A.D. 74-78), when a new legionary fortress was established at Caerleon, that a determined and final assault on the Silures was actually undertaken.[50] Throughout south-east Wales and beyond, a series of forts manned by auxiliary troops and linked by a system of roads was built to ensure the subjugation of native tribes.

Auxiliary forts had been established by the end of the 1st century A.D. at a number of locations including Cardiff, Neath, Loughor, Abergavenny and Gelli-gaer. Another fort, called Bovium, or Bomium, in written sources, also existed somewhere between Cardiff and Neath.[51] Recent excavations in Cowbridge by the Glamorgan-Gwent Archaeological Trust have brought to light tiles bearing the official stamp of the 2nd Augustan Legion and pieces of military-style metalwork. This strongly suggests that Cowbridge is the missing fort. The discovery of a substantial bath-house to the north of the town reinforces this hypothesis.[52]

From about A.D. 120 onward many of the forts were being abandoned and the troops stationed elsewhere, especially in north Britain, to take part in the construction and manning of Hadrian's Wall. A more or less permanent presence was, however, maintained for some time at Caerleon, the base of the 2nd Augustan Legion.

In the second half of the 3rd century A.D., perhaps coinciding with the reign of the usurper Carausius (*c.* A.D. 287-293) and his deputy Allectus, a new fort had already been constructed at Cardiff, similar in many respects to those forts such as Portchester or Pevensey on the south coast of England, commonly referred to as 'Saxon Shore' forts.[53] It has been argued that these were constructed in association with the British Fleet to act as a defence against Saxon raiders, and also as a response to the threat of invasion to Carausius' domain by the legitimate emperor, Constantius Chlorus. The fort at Cardiff might have been built in response to Irish raiders threatening the civilian population along the coasts of the Bristol

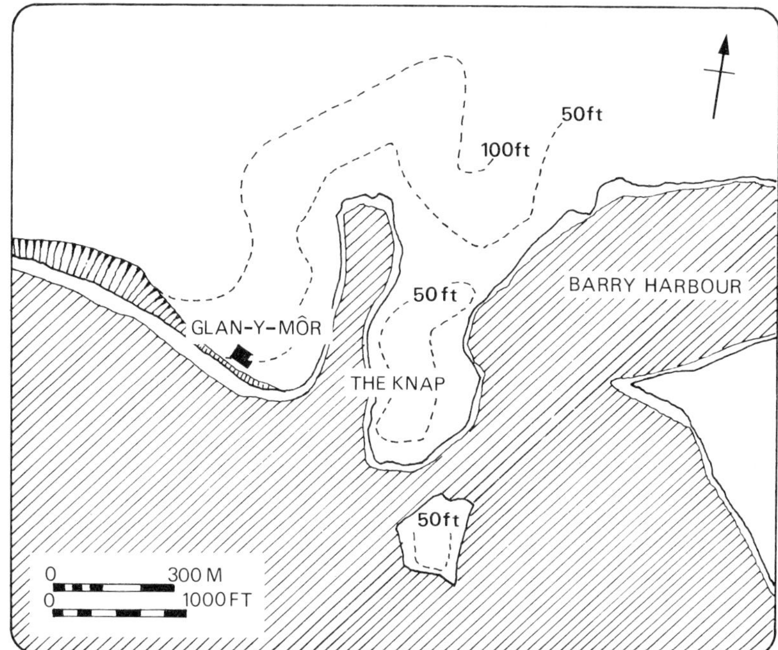

Fig. 15. Location map of Glan-y-môr, Barry, with coastline as it might have appeared in Roman times. *C. Farrow, after G. Beaudette.*

Channel. Elsewhere in Wales, the high incidence of coin hoards of this period suggests either a period of instability, perhaps arising as a result of resistance by the population to Carausius' reign or as a consequence of uncertainty through increased military activity. It is roughly about this time that the building at Glan-y-môr, Cold Knap, was constructed.[54]

On present evidence it would appear that by the end of the 4th century A.D. the Roman military presence in Wales was at an end. Roman troops were needed to repel enemies confronting the Empire elsewhere in Europe, and the last departure was the culmination of a process in which manpower had been drained from the province of Britain by successive usurpers laying claim to the title of Emperor.

Not only forts were constructed in Wales. Civilian settlements were established—a tribal capital at Caerwent for the Silures,[55] and one further west at Carmarthen for the Demetae, the tribe who inhabited Dyfed.[56] Small towns may well have developed at other centres; Cowbridge has been suggested as a possible township. A type of civilian settlement more than adequately attested is the farmstead. The examples at Biglis[57] and Dinas Powys were scarcely distinguishable from their Iron-Age counterparts.

There were well-built villas of the Roman type with central-heating systems, bath blocks and decorated walls and floors, such as those at Llantwit Major and Ely. Between these two extremes lies yet another type of site exemplified by Whitton (occupied probably continuously from A.D.

30 to 340), which displayed certain elements of Roman taste but cannot be regarded as a true villa, although it undoubtedly served the same function, that of a Romanised farm.

In Barry proper, farmsteads are known to have existed at Biglis and on the site of Barry Castle. A larger settlement, probably representing a number of farmsteads, was situated within and without the modern boundaries of Victoria Park, Cadoxton. At those sites occupation probably commenced towards the end of the 1st century A.D. and lasted certainly until the middle of the 4th century A.D., and may well, in the case of Biglis, have continued for some time afterwards. Similar farmsteads are known from a variety of locations, including Dinas Powys Common, partially examined in recent years, Swanbridge,[58] Pop Hill[59] and Little Greave near Wenvoe. At all these the archaeological evidence suggests an economy based on cattle-rearing and crops, perhaps only slightly above subsistence level. At the other end of the scale the occupants of the villas at Llantwit Major and Ely, and most probably Llandough, enjoyed a much higher standard of living. One view recently put forward is that the inhabitants of the poorer farmsteads may have been tenants on large estates centred upon the villas.

Irrespective of the organisation of land division, tenancy and ownership, it is clear that the Barry region was well populated and its agricultural resources well utilised during this period. In addition to agricultural production, there is evidence to show that mineral resources were also being exploited; the presence of iron ore and slag on many sites in the area and in particular at Cowbridge, together with actual iron objects, shows that iron deposits were being extensively utilised. The presence of Roman coins and pottery from the galena-rich area of Goldsland Wood, near Wenvoe, argues for the mining and smelting of lead, an activity attested for this period at Lower Machen.[60] To these can be added the use of coal, as was discovered at the villa at Ely and to a lesser degree at Pop Hill. Elsewhere in Wales gold, silver and copper were being commercially exploited.

Apart from civilian settlements and mineral extraction, chance finds from Barry other than the Sully coin hoard (A.D. *c.* 211-296)[61] include Roman building materials, tiles and bricks in the mud of the Old Harbour. There are tantalising, albeit verbal accounts suggesting the existence of a cemetery on ground now occupied by the Atlantic Trading Estate. Here during the construction of the former Supply Reserve Depot (now the trading estate) workmen unearthed human remains, some of which were contained within lead coffins bearing scallop-shell impressed decoration, identical with Roman types from many sites in Britain. Regrettably, no proper record of this important discovery was made; the lead was cut up and sold for scrap. The evidence concerning the discovery of the Sully coin hoard has also been used to suggest that the hoard was found in the same general area as the above objects. The presence of skeletal remains found with the hoard further strengthens this possibility.

Evidence for Roman occupation in Barry has been observed at both St. Barruc's Chapel and St. Nicholas' Church, where re-used Roman tiles and bricks were incorporated into the fabric of both buildings.[62] To this can be added the partial excavation of a drystone building in Victoria Park Road, found during housebuilding, and provisionally dated to the 2nd and 3rd centuries. Pottery of this date has been found near the King William IV Hotel in Cadoxton, once again during building operations, while Roman coins were also noted by John Storrie during his programme of excavations on Barry Island between 1894 and 1895.[63] Excavations of more recent date, but of limited scale, within the Iron-Age promontory fort of the Bulwarks demonstrated that the site was occupied during the late 1st and 2nd centuries. It may have been a farmstead contained within earlier defences but absence of large-scale investigation makes interpretation difficult.[64] The evidence, however, from the Cae Summerhouse (Tythegston) homestead would incline towards confirming such a suggestion. Here excavation revealed a number of features, including a corn-dryer and pens for livestock, demonstrating the type of settlement which appears to have continued from the latter years of the 1st century A.D. until the middle of the 4th century A.D.[65] Similar activity is also suggested at Castle Ditches, near Llancarfan and at Caer Dynnaf, near Cowbridge.[66]

Fig. 16.
Roman tile with impression of stud marks of military footwear, from St. Nicholas' Church.
Simon Prosser.

One problem which has yet to be resolved satisfactorily is the reason for the abandoning of the villas of Ely, Llandough and Whitton, the first two within the first quarter of the 4th century and the latter by about A.D. 340. At Llantwit Major, however, it now appears that the villa was enjoying a period of prosperity in A.D. 340-50, which enabled the occupants to continue villa life in some form until the end of the 4th century. Why this situation arose is difficult to understand; the answer may lie in the reorganisation of the agricultural and/or administrative area, possibly an effect of the manpower shortage felt elsewhere in the Western Roman Empire during the 4th century, or simply a reflection of successful private enterprise by the occupants of the Llantwit Major villa. Lower down the social scale the people at Biglis appear to have continued to farm successfully after those at Whitton and Ely as well as Llandough had succumbed.

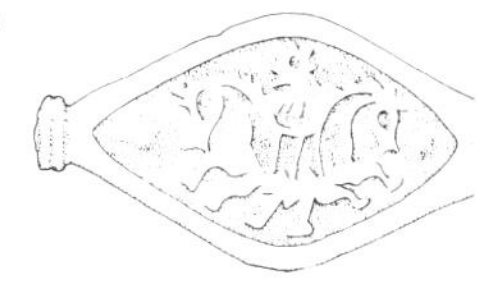

Fig. 17.
Celto-Roman brooch from Biglis.
J. Daly.

In contrast to farmsteads, villas and re-occupied hillforts there is another site in Barry that is perhaps unique in Roman Wales and in Britain as a whole, the Roman building (now preserved) at Glan-y-môr, Cold Knap.

Overlooking Pebble Beach and the boating lake, which was once a small harbour, the site was first discovered in 1960 during the construction of the Waters Edge Hotel.[67] It was not, however, until twenty years later, during the summer of 1980, that the extent of the building was at last realised.

Fig. 18.
Potter's stamp: DOCILIS (2nd century A.D.) from Glan-y-môr.
J. Daly.

Excavation then, and in the following year, showed that the building was originally composed of 22 rooms and cellars, divided into four ranges around a central courtyard, within which was a stone-built verandah. The entire building had been planned as one integral unit and was constructed of local Lias Limestone bonded with a characteristic pinkish mortar. The roofing, unlike other Roman buildings in the area, was exclusively of pottery tiles. Access to the building was *via* the south side, along which ran a trackway that had been constructed in front of the building and was supported by a retaining wall of large pebbles and limestone blocks.

The absence of any refinements such as a bath-block, heating system, water supply, or domestic apartments, i.e. a kitchen or accommodation range, and the fact that the building was not a piece-meal development, like so many civilian enterprises, argues that the building had some official use. If so, the date of construction is of paramount importance to its interpretation. All the evidence points to its having been erected towards the end of the 3rd century A.D., a period noted for the emergence of the usurper Carausius, and it is tempting to interpret the Cold Knap building as belonging to his reign. We know from other locations in Wales, especially at Cardiff, that there was considerable activity by the military at this time and it may well be that Barry figured in a re-organisation of the defences of the area. Carausius undoubtedly based his main line of defence on the sea to counter any invasion by the legitimate emperor—he was a capable naval

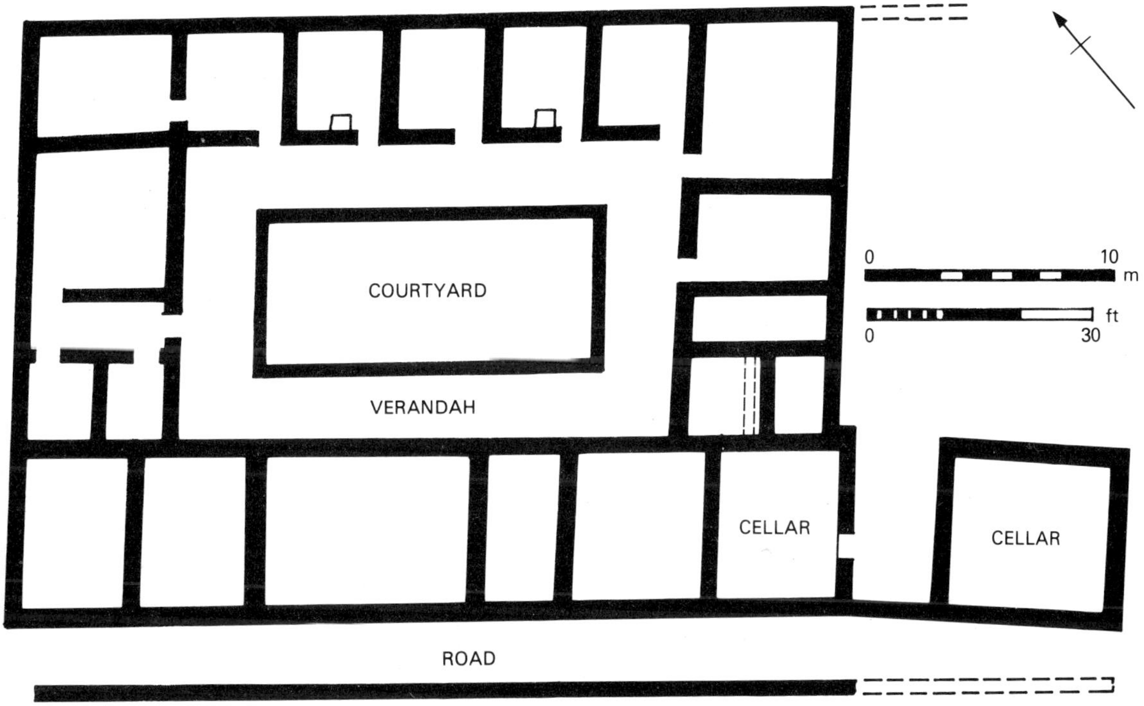

Fig. 19.
Glan-y-môr, Barry. Plan of Roman building.
H. J. Thomas, after G.G.A.T.

commander and it is unlikely that the excellent harbour afforded at Barry would have escaped his or his local commander's attention. The building was probably a store. Given its location, adjacent to a small harbour, sited in the most southerly part of Wales and commanding excellent views of the Bristol Channel, it was possibly connected with naval activity. Whatever the case may be, and we can never be absolutely sure, the building was constructed quickly and might never have been completed, indications that can be interpreted to support the connections with Carausius. We can also be certain that within a short time, perhaps only a few years, the building was systematically stripped of its fittings and deliberately demolished, its ruins being later occupied, probably by squatters, during the second half of the 4th century and again later.

Fig. 20. Coin of Roman Emperor Allectus (A.D. 293-6). *J. Daly.*

Fig. 21. Conjectural reconstruction of Roman building at Glan-y-môr, Barry. *J. Daly.*

The archaeological record for Barry and the surrounding area in the Roman period can thus be seen to be full and varied, ranging from native farmsteads to luxurious villas, and also containing a unique, if enigmatic building, without parallel in the province of Britannia. From the beginning of the conquest in the second half of the 1st century A.D. to the end of the 4th century at least, the area participated in virtually every aspect of Romanised life, and if the archaeological record for the post-Roman settlement of Dinas Powys is correct, it continued in some form even after direct imperial rule had ceased.

Celtic saints and early Christianity

The ending of Roman rule in Britain early in the 5th century A.D. heralded a new era, called by some historians 'The Dark Ages' and by others 'the Early Christian period'. It continued in Wales up to the Norman invasions in the 11th and 12th centuries. Thanks to the work of historians and archaeologists during the last thirty years, major advances have been made in our knowledge of this obscure period. The Barry area has itself received attention, notably with the archaeological investigation of sites at Dinas Powys, Llandough, near Penarth, and Glan-y-môr at Cold Knap, Barry.

Christianity had reached Britain during the Roman period and was well established in many places, though there is no direct evidence of its presence in the Barry area. Romano-British Christianity received a severe set-back when Rome relinquished control of the British provinces; by the 7th century pagan Anglo-Saxons had settled in much of England, making it difficult for Wales and south-west Britain to maintain contact with the catholic mainstream of Christianity on the Continent. In this situation distinctive forms of Christian observance grew up in the Celtic west—in Wales, Ireland and Scotland, and these practices lasted in Wales until the Norman Conquest.

The faith was spread in the early days by some remarkable individuals, well versed in Christian doctrine, who were known as 'saints'. They were often skilled in worldly knowledge too, and could exercise great influence on the course of secular events by their force of character and their personal connections. Many stories of their adventures and achievements were embodied in biographies which were not written down until several centuries after their lifetimes. Miraculous elements were woven in, and by today it is hard to distinguish fact from fable. Churches were dedicated to these saints rather than to apostolic saints, and their personal names became part of the place-name, often prefixed with 'Llan'. This was applied originally to the religious establishment, but later to the settlement which grew up in the vicinity. 'Llantwit Major' is a form of 'Llanilltud Fawr'—'the principal church of St. Illtud'. This saint had a reputation for a profound knowledge of the scriptures, the classics and Celtic lore, and was said to have kept a monastic college at Llantwit Major in the 5th century. Another monastic establishment was traditionally sited at Llancarfan, though here the place-name is misleading—it originated as 'Nantcarfan', 'the Carfan brook'. The founder was St. Cadoc, whose name appears in 'Cadoxton', (Welsh 'Tregatwg'—'the settlement of Cadoc'). In Breton tradition Cadoc is said to have been a 'prince of Glamorgan'. Certainly these Celtic 'saints' travelled widely by sea in the west, and dedications of churches to them fall into patterns which could indicate their respective spheres of influence The name 'Merthyr Dyfan' indicates the shrine of

St. Dyfan (*merthyr* or *martyrium* does not mean a 'place of martyrdom', but a 'shrine' where some of the saint's bones were preserved).

The place-name 'Barry' is held by some to be derived from a St. Baruch or Barruc, possibly an Irishman. The remains of a medieval chapel named after him are to be seen on Barry Island; they were excavated in the late 19th century by John Storrie and more recently re-examined by J. K. Knight on behalf of the Welsh Office.[68]

There has been much discussion over the origins of the place-names of the area. Many of them undoubtedly came into existence in this period, but they are not necessarily Welsh. Scandinavian influence was evident at times. Two islands in the Bristol Channel—Flat Holm and Steep Holm—have a Scandinavian second element, and a local writer, D. R. Paterson, earlier in the present century saw Viking and Danish elements in many Glamorgan place-names. 'Cog' and 'Cogan' he derived ftom a Danish word meaning 'a piece of marsh land'. He suggested that Scandinavians had come not only to raid but to settle.[69]

Monastic establishments and churches are often mentioned in the *Lives* of the saints, but no tangible remains have been found locally. No doubt buildings were usually made of perishable materials such as wood, wattle and daub, which would decay without trace or could easily be cleared away for building in stone on the site at a later date. One curious survival in the Vale of Glamorgan may embody a Dark-Age building tradition—the circular pigsty, made of dry stones.[70] This resembles the round cells made by Irish monks in Irish monastic sites known to belong to the Dark Ages.

The apparent lack of identifiable ecclesiastical sites has long puzzled archaeologists. In a recent study a possible solution has been offered. The Roman villas at Llantwit Major and Llandough have yielded evidence that their sites were used as cemeteries in the post-Roman period, an occurrence widely noted elsewhere in Britain, particularly in the West Country. It is tempting to suggest that settlements developed after the Roman period adjacent to the villa sites, and that some of these represented early Christian foundations, i.e. the monasteries of persons such as Illtud or Dochdwy. Of particular importance in this context is a recent contribution by Dr. Wendy Davies, who draws upon documentary evidence to suggest that Celtic monasteries might well have their origins in villa estates.[71] Such a possibility has long been argued in England in respect of Anglo-Saxon estates.

Fig. 22. Cross of Irbic, Llandough-juxta-Penarth. *G. Beaudette.*

Early Christian memorial stones bearing inscriptions or carved designs exist in many places in Wales; two important groups are at Llantwit Major and Margam. The stones range in date from the 5th to the 11th centuries. An incomplete carved cross bearing the name 'Irbic' stands at Llandough, near Penarth, within the churchyard of St. Dochdwy's church. It has been dated to the late 10th or early 11th century.[72] No example, however, has come to light in Barry or its immediate vicinity.

In the Barry area archaeological investigations have revealed the existence of two secular settlements of the Dark Ages. At Cwrt-yr-ala, near Dinas Powys, excavations in the 1950s revealed the remains of a fortified settlement occupied from the 5th to the 7th century A.D.,[73] while at Glan-y-môr, Cold Knap, the remains of a building constructed some time between A.D. 830 and 950 were found overlying the late 3rd-century Roman building. Radio-carbon dates obtained from samples taken from another part of the Roman building suggested some form of occupation in the 6th and 7th centuries A.D.

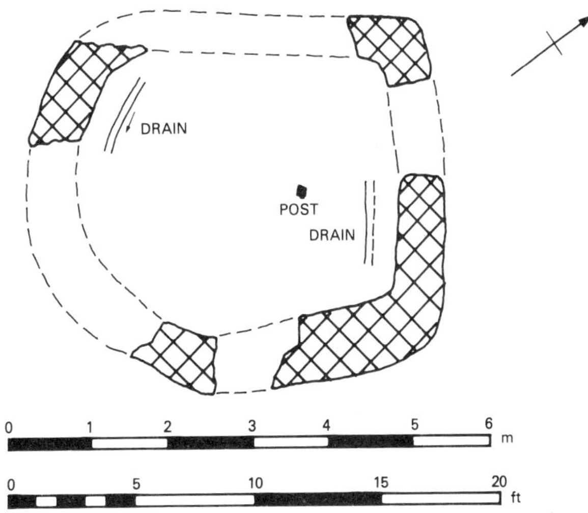

Fig. 23.
Glan-y-môr, Barry.
Plan of 10th-century hut.
H. J. Thomas, after G.G.A.T.

Over twenty-five years after its excavation, the Dinas Powys settlement remains the most comprehensively examined and best understood Dark-Age site in Wales. Dr. Leslie Alcock in his masterly study of the evidence obtained from his excavation concluded that the site was the residence of a petty king or prince. Living within a drystone-built hall, covered with a thatched or turfed roof, the occupants enjoyed a 'sub-Roman' style of life. Pottery vessels (some probably containing wine or olive oil) were imported from France, North Africa and western Asia Minor, as is testified by shards found among the rubbish. The site was defended by a simple bank and ditch, located on a steeply-sloping spur of high ground. In addition to the pottery evidence, metal-working debris, including scrap-metal and glass, indicated the existence of a jeweller working on the site, no doubt enjoying the patronage of the prince. Iron-making and the working of leather and bones were also noted among the many activities conducted there during the period of the 5th-7th centuries A.D.

The large quantity of young animal bones found within the settlement, especially those of pig, led Alcock to identify them as tribute paid in kind by the local peasantry to their ruler. These, along with goats or sheep, and cattle, apparently constituted the staple diet of the occupants.

With the exception of the Glan-y-môr radio-carbon dates referred to above, there exists a gap in our knowledge of settlement in the area until the 9th century A.D. During the excavation of the Roman building at Glan-y-môr, on the site of the former Y.M.C.A. Hostel grounds, the remains of a dry-stone sub-rectangular building were found overlying part of the 3rd century courtyard and verandah. Internally there were traces of a slabbed floor in which there was a setting for a post to support a roof, presumably of turf or thatch. As well as the paving, drains were located alongside two of the walls. Animal bones from the deposits lying on the floor of the building provided the material for radio-carbon dates to be calculated. Unfortunately no other finds were made that could be attributed to this period. It remains to mention one other possibility. The 'porch' of St. Barruc's Chapel on Barry Island, may represent part of a structure pre-dating the medieval chapel and adjacent priest's house.[74]

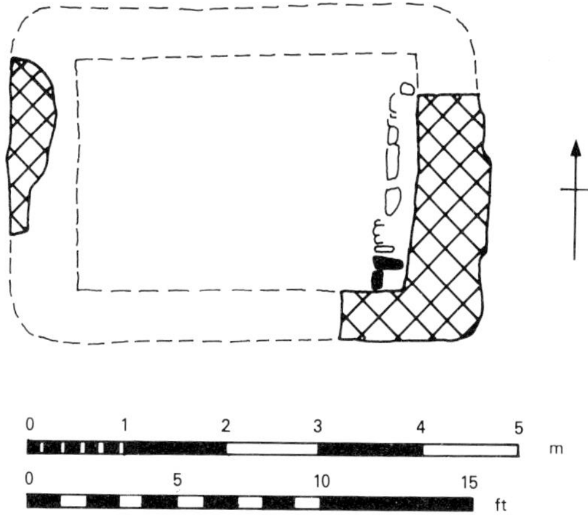

Fig. 24.
St. Barruc's Chapel, Barry Island. Plan of (?) 11th-century church.
H. J. Thomas, after J. K. Knight.

Despite the apparent paucity of evidence for the history of this long and significant period, Barry's share is rich in comparison with that of many other places in Wales and beyond. A generation ago it would have been impossible to cite any archaeological information relating to ecclesiastical or domestic settlements. In addition, much critical work on the Celtic saints and Dark-Age history generally has been accomplished. The historian of the Norman invasion and the medieval period has much more evidence of all kinds available, and many of the stone buildings begun at that time are still standing for all to see.

References

1 R. M. Jacobi, 'The Upper Palaeolithic of Britain with special reference to Wales', in J. A. Taylor (ed.), *Culture and environment in prehistoric Wales*, British Archaeological Reports, British series, 76 (Oxford, 1980), pp. 15-100.

2 'A Palaeolithic handaxe from Rhossili, Gower', *G-GAT Annual Report 1977-78*, p. 50.

3 RCAHM (Wales), *Glamorgan*, I (part i), p. 5.

4 H. Stephen Green, 'A Palaeolithic flint handaxe from Rhossili, Gower', *BBCS*, XXIX (1981-82), pp. 337-9.

5 RCAHM (Wales), *Glamorgan*, I (part i), p. 16.

6 The expression 'b.c.' denotes a radiocarbon date, which is not necessarily the same as a calendar date B.C. There is still uncertainty over the conversion of one to the other.

7 Recent excavations at Pontnewydd in the Vale of Clwyd have produced some evidence to substantiate the presence of Neanderthal Man: H. Stephen Green, *Pontnewydd Cave: a Lower palaeolithic hominid site in Wales* (Cardiff, 1984), pp. 159-70.

8 W. F. Grimes, *The prehistory of Wales* (Cardiff, 1951), p. 146.

9 For finds of microliths at Coldbrook Fach and Vianshill see G. Dowdell, note in *Archaeology in Wales*, 11 (1971), pp. 10-11.

10 G. Dowdell, note in *ibid.*, 5 (1965), p. 9.

11 See ref. 9.

12 J. G. D. Clark, *et al.*, *Excavations at Star Carr: an early Mesolithic site at Seamer near Scarborough* (Cambridge, 1954), pp. 12-17.

13 H. N. Savory, 'Axes of Pembrokeshire stone from Glamorganshire', *BBCS*, XIII (1948-50), pp. 245-6.

14 G-GAT, note in *Morgannwg*, XXIII (1979), pp. 83-4.

15 H. N. Savory, 'Recent archaeological excavation and discovery in Glamorgan', *ibid.*, IX (1965), p. 88.

16 H. N. Savory, 'The excavation of a Neolithic dwelling and a Bronze Age cairn at Mount Pleasant Farm, Nottage (Glam.)', *CNST*, LXXXI (1950-52), p. 75 ff.

17 RCAHM (Wales), *Glamorgan*, I (part i), pp. 36-7.

18 J. Romilly Allen, 'A description of some cairns on Barry Island, Glamorganshire', *Arch. Camb.*, 4th series, IV (1873), pp. 189-91.

19 'The Distribution of Neolithic and Bronze Age flints in Glamorgan and Gwent', *G-GAT Annual Report, 1981-82*, pp. 73-85.

20 Aileen Fox, 'An account of John Storrie's excavations on Barry Island in 1894-5', *CNST*, LXIX (1936), pp. 12-38; H. N. Savory, 'Recent archaeological excavation and discovery in Glamorgan', *Morgannwg*, III (1959), p. 101; Jeffrey L. Davies, 'Excavations at Cae Summerhouse, Tythegston, Glam.: second interim report', *Morgannwg*, XI (1967), pp. 75-7.

21 Aileen Fox, *loc. cit.*

22 H. N. Savory, 'The excavation of a Bronze-age farm at Sant-y-Nyll, St. Brides-super-Ely (Glam.)', *CNST*, LXXXIX (1959-60), pp. 9-30.

23 RCAHM (Wales), *Glamorgan*, I (part i), p. 23.

24 *Ibid.*, p. 8.

25 O. G. S. Crawford and R. E. M. Wheeler, 'The Llynfawr hoard and other hoards of the Bronze Age', *Archaeologia*, LXXI (1920-21), pp. 133-7; Sir Cyril Fox and H. A. Hyde, 'A second cauldron and an iron sword from the Llynfawr hoard, Rhigos, Glamorganshire', *Antiquaries Journal*, XIX (1939), pp. 369-404; H. N. Savory, 'The later Bronze Age in Wales: some discoveries and new interpretations', *Arch. Camb.*, CVII (1958), pp. 38-40; W. F. Grimes, *The Prehistory of Wales*, pp. 221-3.

26 D. Benson, note in *Archaeology in Wales*, 17 (1977), pp. 27-8.

27 Margaret Ehrenberg, Jennifer Price and Vanda Vale, 'The excavation of two Bronze Age round barrows at Welsh St. Donat's, South Glamorgan', *BBCS*, XXIX (1981-82), pp. 776-842.

28 David M. Robinson, *Cowbridge: the archaeology and topography of a small market town in the Vale of Glamorgan* (Swansea, 1980), p. 9.

29 Michael G. Jarrett and Stuart Wrathmell, *Whitton. An Iron Age and Roman farmstead in South Glamorgan* (Cardiff, 1981), p. 3 and *passim*.
30 [H. S. Owen John], 'Llandough: a late Iron Age farmstead, Romano-British villa and medieval monastic grange', *G-GAT Annual Report, 1978-79*, pp. 27-38.
31 Howard Thomas, 'Current work in Welsh archaeology. Excavations and discoveries: Roman period', *BBCS*, XVII (1956-58), p. 294.
32 [J. Parkhouse], 'Biglis—a late Iron Age and Romano-British settlement site', *G-GAT Annual Report, 1978-79*, pp. 1-12.
33 Barry Cunliffe, *Iron-age communities in Britain* (2nd edition, 1978), pp. 273-86.
34 RCAHM (Wales), *Glamorgan*, I, (part ii), no. 615, p. 20 (Castle Ditches, Llancarfan).
35 J. L Davies, note in *Archaeology in Wales*, 8 (1968), pp. 7-8 (The Bulwarks, Porthkerry).
36 G. Guilbert, note in *ibid.*, 12 (1972), pp. 13-14.
37 H. N. Savory, 'The Vale of Glamorgan in archaeology', in Stewart Williams (ed.), *History on my doorstep* (Barry, 1959), pp. 53-63.
38 H. J. Thomas and G. Davies, note in *Archaeology in Wales*, 5 (1965), p. 25.
39 G. Dowdell, note in *ibid.*, 11 (1971), pp. 17-18.
40 R. E. M. Wheeler, *Prehistoric and Roman Wales* (Oxford, 1928), pp. 208-10.
41 Stuart Piggott, The Druids (1968), pp. 113-5.
42 Tacitus, *Annales*, XII, 39.
43 John Storrie, 'Archaeological notes and queries: find of Roman coins, etc., on Sully Moor', *Arch. Camb.*, 5th series, XVII (1900), pp. 60-5.
44 John Storrie, 'Ancient remains on Ely Racecourse', *CNST*, XXVI (1893-94), pp. 129-31 (*cf.* Sir Mortimer Wheeler's re-excavations at Ely described in *ibid.*, LV (1922), pp. 19-45); RCAHM (Wales), *Glamorgan* I, (part ii), pp. 115-8.
45 John Storrie, 'Report on excavations near Llantwit Major', *CNST*, XX (part i), (1888), pp. 49-61; V. E. Nash-Williams, 'The Roman villa at Llantwit Major', *Arch. Camb.*, CII (1953), pp. 89-163; RCAHM (Wales), *Glamorgan*, I (part ii), pp. 111-13, where the 1971 excavation by Dr. A. H. Hogg is summarised.
46 *Ibid.*, pp. 90-4 for Cardiff.
47 See ref. 30.
48 See ref. 29.
49 For the recent excavations at Usk see W. H. Manning, *The fortress excavations, 1968-71* (Cardiff, 1981).
50 V. E. Nash-Williams (revised M. G. Jarrett), *The Roman frontier in Wales* (Cardiff, 1969), pp. 4-8.
51 For a discussion of the evidence of *Iter XII* of the Antonine Itinerary relating to 'Bomium', see RCAHM (Wales), *Glamorgan*, I (part ii), pp. 121-2; see *ibid.*, pp. 82-104 for descriptions of Roman military sites in the county.
52 David M. Robinson, *Cowbridge* (Swansea, 1980), p. 23.
53 Stephen Johnson, *The Roman forts of the Saxon Shore* (1976).
54 G Dowdell and E. M. Evans, 'Glan-y-môr, Cold Knap, Barry', *G-GAT Annual Report, 1980-81*, pp. 1-3.
55 John Wacher, *The towns of Roman Britain* (1974), pp. 375-89.
56 *Ibid.*, pp. 389-93.
57 See ref. 32.
58 G. Dowdell, note in *Archaeology in Wales*, 11 (1971), no. 32, p. 18 and no. 38, p. 20.
59 RCAHM (Wales), *Glamorgan*, I (part ii), no. 769, p. 120.
60 G-GAT, Sites and Monuments Record, no. 902s.
61 See ref. 43.
62 David M. Robinson, *The Romans in south-east Wales*, forthcoming.
63 Aileen Fox, *loc. cit.*
64 Willoughby Gardner, 'The Bulwarks: a promontory fort at Porthkerry, Glamorganshire', *Arch. Camb.*, XC (1935), pp. 135-40; J. L. Davies, note in *Archaeology in Wales*, 8 (1968), pp. 7-8; *ibid.*, 'An excavation at the Bulwarks, Porthkerry, Glamorgan, 1968', *Arch. Camb.*, CXXII (1973), pp. 55-98.
65 RCAHM (Wales), Glamorgan, I (part ii), no. 691, p. 57.
66 *Ibid.*, no. 670, p. 110.

[67] See ref. 54.

[68] Jeremy K. Knight, 'Excavations at St. Barruc's Chapel, Barry Island, Glamorgan', *CNST*, XCIX (1976-78), pp. 28-65.

[69] D. R. Paterson, 'Scandinavian influence in the place-names and early personal names of Glamorgan', *Arch. Camb.*, 6th series, XX (1920), p. 40. This interpretation of 'Cogan' is, however, disputed by Gwynedd O. Pierce in his authoritative *Place-names of Dinas Powys hundred* (Cardiff, 1968), pp. 31-5.

[70] I am grateful to Mr. Donald Moore for making this point.

[71] Wendy Davies, 'Roman settlements and post-Roman estates in south-east Wales', in *The end of Roman Britain*, ed., P. J. Casey, British Archaeological Reports, British series, 71 (Oxford, 1979), pp. 153-73.

[72] RCAHM (Wales), *Glamorgan*, I (part iii), pp. 18-68, *passim*; for the 'Irbic' stone, see *ibid.*, no. 938, pp. 61-2.

[73] Leslie Alcock, *Dinas Powys: an Iron Age, Dark Age, and early medieval settlement in Glamorgan* (Cardiff, 1963), pp. 23-93.

[74] I am grateful to Mr. Howard J. Thomas for drawing this to my attention.

CHAPTER III

Castle, Church and Village Medieval Barry, 1100-1500

HOWARD J. THOMAS

Medieval funerary paten from Uchelolau church. *H.J.T.*

THE modern town of Barry lies over a once rural landscape which has been continuously occupied and cultivated for at least eight hundred years. Before the building of the town the principal geographical feature of the area was an island in the Bristol Channel, divided from the mainland by a sheltered tidal estuary fed by the Cadoxton River. The semi-circular hinterland stretching from Porthkerry Bay on the west to Sully Moors on the east somewhat resembled the inside of a shallow half-bowl, enclosing the northern side of the island, and rising from the shoreline to about 200 feet (61 metres) above sea level. Above the 150-foot (46-metre) contour the soil was well drained, composed of fertile lias loam or loamy clay, gradually developing eastward into areas of heavy clay surrounding 'islands' of shallow rocky soil.

The place name 'Barry' (modern Welsh, 'Y Barri') was certainly in existence from the 11th century and probably much earlier. Its origin, however, remains uncertain. The name could have been derived from three sources; possibly from a Celtic saint Barruc, *alias* Barrog, Barrwg, or Baruch; or an old Welsh word 'Bar' meaning 'hill' or 'rise'; or (which is less likely) from an old Norse word meaning 'barley', 'shore', 'island'. Whatever its origins the name originally described the island, but by the 12th century was applied also to much of the mainland of the coastal area within the parishes of Barry, Merthyr Dyfan and Cadoxton. From the middle of the 13th century the place-name became restricted to Barry Island and the parish of Barry which lay close to its western mainland shore.[1]

Plate VIII. Barry Castle, gatehouse ruins. *B. Daly.*

Barry Island is mentioned by three medieval travellers and it figures in a eulogy by Ralph Higden (1300-64) as one of the wonders of ancient Wales.[2] The earliest account occurs in Latin in the travel diary of Gerald de Barri or Gerald of Wales (Giraldus Cambrensis), describing his preaching tour of Wales in the company of Archbishop Baldwin in 1188:

> 'Not far from Cardiff there is a small island just off the shore of the Severn Sea which the local inhabitants call Barry. It takes its name from Saint Baroc, who used to live there. His remains have been placed in a coffin, and they can be found there in an ivy-clad chapel... It is an odd thing that in a rock by the sea where one first lands on the island there is a small crack. If you press your ear to it, you can hear a noise like that of blacksmiths at work, the blowing of bellows, the strokes of hammers and the harsh grinding of files on metal . . . One could well imagine that a sound of this sort would come from the sea-waters rushing into hidden orifices beneath the island, but it is no less loud when the waves draw back, and it can be heard just as well when the shore is dry as when the tide is up.'[3]

Gerald was at Cardiff when he wrote this, but it is doubtful whether he actually visited the island; his information was taken more likely from family tradition and hearsay. The description of the chapel seems fairly reliable and there is a deep fissure leading into the rock on Nell's Point, but his account of a blow-hole may result from a confusion with Worm's Head in Gower or some other island, perhaps off the Pembrokeshire coast.

Barry and Sully are noted in a list of the islands of Wales compiled by the antiquarian William Worcestre in 1478. He derived his somewhat garbled information from the mariners of Bristol. After describing Burry Holms and Lundy he states:

> 'The next island of Wales is Barry Island, following the island called Little Sully; it is a mile long and half a mile wide and is not inhabited but cattle are grazed there. There is a chapel of St. Nicholas. Sully Island follows Barry Island, 9 miles off, and is 3 bowshots across in all directions.'[4]

It is uncertain from Worcestre's account whether 'Little Sully' was Sully Island or whether it was the same place as 'Little Island' on the west side of Barry Island, which seems at one time from map and geological evidence to have been a separate island before being joined to Barry Island proper by a narrow spit of sand. The dedication of the chapel is clearly mixed up with the parish church of Barry on the mainland, familiar to medieval mariners from its prominent position as a navigational landmark.

The most informative topographical description is bequeathed to us by John Leland who was appointed by King Henry VIII to make a systematic antiquarian survey of the realm in about the years 1536-39. Unlike the earlier authors, Leland's information was based on first-hand observation rather than hearsay, and written in English. His itinerary followed the Glamorgan coast and included several excursions inland into the uplands. The following is his account of the coastal area from Sully to Aberthaw:

> 'From Scylley mouthe to Aberbarrey, wher cummith a litle rylle of fresch water to the Seven, is about a mile. The hedde of this rylle is scant a mile of by north est in a playn ground.

On this bekke stondith the castelle of Barrey aboute a quarter of a mile beyond the west ripe of it. This castelle stondith on a litle hil, and most of it is in ruine. Master S. John of Bedfordshir is lorde of it. Maurice S. John, uncle to Syr John S. John, was owner of it.

Right againe this brooke mouth lyith Barry Isle. The passage into it at ful se is a flite shot over, as much as the Tamise is above the bridge. At low water ther is a broken causey to go over, or els over the shalow stremelet of Barrey brooke on the sandes.

The isle is about a mile in cumpace, and hath very good corne, grass and sum wood. The ferme of it worth a x.li. (£10) a yere.

There is no dwelling in the isle, but ther is in the midle of it a fair litle chapel of S. Barrock, wher much pilgrimage was usid.

Half a mile and more beyonde Aber Barrey is the mouth of Come Kydy. This broke risethe flat north a mile and an half from the place wher it goith ynto the Severn Se. There is no notable building on this rylle. The soile of boothe side of the ril in this valley hath good corn, grasse and wood.

From Kiddey mouth, wher no enteraunce is for shippes, to the mouthe of Thawan a 3. miles by very principal good corn ground. At the mouth of Thawan shippe-lettes may cume ynto the haven mouth.'[5]

The manors of the district

The five villages of Barry, Cwmcidy, Cadoxton, Merthyr Dyfan and Uchelolau (Highlight), all within the town's boundaries, owe their foundation to the Norman conquest and colonization of Glamorgan in *c.* 1091. Soon after the conquest the most fertile land was retained by the chief lord, Robert Fitzhamon, and the remainder allocated among his baronial followers. Each 'manor' was held in return for military services assessed at a number of knights' fees. The barons had to provide the service of an armed horseman or knight in respect of each 'fee'. In Glamorgan this service was for forty days annually at Cardiff Castle, commuted in peacetime for the sum of six shillings and eight pence 'wardsilver' for each 'fee'. In the case of the larger holdings held by the service of several knights the solution was to create 'sub-fees', namely to sub-divide the land among the barons' own military followers to make up the number of knights required for the services owed. Each of these in turn was endowed with sufficient land for their sustenance. The lands held by military service were organised as manors and settled with peasants to work the land.

The Barry area became incorporated into two large lordships held under the Chief Lord of Glamorgan; Penmark in the west and Dinas Powys in the east; held respectively by the families of de Umfraville and de Sumeri. Penmark, held for the service of four knights, was split into four manors; one was retained by its lord, the remainder were held as sub-manors; there were Fonmon held by the St. Johns, West Penmark by the Odyns, and Barry by the de Barris. Dinas Powys, valued at three-and-a-half knights' fees, had locally two sub-manors; Cadoxton held for the service of two knights, and

Uchelolau (Highlight) which was judged to be half a knight's fee (or three shillings and four pence for twenty days' service at Cardiff Castle).[6] It must be borne in mind that the knight occupying the lowest rung in the chain of services and 'wardsilver' payments owed to a succession of superior lords was the actual owner of the land, in most cases the resident lord.

Barry manor

The sub-manor of Barry or 'Westbarry' as it was sometimes called, was granted not long after the Conquest by the de Umfravilles to the de Barri family. Within the first or second generation of their acquiring Barry there issued a younger branch which migrated westward to participate in further conquest, settling at Maenorbir (Manorbier) in Pembrokeshire. Gerald de Barri, the most renowned of this branch, explained the origins of their surname:

Fig. 25.
Map of Barry area, *c.* 1300.
H.J.T.

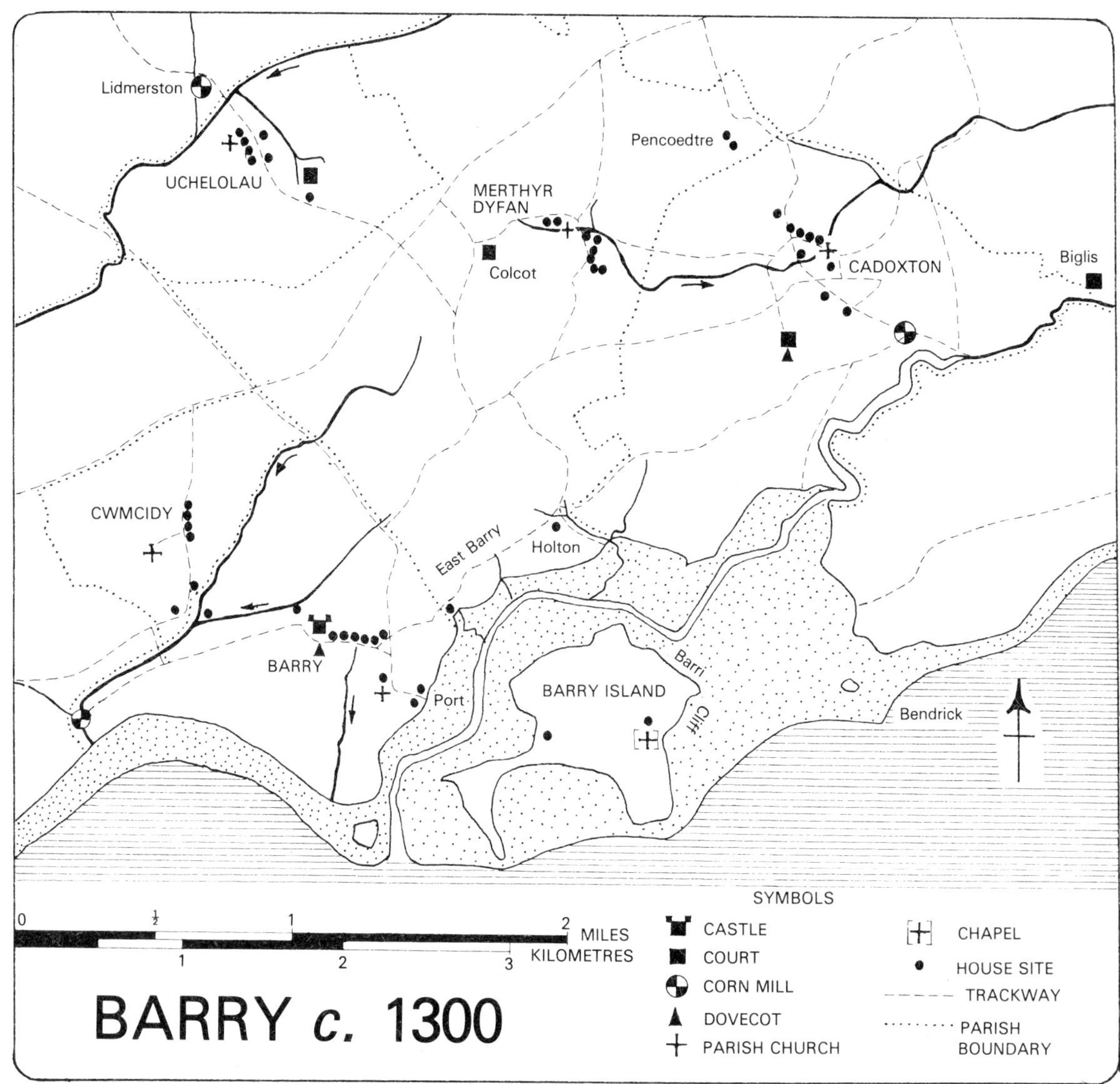

> 'A noble family resident on the coast of South Wales has taken its name from the island (Barry), because it owns it and the neighbouring estates. Barry was first of all the family's forename, and then its surname became de Barry.'[7]

The elder Glamorgan branch held other lands under the Umfravilles as portions of knights' fees at Bychenstoke in Somerset, and Culm Reigny (or Culm-by-Silverton) in Devon. The family's possessions included also the sub-manor of Walterston in Gower. In the early 13th century they were busy consolidating their West Country properties when Walterston was exchanged with Neath Abbey for their grange at Hornblotton in Somerset. About 1300 they invested in the purchase of a town house in Cardiff which was afterwards sold to one of the townspeople.[8]

Members of the de Barri family frequently appear as witnesses to deeds issued by their manorial neighbours, and attended the Glamorgan Shire Court in the capacity of jurors and inquisitors. A William de Barri was living between 1180 and 1233. He was on military service for King Henry III in Ireland in 1225, and in 1233 followed in the steps of his overlord Umfraville in the rebellion of the Earl Marshal against the King. William had a son named Thomas and other children probably including a Luke and Richard. Another William occurs about the middle of the 13th century. There was also a Walter in 1281, and a Lucas in 1299. At the close of the 13th century there lived a William de Barri 'junior'. He attested a Michaelston deed in *c.* 1280, and a Merthyr Dyfan deed in 1304; and in 1316 he sat on a panel which gave evidence at an inquiry into the uprising of Llywelyn Bren. About the same date he purchased a town house in Cardiff which was inherited by a son named John.[9]

The last male member of the family was Thomas de Barri (*fl.* 1330-49) whose daughter Isabella married John de Avene, lord of Afan and Sully. The family disappears from the Glamorgan records after 1349. Barry manor seems not long afterwards to have passed to the St. Johns of Fonmon through an unredeemed mortgage and failure of the male line. By their acquisition the St. Johns became possessed of two knights' fees or 'half' of the four fees of Penmark, their ownership of which was confirmed by a deed of settlement in 1371 followed by a deed of partition in *c.* 1373-1385 in which their status was elevated from sub-lords to co-heirs of the lordship. They inherited the other 'half' in 1415 after the death of Alice Blount, the heiress and granddaughter of Alice Umfraville.[10]

Before 1371 Barry manor was held by Oliver St. John who had leased it for life to John Andrew of Rhoose, during whose tenure the manor was valued at 10 marks (£6 13*s.* 4*d.*). In the 1390s Barry was settled by trustees upon Oliver's younger son Alexander in tail male. Alexander St. John entered into possession and was 'dwelling in Wales' in 1398, but he does not appear to have been succeeded by male heirs as the manor subsequently (before 1424) escheated to his elder brother John. In about 1500 the manor

Plate IX.
Barry Castle, as it might have appeared in the mid 14th century.
David Crouch after H.J.T.

and castle were 'owned' by, or more probably leased to, Maurice St. John. He was another junior member of the family and was also lessee of Ogmore lordship between 1506 and 1508. The St. Johns continued in possession until 1660 when Barry was sold by Oliver St. John, Earl of Bolingbroke, to Evan Seys, Serjeant-at-law of Boverton for £1,740.[11]

The seat of the manor was Barry Castle, located on high ground overlooking the Bristol Channel on a site which had been occupied in Roman times by a native homestead. The presence of hearths and pits containing twelfth-century potsherds shows that the castle had been established by that date, probably in the form of a ditched and embanked ringwork with drystone or timber buildings, the circular outline of which survived later re-buildings until the 17th century.[12] By the late 13th century two stone buildings had come into existence, forming the east and west sides of a small quadrangular courtyard. The building on the east contained two chambers of unequal size, the larger possessing a garderobe in a buttress projecting beyond its outer wall. The first half of the 14th century saw the addition on the south side of the courtyard of a sizeable hall with a gatehouse attached to its east gable, the three buildings linked together by a crenellated curtain wall pierced by arrow slits, the whole occupying an area of about 29 metres (95 feet) square. These building works may have followed devastations caused by the rebel Llywelyn Bren and must have been a considerable financial burden for a minor lord, possibly the reason for the de Barris selling off their town house and raising money by mortgage.

All that now survive are the gatehouse ruins and the scanty remains of the 14th-century hall. The spacious banqueting hall, 16 × 6 metres (52½ × 20 feet), situated on the first floor was heated by a hooded fireplace in the side wall facing the courtyard. This was surmounted by a tall circular chimney of Sutton stone. The ground floor was lit by small arrow slits and probably served as a storage room. A narrow stair in the wall in the south-east corner of the hall led to a wall walk which communicated with an angle turret on the south-west, now completely destroyed.[13] In the east wall of the hall another door led into a portcullis chamber. The hall roof was of Cornish slates capped by a green-glazed serrated tile ridge.

Plate X. Barry Castle, courtyard. *B. Daly.*

The gateway was defended by a drawbridge, the base of which was hinged on the door threshold. Behind the drawbridge was a portcullis and heavy two-leaved door. Above the vaulted entrance passage was a small chamber which contained the windlass gear. The chains of the drawbridge were drawn through two holes flanking the sill of a large lancet window above the entrance. The presence of a broken piscina (a stone basin with a drain used for rinsing the chalice after Mass) and an aumbry (a wall cupboard for storing the chalice, paten, cruets, etc.) shows that the chamber also served as a small private chapel, with its altar stone set within the sill of a recessed east window. The lord's household doubtless included an unbeneficed priest or chaplain whose function was also that of private tutor to the lord's children. To the south of the gateway stood a stone dovecot which would have provided fresh pigeon meat in winter for the lord and his family.[14]

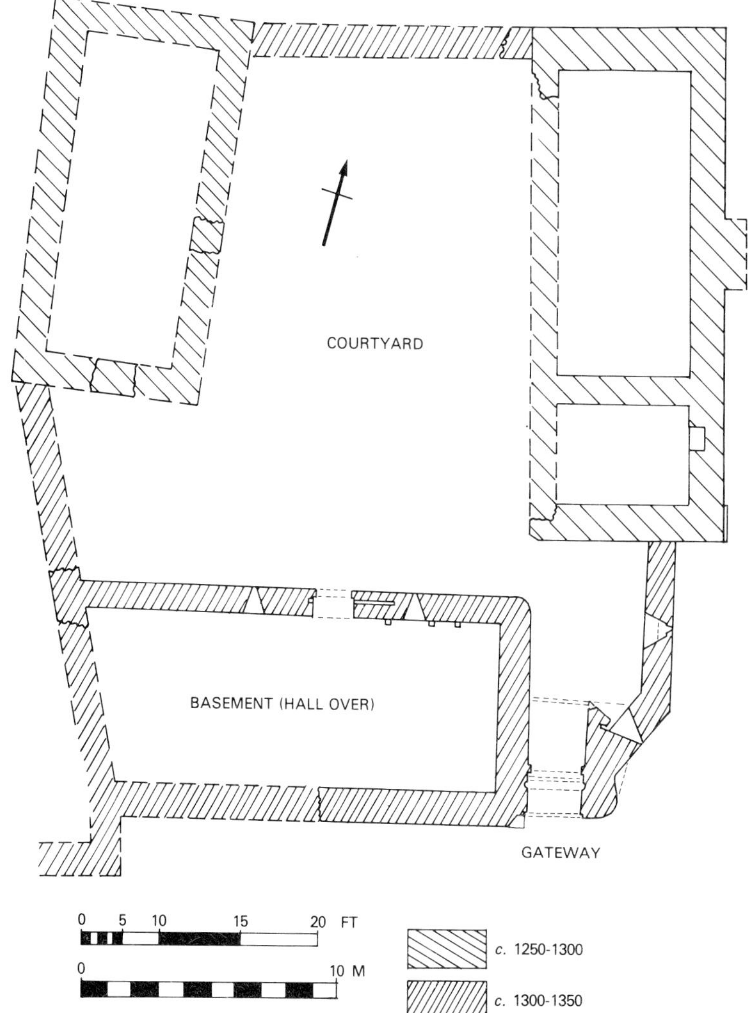

Fig. 26.
Plan of Barry Castle, ground floor.
H.J.T.

Plate XI.
Barry Castle, arrow slit in curtain wall.
B. Daly.

The castle had become ruinous before Leland's visit in 1536-39. During the reign of Elizabeth, the south wall of the hall was demolished and a small cottage built within the shell of the remaining walls. The cottage once served as a tavern kept by a William Wilkyn (*fl.* 1582-1615). It was still standing in the 18th century, when it was called the Castle House. The gateway probably owes its preservation to the fact that it was used as a meeting place for the manorial courts in the second half of the 17th century.[15]

The boundaries of Barry manor were coterminous with those of the parish of the same name. Its area (exclusive of brake and shingle) is given as 460 statute acres in manorial surveys of 1622 and 1773. Barry Island, if the statement by Gerald de Barri is correct, originally formed part of the de Barri possessions. It may have come into the hands of the lords of Sully in the 1300s with the marriage of Isabella de Barri to John de Avene.[16]

Cadoxton manor

Cadoxton manor *alias* East Barry appears originally to have been an extensive tract of about 2,000 acres embracing the whole of the parishes of Merthyr Dyfan and Cadoxton. Its early sub-lords were the de Mitdehorguill family, who also held a sub-manor located in the western part of the lordship of St. Nicholas. The male line failed at the close of the 12th century when the heiress Milisant, daughter of William de Mitdehorguill, married her overlord Adam de Sumeri. Through this match the St. Nicholas sub-manor came into the possession of the de Sumeris (which they still retained in 1280).[17]

By the early 14th century Cadoxton seems to have been divided into three portions, each apparently under different ownership, comprising East Barry, Cadoxton and Merthyr Dyfan. The precise topographical locations of these portions remains obscure, 'East Barry', for example, being later on the name of an isolated farmstead of 12th-century origin in the south-west corner of Merthyr Dyfan parish, seems also from 16th-century sources to refer to lands in Cadoxton parish extending as far east as Sully Moors. Possibly the lands were intermixed throughout the two parishes.[18]

A feature of the larger Vale lordships of Dinas Powys, Ogmore, Llantwit Major and elsewhere, was the sub-division of outlying areas into self-contained agrarian units connected with farming of the lord's demesne, which had not been sub-enfeoffed but retained by the lord. Each of these resembled a small manor with its demesne and customary lands, open fields and granges worked under the supervision of a reeve or bailiff. Such an arrangement seems to have been the case with the lands around Merthyr Dyfan village, one of the portions of Cadoxton sub-manor, which contained two carucates or 240 customary acres of arable, with a court or grange situated at Colcot. The lords of Dinas Powys also had another grange at Biglis which had 210 acres attached, perhaps specialising (as the place-name element suggests, *bugail* = 'shepherd', 'herdsman') in sheep farming.[19]

The manor of Cadoxton also contained a freehold with a house situated in the hamlet of Holton in Merthyr Dyfan parish, held under the de Sully family for an annual rent of 20*s*. About the middle of the 13th century this belonged to Maurice de Cantelupe, lord of Candleston, from whom it went by inheritance to his son-in-law, Mathew Everard. In 1304 the freehold was exchanged by Mathew's son William with Sir Simon de Raleigh for lands at Pilton in the West Country. The name of the former owners was perpetuated by the place-name 'Everard's tenement' in rentals until the end of the 16th century.[20]

At the end of the 14th century the manor of East Barry with Cadoxton came into the hands of a family called Andrew, who arose from unknown origins in the late 14th and early 15th centuries, when they bought a number of small freeholds in the parishes of St. Andrew's, Gileston, St. Athan, Porthkerry and Barry. The family perhaps originated from the north of England, for, in 1593, one of the Andrews of Cadoxton delivered, for genealogical purposes, some of his ancestral evidences to the York Herald, namely a deed of 1425 and an ancient heraldic seal inscribed '+ S[IGILLUM] . ANDREE . DE CAMBERONE . MILITIS' (The seal of Andrew of Camberone, knight). Their arms consisted of three bars, and bear a close similarity to those of the de Sullys and the de Barris.[21]

Their earliest Glamorgan ancestor was certainly John Andrew (*fl.* 1362-98) who was resident at Rhoose, in the lordship of Penmark, where he had a house standing upon a substantial freehold, the site of which later became known as 'Rhoose Castle'. John was also lessee for life of the manor of West Barry. In the following generation there was a William Andrew (*fl.* 1401-1425) now designated as 'of East Barry', which seems to show that the family had lately obtained that manor. William had a son Richard and probably another son named Robert. In 1478 a William Andrew of East Barry was witness to a Cogan deed. A Nicholas Andrew and Joan his wife were living in *c.* 1480. Their son John was lord of the manor of East Barry in 1503, and about the same date sold the Rhoose freehold to James ap Morgan Mathew.[22]

Cadoxton, together with a third portion of St. Nicholas, is returned in Beauchamp's Survey of 1429 as held by a Thomas ap Watkin, acting probably as a clerical trustee of the Andrews. In the same survey East Barry is recorded as being divided between Alexander Langley and the Earl of Warwick. The Andrews residing at Cadoxton Court retained their share of the manor until the death of William, last of the male line, in 1683. The demesne lands belonging to the Court are described in an enrolled deed of 1545 as lying within 'Est Barry. . . in the lordship of Cadoxton'. This deed recorded a transaction whereby James Andrew son of William Andrew lately deceased, purchased half of the demesne freehold from his overlord Walter Herbert. The deed mentions a 'little tower' (perhaps a watchtower) which was located on the west side of 'Courte hille' and a mill called the 'More Mill'.[23]

The manor house lay in an isolated position some distance beyond the south-western perimeter of Cadoxton village on a rocky knoll overlooking Sully Moors. It had been long abandoned by the middle of the 19th century when it was described as the 'extensive ruins of a castellated mansion'. Unfortunately, no early prints or drawings of it exist nor any detailed antiquarian description recording its appearance. The site was bought in 1871 by the Rev. John Hughes who built the present Cadoxton Court alongside the medieval ruins. Ordnance Survey maps suggest that the foundations were extant until about the 1890s, when they were swept away and the site incorporated in a garden layout. A few fragments of late medieval dressings in the rockeries confirm that it was a building of some architectural pretensions. A well-preserved 13th-century dovecot still stands in the grounds, noteworthy as the largest of the five surviving medieval dovecots in Glamorgan. The building is circular with a domed roof constructed from small overlapping stones. The inside is lined with the remains of 700 nesting holes which would have provided a total capacity for 1,400 pigeons.[24]

Uchelolau (Highlight) manor

'Uchelolau' or Highlight manor was held under Dinas Powys for the service of half a knight's fee. No early record survives as to whom the manor was sub-enfeoffed, though a David de Sumeri, probably a younger son of the family, is named as its lord in 1291. In the beginning of the 15th century the

Fig. 27. Uchelolau (Highlight), manor house of St. John family, as it might have appeared in *c.* 1550. *Simon Prosser after H.J.T.*

manor was in the possession of Sir John St. John, lord of Fonmon, who granted it to his second son Alexander.[25]

Alexander St. John is returned as holding the fee of Uchelolau in 1429 and was still living in about 1480. Before his death he had conveyed the property to a group of trustees who afterwards made a settlement upon his son William and Catherine his wife. Alexander's descendants retained Uchelolau and were resident there for eight generations until the death of Oliver the last male heir in 1728. The manor then went to his wife's nieces, Francis and Mary Kemys, and from them to their kinsman Sir Charles Kemys-Tynte of Cefn Mably.[26] This manor was coterminous with the parish of Uchelolau except on the northern side, where it extended into the parish of Wenvoe to include Lidmore mill. Its area was 418 acres.

The medieval manor house at Uchelolau was sited on marshy ground within a fork formed by two small streams. The site had a long history involving gradual structural improvements reflecting increasing prosperity over a period of three hundred years. The manor house in its earliest 12th-century phase consisted merely of a crudely built drystone hall with rounded corners 10 × 7 metres (33 × 23 feet) built on a clay platform. The inside contained two rooms divided by a timber partition, the larger chamber heated by an open hearth. In the 1200s the building was extended further and the partition resited in order to provide additional living space. To the south there was now a timber structure and another smaller drystone building, also with rounded corners. A surrounding ditch was dug, the clay spoil thrown into the interior, slightly raising the ground level, and thus creating a typical quadrangular moated homestead of about 30 metres (33 yards) square.

In the period *c.* 1280-1350 the hall and its outbuildings were demolished and the site levelled off. A more substantially constructed drystone hall with plastered walls was built in the centre of the enclosure. A barn containing a threshing floor between the doors was then tacked onto the hall's east gable and a small outbuilding built against the north side of the enclosure on the site of the 12th-century hall. The area between became a small, muddy courtyard enclosed on the east by a timber shed. An open space south of the hall and barn probably served as a rickyard. The moated manor continued in occupation until the 15th century, when it was eventually abandoned.

Between *c.* 1450 and *c.* 1500 the St. John family built a brand-new manor house on a different site close by, replacing its by now somewhat rundown and squalid predecessor. The second house was of H-shaped plan of two-storeyed wings between an open-roofed hall. The building had dressed stone doorways and mullioned windows. The ground-floor rooms were properly heated by fireplaces. Nearby stood a pigeon house. After the departure of the family, the 15th-century house became ruinous and it in turn was demolished and replaced by the present farmhouse in the 18th century.[27]

Plate XII. ► Barry village, as it might have appeared in *c.* 1340. *David Crouch after H.J.T.*

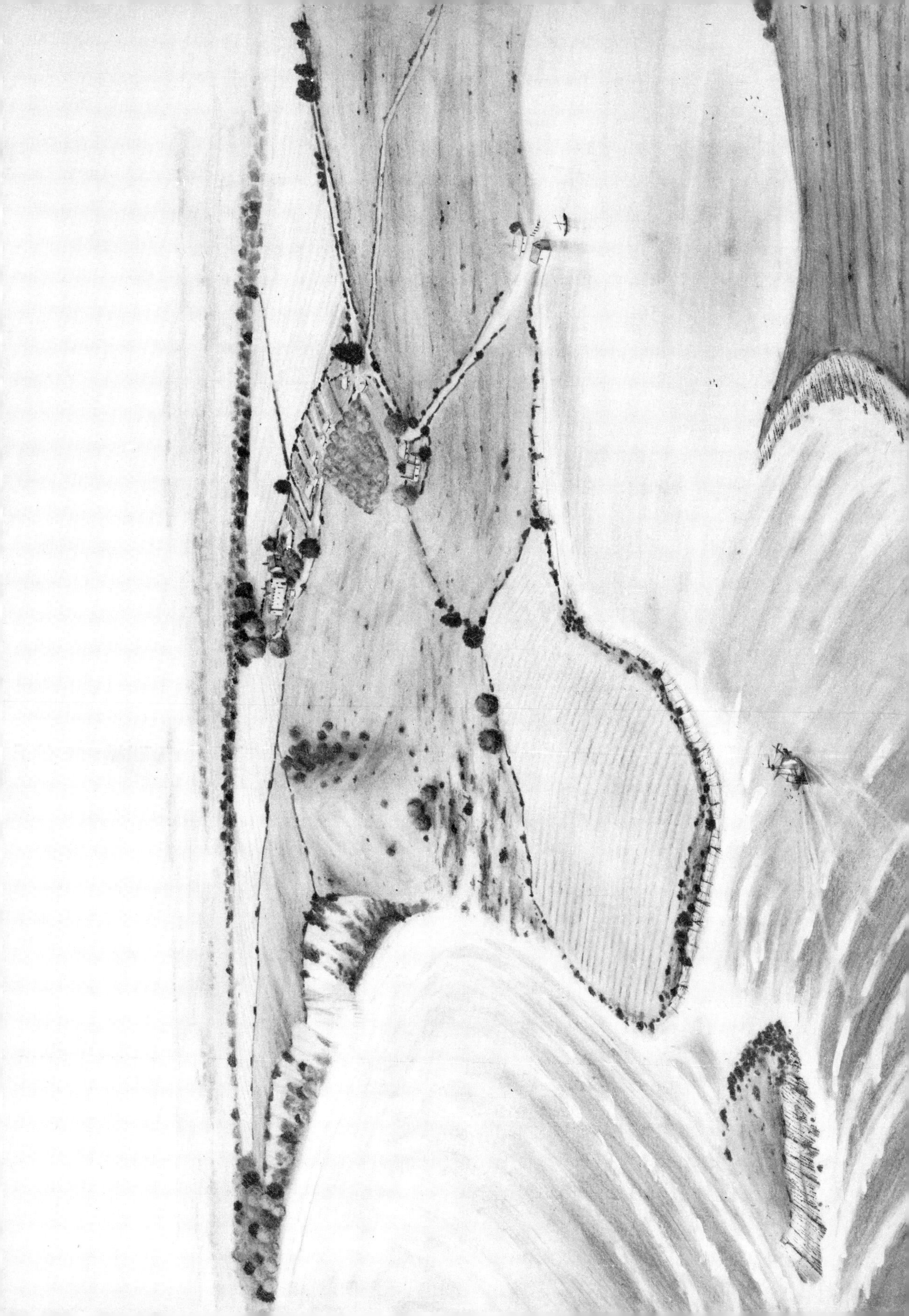

The villages: Barry

From archaeological fieldwork and excavation, combined with the somewhat meagre documentary sources, it is possible to reconstruct in outline the general form and development of these villages in the middle ages. Barry village in the 12th century and during the early part of the 13th century was very small and semi-dispersed with the main settlements situated at Cwm Barry, an eastern tributary valley of the Cidi or Cidy valley. Here alongside the banks of a small stream, close to springs, were a half-dozen scattered homesteads, evidently originating as piecemeal colonization of uncultivated wasteland, extending for about three-quarters of a mile to the head of the valley at Eagers (Beggars) Well. The westernmost of these, at the junction of the valley with Cwm Cidy was situated in a woodland clearing. On high ground overlooking the sea, about a quarter of a mile south of Cwm Barry, also in close proximity to springs, was a tiny group of dwellings adjacent to the castle.

A century later a considerable change had occurred in the settlement pattern, perhaps reflecting a deliberate manorial policy of consolidation and re-settlement following a period of warfare and famine in the early 13th century. The Cwm Barry hamlet was abandoned, with the exception of the western farmstead, which survived into post-medieval times as a freehold. The settlement on the higher ground eventually grew into a loose nucleus which became Barry village proper.

Thus Barry village had evolved by *c.* 1300 into a linear settlement that followed the line of an east-west trackway along the brow of a hill. It is known that a minimum of six houses and crofts extended for a distance of 300 metres (328 yards) along the north side of this track. The village was bounded on the east by a green, or small common, which served as a crossroads while the western limit was marked by the castle and its dovecot. There were, in addition, several isolated dwellings, including a priest's house close to the churchyard, a corn mill, and a habitation area on the edge of the harbour connected with a small seaport. The whole parish at this date contained a total of about twenty houses.

Ground plans of three of these houses have been recovered by excavation, thus providing a detailed picture of a part of the village. The houses, designated from east to west as houses A, B and C, occupied the north side of the street which still survives as Old Village Road. Four main periods of buildings and occupation have been identified extending from the 12th to the middle of the 14th century.

In period I (*c.* 1180-1250) the site of House A was occupied by a timber building, measuring, to judge by the slight remains that survived, 8 × 3 metres ($26\frac{1}{4}$ × $9\frac{3}{4}$ feet). House B stood on a platform cut into sloping ground. It measured about 10 × 4 metres (33 × 13 feet) externally and had rounded corners. The inside had been divided by a wooden screen into an

Fig. 28.
Plans of medieval peasant houses in the Barry area.
H.J.T.

Barry, House B

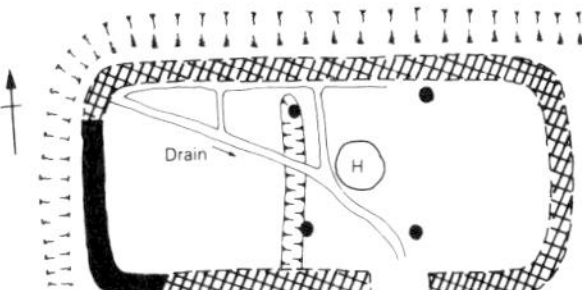

Phase I, *c.* 1200.

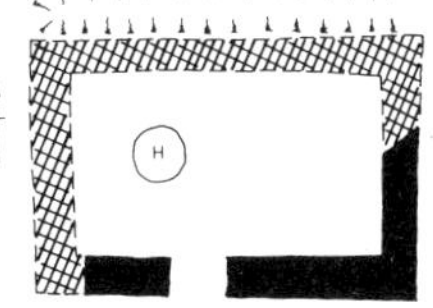

Phase II, rebuilt *c.* 1250.

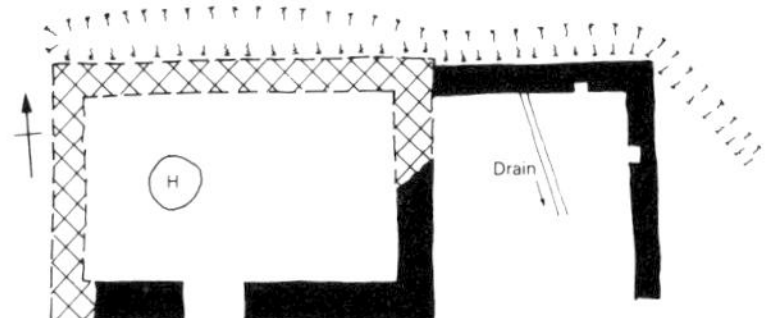

Phase III, enlarged *c.* 1300.

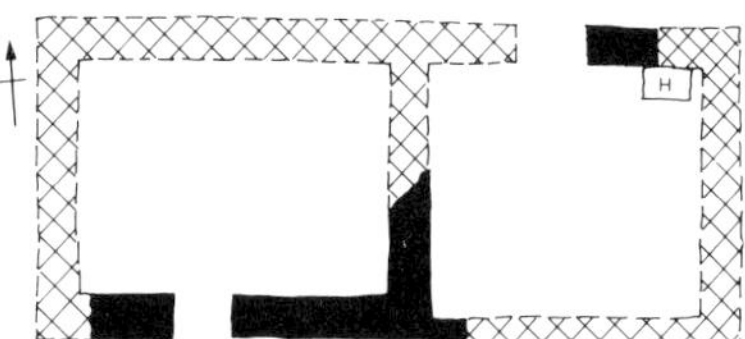

Phase IV, further enlarged *c.* 1350.

Barry, House A

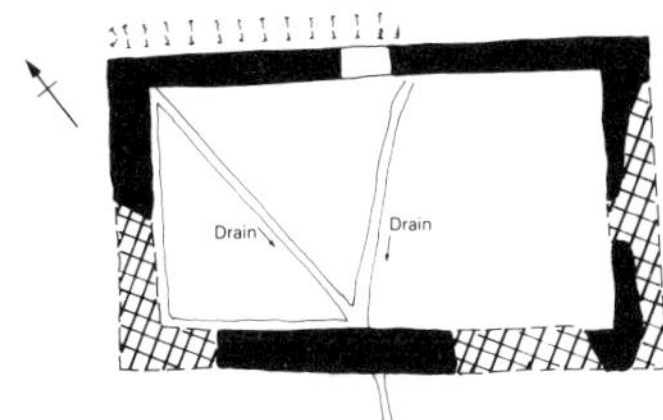

Barry, House C

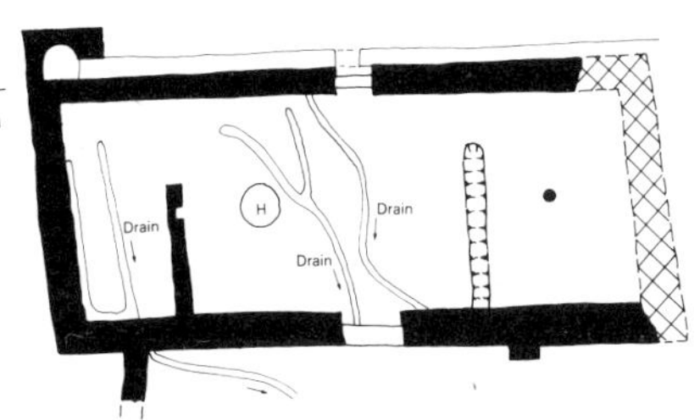

Note entry by opposed doors.

Merthyr Dyfan, House

House at Ffynnon John Lewis site, Merthyr Dyfan.

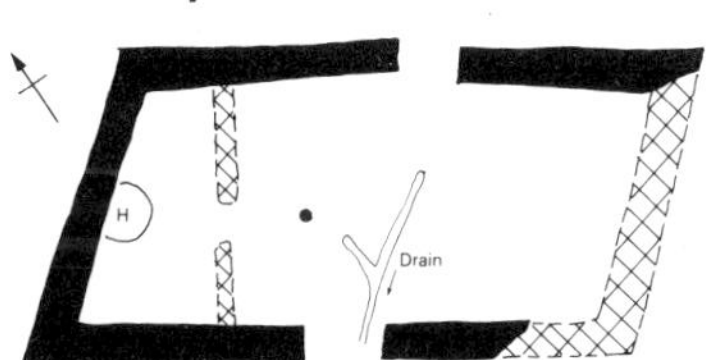

Note entry by opposed doors.

Priest's house, Uchelolau (Highlight).

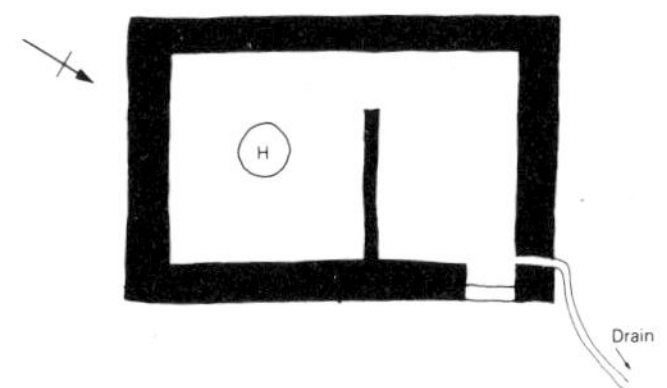

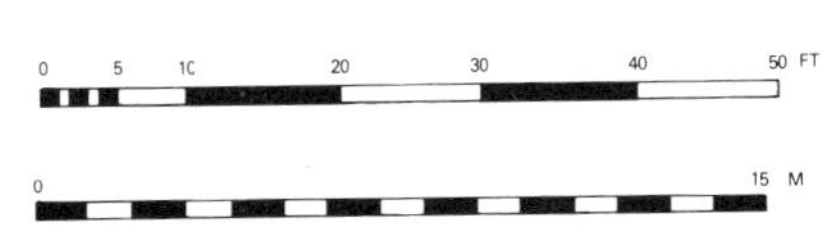

upper and lower chamber, the lower being the 'hall' (i.e. living room) entered from the outside and heated by a central hearth marked by a burnt area in its clay floor, around which was an arrangement of posts about 2 metres (6½ feet) square. A stone drain traversed the interior. Outside, to the north and north-west were rubbish pits (one containing a quantity of limpet shells), what was probably a shallow well and a garden or yard.

In period II (*c.* 1250-1300) House A was solidly rebuilt in stone. It measured 11 × 6 metres (36 × 19½ feet) externally, its walls built of beach stones with good dressed quoins, mortared with a distinctive red clay which may have been brought from the channel between Barry Island and the mainland. It consisted of a single room, and seems originally to have been entered through a doorway on the side away from the village street, though this may have been superseded by an entry on the street side. The upper half had a clean, clay floor with a stone drain, but the floor of the lower half had a layer of occupation debris; no traces of a hearth were found.

At around the same date house B was demolished, and a smaller cottage, measuring 8 × 5 metres (26¼ × 16½ feet) externally, was built over its eastern half. It consisted of a single room entered from the street. The hearth and drainage system of the previous house seem to have been retained in use. Building debris included dressed stone, whose detail suggested that the building had internally splayed window openings with broad-chamfered jambs. House C was erected, its masonry resembling that of Houses A and B. This house was 15 × 6 metres (49 × 19½ feet) overall, and had dressed and chamfered window openings. The interior was partitioned into three chambers, these being a hall heated by a hearth and entered by opposed doors, and two smaller rooms. The floors contained an elaborate system of slabbed drains. Water supply was obtained from a drystone lined well set against the north-west corner, its outflow leading into a large gutter running alongside the outside of the north wall. To the south of the house was a metalled yard enclosed on the west by a stone wall. The find of a bronze spur of a type closely datable to the middle of the 14th century, in the debris filling the gutter, shows that the house had been abandoned by the second half of the century.

In period III (*c.* 1250-1300) House B was extended by a drystone and timber shed built against its east wall. This was at first completely open to the street, though later its entrance was narrowed by the building of a wall, and to judge by its worn floor, it may have been a stable or a byre. Further trodden ground behind the building suggested a farmyard. A ditch was dug between Houses A and B, which served for drainage as well as a boundary. When this became silted up, the metalling of the street was extended into the space between the houses to form an entrance to the yard at the back.

In period IV (*c.* 1300-60) House B's 'annexe' was demolished and the house properly extended by the addition of a room 5 metres (16½ feet) square. At the same time, the whole house was widened through the rebuilding of its north wall, to become a sizeable peasant house of two rooms, 14 × 6 metres (46 × 19½ feet) overall. The east room had lime-plastered walls and a (much renewed) hearth in the corner with a circular bakestone. Amidst the occupation rubbish thrown into a gully behind the house, and in a situation which indicated that it had been lost towards the end of its occupation, was found a halfpenny of Edward III, minted in London between 1344 and 1357.

Scanty remains of another stone house with a backyard, designated as House D, lay 40 metres west of House C. The Barry village site was finally abandoned in the second half of the 14th century. Between this date and *c.* 1600 there was a change in the line of the road west of House C to higher ground, where it encroached on the sites of abandoned houses and crofts. Most of the walling of the last phase of House B was robbed, probably in the 1600s when the area was enclosed for agricultural improvements. The site of the four houses remained a corn field until the end of the 19th century.[28]

The villages: Merthyr Dyfan

The village of Merthyr Dyfan was located in a sheltered valley where four trackways converged near the church. Sites of six houses, all occupied in the period *c.* 1250-1350, have been found, three of which bordered a main north-south way which may have been the village street. Four of these dwellings were partially excavated between 1968 and 1978.

At Ffynnon John Lewis on the southern perimeter of the settlement was a farmstead within an embanked croft. The house, 14 × 6 metres (46 × 19½ feet) overall, was dry-built of lias rubble. It contained two rooms, the larger 'hall' chamber having opposed doors between which was a slabbed drain. Against the wall of the smaller room was a hearth. A short distance to the north-east was an outbuilding with externally rounded corners, bounding a yard, while further away in the same direction was another building.

Another house stood in a low-lying position near a stream, bordering a track which led eastwards towards Cadoxton. This house, 12 × 6 metres (39½ × 19½ feet) in area, had dry-built foundations with traces of lime plaster adhering to the inner face. The total absence of building debris suggested that the superstructure was half-timbered. The house was entered by a single door on the side facing the track. An unusual feature was a corn-drying kiln of oval plan with a projecting flue placed within the west end. Heating and cooking were provided for by a hearth in the opposite end of the house.

Two further stone houses lay along an east-west track running parallel with the north side of the church towards the Colcot. One of these was substantially built, with a north porch, plastered walls, and roof of Pennant Sandstone slabs capped by green-glazed ridge tiles. The other house which lay further to the west was 12 × 7 metres (39½ × 23 feet) and had a croft adjoining its west side which contained a corn-drying kiln.[29]

Within the bounds of the parish in the 13th century were the two hamlets of Pencoedtre and Holton, and an isolated farmstead at East Barry. Pencoedtre included among its buildings a very large, possibly aisled, peasant house, containing stone drains.[30]

The villages: Cadoxton (Tregatwg)

At Cadoxton the form of the village was influenced by a rocky whaleback hill of Carboniferous Limestone. The shallow soil cover there led to the formation of a large open common or waste. Here sites of nine medieval habitations are known from archaeological fieldwork, distributed in two distinct clusters skirting the northern and southern bounds of the common; the northern settlement, which lay close to the church, seems to have been the more substantial. In post-medieval times there was considerable infilling by the small dwellings of cottagers and artisans on the wasteland around the common. The result was a dramatic rise in population from 14 families in 1543 to 38 in 1673. These trends were to continue at Cadoxton until the 1800s, when it was one of the largest villages in south-east Glamorgan.[31]

The villages: Highlight (Uchelolau)

The settlement of Uchelolau on the northern outskirts of the town, overlooking the Waycock valley, was founded on marginal land as a manorial enterprise in the late 12th century. At the close of the following century it had developed into a small linear village following a ridgeway, of about half a dozen houses, together with a parish church and the manor house already described. The village, with the exception of the manor house, became completely depopulated before the mid 16th century.

The villages: Cwmcidy

On the western side of Barry town was another deserted village, at Cwmcidy, which lay in the lordship of Penmark. This village had come into existence before the middle of the 13th century, its fertile land of 280 acres producing sufficient surplus to just about support a parish church. The settlement suffered some shrinkage in the late medieval period as a result of which it was joined for ecclesiastical purposes with Porthkerry and Barry and its church abandoned.

In 1622 Cwmcidy contained five houses bordering 'Comkedye Street' interspersed with a number of tofts including a 'croft whereuppon in tyme past theare was seated a howse'. There were a further three scattered dwellings, one of which had been built on the site of the church. Further depopulation took place in the 18th century, when the tenements were incorporated into larger units. By 1812 there remained only three cottages and a farmhouse. These, with the exception of the farmhouse, were finally swept away in the 1840s when the area was landscaped by the Romilly family to form the now familiar Porthkerry Park.[32]

The villages: depopulation

Unfortunately virtually nothing is known of the lives of the ordinary people who lived in these villages. Only a handful of their names has escaped oblivion, inscribed on parchment documents; there lived, for instance, a John and Mabil Val, both of Cadoxton, who were excommunicated in 1263 for contempt of the Bishop's Court. There was also an Adam of Pencoedtre who was living in *c.* 1280; a Thomas of East Barry who was living in 1339; and a Robert Mayo and Maud, his wife, who held a small freehold in Barry in the 1400s.[33]

The archaeological record gives clear indications that the local villages suffered depopulation in the later medieval period. Shrinkage may have been brought about through a complex combination of different factors rather than by a single cause. The late 13th century saw a considerable rise in population throughout the British Isles. Small villages like Barry, Cwmcidy and Uchelolau, in spite of their limited territory, certainly expanded during this period, possibly to such an extent that they outstripped their food resources. The period also coincided with a climatic deterioration into colder, wetter summers which caused a series of crop failures, one of which prompted the local Llywelyn Bren rebellion in 1316. Moreover, settlements such as Uchelolau, which were located on heavy clay soils, were particularly susceptible to increasingly waterlogged conditions which came about through the rise in the water table. Such decline as may have already taken root by the second decade of the 14th century would certainly have been accelerated by the three pestilences which swept into south-east Wales in 1349, 1361 and 1369.

The bubonic plague, or Black Death, is thought to have been first introduced into Britain by sailors using the Bristol Channel ports, in which case Barry, by virtue of being a seaport, would have hardly escaped the catastrophe. A few confirmatory clues to the local effects of these disasters are provided by the scanty documentary evidence. For example, the unexplained disappearance of the de Barri family after 1349; the drop in value by as much as a third of the combined manorial revenues of the four Penmark fees (which included Barry) between 1349 and 1376; and the union of the three parishes of Barry, Cwmcidy and Porthkerry in the 15th century.

The economic recovery which followed in the late 14th century was shattered by the Glyndŵr Rising which devastated the Vale of Glamorgan between 1402 and 1405. The Ministers' Accounts of 1428 for the Lordship of Ogmore remind us of the local effects of the rebellion there; it was recorded that more than half the tenements had been wiped out and three hamlets destroyed as a result of the warfare. At Llantwit Major in 1490 the manorial accountants were still blaming the Glyndŵr insurrection for low revenue 'because many tenants departed from the country, and their tenements burnt through the rebellion of Wales'. In this context it is worth noting that the manorial accounts for Dinas Powys for 1425-26 refer to a large number of tenements in the hands of the lord which had become vacant. Among these was 'one acre of land formerly a *curia* (court) at Caldecote (Colcot)', implying the existence there of an abandoned manorial complex of farm buildings around a courtyard, enclosed with a stone wall, similar to that which survived until recently at Biglis on the eastern outskirts of the town. The after-effects of the rebellion also created a cheap market in land, advantageous to the less wealthy purchaser, which resulted in the creation of several freeholds in Penmark lordship in the time of Sir John St. John (*fl.* 1400-25), at Barry, Rhoose and Porthkerry.[34]

Agriculture

The medieval economy of the Barry area was essentially based on mixed farming. Wheat and oats or barley were grown in rotation in large, open fields divided up into a number of narrow unenclosed strips, each about 5 metres (16½ feet) wide and varying in length according to the lie of the ground. These open fields had been completely enclosed with hedges in Barry parish by the 1600s, and in the parishes to the east, enclosure was completed in the following century, marking the end of a process which may have begun in the 15th century. Traces of medieval cultivation became fossilized in the elongated forms of the early modern fields, created when two or three strips had been joined together and enclosed; these survived throughout the Barry area until they were swept away by the building of the modern town.

A survey of the ploughlands of the shire fee of Glamorgan undertaken in 1320 for taxation purposes gives some rough pointers to the extent of arable. There is some evidence that the areas quoted in this survey and in other medieval documents of Glamorgan were reckoned in terms of the customary 'Gwentian' or 'Hereford' acre (3,240 square yards to the acre), and that the ploughland or carucate was the equivalent of 120 customary acres, or 80 statute acres. Thus, when converted to acres and deducted from the total statute area in each parish we find that Barry's four ploughlands represent approximately 59% of the total. This would seem to indicate that almost all the available land capable of cultivation in the small parish had been fully exploited by the early 14th century, as it was in the period of high farming in the Napoleonic Wars, when 63% of the land in Barry was arable. Cadoxton and Merthyr Dyfan were located on less fertile, impeded clay subsoil and had three and five ploughlands respectively, representing only about 28% of land used for cultivation. In the little manor of Uchelolau the position resembled that in Barry; its two ploughlands suggesting that 40% of its area was arable.[35]

In Barry the presence of abraded potsherds scattered in plough soil, notably in the fields north of Cwm Barry and at Westward Corner, carried there as a result of manuring, confirm that these areas of the parish had been brought under cultivation in the Middle Ages. In the valley bottoms of Cwm Barry and Cwm Cidy exist thick layers of white loamy calcareous marl (its local name 'gypsy soap'), deposited there by stream action. There is some evidence that these deposits, as well as those in other places in the Vale of Glamorgan (for example, Marcross), were not overlooked, being quarried for use as fertiliser and as a fuller's earth in cloth preparation.

The series of wet summers, known from general historical sources to have occurred throughout western Europe from the end of the 13th century, created difficulties in grain storage, making it necessary to dry the corn in kilns before threshing and milling. The well-preserved remains of such a kiln discovered at Barry village consisted of a sunken drying chamber 1 metre (39 inches) square, with an arched flue running out from its base. Kilns of similar design have also come to light at Uchelolau and Merthyr Dyfan. From modern examples in upland areas of the British Isles and Ireland, it is possible to reconstruct the drying process. A small fire was lit at the entrance of the flue, the hot gases being sufficient to dry the grain. The drying chamber had a floor of sticks supported by rafters over which was a primitive thatched loft. The corn was dried on the floor and the sheaves laid inwards; the whole process lasted 24 hours.[36]

From the bones recovered from excavations, discarded in the routine processes of butchery and cooking, it is possible to estimate the rough relative proportions of the domestic animals kept by the peasantry of Barry village on the one hand, and on the other by a manorial family or their servants at Uchclolau moated homestead. The identifiable specimens are as follows:

Table 1.
Analysis of animal bones excavated at Uchelolau (Highlight).

	Barry village	Uchelolau moat
Sheep	49·50%	33·10%
Cattle	25·74%	45·95%
Horse	00·99%	04·05%
Pig	23·76%	16·89%

The amount of meat supplied by each was:

Sheep	17·73%	07·94%
Cattle	66·38%	79·35%
Horse	02·26%	06·22%
Pig	13·61%	06·24%

The sheep were of an intermediate size between the Soay and the North Welsh Mountain breeds, and had been kept into maturity for wool; only a few surplus females were slaughtered young as lamb. The bulk of the meat came from small cattle which were used as plough oxen and milking cows, with the occasional calf producing veal. The majority of the pigs were slaughtered while still immature. At Barry village the beasts were killed on the spot, one cow having been decapitated by a downward and forward-directed axe blow. A few chickens were also kept. The diet was supplemented by oysters, limpets, winkles, whelks and mussels, occasionally gathered from the foreshore. The meat supply provided by wild animals was of little significance.

Dairying and cheese-making is hinted at by the presence of wide-mouthed earthenware pans and large, flat dishes with incurved sides, perforated with holes in the walls and base. These latter utensils were perhaps used for draining the curd, as are vessels of a similar shape that are still used in the La Bourne area of central France.

Rabbits are known to have been farmed on the islands of the Bristol Channel from the 13th century. This was certainly the case on Barry Island, for in 1491, there is a reference under 'New Rents' in a Minister's Account of the manor of Sully, to a payment by Nicholas Button of 26*s.* 8*d.* for the island 'with its rabbits'. In the reign of Richard III, John Wrexham was Royal keeper there, Sully then being in Royal hands. In 1485 Henry VII appointed Robert Jones, Groom of the King's Chamber, to a sinecure, this being the keepership of the warren of Barry Island, a post which he retained until 1511. Rabbits were still the principal produce of the island in the early 19th century, when they were exported in great quantities to Bristol. The sandy soil which covered the south part of the island provided ideal terrain for burrows. The presence of a pillow mound on Friars Point shows that natural rabbit breeding was supplemented by artificial means.

About 78 acres, or 15%, of the parish of Barry was woodland. This included the lord's wood, called 'Barry Wood' (now Cliffwood in Porthkerry Park). This wood contained twenty acres and was noted by Rice Merrick in 1578 because it was one of the largest in the Vale of Glamorgan. This wood was retained by the lord of the manor as his private reserve on account of its valuable timber. The trees and undergrowth, in addition to contributing wood for house- and ship-building, poles for fences, bark for tanning and acorns for pig food, provided an ideal habitat for game.

The peasants were forbidden to cut live timber or graze their animals in the lord's wood, but were allowed, under licence, to take timber for repairs and to collect dead wood for firewood. Charcoal samples from one of the hearths in Barry village show that the composition of the tree species in the local woodland was as follows: oak (40%), birch (28%), hazel (9%), beech (7%), ash (7%), alder (4%) and elm (2%). Mature oaks from the lord's wood would have provided the eleven great timber beams, each 6 metres (19½ feet) long, which were used in the construction of the floor of the hall of Barry Castle early in the 14th century.[37]

Manorial mills

The right to mill grain was the monopoly of the lord of the manor. Peasants were obliged to grind their grain at the lord's mill upon payment of a 'multure', usually a proportion of the grain fixed by custom. Failure to render suit was usually subject to a heavy fine, 13*s.* 4*d.* in the case of Penmark and its dependent manors. The Barry area was served by three mills; at Barry, Cadoxton and Uchelolau. The villagers of Porthkerry and Cwmcidy were without mills and had to take their grain to Penmark. Likewise, the inhabitants of Merthyr Dyfan were dependent upon the Cadoxton mill.

The mill at Cadoxton was in existence from as early as the first half of the 12th century when a grant of 20*s.* out of the rent of the mill was made by Adam de Sumeri to the monks of Margam Abbey. In late 12th century documents it is described as the 'mill of the moor' and, in the 16th century, was still referred to by the same name. Its site lay on the edge of marshy ground near the north bank of the Cadoxton river. The power was derived from water fed through a long leat which joined the river upstream near Ferlon Farm. When this mill became ruinous in the 1760s it was replaced by a new one, built downstream on a dam near the mouth of the river.[38]

Uchelolau's mill was located at Lidmore within a bend of the Waycock river. Here the stream had been dammed to form an elongated pond, 45 × 12 metres (49 × 16½ yards), which provided a head of water for an undershot wheel. The building still stands as a dwelling house and retains a Tudor doorway.[39]

The Barry mill stood in woodland within Porthkerry Park, near the westernmost limit of the manorial boundary. Here a small stream had been diverted into an embanked leat 450 metres (492 yards) long which terminated in a narrow pond. Trial excavation has shown that the mill was a drystone, two-roomed structure, 10 × 7 metres (33 × 23 feet) overall, placed so as to abut the end of the pond at a right angle. Between the side wall of the mill and the pond was a strongly revetted pit, still partially visible, which housed an overshot or breastshot wheel. The mill was in use in the 13th and early 14th century. It was probably destroyed during the Glyndŵr revolt in the early 15th century, and was never rebuilt owing to loss of suit caused by depopulation. By 1622 its site was overgrown with woodland and completely lost.[40]

Finds of small hand-querns (grinding stones) in the peasant houses at Barry and Porthkerry and elsewhere indicate that there had been fairly widespread evasion of the obligation to grind at the lord's mill. Perhaps the

Fig. 29.
The corn mill of Barry manor, as it might have appeared in *c.* 1350.
Simon Prosser after H.J.T.

manorial laws against hand milling were never rigorously enforced, provided the peasants put in a regular appearance at the manorial mill, or when the local mills (comparatively few in relation to the density of population) were under repair. The find of a hand mill at Barry Castle itself would suggest that the local mill was not always reliable.

The port and fisheries

From medieval times Barry was one of a number of tiny ports on the creeks of the Glamorgan coast which included Penarth, Sully, Aberthaw, Ogmore and Newton. The site of the ancient port of Barry lay in the western part of the tidal channel or sound which divided Barry Island from the mainland, in the area now occupied by the 'Old Harbour'. The landing place was on the northern shore, in the parish and manor of Barry. Here, a low promontory extended into the harbour, against which was a bank of shingle which provided mooring for ships, sheltered from the prevailing south-west winds by a ridge of land on the west. In the 16th century and probably much earlier, the port facilities included the Ostry tavern and a warehouse, while the 1878 Ordnance Survey Map marks the position of mooring-posts. From the harbour's edge there was good road communication inland with the medieval borough of Llantrisant.[41]

In Lifris' *Life* of St. Cadoc, compiled in *c.* 1090, *Barren* (Barry) is named as the location of a harbour which served the district belonging to the Celtic monastery of Llancarfan, a legend perhaps derived from some memory of maritime trade there in the Early Christian period. However, a port at Barry which continued to be used into the Norman period would explain the choise of St. Nicholas, the patron of sailors, for the dedication of the parish church.[42]

The earliest reliable reference to trade at Barry occurs as the subject of a lawsuit in the King's Assize Rolls of 1274. The proceedings record that

Robert le Veel, the bailiff of the Earl of Gloucester, on Tuesday 10 April 1274, seized a ship and its cargo in the port of *Barri,* which was valued at 26 marks (£17 6*s.* 8*d.*), the property of a French merchant, Henry of Caen. The owner suffered further losses by being taken away and imprisoned in Cardiff Castle until he paid a fine of 100 marks. The involvement of the Earl's bailiff is explained by the fact that the tolls of the port of Barry, together with those of Aberthaw and Ogmore, formed part of the revenue of the Lords of Glamorgan. These continued to be collected and accounted for by the bailiff from 1307 to 1375. This fact in itself implies that there was early maritime trade at these places, of sufficient potential to have been reserved by the conqueror of Glamorgan when the Vale was parcelled out among his followers. However, local trade was troubled by pirates as early as 1291, when it was recorded that Welshmen had stolen goods from merchants off the island of Sully. Before the beginning of the 17th century the port rights of Barry had been somehow transferred from the Chief lord to the St. John family, lords of the manor of Barry.[43]

Unfortunately, no medieval records survive relating to the nature of the goods exported and imported, though these must have included consignments of French wine. Finds of potsherds of freshly broken appearance from the mud of the harbour up to 100 (109 yards) metres from the shoreline represent damaged goods thrown overboard from vessels and point to ceramic imports in the 13th and 14th centuries, mostly green-glazed jugs from the Bristol region. It is also interesting to note that, in the last century, what was described as a complete '16th-century crock' was dredged from the harbour.[44]

In 1598 there existed, at the edge of the harbour, a building referred to as the Storehouse which combined the function of a warehouse-cum-customs house. A quarter of a century later it was described as 'a howse lately newe buylte' containing 'divers Loftes and Sellors'. At this date the 'Ancient Customs belonginge to the Haven of Barrey' were collected at the Storehouse by an official called a Water Bailiff. Each ship entering the haven was required to pay 2*d.* keelage, or 4*d.* if accompanied by a cockboat. On cargoes there was a levy of two bushels for every shipload of salt, 4½*d.* for every tun of wine and, 'if anye Straunger as Frenchman, Spaniard, Portingall or such like bringe in any Shippe into the Sayde Haven beeinge laden with theire owne propper goods, shall paye dobble the Keelage and double the Customs or Ancourage of Salte and Wyne'.[45]

The Barry Sound and the adjacent coastline abounded with many varieties of sea fish, including bass, plaice, skate, thornback, gurnet, brill, mullet, turbot and sole. Remains of fish bones, with a clinch nail from a boat, found in a medieval midden near the priest's house at Barry, confirm that these resources were exploited from an early date.

The rights to take sea fish were the exclusive franchise of the local landowners, the coast between Sully and Porthkerry being divided into four fisheries. From at least the later Middle Ages these were leased or farmed to various private individuals. The fishery of Barry occupied the western half of the haven of Barry westward around Cold Knap to Porthkerry. From about the first quarter of the 15th century the Barry fishery seems to have been parcel of a small freehold which had been granted by John St. John to a Robert Mayo. In 1556 what may have been the same property, its freehold now extinguished, identified as the Ostry, was let as a tenement with its fishing rights to Lewis David; and in 1598 it was let to Reynold Portrey for 5*s*.[46]

The fishing in the eastern part of the haven belonged to the manor of Sully. In 1491 this was let for 8*s*. Further east were two other fisheries each let for 6*s*. One of these lay in the eastern entrance of the sound between Bendricks and 'Barri Cliff', a place noted for sprat fishing until the last century. The other lay around an island called 'Litell Sully' which could be Sully Island or, perhaps, 'Little Island' once a separate island between Cold Knap and Barry Island.[47]

Churches and parishes

The area of the town and its environs contains the sites of seven medieval churches. These were founded as places of worship for small parishes that matched the knights' fees of the district. There were, in addition, a pilgrimage chapel on Barry Island and small private chapels in the manor houses.

The presence of Celtic dedications unsupported by early literary references or by the survival of Early Christian memorial stones at Cadoxton, Merthyr Dyfan and Porthkerry remains a puzzle. The most likely explanation is that these dedications bear testimony to the continuing post-Norman popularity of local saints among a surviving residual Welsh population rather than that they are evidence of actual Celtic foundations. These churches would have been erected and endowed at the expense of the manorial lords to meet the spiritual needs of themselves and their tenants. The lords also retained the right of advowson, namely the privilege of presenting a priest (sometimes a younger son) to the benefice.

Barry church was doubtless founded by the de Barris; Porthkerry and Cwmcidy, which lay within the demesne lordship of Penmark, by the de Umfravilles, while Cadoxton and Merthyr Dyfan may have been de Mitdehorguill creations. Their status originally would have been that of manorial chapelries subordinate to a mother church, but distinguished from chapels of ease by possessing rights of baptism and burial. All eventually acquired full independent parochial status before the middle of the 13th century.

The plans of the parish boundaries and their relationship to each other provide some clue as to parochial origins. The parishes of Barry, Porthkerry and Cwmcidy were carved out of Penmark, itself taken from the former territory of the Celtic monastery of Llancarfan. The rights of mother churches were jealously guarded, hence the complaint by Theobald, archbishop of Canterbury, to Uthred, bishop of Llandaff, in *c.* 1140, that 'chapels had been lately built in the parish of St. Cadoc of Lancarvan', thus diverting revenue from the mother church, certainly includes the aforementioned churches in the broader territorial context. At Merthyr Dyfan a primary parish church seems to have been founded perhaps not long after the conquest of Glamorgan and its territory subsequently sub-divided in the later 12th century with 'daughter' churches at Cadoxton and Uchelolau.[48]

There survive for Llandaff Diocese three ecclesiastical returns, namely the *Taxation of Norwich,* 1254, the *Taxatio* of Pope Nicholas IV, 1291, and the *Valor Ecclesiasticus* of Henry VIII, compiled in 1534, made for the purpose of Royal and Papal taxation whereby a tax was levied on the revenue of each benefice. These provide valuable information as to the state of local parish finances throughout the later medieval period. The relative value of the six rectories in the Barry area is shown by the following table:

Table 2.
Value of medieval rectories in Barry area.

	1254			1291			1534		
	£	*s.*	*d.*	*£*	*s.*	*d.*	*£*	*s.*	*d.*
Porthkerry	6	0	0	3	6	8	8	3	0
Cadoxton	4	13	4	3	6	8	5	2	1
Merthyr Dyfan	3	0	0	2	13	4	5	2	4
Barry	2	10	0	2	13	4			
Uchelolau	1	6	8	1	0	0			
Cwmcidy	1	0	0						

The priests' stipends would have been based upon the farming of the glebeland, gifts, offerings and tithes of the parishioners' agricultural produce. The above estimates of 1254 and 1291, however, represent only the value of the benefice let to farm, i.e. the rental value which was considerably lower than the gross value.

The 1254 figures, with the exception of Porthkerry, reflect modest or poor livings, among some of the poorest in the diocese. In 1291 there had been a slight decrease in four of the churches while Barry was worth 3*s.* 4*d.* more, the whole showing a sharp contrast with the staggering increase in values of benefices throughout Wales which occurred between 1254 and 1291. All would have been classed as 'lesser benefices', namely churches under the value of 6 marks (£4), while Cwmcidy was omitted altogether from the

1291 taxation on grounds of extreme poverty. The distribution of these churches forms a compact geographical cluster surrounded by wealthier churches, highlighting the areas of less productive land which had been divided up as sub-fees.[49]

There is also a useful list of Synodals compiled in *c.* 1348 which shows that in the first half of the 14th century there had occurred a slight shift in the relative order of prosperity, the churches contributing the following amounts: Porthkerry 2*s.* 5*d.*, Cadoxton 2*s.* 5*d.*, Barry 17*d.*, Cwmcidy 17*d.*, Uchelolau 15*d.* and Merthyr Dyfan 12*d.* The synodal represented a fixed proportion of the value of each church which was paid to the bishop for his visitation and synod. The churches of the Barry area also figure in an account roll attached to a Clerical Subsidy certificate of 1433 (which was based on the estimates of 1291). In a clerical taxation return of the following year we are again reminded of poverty when it was reported that Cadoxton was in arrears of tithe subsidy.[50]

The effects of depopulation on church revenues is vividly illustrated by the cases of Barry and Cwmcidy, which were united with Porthkerry between 1433 and 1534 and demoted in status to parochial chapelries served by rectors of Porthkerry. Barry was afterwards separated from Porthkerry in 1674, and again united for the second time on grounds of insufficient population in 1839. Cwmcidy had become defunct long before 1591, when all that was left to mark the site was 'a vacant parcel of land where the church was formerly built'.[51]

The 1534 return, based on the gross values, shows that the local churches were still poor and among the 45% of churches in the diocese which were worth between £5 and £10. Uchelolau, or Highlight, survived the abandonment of the village there for a short period after the Reformation, virtually as a private chapel and burying place for the occupants of the nearby St. John manor house. In *c.* 1570 its tithes, then worth 20 marks (£13 6*s.* 8*d.*), were seized by Christopher St. John who refused to appoint a priest. The church was abandoned and, in 1603, was described as 'almost fallen down'.[52]

A few references to the medieval clergy who served these churches have survived. Among them was a 'Thomas, Rector of Barry' who assisted in the compilation in Llandaff deanery of the estimates for the 1254 taxation. There is a record that a certain Richard Russel, clerk, was presented about 1390 by trustees to a church (probably Barry) belonging to the St. John 'moiety' of Penmark. The register of Archbishop Peckham records the institution, on 6 July 1291, of Richard de Torvesmere to the church of *Highanwole* (Uchelolau).[53]

In 1371 a Thomas Michel, 'parson of the church of *Pourkerrye*' was one of the trustees for the St. John manors in Penmark, and in *c.* 1390 he appears in the same capacity when settling Barry manor upon Alexander St. John.

(This led to a suit in Chancery whereby Thomas Michel's niece, the 'bedewoman' Joan, widow of Robert Trenchmere, disputed Alexander's title, a tenuous claim probably connived at to extort a fee for a deed of quitclaim.) Thomas Michel may have been the person of the same name who, in retirement and aged 60, served St. Catherine's chantry at Ilminster, Somerset, in *c.* 1400.[54]

Exchanges and the pluralistic acquisition of additional benefices in the search for increased clerical income were common in the later Middle Ages, as is illustrated by the movements of Thomas Gosselyn, rector of Stauley in the diocese of Bath and Wells. He exchanged benefices with Thomas Cotynham, vicar of Swansea, on 14 November 1401, and then exchanged with William Gowrda, rector of Porthkerry, in the following May. Another case was John Thomas, rector of Porthkerry, who in 1495 received a Papal dispensation to hold another church in plurality in the Diocese of Bath and Wells. At the time of the Reformation three of the parishes had rectors who signed the Oath of Allegiance to King Henry VIII, namely Lewis Thomas at Cadoxton, William Thomas at Merthyr Dyfan and Robert Hewys at Uchelolau.[55]

St. Barruc's chapel

The pilgrimage chapel on Barry Island stood on the reputed grave of a Celtic saint, thought to be of an itinerant Irishman, Barruc *alias* Finbarr, the patron saint of Cork. There is an early legend that the saint was a disciple of St. Cadoc of Llancarfan and was drowned while fetching a manual book from a Lenten retreat on Flat Holm. His body was afterwards washed up on the shore of the island and there buried. Veneration of the saint's burial place received further impetus in Norman times when a chapel was built over the spot.[56]

Gerald de Barri, in 1188, testifies to the existence in his day of an ivy-covered chapel housing the saint's relics, which had been transferred to a shrine. The chapel is omitted from medieval taxations because it was technically a free chapel not affiliated to a parish church or religious establishment, but supported entirely by the offerings of pilgrims.

The chapel flourished during the pilgrimage revival of the 15th century when the cult of St. Barruc achieved fairly widespread popularity. At Wenvoe church, a few miles inland, there existed a side altar adorned with an image of St. Barruc, and on the island itself was a votive well dedicated to the saint, noted for its curative powers. In a letter dated March 1476, sent by Sir Harry Stradling from Rome to his wife Elizabeth at St. Donat's, reference is made to a religious vow to be kept at an unnamed shrine in Barry. Sir Harry instructed his wife 'I pray yowe to se my dayes kept at Barry, for ye dayes must nede be kept or ellse I must be schamyd'. The chapel was abandoned in the early 16th century and the ruins gradually engulfed by sand dunes.[57]

Fig. 30.
St. Barruc's Chapel, as it might have appeared in its final phase, *c.* 1500.
Simon Prosser after H.J.T.

The chapel occupied high ground on the eastern side of the Island, commanding the Bristol Channel. The foundations were discovered and exposed in 1894 and again excavated in 1968. The results show that the building was a tiny Norman church of a nave and apsidal chancel which had been constructed along the north side of an earlier single-celled chapel with rounded corners only 5 × 3 metres (16½ × 9¾ feet) overall, itself built over the site of an older burial ground. The inside contained two altars and a shrine housing the saint's relics in a stone box. In the 1300s the chancel was extended with buttressed walls and square east end and the Pennant Sandstone roof replaced with Cornish slates. About this period the pre-Norman church was allowed to fall into ruin and its site incorporated into the graveyard.

Against the north side of the church had been built a two-roomed priest's house which was of later date than the extension of the chancel. It comprised a hall lined with stone benches and a small inner room heated by a raised fireplace in its north-east corner. Numerous burials inside the church and an extensive graveyard are a reminder of the special sanctity in which the site was regarded in the Middle Ages.[58]

St. Nicholas's church

The parish church of Barry was located on a prominent spur of land overlooking the harbour. The survival of a plain Norman font of Sutton stone would seem to indicate that the church had been founded by the 12th century. In the 13th century a small church was built, probably replacing an older structure. It consisted of a chancel and nave, only 14 × 6 metres (46 × 20 feet) overall. Its walling incorporated some re-used tiles robbed from the ruins of the Roman building at Cold Knap. Over the west end was a gabled bell-cot for two bells.

The only late medieval addition was a rather poorly constructed porch which had a Perpendicular door. Above the south door of the nave there was inserted a carved stone corbel which probably supported an image of the patron saint. About this date the church had a roof of Cornish slate with glazed ridge tiles. The revival of piety in the 15th century was here reflected by the erection of a churchyard cross, of which only the octagonal socket stone on three steps remains. In the early 16th century the chancel arch was rebuilt to allow the insertion of a rood screen. The archaeological record chronicles a mysterious incident in the church's history. From signs of reddening on the walls and floor it is apparent that a bonfire had been kindled within the newly-constructed porch, the object of which must have been forcible entry through burning down the door![59]

At the time of the Reformation Barry church was fairly well endowed with liturgical goods, including a cope of blue satin of Bruges and two pairs of vestments, respectively of green damask and green silk. Brass vessels comprised a pix (a small box for the reserved sacrament, sometimes suspended over the altar), a holy-water pot and a censer, while the stone altar was adorned with a copper gilt cross flanked by two brass candlesticks. In 1572 one of the bells, worth 40 shillings, was lost through theft. The surviving medieval bell was replaced in 1630 by a new one inscribed 'FEARE GOD'. The church was demolished in 1874 and replaced by a larger edifice in Early English style, designed by a noted antiquarian, John Romilly Allen.[60]

Against the northern boundary of the churchyard there once stood a priest's house. This building was built of stone bedded in red clay brought from the harbour. Rubbish deposits lying around the building contained a quantity of food refuse and potsherds of late 13th-century and early 14th-

Fig. 31.
Barry church
(St. Nicholas) in 1873,
before demolition.
J. Romilly Allen.

century date. It had been abandoned early, probably long before the parish was amalgamated with its neighbours, and its site subsequently used as a butts for archery practice.[61]

St. Cadoc's church

Cadoxton parish church was located on a low-lying stream bank near the northern perimeter of the common. The presence of a small, plain, roll-moulded Norman font and an Early English piscina point to the existence of a church here in the 12th century. In the 15th century there took place considerable structural alterations, responding to the expense and patronage of the resident lords, the Andrew family, at which period the nave was rebuilt and lengthened and a west tower with saddleback roof added. The interior was further embellished by the insertion of a rood loft and screen within a renewed chancel arch, and the roofs covered with handsome waggon trusses of Somerset craftsmanship. A cross was erected in the churchyard. In close proximity to the churchyard existed a parsonage house and tithe barn.

By the middle of the 16th century the church's goods included a vestment of blue velvet valued at 40*s.* and a vestment of red silk with a blue satin cope, together valued at 15*s.* There was also a silver chalice, its paten cover weighing 3½ ounces, a brass censer and eleven brass candlesticks which may have adorned the rood loft as well as the altars, the brass items valued in all at 22*s.*[62]

Plate XIII. Cadoxton church (St. Cadoc). *Matthew Griffiths.*

Fig. 32.
Plans of medieval churches in Barry area.
H.J.T.

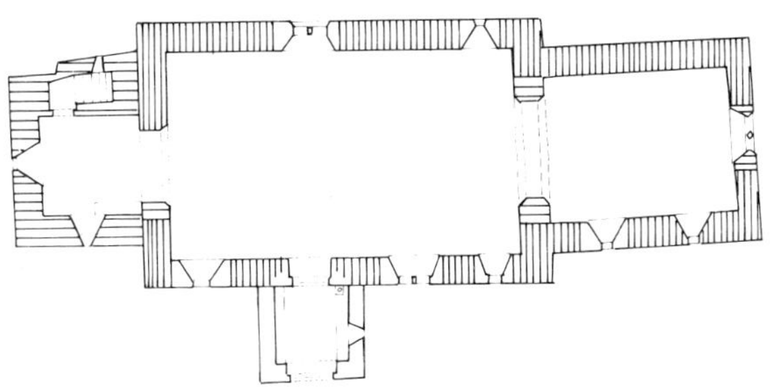

Merthyr Dyfan

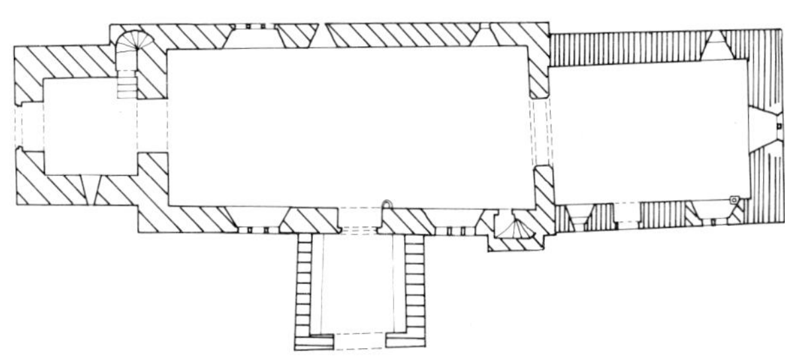

Cadoxton

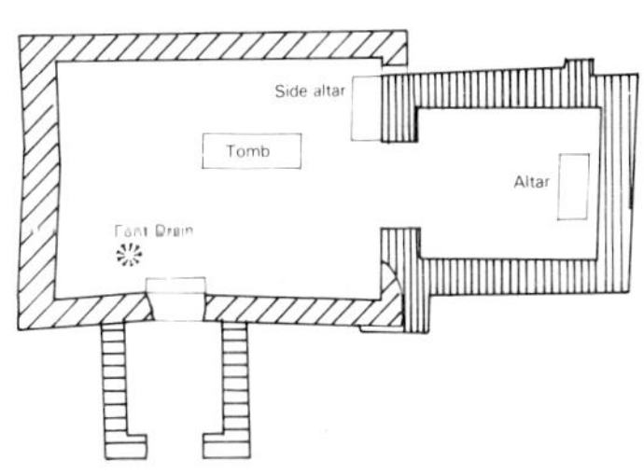

Uchelolau (Highlight)

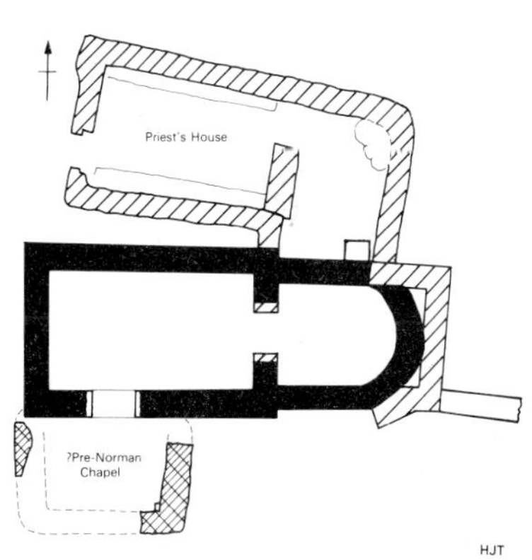

St. Barruc's Chapel

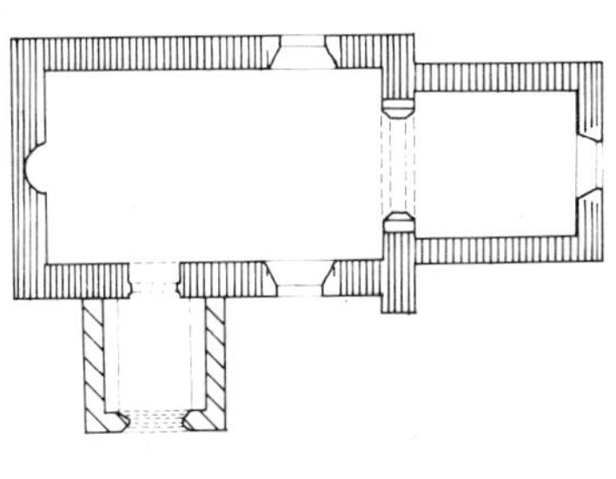

Barry

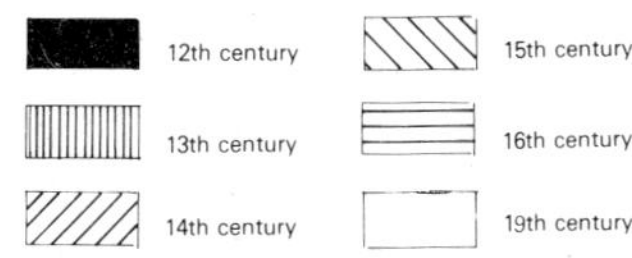

0 5 10 20 30 40 50 FT

0 10 15 M

Plate XIV.
Merthyr Dyfan church
(St. Dyfan).
Matthew Griffiths.

St. Dyfan's church

The parish church of Merthyr Dyfan was picturesquely sited in a sheltered ravine within an unusually large churchyard containing a holy well. In the 12th or early 13th century a fairly sizeable church was erected, consisting of a nave and chancel and possessing a stone altar and a bowl-shaped Norman font. Throughout the three centuries after its building there were only minor alterations, but in the early 16th century a crenellated tower was built on to the west end, a porch added, and the chancel arch rebuilt for a rood screen and loft. A late medieval cross stood in the churchyard.

In 1553 the Commissioners of King Edward VI took from this church a cross of copper gilt worth 20*s.*, a vestment of white fostian worth 6*s.* 8*d.*, a cope of white damask valued at 20*s.* and a vestment of green damask valued at 33*s.* 4*d.* The church was drastically restored and gutted of its screen in the middle of the last century.[63]

Uchelolau church

The foundations of Uchelolau church, excavated in 1964, survive on a brow overlooking the Waycock valley. This church, its dedication lost, had been constructed in the late 12th or early 13th century, partly with re-used Roman building material. It comprised a small chancel and nave, roofed

Fig. 33. Uchelolau (Highlight) church, as it might have appeared in c. 1500. *Simon Prosser after H.J.T.*

with Pennant Sandstone slabs. In the 14th century the nave collapsed owing to subsidence, and the Norman font was damaged. The nave was subsequently rebuilt with a Cornish slate roof. The final phase of the building saw the addition of a south porch with pitched stone floor in the early 16th century. In the early part of the following century the abandoned church was occupied by squatters who lit a cooking fire on the floor.

The inside contained a stone altar against the east wall of the chancel (which did not possess an east window). The position of the font was marked by a sand-filled drainage hole in the nave to the left of the door. Many shallow burials, some representing members of the local manorial family, had been inserted in the clay floor over the centuries. Most of these bodies had been interred without coffins, extended full length with their arms placed alongside the trunk. The most interesting burial was identified by the accompanying grave goods as a priest. He had been buried in a wooden coffin in front of a side altar. The body, which had been dressed in linen garments bound by a belt, was fully extended with the forearms positioned across the chest, the hands placed together in prayer, and the left foot placed over the right foot. On his abdomen had been placed a lead funerary chalice and paten. Another chalice of pewter had been put near the feet. The nave contained also the mortared foundation of a rectangular tomb erected over the grave of William St. John, lord of Uchelolau, who died in 1562. The majority of the corpses in the churchyard had been buried with their arms crossed on their chests.

Other finds included sherds of an earthenware cruet, a bronze book clasp from a missal, a piece of bronze chain, probably from a censer, and an iron key. Iron arrowheads found on the floor show that there had been archery practice in the vicinity.[64]

A small 13th-century priest's house stood on the north-east boundary of the churchyard. This house measured 9 × 5 metres (29½ × 16½ feet) and contained two rooms, the larger inner room heated by an open hearth. The house had been abandoned in the later Middle Ages and was in an advanced state of ruin before the 16th century.[65]

Today only two of the half-dozen medieval churches in the Barry area are still standing—at Cadoxton and Merthyr Dyfan. The fate of the others was less fortunate. The parish church of Cwmcidy, together with St. Barruc's chapel, became defunct at the Reformation. Uchelolau (Highlight) was closed down by its patron in the reign of Elizabeth I, while Barry church was demolished in 1874 and a new church built on its site, which in turn became redundant when replaced by All Saints' Church in 1908.

The discovery of Medieval Barry

The foregoing story of medieval Barry was largely drawn from the results of archaeological investigations carried out since the close of the last century. The first of these excavations was undertaken by John Storrie of Cardiff Museum at St. Barruc's chapel in 1895. He also located and partially dug two medieval settlements on the Island. His work was re-assessed by Aileen Fox in 1936 and the site of the chapel was re-excavated by Jeremy Knight in 1967-8, resulting in a further valuable contribution to our knowledge of Barry's early ecclesiastical history. The site of the shrunken medieval village of Barry, which lay off Park Road, fortunately escaped being built over when the town was founded, by being incorporated in the grounds of a large private house, later St. Baruch's School. Here, excavations by the Barry and Vale Archaeological Group in 1962, and by the Glamorgan-Gwent Archaeological Trust prior to building development in 1977, brought to light part of the village street with foundations of four houses, croft boundaries and ancillary structures. Between 1964 and 1972 portions of a deserted village were excavated by the Barry and Vale Archaeological Group at Highlight farm on the town's northern outskirts. The Group's work here revealed the footings of the parish church, a priest's house, and a moated manor house. Meanwhile, at the same time, Mr. Gareth Tyley recovered plans of foundations of four medieval dwellings belonging to the shrunken village of Merthyr Dyfan.

Excavation has been supplemented by intensive fieldwork carried out by local archaeologists, among them Gareth Dowdell, Gerald Davies, Gerald Beaudette and the author of this chapter. In the past twenty years they have recorded and plotted each discovery of potsherds and traces of buildings

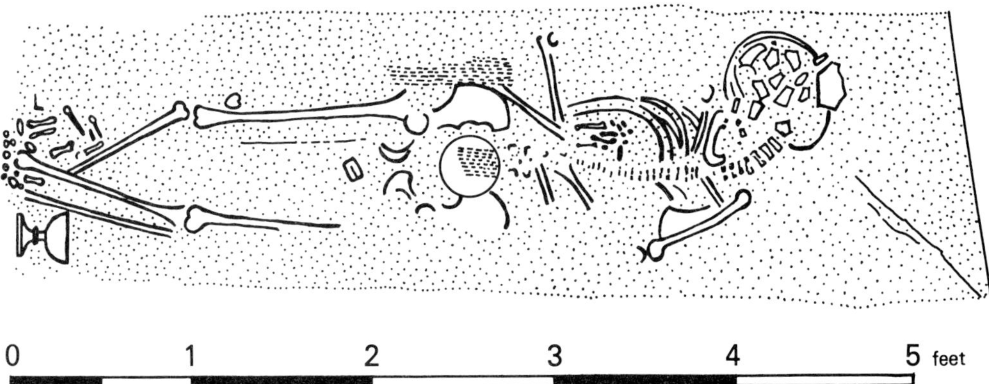

Fig. 34.
Burial of medieval priest in nave of Uchelolau (Highlight) church.
H.J.T.

accidently made, particularly during the building boom of the 1960s. These discoveries have contributed some fifty previously unrecorded habitation sites belonging to the period between the 12th and the 14th centuries. These sites, when taken with documentary evidence, for instance the 1622 Manorial Map of Barry, which shows the positions of the medieval roads, have enabled a fairly reliable reconstruction of the medieval topography, notably that of Barry parish. Probably no other small area in Wales has been so studied in detail for the medieval period. It is, therefore, with some confidence that we can reconstruct the scene as it might have appeared 650 years ago.

A walk around Barry in 1340

Let us imagine ourselves transferred back in time to the autumn of the year 1340, about to commence a short perambulation of medieval Barry. The walk will take us from the site of the port (opposite the Ship Hotel, near the Parade Gardens), through the village (now Old Village Road), to the place where the manorial mill once stood (near the golf course in Porthkerry Park), a distance in all of about one and a half miles.

From our starting point at the harbour, we note a low foreshore of rocky cliffs with two Bristol or French merchant sailing ships beached on the shingle. Cargoes of salt, earthenware pots, and barrels of wine, destined for the townspeople of Llantrisant, are being unloaded and transferred to a strongly-built warehouse located on the cliff edge. Here we also see a group of merchants arguing with the waterbailiff over the payment of customs dues, while stevedores are stacking bales of Welsh wool destined for the outgoing voyages. The only other building of note in the immediate vicinity is a stone-built tavern called the Ostry, providing overnight lodgings for merchants and the occasional pilgrim *en route* for the shrine of Saint Barruc.

Looking to the south and east, we see Barry Island separated from the shore by a muddy tidal sound across which runs a shingle causeway. Close to the low island foreshore opposite (the site of the present Island fairground), a group of farm buildings is visible. To the south lies the entrance of the harbour bounded by a promontory (Friars Point) on the east, and by a small rocky islet of Cold Knap on the opposite mainland side, with the grey turbulent waters of the Bristol Channel beyond.

Turning to the north west, we find a rutted trackway ascending a gentle slope (Ship Hill). Following its route, we soon reach the brow of a hill surmounted on the left by the small parish church. A sharp fork of the road turns into the graveyard past a thatched priest's house set against the hedged boundary of the churchyard. From the church we see a broad view over the Bristol Channel across to the Somerset coast. On the landward horizon to the east the keep of Sully castle is visible, while just below is the treeless terrain of Barry Island, with the whitewashed chapel of Saint Barruc, perched just below its highest point. To the north-west there is a shallow bowl-shaped valley (now occupied by Romilly Park) with meadowland in the bottom, and the castle and village of Barry on the brow opposite. Travelling northwards from the churchyard (St. Nicholas Road), we come in a few minutes to a triangular village green with a few sheep grazing on it. From here the track continues as a merchants' 'highway' (Park Crescent) that leads eventually to the towns of Llantrisant and Cardiff. To the east a track down a steep hill (Canon Street) leads to the farmstead of East Barry (Broad Street), continuing further for about three-quarters of a mile on low-lying ground until it reaches the hamlet of Holton, also close to the shore of the tidal sound.

Taking the track to the west through the green (Old Village Road), we can see on our right a row of some half-dozen widely spaced drystone dwellings, all low and thatched with both gabled and hipped roofs (reminiscent of 19th-century Scottish crofters' houses), with trails of smoke drifting from holes in their roofs. Surrounding the houses are muddy farmyards containing pigs and chickens. To the rear are several gardens and rickyards with stacks of unthreshed corn still in the sheaves. Looking inside one of the doorways we catch a glimpse in the dark smokey interior of an old woman furtively grinding grain with a small hand-mill. Peasants are flailing and winnowing corn. Behind the first house billowing smoke issues from a corn-drying oven. To the north, behind the village, is a rather bare, hedgeless landscape made up of a patchwork of open-field strips, some fallow and grazed by sheep; others are being ploughed by pairs of oxen managed by boys.

After a few hundred yards the track reaches a crest and then turns to the right (Park Road). Here, against its northern angle there stands, in stark contrast to the mean dwellings just passed, an imposing castle, or rather fortified manor house, its stonework new and crisp, surrounded by hedged paddocks and fronted by a circular, domed pigeon house. Passing over the drawbridge, beneath the portcullis, and through the gate passage, we enter a small courtyard enclosed by a high crenellated wall. The open space is hemmed in by various buildings, including the lord's residential block, distinguished by its tall, circular chimney, outbuildings and stables, all substantially built with crenellated eaves and slated roofs.

Returning to the road, we proceed for a few hundred yards in a north-westerly direction passing more open fields on both sides of the road, until reaching a steep-sided valley called Cwm Barry which opens into a larger valley called Cwm Cidy. The track turns westwards skirting the edge of a north-facing wooded slope, the track dividing the wooded ground from arable land on the south. In the valley bottom below the bend in the road the presence of smoke points to another habitation, perhaps a fulling mill. Further to the west we find that the road (Lovers' Lane) descends steeply down into the lord's wood flanking the southern slope of the Cidy valley. Through the trees we see a low-lying farmstead in a clearing. Beyond the stream that marks the manorial boundary lies the village of Cwmcidy nestling in a ravine with its little church prominently visible on the open brow opposite.

Walking downhill through a great oak wood that is enclosed by a strong hedge, we reach a stream blocked by a dam (opposite Nightingale Cottage in Porthkerry Park). Here the road divides in two directions; one to the north crossing the dam through lush meadowland called Barry Moor to join with another track leading from Cwmcidy village to Porthkerry and Penmark; the other continuing to the west, diminishing to a small trail that runs along the base of a wooded slope parallel with an embanked leat or watercourse leading to a mill. As we walk along this track we pass a peasant leading a pack-horse loaded with bags of grain. Near the mill we pass a sluice, and gradually we become aware of the creaking, clacking noise of primitive machinery. We now find ourselves standing by a deep embanked pond next to a small thatched mill, its door being the termination of the track. There is another sluice on the streamward side of the pond; the water is conveyed through a wooden trough on to the top of a large wooden wheel housed in a deep walled pit on the side of the building. We have now reached the end of our journey and are standing on the bank of the stream which turns around the bottom of the slope, discharging into the sea at Porthkerry. The spot marks the western limit of Barry, the area beyond lying in the lordship of Penmark.

Conclusion

The early topography and history of the villages of Barry, Cadoxton, Cwmcidy, Merthyr Dyfan and Uchelolau, represent an excellent example in microcosm of the general developments which occurred in hundreds of small medieval settlements which existed throughout the lowland zones of England and Wales. These little farming communities came into existence in the 12th century as a result of Norman conquest and feudal exploitation. Following an initial period of colonial expansion into wasteland there emerged towards the end of the 13th century a period of prosperity combined with a maximum use of land resources. The result was the rebuilding and enlarging of peasant houses on a more substantial scale throughout the district, and the rebuilding of manor houses, including the reconstruction of Barry castle.

The Barry area, as elsewhere in the Vale of Glamorgan, was severely affected in late medieval times by depopulation, probably caused by a combination of crop failures, epidemics and warfare. The settlements possessing smaller territories were particularly vulnerable. In consequence, Barry village lost half of its houses, its mill went out of use, the castle there became ruinous, the priest's house abandoned, and the parish merged with two of its neighbours. The villages of Cwmcidy and Uchelolau shrank, eventually to the point of total extinction. The striking absence of any major structural alterations to the parish churches bears testimony to the late medieval poverty which prevailed, with two of the parochial churches becoming defunct before the middle of the 16th century.

In early modern times there was a gradual recovery in the parishes of Barry, Porthkerry and Merthyr Dyfan, though they never regained their former population. Thereafter they remained fairly prosperous, though static, until the building of the town at the close of the 19th century. Only at Cadoxton, which had a different geography and retained a resident lord, was there a major change. This wretched place, while not being relatively wealthier than its westerly neighbours, witnessed a rapid increase in its population until it became one of the largest villages in south-east Glamorgan.

References

1 Gwynedd O. Pierce, *The place-names of Dinas Powys hundred* (Cardiff, 1968), pp. 1-16.
2 Quoted in G. T. Clark, *The land of Morgan* (1883), pp. 14-15.
3 Gerald of Wales (Giraldus Cambrensis), *The Journey through Wales (1188) and the Description of Wales,* trans. and ed. Lewis Thorpe (Penguin edition, 1978), p. 125.
4 William Worcestre, *Itineraries,* ed. John H. Harvey (Oxford, 1969), p. 139.
5 *The itinerary of John Leland in or about the years 1536-1539,* ed. Lucy Toulmin Smith (1964 edn.), VI, pp. 23-4.
6 John Stuart Corbett, *Glamorgan: papers and notes on the lordship and its members,* ed. D. R. Paterson (Cardiff, 1925), pp. 94-107, 217-21.
7 Gerald of Wales, *op. cit.,* p. 125.
8 G. T. Clark, *Cartae et alia munimenta quae ad dominium de Glamorgancia pertinent* (2nd edn., Cardiff, 1910), II, p. 315 *et seq.,* p. 466 *et seq.;* III, pp. 570-1, p. 800; *Trans. Somerset Record Society,* III, p. 51; VI, p. 307; XI, p. 201; PRO, *Index of Placita de Banco 1327-8* (1910), I, p. 106.
9 Amy G. Foster, 'Two deeds relating to Neath Abbey', *South Wales and Monmouthshire Record Society Publications,* 2 (Cardiff, 1950), p. 206; *Trans. Somerset Record Society,* XI, p. 31; *Calendar of Close Rolls, Henry III, 1231-34,* pp. 354, 447, 538; Clark, *Cartae,* II, pp. 565-6; III, pp. 800. 850, 911; PRO, C. 49/1/20; Som. RO, DD/WO MTD/II/11a.
10 Clark, *Cartae,* III, pp. 981-2; IV, pp. 1213 *et seq.,* 1225-6; P. C. Bartrum, *Welsh genealogies A.D. 300-1400* (Cardiff, 1974), VIII, p. 899; C[ardiff] C[entral] L[ibrary], MS 3.464, p. 69; British Library, Lansdowne 860A, f. 286; 'Contribution towards a cartulary of Margam Abbey', *Arch. Camb.,* 3rd ser., XIV (1868), pp. 39-40.
11 NLW, Floyd 3784D (*inquisitio post mortem*) of Edward le Despencer, 49 Edward III); PRO, C. 1/6/322, 1/1069/10; CCL, MS 3.464, pp. 126-7 (Beauchamp's survey of the lordship of Glamorgan); GRO, Fonmon Deeds 694, 695; D/DF E/67.
12 RCAM (Wales), *Glamorgan,* III (part ii), p. 120; GRO, manorial map of Barry manor surveyed by Evans Mouse (1622).
13 The foundations of the SW angle turret are shown on a plan of Barry Castle by G. T. Clark, *c.* 1835, in NLW 5198.
14 Court roll entries of 1591 and 1615 mention the ruins of the castle and dovecot, both lying W of a parcel of wasteland. From the topography it seems that the dovecot lay S of the castle. A circular patch of rough ground is marked in this position on the 25-inch OS map of 1878. This was described in 1891 as 'immediately opposite the gateway. . . a mound covered with trees. . . said to be a cromlech or burial place of an old Welsh chieftain.' The area is now contained within the garden of a house. GRO, D/DF Court books, 1590-6 and 1604-15 (formerly D/DF vol. 40); The *Barry Dock News,* 13 March and 17 April 1891.
15 GRO, D/DF Court books; D/DF M/5; D/DF vol. 50 (Fonmon rental, 4/393); unscheduled estreats from Barry court rolls in Fonmon MSS, 1663, 1686 and 1719.
16 Beds. RO, GY 10, pp. 73-87; GRO, D/DF vol. 44, pp. 101-25; D/DF vol. 29.
17 In *c.* 1186-91 Milisant, daughter of William de Mitdehorguill, sold twelve acres of land in her fee of St. Nicholas to Margam Abbey in exchange for the sum of 13*s.* 4*d.,* so that she could pay a relief (or death tax) for her 'land of Barri'. The relief would have been in respect of two knights' fees, in which case her land at Barry was Cadoxton rather than West Barry. This transaction, together with other grants to Margam, was confirmed by her husband, Adam, son of Roger de Sumeri, lord of Dinas Powys (of which Cadoxton was a sub-fee). See J. Conway Davies (ed.), *Episcopal acts relating to Welsh dioceses, 1066-1272,* II (Historical Society of the Church in Wales, Nos. 3 and 4, 1948), pp. 671, 672, 675-6; J. Conway Davies (ed.), *The Welsh assize roll 1277-1284* (Cardiff, 1940), pp. 182-3, 288.
18 CCL, MS 3.464, pp. 62-3 (Hugh le Despencer's survey of the lordship of Glamorgan): College of Arms, MS 36/25, p. 6.
19 NLW Bute 106; RCAM (Wales), *Glamorgan,* III (part ii), p. 61; Gwynedd O. Pierce, *op. cit.,* p. 211.
20 Clark, *Cartae,* III, p. 976; Som. RO, DD/WO MTD/II/10, 11a.

21 *Ibid.,* VI, p. 2382.

22 PRO, C. 1/1069/10, 1/831/28, 1/940/23-4; GRO, Glamorgan Deeds 18.

23 CCL, MS 3.464, p. 126; NLW, Wales 22/8 (Glamorgan Plea Rolls), June 37 Henry VIII.

24 RCAM (Wales), *Glamorgan,* III (part ii), pp. 196, 378.

25 C. T. Martin (ed.), *Registrum epistolarum Fratris Johannis Peckham, Archiepiscopi Cantuariensis* (1885), III, p. 1011; PRO, C. 1/1059/66.

26 CCL, MS 3.464, p. 126; MS 5.6; NLW, Wales 22/7, 10, 57, 100, 130, 150; NLW, Add. MSS 7A, 8A; MS 5211; G. T. C[lark] and R[obert] O[liver] J[ones], 'Some account of the parish of Penmark', *Arch. Camb.,* 3rd ser., VII (1861), p. 7.

27 H. J. Thomas, 'Uchelolau (Highlight) Deserted Medieval Village', *Morgannwg,* XIV (1970), pp. 88-92; RCAM (Wales), *Glamorgan,* III (part ii), pp. 107-110.

28 H. J. Thomas, 'Barry, Old Village Road', *Morgannwg,* XXI (1977), pp. 92-5; RCAM (Wales), *Glamorgan,* III (part ii), pp. 231-33.

29 RCAM (Wales), *Glamorgan,* III (part ii), pp. 234-5.

30 *Ibid.,* p. 61.

31 Entries by G. Dowdell in *Archaeology in Wales,* 5 (1965), pp. 24-5; PRO, E. 179/221/237, 297.

32 RCAM (Wales), *Glamorgan,* III (part ii), pp. 224-8.

33 J. Conway Davies (ed.), *Episcopal acts,* II, p. 746; Clark, *Cartae,* III, pp. 783, 976; PRO, C. 1/1069/10.

34 William Rees, *South Wales and the March, 1284-1415* (Oxford, 1924), pp. 241-73; Corbett, *Glamorgan,* p. 205; T. B. Pugh (ed.), *Glamorgan County History,* III (Cardiff, 1971), pp. 302-4; NLW Bute 106.

35 CCL, MS 3.464, pp. 62-3, 116-7.

36 RCAM (Wales), *Glamorgan,* III (part ii), p. 377.

37 *Ibid.,* pp. 344-5; NLW 5215E; Howard J. Thomas and Gerald Davies, 'A medieval house-site at Barry, Glamorgan', *Trans. Cardiff Naturalists' Society,* XCVI, p. 22.

38 Corbett, *Glamorgan,* pp. 95-6; NLW, Wales 22/8.

39 At Uchelolau (Highlight) a fragment of a conglomerate millstone was found incorporated in the wall of a 13th-century corn-drying kiln, implying the existence there of a mill. The 16th-century plea rolls (NLW, Wales 22/10, 39) mention a corn mill at Uchelolau which is certainly the one at Lidmore.

40 RCAM (Wales), *Glamorgan,* III (part ii), pp. 372-5.

41 G. Dowdell and H. J. Thomas, 'Some evidence for the sea-borne carriage of medieval and later pottery in the Bristol Channel', *Medieval and later pottery in Wales,* 3 (1980), pp. 5-11.

42 A. W. Wade Evans (ed.), *Vitae sanctorum Britanniae et genealogiae* (Cardiff, 1944), p. 71.

43 PRO, K. B. 27/11, 15; *Calendar of inquisitions post mortem,* IV, p. 323; V, p. 334; IX, p. 332.

44 *Arch. Camb.,* 4th ser., IV (1873), p. 191.

45 GRO, D/DF vol. 40; Beds. RO, GY 10, pp. 85-6.

46 PRO, C. 1/1069/10; NLW, Wales 22/1, 2, 3; GRO, D/DF vol. 40.

47 NLW 5215E.

48 J. Conway Davies (ed.), *Episcopal acts,* II, p. 642.

49 W. E. Lunt (ed.), *The Valuation of Norwich* (Oxford, 1926), pp. 315-6; Clark, *Cartae,* III, pp. 946-7, 952 *et seq.; Valor Ecclesiasticus* (Record Commission, 1821), IV, p. 349.

50 J. Rhys (ed.), *The Book of Llan Dav* (Oxford, 1893), pp. 323-4; David Crouch, 'An unknown medieval church survey', *Morgannwg,* XXVI (1982), pp. 8-14. The author is indebted to Dr Crouch for supplying him with transcripts of the clerical subsidies in advance of publication.

51 NLW, LL/OC/6; GRO, D/DF vol. 40.

52 Clark, *Cartae,* VI, pp. 2144-9.

53 CCL, MS 2.1148, III, p. 63; C. T. Martin (ed.), *Registrum epistolarum,* III, p. 1011; British Library, Lansdowne 860A, f. 345.

54 PRO, C. 1/6/322, 1/1069/10; W. A. Pantin, 'Chantry priests' houses and other medieval lodgings', *Medieval Archaeology,* III (1959), p. 231.

55 R. F. Isaacson (ed.), *The episcopal registers of the diocese of St. David's, 1397-1518,* Cymmrodorion Rec. Ser., 6 (1917), p. 215.

56 A. W. Wade-Evans, *Vitae sanctorum,* pp. 91-3.

57 Thomas Nicholas, *The history and antiquities of Glamorganshire and its families* (1874), p. 102.

58 Jeremy K. Knight, 'Excavations at St. Barruc's chapel, Barry Island, Glamorgan', *Trans. Cardiff Naturalists' Society,* XCIX (1980), pp. 28-65.

59 H. J. Thomas, 'The old parish church of St. Nicholas, Barry, Glamorgan', *Arch. Camb.,* CXXI (1972), pp. 108-10.

60 CCL, MS 2.1111, XXXI, p. 87 (transcript of Church Goods return, 1556); NLW, Wales 22/53.

61 The *Barry and District News,* 26th August, 1976.

62 CCL, MS 2.1111, XXXI, p. 95.

63 *Ibid.,* p. 95.

64 Howard J. Thomas, 'Uchelolau (Highlight) Deserted Medieval Village', *Morgannwg,* X (1966), pp. 63-4.

65 RCAM (Wales), *Glamorgan,* III (part ii), p. 228.

CHAPTER IV

Families and Farms, 1500-1700

MATTHEW GRIFFITHS

Pipeclay figurine from Cwm Barry. 17th century.
J. Daly.

ARCHAEOLOGY can tell us more than written documents about life in the Barry district in the Middle Ages and before. Even the names of almost all its inhabitants are lost to us. However, from the later years of King Henry VIII's reign onwards, documentary evidence for the activities of ordinary people becomes slowly more abundant. This chapter is largely based on the various tax records, deeds, estate rentals and surveys, wills and probate inventories, together with the evidence of surviving houses and hedgerows. We shall explore the physical landscape of this corner of the Vale of Glamorgan, the farms and houses of local people, and the trade of the little port that took their produce to the markets of Bristol and the West Country. It will become apparent that patterns of land-ownership and agrarian organisation laid down in the 12th and 13th centuries continued to shape the lives of our predecessors throughout this period, and even to the brink of modern times, right down to that grey November day one hundred years ago, when the first sod was turned at Barry Docks.

It is this underlying continuity that has determined the structure of this chapter and the one which follows; they will take affairs from the early 18th century up until the middle years of Queen Victoria's reign. From the 1750s certain types of document which are vey helpful to writers on Tudor and Stuart times—notably probate inventories, which describe in often minute detail the contents of houses and farms—become scarcer; at the same time a great volume of information, much more personal and anecdotal than that available for earlier centuries, becomes available. A decision has been taken to leave out many of the curious stories that could be told about local families in the later 18th and early 19th centuries, and to concentrate on taking the argument and themes of the present chapter up to the advent of the docks. It

Plate XV. Medieval dovecot, Cadoxton Court. *Matthew Griffiths.*

is hoped that, in so doing, a structural framework of social and landscape history will have been provided for the narratives that will be written about the people of the villages of Barry, Merthyr Dyfan and Cadoxton.

Local society in the mid 16th century

The Lay Subsidy returns of the 1540s enable us to examine the structure of society in the Barry area in the widest context: that of the county and the nation. The Lay Subsidy returns contain the first firm statistical evidence for the social and economic structure of Welsh society, and they allow us also to form a reasonable estimate of the size of the local population. The Hearth Tax returns, drawn up 130 years later, can be directly compared with the earlier source.[1]

The Subsidy Act of 1543 was passed by Parliament in order to provide King Henry VIII with money to prosecute his war with Scotland. The people of England and Wales were to be taxed each autumn for a period of three years. All lay persons (*i.e.* those not in only holy orders) who had cash, crops and goods worth £1 or more, or an annual income from land worth £1 and upwards, came into the Exchequer's far-flung net—and that was the great majority of the adult population. The autumn collection meant that assessments were made just after the harvest had been gathered in, when people were most well off, before the hardships of winter depleted their stocks of corn or their savings.[2] The surviving assessments give the names of every taxpayer in each parish or township. By the recent Acts of Union—the measures by which Henry VIII and his chief minister, Thomas Cromwell, integrated Wales into the structure of the Tudor state, and created modern counties out of the medieval marcher lordships— Barry now lay within the administrative division of the new county of Glamorgan known as 'Dinas

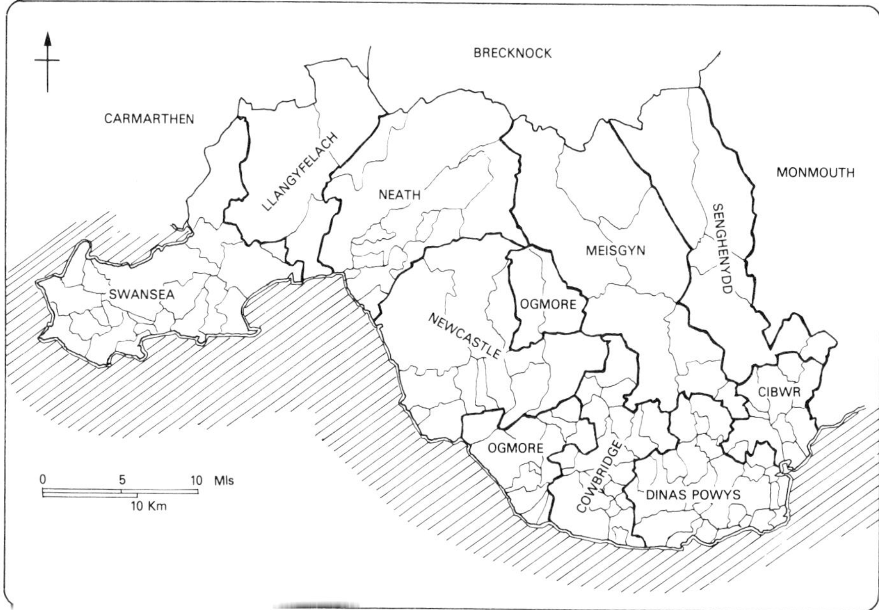

Fig. 35. The hundreds of Glamorgan. *M.G.*

Powys hundred' (Table 3). The assessments for the hundred have survived for each year of the Subsidy, 1543, 1544 and 1545.[3] As the following table shows, the number of people listed in each of our three parishes varied from year to year; for Barry and Merthyr Dyfan most names are given in 1543, but the best return for Cadoxton is that of 1545.

Table 3. Local taxpayers, 1543-45.

Parish	1543	1544	1545
Barry	10	8	7
Merthyr Dyfan	23	16	15
Cadoxton	14	14	16

Why do these numbers differ? In each year of the subsidy the tax collectors drew up a new list of taxpayers; all the evidence is that they did so quite conscientiously. The reason why the number of contributors fluctuated is less likely to do with carelessness or corruption on the part of officials than with changing economic circumstances. For ordinary folk in the countryside the harvest was, in W. G. Hoskins's words, 'the heartbeat of the economy'; people's circumstances varied from year to year according to the quality of the harvest, dependent then, as now, on the weather during the spring and early summer months when the crop was in the fields. The harvest of 1543 was poor and those of 1544 and 1545 worse still; lower yields meant higher prices and increasing hardship. It is probable that some of those who paid the tax in 1543 became too poor to do so in succeeding years; the general pattern, to which Cadoxton is an exception, is that the 1543 tax lists are the fullest.[4]

The Lay Subsidy assessments give the name of each taxpayer, the basis of his contribution (whether he was taxed on his personal estate or on his income from land—whichever would yield most to the Crown), his assessed wealth, and the amount of tax he paid. These facts, especially when we compare the local position with information for the rest of the county, can be made to yield a surprising amount of detail.

Local society: size of population

It is unlikely that even the fullest list for each parish contains the name of *every* householder living there in the year in question; probably there were some very poor folk in the community who were not liable to contribute the tax. In addition, we have the problem that some names listed in 1544 and 1545 are not mentioned in 1543, so that we have a total of eleven names for Barry parish, 25 for Merthyr Dyfan and 27 to 29 for Cadoxton. Even over a short period of three years, death and migration could lead to significant changes in personnel. At the very least, however, assuming that, on average, households contained 4·5 people,[5] it is possible to suggest *minimum* population figures for each parish. Barry probably had about 45 inhabitants, Merthyr Dyfan about 100, and Cadoxton at least 70. Porthkerry, in 1543, had 20 taxpayers, suggesting a population of about 90 people in that small parish.

Perhaps a more useful procedure is to use the numbers of taxpayers in each parish as a basis for comparing the *density* of the local population with that elsewhere in the county. The density of population in Glamorgan was, as one would expect, closely related to the quality of land and to the historic pattern of settlement. There were far fewer taxpayers in the hill country than in the more fertile lowlands of Gower and the Vale of Glamorgan, where many people lived in villages and hamlets rather than in scattered farmsteads. Within the Vale, the parishes in the northern, 'Border Vale' zone supported fewer people in relation to their area than those in the Ely Valley and in the southerly part of the Vale, below the 'Portway', the modern A48. South of this road lias soils make for a richer husbandry than the glacial drift that covers parishes such as Ystradowen or Pendoylan. In the south-eastern Vale, between the river Thaw and the river Ely, the density of population was normally between 50 and 74 acres per taxpayer, and Barry and Cadoxton come into this category. Merthyr Dyfan, with 82 acres per taxpayer, was more thinly settled; Porthkerry, with 57 acres per taxpayer in 1544, was one of the most densely populated parishes in the region.

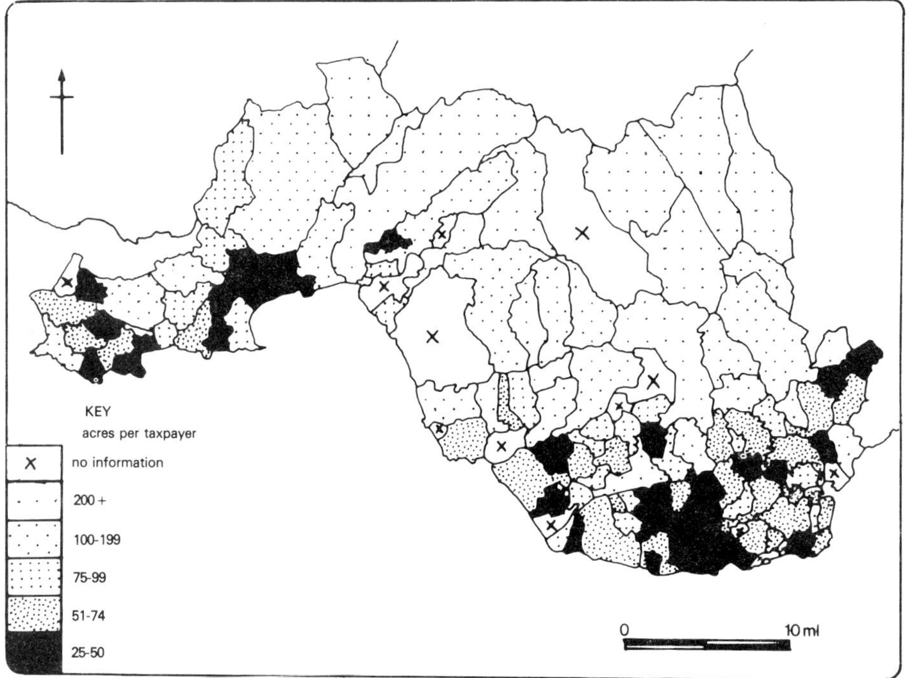

Fig. 36.
Population density in mid 16th-century Glamorgan, based on Lay Subsidy returns, 1543-5 (Cardiff and Swansea boroughs included; other boroughs omitted).
M.G.

By the 1540s, many parishes in the Vale were as well peopled as some of the more prosperous counties of lowland England. Yet as we have seen, communities in the Vale of Glamorgan, including Barry, suffered severe depopulation in the later Middle Ages, perhaps beginning in the early 14th century. Repeated visitations of bubonic plague (starting with the Black Death in 1348) were followed by the disasters of war, when in the years after 1400 the rebellion of Owain Glyndŵr spread to South Wales. Owain, in revolt against the Crown, was seeking independance for Wales and his marauders brought devastation to many villages in the rich coastal lowlands—it was then that Barry's mill may have been burnt. The population of England fell markedly in the 14th century; it is possible that in South Wales the decline was greater, although it is impossible to give statistics, and many villages, Barry included, shrank or were deserted in consequence.[6] However, the Lay Subsidy returns suggest that there had been, by the mid 16th century, a substantial recovery.

Local society: distribution of wealth

The Subsidy returns tell something, then, about the size of the local population. We shall set this evidence later on against that of the Hearth Tax, to see how matters had developed by the latter part of the 17th century. But we can use the Subsidy returns in other ways as well, to examine the social structure of the local community and the wealth of its people.

The richest man in the Barry area in the 1540s was undoubtedly William St. John, lord of Highlight, and a relation of the St. John family who owned the manor of Barry and the neighbouring manors of Penmark, Fonmon and Llancadle, but lived at Bletso in Bedfordshire. William St. John, who was buried in Highlight Church in 1563, was taxed on a landed income of £20 a year in 1543, and listed under Porthkerry where he had a farm.[7] Nearest to him in personal wealth was James Andrew of Cadoxton, whose family, like St. John's had long been connected with the area. He held part of the manors of Cadoxton and East Barry from the absentee lords of Dinas Powys, and probably dwelt at Cadoxton Court (where only the dovecot now survives of the building connected with the medieval manor house). Andrew was rated at £8 in lands in 1543, £9 in 1544; an assessment presumably based on the rents he took from farms in Cadoxton and Merthyr Dyfan. Alone amongst the taxpayers of the 1540s, St. John and Andrew might lay claim to 'gentle' status and only St. John had an income (and connections) which might have ranked him on the lower rungs of the 'county' gentry, the landowners who governed the new county of Glamorgan as sheriffs and justices of the peace. Andrew was smaller fry, with an income in real terms comparable with that of the higher ranks of the newly emerging yeomanry, the wealthier farmers in the countryside.[8] In our three parishes, as throughout the Vale, the majority of taxpayers were assessed on personal estate worth one or two pounds only. Men in this category were small farmers, mainly customary tenants, the successors of the villein tenants of the Middle Ages, but now freed from work services on the lord's demesne and paying cash rents for their holdings. This group may also have included a number of small craftsmen and cottagers, but by and large the majority of such taxpayers managed holdings of twenty acres and less. Six taxpayers in Barry in 1543 came into this group, including Robert Gyles, possibly of the 19-acre Marsh Farm. This group includes also 13 out of the 23 taxpayers in Merthyr Dyfan. Only in Cadoxton were such contributors in the minority.

Between taxpayers on one or two pounds and those worth £20 in goods or £10 in land, the point at which, as we have seen, better-off yeoman farmers shade into the minor gentry, were ranged tenant and freehold farmers with farms from around 20 acres to several hundred. In Barry four men rank as middling farmers in this class, including William Morgan, probably tenant of Ostry Farm at Barry Harbour, and Thomas Yever, conjectually of Greenhouse Farm, sited in the Old Village Road. Merthyr Dyfan also contained an even spread of farmers whose personal estate ranged from £3 up to £15, but it is hard to say anything about these men as individuals. Cadoxton was exceptional in that men in the lowest category of taxpayers were a minority; all but four taxpayers in 1543 had £5 and upwards in goods, suggesting either that Cadoxton was by and large the wealthiest community in the mid 16th century, or that its smallest farmers escaped the tax. In the wider region, Barry and Merthyr Dyfan rank amongst the poorest parishes in the Vale; their taxpayers contributed less than average to the subsidy (an average of 5*d.* in Barry compared to 11.7*d.* in Porthkerry and 12.8*d.* in Llancarfan) and their tax yield per acre of land was low (0.08*d.* from Barry and 0.05*d.* from Merthyr Dyfan as against 0.14*d.* from Penmark). The average Cadoxton taxpayer contributed 7.8*d.* to the subsidy, and the parish yielded 0.12*d.* per acre.[9]

Estates and landowners

Careful analysis of taxation records, therefore, gives insights into the size and social complexion of the mid 16th-century community. This understanding can be deepened when, from the early years of Queen Elizabeth I's reign it becomes possible to reconstruct the social and economic structure of the locality in much greater detail. From *manorial* records—surveys and rentals and the like—we can study the size and make-up of farms in the three parishes and gain an idea of the resources of individual farmers. We can also study the changes in the local landscape which accompanied the far-reaching economic developments which permeated local and regional society under the Tudors and early Stuarts.

In the high Middle Ages, lowland South Wales had been unmistakably a feudal society, the majority of the population forming a class of peasant farmers, many of whom were personally and economically unfree. It was peasant society which throughout western Europe provided, in Rodney

Hilton's words, 'the necessary support for the whole social and political superstructure of nobles, clergy, towns and state'.[10] The manor was the body through which lords extracted the economic surplus of peasant holdings, in the form of rent, which could be in cash, in kind, and in the form of labour services on the demesne farm of the manorial lord. By the later 14th century the old order in the countryside was on the wane, and the period from the Black Death until the 18th century saw a gradual transition from feudal to capitalist relations of production in the countryside, a transition that created the basis for the Industrial Revolution in Britain after 1700. With economic crisis and population decline, manorial lords were unable to resist peasant demands for personal freedom; in the later Middle Ages land became cheap and labour scarce, and the demesne economy decayed as the medieval villein became transformed into the customary tenant, paying a cash rent to his landlord. The coercive function of the manor slowly declined, faster in some areas than in others, as the institution gradually changed into the landed estate that was characteristic of the 18th and 19th centuries. More particularly, the 15th and 16th centuries witnessed many peasant farmers laying the foundations for greater prosperity as, under the Tudor and Stuart monarchs, population rose again, demand increased, and internal trade quickened. The ruling class—the gentry and nobility—now exercised their control less through the manor than through new institutions such as the Sessions of the Peace, though their income depended, as before, on rent.

At the local level we can only trace specific aspects of these developments, but it is important to bear this context in mind as we examine the *minutiae* of economic and social organisation in a small corner of south-east Wales. In many respects Barry took a different path from its neighbouring parishes to the east in the early modern period; as in the Middle Ages its development bears more comparison with that of Penmark and Porthkerry, while Merthyr Dyfan and Cadoxton go a different way, their ultimate focus being the manor of Dinas Powys.

Estates: manors and their lords

The manor of Barry, co-terminous with the parish, remained in the hands of the St. John family, its medieval lords, until the 1650s. Despite the fact that they were absentee landlords, the St. Johns seem to have kept a close supervision over their small Glamorgan estate, the manor of Barry being managed as a unit within their lordship of Penmark, which also comprised the manors of Penmark and Fonmon. The St. Johns supported Charles I during the Civil Wars, and financial necessity meant that they were forced to sell off their South Wales lands. Barry manor passed to Mr Evan Seys of Boverton Castle, whose family rose to prosperity as lawyers in the intensely litigious society of Elizabeth Glamorgan, while the other St. John lands were acquired by Col. Philip Jones, the influential friend of Oliver Cromwell, who had been a signatory of Charles I's execution warrant. Barry remained with the Seys family until 1762, when on the marriage of Jane Seys to Robert Jones, the estate was reintegrated with the lands of Fonmon.[11] Reconstruction of the history of Barry's farms and landscape is made easy by virtue of the fact that its ownership remained undivided; above all, the St. Johns were careful to preserve the records of their rights.

Landownership in the parishes of Merthyr Dyfan and Cadoxton was a much more complex matter. As far as lordship is concerned, the medieval ties with the lordship of Dinas Powys were maintained. However, for all but a few years in the early 17th century, ownership of that large manor was divided. Moreover, it contained within it several sub-fees, amongst which were the sub-manors of Cadoxton and East Barry, the ownership of which was also divided, and the manor of Highlight. Because of this situation, manorial control in the parishes of St. Andrew's, Cadoxton and Merthyr Dyfan was by the 16th century, if no earlier, much weaker than in Barry, a state of affairs that the existence of extensive freeholds from an early date can only have compounded.

Dinas Powys manor became divided after the death of John de Someri in 1322, who left two sisters as co-heiresses. By 1373 one part (or moiety) of the manor was in the hands of the lord of Glamorgan. After the death of Henry VII's uncle, Jasper, Duke of Bedford, this moiety reverted to the Crown. In 1514 it was leased to Sir Mathew Cradock of Swansea, receiver of Glamorgan, but was back in Crown hands under Elizabeth I, until in 1600 it was purchased by Sir William Herbert, the owner of the other moiety. The latter had been held in the later Middle Ages by the Suttons of Dudley, and was bought from them by Sir Mathew Cradock between 1514 and 1529. It passed from him to his elder grandson, Sir George Herbert of Swansea (*d.* 1570), who was Knight of the Shire in 1542, and Sheriff of Glamorgan in 1540 and 1552. From him, this moiety of Dinas Powys passed to his grandson, the Sir William who was to unite the manor in 1600. By this last year of the 16th century, then, the manor was under the sole control of a branch of the leading family in Elizabethan and early Stuart Glamorgan. Sir William Herbert, who died in 1609, had his principal seat at White Friars in Cardiff, where he built a house in the ruins of the Grey Friars' monastery, He was a Justice of the Peace from 1554 until his death, Deputy Lieutenant of the county from 1579 and five times Sheriff of the county. The cousins of this family were earls of Pembroke, the largest landowners in the shire and leading officers of state. After 1609, however, Dinas Powys was again divided. The old Sutton moiety passed to Sir William Doddington, who married Mary, daughter of Sir William Herbert's brother Sir John Herbert of Neath, a courtier and second secretary to Elizabeth I and James I. By the 1670s, this estate had passed, again by marriage, to Lord Brooke of Warwick. The other moiety, which had been the Crown's, passed to Sir

William's nephew, William Herbert of Cogan Pill (*d.* 1628), thence to his royalist heir, who was killed at the battle of Edgehill in 1643, and to the Herberts of White Friars, Cardiff, until the early 18th century.[12]

The lands of both parts of these moieties were inextricably intermingled, so that some of the tenements in Merthyr Dyfan parish belonged to one part of the manor, others to the second moiety. Some tenants owed rent to both lords of the fee. Held as sub-manors of Dinas Powys were Cadoxton, East Barry and Highlight. Highlight was held by a cadet branch of the St. Johns. Thus in 1566 when the Queen's moiety of Dinas Powys was surveyed, Christopher St. John held Highlight for an annual rent of 1*s.* 8*d.* as tenant by knight service. Christopher was a descendant of Alexander St. John, the second son of Sir John St. John of Fonmon, who flourished in the early 15th century. Two of his sons, William and Oliver, became admirals in the service of James I and Charles I, while the middle brother, Thomas, stayed at home, leasing the estate of Highlight from, first his father, then from his brother William. Thomas also rented land at Tredogan from the Bletso St. Johns, and the storehouse at Barry Harbour.[13]

The 1566 survey of Dinas Powys also helps to clarify the relationship between the sub-manors of Cadoxton and East Barry. Cadoxton manor seems to have comprised much of the ecclesiastical parish of the same name, but also included land in neighbouring St. Andrew's. East Barry included land in Cadoxton and in Merthyr Dyfan. In 1601 the manor of Cadoxton, regarded as one knight's fee, was divided between Sir John Popham (5/8ths) and Nicholas Andrew (3/8ths). East Barry was divided amongst Popham (4/16ths of a knight's fee), Andrew (11/16ths) and Elizabeth Morgan of Coed y Gores (1/16th). Despite those legalities, in practice the Popham estate was administered as one unit, generally known as the 'manor' of 'Cadoxton East Barry', as were the lands of the Andrews of Cadoxton Court.[14] The rationale of estate management cut across the legal complexities of sub-infeudation.

The Pophams were absentee landlords, as were the St. Johns of Bletso, and lived at Littlecot in Somerset. Sir John Popham, who became Chief Justice of England in the later years of Elizabeth's reign, derived his Welsh connections from his mother, Jane Stradling, daughter of Sir Thomas Stradling of St. Donat's, and from his wife, the heiress of Castleton, St. Athan. He acquired his estate in Cadoxton, Merthyr Dyfan and St. Andrew's in 1584, purchasing it from Sir William Herbert of St. Julian's, another scion of that powerful family.[15] The Andrews were, of course, resident locally, having moved their seat from East Barry to the Court by 1543. By the early 17th century this petty gentry family seems to have been in decline, for it must have been straightened circumstances that led Nicholas Andrew, between 1628 and 1631, to sell a total of 32 messuages and 700 acres to William Herbert of Cogan Pill and to Edmund Thomas of

Wenvoe Castle, thus initiating the gradual fragmentation of the Court estate.[16]

Because the ownership of land in Cadoxton and Merthyr Dyfan was so fragmented it is impossible, in contrast to Barry, to reconstruct in full the distribution of land in those two parishes at any particular time. The Andrew estate in particular is very poorly documented and we are reliant in the main on surveys and rentals drawn up for the Pophams of Littlecot and the several owners of Dinas Powys manor.

Estates: the manor of Barry

In 1622 the Glamorgan estates of the St. Johns of Bletso were surveyed and mapped by Evans Mouse. It is probable that Mouse was a Dutchman

Table 4. Farms on the manor of Barry in 1622.

	Tenement[a]	Tenant	Rent	Acres
A	Ostry Farm	Reynold Portrey	£2 4*s*.	44½
B	Marsh Farm	Michaell Gyles	£1	19½
C	Burroughes Farm	Anne Strowde	13*s*. 4*d*.	10¾
D	Greenhouse	John Yvor	19*s*.	16¾
E	Westercloses	John Yvor	£1	20¼
F	Westercloses	Thomas Williams	£1	20½
G	Wellhouse	William Morgan	£1 6*s*. 8*d*.	26
H	Castle Farm	Thomas Williams	£2 13*s*.	57¾
I	Cwm Barry	Oliver Mathewe	£6	83
K	Cole Farm (Cold Knap, or Colehole)	Thomas Williams	£3	67
L	Barry Wood	Thomas Williams[b]	£1 9*s*. 3*d*.	20
M	Site of castle	George Wilkin	16*s*. 5*d*.	cottage, orchard and garden
N		Joan Yvor	12*s*. 5*d*.	cottage, garden and croft
O		Alice Kewe	2*s*.	house and orchard
P		Joane Owyn	2*s*.	house, orchard and croft
	the ore[c]	Lewys James	3*s*. 4*d*.	
	Storehouse	Reynold Portrey	—	
	fishing between Barry & Aberthaw	Reynold Portrey	—	

[a] The index letters in this table are those used by Evans Mouse on his map.
[b] Tenant at will.
[c] Seaweed on the rocks and cliffs within the manors of Barry, Penmark and Fonmon that was gathered and used as fertiliser.

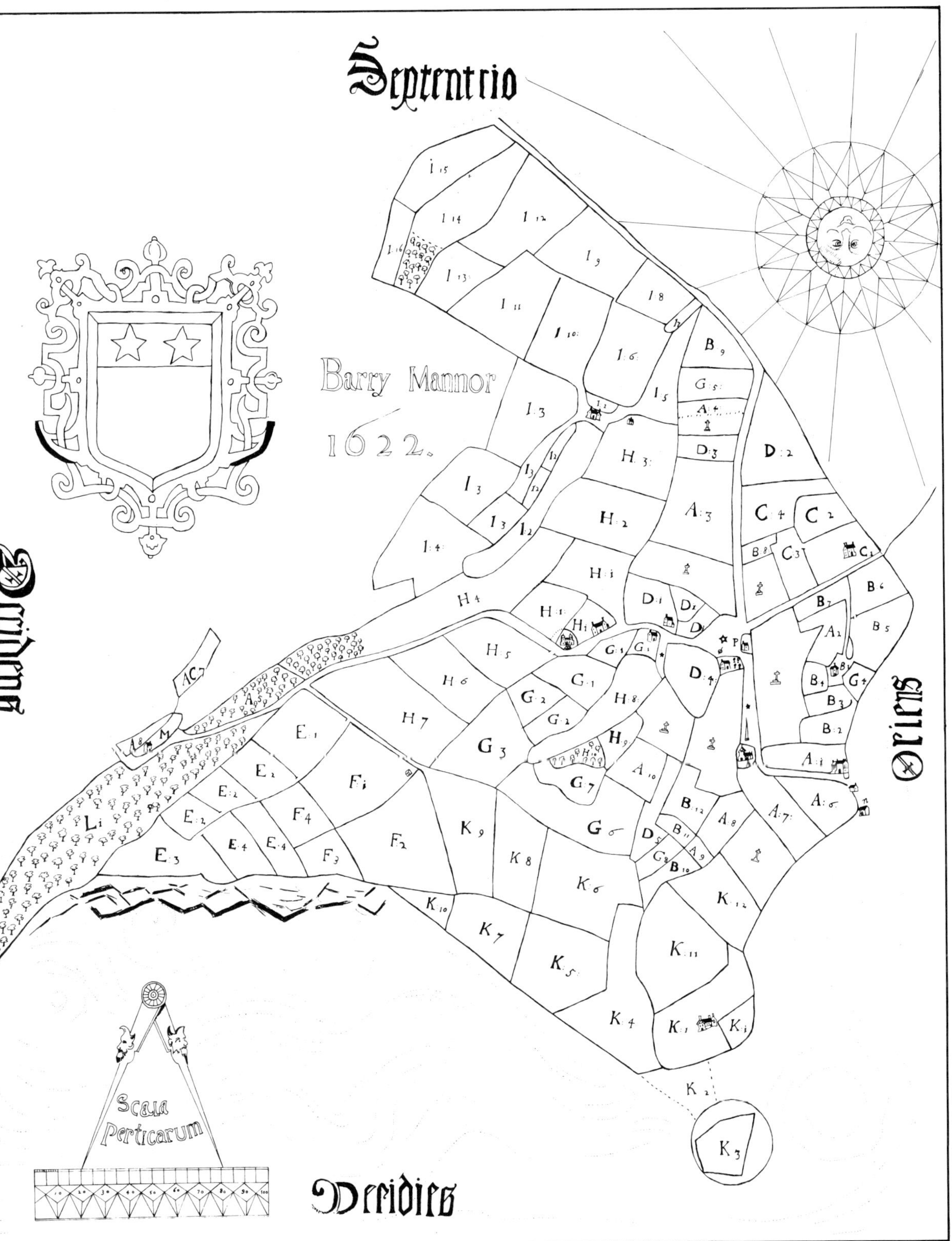

Fig. 37. Map of Barry manor in 1622 by Evans Mouse, based on original in Glamorgan Record Office. *H. J. Thomas.*

who, like many of his compatriots, had come originally to England to work on the land drainage schemes under way in the Fens. His plans of Barry, Penmark, Fonmon and Llancadle form the earliest accurate large-scale survey of any part of Wales.[17] They present a vivid picture of the early 17th-century landscape of the St. John estates, while the accompanying terrier, which describes field by field the tenant farms and other resources belonging to the St. Johns, provides the basis for a precise analysis of the structure of landholding on the manor of Barry and on the other St. John manors.

There were eight farms in the manor, ranging from the 10¾-acre Burroughes Farm, rented by Anne Strowde, to Oliver Mathew's farm of Cwm Barry, which had 83 acres of land. Several tenants combined more than one tenement. Thomas Williams was tenant of Castle Farm (57 acres) and 'Colehole' (Cold Knap Farm, 67 acres), and also held part of Westercloses (20½ acres) and the lease of Barry Wood; John Yvor rented Greenhouse Farm—which still stands in Old Village Road—and the other part of Westercloses; and Reynold Portrey held Ostry Farm at the Harbour, the nearby Storehouse and the fishing rights between Barry and Aberthaw. In addition there were four cottages, including the inn which George Wilkin kept within the Castle precinct.

All the tenements belonging to Barry Manor, with the exception of Barry Wood, which was held as a tenancy at will from year to year, were rented to *copyholders*. Copyholders were the legal descendants of the medieval villeins. During the later Middle Ages the servile obligations owed by unfree villein tenants to lords of the manor had been by and large commuted to money rents, and such tenants had acquired personal and economic freedom, though still often owing certain more than residual obligations. Copyholders were known as such because the proof of their tenure was the copy of the roll of the manor court at which they had formally taken up their tenements. They were still bound to hold their farms and cottages according to the *custom* of the manors; and copyhold was therefore a *customary* tenure, regulated by the manorial court rather than common law. In the early 17th century the majority of tenant farmers in the Vale were customary tenants, although leasehold was becoming increasingly common, and the custom of the manor varied from estate to estate. Thus, on the manors of Llanblethian and Llantwit Major, customary tenants inherited their holdings and passed them on from heir to heir, having in practice as great an interest and as much control over such land as any freeholder; on the St. John manors, as Evans Mouse's survey book makes clear, tenants held their tenements for a maximum of three lives only, after which time the lord regained control over such property and could, if he wished, put in another family. At Barry, as on the other St. John manors, custom forbade a copyholder to live away from his holding without permission of the lord. Copyholders were forbidden, too, to fell timber on their tenements without licence. They were liable to forfeit their tenancies if they allowed their buildings to fall into disrepair or sold or gave away firewood collected on their land. Each was liable to a *heriot*, or tribute on his death. On most farms this meant that the lord would take the 'best beast' of the dead man; if there were no cattle from which the lord could make his choice, then he could take an item of clothing or furniture, or cash. Cottagers paid a heriot of 5*s*. Strangers and undertenants were also liable to pay a heriot if they died within the manor. Another important obligation was that of grinding corn at the lord's mill, on pain of a fine of 6*s*. 8*d*. Since Barry's mill had been abandoned in the early 15th century, the nearest mill available to Barry tenants was Cow Cliff Mill on Penmark manor.[18]

Most of the manor of Barry was customary land, with the exception of the twenty acres of woodland let to Thomas Williams that sloped down from Westercloses above Bull Cliff to the meadowland that occupied the modern Porthkerry Park. The remainder of the ecclesiastical parish was a freehold farm, loosely attached by virtue of a nominal rent to the manor, of some 50 acres, belonging to William Griffith, esquire. This property later became known as Cwmcidy Farm, its farmhouse sited on low-lying land within the angle of the Barry Brook and Nant Talwg (to the east of the railway bridge in Porthkerry Park). In 1661 this farm was sold to the Fonmon estate.[19]

Nearby lay the hamlet of Cwmcidy itself. This settlement comprised five farmhouses and a cottage, and was also mapped by Mouse in 1622, as part of the manor of Penmark. Cwmcidy had once been a parish in its own right, but the population decline of the 14th century had led to its amalgamation with Porthkerry, the cure that was held jointly with Barry. Mouse's map is vivid evidence for the shrinkage of the medieval village. One of the farmsteads, that held by Richard Love, was built on the site of the medieval church of Cwmcidy on the ridge above the village street; and belonging to one of the tenements was, according to the 1622 terrier, a croft 'whereupon in time past there was seated a house'.[20] Like the tenants at Barry, Cwmcidy farmers were copyholders, paying their rents to the St. Johns and bound by the same customs.

The 17th-century village of Barry lay along a lane known as 'Barry Streete' that extended from the ruins of the castle to the green at the junction of the modern Old Village Road and St. Nicholas Road, where stood the cottages of Alice Kewe and Joan Yvor. A little way to the south, in the middle of the wide, rutted track that led to the harbour, stood the archery butts, where by law able-bodied men were still supposed to practise their skills with the long-bow that had once dominated the medieval battlefield. At the top of Ship Hill stood the church and churchyard of St. Nicholas, overlooking the harbour, where there were three buildings. Ostry Farmhouse, to which was attached a tenement of 44 acres, was also a tavern; and nearby there was a little barn and a Storehouse. The first mention of the latter building is in 1598; Mouse describes it as newly built. Here, goods brought ashore from ships in the harbour were stored until customs dues had been paid and local merchants came to collect their wares.

Perhaps it is flattering to describe this little settlement as a village. After all, only six dwellings stood on Barry Street itself, and the other houses in the parish were widely dispersed, lying either at the harbour or in isolation away from the medieval focus of settlement. Burroughes Farm lay on the eastern boundary of the parish, on the lane leading past the farmhouse of East Barry to the next hamlet of Holton. Slightly to the south was Marsh Farm, a stone's throw from the marshes that fringed the northern side of the estuary between mainland and island. Three other farmhouses stood amidst their fields away from the village. These were William Griffith's farmhouse at Cwmcidy; Cwm Barry Farm to the north of the castle; and Coldknap Farm, then known as 'Colehole'. Finally, on the extreme western edge of the parish, nestling against the wooded slopes of Barry Hill, was a small cottage occupied by Joan Owyn.

Table 5. Farms at Cwmcidy in 1622.

Tenement[a]	Tenant	Rent	Acres
y	Richard Love	£1 9*s*. 6*d*.	32¼[b]
z	Eliza Harry	12*s*.	15½
AB	Richard Love	£4 16*s*.	53½[c]
AC	Mawde Harry	18*s*.	14
AD	Robert Nicholas	£1 18*s*.	50½
AE	Hugh Griffith	£1 16*s*.	31½
AF	Hugh Merrick	3*s*.	cottage & ½[a]

[a] Mouse's index letters are followed here.
[b] Field y1 is described by Mouse as 'a croft whereupon in time past there was seated a house'.
[c] The farmhouse (AB1 on the map) stood in the *Chappell Close* on the site of the former parish church of Cwmcidy.

By 1622 the pattern of fields around Barry village had attained the shape it was to retain, by and large, until the growth of the modern town. They were essentially those depicted on the first edition of the Ordnance Survey six-inch survey of the 1870s. All appear to have been hedged apart from one small strip, or *landsett*, of glebe land and an adjacent plot belonging to Ostry Farm. These two tiny fields represented the last traces of the former open fields of the manor. Rice Merrick, squire of Cottrell near St. Nicholas and author of a historical and topographical account of his native county of Glamorgan in the 1570s and 1580s, wrote that the countryside between his

Fig. 38.
Map of Cwmcidy in 1622, from map of Penmark manor by Evans Mouse, based on original in Glamorgan Record Office.
H. J. Thomas.

home and Barry had once been largely an unhedged landscape, 'a champion and open country, without great store of enclosures'. Old men of his day could remember that when they were young, cattle could run from the Portway the four miles to Barry seeking shade from the summer sun. Yet even these old men lived at a time when much of the Vale had already been enclosed.[21] Merrick seems to be suggesting that it was a period of agrarian re-organisation that followed the decay in population and the raids of Glyndŵr that witnessed the disappearance of the open fields in the Vale. We have little detailed evidence by means of which to chart this process, or even to confirm Merrick's chronology. However, it seems probable that at Barry the modern field pattern was largely in existence by the 1570s.

With only two certain exceptions, the tenements described by Mouse in 1622 were all in existence by 1570, and we can trace the history of these holdings with reasonable continuity through the later decades of the 16th century, using the books that record the proceedings of the manorial court. Most importantly, the two largest copyhold farms, both isolated from the medieval village, were both in existence by the third quarter of the 16th century; Cold Knap and Cwm Barry. Cold Knap was acquired in 1570 by William Andrew, bailiff of Barry manor, while Cwm Barry is also mentioned in that year, when John Mathew, *alias* John Gogh, held it in the right of his wife. There is some doubt, however, as to whether the fields belonging to Cwm Barry had the same layout in 1570 that they did in 1622, when this 83-acre farm was divided into sixteen closes, some of which still survive unsullied to the west of Pontypridd Road. In 1595, when Maurice Mathew, John's son, was tenant, the farm was described as comprising 'one close called the North Close, and another close late in the tenure of John Giles, containing altogether 80 acres', phraseology repeated in 1614 when Maurice renewed his copy. It is possible that in 1595 and 1614 the court books were recording the actual position at those times, but more likely, especially in 1614, that they were repeating phrases then out of date. What they do make clear, however, is that at some fairly recent point in the history of the tenement, Cwm Barry had been organised in a way that was intermediate between the position in 1622 and the existence of open field. The field name 'North Close' suggests strongly that the farm was carved out of an earlier 'North Field'. This theory is reinforced by the existence on the 1622 map of a clearly defined continuous boundary of hedges running from N.E. to S.W. of Barry village, separating Cwm Barry, Castle Farm and Westercloses from the remainder of the manor, and probably representing the boundary of a medieval open field.[22]

Cold Knap Farm also has the appearance of a holding created out of former open field land; in structure it is very similar to Cwm Barry, an isolated farmstead standing in its own fields at a distance from the primary settlement. Westercloses tenement also seems not to have achieved its final

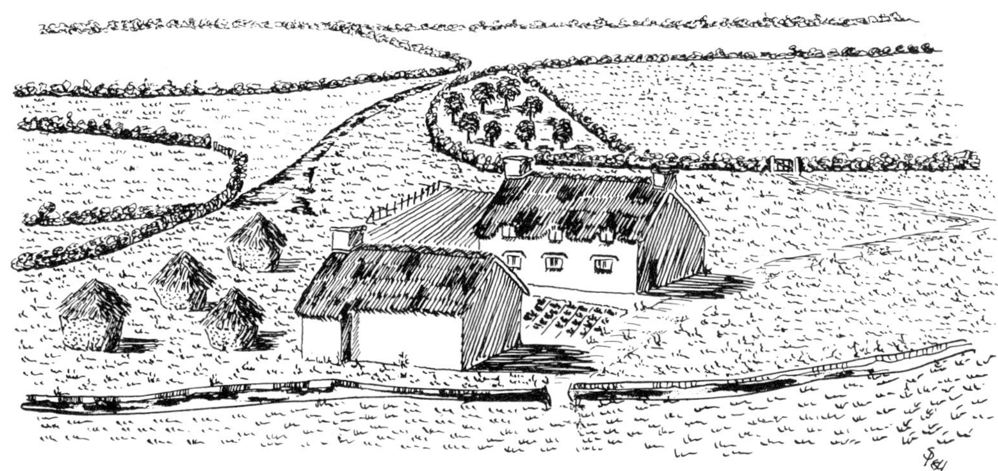

Fig. 39.
Cwm Barry in *c.* 1622, reconstruction drawing.
Simon Prosser after H. J. Thomas.

form until the early 17th century, and this too appears to be a unit that was carved out of open arable fields in the later 15th century or the first half of the 16th. In 1606 Mark Love surrendered his tenancy of two closes called 'Westercloses', suggesting that the two portions into which the tenement was subdivided in 1622 originated as two large fields enclosed out of a common field, later being divided into the eleven closes drawn by Mouse. Possibly, just as Cwm Barry was created from a hypothetical North Field, Westercloses originated in another open field unit, and Cold Knap in another, perhaps a 'South Field'.[23]

In 1622 enclosure was almost complete in Barry; it was less advanced elsewhere on the St. John estate in the Vale, especially at Fonmon and Llancadle, where small areas of open field strips still survived in the 1620s and were mapped by Mouse. There is no evidence that enclosure on these manors, or elsewhere in the Vale, was as contentious an issue as it was in Elizabethan England. The agent of change locally was not an aggressive landlord, out to maximise profits by dispossessing small peasant farmers and consolidating their holdings into larger farms, or turning their land into sheep pasture. Enclosure at Barry, Penmark, Fonmon and Llancadle must have taken place on the initiative of the larger customary tenants, with the agreement of the lord of the manor; as such it was, as the Mouse maps suggest, a gradual, piecemeal and, presumably, peaceful process, carried through in the name of more efficient farming.[24]

The only two tenements certainly created afresh after 1570 were both cottages. In 1588 Owen Williams was granted a vacant plot of ground measuring half an acre 'lying below Barry Hill next to the stream' on which to build a cottage. The foundations of a later rebuilding of a cottage on this site can still be seen at the foot of Lover's Lane, just before the track crosses a footbridge and enters Porthkerry Park. This road was once the main highway from Barry to Porthkerry. Williams was to pay 2*s.* rent each year, to owe suit of court and suit of mill and to be liable for a heriot of 5*s.* on his death. This was the cottage occupied in 1622 by Joan Owyn. The other cottage was erected likewise on waste ground, east of the ruined castle. It was built between 1591 and 1596 by William David, tenant of Castle Farm, and it is described in 1622 as lying between the orchard of Castle Farmhouse and the castle itself. Two other cottages should be mentioned. It is likely that the cottage on Barry Green granted in 1594 to Joan Yvor was recently established, and that the cottage of George Wilkins within the site of Barry Castle, first mentioned *c.* 1582, had been erected between 1545 and 1570. This latter cottage was rented in 1622 by Wilkins at 16*s.* 5*d.* *per annum* and was used as a tavern.[25] Thus, by 1622, the parish of Barry contained thirteen houses, excluding the Storehouse, the same number as listed in the 1673 Hearth-Tax list.

Estates: Cadoxton and Merthyr Dyfan

By contrast with the superb map and terrier that allow such a precise picture to be drawn of early 17th-century Barry, the evidence for Cadoxton and Merthyr Dyfan is fragmentary. We are dependent on surveys of the different estates that owned land in these parishes, surveys that were made at widely separated times. No map was drawn, of even a portion of these parishes, until the middle of the 18th century.

The earliest document to give a systematic account of some of the tenancies and freeholdings in these parishes is a survey of the Crown's moiety of Dinas Powys manor, drawn up in 1566.[26] Unlike Evans Mouse's survey of Barry, which involved the accurate measurement and description of each plot of land, this was accomplished along more traditional lines. Under the authority of a royal commission, a jury of the leading tenants, headed by Rice Flemynge and Nicholas Andrew, gentlemen, was empanelled, before which each freeholder and copyholder gave evidence of title. Amongst these freeholders and copyholders, several can be identified who held land in Merthyr Dyfan (Table 6). Almost certainly some tenements have been missed; at most one can positively recognise only 129 acres of copyhold land, and an unquantifiable area of land held in 'free socage' (more or less the same as a modern freehold, but still liable to a nominal rent charge) as being in Merthyr Dyfan. The Coldbrook tenement mentioned is probably Great Coldbrook farm. Despite this sparse information, the document is important, partly because it allows comparisons to be made with other records. It tells us, for example, that Nicholas Andrew of Cadoxton Court, son of James Andrew (who is listed in the 1543 subsidy returns), held not only part of the sub-manor of East Barry from Dinas Powys, but also a freehold interest in lands called 'Mancheldowne' and 'Crosland'. Mancheldowne—?great hill[27]—we know from the 18th-century Wenvoe estate maps to be the ridge along which Jenner Road runs; Crosland was nearby. It is tempting to connect Robert

Table 6. Land held in Cadoxton and Merthyr Dyfan from the Queen's moiety of Dinas Powys manor in 1566.

Tenant	Description	Rent
By Knight Service		
Christopher St. John	Highlight sub-manor	1*s.* 8*d.*
Nicholas Andrew	3 parts of East Barry	5*s.*
William Herbert	1 part of East Barry	1*s.* 8*d.*
Freehold		
William Bassett	at Colcot	6*s.* 8*d.*
William Mathew	at *Colebrook* [a]	5*s.*
Christopher Flemynge	*Barry* in the tenure of Mary Ragland, widow	5*s.*
David Carne	in Merthyr Dyfan, late Thomas Adams	5*s.*
Thomas Kewe	in Merthyr Dyfan	3*s.*
Davyd Grange	in Merthyr Dyfan	—
Lewys Philpot & William Kemys	in Merthyr Dyfan, 11 acres	5*s.* 6*d.*
Nicholas Andrew	*Mancheldowne*	4*s.*
Nicholas Andrew	*Crosland*	4*s.*
Copyhold		
Robert Yeroth	in Merthyr Dyfan, 42¼ acres of former demesne land, held from 1553/4	18*s.*
William Thomas, clerk	in Merthyr Dyfan, cottage, garden and 30 acres; cottage called the *Pirhey*. Held from 1565	8*s.* 6*d.*
Margaret Willy, widow	two tenements and 27 acres late John Willy in Merthyr Dyfan, held from 1565	£1 2*s.* 10*d.*
John Tromp	tenement and 30 acres in Merthyr Dyfan, late William Kewe. Called *Everodes* tenement and held from 1566	10*s.*

[a] Probably Great Coldbrook Farm, and strictly speaking in the parish of St. Andrew's Major. We should possibly also include Richard Best's copyhold: a messuage and 5 acres *Aylwards lands*, 1a called *Lechehull*, and ½a called *Walbreds lands*. Rent 5*s.* 7*d.* Copy dated 1553. Probably in Merthyr Dyfan.

Yeroth and his 42½-acre tenement of former demesne land with the John Yoroth who was assessed at £2 in goods in 1543. John Tromp's 30-acre tenement 'late Everodes' may be traceable back to the early 14th century. In 1302 Mathew Everard and his wife Joan are named as tenants of a farm at 'Holeton' in the lordship of Dinas Powys.[28] It was by no means unusual for the name of an occupier of a tenement to be used to identify it centuries after his death.

However, for a more extensive account of those farmers in Merthyr Dyfan and Cadoxton who held land from Dinas Powys we must turn to the survey of the manor made for Sir William Herbert in 1601. As we have seen, for a brief time Herbert combined both the long sundered parts of the manor in his hands. As a result this survey, though drawn up in the same fashion as that of 1566, is much more informative; with its help we can establish a fairly

Table 7. Merthyr Dyfan tenants of Dinas Powys manor in 1601.

Tenant	Holds[a] (acres)	Rent
Freehold		
John Popham	13, part of *Kews lands*	2*s.* 1*d.*
	7, late Adams	3*s.* 6*d.*
	200, the *faremes*[b]	
Catherine Kemis	9, late Wenllian Andrew	4*s.* 8*d.*
William Mathew of Llandaff	60 in Coldbrook	5*s.*
Nicholas Andrew	10 called *Mychelldore*	4*s.*
	10 called *Crosland*	4*s.*
	16 of lands called *the buttrill*	4*s.*
John Love	30 in Colcot [N.B. low rent figure]	6*d.*
Hugh Adam	7½	3*s.* 6*d.*
Christopher Flemynge	about 30 at Holton called *Prides lands*	8*s.* 8*d.*
William John Richard	5½ late Thomas Kew	11*d.*
John Norman	2½	—
David Stasy	22 in the *Collcot*	5*s.* 4*d.*
Copyhold		
Thomas William Ball	30	8*s.* 6*d.*
	Sheeping moor	3*s.*
William Richard	30 called *Trompse Lands*	10*s.*
	21	3*s.* 6*d.*
Thomas Prouting	4	—
Joan Andrew	42 of demesne land	18*s.*
Lewis Morgan	22 in Holton	11*s.* 8*d.*
Catherine Morgan	21 in Merthyr Dyfan	8*s.* 4*d.*
Felis Hughe	27 in Merthyr Dyfan	£1
Lewis Adam	22 in Holton	11*s.*

a The survey is not explicit as to whether messuages accompanied each of these holdings.
b Probably White Farm and Walters Farm, leased by Popham as from his manor of Cadoxton East Barry.

complete picture of the distribution of land held directly from Dinas Powys manor in Merthyr Dyfan parish. Freehold and copyhold tenements so held are listed in Table 7; the distribution of freehold and copyhold land is summarised in Table 8. Excluding land held by knight service, we can account for 577½ customary acres, about 700 statute acres, of which 362½ customary acres were freehold.

Table 8. Land in Merthyr Dyfan held from Dinas Powys manor in 1601, excluding sub-manors held by knight service (in acres).

Freehold	Copyhold	Copyhold (former demesne)	Total
Crown moiety			
142½	85	42	251½
Herbert moiety			
238[a]	88	—	326
362½	173	42	577½

[a] Includes White Farm and Walters Farm held as freehold by John Popham.

The majority of the tenements listed in 1566 are identifiable in 1601, but only in the latter year are the acreages of the majority of freeholds given. Thus 'Mancheldowne' (or 'Mychelldore', in the more corrupt 1601 form) and 'Crosland' were each of ten acres. The later survey tells us also that, in addition to these freeholds, Nicholas Andrew had a 16-acre farm called the 'Buttrill' (from *butter-hill,*[29] i.e. a hillside that had rich pasture land producing good butter), which, of course, ultimately gave its name to Buttrills Road. John Love's 30-acre farm at Colcot (held by William Bassett forty years before) was probably that later known as Colcot Fawr; this farm is mentioned in a number of 17th-century wills, and stayed in the Love family into the 18th century. If John Love's farm is Colcot Fawr, on the west side of Colcot Road, then David Stasy's freehold may be one of the tenements that later lay on the other side of Colcot Green: Colcot Fach or Colcot Ganol.

Several of the copyhold tenements can be traced back to earlier occupiers; thus William Richard held the Holton tenement that had been John Tromp's and Joan Andrew the farm that had been Robert Yeroth's. The majority of the copyholds were between 20 and 30 customary acres in extent, the exceptions being a small parcel of four acres held by Thomas Prouting, who also rented Dinas Powys mill, and the 42 acres of former demesne that was Joan Andrew's.

What of the lands of the sub-manors of Cadoxton and East Barry? The indenture recording John Popham's purchase of 1584 lists the tenants by copy and by lease of his new estate.[30] Altogether, Popham was lord of some 600 acres of tenanted land, together with a number of freeholds of which the acreages are unknown (these included Greenyard Farm and four other tenements, all in the possession of Sir John Thomas of Wenvoe Castle, and all probably in St. Andrew's Major parish). It is by and large impossible to distinguish in this document farms which lay in Merthyr Dyfan from those lying in Cadoxton. However, White Farm at Merthyr Dyfan is said to be leased by Oliver St. John, one of the Highlight family, with 200 acres of land. This 200 acres clearly included more than White Farm alone, for in 1586, when Popham leased this holding to Owen ap Jevan, gentleman, of Merthyr Dyfan for three lives, its acreage was estimated to be no more than 86 acres, for which Owen was to pay £4 10*s.* *per annum.*[31] Included with White Farm in 1584 must, therefore, have been either Great Brynhill farm or Walters Farm. In the same document Christopher Fleming is listed as the tenant of a messuage and 100 acres of land by copy for 99 years, of which 60 years were left to run. Conceivably, this was in fact Great Brynhill, which in later documents is described as having 111 acres of arable, meadow and pasture land.

Great Brynhill, White Farm and Walters Farm were of exceptional size. The great majority of holdings on both the Popham estate and Dinas Powys manor were much smaller. Out of the 17 tenements on the Cadoxton East Barry estate of John Popham in 1584 that had messuages associated with them and were therefore clearly farming units, six were of between 10 and 13 acres, four of between 20 and 30 acres. Seven of the eight copyholds listed in Merthyr Dyfan in 1601 were of between 21 and 30 acres. Farms in this latter range may be representative of the standard tenement of the Middle Ages; if those of 21 to 30 acres represented a full, *virgate* holding, those of 10 to 15 acres may represent the medieval half-virgate tenement.

In addition one must distinguish a further class of customary tenement on the Popham estate, smallholdings of one to four acres, of which there were six. Whereas a farm of 20 to 30 acres might reasonably have been expected to produce sufficient food to feed a family in a year when the harvest was adequate, smallholdings of this kind, such as the messuage and 2¾ acres occupied by John Prouting, must have been managed by folk who supplemented their meagre incomes from farming by wage labour on larger tenements. At Barry in 1622, though there were four cottage tenements, smallholdings of this type were absent; indeed, in that parish only two of the farms had less than 20 acres. In Cadoxton and Merthyr Dyfan the average copyholding was half the size of that in Barry and on the other St. John manors in the Vale of Glamorgan. Cadoxton and Merthyr Dyfan farms were by and large smaller than those in Barry and their soil was heavier and less fertile.

Table 9. Tenants of the Popham manor of Cadoxton East Barry in 1584.

Tenant	Description (figures in acres)
Copyhold	
Nicholas Androwe	4 of meadow
Lewes Thomas	messuage and 28
Jane Gebon	messuage and 30
John Wylly, tailor	messuage and 20
Margaret Wylly	messuage and 20
Thomas Taylor	messuage and 10
Joane Hopkyn	messuage and 10
William Madock	messuage and 10
Robert Yoroth	$1\frac{1}{2}$ of meadow
John Wylly, junior	pasture of 10 of woodland
Jenkin ap Poel	messuage and 4
Thomas Androwe	messuage and 1
Morgan David	messuage and $1\frac{1}{2}$
Lewes Hawkin	messuage and 10
Joan Tracye	messuage and 10
John Prouting	messuage and $2\frac{3}{4}$
William White	9 of land, meadow and pasture
John Nicholl	1 of meadow
Christopher Fleming[a]	messuage and 100
Jane Gebon	9 of land, meadow and pasture
Hoel ap Poel	messuage and 13
John Wylly	pasture of 10 of wood
Evan Richard	16 of land and pasture
Andrewe Madock	messuage and $4\frac{1}{2}$
Thomas Taylor	8 of land and pasture
Lewes Thomas[b]	one quarter of a marsh
Leasehold	
Oliver St. John	White Farm and 200[c]
Jenett Thomas	17
Lewes Thomas	certain lands

a Copyhold for 99 years rather than three lives, suggesting this holding was former demesne. Probably Great Brynhill, Merthyr Dyfan.

b Copyhold for 99 years.

c Probably includes Walters Farm as well as White Farm. Again, perhaps former demesne land.

However, as in Barry, certain farmers combined a number of tenements to form larger units. In 1584, Jane Gebon rented a messuage and land amounting to 30 acres, together with a further 9 acres of arable, meadow and pasture. John Wylly, a tailor, had a messuage and 20 acres and the pasture of 10 acres of wood.[32]

Of the Andrew estate, centred on Cadoxton Court, we have little knowledge. However, we can form an impression of the overall extent of this estate before, in Charles I's reign, the Andrews began to sell off portions of their inheritance. We can take the known acreages of the Popham and Dinas Powys interests in Cadoxton and Merthyr Dyfan in Elizabethan times, convert them into statute measure, and compare them with the acreage of the two parishes combined as given in 19th century Census statistics (2,424 acres, which included some foreshore). Excluding unquantifiable freeholds, the Popham and Herbert estates amounted to some 1,388 acres. The Andrew estate must, therefore, have occupied the greater part of the balance of 1,036 acres, of which over 700 (statute) acres were sold in 1628 and 1631.

Estates: the appearance of the landscape

We have seen that by the early 17th century, Barry parish had been enclosed. It has been suggested that this process was essentially complete by 1570. However, we know that elsewhere in the Vale, on Fonmon manor, for instance, the process of enclosure took longer to complete. What evidence have we for the physical organisation of Elizabethan and early Stuart farms in Cadoxton and Merthyr Dyfan?

When James Andrew purchased a moiety of the freehold of the demesne of Cadoxton and East Barry from Walter Herbert of Dunraven in June 1545, he acquired a total of 93½ acres, described in detail in the enrolled deed.[33] It is clear from this document that part of the demesne land concerned lay in enclosed fields, part still in open arable. Thus, alongside references to closes called the 'hygher horse crofte', 'Russhe close', 'the Vocay', 'Castell lands', and so forth, we have reference to two acres of arable 'in the west part of West feld' and fifteen acres of arable 'in the West Fylds in the lordship of Cadoxton'. The deed also refers to one acre of arable land lying to the south of Katheryn Fleming's house and to two acres of land adjacent to the lands of James Andrew and the acre of arable mentioned above; the intermixed character of these plots of land also suggests that they were common field strips.

The Wenvoe estate map of 1763-4 allows a number of the closes named in 1545 to be located on the ground.[34] The majority lay in the south-eastern part of Merthyr Dyfan parish and in the south-west of Cadoxton. The name West Field still survived also in 1763 as the common denomination of several enclosures; it lay, as its name suggests, in the western part of Cadoxton parish, in the vicinity of the modern Barry Road. Later maps allow us to indicate areas in Cadoxton and Merthyr Dyfan which were formerly open

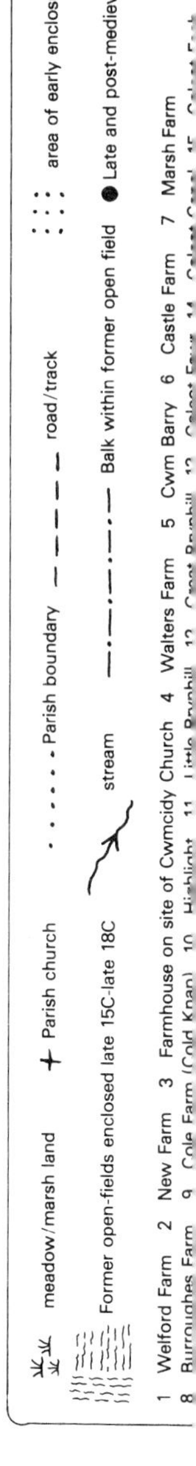

Fig. 40. Map of former open-field and post-medieval farmsteads in the Barry area, based on 17th- and 18th-century estate maps. At one time most of the locality was cultivated in open fields, but by *c.* 1750 these had virtually disappeared. In the late Middle Ages and the 16th and 17th centuries new farmsteads appeared, some on previously uncolonised land, others on former open field (Cwm Barry) or manorial demesne (Colcot). *M.G.*

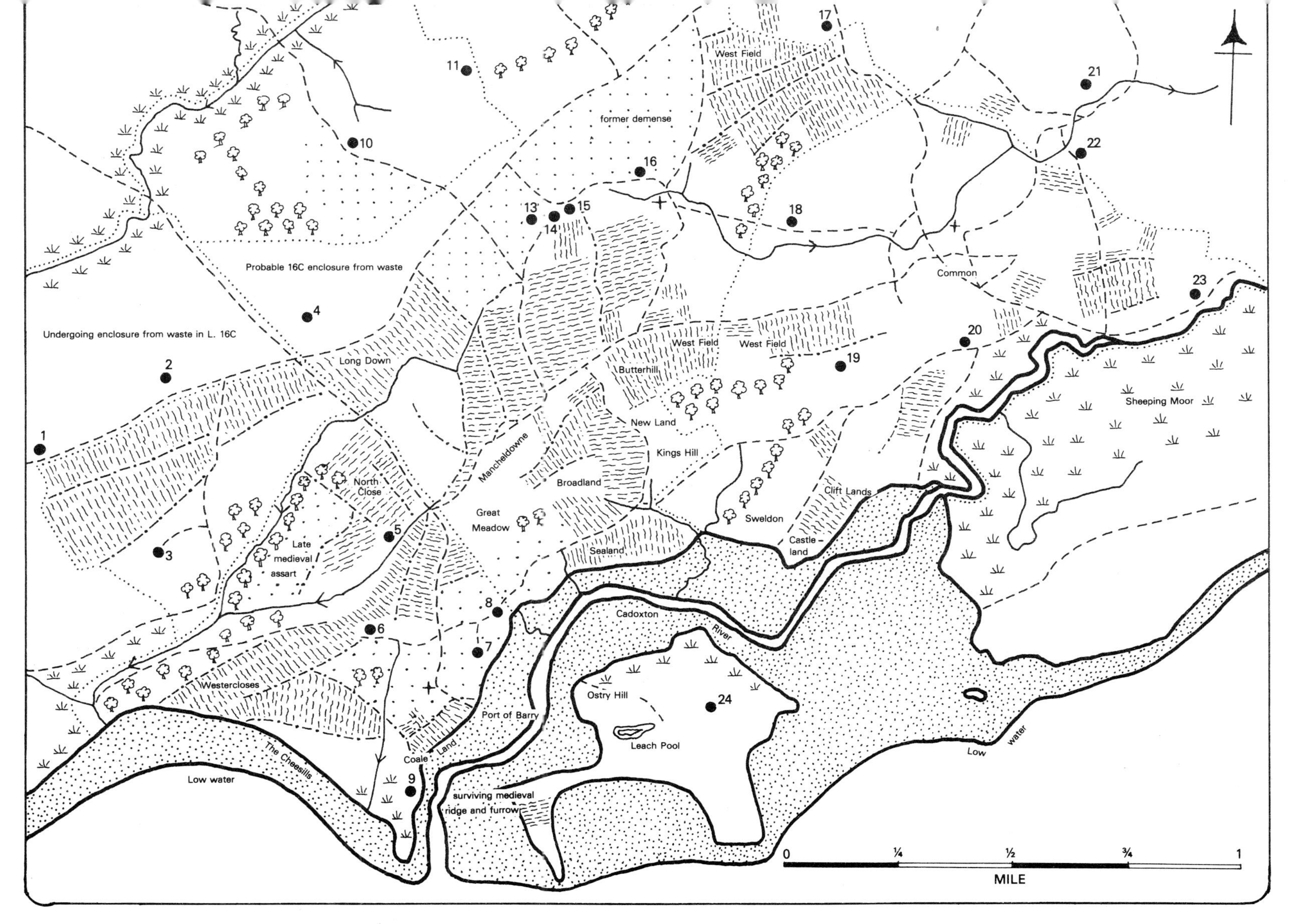
West Field
former demense
Probable 16C enclosure from waste
Undergoing enclosure from waste in L. 16C
Long Down
West Field
West Field
Butterhill
Common
Sheeping Moor
New Land
Kings Hill
Mancheldowne
Broadland
North Close
Great Meadow
Clift Lands
Sweldon
Castle-land
Late medieval assart
Sealand
Cadoxton
River
Ostry Hill
Leach Pool
Westercloses
Port of Barry
Coale Land
The Cheesills
Low water
surviving medieval ridge and furrow
Low water
0
¼
½
¾
1
MILE
1
2
3
4
5
6
7
8
9
10
11
13
14
15
16
17
18
19
20
21
22
23
24

arable, although we cannot attach specific names to any common field other than West Field. Using the Wenvoe estate maps of the 1760s and 1798,[35] the tithe maps of the two parishes and the first edition of the O.S. six-inch map, we can plot these areas of open field, which are suggested by the appearance of fossilised open field strips in the form of long narrow closes, and by the survival in the 1760s of unenclosed strips south of Cadoxton common and on the flanks of Weston Hill. The latter were finally enclosed between 1763 and 1798.

The pace of enclosure, however, is difficult to judge. By 1763 Merthyr Dyfan was wholly enclosed and only bare remnants of open field survived in Cadoxton, but we have little hard evidence of the extent of enclosure in the 16th and 17th centuries. Clearly enclosure was well under way, on the demesne at least, in the first half of the 16th century, if not before. By the 1580s, White Farm and Great Brynhill, and probably also Walters Farm, were recognised units and this would imply that their fields were largely enclosed by this date. Some clues to the state of affairs by the end of the 17th century are supplied in a survey made in 1693 of the moiety of Dinas Powys manor that was in the possession of William Herbert of White Friars, Cardiff, and had formerly been the Crown's.[36] This survey accounts for 181 acres of copy or leasehold land, mainly in Merthyr Dyfan, and each tenant's farm is described in some detail. The evidence is ambiguous as to how many parcels were closes in severalty and how many were surviving open-field quillets, perhaps very few, though we have one reference to a half-acre in 'West Field' (?Cadoxton). What is clear, however, is that, even though enclosure must have been virtually complete, many farms were fragmented, with the fields of one tenement often widely dispersed and surrounded wholly or partly by the fields of other farms. Many parcels mentioned in 1693 were of no more than one or two acres. Thus, though enclosure was well-advanced, and complete in Merthyr Dyfan 70 years later, the process had not been taken to its logical conclusion: the re-organisation of farms into compact units. Here, the situation in Merthyr Dyfan and Cadoxton must again be contrasted to that in Barry, where 17th-century farms were much more conveniently organised. The process of modernisation in Cadoxton and Merthyr Dyfan was almost certainly retarded by the complicated pattern of landownership. Whereas Barry manor remained undivided, the manors of Dinas Powys and Cadoxton East Barry were fragmented, and the position was further complicated by the existence of extensive freeholds such as that of the Love family at Colcot. There was never an opportunity for a landlord to institute an effective rationalisation of the farms on his estate, for the co-operation required with other landlords and their tenants would have been far too complex to arrange. Proper rationalisation of the structure of tenements would have required a large measure of consensus between landlord and landlord and also amongst the tenantry, most of whom held copies for lives and were therefore difficult to manipulate; in addition it would have needed capital to grub up and lay-out hedges, dig ditches and erect walls and gates, and we see little sign of such investment until the Thomases of Wenvoe took matters in hand in the 1750s.[37]

Estates: population growth

Between the later 15th century and the Civil Wars between Charles I and Parliament in the 1640s the population of England and Wales grew considerably. There were probably about two million people living in the two countries in 1500, increasing to about 4½ million by 1640. The pace of population growth varied from region to region, and the upward trend was not continuous, but could be temporarily halted by epidemic and harvest failure. In Wales we lack the information that could help us chart the rate of population growth, though we suspect that from a base of about 250,000 people in the 1540s, the population increased to about 380,000 by 1670.[38] We can get some idea of the local picture by comparing the Lay Subsidy evidence (previously discussed) with the information provided by the Hearth Tax returns of 1670 and 1673.[39] With the aid of the latter documents also, we can form an impression of the pattern of social change in our three parishes which can be set alongside the evidence of terriers and rentals.

The Hearth Tax was instituted by parliament shortly after the Restoration of Charles II in 1662. It was a tax based on the number of hearths, fires and stoves in each household, a tax which, though very unpopular, continued to be levied until the 1680s. The local constable in each parish or township, who was chosen by the vestry or at a manor court, according to the practice of each community, counted the number of hearths in each house within his jurisdiction. For each hearth the householder paid at the rate of 2*s*. *per annum.* In some years there was considerable evasion; however, the 1670 and 1673 returns for Glamorgan allow a generally accurate listing of households in the county to be compiled. For our three parishes the 1673 return is the fullest, almost certainly naming every householder. These lists indicate not only those who paid the tax, but also those exempted through poverty.

A quick comparison of the names of householders alive in the 1670s with the names given in the Lay Subsidy return is revealing. A significant number of families present in the 1540s were still settled in the area 130 years later. The continuity of families such as the Gileses and Evors of Barry or the Stacies, Willys, Beasts, Adamses and Yoroths of Merthyr Dyfan and Cadoxton is remarkable in an age when people were increasingly mobile. We shall return to this point again. More important for our present purpose is to gain some idea of the extent of local population growth.

Thirty-four households are listed in 1673 for Merthyr Dyfan, thirty-eight for Cadoxton and thirteen for Barry, figures which suggest a total population for each parish of 150, 170 and 60 respectively. Porthkerry had

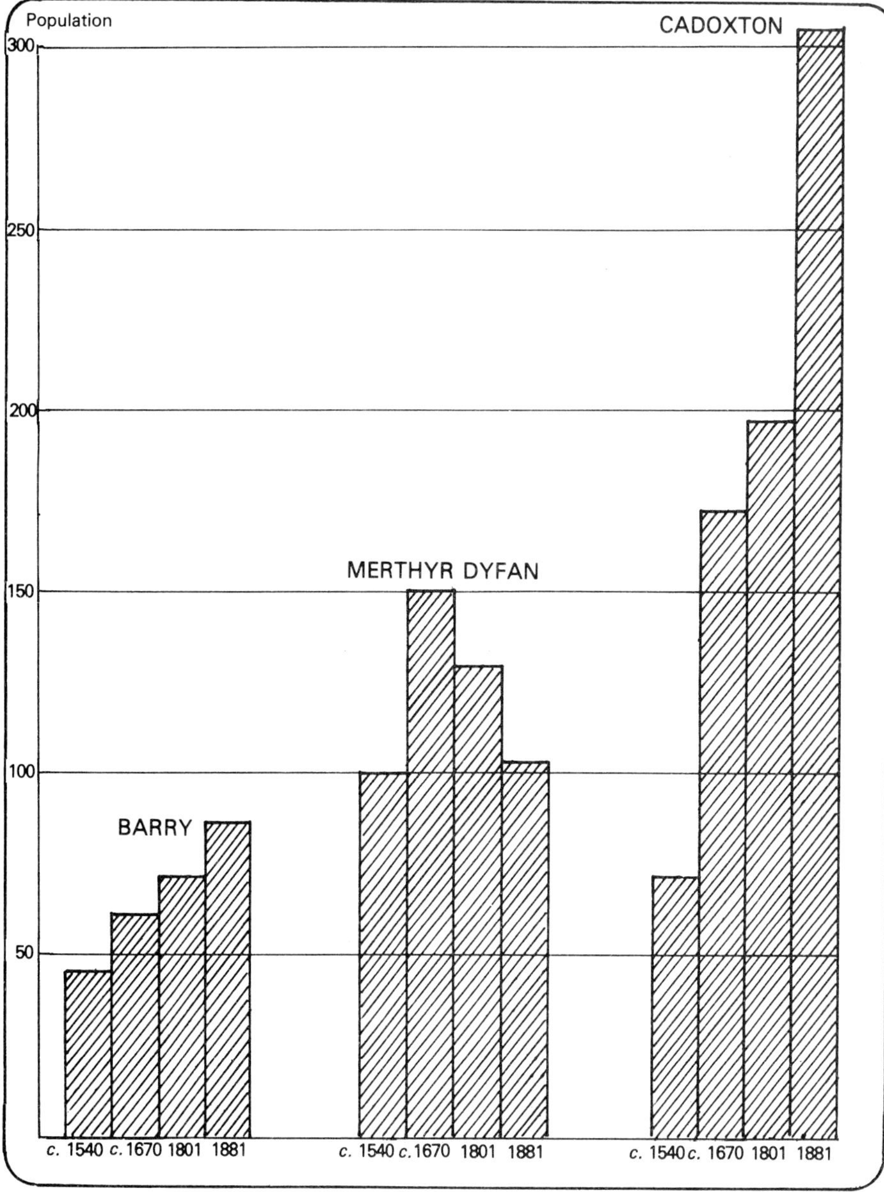

Fig. 41. Population growth in Barry, Merthyr Dyfan and Cadoxton from 16th to 19th century (figures for *c.* 1540 and *c.* 1670 are estimates). *M. G.*

eighteen taxpayers representing about 80 people. We cannot be sure how many people were exempted from paying the Subsidy in the 1540s, but these figures suggest that the population of each parish had increased over the intervening decades. Cadoxton seems to have grown most dramatically, by a *maximum* of 137%. This figure represents real and substantial growth; no parish in Dinas Powys hundred increased its population by so much, save St. Nicholas. Less dramatic was the 48% increase in the population of Merthyr Dyfan. The size of Barry seems to have increased from about ten households in the 1540s to thirteen by the later 17th century. In practice, we know that this figure of thirteen dwellings had been achieved by 1622 and that two new cottages were erected in the parish in late Elizabethan times. In terms of population history, Barry's experience more nearly resembles that of Penmark and Porthkerry, which also grew only slightly in the 16th and 17th centuries, than that of Merthyr Dyfan and especially Cadoxton. Cadoxton's increase in population is more comparable with the growth of parishes in the Border Vale than with the experience of the south-east.[40]

The number of householders exempted from payment of the Hearth Tax through poverty in Cadoxton in 1673 was also much greater than in Barry and Merthyr Dyfan, where the exemption rate was 38% and 24% respectively. Twenty-one out of the 38 Cadoxton householders—55%—were recorded as 'under the value and poor'; a much higher figure than was usual in the Vale of Glamorgan. The exceptions were communities such as Llantwit Major and Cowbridge, which were by and large urban in character and social structure; and settlements which had extensive areas of common land and may have attracted squatters and poor cottagers to settle there. Cadoxton falls into this latter category, and may be compared with places like Llanblethian and Wick, where also the 'poor' were in a majority. However, one must be guarded in one's use of the word 'poor'; in the context of the Hearth Tax this was always a subjective term, for while the poor would include all those families who were in receipt of poor relief from the parish, their number would also include those whom the parish constable himself judged to be on hard times—he was not immune to favouritism and local pressure. Moreover, the fact that amongst those exempt in Barry in 1673 was Mr Evan Seys, then lord of the manor and resident at Boverton Castle, is also a warning against a too literal interpretation of the documents; Seys was exempt probably because he was owner of a house which was temporarily vacant, almost certainly Ostry Farm.

Estates: management

The greater extent of population growth in Cadoxton and Merthyr Dyfan can be at least partly understoood in relation to the different conditions of landownership in those parishes, and the way in which this ownership was exercised. In Cadoxton and Merthyr Dyfan, as we have seen, landownership was much less concentrated than in Barry; as a result they were more 'open' in character, it being difficult for any landlord to control immigration or restrict new building of houses to accommodate the increased population.

In the reign of Elizabeth the great majority of tenant farmers in the Barry area—whoever the landlord was—were copyholders, customary tenants freed from the onerous labour services of the medieval villein. Tenants paid a cash rent for their farms and, in addition, owed a *heriot*, or tribute. Details of the administration of the local estates are few and, in general, have to be inferred from successive rentals and surveys. However, in the case of the St. Johns, lords of Barry, some correspondence dating from the middle years of Queen Elizabeth's reign has survived; letters through which Oliver and John St. John communicated with the high steward of their Welsh estate, Sir Thomas Stradling of St. Donat's.[41] These letters show that the Bletso family kept in close touch with affairs locally, through regular correspondence with both Stradling and their manorial bailiffs. The latter apparently sent regular reports to Bedfordshire and from time to time themselves journeyed to Bletso. In addition to these contacts, the engrossed records of the manor court, held at Penmark five or six times in the year, were sent regularly to the lord. By these means the St. Johns obtained detailed knowledge of the management of their estate and they were able as a result to give precise instructions as to how their tenants should be handled; in one case, Oliver St. John refused to repeal the forfeiture of his tenement by an Irishman because he objected to his 'lewd and disordered behaviour', distrusted his loyalty to the Queen, and feared that he might be cheated of his heriot when it fell due.[42]

The authority of the St. Johns was also exercised through the steward and understeward at meetings of the manor court; their supervision made the court a body which efficiently oversaw the estate and its affairs and was the effective focus of local government and social control. The court intervened continually in the lives of the villages of Penmark, Porthkerry, Cwmcidy and Barry.

Estates: the manor court

The court met on five occasions in the year as a rule, to register changes in the tenure of customary and freehold land, to settle disputes between tenants and to fine those who had infringed custom in some way. Two or three times a year, the court functioned also as a *court leet*, and in this role it exercised a petty criminal jurisdiction over not just tenants of the manor but all other inhabitants in the parishes of Barry, Porthkerry and Penmark. For the ordinary farmer, craftsman and labourer and their families, the court was, in the 16th and early 17th centuries, the most important organ of local government; contact with higher, common-law courts must have been much rarer. Sessions of the court leet, particularly, must have seen the majority of the local adult population in attendance in Penmark, and on these occasions the court was a genuinely communal gathering, presided over by the lord's steward or his deputy. As Oliver St. John wrote to Sir Thomas Stradling in 1578, a skilful steward was needed 'to govern such a great number of rude and forward people as appeareth before him at every court and leet'.[43] Punitive fines were imposed from time to time to quell sporadic acts in defiance of the lord's authority; in 1573, for example, Thomas Wilkin, rector of Barry and Porthkerry, was fined 20*s.*—a sum equivalent to the entire worldly wealth of some poorer folk—for disturbing a meeting of the court.[44] In general, however, for the period for which records survive for the Penmark court, 1570-1615, the impression is of co-operation rather than conflict between steward and community.

Many matters were in any case a matter of routine in which the court could be said to be taking action for the good of the community. Jurors, chosen from amongst the leading copyhold tenants, were regularly instructed to inspect and put to right boundaries and rights of way. At many courts it was reported that the archery butts at Penmark, Barry and Porthkerry were in decay, although all men were supposed to practise weekly with the longbow. Local folk, as had most Elizabethan villagers, had become apathetic to this duty: the longbow by the end of the 16th century had effectively been superseded by the musket and harquebus as a weapon of war. More concern was shown about the maintenance of the stocks; in June 1590 the entire parish of Barry was threatened with a corporate fine of 30*s*. unless stocks were provided. Responsible for the keeping of the peace was the parish constable; in some communities he was elected or nominated by the vestry, but locally—a measure of the strength of the manor court as an institution—he was elected at the Michaelmas court. The constable was responsible for keeping the peace in the community, appointing the watch, carrying out warrants from justices of the peace and passing on vagrants. It was an unpaid office, and not necessarily a popular one: in 1584 William Evor of Greenhouse Farm was fined 3*s*. 4*d*. by the manor court for refusing to serve as constable of Barry.[45]

The leet had a number of important functions relating to the maintenance of order in the local community. Each meeting saw the jurors presenting a series of minor assaults and affrays—petty quarrels that ended in blows. In 1604 an affray is reported between an alehouse keeper, William Wilkin, and a 'traveller called a tinker' (*peregrinus anglice vocatus* a tinker). A number of these quarrels must have begun, as today, in a tavern, and Elizabethan and Jacobean Barry was extremely well-provided with alehouses. The court rolls indicate that as a rule, there were two or three taverns trading regularly in the parish; occasionally this number was augmented by other housekeepers brewing and selling ale. In 1607 four alehouses are recorded in Barry, as against one in Penmark. The Barry taverns were kept by William Wilkin, Thomas Jones, Alice Duke and Elizabeth Jones, and Richard Portrey—the latter probably at Ostry Farm. William Wilkin may have used a cottage adjacent to Barry castle. Alehouse keepers in Barry are sometimes presented at the manor court for failing to sell beer in the legal measure (a quart pot) or for charging above the legal price; in 1610 it was reported that Thomas ap Owen of Barry 'doth not usually sell a quart for a penny'. The local alehouse was not just a drinking den; in 1588 it was said of William Wilkin that he kept in his house women of ill-fame (*suspectas esse inhonestas*).

Barry, a community of some seventy souls, no doubt had so many taverns because of its port; alehouse keepers catered not only for locals but for ships' crews and local merchants. Otherwise, the maritime importance of Barry is hardly reflected in the manor court records, although in 1597 the bailiff of Barry manor was said to be in possession of a frying pan and a hatchet, said to be 'pirates' goods'.

The majority of entries in the court books are less colourful. Year after year there are lists of tenants who failed to keep their tenements in good repair, of others living away from the manor without licence, and of those who had encroached on other men's land or cut timber without permission. Deaths of tenants and residents are recorded and their heriots noted. Occasionally, a note of tragedy is struck. In 1593 Nicholas Walter 'hanged himself within the manor', and the lord of the manor claimed his goods, as he was entitled to: four cows valued at £1 each, 7*s.* borrowed from Walter by William Wilkin, and £1 that had been loaned to the deceased by John Thomas of Cwmcidy. Most courts, too, acted to settle petty pleas of debt and trespass—at the manor court damages of up to 40*s.* could be claimed. Little detail is given, but the following cases are probably typical: in 1601 Nicholas Harry sued the miller William Hopkin for a debt of 4*s.* 10*d.*; in 1602 John Rees claimed that John Hopkin had allowed his horses to damage his growing corn and sought 39*s.* 11*d.* compensation.[46]

The information that the court books contain concerning the transfer of farms, both freehold and copyhold, is immensely useful, for it enables us to trace the history of tenements and the families asociated with them. This information can also be combined with rentals and surveys to give a picture of the St. John family as landlords.

Fig. 42. Barry Castle and surroundings in *c.* 1622, reconstruction drawing. Farmhouse on extreme right. Alehouse kept by Wilkins family, within castle ruins. *Simon Prosser after H. J. Thomas.*

Estates: rents and 'fines'

The St. Johns were in many ways conservative in the way they ran their Welsh estate, despite their close control over affairs. In an age of steep inflation rental income from their Glamorgan manors remained static until the 1630s, and copyhold for three lives remained the dominant tenure until the reign of Charles II. This conservatism undoubtedly worked in the interest of the tenant farmer, whose copyhold gave him reasonable security of tenure and whose low rent gave him the opportunity to save, providing he was able to generate a regular surplus from his farm. This situation must have helped families to retain the same holding for several generations; farmers who prospered were also able to increase the number of tenancies they held.

The St. Johns, after 1580, sought to increase their revenue not by raising rents—very difficult when farms were let for three lives and rents regarded as customary—but by increasing the value of *entry fines*, levied from tenants when they took over their farms. In 1611 a fine of £200 was levied on Cole Farm when it was taken over by Thomas Williams (this figure being only £15 less than the rental income of the whole Welsh estate in 1622). However, the following year a mere £5 was taken as an entry fine from Maud Harry when she took over her 14-acre copyhold at Cwmcidy.[47]

Unlike some contemporary landlords the St. Johns do not appear to have attempted to use exorbitant entry fines to force potential tenants to compete for a holding after the expiry of the third life in a copy; rather, the level of fine charged appears to have reflected the amount of capital a potential tenant could raise, and local families were allowed to remain on their holdings provided they were likely to be reliable tenants. Nonetheless, some of the larger farms did attract men from some distance away who were ready to invest their capital in acquiring a Barry copyhold. In 1593 James Andrew of Bletso took over a fifty-acre farm at Porthkerry on the death of John Slugge; the following year he acquired Cole Farm at Cold Knap. Once established, a high level of entry fines persisted at Barry, £230 being raised on Cwm Barry farm when George Mathew succeeded his father Oliver in the 1640s; £220 on Castle Farm when Ralph Dawkins succeeded Lewis William.[48] By the 1660s, however, some rents had been raised to a more economic level, Cwm Barry being let for £23 per annum compared to the £6 it yielded in 1622, but the St. Johns had not emulated other Glamorgan landlords by replacing copyholds by leases save on a handful of farms. The introduction of leases on a large scale was left to their successors, the Joneses of Fonmon (in the case of the manors of Penmark, Fonmon and Llancadle) and the Seys family of Boverton (in the case of Barry). By the 1670s Marsh Farm and Greenhouse Farm were being let by lease for 99 years determinable on three lives; they were no longer held by restrictive custom and therefore had greater potential value to the lord.[48]

Despite these changes the distribution of farms in late 17th-century Barry had altered little, and a number of families were still in possession of farms that they had held for three or four generations. One must be careful, however, not to equate possession with occupation, for there is some evidence that all or part of a farm could be sublet. The court books of the late 16th and early 17th centuries show that while some tenants sublet their farms illegally, without licence, others obtained permission from the lord to do so. At most, however, half-a-dozen tenants on the St. John estate were living away from the manor without licence at any one time in this period; equally licences to sublet were rarely granted, although it is probable that James Andrew of Cole Farm sublet this tenement to Jenkin Cradock in the 1590s. Close comparison of the Hearth Tax lists of the early 1670s with contemporary rentals suggests that several Barry tenements were then sublet, since the householder who paid tax on his dwelling sometimes does not match with the name of the known tenant. Robert Morgan of Wellhouse, Lewis Alexander of Burroughes and Thomas Jones of Lower Green cottage almost certainly were subletting their holdings, while at the very end of the 17th century we know that Rees William of Cole Farm had sublet it to a kinsman, Meredith Howell of Porthkerry.

All the evidence is that the Herbert and Popham estates in Cadoxton and Merthyr Dyfan were managed in an equally conservative fashion. Successive late 17th-century and early 18th-century rentals for the Popham manor of Cadoxton East Barry show that during the course of time copyholds were replaced by 99-year leases. Rents, however, as they stood in 1663, were the same nearly sixty years later in 1721.[49] They were far cheaper at this date than the rents levied on Barry farmers by the Seys family, and lower in many cases than the 1*s.* per acre characteristic of the St. John estate at the time of Evans Mouse's survey forty years previously. In 1663 Thomas Taylor owed a mere 21*s.* 2*d.* on Watts House tenement in Cadoxton, which comprised a messuage and 28 acres of land; in the same year David Spencer was rated at £4 6*s.* for his 111-acre farm of Great Brynhill. Rents on the Popham estate were low even in the early 17th century and remained so into the 18th century. Rents on the Herbert estate in Merthyr Dyfan, surveyed in 1693, seem to have been comparably low; Thomas Willy, who held by copy two tenements and 37 acres, was expected to pay only £1 2*s.* 10*d.* annually. Miles Williams paid only 10*s.* a year for the 30-acre Croft Way Farm.

This stability in rent, along with the system of three-life copyholds and 99-year leases, contributed as it did at Barry to stability amongst farming families. Families named in the Lay Subsidy assessments of the 1540s survived in the locality often into the 18th century; through the Popham rentals we can trace the handing down of farms from generation to generation in the half-century after the Restoration of Charles II in 1660.

Because the 1584 list of tenements is so brief and lacking in detail it is difficult to match it with later rentals, but there seems by the 1660s to have been little amalgamation or subdivision of farms. The most notable feature of the 1663 rental of the Popham estate, and more especially that for 1671, is the increased number of cottages on the manor. Some of these had been erected on land belonging to existing farmsteads, others were built on patches of waste or common land. In 1671, for example, Henry David's leasehold tenement comprised two cottages, nine acres of arable and meadow land; one further acre of meadow; and two more cottages and a house nearby. Assuming he and his family lived in the house, David may have sublet his four cottages. In 1663, John Langton was said to hold sixteen acres of arable and a 'newly erected house' called 'Cowlins Down'. Amongst the regular cottages and farms, the 1671 rental lists three cottages that had been built on the waste; each was let at 1*s*. a year and neither had more than a garden in terms of land. Two of them had been built by Richard Petre and Edward William.

The erection of cottages appears to have been a response to the growing population of the local community; manorial control, unlike in Barry, seems to have been too weak to exclude migrants or prevent illegal cottage-building on common land. We can match the Cadoxton examples with two others revealed in Merthyr Dyfan by the 1693 rental, occupied by Francis Leyshon and Morgan Harry. This document also appears to include the Cadoxton cottages noted in 1671; the jury of survey claimed that none of their occupants acknowledged any lord or paid any rent—the 1*s*. *per annum* claimed by the Pophams rental may, then, have been mere wishful thinking. The erection of such dwellings indicates how the increased populations of Merthyr Dyfan and Cadoxton were housed; apart from documented examples we also have the evidence of the 1763 Wenvoe estate maps to show the extent of encroachment by that date by illegal cottage-builders on the south and south-eastern margins of Cadoxton Common. In Barry strong lordship and the absence of common land prevented such squatting.

The local economy

The rentals and surveys of the various estates in the area of Barry tell us the names of farmers and the acreages of their farms; by the mid to late 17th century we have also increasing evidence for growing numbers of cottagers, particularly in Cadoxton and Merthyr Dyfan. Such landless or near landless folk eked out a meagre living by working on the farms of their more fortunate neighbours. There is considerable information available concerning the type of agriculture favoured by these farmers, both large and small, derived mainly from the probate inventories that describe the possessions of deceased members of local families. Inventories are associated with the wills of such people; a good inventory will often contain a room-by-room description of the contents of a house and detailed valuations of livestock and crops. Not everyone by any means made a will, however, and because of the disruption caused by the Civil War, few probate records survive from before 1640. Most of our information from this type of source relates to the period from 1660 until the mid 18th century (thereafter wills continue but inventories become much rarer) and to the middle and upper ranks of the farming community. The very poor had little furniture and few animals, and, for them, there was little point in will-making; it is also the case that many of the better off had no need to make a will because they were able, during their lifetimes, to make arrangements for the disposal of their property amongst their children and relatives. Amongst the farmers, family circumstances would indicate whether a will were made or not. In total, 34 inventories and 36 wills have survived from the 17th century. The earliest will is that of John Willy of Merthyr Dyfan, dated 1622, the earliest inventory belongs to Margaret Spenser, widow, of the same parish and is dated 1636; the earliest probate records for Barry are the will and inventory of Oliver Mathew of Cwm Barry Farm (1641). Apart from probate records relating to Barry, Cadoxton and Merthyr Dyfan, a handful have survived also for Highlight and for Cwmcidy, the latter amongst the records for Porthkerry parish.[50]

Most inventories describe the personal estate of men and women actively engaged in farming at the time of their deaths; others seem to document the possessions either of craftsmen and labourers, or of folk who had retired from the land and were supported up to their deaths by income saved over the years or by their grown-up families. John Llewelyn of Cadoxton, who died in May 1699, had goods worth over £50. Of this, £22 10*s.* was accounted for by money he had lent out at interest; he still had a few cattle but was no longer fully engaged in running a farm. Llewelyn was one of the wealthier in the area to make a will in the 17th century; at the opposite end of the social scale was Abel Hoskins of the same parish, whose estate totalled only £3 15*s.* Although he had ten sheep (worth £1), he may, in fact, have been a blacksmith, since his inventory mentions 'tools in the forge', also worth £1. The remainder of his goods was made up of clothing (7*s.*), a bed and bedding (10*s.*), two pewter platters (2*s.*), some salted meat (8*s.*), and a chair, pail, tub and cauldron (10*s.*).

In the early modern Vale of Glamorgan farming was mixed in character. Most farmers grew crops as well as kept cattle, sheep and other animals. Writing in 1578, Rice Merrick, squire of Cottrell near St. Nicholas, depicts the Vale as having 'pleasant meadows and . . . pastures, the plains fruitful and apt for tillage, bearing abundance of all kind of grain'.[51] In some Vale parishes, such as Penmark, Porthkerry, Llantwit Major and St. Athan, many farmers had nearly as much capital invested in corn-growing as in dairying, fattening and sheep-rearing; on some of the larger farms in the latter two parishes cereal production was probably even more important.

According to Rice Lewis, the manor of Boverton and Llantwit Major had between 'eight and nine hundred acres of good arable lands'.[52] In other parts of the Vale, however, the tendency seems to have been for the pastoral element in farming to predominate in terms of investment; corn there being grown for domestic needs as it was in the uplands, for bread and fodder rather than for market. The inventories enable us to get quite an accurate picture of farming in the Barry area. It is clear from them that livestock dominated the local economy, on both large and small farms; however, arable crops were only of any significance in the personal estate of men and women who had possessions worth £20 and upwards. Smaller farmers may have grown less and may have depended on buying in wheat and barley to meet the needs of their households. People at this level—men like John Thomas of Merthyr Dyfan, who had five cattle, some hay, a few pigs and poultry, and 16*s.* of oats and wheat in the ground (in all, part of an estate of only £18 9*s.* 4*d.*)—must have supplemented their income from their own land by work on the farms of others. Contrast Thomas's position with that of James Robins, who died a year before him in 1691, and lived in the same parish. Robins had personalty worth over £78, including livestock, fodder and provision worth £30 9*s.*; that his was a profitable concern is demonstrated by the fact that he had loaned £21 13*s.* to other people.

On only four 17th-century farms was over 30% of capital invested in growing corn,[53] although since we have few inventories drawn up in summer or early autumn, when it was possible for the appraiser of a person's farm to know more accurately the value of a crop, it is possible that in the case of some farmers the extent of investment in cereals is understated by their inventories. Table 10 summarises information from the inventories as to relative investment in stock and crops. Although we have only four examples of 'small' farmers' inventories—those whose possessions were valued at under £20—the same pattern is repeated in 18th-century Merthyr Dyfan and Cadoxton inventories. The picture revealed by Table 10 is very different from the results of a similar analysis of Penmark and Porthkerry inventories; in the latter parishes the balance between arable and pastoral production was somewhat closer. It is possible that, in the century before 1640, for which we have much less evidence, more effort was put into growing corn in our three parishes. Before the Civil War cereal prices were much higher than they were to be between 1660 and 1760. Larger farmers might have grown more wheat and barley in Elizabethan and Jacobean times, when it was more profitable, but shifted towards livestock after the Restoration when arable prices slumped. The decades after the Restoration saw a growing regional specialisation in agriculture; successful arable farming increasingly required a large farm and light soils, while heavier-soiled lowland areas and the uplands concentrated on livestock, for which prices were more stable.[54]

It is possible that a shift in the balance of production on Cwm Barry Farm may have been symptomatic of this trend. In 1641 Oliver Mathew left stock and crops worth £75 6*s*. 8*d*. Of this figure, 60% was represented by cattle and oxen (£30), sheep (£5), horses (£6), pigs, poultry and hay. Corn in store and in the ground was valued at £30, 40% of the investment on a farm of 83 acres, one of the largest in the locality. By September 1683, when the inventory of Oliver's grandson Philemon Mathew was drawn up, the organisation of the farm was very much altered. Crops now represented only 14% of investment, £8 10*s*. as opposed to the £53 6*s*. 8*d*. which was the value placed on the livestock.

In the case of those Barry farms for which inventories have survived we can make a direct comparison between farm-size, investment and personal wealth. The two 17th-century inventories for Cwm Barry have already been mentioned; Oliver Mathew's total personal estate was valued at £95, his grandson's at £93. We have a single inventory for the 67-acre Cole Farm, that of Wenllian Reese *alias* Rosser, who left property worth £88 in 1684. Castle Farm was also of 67 acres; Lewis William, who died in 1688, left goods and farmstock worth £28 12*s*. Two inventories represent somewhat smaller farms; Thomas Evers of Greenhouse Farm (36 acres plus 20 acres at Westercloses) left estate worth £67 10*s*. in 1687, and William Richards, described as a 'seafarer', left property worth £35 10*s*. on 'Marsh Farm (19½ acres) in 1698.

Table 10. Investment in livestock and crops on 17th-century farms.

Parish	Stock %	Crops %	Mean value of inventories
Merthyr Dyfan			
larger farms (11)[a]	78	21	£77·18
smaller farms (4)	96	4	£18·49
Cadoxton			
larger farms (8)	84	16	£66·85
Barry			
larger farms (8)	82	18	£68·10

[a] 'larger' farms are defined as those units where the deceased is recorded in his inventory as possessing £20 or more in personalty.

The organisation of Cole Farm in 1684 was very similar to that of Cwm Barry the year before. The main investment was equally in livestock. At Cole Farm, animals and fodder were valued at £52 5*s*. 10*d*.; at Cwm Barry

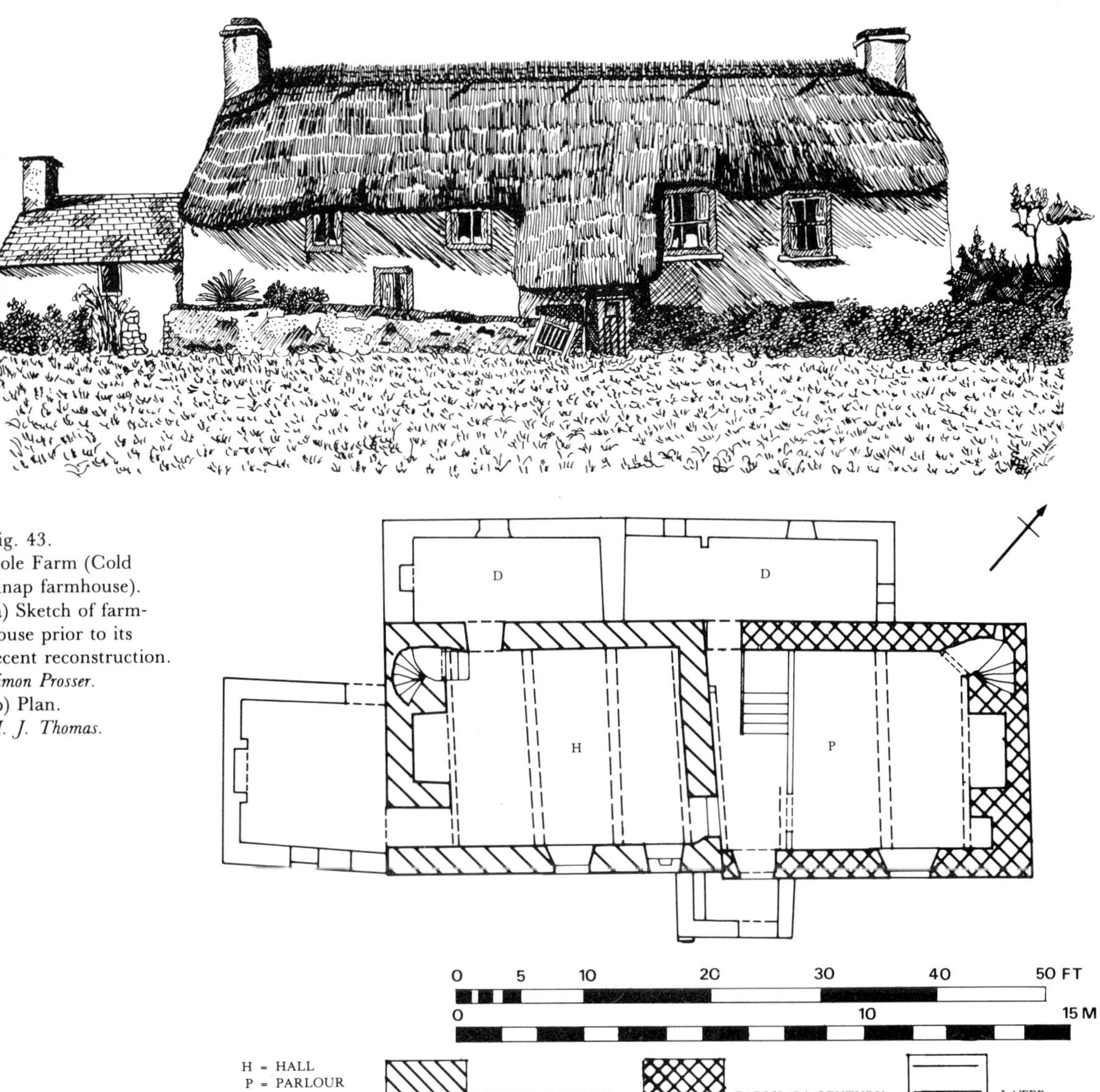

ig. 43.
ole Farm (Cold
nap farmhouse).
) Sketch of farm-
ouse prior to its
cent reconstruction.
imon Prosser.
) Plan.
. J. Thomas.

they were worth £53 6*s.* 8*d.* Whereas Philemon Mathew had corn valued at £5, Wenllian Rosser's crops were valued at £6 10*s.* As at Cwm Barry the emphasis was on dairying and rearing young cattle for sale, Wenllian having four oxen, three steers, three yearling cattle, seven milk cows, seven calves and, usually, a bull. Sheep were more important at Cole Farm than at Cwm Barry; Wenllian Rosser had a flock of 30 sheep and 20 lambs, worth in all £5 16*s.* 4*d.* whereas Philemon Mathew had only seven ewes and lambs, worth £1 15*s.*

Cole and Cwm Barry farms are good examples of the medium-sized yeoman farms that were the mainstay of agriculture in the lower Vale, rearing cattle, probably Glamorgan 'reds' rather than the smaller black cattle of the uplands, for cheese and butter, and raising beef animals until they were three or four years old, when they could be sold to dealers or drovers. Sheep flocks in Barry were small, probably because there was no common pasture, unlike the extensive sheep commons of parishes such as St. Hilary, Ewenny and St. Bride's Major. Castle Farm, although the same acreage as Cole, cannot be directly compared with Wenllian Rosser's tenement. Lewis William was aged about 95 at his death in 1688 and, from 1660 at least, he had shared Castle with his brother-in-law Randolph Dawkin. At Marsh and Greenhouse Farms cattle again predominated. William Richards of Marsh Farm, who died in 1698, had been tenant since 1674. Household goods account for two-thirds of the value of his inventory; of the remainder, a cow, three heifers, two yearlings, a horse and a pig were collectively worth £10 10*s*. and, in addition, he had two acres of wheat, beans, peas and oats, valued at £1 10*s*.

Amongst Cadoxton and Merthyr Dyfan farmers Mary Tucker of Cadoxton was something of an exception, for hers was one of the few farms on which crops were as important as they were further west in the Vale. Mary was the wife of Hugh Tucker, who died in 1676, twenty-four years before his widow. Mary's estate totalled £81 7*s*. She had continued to farm her late husband's tenements: a close of pasture in St. Andrew's of eight acres; a messuage and twenty acres of land, with pasture for sheep on Sheeping Moor, the extensive area of common land bordering on the sea which Cadoxton farmers shared with those from Sully and Dinas Powys; and a messuage and ten acres, together with a cottage 'near the Pinfold' in Cadoxton. In 1671 she also held in her own right a further house and 22 acres of land. Aged 72 when she died in 1691, she may have farmed some 52 acres in Cadoxton and an additional eight acres in St. Andrews. In September of that year crops represented 37% of her farmstock. She had seven acres of wheat, four acres of oats and two acres of beans and peas ready for harvesting, valued at £21 10*s*. Cattle comprised her major investment in livestock—five cows, four oxen and eight 'young beasts'—but she also had one of the largest sheep flocks in the district. Her flock was worth £5 10*s*. and must have numbered about fifty animals (John Lewis, three years later, had eighteen sheep worth £2, about 2*s*. 2*d*. each). The presence of a significant sheep flock, though less valuable than her cattle or crops, demonstrates the relationship between sheep-rearing and the availability of common pasture. Many Cadoxton farmers, and some from Merthyr Dyfan, had access to the grazing on Sheeping Moor and sheep consequently figure more prominently in their inventories than in those from Barry. Flocks were generally small, however; in Cadoxton only Mary Tucker and John Stephens (*d*. April 1685) had more than twenty animals. Seven out of fifteen Merthyr Dyfan inventories include sheep, but only three of the farmers had twenty sheep or more.

The local economy: money-lending

Judging from the contents of their inventories, farmers of medium-sized tenements—say thirty acres or more—had attained more than a modest prosperity by the later 17th century, though few were as wealthy as the leading farmers of Penmark and Porthkerry or of Llantwit Major. Several put their savings from farming to work by lending money at interest. Eleven of the farming inventories contain lists of debts owed, as do those of a number of people who had at least partly retired from the land. John Llewelyn, yeoman of Cadoxton, had £22 10*s.* lent out 'by bonds and bills or otherwise' at the time of his death in 1699. This sum represented nearly half of his personal estate.

In the absence of a developed system of local banking—not to be a feature of the South Wales economy until the end of the 18th century—lending money at interest could be a profitable way of using one's money; it was far preferable to keeping it under the mattress. Ideally it could be called in when needed to recover from a bad harvest, or to invest in land or stock, or in improving a farmhouse and its outbuildings. For some farmers, such as John Llewelyn, this was a good way to provide for one's retirement. Occasionally inventories contain detailed lists of such loans and these point to a quite extensive network of local credit, linking farmers from our local parishes to folk quite far afield. Ann Love of Colcot, who died in 1690 worth £41, was owed a total of £29 3*s.*; amongst her creditors were Philip David of Wenvoe (10*s.*) and Ann Smith of Colcot (3*s.*). Philemon Mathew of Cwm Barry had lent £27 to Mr Evans of Castleton Farm in St. Athan. Sometimes, however, this system broke down. Margaret Love's credits were listed as 'desperate' in April 1681, These were debts that the appraisers of her estate doubted could be recovered. She had loaned £5 to Richard Mathews of St. Fagans; £9 6*s.* to Arthur French of Wenvoe, £4 19*s.* to Thomas William of Carmarthen and £4 9*s.* to Thomas Griffith of St. Nicholas.

Local farmers borrowed as well as lent large amounts of money. John William of Cadoxton (*d.* 1682) had borrowed a total of £15 7*s.* from nine persons, including John Stephens of the same parish, to whom he owed £6 13*s.* 4*d.*

These references remind us that local farmers did not follow their calling in isolation but operated within the context of a well-developed regional economy. No farmer, however small, was solely concerned to produce food for his own family's needs; to some extent all were involved in marketing their produce. The small farmer who ran an almost exclusively livestock unit depended on the markets of Cardiff and Cowbridge, or on his larger neighbours, for his bread-corn, which he bought from the proceeds of sales of meat, animals, cheese and butter. Even if it was only the farms of thirty or forty acres or more which could yield regular profit, and allow their proprietors to accumulate capital, every farmer and every inhabitant operated within the context of a cash economy and was dependent on the fluctuations of prices in the market. For the larger farmers especially, there was a wide market available for their produce.

The local economy: the port of Barry

The major local markets were at Cowbridge and Cardiff. At Cowbridge market days were Tuesday and Saturday; at Cardiff a corn market was held on Wednesday and Saturday. Fairs were also important, held twice a year in Cowbridge and three times a year in Cardiff; other nearby fairs were those of Bridgend, Ely Bridge, St. Nicholas and St. Mary Hill. Vale farmers, however, produced for a market much wider than that of local demand; by 1600 they were integrated into a market that encompassed the west of England, Ireland and France. In the service of this market Barry played a small but significant part, alongside the other local ports of Cardiff, Penarth, Sully, Aberthaw and Newton. The 'Port Books', which record from the early years of Queen Elizabeth's reign the inward and outward voyages of local ships, show that Bristol and the smaller West Country ports received regular cargoes of hides and dairy produce, livestock and corn, wool, stockings, gloves, flannels and kelp from the ports of the Vale.[55]

Thomas Phaer, commissioned by the Crown in 1552-3 to compile a report on the Welsh ports and their administration, has left a brief description of the port of Barry:

> Barry from Cardiff road six miles a good road at four fathom low water and a dry haven to come into with northerly and westerly winds; it lieth against Minehead and Bridgwater in Somersetshire.[56]

The quayside at Barry was located at the bottom of Ship Hill, below the parish church of St. Nicholas, which was a good landmark for sailors in the difficult waters of the Severn estuary. By the quay stood Ostry Farm, where a tavern serving the port had been kept for many years. Nearby, in existence by 1598, was a storehouse, which Evans Mouse described in 1622 as having 'divers lofts and cellars'. In 1622 the storehouse was let to Reynold Portrey, also tenant of the Ostry, for 26*s.* 8*d.* a year, together with the 'water bailiwick unto the manors of Barry, Penmark and Fonmon', and the right to levy and retain the customary duties that the St. Johns could levy on ships coming into the harbour. Portrey could also claim for his own, all casualties from wrecks up to the value of 40*s.*, and his storehouse was said to have 'convenient room to lay the same wrecks and casualties by sea until convenient sale thereof by the lord of the said manors'. Duties levied on ships included 2*d.* 'keelage'; two bushels out of every cargo of salt and 4½*d.* on every tun of wine. Foreign ships paid double these rates.[57]

Even today, despite all the changes in the shoreline that have taken place since the building of the docks in the 1880s, archaeologists can find traces in the mud of the old harbour of the activities of the old port. Broken medieval and post-medieval pots discovered there are the remains of damaged goods thrown overboard from vessels moored at the quay; they demonstrate that the harbour had some importance as early as the 13th century, when it served the newly established town of Llantrisant.[58] Documentary evidence of its trade survives, however, only from the middle of the 16th century, when, for the first time, the Crown began to get a grip on the customs administration of the Welsh side of the Bristol Channel, in the teeth of opposition from the aristocratic landlords who controlled most of the harbours of Glamorgan and Monmouthshire. Much of this evidence arises out of the activities of two men: Henry Morgan, appointed searcher of customs at Cardiff in 1559, and John Leek, royal customs collector in the Glamorgan ports from 1564 until 1571, when he was dismissed for corruption. Neither man had an efficient network of deputies or informers to aid them and they met fierce opposition both from the local owners of ports and the masters and merchants trading from them. Both attempted to bring prosecutions for the evasion of royal customs dues; the records of these prosecutions give us some idea of the ships and shipowners who traded through Barry. While the finer details of the allegations made by Morgan and Leek may be dubious, their general accounts of ships and their cargoes have the ring of truth.[59]

ig. 44.
'he old port of Barry, ɿowing quayside as it ɿight have appeared ɿ the late 17th and 8th centuries. Ostry ɿrmhouse on left;)stry barn at centre, 'ith limekiln behind; torehouse in right ɔreground; shoreline urving away to East ʒarry.
imon Prosser
fter H. J. Thomas.

On 5 April 1560, for example, Morgan attempted to take possession of the *Saviour*, then lying in Barry roads. She was from Minehead, but was part-owned by Maurice Mathew, owner of a large Rhoose freehold and father of John Mathew of Cwm Barry. Morgan claimed that Mathew, his partner William Bawdren, and one Jevan Jones, had transported 150 barrels of butter overseas without a licence, and gave evidence that when he boarded the ship, James Mathew, Maurice's son, drew a dagger and threatened to pin him to the mast. Another crewman, Richard Jones, tried to throw the customs man overboard, but Morgan nonetheless gained control of the ship, which he left at Barry in the charge of the local constable, Thomas John Dee. In their answer to Morgan's charges, Mathew, Bawdren and Jones claimed that three barrels of butter were necessary victuals for the ship's crew of 24 and they denied knowledge of the other 147 barrels. The *Saviour*, they said, was to carry goods belonging to Taunton merchants to Lisbon in Portugal.

This story contains useful information, whatever the truth of claim and counterclaim. The *Saviour* must have been a largish vessel, fit both for the Bristol Channel and the long crossing of Biscay. Her main cargo was probably butter, as Morgan alleged, for butter was the principal export of the Vale, sent legally and illegally across the channel, and to Ireland and France. It was typical, too, for ships to be owned by partnerships of the wealthier yeoman and gentlemen of the Vale, men who sank their profits from agriculture into the expanding trade of Tudor Glamorgan. The mention of Taunton merchants, however, reminds us of the significant and increasing role that West Country capital played in the local economy, providing the finance and the goods for many overseas voyages.

Other prosecutions also reveal the names of ships using Barry in the 1560s, a decade for which our information is very full. In 1561, for example, Jevan Jones, part-owner of the *Saviour*, was accused of exporting 60 barrels of butter from Barry and Cardiff in the *Michael* of Sully. In 1568, Leek's agent, Jerome Westall, claimed that the *Katherine White* of Barnstaple had carried twelve barrels of butter, 1,200 measures of wheat, and 60 woollen cloths (a cargo worth £764) from Barry without paying duty. This cargo had been put together by six men, the principals being John Askott of Barnstaple and John Thomas, a gentleman farmer of Flemingston, near St. Athan. It was later claimed that the 'kaykeeper' at Barry, John 'ap Jones', had stolen a barrel of butter from this cargo after it had been placed in his custody, and put it on board a ship sailing from Barry. Meanwhile, the *Katherine White* is named again in Exchequer proceedings in the same year, when it was alleged that Lewis Frowde, a Cardiff merchant, had exported twenty barrels of wheat, each worth 40*s.*, from Barry aboard her.

From this decade we also learn of the *Julian* of Barry. In 1569 Leek claimed that she had evaded the customs men at Southwark with a cargo of

40 barrels of butter. She was seized by Leek, probably at Barry, on 17 November 1569. Her cargo belonged to David Stacy of Cosmeston, John Dyer of Cogan, and John Nycholl and John Taylor of St. Andrew's Major. That same month Leek also claimed to have discovered 300 measures of French salt valued at £20 in the house of John ap John, which also belonged to John Dyer; and in December 1569 Leek laid yet another claim, this time that Dyer, Stacy and their associates had sent overseas twelve barrels of butter and thirteen tons of lead from Barry on board the *Julian* in the previous October.[60]

In the 1560s, then, Barry's trade was quite active, the port being used regularly by ships trading both across the channel and further afield. Voyages were financed by merchants from Cardiff and the West Country, and by the wealthier farmers of the Vale, who were also shipowners, usually in partnership. Later evidence for the trade of Barry is harder to come by, mainly because of deficiencies in the documentary record. It is clear that there was no decline in trade; the storehouse on the quay was rebuilt to serve local merchants, but it is likely that in the Port Books ships trading from Barry are concealed in entries for Cardiff and Sully. Probably the customs men at Cardiff found it unnecessary to distinguish Barry from its neighbouring ports. However, we do learn the names of some of the ships using Barry in the later 16th century. In 1589, for example, the *Gifte* brought in a cargo of French salt, and between 1586 and 1595 there are frequent references to the *Primrose*, a ship of thirty tons that was based at Barry and captained in succession by Richard Richards, Thomas Clement, Richard Hardy, John Clement and Nicholas Selephant. On her outward voyages from Cardiff and Barry the *Primrose* carried butter, cottons and coal to La Rochelle; she brought home pitch, salt, honey, raisins, paper, wine and rosin.[61] A document dating from the reign of James I suggests that Barry was the home port of two vessels, Aberthaw of five, Cardiff of three and Penarth of one. Since Sully and Newton are omitted, the accuracy of this document is dubious,[62] but it gives an idea of the comparative importance of each of the local ports, and confirms, in particular, the pre-eminence of Aberthaw, which by 1636 was even trading with the West Indies.[63] Occasional late 17th-century references to Barry occur in the Bridgewater Port Books, and in a manuscript kept by an Aberthaw customs man. These are sufficient to show that the cross-channel trade of Barry continued in the early 18th century to be of some importance, probably dwindling in the latter half of the century, when the expansion of iron-founding and coalmining in Glamorgan created a massive increase in local demand for the produce of Vale farms. By 1800 ships using Barry harbour were mainly concerned with the carriage of limestone. On 18 November 1698 the *Richard and Jane* of Barry carried 300 strikes of wheat, 30 strikes of oats, 30 strikes of beans and a cask of butter from Aberthaw to Bristol, with William Bevan as her master and merchant. This vessel is mentioned three times in the following year, when her master was Daniel Luckas, and one of her cargoes was provided by Charles Mathew of Cwm Barry. In 1699 she carried cargoes of corn, butter, kelp, oatmeal and herrings to Bristol and Minehead. Other ships working from Barry in these years were the *Endeavour* of Barry, captained by Richard Spenser; the *Mary*, mentioned in 1707, also captained by Richard Spenser; and the *Laurell*, which was captained by William Bevan in 1701, when she carried coals and culm to Bridgwater.[64] Bevan was tenant of the Ostry in the 1690s and, in 1705, he was described as a mariner when he took up the tenancy of Cole Farm from Richard Seys of Boverton, a holding he forfeited in 1712 for non-payment of rent.

Although the evidence for Barry's maritime trade is limited, there is no doubt concerning the importance of the sea in the local economy. Barry farmers and their fellows from Cadoxton and Merthyr Dyfan, were probably as familiar with the markets of the West Country and Bristol as with those of Cardiff and Cowbridge. In the 16th century the wealthier farmers of the Vale, including the Mathew family of Cwm Barry and Rhoose, financed voyages to export not only their own produce but the butter and corn of smaller farmers which they brought up either at market or by private dealings. By the 1630s, however, English dealers and merchants had come to dominate this trade, especially from Bristol, which exercised a strong grip on the butter market. Nonetheless it is arguable that Vale farmers, putting their profits from commercial farming to good use, continued to play an important subsidiary role in the cross-channel trade in the later 17th century, whether as the part-owners of ships or merchants sponsoring voyages, despite the increasing hold of Bristol on the marketing of butter and wool. Increasingly, too, the city of Bristol, whose population grew from about 10,000 in 1600 to some 20,000 a century later, provided an important market for the Vales's produce as it developed into a leading international port.

Home and family: the Great Rebuilding

The later 16th and 17th centuries were a time of economic growth and expanding markets, nationally and locally. A rising population generally and the rapid growth of London and of provincial towns and ports provided considerable benefits for those farmers who were placed to take advantage of price trends. The mixed farmers of the Vale were in a position to benefit from the high corn prices that prevailed until the 1640s. After the Restoration of Charles II corn prices slumped, but prices for livestock and dairy prices held up well, which also placed these farmers in a favourable situation. It has been argued that better-off farmers—those whose holdings were large enough to return a regular profit—could make use of their capital to invest in improving their houses. W. G. Hoskins coined the phrase 'the

Great Rebuilding' to describe this process. It involved 'first, the physical rebuilding or substantial modernisation of the medieval houses that had come down from the past; and . . . almost simultaneously, a remarkable increase in household furnishings and equipment'.[65] Money was invested in the building of more permanent dwellings which afforded greater privacy, were better heated and lit, and which contained more rooms, particularly rooms with more specialised functions. Although Hoskins suggested that the rebuilding was most intensive between the early years of Elizabeth's reign and the outbreak, in 1640, of the English Revolution, his view has since been qualified as historians have become aware of both regional and local variations in the timing of the rebuilding.[66] In particular, in upland and pastoral areas, such as Wales and the north of England, the seventy years after 1660 are now seen as the more important period.

In Wales, the meaning of the rebuilding is clear enough. As Hoskins indicated, medieval houses, whether of timber or of stone, with their halls open to the roof, were either replaced or extensively modified. Fireplaces and chimneys replaced open hearths whose smoke escaped through a hole in the roof, and permanent staircases gave access to rooms or lofts on an upper floor. In some parts of Wales, such as Cardiganshire, this development was very late, not until the second half of the 18th century; elsewhere it is the later 17th century and the first half of the 18th century that was important. In Glamorgan as a whole, the major period of rebuilding was after 1660, but in parts of the Vale, especially in the southernmost parishes, there is evidence for substantial rebuilding of the houses of middling and larger farmers much earlier.

In the Barry area information on the development of housing in this period takes two forms. First there is the physical evidence of a small number of surviving houses of 16th- and 17th-century date. Secondly, there is the evidence of documents: the Hearth Tax assessments of the 1670s and the probate inventories of local farmers.

The fact that Hearth Tax lists indicate the number of hearths belonging to each householder means that we can obtain from them a general impression of house size in the local community; standing houses and probate inventories help us to interpret this evidence and to understand what kind of house may be indicated by a one-hearth, two-hearth or three-hearth dwelling. In Cadoxton, Barry and Merthyr Dyfan, houses of one or two hearths predominated. In Cadoxton over half of all dwellings had a single hearth; in Merthyr Dyfan over two-thirds; whereas in Barry such houses were slightly in the minority. Houses of three hearths or more were very few and there were no large mansions in the area—Cadoxton Court, the residence of the petty squire William Andrew, had four hearths, William St. John's house at Highlight three. By contrast, Boverton Castle had fifteen hearths in 1673.[67]

There is a close correlation in the lower Vale between 'poverty'—as subjectively defined by the local officials who drew up the Hearth-Tax lists—and one-hearth dwellings. The houses of the poor have not survived to the present day, but we know that they were often no more than crudely built one- or two-room cottages. The simple structure recently excavated at Greencliff near Barry may be a representative example of the better type of labourer's dwelling. A single-roomed structure, 25 × 10 feet internally, with a floor of pitched cobbles, it at least had a hearth and chimney.[68] Not all one-hearth dwellings, however, were poorly built and impermanent.

The houses of farmers, of whatever size, tended to be of better quality than the labourer's hovel, and thus had more chance of surviving to the present day. Two farmhouses survive in the old parish of Barry; one other was destroyed only within the last thirty years.[69] Together with the probate inventories they provide a guide to housing conditions in the late 16th and 17th centuries. Cold Knap farmhouse—or Cole Farm—originated in the later 16th century as a house that was well-built out of local stone, with a fireplace and chimney but only a single room on the ground floor. By about 1600, however, it had been enlarged with the addition of a parlour on the gable opposite the fireplace, which had walls decorated with multi-coloured floral designs and a separate outside entrance through a dressed-stone doorway with a 'Tudor' arch. Its plan follows a pattern very common in South Wales, with the main entrance to the house backing on to the fireplace. This is now the oldest surviving house in Barry. In 1673 its occupier, William Rosser, was rated at two hearths. As the plan shows, one of these was in the 'hall'—the main living accommodation, the other in the parlour or kitchen. Although further altered in the 18th century, the present thatched and white-washed appearance of Cold Knap farm gives an impression of the dwelling of a fairly-well off 17th-century farmer. Rosser farmed 67 acres, a good size for the area.

Cwm Barry Farm, demolished following a serious fire in the 1950s, was a house of similar plan, though it had been more drastically altered from its 17th-century appearance. The house dated from about 1570 and originally composed a hall with a small inner room used as a kitchen, with three bedrooms on the upper floor separated by a pair of roof trusses. Nearby was a bakehouse. This was the home, from the mid-16th century until the early 18th, of the Mathew family. In 1673 George Mathew was rated at three hearths, two in the house itself, in the hall and kitchen, and the third in the detached bakehouse. With 83 acres, this comprised the largest farm in the parish.

Greenhouse Farm still stands in Old Village Road. It is a much less impressive dwelling than Cold Knap, consisting in the 17th century of a single unit, with a fireplace in the hall alongside a spiral stone staircase

a. Cwm Barry (restored)

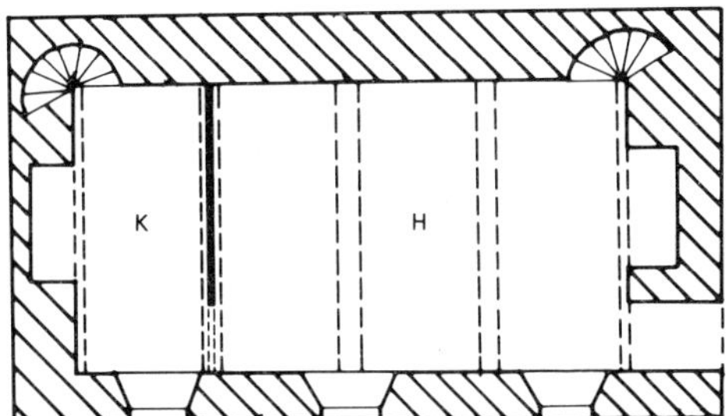

b. Greenhouse, Old Village Road

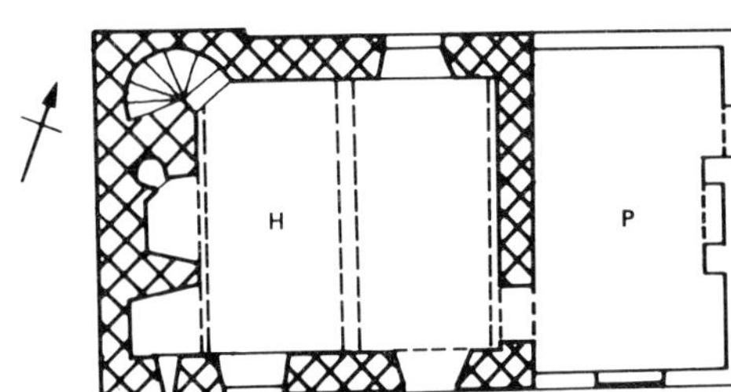

c. Old Mill Farm, Cadoxton

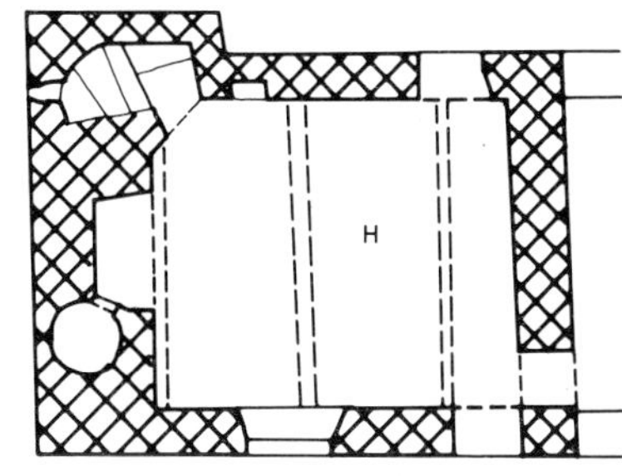

d. Great Brynhill, Merthyr Dyfan.

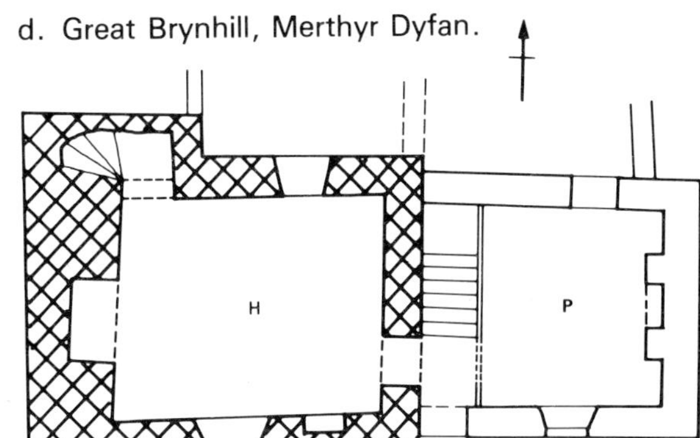

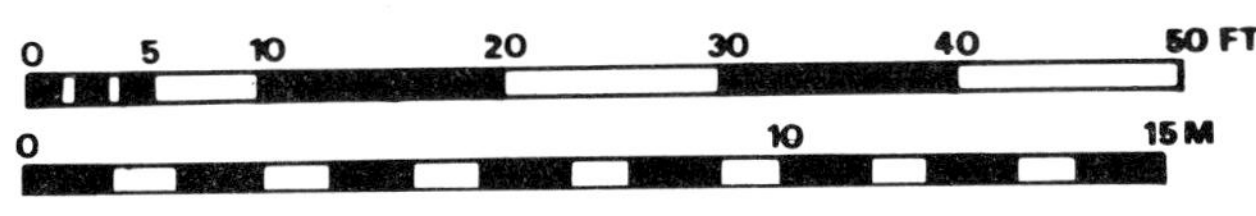

LATE 16th CENTURY

EARLY 17th CENTURY
LATER

H = HALL
P = PARLOUR
K = KITCHEN

Fig. 45.
Plans of houses in Barry area.
(a) Cwm Barry (restored).
(b) Greenhouse, Old Village Road.
(c) Old Mill Farm, Cadoxton.
(d) Great Brynhill, Merthyr Dyfan.
H. J. Thomas.

giving access to a low loft space. Its plan is very unusual in that the entrance is in the gable wall opposite the fireplace—a feature shared by Old Mill Farm, Cadoxton, and Great Brynhill in Merthyr Dyfan. Greenhouse was a one-hearth dwelling, occupied in 1673 by Thomas Evor, son of John Evor, who had been tenant in 1622. Evor farmed a total of 36 acres, 16 of which belonged to the Greenhouse tenement. He was in fact rated at two hearths, the second being represented by the Storehouse at the harbour.

Although Cwm Barry was the largest and wealthiest farm in Barry parish, the largest house was Castle Farmhouse, whose tenant, Lewis William, was rated at four hearths in 1673. Like William Rosser, he held 67 acres, but he sublet these to his brother-in-law Randolph Dawkin. The house itself had three hearths. Surviving photographs show it to have been similar in plan to Cold Knap and Cwm Barry, but with three units rather than two. An outer kitchen was separated from the small inner parlour by the main fireplace gable. Each room was heated, and, as at Cwm Barry, there was a detached bakehouse.

Table 11. Analysis of the Barry Hearth Tax assessment in 1673[70].

Householder	Hearths	Tenement	Acres
Arnold Spencer[a]	2	Burroughes	12[b]
George Mathewe	3[c]	Cwm Barry	83
Lewis William	4[d]	Castle	52
Joan William	2	Marsh	16
John Thomas	1	? Cliffwood Cottage	
Thomas Evor	2[e]	Greenhouse	36
William Rosser	2[f]	Cole Farm	60
William Crosse	2	Cwmcidy	56
Not chargeable			
John Jenkin	1	Upper Green Cottage	
William David	1	? Lower Green Cottage	
Evah Thomas widow	2	Wellhouse	26
Evan Seyse Esquire	3[g]	Ostry	44
Lewis William	1	? Castle House	

a Appears as a sub-tenant.
b Acreages derived from a near contemporary rental, GRO, D/DF M14 and from Evans Mouse.
c A two-hearth house, the third being represented by a bakehouse.
d A three-hearth house, the hall, parlour and kitchen being heated; the fourth hearth was in a detached bakehouse. William sub-let this property to his brother-in-law, Randolph Dawkin.
e Greenhouse had one hearth, but Evor was taxed also on the Storehouse at the harbour, which he let.
f Hearths in hall and parlour or kitchen.
g Lord of the manor; this tenement was in hand.

We have less precise information for the other houses listed in Barry parish. Burroughes Farm and Marsh Farm both seem to have been two-hearth dwellings; Cwmcidy Farm, a former freehold, but by the 1670s a 56-acre tenement occupied by William Cross, had a one-hearth house associated with a bakehouse. Ostry Farm was, in 1673, in the hands of the landlord, Mr Evan Seys of Boverton, it was rated at three hearths. In contrast to the dwellings we have been discussing were the houses of the poor. Amongst these was John Jenkin, tenant of Upper Green cottage, a one-hearth structure on the east side of Barry Green. Two other one-hearth householders were also exempted from the tax in 1673, as was Eva Thomas, widow, who was assessed at two hearths. This sounds more like a farmhouse rather than a cottage, and may have been Wellhouse Farm, a tenement of 26 acres. Perhaps age and widowhood accounted for her poverty.

Probate inventories tell us most about houses when they supply, not a generalised description of their contents, but a room-by-room account. Only one 17th-century inventory of this kind survives for Barry, the inventory of William Richards, 'seafarer', of Marsh Farm who died in 1698. Three rooms are mentioned: an 'inner room', which contained a bedstead, feather bed, four chairs, one 'drawer', and a chest; an 'outward' room, with a table, pewter dishes, plates, four chairs, earthenware utensils and other small stuff; and a 'chamber', with a feather bed, dust bed and some lumber. The chamber was probably an upstairs room reached from the hall, which is what we should understand by the 'outward' room on the ground floor, the inner room being partitioned off at the end of the hall furthest from the entry. Since Marsh Farm had two hearths in 1673, both ground-floor rooms were probably equipped with fireplaces. The Evans Mouse map of 1622 shows only one chimney, suggesting that some improvement had taken place at Marsh Farm by the end of the century. By 1700, Marsh Farmhouse may have resembled a less well-appointed version of Cwm Barry.

Our information regarding early modern housing in Cadoxton and Merthyr Dyfan is more rudimentary. No buildings survive which can be related directly to documents; although two houses retain 17th-century fabric—Old Mill farmhouse in Cadoxton and Great Brynhill in Merthyr Dyfan—and can be seen to be similar in plan to Greenhouse, we can identify neither with a particular occupier. All other houses in these two parishes which pre-date the Docks are either late 18th- or 19th-century in date. We must therefore rely on the inventories to gain some idea of the character of local housing.

The meanest dwelling so recorded is probably that of Nebuchadnezar Turbervill of Cadoxton, who was listed, with one hearth, amongst the poor of Cadoxton in 1673. The rental of 1671 identifies him as tenant of a cottage, garden and orchard at a rent of 1*s.* 8*d.* a year. He may have sub-let additional land from another farmer, for when he died eight years later, he was clearly a small farmer with a flock of nineteen sheep, twelve cattle, two horses and, unusually, a bull. Perhaps he was able to graze some of this livestock on the commons of the parish. Although his circumstances may have improved between 1673 and 1679, his cottage may have been a simple enough building, for his inventory mentions only a hall. In contrast, Mary Tucker's Cadoxton inventory of 1691 probably relates to the two-hearth house she and her husband occupied in 1673. This was a more impressive structure, with a hall and kitchen on the ground floor and two chambers over—either a recently-built storeyed house, or a converted open hall. As has been noted, Mary and her husband had an exceptionally large farm. The one-hearth house of Elizabeth Hawkins of Cadoxton, a widow who died in 1679, contained a chamber and two other rooms, perhaps representing a kitchen and chamber on the ground floor, with an additional room in the loft space. The inventory of John Llewelyn (1699) may relate to a two-hearth dwelling. It lists a kitchen, a chamber over and a milkhouse, and we can perhaps assume that it also contained a hall and that the milkhouse was either in an outshut or a detached building. Probably this was a two-unit dwelling, with a ground-floor and kitchen, both with fireplaces, and a chamber upstairs. Margaret Love of Merthyr Dyfan (*d.* 1681) was the widow of John Love, assessed on three hearths in 1673. Her inventory lists a hall and lower room, with a chamber above stairs and a dairy (perhaps detached or in an outshut). Her mother, Eleanor Phillips, who died three years later, had a hall, kitchen, crogloft and upstairs chamber. Edward Adam, assessed at two hearths, had, on his death in 1692, a hall, kitchen, upper chamber and dairy.

There is one other 17th-century house in the Barry area which *can* be related to an inventory, however. An inventory for Little Brynhill, in Highlight, like Greenhouse at Barry, gives us a clue to the layout and character of the better one-hearth dwelling. Gilbert Ford, its tenant in 1673, died nine years later, leaving goods and stock worth £34 17*s.* 6*d.* His inventory lists a hall, a chamber over and a chamber over the dairy. The dairy was probably an inner room within the hall, partitioned from the main living-space and away from a gable fireplace.

A one-hearth house, then, could locally be anything from a roughly built, open-halled cottage, to a modest storeyed farmhouse; it could be the home of a poor labourer or a small farmer. A two-hearth house was normally a more substantial dwelling, with between three and six rooms and a proper upper floor—the home of a more prosperous farmer. In Cadoxton and Merthyr Dyfan a number of tenants of small ten- to twenty-acre farms lived in one-hearth houses, which may have been small, but were probably relatively comfortable. The conditions of the many poor who were also rated as occupying one-hearth dwellings must have been very different. Daniel David, a pauper in Cadoxton in 1673, is said in a rental two years before to have lived in a 'decayed cottage' for which he paid 3*s.* 4*d.* a year;[71] Morgan Williams and Morgan Harry, amongst the poor in the Hearth Tax list, occupied cottages that had been built on the waste.[72]

In Barry parish, as in sea-board parishes further west in the Vale, the Great Rebuilding seems to have taken place between 1570 and 1640; the solid and comfortable dwellings of the farmers of the community—and even a simple house such as Greenhouse was an improvement on the medieval hall—reflect the attainment of a reasonable level of prosperity, fuelled by the profits of farming in a period of buoyant prices. Of the thirteen houses and cottages in Barry in 1670, nine were houses of the Rebuilding. These solid houses dominated Barry, but Merthyr Dyfan and Cadoxton, though they evidently contained a number of similar dwellings, were characterised more by small, one-hearth farmhouses and poor cottages; a modern visitor would have been struck as much by the presence of tiny cottages on common and roadside as by the homes of the tenant farmers. Perhaps few of the latter were of the quality found in Barry or Penmark, since so few survived the 18th century, when housing conditions improved. This contrast in building history no doubt reflects the fact that farms in Merthyr Dyfan and Cadoxton were generally smaller and less profitable units than those found further west; they were parishes, too, unlike Barry, that were open to poor settlers, who could erect cottages free from manorial restrictions.

Home and family: house interiors

The *hall* was the main room (sometimes the only room) in the 17th-century house. Dominated by a large ingle-nook fireplace, it was used for eating and living, often for cooking, and more often than not for sleeping, since it could be the only heated room in a house. It was the focus of the life of the household. Mary Tucker of Cadoxton (1691) had in her hall a 'standing bed with its appurtenances', together with a 'great cobertt, one table, one round table, one chair, one settle, and five joynt (i.e. 'joined) stooles'. Edward Adam's hall (Merthyr Dyfan, 1695) contained similarly a 'standing bed with one feather bed and all the appurtenances thereunto belonging . . . one table board and frame and stooles, one coffer, one chest, and lumber stuff . . . one fowling peace'. The *chambers* on the upper floor of a farmhouse were also used as sleeping accommodation—often for servants, since they were colder and less comfortable than a room downstairs—and as storage space for furniture, lumber and provisions. In the chamber over the hall Mary Tucker had 'one feild bedsteed' and two feather beds; in the chamber over the kitchen 'two ould beds'. Katherine Taylor of Merthyr Dyfan's inventory mentions, unusually, a *parlour*. This term was coming into vogue in the later 17th century, not for a sitting room, but generally for the best bedroom in the house, the one which would be offered to a favoured guest. Katherine Taylor had beds both in her hall and in the chamber over; in the parlour, which was a ground-floor room, she had 'one standing bedstead and featherbed . . . two chests and two chaires', valued together at £3 15*s*.

Fig. 46.
Fireplace at Greenhouse Farm, C Village Road.
Fireplace and beam late 16th-century; oven later.
Simon Prosser.

Most inventories, save very early examples, list the main items of furniture in a house; smaller items, such as cutlery, cooking pans, fire tools and so on, are seldom listed in detail. Better-off farmers in the second half of the 17th century usually had some items in brass or pewter. At Cold Knap, Wenllian Rosser (1684) had linen (£4), six silver spoons (£1 6*s.* 8*d.*), brass and pewter (£3 10*s.*), and 'tables, joynt stools, chests, coffers, binches and all other lumber stuff' worth £3 5*s.* In her kitchen, Katherine Taylor had 'fower brass crocks, two brass panns, one brass kittle, six pewter platters, two pewter candlesticks, one brass skillett, one brass morter and pessell' valued at £8, and three silver spoons worth £1 6*s.* It is striking that in 17th-century inventories we find few of the luxury items such as mirrors, clocks, napkins and dressing tables that are itemised in loving detail in their 18th-century counterparts. Even the larger farmers seem to have had little cash to spare for conspicuous consumption, and their homes, even in Barry, seem less well appointed than are those of their contemporaries in Penmark. Nonetheless, standards of domestic comfort in the average farmhouse much improved between 1550 and 1650; equally, the contrast between the inventories cited above and examples from lower down the social ladder is striking. Elizabeth Williams of Cadoxton (*d.* 1697) left personal estate valued at a mere £2 10*s.* 3*d.*, less than the value of Wenllian Rosser's brass and pewter alone. She had clothing worth 5*s.*, a bed, bed clothes, pillow, bolster, blanket and rug, with the outer casing of a dust bed and a sheet (£1 5*s.*); an old bedstead, two boards, two old coffers, an old chair, an old trunk and bellows (10*s.*); two small kettles, a little pewter plate, an earthenware pan, a trunk and a bakestone (7*s.* 9*d.*); and an 'old Bible' valued at 2*s.* 2*d.*

The inventories record the possessions, by and large, of the farming families in the locality. Although we have some documents that relate to widows and elderly persons, who perhaps ended their days in reduced circumstances, we are unable to penetrate the conditions of the genuinely poor; of their lives, harsh as we may imagine them to be, the record is silent.

Community, family and inheritance

If inventories give us some insight into the material condition of sections of the local community, the wills with which they are associated reveal to us something about family relationships, attitudes and loyalties; they explain, too, how possessions, savings and land were transmitted from one generation to the next. At one level, we can approach through testaments the mentality of local people, insofar as it is revealed by the concerns they voiced when they were near death.

Tudor and Stuart society, even at the village level, was highly stratified; the status of a person was even reflected in the place of his or her burial. Burial within the parish church was an aspiration of the wealthier farmers in the community, an aspiration that sometimes finds voice in a will. John Love, a relatively prosperous farmer and the owner of the freehold of his farm at Colcot, specified particularly that he be buried in the church of Merthyr Dyfan, when he made his will in 1667. Only a clergyman or a gentleman could claim the right to burial in the chancel of a church, close to the altar, as did William Andrew of Cadoxton Court in 1684, who wished his body 'to be in a Christian manner interred within the chancell of the parish church of Cadoxton . . . being the burying place of my ancestors'. For the majority of parishioners, burial took place in the churchyard, although Evan David of Merthyr Dyfan, who died in 1645, left the matter open, hoping in his will to be interred in either the church or the churchyard of St. Cadoc's.

Willmakers, as a group, were among the fortunate in the parish community, and a large minority of them made over small legacies to the use of the poor, although, except in Cadoxton, this practice was in decline by the end of the 17th century.[73] Oliver Mathew of Cwm Barry (1641) gave two pecks of wheat each to three poor cottagers: Nicholas Borough, George Wilkin and Alice Kewe. John Llewelyn of Cadoxton (1699) left 20*s.* to the poor of his parish 'namely Mary Miles, Jenet Turbervill, widow, and Mary Matho, widow . . . to be equally divided between them within [a] few days after my interment'. John Yorath of Merthyr Dyfan (1660) neglected the poor of the parish where he died, but gave 5*s.* to the poor of Sully, to which he presumably felt a stronger tie.

A sense of loyalty and duty to the parish community was sometimes also expressed in bequests to the parish church, although, again, by the later 17th century this was apparently customary only in Cadoxton. Most generous, as befitted his rank, was William Andrew, who left 2*s.* 6*d.* to Llandaff Cathedral, 2*s.* 6*d.* to the church of St. Andrew's Major and 5*s.* to St. Cadoc's, together with 5*s.* to the poor of St. Andrew's and £1 to the poor of Cadoxton. Sometimes testators specified that their gifts were specifically to help maintain the fabric of the church; John Llewelyn, whom we have mentioned above, generously set aside 10*s.* for that purpose.

The way in which willmakers disposed of their property bears out the now well-attested assertion that the nuclear family household of parents and children (and perhaps servants) was the basic social unit in the community; in their wills provision was made for members of the immediate family circle; little concern was likely to be shown for other kin, or neighbours, unless a testator was especially well-off, or if such family needs were absent—in the case, for example, of a spinster or an elderly parent whose children had grown up and had been already provided for. The main intent of men and women with under-age or unestablished children was to provide for a surviving spouse and for sons and daughters who had not received, during the lifetime of the testator, portions of money, goods, stock and land. Thus, while Oliver Mathew of Cwm Barry, who died in 1641, aged 57, mentioned his maid servant Catherine William, to whom he gave 40*s.*, and his sister, Joan Mathew, to whom he left £1, he was mainly concerned to settle his estate on his daughter Gwenllian and his five sons, Morris, George, Edward, William and John. Gwenllian, under 18 when her father died, was given a generous portion of £60 in cash, a 'french bedstead', the best feather bed and bolster, a pair of the best linen sheets, the best coverlet and a pair of the best blankets; Morris, George and Edward, all three under 21, were to have £20 apiece, payable, like their sister's portion, within one month. More detailed provision was made for William and John. William was to have a messuage and dwelling house and six acres of land in St. Bride's Major, provided he allowed his brother John quiet occupation of two tenements in Llantrithyd; John, the eldest son, was to have his father's free land in the parish of Bettws, and to discharge out of this his father's debts and cash legacies. John and William must have been already established on their own farms; if their three brothers seem less generously treated, it may be that additional provision had already been made for them. We know that George was the successor to Oliver's prosperous copyhold at Cwm Barry. In part, this wealthy yeoman farmer was using his will to tie up the loose ends in the disposal of his estate. Margaret Spenser of Merthyr Dyfan, who died a widow in 1636, was outlived by at least five children, two of whom were bequeathed substantial legacies that suggest they were unestablished at their mother's death. John Spenser was to have £30 in cash, a pair of blankets, a pillow, a chair, a rug, a cow and a calf, a bushel of wheat, and the residue of the estate; his brother Robert was to get £28, two blankets, a bushel of wheat, a flitch of bacon, a rug and a pail. Three daughters, Catherine, Mary and Margaret, appear to have already been married with their own families and received lesser bequests. Catherine was to have a cow, a couple of ewes, all her mother's clothes, a coffer and its contents, a platter and a hat; her eldest daughter was to have a cow, her youngest children two one-year old bullocks between them.

The will of Thomas Evor of Greenhouse Farm, Barry, illustrates how a person might dispose of his property if he had no close family to provide for. Thomas, who made his will in 1687, appears to have been survived only by his wife. To his maid-servant Margaret Llewelyn he gave 5*s.*; his brother Lewis Evor of Cowbridge was to have a heifer, a steer and six wethers; his niece, Elizabeth Evor of Cadoxton £5. John Lewis of Cadoxton was unmarried. He made his sister Cissell his executrix, and left her the residue of his estate, knowing that these goods would 'surmount in value the portion bequeathed unto her from her parents'. In addition, he left cash and clothing to his sister Jane, his kinsmen Craddock Griffith of Cadoxton and Jenkin Stacy of Merthyr Dyfan, his cousins John and Elizabeth Gwillim, and his uncle Thomas Gwillim, all of Pencoetre, and Mary Gwillim 'living in my family'.

As these examples demonstrate, bequests could take the form of cash, stock, household goods and land. Land, of course, was the basis of most people's wealth and the determinant of ranking within the local community. Not all wills, by any means, mention land, however. This was because most 17th-century farmers in our three parishes held by copyhold, and usually the descent of such property was already governed by a tenant's copy of court roll. The references to land, however, that are contained in thirteen local wills, remind us that some farmers combined holdings of more than one tenure, and might control property outside the parish in which they lived.

Land passed most often to a single heir. John Love of the Colcot (1668) was mainly concerned to cater for his grand-children and a niece. He declared the rightful heir of all his freehold land to be his grandson Thomas Love, but gave Thomas's father John the use of all the household stuff in his lifetime. John would manage the farm until his death, perhaps jointly with his sister Elizabeth, sharing the house with their mother. A different sort of arrangement might be made where a testator had several tenements to his name. Perhaps the most complicated arrangement of this kind was made in

1675 by David Spenser, farmer of Barry Island. He was survived by his wife, Margaret, three daughters and three sons. Of the children, the three boys were minors at the time of their father's death. Jane, Margaret and Martha, the daughters, were to receive, successively, over a period of seven years, the profits of the farm on the Island and of the leasehold lands held by the middle brother, David, in Llanbethery. After the seven years were up, the eldest brother, Thomas, was to inherit all his father's freehold, with the exception of three acres of land in St. Andrew's Major. Thomas was also to have the lease of the lands at Llanbethery, and of Brynhill Farm in Merthyr Dyfan, whose 111 acres were rented from the Popham estate. In 1671 Thomas was aged fourteen,[74] so he would have been aged about 25 before he inherited. David was to have 'all the island of Barry . . . during the term of one thousand years', and if Thomas died before he inherited, was to pay £40 to each of his sisters out of the land that would then come to him. Although David got the farm on Barry Island, his younger brother, Philip, was to have all the stock there. To the widow Margaret went the Sound Farm in Sully, a 30-acre copyholding; to Jane and her sister Margaret, jointly, another Sully farm called the Hill. If Jane would not 'suffer Margaret to hold it' she was to pay her sister £40 on demand. Martha was to have the three acres in St. Andrew's, and in addition the three sisters were to 'maintain their three brothers [in] meat drink and clothing that is fitting during the space of seven years upon forfeiture of their portions . . .'.

A farmer who held or owned more than one tenement would often allocate integral holdings to each of several children; it seems to have been rare, on the other hand, to divide up an individual farm in order to provide for heirs, although one testator, William Richards of Merthyr Dyfan (1663), did adopt a procedure resembling partible inheritance. William had a widow and three young children, Mary, Jane and William. He divided his personal estate equally amongst his wife and children, their mother to have the management of each child's portion until the age of sixteen. The same was done with his farm, a messuage and 14½ acres of land leased from the Popham estate at a rent of 12*s.* 4*d.* a year.[75] William's wife, Mary, aged 35 in 1663, was to enjoy the whole farm for ten years, after which Jane, aged seven at her father's death, was to be paid one quarter of the value of the premises, to be put out at interest for her until she became 21. The same arrangement was to apply after twelve and fourteen years respectively with Mary and William. One quarter of the tenement was to be William's widow's for her life. In practice William was probably expected to gain control of the whole farm after his mother's death, but from the age of nineteen he would be able to manage it in the interest of his mother and sisters. In fact, these arrangements may never have been carried out. The 1671 Popham survey indicates that Mary Richard remarried, to Thomas Howell, who held the tenement in the right of his wife. Jane, aged 14 in

1671, had the last life in the lease and she surrendered her right in the farm in 1696, when it was leased to William Richard, who was probably her brother, on payment of a fine of £5.[76]

While a willmaker might make a division of his land amongst several heirs, these examples show that he would try to avoid a situation where a tenement itself would be split up; the intention was to hand on holdings that had a chance of economic viability. Personalty, like land, might also be shared amongst several heirs, in an effort to provide adequately for the well-being of offspring. Local farmers in the Barry area and elsewhere in the Vale of Glamorgan seem backward in comparison to parts of England in that, even in the second half of the 17th century, bequests were made in kind as well as in cash. Only three testators made legacies in cash alone, although this arrangement had the advantage that it avoided depleting a family estate of valuable fixed capital in the form of livestock, implements and furniture. This fact may be an indication that local farmers, running small units in the main, found it hard to accumulate large amounts of cash.

Only the larger farmers, perhaps those farming forty acres or more, could save and dispose of substantial amounts of money. Philemon Mathew of Cwm Barry, grandson of Oliver, was able to leave his only child, Charles, £50, which was to be paid to his 'supervisors', Howell Thomas, the boy's grandfather, and the rector of Barry, Evan Howell, who were to set out the money at interest to maintain the child 'in school with meat, drink, clothes, and lodging sufficient, till he comes to the age of fourteen'. From then until the age of 20, the money was to be used to settle Charles as an apprentice. Like other children, however, Charles was also left a bequest of furniture—his father's featherbed and the bedstead in the hall. Beds and bedclothes were in fact prominent amongst the bequests in 17th-century wills, indicating that these were prized possessions, especially where a feather bed rather than a dust bed, stuffed with powdered wool or cloth was concerned. Clothing is rarely described in detail save where a willmaker had no direct heirs and divided his possessions amongst large numbers of his family. Thomas Love of the Colcot (1683) gave cash totalling £20 to his sisters Anne Love and Margaret Richard and to his nephews and nieces. To his brother Arnold he left his 'best hat, my best coat, my wedding shirt and best suit of apparel, my best shoes, my boots and my great gun'.

As a comparison with the provisions made by these farming families we may look at the will of William Andrew of Cadoxton Court. Although the Andrew estate was much depleted by the 1680s, William Andrew's legacies indicate the wide social gulf that separated even a very minor gentleman from most of his fellow parishioners. William had three under-age children, Jane, Anne and William, who were to have cash portions of £200, £200 and £250 respectively, to be paid when they were 21. In the meantime the children were placed under the guardianship of four other members of the lesser Glamorgan gentry: William Herbert of the White Friars, Cardiff, owner of half of Dinas Powys manor; Philip Herbert of Cogan; Reynold Deer of Wenvoe; and Matthew Deere of Rhoose. An adult daughter, Elizabeth, had already been given some land while her father lived; to this he added half an acre in Northmead in Cadoxton, a feather bed, three pewter platters, a brass cauldron, a pan and a chest, as additional tokens of his affection. William's eldest son, Nicholas, was to have two tenements in Cadoxton, 'Brooks' and the 'Bowa', two fields totalling 13 acres, and a tenement in the hands of Gabriel Morse. These were to be used to discharge his father's cash legacies, probably by selling the land. Other land may have been due to Nicholas under the terms of a jointure settled on his mother, Elizabeth, sister of Sir Richard Bassett of Beaupre; in addition to this, Elizabeth was to have a tenement her husband had bought from John Rosser of Swansea, in case her brother did not pay her £400 due under her jointure. She was also to have a farm in Marcross. In his will her husband also made provision for his five servants: Edward Turbervill, who was to have £2, George David (5*s.*), Anne Lewis (5*s.*), Avice Evan (5*s.*), and William Richard (10*s.*).[77]

General conclusions

By the reign of William and Mary the farming families of the Barry district, many of whom had been established there for well over a century had, in material terms, achieved a level of modest prosperity; this was to be further augmented in the first half of the 18th century. The pace of social and economic change had been slow and undramatic; after 1750, however, the actions of landowners were to transform the social character of the local community, beginning when the old pattern of estate ownership and tenant farms was broken up by the dissolution of the Popham estate and the sale of the lands of the Thomas family of Wenvoe Castle to a Yorkshireman, Peter Birt. At the same time, in Barry, sweeping changes were initiated by the Joneses of Fonmon. The following chapter will concentrate on these changes, leading to an analysis of the make-up of the community on the eve of industrialisation.

Let us remember the essential differences between Barry, on the one hand, and Merthyr Dyfan and Cadoxton, at this stage in their story. The economic conditions in the 16th and 17th centuries, coupled with the innate conservatism of landlords, had enabled farmers in each of these three parishes to acquire and retain in their families modestly sized, but adequately profitable, tenements over several generations. Yet the experience of Barry in the 16th and 17th centuries was largely static, a characteristic it appears to share with Porthkerry and Penmark to the west. The experience of Merthyr Dyfan and Cadoxton was dynamic: fragmented landownership made for communities that were more open in character, which sustained a higher level of population growth and perpetuated an economic structure in which farms tended to be smaller and less profitable and in which the number of poor and labouring families was proportionately greater. Barry, its land controlled almost wholly by a single family—initially the St. John's, later the Seyses of Boverton—changed very little structurally. Its population remained stable and, following the completion of enclosure of its fields (by 1622 at the very latest), the 17th century saw no changes in the distribution of farmland in the parish. While the later 18th century was to see the initiation of significant changes in all three parishes, the nature of such change would be heavily influenced by the pattern of life established between the reigns of Henry VIII and Anne.

References

1 Matthew Griffiths, 'The Vale of Glamorgan in the 1543 Lay Subsidy returns', *BBCS*, XXIX (1981-2), pp. 709-10, and *passim.*
2 *Statutes of the Realm*, III (Record Commission, 1810-22), pp. 938-51: 34-5 Henry VIII, c. 27.
3 PRO, E. 179/221/237, 238 and 239.
4 Matthew Griffiths, 'The Vale of Glamorgan', pp. 714-6.
5 P. Laslett in 'Mean household size in England in the sixteenth century', in *Household and family in past time*, ed. P. Laslett and Richard Wall (Cambridge, 1972), p. 126, suggests 4.75 as an appropriate multiplier. This figure is now felt to be too high and in consequence a slightly lower rule of thumb has beeen adopted here.
6 RCAM (Wales), *Glamorgan*, III (ii), pp. 215-43.
7 PRO, E. 179/221/237. William St. John died in 1563 and was succeeded as lord of Highlight by his son Christopher.
8 Matthew Griffiths, 'The Vale of Glamorgan', pp. 737-43.
9 *Ibid.*, tables 5 and 6, pp. 731-5.
10 R. H. Hilton, 'A crisis of feudalism', *Past and Present*, 80 (1978), p. 5.
11 See below, p. 166.
12 J. S. Corbett, *Glamorgan: papers and notes on the lordship and its members*, ed. D. R. Paterson (Cardiff, 1925), pp. 98-101; Glanmor Williams (ed.), *Glamorgan County History*, IV (Cardiff, 1974), pp. 162ff.
13 NLW, D[inas] P[owys] 111 (1566); H. J. Thomas, 'Sir William St. John, admiral and adventurer', *Barry and District News*, 14 October 1976.
14 NLW, DP 88.
15 NLW, DP 65.
16 GRO, D/D MS 83.
17 GRO, manorial maps, 1622. Copies of the terrier are Beds. RO, GY 10 (the original Bletso copy) and GRO, D/DF vol. 44 (a copy probably kept at Fonmon).
18 See Chapter III on Porthkerry mill.
19 GRO, Fonmon Deeds 714, 694. See H. J. Thomas, 'Cwmcidy—a lost farmstead', *Morgannwg*, XVII (1973), pp. 64-5.
20 Beds. RO, GY 10.
21 Rice Merrick, *Morganiae archaiographia: a book of the antiquities of Glamorganshire*, ed. Brian Ll. James (Barry, 1983), p. 14.
22 Matthew Griffiths, 'Manor court records and the local historian: Penmark, Fonmon and Barry 1570-1622', *Morgannwg*, XXV (1981), pp. 56-7.
23 *Ibid.*, p. 54.

[24] *Ibid.*, pp. 58-9.
[25] GRO, D/DF Court books, 1582-5, p. 11; 1590-6, p. 15; 1596-1604, p. 1; 1604-15, p. 128.
[26] NLW, DP 111.
[27] G. O. Pierce, *Place-names of Dinas Powys hundred* (Cardiff, 1968), pp. 144-5.
[28] Som. RO, MTD/II/10, 11a.
[29] G. O. Pierce, *op. cit.*, p. 137.
[30] NLW, DP 65.
[31] Som. RO, DD/Pot 87.
[32] NLW, DP 65.
[33] NLW, Great Sessions, Wales 22/8, June 37 Henry VIII.
[34] GRO, D/D We 1.
[35] GRO, D/D We 2.
[36] NLW 6947E.
[37] Brian Ll. James, 'Contributions towards a history of Wenvoe Castle', *Trans. Cardiff Naturalists' Society*, XCVIII (1978), pp. 7-11.
[38] Frank Emery, 'The farming regions of Wales', in *The agrarian history of England and Wales*, IV, *1500-1640*, ed. Joan Thirsk (Cambridge, 1967), pp. 142-3.
[39] PRO, E. 179/221/294 and 297.
[40] *Cf.* table 4 in Matthew Griffiths, 'The Vale of Glamorgan', pp. 728-9.
[41] J. M. Traherne (ed.), *The Stradling correspondence* (1840), *passim.*
[42] *Ibid.*, pp. 95-6.
[43] *Ibid.*, pp. 113-4.
[44] GRO, D/DF Court book, 1568-?75, p. 87.
[45] GRO, D/DF Court book, 1528-5, p. 36.
[46] GRO, D/DF Court books, *passim.*
[47] Matthew Griffiths, 'Manor court records', p. 61.
[48] GRO, D/DF M14; Fonmon Deeds 405, 697.
[49] NLW, P[enrice] and M[argam] 5655 (1663); NLW, BRS (Frere and Chomeley) 122 (1671); P and M 6599 (1721); BRS (Frere and Chomeley) 126 (1723).
[50] Probate records for the three parishes are to be found amongst the Llandaff diocesan records in the NLW, filed under the name of each testator and the date of the grant of probate (LL/PR).
[51] Merrick, *op. cit.*, p. 14.
[52] Rice Lewis, *A Breviat of Glamorgan*, ed. William Rees, in *A Breviat of Glamorgan and other papers*, South Wales and Monmouthshire Record Society Publications, 3 (Cardiff, 1954), p. 102.
[53] These were: John Love, yeoman, of Merthyr Dyfan (1667)—43%; Eleanor Phillip of Merthyr Dyfan (1684)—32%; Mary Tucker of Cadoxton (1691)—37%; and Oliver Mathew of Cwm Barry (1641)—40%. All owned more than £20 in personalty.
[54] Matthew Griffiths, *Penmark and Porthkerry: families and farms in the seventeenth-century Vale of Glamorgan* (Cardiff, 1979), pp. 33-4.
[55] Extracts from and analyses of the relevant Port Books are to be found in E. A. Lewis (ed.), *The Welsh Port Books 1550-1603*, Cymmrodorion Record Series, XII (1927); William Rees (ed.), 'A Port Book of the Port of Cardiff and its members . . . 1606-10', in *A Breviat of Glamorgan and other papers*, op. cit., pp. 69ff; M. I. Williams, 'A contribution to the commercial history of Glamorgan, 1666-1735', *National Library of Wales Journal*, IX (1955-6), pp. 188-215, 334-53; M. I. Williams, 'A further contribution to the commercial history of Glamorgan', *ibid.*, XI (1959-60), pp. 330-60; XII (1961-2), pp. 58-81, 265-87, 353-69.
[56] W. R. B. Robinson, 'Dr. Thomas Phaer's report on the harbours and customs administration of Wales under Edward VI', *BBCS*, XXIV (1971-2), p. 495.
[57] Beds. RO, GY 10.
[58] G. Dowdell and H. J. Thomas, 'Some evidence for the sea-borne carriage of medieval and later pottery in the Bristol Channel', *Medieval and later pottery in Wales*, 3 (1980), pp. 5-20.

[59] W. R. B. Robinson, 'The establishment of royal customs in Glamorgan and Monmouthshire under Elizabeth I', *BBCS*, XXIII (1969-70), pp. 347-96, *passim*.

[60] *Ibid.*, pp. 352-69, *passim*; 371-2, 381-4, 395-6.

[61] E. A. Lewis (ed.), *op. cit.*, pp. 8-10, 20-21.

[62] R. G. Marsden, 'English ships in the reign of James I (1603-25)', *Trans. Royal Historical Society*, new series, XIX (1905), p. 336.

[63] M. Griffiths and H. J. Thomas, 'Marsh House, East Aberthaw', in *Glamorgan-Gwent Archaeological Trust Annual Report 1981-2*, ed. H. N. Savory and G. Dowdell (Swansea, 1982), pp. 64-9.

[64] M. I. Williams, in *NLWJ*, IX (1955-6), pp. 341, 343-4, 347; XII (1961-2), pp. 357, 366. GRO, Fonmon Deeds, 703, 705.

[65] W. G. Hoskins, 'The rebuilding of rural England, 1570-1640', *Past and Present*, 4 (1953), p. 44.

[66] R. Machin, 'The Great Rebuilding: a reassessment', *ibid.*, 77 (1977), pp. 33-56.

[67] PRO, E. 179/221/294 and 297.

[68] H. J. Thomas and M. Griffiths, 'Penmark: Greencliffe', *Morgannwg*, XXVII (1983), pp. 74-7.

[69] The information that follows on 16th- and 17th-century houses in the Barry area is based on surveys by Howard J. Thomas, filed with RCAM (Wales).

[70] Based on PRO, E. 179/221/297.

[71] NLW, BRS (Frere and Chomeley) 122 (1671).

[72] NLW 6947E.

[73] Brian Luxton, *A history of the old village church, Cadoxton-juxta-Barry* (Barry, 1980), p. 30.

[74] NLW, BRS (Frere and Chomeley) 122; gives tenants' ages in 1671.

[75] NLW, P and M 5655.

[76] NLW, BRS (Frere and Chomeley) 126.

[77] NLW, LL/PR, will of William Andrew of Cadoxton-juxta-Barry, 15 March 1684/5.

In the name of god Amen the thirteenth day of June in ye yeare of
our Lord god one thousand seven hundred & five I John Smith of the psh
of merthir dovan in ye County of Glamorgan yeoman and diocess of Landaffe
being sick and weake in body but of perfect memory & mind thanks be to the
All mighty god for it Calling unto minde ye Mortalyty of my body and knowing yt
tis appointed for all men once to dye doe make & ordaine this my Last will and
Testamt that is to say principaly and first of all I give and recomend my soul into
the hands of Allmighty God that gave it and for my body I comend it to the Earth to be
Buried in a Christian Like mann^r at the discretion of my Executrix nothing doubting but
at ye Generall Resurrection I shall receive the same againe by the mighty pow^r of god and as
Tuching such worldly Estate wherewith it hath pleased God to bless mee in this Life I give
and dispose of the same in following mann^r and forme
Imprimis I give and bequeath unto my Cozen Nathaniell Lewis senio^r the sume of two shillings
It I give and bequeath unto Thomas Lewis one shilling It I give and bequeath unto Nathan
Lewis Junio^r one shilling It I give and bequeath unto Georg Lewis one shilling It I give &
bequeath unto Mary Dixon the sume of one shilling Item whereas now I am possessd of one
Mansion or dwelling house Barne orchards and Gardens together with nine acrs of Lands
be it more or less arrable meadow and Pasture Lands there unto adjoyning Comonly
Called and Knowen by the name of Merthir Dovan in ye parish of Merthir Dovan all
the aforesaid [illegible] house barne orchard and gardens with the nine acrs of
Lands afore sd mentioned withall my goods Chattels and Cattels Item I give and
bequeath unto my deare and supposed daughter Anne Smith whome I likewise
Constitute and ordaine my only sole Executrix of this my Last will and Testamt
Item I doe utterly dissalow revoke disanul all and Every other former Wills
Testaments Legacies Executors & Executrices by me in any wise made before
this time and Confirming this my Last will and testament and noe other
In Wittness hereof I have put my hand and seale the day and yeare above
Written

Sealed Signed and Delivered
in the presents of us

William Matthew
Wm Pettitt
Jno Wilkins

Sig
John [mark] Smith

7 mo Martij Anno Dni 1705/6
Anna Smith filia nrals defunct
Exix in huiusi Testamento noiat Jur^t &c
Coram me
Johan Jones

CHAPTER V

Landlords and Tenants, 1700-1880

MATTHEW GRIFFITHS

Copper-alloy buckle, 1750, from St. Nicholas churchyard, Barry. I. J. Thomas.

BY the middle years of the 19th century the population of Barry, Cadoxton and Merthyr Dyfan, together with the tiny extra-parochial district of Highlight, stood at a little over 500.[1] On the eve of the creation of Barry Docks this was still an agricultural community, with a residual interest, through the limestone trade, in the sea. On the face of things it might seem that little change had occurred in the district since the end of the 17th century and that a 17th-century farmer, suddenly transported to early Victorian Barry, would hardly have been surprised by what he discovered; the main difference would be the nonconformist chapels—Sion and Bethel, Philadelphia and Tabor—that had sprung up in Cadoxton after 1810. Elsewhere in South Wales the Industrial Revolution had wrought massive changes in landscape and society, and canals, railways, new roads, docks and towns had developed to serve the expanding economy of iron and coal. Had the Barry district been passed over by this tide of modernity?

While the villages of the Vale might have seemed little changed at first sight to our 17th-century visitor, he would have found as he tramped the lanes from farm to farm, and talked to the locals in the public houses, that this was a very different society from his own and was still in a process of rapid change. The 150 years from 1700 to 1850 had seen a quieter revolution in the countryside of the Vale than that which took place in the Valleys, but it was a revolution nevertheless.

Fig. 47. The Will of John Smith, yeoman, of Merthyr Dyfan, 13 June 1705. National Library of Wales.

Landowners and their estates

The early 18th century throughout Glamorgan witnessed the dissolution of estates and the disappearance of families that had dominated local society since the 15th century. As old families such as the Stradlings, the Bassetts and the Thomases died out—often as the result of a failure to produce a male heir, or frequently as the consequence of a massive burden of debt—they were replaced by outsiders, usually of English origin. A simultaneous and concomitant process witnessed the gradual concentration of landed estates in fewer hands, so that by 1780, 47 families in Glamorgan owned 80% of the land.[2] Under the stimulus of emerging industry and the growth in population of the northern and western parts of the county, landowners and wealthy gentlemen farmers became addicts of the philosophy of 'improvement', and paid closer attention both to the structure of their estates and to the practices of their tenant farmers. Following the long depression in agriculture, and the period of low rents that marked the century after 1650, the second half of the 18th century saw rapid growth in the countryside, associated, in many communities, with a transformation in social relations.

In the Barry area, the Jones family of Fonmon reorganised its estate in Barry, Porthkerry and Cwmcidy in a way that left little untouched, and no family unaffected; in Merthyr Dyfan and Cadoxton notable opportunities were created by the bankruptcy of the Thomases of Wenvoe and the breakup of the old Popham estate. In Barry, as a result, the classic triad of landlord, tenant farmer and agricultural labourer came to typify the social structure as it did that of many Vale parishes. At the opposite pole stood Cadoxton, where landownership remained fragmented, and complicated patterns of kinship linked farmer and labourer; Merthyr Dyfan came to stand somewhere in between these extremes.

Barry

Barry manor was in the hands of the Seys family of Boverton—Elizabethan lawyers who had profited from their involvement in the Cromwellian *régime* after the Civil Wars—from 1661 until 1762. In the latter year Robert Jones III (*c.* 1737-93), the descendant of the regicide Col. Philip Jones, who, like Evan Seys, had benefited from the collapse of the Bolingbroke estate in South Wales, married the heiress Jane Seys, and the manor reverted to the Fonmon estate, of which it had for so long been a part. The acquisition by marriage of the Seys estate, comprising some 2,000 acres in the Vale, followed by Robert Jones's second marriage, eight years later, to the daughter of Edmund Lloyd of Cardiff, made the Fonmon Castle estate the largest in the Vale; by 1780 it controlled some 8,900 acres.[3] Under the Seys family little had altered in the way in which Barry manor was run and organised. A rental of 1749 shows that the distribution of tenanted farms and cottages was then much the same as it had been in the second half of the 17th century.[4] Indeed, every holding mentioned in 1749 can be identified with one of the tenements surveyed by Evans Mouse in 1622, save for Cwmcidy Farm, the freehold of which had been acquired in 1661.[5] The major change by this date was the replacement of copyhold by leasehold tenure, but in a form that differed little as far as tenants were concerned from customary tenure for three lives. In 1749, only Ann Jenkins's little cottage at the foot of Barry Hill was held by copy.[6] The other holdings, with the exception of Cwm Barry, the Ostry, and Barry Wood, were held by long leases for three lives. These three exceptions seem alone to have been held by the more advanced form of tenancy at will, at rents considerably higher than the level of 1622. Cwm Barry had been occupied since 1746 by the Reverend Jeffrey Beynon (instituted to the parish in that year, but with no rectory to occupy). On the other farms and cottages, the early 17th-century rents persisted, or had been only marginally improved. Burroughes Farm, for example, still cost its tenant only 13*s.* 4*d.* a year. By 1686, the rent of Wellhouse Farm had been improved from £1 6*s.* to £2 10*s.*, and then remained stable until the second half of the 18th century. Annotations to the 1749 rental indicate that it was thought that shorter tenancies could be profitably substituted for three-life leases when the chance arose, Cole Farm being assessed at an improved rent of £35 *per annum* rather than £5 2*s.* 6*d.* Nonetheless, on 18th September, 1749, Arnold Hawkins was granted a lease for three lives at the traditional rent in exchange for an entry fine of £220.

At the end of the first half of the 18th century, tenure for three lives persisted on the Seys estate in Barry just as it did on the lands of the Popham and Thomas families in Merthyr Dyfan and Cadoxton, and rents were little changed from the level of the mid 17th century or much earlier. This phenomenon was only partly due to the conservatism of landlords, for the land market during the century after Charles II's restoration favoured the tenant; with agricultural prices low, demand for land was also depressed, and a three-life lease was more attractive to a potential tenant because it gave him and his family a long-term interest in a farm, together with total control over the property, in exchange for a large lump-sum entry fine and a low annual rent. Families were thus enabled to retain control of their farms over several generations. During the second half of the 18th century the number of long leases dwindled, as the competition for land increased, and landlords found themselves able to substitute short leases for years, or tenancy at will, for the older, less profitable system. They would be assured of a regular and larger income, and the opportunity to adjust rents in response to the market. They could also rid themselves of inefficient tenants in favour of better farmers who had greater working capital, and could take the opportunity to reorganise their farms and their methods of estate management.[7] The Joneses of Fonmon were leaders amongst the landlords of Glamorgan in improving their estates and replacing old-fashioned tenures. In consequence, the period between 1762 and 1810, when Barry and Porthkerry were sold, to pass shortly into the hands of the Romillys, was marked by a major reorganisation of Barry manor. In 1749, there were nine farms and several cottages but, by 1810, only four farms remained and long leases had disappeared for ever. Castle Farm was merged with Cwmcidy

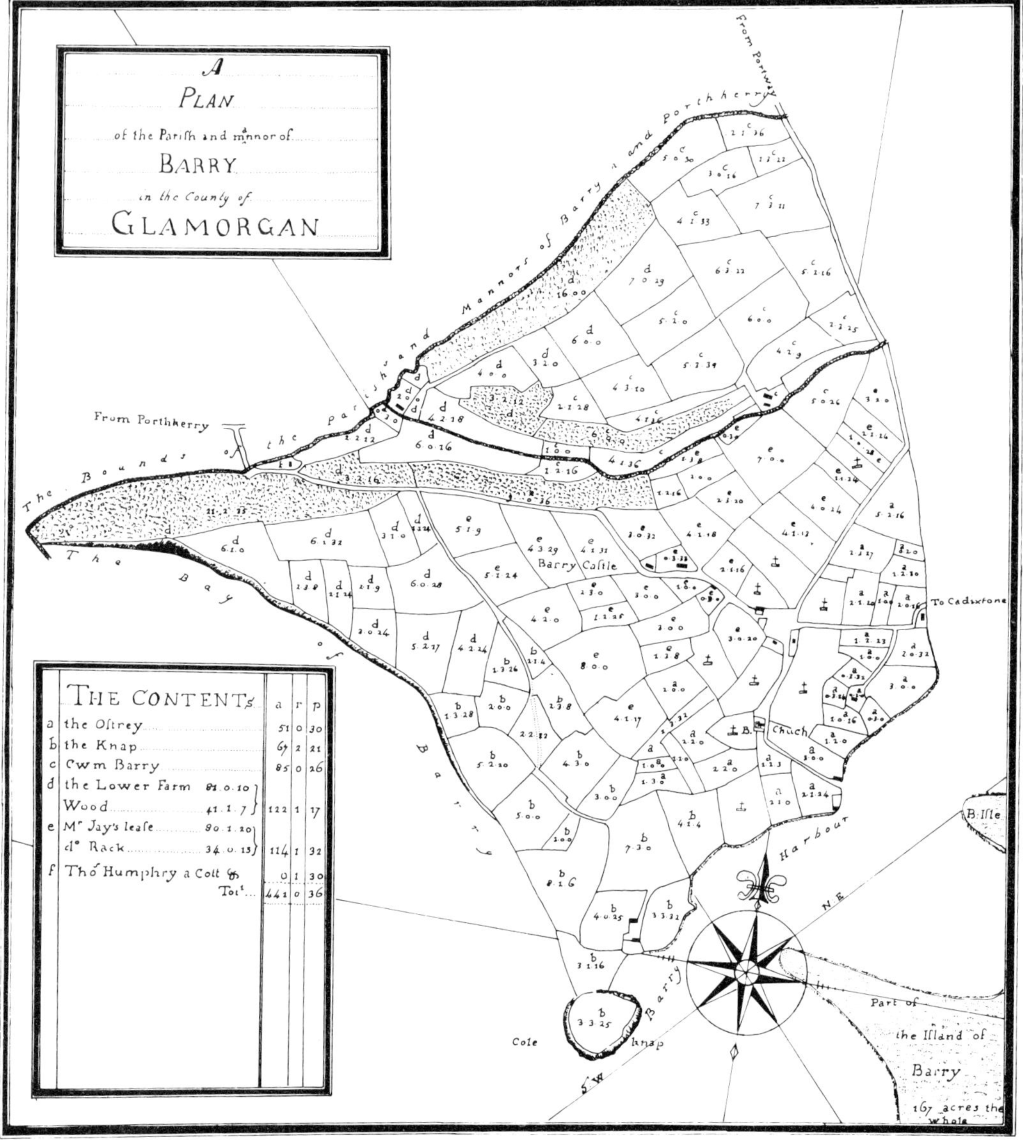

Fig. 48.
Map of Barry manor in *c.* 1780, copied from original in Glamorgan Record Office.
H. J. Thomas.

Farm in that year to become, with 236 acres, the largest tenement in the parish, let at £180 a year; Cwm Barry was let jointly with 91 acres in Porthkerry, bringing it up to 175 acres, at £105; the rent of Cole Farm had been improved to £65; and Ostry Farm, now of 56 acres, was worth £52 10*s*. All four farms were held at will, their tenants replaceable annually if need be. Gone were Marsh Farm, Burroughes Farm, Wellhouse and Greenhouse. Ostry Farm had swallowed Burroughes and Marsh by 1775; Castle Farm had absorbed Wellhouse and Greenhouse. The second half of the century saw some experimentation with tenures, seven-year leases at improved rents at first being favoured for the larger farms. But by 1775-6 Cwm Barry, Marsh farmhouse and Castle House, run as a pub by its tenant John Thomas, were already let at will.[8]

Barry was not alone amongst the Fonmon Castle estates in undergoing such a thorough reorganisation. Elsewhere, too, farms were amalgamated to create larger, more efficient and more profitable units. Despite their profligacy and wanton expenditure, which forced the Joneses ultimately to sell most of the property which they acquired in the 1760s and 1770s, Robert Jones III and his son Robert Jones IV (1773-1834) were to the forefront in 'improving' their estates. At Wrinstone, near Wenvoe, they initiated an even more drastic reorganisation, reducing the number of farmsteads from 20 in 1686 to nine by 1762; this process was taken to its logical conclusion by the Jenners of Wenvoe when they acquired the estate: by 1839 only one farm and four labourers' cottages remained at Wrinstone.[9]

Similarly, the sale of Barry in 1810 initiated a further phase of reorganisation, which was to culminate after 1850 in the wholesale remodelling of Barry as an 'estate village' by the Romilly family. In 1810, as we have seen, Castle and Cwmcidy Farms were united, under the management of Llewelyn Iorath, tenant of Castle Farm since about 1800.[10] By 1812, the farmhouse at Cwmcidy had been reduced to a labourer's cottage and Iorath had been replaced by John Spickett. This was in the year the great jurist Sir Samuel Romilly (*d.* 1818) bought the Barry and Porthkerry estate, a total of 1,950 acres, as an investment for his savings.[11] This initiated a remarkable changeover in the personnel of the estate,

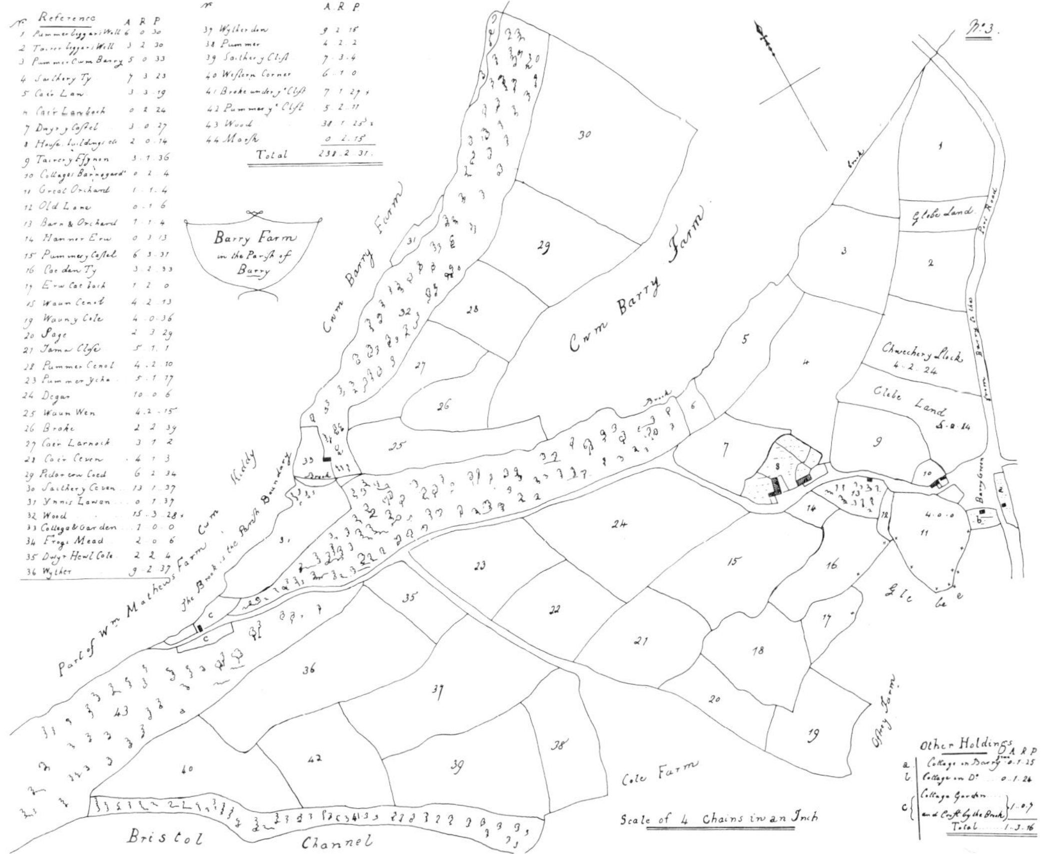

ig. 49.
state plan of *c.* 1812,
nowing Barry Farm,
reated by merging
astle and Cwmcidy
arms; based on
riginal in Glamorgan
ecord Office.
I. J. Thomas.

perhaps in an attempt to replace inefficient farmers and raise rents still further. Further experiments were undertaken in the organisation of the tenant farms. In 1818, Cole Farm and Ostry were held jointly by David Morgan, to create a unit of 142 acres,[12] but by 1831 they were once more in separate hands, and Cwm Barry had been (temporarily) combined with Castle Farm, to create Barry Farm, an impressive holding of 420 acres, still run by John Spickett. At Cwmcidy there was equally a process of engrossment. By about 1760 three farms remained where six had been recognisable in 1622; by 1800 Cwmcidy had dwindled to a single farm, accompanied by a small freeholding.[12]

In 1841 there were twelve households in Barry, representing the four farms of Cwm Barry, Cole Farm, the Ostry and Upper Barry (Castle), together with the cottages of four labourers, a gamekeeper, a publican (at the Ship Inn) and a widow. Cole Farm had a mixed succession of occupants in the first half of the 19th century, which included a smuggler, Richard Garby, a farmer, Evan John, and in 1851, the households of two master mariners, Henry Thomas and William Parker; by the 1850s it had become, like the Romilly's model farm at Cwmcidy, a home farm for the Porthkerry estate.[13]

The first half of the 19th century had already seen some new building in this small community. Jordan's Cottage had been erected in about 1800 by the Jones estate, in a style similar to ironworkers' houses to be found in the valleys; in about 1840, a sawmill was erected in the Millwood to serve the Porthkerry estate, now based on the Romillys' new mansion, Porthkerry House. The middle years of the century also saw the landscaping of Porthkerry Park—a process which entailed the demolition of the old Cwmcidy farmhouse. These changes, however, were marginal compared to the new building undertaken by the Romilly family after 1857. Between 1857 and 1862 thirteen new buildings were erected, to be followed shortly after by yet more dwellings and, by 1876, by the rebuilding of St. Nicholas Church. By the early 1870s there were twenty-two households in the parish and 98 inhabitants. The experience of Barry is perhaps the perfect example in miniature of the impact that the control of a community by a single family could have; it was a 'closed' community, with the economic lives of its inhabitants, its growth and development, dominated by one landlord. In consequence, the changes that took place are relatively straightforward to explore. However, as before 1700, the very different structure of landownership in Cadoxton and Merthyr Dyfan makes the history of these communities much more complex.

Cadoxton and Merthyr Dyfan

In the middle years of the 18th century five principal estates had an interest in these parishes. There was the Wenvoe Castle estate of the Thomas family, whose lands there formed part of a larger estate of some

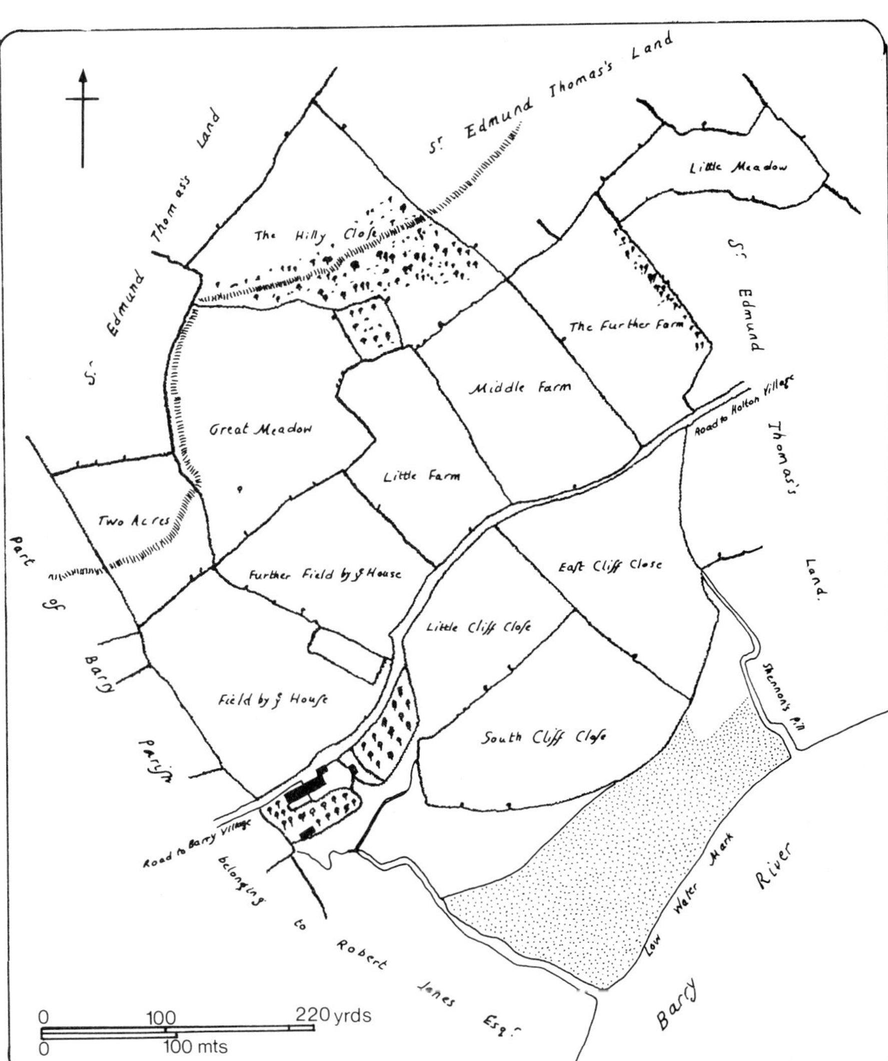

g. 50.
an of East Barry
rm in 1767, based
original in
amorgan Record
fice.
G.

3,500 acres in the south-east Vale; the Cadoxton East Barry estate of the Pophams of Littlecote in Wiltshire; the manor of Dinas Powys, divided between the Earl of Warwick and the Herberts of the Friars and Cogan Pill; and the fifty-acre farm of East Barry, alone amongst these properties in that it formed a compact parcel of farmland in the south-east corner of Merthyr Dyfan parish astride the lane from Barry to Holton and Cadoxton, which belonged to the Earl of Plymouth.[14] The 1760s and 1770s saw the transformation of this pattern of landownership, as successively the Warwick, Thomas and Popham estates were put up for sale, and the Herbert estate became divided.

The Wenvoe estate

This estate was professionally mapped and surveyed for the first time in the early 1760s, for Sir Edmund Thomas.[15] In the two parishes of Cadoxton and Merthyr Dyfan Sir Edmund then seems to have had between 380 and 400 acres. In Merthyr Dyfan there were nine tenements, including five farms of between 9 and 45 acres, the whole amounting to between 126 and 159 acres. In Cadoxton there were at this date some 270 acres, the larger part of which comprised holdings independent of farmhouses. Tenure for three lives predominated, although two tenements in Merthyr Dyfan and one in Cadoxton were held at will. In 1765 the Earl of Warwick's moiety of Dinas Powys manor was put up for sale, as it represented, to a man whose interests lay firmly in England, an 'outlying encumberance, as much a liability as an asset', whose administration at a distance was needlessly expensive.[16] Sir Edmund Thomas bought *en bloc* the 500 acres or so that belonged to this moiety, and this included 162 acres in Merthyr Dyfan, amongst which were farms at Holton and Felonsway.[17] With this purchase Sir Edmund stretched his resources to breaking point. His estate had become burdened with debts incurred in his pursuit of a political career—he was a client of the Prince of Wales, later of the Princess Dowager, sat for Glamorgan in the House of Commons, and secured office at the Board of Trade; at the same time he was extending and landscaping his park at Wenvoe. In October 1767 he died while canvassing electors in Gelligaer. His son, the fourth baronet, was forced to sell the estate to relieve his debts. The earl of Verulam, who stayed at Wenvoe during a tour of Wales in August 1769, records that the father

> fired with the zeal of electioneering and improving his place, spent here more than the income of his estate would allow; the ill consequence of which the son now experiences in such a manner that he is obliged to pay off the debts his father contracted by parting with his inheritance.[18]

The Wenvoe estate, which brought in an annual income of only about £1,240, 'must have been quite inadequate for a man who was a member of Parliament for many years and who held offices at court and in the government'.[19] Put up for sale in 1769, after 'long lingering',[20] it was sold in 1775 for £41,000, to one of the numerous outsiders who acquired land in Glamorgan at this period, Peter Birt of Airmyn Hall in Yorkshire. Birt, unpopular through his exploitation of the tolls on the Aire and Calder Navigation, saw Wenvoe as a suitable place for his retirement, an escape from his native Yorkshire, and was responsible, in 1776-7, for the complete rebuilding of Wenvoe Castle.[21] Acquired relatively cheaply, the Wenvoe estate was a fine investment offering him ready opportunities to increase its rental. The 1769 sale catalogue claimed that the rent of only one farm had been improved since 'almost time immemorial'—something of an exaggeration, but a remark which indicates that the majority of farms were on long leases and were 'capable of very great improvement'.

> The tenants at will are very desirous of taking leases at considerably improved rents, to the amount of several hundred pounds a year; but the owner did not care to raise 'em as he was going to sell the estate, and there are a great number of other tenants ready to take the farms, if the present tenants were to decline it.[22]

It was foreseen that a new owner would be able to institute a lucrative campaign of improving rents and substituting short leases for lives. A further major survey of the Wenvoe estate was undertaken in 1798, by which time it had passed through Birt's heiress to the Jenner family.[23] By this time the Wenvoe property in Cadoxton and Merthyr Dyfan had been considerably augmented; in Cadoxton it now amounted to 435 acres, in Merthyr Dyfan to 876 acres. How did this come about?

The Popham Estate

Some of this additional land came from the disposal of the Popham estate, whose 776 acres or thereabouts, in Cadoxton, Merthyr Dyfan, St. Andrew's and St. Athan, were put up for sale in 1775. This estate had, like the Wenvoe estate, been managed in a conservative way, with the added disadvantage that it was supervised from a much greater distance. Like the Earl of Warwick's estate, it was an outlier to a more considerable property and its rental did not justify the costs of administration.[24] The Popham estate records support this view. The total annual income from their Cadoxton East Barry estate seems to have been, net, little more than the Seys family could expect from the rent of one farm at Barry. In 1714, the bailiff, Thomas Wilkins, accounted for income of £95 1*s.* 3*d.*, nearly £43 of which was represented by rents from Brynhill, White Farm and Cae Warr tenement, which were being let from year to year, probably experimentally, since they soon reverted to being held by long leases. Expenditure amounted to £68 2*s.* 5¼*d.*, and arrears of rents to over £12, leaving a balance to be handed over of a meagre £14 13*s.* 4¼*d.* Once Brynhill and White Farm had been let out again for lives, the total rental dropped alarmingly; in 1763 Miles Spickett announced receipts of £45 15*s.*, and expenses of £15 5*s.* 1½*d.*; the latter included repairs on tenements held at will, the costs of holding a manor court, and his own salary). By the 1750s this estate was in addition encumbered with arrears of over £400 in rent, a result, probably, of the widespread hardship experienced by small farmers in the hard years of the 1740s. This was a heavy burden for the estate to bear, which could not be alleviated by occasional sales of timber.[25] Against this background of conservatism and inefficiency, the immediate motive for the sale of the Popham estate was the huge debt of nearly £50,000 with which the estate as a whole, not just its Welsh lands, was saddled by 1773, as a result of mortgages taken out to raise marriage portions for the daughters of Alexander Popham in 1692. It was therefore arranged that, on the marriage of Edward Popham, heir to the estates, in 1772, the Welsh lands would be sold to help reduce the charge on the Somerset estate.[26]

Precise details of the disposal of the Cadoxton East Barry lands are difficult to establish. It is unclear from the accounts of John Stokes, trustee of the estate, to whom what parts were sold, and when. It was intended originally to sell the manor in parcels to the tenants; in 1772 it was hoped to sell it as a whole either by auction or private contract. In 1775 a particular of the estate was printed to attract interest, though Stokes tried to persuade Peter Birt to buy it *en bloc*. Some land had been sold by early 1776, though not to Birt, with whom negotiations continued for the purchase of the residue. Ultimately, in 1777, the title to the manor of Cadoxton was sold to Peter Birt of Wenvoe. Other purchasers included William Hurst of Gabalfa, who had a share in the Mount estate in Dinas Powys, and Robert Jones III of Fonmon, who acquired 50 acres or so in St. Athan.[27] These were not the only purchasers, however. In Merthyr Dyfan and Cadoxton the Popham estate had comprised some 703 acres, approximately 400 of which lay in Merthyr Dyfan. Not all of this land was bought by Birt and Hurst, for Great Brynhill farm was purchased by its former tenants, the Spickett family, along with three other houses in Merthyr Dyfan and two tenements—'Welshman's Grounds' and Witchell—which had also been Popham land. The Spicketts held on to Brynhill, despite the unfavourable conditions for small freeholders that prevailed in the depression following the war against Napoleon, until the 1830s, when it was sold to the Lees of the Mount, Dinas Powys.[28] In Cadoxton, the house later known as Golden Grove, together with ten acres of land and two cottages, was bought by William Jenkins; his money-lending activities and reputed abilities as a 'wizard' contributed to his unpopularity as a man from humble origins in Barry (he had been born in his mother Ann's cottage at the foot of Lover's Lane). He profited in the later 18th-century land market and built up a small estate. It is probable that other small freeholders and some of the tenants of the Pophams in Cadoxton were also able to benefit in the same fashion from the break-up of the estate.

The land tax assessments of the later 18th and early 19th centuries and, a little later, the tithe schedules of the 1840s reveal Merthyr Dyfan and Cadoxton as communities that, in terms of the distribution of land-ownership, were successive stages away from the 'closed' parish that was Barry. The only land in Barry that was not in the hands of the Joneses, and later the Romillys, was the small amount of glebe land that belonged to the church. By 1800, the Wenvoe estate had a clear, but by no means total predominance in Merthyr Dyfan, where it controlled 879 acres out of a total of 1,396 acres (63%), and was liable for 62·8% of the land tax assessment. The remainder was in the hands of a combination of small gentlemen or yeomen such as the Spicketts (11%), the Plymouth estate (East Barry—2·1%), and minor squires such as Anthony Deere and William Hurst. By 1831, the Jenner estate had acquired additional land, bringing their proportion of the land tax liability to 69·9%, while a number of the smaller freeholds had been acquired by gentlemen landlords.[29] This is the position reflected in the tithe schedule of 1840.[30]

Table 12. Landownership in Merthyr Dyfan parish in the mid 19th century (area in acres, roods and perches).

Owner	a. r. p.	% (approx)
R. F. Jenner (Wenvoe)	971.1.14	72
E. H. Lee (Mount)	153.3.09	11
R. H. Clive (Plymouth)	31.0.14	2
David Jones	67.2.27	5
Rev. J. Simons	30.2.31	2
Glebe	24.1.14	2
R. Bassett	8.3.06	0.7
John Watkins	3.3.20	0.3
Francis John	2.05	0.04
David Thomas	2.14	0.04
John Morgan	1.12	0.02
Elizabeth George	.15	0.007

Of the above owners of land, only Francis John, Elizabeth George and John Watkins owned the houses or cottages in which they lived.

Merthyr Dyfan, then, was a parish not dominated wholly by a single family, but one nonetheless where nearly all the land was in the hands of gentlemen. Structurally, Cadoxton had different characteristics.

Comparison of the 1798 land tax assessment with the schedule in the tithe apportionment for Cadoxton of the 1840s reveals a very similar picture, one in which the control of gentry landowners over the resources of the community was much less marked and where a considerable acreage was in the hands of minor, non-gentry proprietors, a position which is the legacy of centuries of fragmented landownership. The effects of this legacy were reinforced by the break-up of the Popham estate in the 1770s. The tithe schedule provides the clearest breakdown of the situation in the early years of Queen Victoria's reign.[31]

Gentry landlords were present, of course, the Jenners owning over a third of the acreage, including Weston Farm, the Old Mill, and Sweldon tenement; smaller estates were also controlled by the Lees of the Mount, Richard Bassett of Bonvilston (Brooks Farm, etc), Sir S. Britain (Verlon Farm) and Llewelyn Traherne, esquire (part of the Court lands). But equally marked is the presence of local families such as the Spicketts and Jenkinses amongst the more significant proprietors, and the tiny freeholds, often in owner-occupation, that belonged to families such as the Brocks and the Griffithses, folk who, despite the tendencies of the age, had been able to preserve their land from the clutches of gentry owners, and were often able to augment their income as publicans, small farmers, or craftsmen with the rent obtained from the letting of cottages. Ann Griffiths, for example, who died in 1828, was able to leave two houses to her sons John and Rees, the Orchard House and the Pound House, both in Cadoxton. When Robert Jenkins, son of William Jenkins the 'extorter', died in 1812 he left a substantial clutch of small properties to his descendants: a messuage and six acres in Cadoxton; Gilhill tenement at Pencoetre in St. Andrews parish; two houses at Playhill in Cadoxton (let to Thomas Vaughan); a house and garden in Dinas Powys (let to John Williams and Morgan Lewis); the Three Bells Inn—left to his daughter Amelia, who married David Griffiths; a number of cottages and gardens to the north of St. Cadoc's churchyard, and several small properties in Dinas Powys village, all seemingly let to agricultural labourers.[32] This class of proprietor, doing modestly well out of a small, carefully accumulated estate, was barely to be seen in Merthyr Dyfan and was totally absent in Barry. This presence, together with the smaller gentry estates, made Cadoxton, unlike Barry, an 'open' community, its growth unrestricted by the control of a great landlord.

Table 13. Landownership in Cadoxton parish in the mid 19th century.

Owner	acres	% (approx)
R. F. Jenner	385	39
R. Bassett	110	11
Common—Sheeping Moor	88	9
E. H. Lee	85	9
Common	56	5.75
Glebe	41	4.2
Catherine Thomas	39	4.0
Robert Spickett	30½	3.1
Miles Spickett	27	2.8
Thomas Spickett	26	2.7
Thomas Edwards	24	2.5
Llewelyn Traherne	24	2.5
Sir S. Britain	8½	0.9
Robert Jenkins	9	0.9
Thomas Jenkins	7	0.7
Oddfellows	2	0.2
Grace Roberts	1½	0.15
David Griffiths	½	0.05
David Jenkins	½	0.05
Mary Evans	¼	0.25

Under ¼acre: Elizabeth Brock, William Brock, John Brock, William David, Mary Griffiths, William Lewis, Mary Miller, Howell Thomas, Llewelyn Thomas, John Williams, Edward Williams.

The changing landscape

In the previous chapter we saw how the largely unenclosed medieval landscape of the Barry area was gradually replaced between 1450 and 1700 by a field pattern that would be familiar to a modern eye. However, it was not until the middle of the 18th century that maps were drawn to show how far this process had actually evolved in Cadoxton and Merthyr Dyfan, and to visualise the shape of the villages and hamlets of these parishes. At Barry, of course, as Evans Mouse's map of 1622 shows, enclosure was complete by that date.

The maps commissioned by the Plymouth and Wenvoe estates in the 1760s allow for the first time a coherent view of the landscape in Cadoxton and Merthyr Dyfan. In 1766, for example, John Edward Eyre mapped East Barry farm for the Earl of Plymouth. The farm was then held on a long lease by Mr John Edwards, who managed a compact block of 45 acres of arable, pasture and meadowland in the south-western corner of Merthyr Dyfan parish, together with five acres of 'slimy ground'. The farmhouse stood a little to the east of the modern railway station at Barry, on the lane from Barry village to Holton; below it, a small stream or pill entered the sound between Barry Island and the mainland, while the eastern boundary of the estate was marked by another stream, Shennon's Pill.[33]

The Wenvoe estate was first mapped in 1762-4 for Sir Edmund Thomas, and it was surveyed again at the end of the 18th century when, much enlarged, it was in the hands of Peter Birt's son-in-law Robert Jenner.[34] Although by the 1760s most of the Wenvoe estate in Cadoxton and Merthyr Dyfan was enclosed, relict features survived from an older landscape. Long, narrow closes, some of them still unhedged, were prominent to the south of the Port Road in Merthyr Dyfan parish, between Colcot and Pencoetre, and to the west of Colcot Road; in Cadoxton there were similar survivals near Weston Farm, and to the south-east of the Common, between Cadoxton village and the old Mill. A much larger area was mapped for Robert Jenner's enlarged estate in 1798, and comparison of the earlier and later plans shows that a number of significant changes had occurred in the landscape. Most of the relict open field strips had disappeared, and there had been a considerable reorganisation of fields and farms. Sir Edmund Thomas had initiated these changes. William Thomas's memorial of that owner of Wenvoe reveals him as a great improver of his estate who 'had much delight in clearing the lands about his place, in planting clumps of trees . . . in drawing down hedges, ditches, levelling lanes, making new ones'.[35] The expenses incurred in these activities were a partial cause of the indebtedness that led to the sale of the estate. It was by him, for example, that the line of the Port Road was diverted east of Stumpy to enlarge Wenvoe Park.

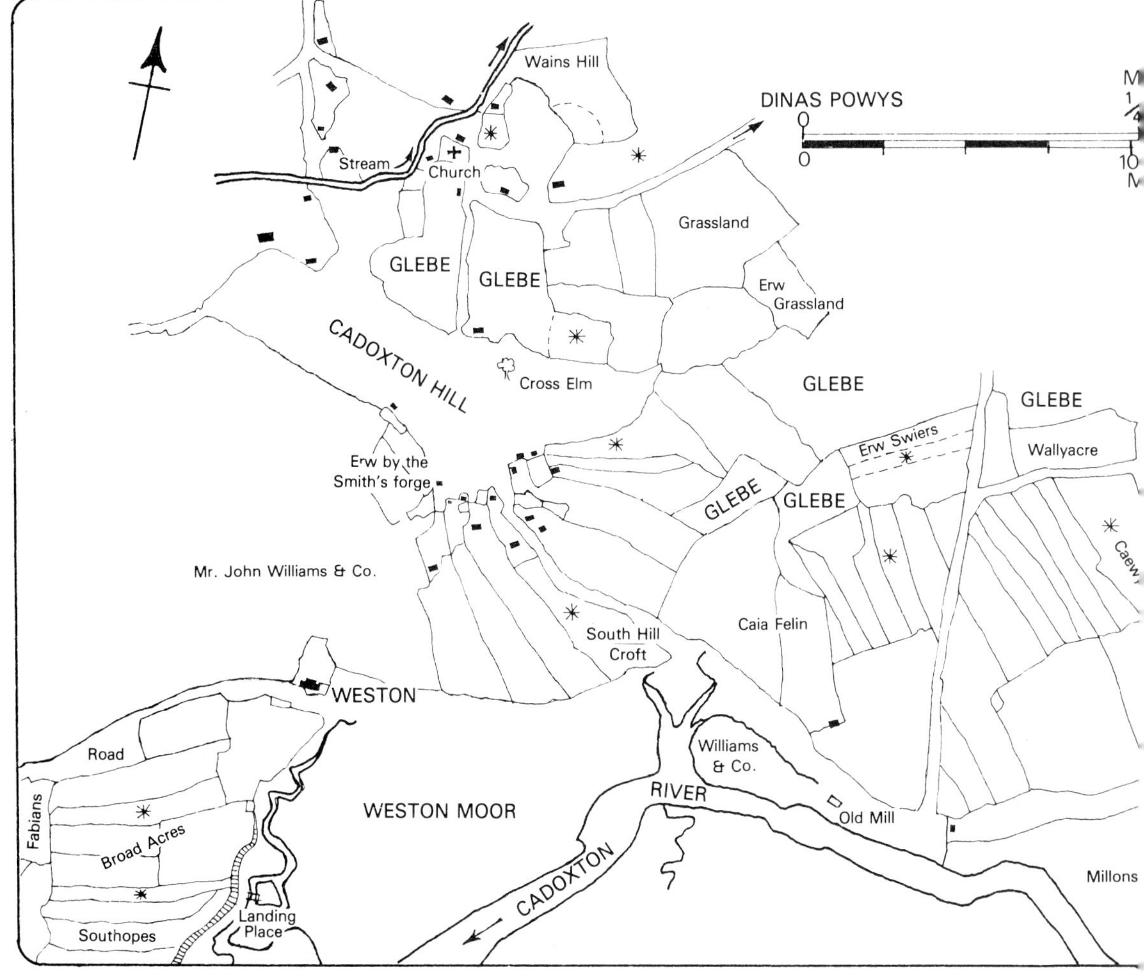

Fig. 51.
Plan of Cadoxton village and surroundings in 1763, based on estate plan in Glamorgan Record Office. Note development of village around common and pattern of open-field strips to S.E. and S.W. (property of Popham estate marked with asterisk) *M.G.*

The later series of estate maps shows, however, that this work had not extinguished all reminders of the earlier landscape of strip and furlong, headland and balk. The lands of the Popham and Brooke estates had not been visited by the hands of an improver. For example, the relatively flat land bounded by Colcot Road, Claude Road and the Port Road, and the high ground between Barry Road and Merthyr Dyfan village was still in the 1790s an unimproved landscape of 'fossilised' strips and intermixed lands, and it remained for the Jenners to undertake the modernisation of these tenements. By the time the Tithe Map of Merthyr Dyfan was drawn in the 1840s, long, narrow closes had largely disappeared and the lay-out of farms had been rationalised to create better organised holdings. In Cadoxton, however, where the Jenners were less powerful, and ownership more divided, such rationalisation was less easy to undertake. By the 1840s, although the major farms—Gibbonsdown, Weston and Old Mill Farm—formed relatively coherent units, other estates were still intermingled—the lands of the Lees of the Mount, for example, which were farmed by David Griffiths and Edward Greatrex, and Brooks Farm, belonging to Richard Bassett. Intermixed fields with the physical characteristics of open field strips were still to be seen south of Barry Road, to the south of Coldbrook Road, and to the east of the common, while the distribution of glebe land indicates well how widely dispersed across the parish the land belonging to other farms may once have been.

We have seen how at Barry in the later 18th and in the early 19th centuries, a concern for 'improvement' found expression in the laying together of farms. Despite the obstacles to this latter course in Merthyr Dyfan and in Cadoxton, the evidence suggests that it did nonetheless take place on a small scale. In the middle of the 18th century tenement farms on the Popham estate (excluding smallholdings of five acres or less) averaged 34 acres in extent; those on the Wenvoe estate, following its acquisition of the Warwick moiety of Dinas Powys manor, 23 acres. By contrast, the mean farm size in Merthyr Dyfan in the 1840s was 65 acres, in Cadoxton, 32 acres.[36] However, the majority of holdings planned by the tithe surveyors were recognisably similar to those of a century or even two centuries earlier.

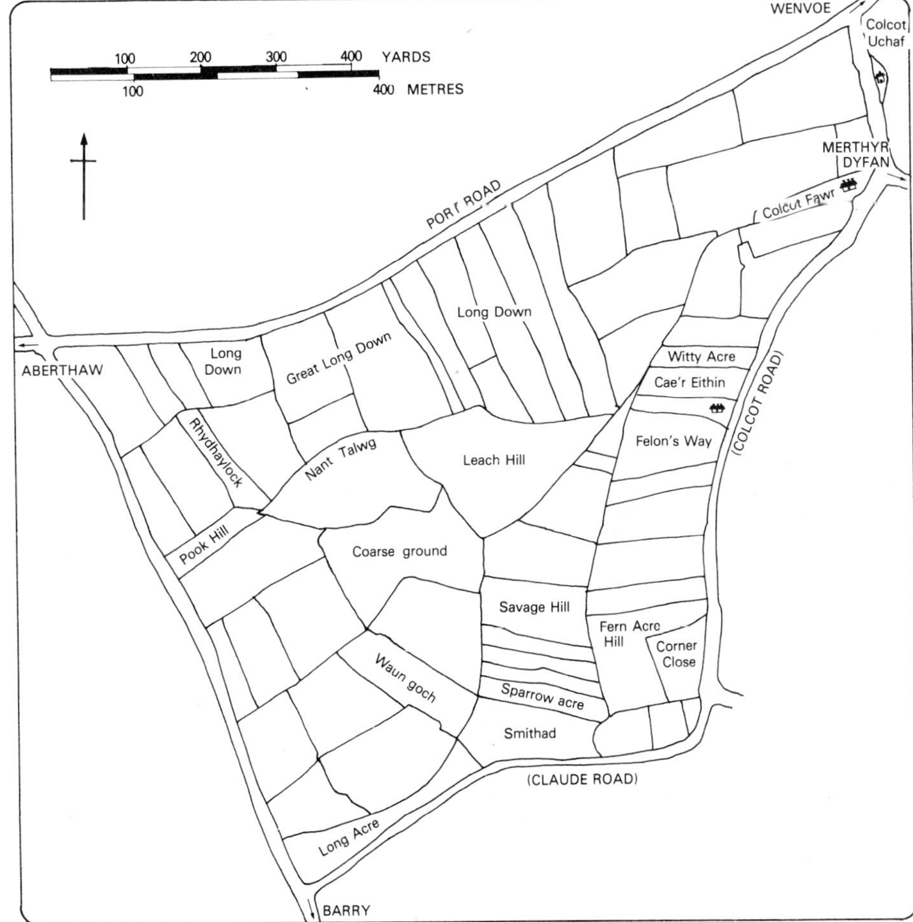

ig. 52. lan of part of Venvoe estate in lerthyr Dyfan parish n *c.* 1790, based on riginal in Glamorgan ecord Office. Note attern of open-field rips, represented by ng, narrow closes nd long, continuous edge lines. *I.G.*

It is unfortunate that we have little information on the economic organisation of local farms in the second half of the 18th century and after to set along the earlier evidence of the probate inventories. Inventories disappear as a source after the 1770s. However, those of the earlier part of the 18th century suggest that little had altered by 1770 in the structure of many farms, and that until the Napoleonic wars, when the pressure was on many farmers to increase corn production, a similar balance obtained between arable farming and livestock as in the later 17th century. Arnold Hawkins of Cole Farm, Barry, was remembered by William Thomas as a 'great farmer and a great fat man'[37] when he died at the age of 65 in 1766 from a sudden fever, and he may stand as a representative of the handful of men who farmed units of over 50 acres in the Barry area at this date. He left farmstock and household goods worth £238, amongst which his crops were valued at £33 8*s.* 6*d.*, his stock at £130 14*s.* 6*d.*, and his household stuff at £74 4*s.* 3*d.* Agriculture on Cole Farm was heavily biased towards cattle and sheep, over three-quarters of his investment being tied up in livestock, although he grew also a reasonable quantity of wheat, barley and oats, supplemented by peas and beans. He had sown clover, copying the example set by innovative gentlemen farmers further west in the Vale, to improve the quality of his grass. In his farmhouse at Cold Knap he had several items of furniture that few men of his rank would have owned a hundred years before: two round tables, a tea table, a looking glass, and a clock, together with a teapot, sugar dish and slop basin, and silver teaspoons among the smaller items.[38] A great gulf continued to separate the few men of this standing amongst the tenantry in the Barry area from the ordinary small farmer who was rather more typical of the locality. While the occasional rich tenant might live like Miles Richard and his mistress Gwenllian of Biglis Farm 'in great pomp and volputuousness'[39] and ape the manners of the gentry by indulging in the new fashion of tea-drinking, conditions had but little improved by the 1760s for smaller farmers, let alone the labourers.

However, the later 18th century seems—though the local evidence is rather thin—to have brought some improvement generally in the standard of living in the rural Vale. This is linked to the expansion of the iron industry in the north of the county, itself part of the more general industrial revolution under way in Great Britain. The production of iron, cloth, and a host of other industries increased to serve new markets at home—in the swelling factory towns—and abroad—in Britain's colonial empire. Locally the market for agricultural produce shifted and the Vale now no longer sent much of its corn and dairy products across the Channel and to Bristol, but to the new iron towns, especially Merthyr Tydfil. The decline of the older pattern of trade is reflected in the decay of the old port of Barry. By the second half of the 18th century, Barry, like Aberthaw, was much reduced in significance; though the occasional small vessel took out small quantities of grain, or a cargo of pigs and cattle, trade was predominantly in the export in coastal vessels of limestone and beach pebbles, for fertiliser and cement, with some importing of coal. It was the growing population of the iron towns that set the new pattern and provided an additional stimulus to improve the efficiency and profitability of Vale farms.

Clover, grown at Cole Farm in the 1760s, was one of the first innovations, aimed at improving the quality of grass, and thereby yields of milk and butter, and at raising the value of fat cattle. Clover had come into the Vale in the later 17th century. Other new crops arrived and spread more slowly—perennial rye grass, sainfoin, turnips and potatoes—while in the later 18th century old rotations of corn and grass were abandoned in favour of systems that would bring higher yields and better grazing. There is some

ig. 53.
lan of hamlet of
olton in 1763, based
n estate plan in
lamorgan Record
ffice.
I.G.

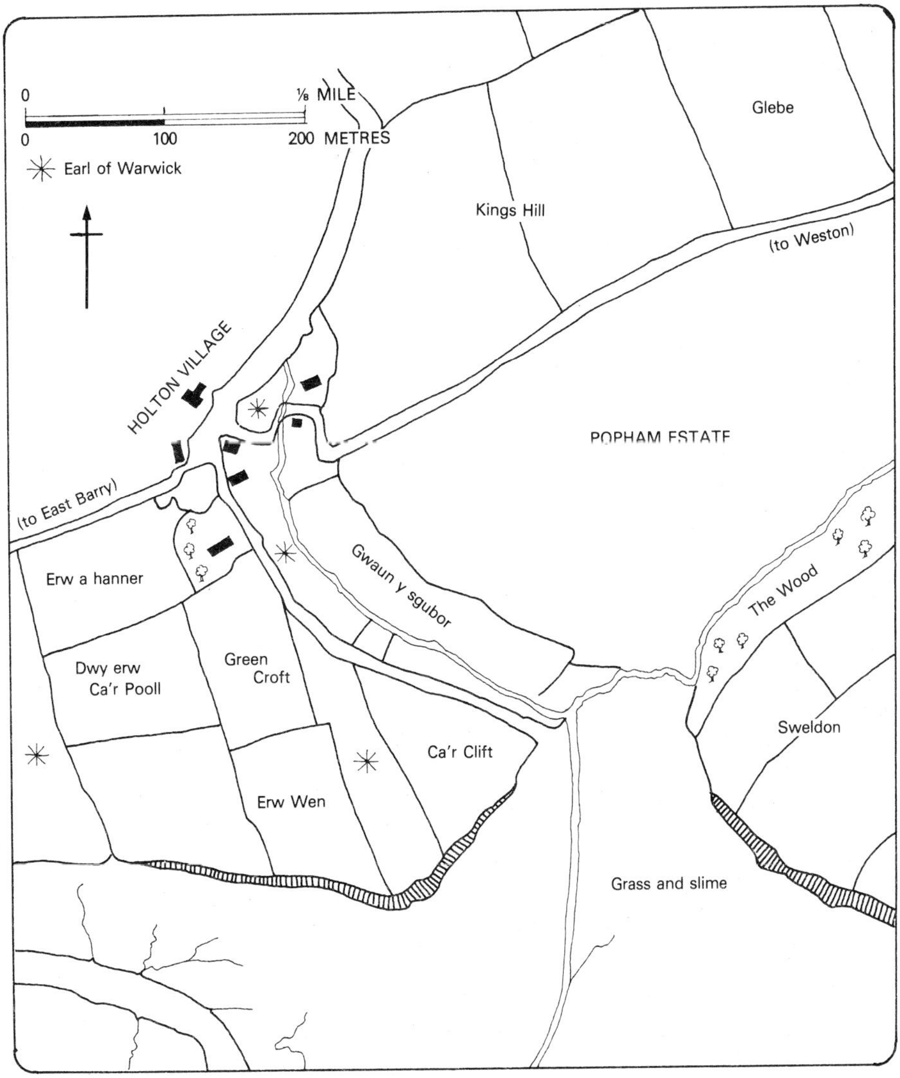

evidence too, that some farmers tried to improve the breeds of sheep and cattle, though generally native Glamorgan sheep, and the local red, brown and black cattle remained adequate into the 19th century.[40] Glamorgan reds were still grazing in Cadoxton in the late Victorian era[41] though they died out subsequently in favour of Friesians and Herefords. According to Iolo Morganwg, the Flemingston stone mason, forger and antiquarian, who wrote valuable accounts of Glamorgan farming practices at the turn of the 18th century, it was the gentlemen farmers, rather than the great landlords, who were the most active innovators, but the Jones family of Fonmon, owners of Barry and Porthkerry until 1810, stood out in their encouragement of better techniques, using covenants in the leases they granted to force improvements on farmers, even before 1750.[42] This type of encouragement was more widespread by the early 19th century, and may be exemplified by the lease of Pencoetre Farm which Robert Jenner granted to Howell Thomas in 1810.[43] Pencoetre had 150 acres (130 in Merthyr Dyfan) and was let by Jenner for fourteen years (the usual term on the Wenvoe estate by this date) for £105 *per annum*. The tenant was not to take more than two crops of corn from any parcel without allowing it to lie fallow and laying twenty crannocks of lime as fertiliser per acre. He was to sow 18 lbs of clover seed or a proportionate amount of another grass with every second cycle of corn, under a penalty of £5 per acre, unless he was intending to plant beans, peas, turnips or clover, which he could do after a summer fallow and a thorough hoeing. Neither beans nor peas were to be sown during the last three years of the lease. This lease was made during the Napoleonic War, when blockade combined with poor harvests led to soaring corn prices and attempts by farmers to maximise yields of corn by sowing poor quality land. In order to prevent the deterioration of the farm Jenner therefore proposed to fine his tenant £5 an acre for every parcel of meadow or pasture converted to tillage.

The gradual reorganisation of fields and farms was not the only significant aspect of change in the local landscape. Comparison of the plans of Cadoxton drawn in the 1760s, 1790s and 1840s indicates how the village, which had developed in the Middle Ages around the edge of an extensive area of common land, continued to expand around the common edge, by means of successive intakes, whether as illegal encroachments or under licence from the lords of the manor. At the same time, land between occupied plots was infilled by cottage building—often by the smaller proprietors such as the Jenkins family—as the community grew in the later 18th and early 19th centuries. A major expansion in population took place in the Vale of Glamorgan in the twenty years after 1770, and between about 1811 and 1830. This growth is attributable in part at least to improved standards of hygiene and housing, which reduced child mortality and prolonged the lives of adults; after 1831, however, the population of many parishes remained stable, or even contracted somewhat, as folk migrated

Fig. 54.
Plan of Cadoxt
1842, based on
map. Compare
Fig. 51, and n
growth of settle
especially arou
common.
M.G.

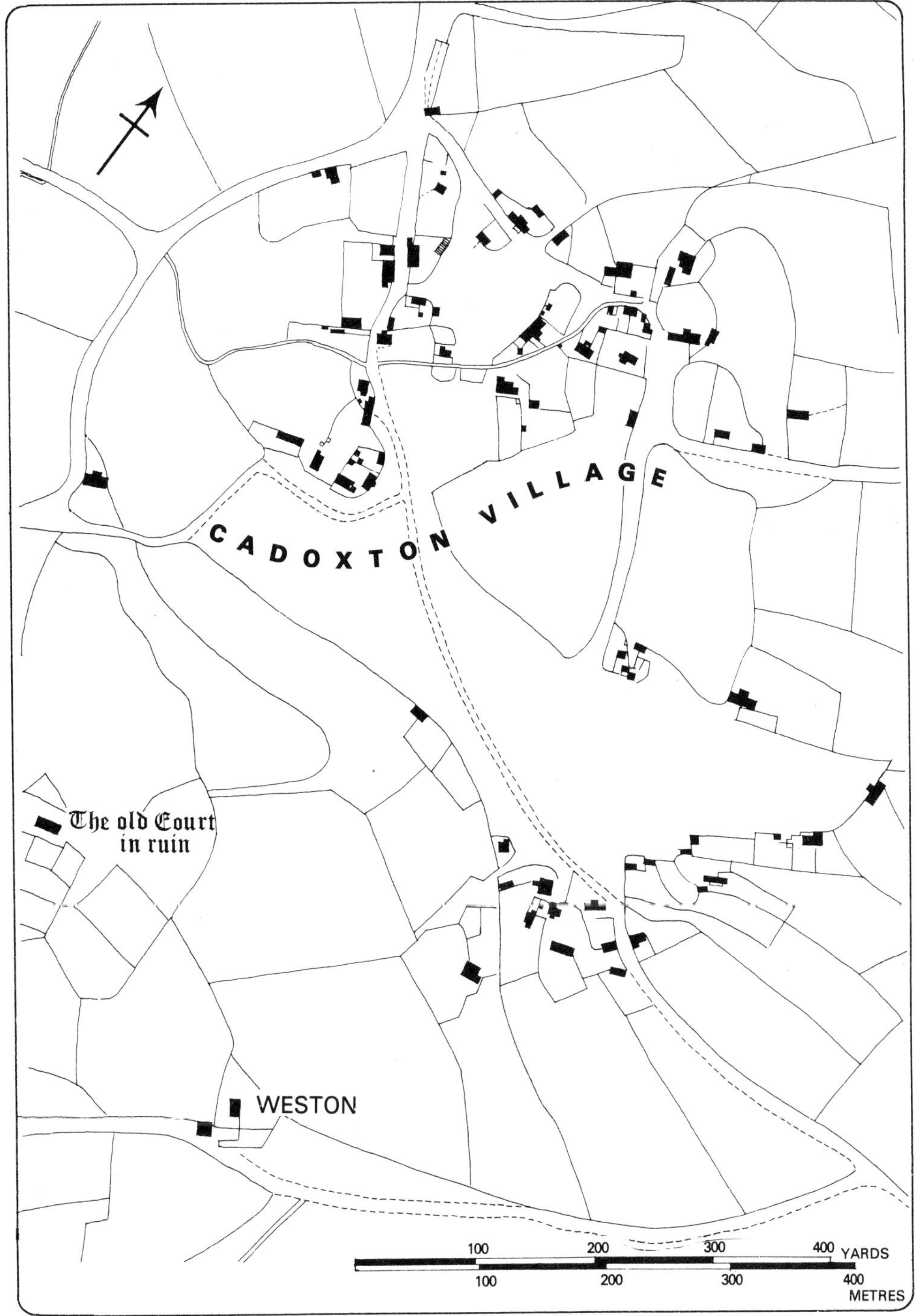

from the countryside to take up the opportunities offered by higher wages in the industrial valleys of Glamorgan and Monmouthshire. In the middle decades of the 19th century, these losses were sometimes made good by the arrival of immigrants from Ireland and from the depressed agricultural parishes of the west of England and west Wales (where expanding population had kept down wages for work on the land), but overall there was little further growth in population. The population of Merthyr Dyfan actually shrank between 1801 and 1861. In fact, locally it was the 'open' community of Cadoxton, with its lack of a dominant squire and its commons, that accommodated the major increase in population between 1780 and 1820 and attracted migrants. Barry, firmly under gentry control, grew little before it was remodelled by the Romillys after 1850.

Fig. 55. Plans of houses Cadoxton, typi rebuilding in la and early 19th centuries. *H. J. Thomas.*

Houses, cottages and chapels

Few houses in Cadoxton or Merthyr Dyfan survive from the 17th century or before.[44] The old village of Cadoxton, as it is today, is of essentially later 18th- and early 19th-century character. The same would have been true of dwellings in Merthyr Dyfan parish before the advent of the modern town. Only in Barry did early modern houses survive in a representative number into the present century—Castle farmhouse being lost before the Great War, Cwm Barry in the 1950s, while Greenhouse still stands in Old Village Road, and Cole farmhouse at the Knap. In Merthyr Dyfan and Cadoxton farmers seem to have taken advantage of their greater prosperity after 1750 to demolish and build anew; it is possible, therefore, that earlier houses in those parishes had not been as substantial or as well built as their contemporaries in Barry, where 18th-century tenants seem to have been content to extend their dwellings rather than replace them. If the 'Great Rebuilding' in Barry took place between 1570 and 1640, this phenomenon must be dated in Merthyr Dyfan and Cadoxton to the period after 1750.

Hillside, at Little Hill in Cadoxton, is typical of the kind of house that might be erected in the middle of the 18th century. It was a dwelling that was still vernacular in style. On the ground floor were four rooms, a hall and a kitchen, backed by a daïry and another room whose function is unclear. The hall and kitchen were both heated, with chimneys in each gable, each fireplace having adjacent to it a newel stair leading to chambers on the upper floor. The entry, which led directly into the hall, was roughly central, making Hillside representative of the 'type A' vernacular house which was an increasingly popular plan in the early to mid 18th century in eastern Glamorgan. Built in 1776—the year of the American Revolution—Hillside was a public house in the 1770s and 1780s. Caerlan (*c.* 1780), Double Cot (*c.* 1800) and Rock Cottage (*c.* 1800), also in Cadoxton, are of similar plan, although at Caerlan and Double Cot the stair is placed adjacent to the kitchen fireplace, while at Rock Cottage it is to be found in a rear kitchen. By the end of the 18th century, Glamorgan houses were losing their individuality and a national style of house and cottage building was emerging in which the only variation from region to region depends on the materials used, local stone still being favoured by builders if cheaper than the ubiquitous brick. Cross Elms in Cadoxton, which was also built about

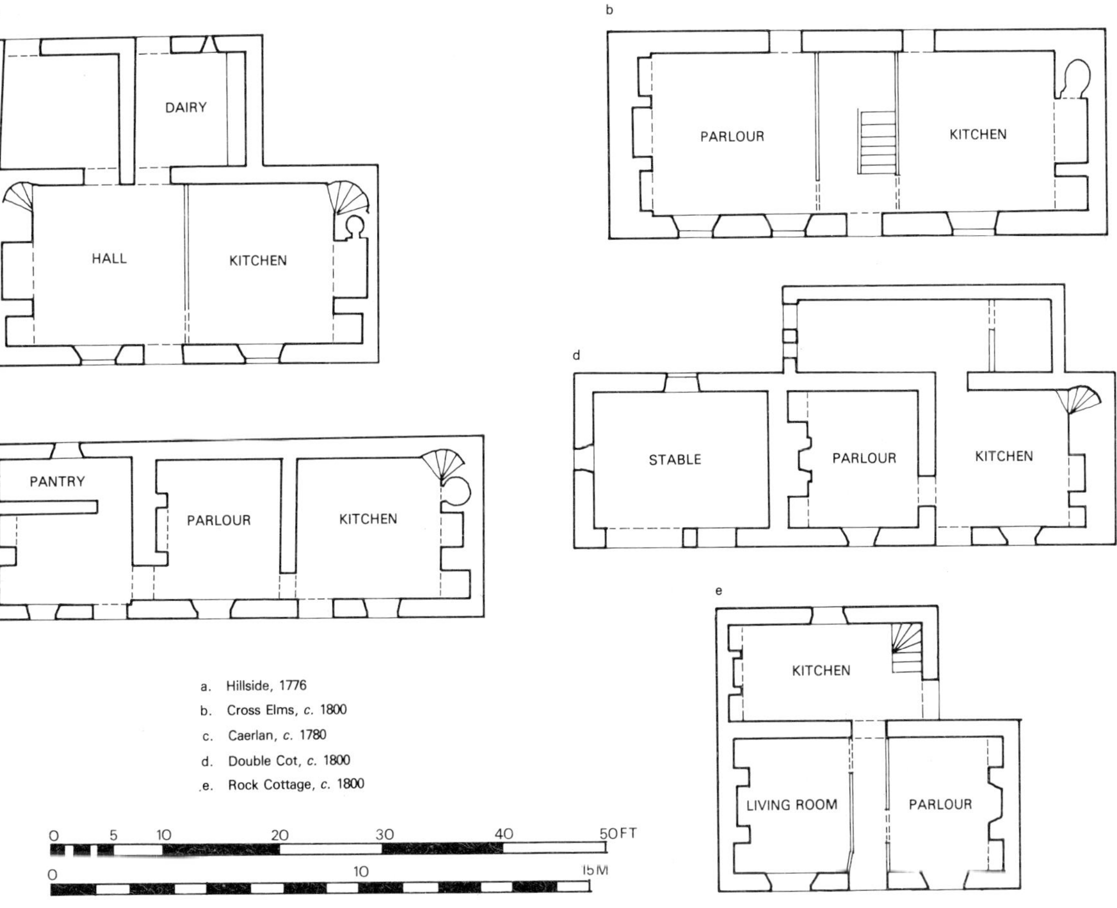

a. Hillside, 1776
b. Cross Elms, *c.* 1800
c. Caerlan, *c.* 1780
d. Double Cot, *c.* 1800
e. Rock Cottage, *c.* 1800

1800, may be said to be transitional between a vernacular and the national style. It is still one room deep on the ground floor, with gable fireplaces in parlour and kitchen, but the stair, which in the vernacular house is normally adjacent to the fireplace, is now to be found located in a central hallway between the main downstairs rooms, setting the pattern for the rather dull dwellings erected in later years. The house at White Farm in Merthyr Dyfan, which still stands today, is a good example of these later dwellings.

In Barry, where there was little demand for new buildings in this period, older dwellings largely sufficed until the 1850s. However, as we have noted, some new building did take place. At the foot of Lovers' Lane, Cliffwood Cottage was rebuilt about 1790, in a style that may be considered an impoverished version of the vernacular, and was quite common in labourers' cottages of this date in the county. More innovatory were the two cottages put up for labourers about 1800 by the Jones estate, later to be known as Jordan's Cottage (No. 12 Old Village Road) until their demolition in the 1960s. Consisting of two semi-detached dwellings, each had only a single room on the ground floor. They resemble early industrial workers' cottages

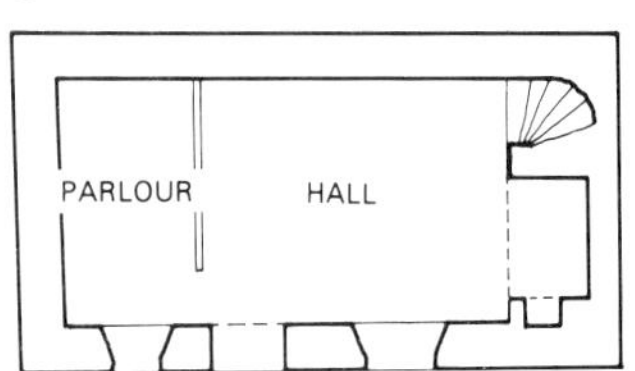

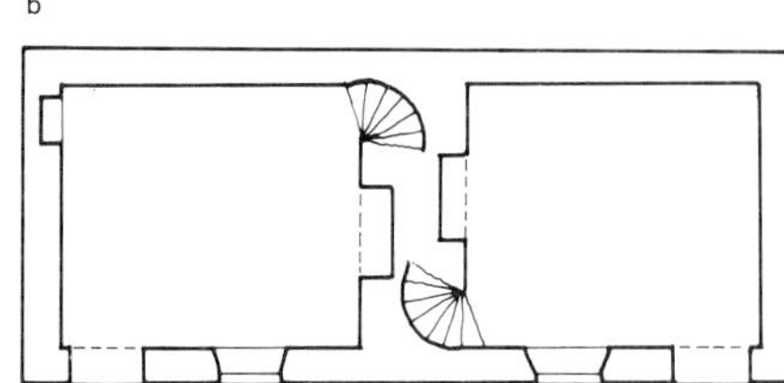

c

LIVING ROOM/
KITCHEN

a. Cliffwood Cottage, *c.* 1790

b. No. 12 Old Village Road, *c.* 1800

c. Nos. 2, 4, 6, 8 Old Village Road, *c.* 1860

Original plans by H. J. Thomas.

Fig. 56.
Plans of houses in Barry parish.

to be found in the Taff and Cynon valleys, but unlike the latter retained a rustic appearance by virtue of their thatched roofs. The design was to be copied in the 1860s when the Romillys put up Nos. 2, 4, 6 and 8 Old Village Road for their estate workers.

If house and cottage building was one aspect of the expansion of Cadoxton in the later 18th and early 19th centuries, so too was the erection of chapels. It is clear that the religious affections of many folk in the Barry district were fired by the nonconformist revival of 1813-15.[45] The apparent disrepair of St. Cadoc's church in the later 18th century—churchwardens in this period were regularly admonished because roof, floor, seats and bells were in poor condition—is an indication of the low esteem in which the Church of England was held. The opportunity for chapel building does not seem, however, to have existed in Barry or Merthyr Dyfan. In Barry neither the Joneses nor Romillys, as controlling landlords, were prepared to countenance the erection of a nonconformist meeting house, although in the 1820s Catherine Evans' house was used by the Baptists, while the gentry landowners of Merthyr Dyfan, with their Anglican loyalties, were similarly reluctant to release land for such a purpose. In Cadoxton, however, where there was no real squire, and where landownership was fragmented amongst many proprietors, conditions were tailor-made for the dissenters. A Baptist chapel, Philadelphia, was the first to be built, in 1813; the shell of this simple place of worship still stands in its little graveyard near the King William IV Inn. Gravestones show that it attracted worshippers not only from Cadoxton, but from surrounding parishes where there was no chapel. Tabor, also Baptist, was built during the same revival, while in 1815 the Welsh Wesleyan Methodists built Bethel on the south side of Cadoxton

Common and the Calvinistic Methodists leased land on which to build Sion. By the time of the 1851 religious census Anglicanism may have undergone its own quiet revival in Cadoxton (some repairs were carried out to the church in the 1820s) for in that year Sunday attendance was claimed to number 35, together with 25 scholars of the National School, who presumably came compulsorily. On Sundays, however, a further 350 or more people may have attended the chapels in the village.[46]

'Stopping the tide'

Some of the 18th century intakes on Cadoxton Common were almost certainly linked to an ambitious, but doomed scheme to drain the Sheeping Moor and Weston Moor. Had this succeeded, it would have changed the area between Barry Island and the mainland, a wide, muddy tidal estuary, with coarse grazing around its edges, out of all recognition.

It was a Bristol baker, a Mr Vowles, who planned these improvements. He must first have identified Cadoxton as a potential source of investment in the mid 1750s, when he purchased large quantities of timber from the Popham estate.[47] By 1762 he had framed plans to erect a sea wall across the moors between Barry Island and the mainland that would hold back the tides and allow the moors to be developed as lush meadowground. He also aimed to build a new mill that would take away the trade of the old mill near the Verlons.

To accomplish this scheme, Vowles had to expropriate the rights of the commoners of Cadoxton, who valued their liberty to graze sheep and cattle on the moors. Not every Cadoxton farmer had common rights, but the leases of many small farmers allowed them to turn out a certain number of beasts on to the commons alongside those of freeholders. To William Thomas, the schoolmaster diarist of Michaelston-super-Ely who knew Cadoxton and its people well, Vowles simply aimed to take away the privileges of the poor. Thomas sympathised with the potential victims of an outsider who aimed to enlarge his purse at the expense of their livelihoods. By 1762 Vowles was negotiating with Sir Edmund Thomas, and trying to persuade tenants to surrender their leases to him. He obtained no financial support from Sir Edmund, but may have enjoyed his active encouragement for a scheme so similar in spirit, if much more ambitious in scale, to his own 'improvements'. The commoners naturally resisted the scheme, but Vowles must have had some success, for work began in August 1763 to 'stop the tide at Barry Island', with a workforce of twenty or more men.

Vowles built his new mill, but the scheme to drain the moors quickly ruined its author and hastened his death. Work could only be undertaken between the spring and the autumn, and when work was halted at the end of October 1763, the baker had already lost a sloop he owned, 'blown from Cadoxton and sunk against Lavernock' in a great storm. The following year

Fig. 57.
View of Holton and Barry Island from N. in 1870s, from early photograph.
Simon Prosser.

gangs of labourers were again brought to Cadoxton, and probably settled in cottages on the common, while Vowles raised money from the sale of houses in Bristol to pursue his scheme. The tide damaged his wall in July 1764, and on the night of 2 September 1764, it collapsed, but Vowles was determined to complete his project 'let it cost him whatsoever'. Indeed his attempts were not halted finally until September 1766. In the summer of 1765 he had 'many workmen on work' according to William Thomas, undeterred by damage by the sea in June and August. In July 1766, labour was again recruited:

> Mr. Vowles gave papers about Dinas Powys and elsewhere for workmen to work on the sea wall in Cadoxton to stop the tide, which had gone down twice after much labour on it, offering them 7*s.* a week.

Storms and high tides that September forced Vowles to admit defeat, and the following month William Thomas recorded that he had been buried in Bristol, noting in his moralising way that his labour, and his 'taking away the privileges of the poor', had come to nothing. Vowles, a 'stout fat man about sixty years of age', had died of a fever, and his son came to Cadoxton to remove equipment and building stone, leaving 'poor workmen and others unpaid'.[48]

The sale catalogue of the Wenvoe estate reveals that half of Sheeping Moor—84 acres of pasture land—was held on lease by the trustees of Vowles's estate, with more than 40 years of the term unexpired.[49] Many small tenants had been deprived of access to valuable grazing, leaving some 56 acres of common land in Cadoxton; in addition it seems that labourers and their families had been attracted to the area to work on the ill-fated sea wall, settling in intakes on the common above Cadoxton village. The latter must have represented a considerable charge on the parish. Only Vowles's new mill, which was acquired after his death by the Wenvoe estate, may have been of positive benefit to the community. Nonetheless, this bold attempt to reshape the local landscape was not to be matched in its

potential impact until the first schemes to build a modern port at Barry were mooted a century later.

Barry Island

Vowles's ill-fated scheme had sought to build a barrier across the marshes between Barry Island and the mainland. What was the island itself like before the docks came? The Wenvoe estate map of 1762 gives a graphic picture of the island's appearance, its most prominent feature being Ostry Hill which faced St. Nicholas Church and Ostry Farm on the mainland, and overlooked Ostry Bay. On the eastern side of Ostry Hill were a farmhouse and three small fields, but the bulk of the island consisted of rough pasture, sand hills and marshy ground. In 1668 Philip Jones of Fonmon Castle, the island's owner, created a thousand-year lease of the property, which was granted to David Spencer, of Merthyr Dyfan, gentleman, with the reservation of a quarter of an acre of ground on the western side of the island should the Joneses wish to put up a cottage for a fowler.[50] David, his son, must have been a gentleman of some education, for he provided a graphic account of the island for the great antiquary, Edward Lhuyd, in the 1690s. This description suggests that the island in the 18th century was not being exploited to its full potential:

> it breeds very good cattle and sheep and there are plenty of rabbits on it. It is also good for corn, wheat, barley, and peas. Also good fishing belonging to it of plaice and soles and mullets and bass. Also good fowling on it.[51]

Whatever its potential as corn ground—and there is the evidence of ridge and furrow on Friars Point to indicate that during the Middle Ages corn was certainly grown on the island—by the end of the 18th century Barry Island was mainly being exploited for its rabbits and the fish around its shores. By this date control of the island was back in the hands of the Joneses of Fonmon. David Spencer's ultimate heir, Thomas Morgan, an excise officer, had sold the lease in 1748 to one Mr Bartholomew, which he in his turn sold to Sir Edmund Thomas of Wenvoe. In 1776 Peter Birt had assigned the residue of the lease to the Joneses. In the 18th and early 19th centuries, the island farm was in the hands of tenant farmers (the rent under the Joneses was £50 a year). In the 1760s the tenant became John Biss junior of Flat Holm, who captained a sloop belonging to 'Esquire Jones' of Fonmon. In 1765 the farmhouse was extended to accommodate Biss and his new wife.[52]

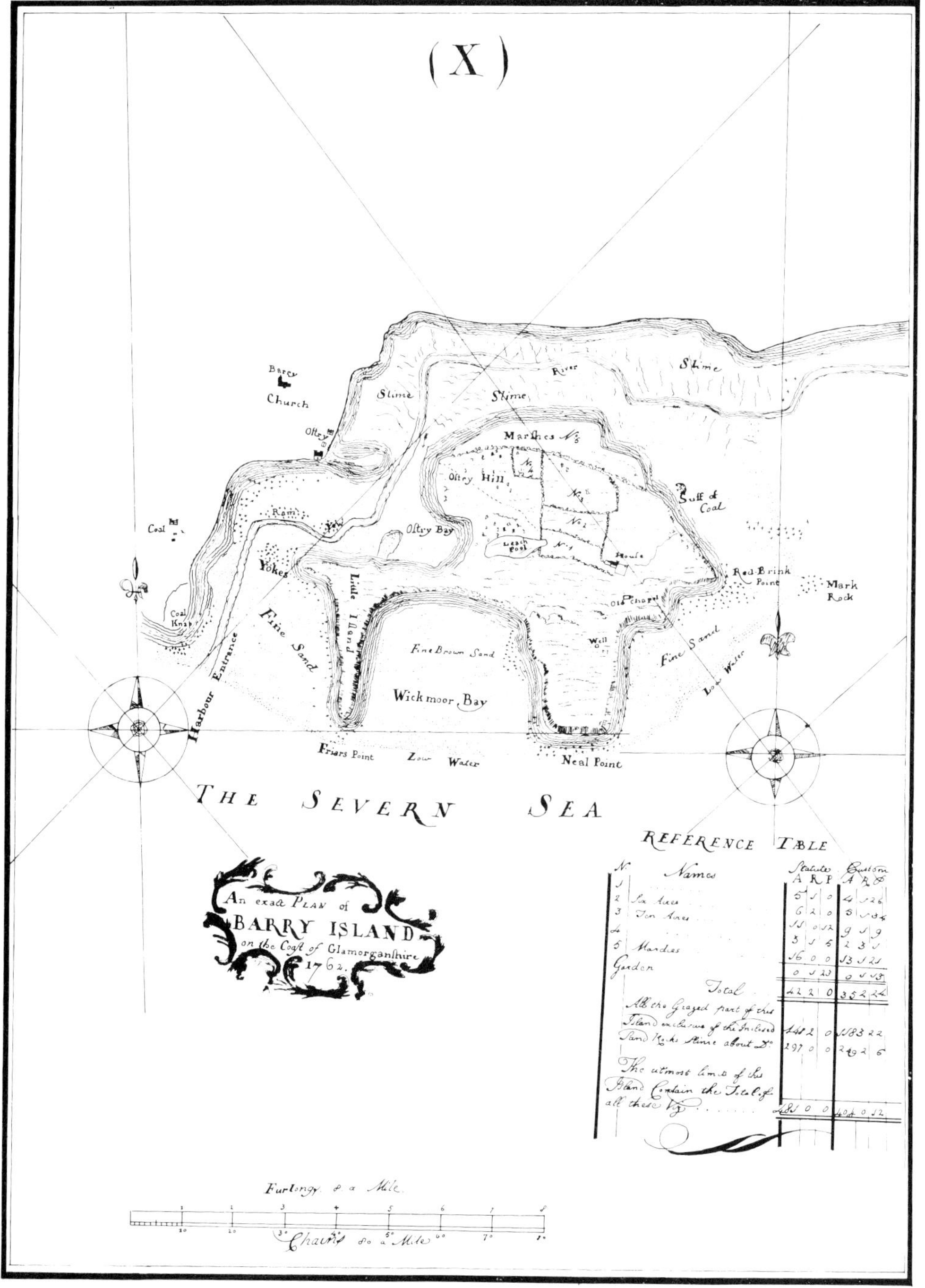

Fig. 58. Map of Barry Island in 1762, copied from original in Glamorgan Record Office. *H. J. Thomas.*

In the latter part of the 18th century the island was occasionally frequented by the 'pirates' and smugglers who haunted the channel, basing themselves on Lundy, but by 1804 the farmhouse took in lodgers who came for the sea-bathing—an increasingly fashionable cure—and the fishing. Barry's isolation prevented the island developing any great popularity—the Reverend J. Evans, in his *Tour of South Wales* (1804) pointed out that the absence of bathing machines made things difficult for 'delicate females'—but it was the potential of the island as a resort that Robert Oliver Jones stressed in 1856 when he put the island on the market, to be sold to Francis Crawshay of Merthyr for £3,200. It was Crawshay who, in 1858, built the Marine Hotel, now Friars Point House, for the more select Victorian visitor.[53]

The Mid-Victorian Community

We have now looked in detail at some of the changes that took place in the structure and management of landed estates in the Barry area in the 18th and 19th centuries. In great measure, it was the character of landownership in each parish that determined the evolution of the social structure and landscape and which explains why Cadoxton became such a different community from nearby Barry. Even in the mid 19th century, thirty years before the engineers and navvies arrived who were to fulfil David Davies's scheme to free ship and coal owners from the Bute monopoly at Cardiff Docks, a pattern of landownership which had its origins far back in the 12th and 13th centuries continued to shape the evolution of the three communities.[54]

Table 14. Merthyr Dyfan farms in the 1840s[a].

Tenant	Acreage	Name/location of farm	Landowner(s)
Will Williams	191	White Farm	Jenner
David Thomas	167	Walters Farm	Jenner/Glebe
Howell Thomas	130	Lower Pencoetre	Jenner
Job Thomas	120	Great Brynhill	Lee
John Morgan	97	Colcot Fach	Jenner
Robert John	94	Felonsway	Jenner
Thomas John	82	Colcot Mawr	Jenner/Jones
Thomas Thomas	79	Holton	Jenner
Jeremiah Richard	66[b]	Kupperd, Holton	Jenner
William Spickett	61	Rectory, Merthyr Dyfan	Jenner/Glebe
Evan Morgan	51	East Barry	Clive (Plymouth)
John Wild	46	Buttrills	Bassett/Jenner/Lee/Simms
Ann Hopkins	25	Clap y Dwndwr, Holton	Jenner/Glebe

[a] Based on the tithe apportionment [b] 150 acres in 1851 census

By the 1840s, there remained only three tenant farms in the parish of Barry. These were Cwm Barry, Castle Farm and the Ostry. Cold Knap (Cole Farm) was now managed as a home farm for the Romilly estate, and in 1851 its farmhouse accommodated two families, both headed by master mariners. In Merthyr Dyfan there were thirteen farms, ranging in size from White Farm with 191 acres, to John Wild's 46-acre farm at Buttrills (Ann Hopkins of Clap y Dwndwr, Holton, had only 25 acres in the parish, but

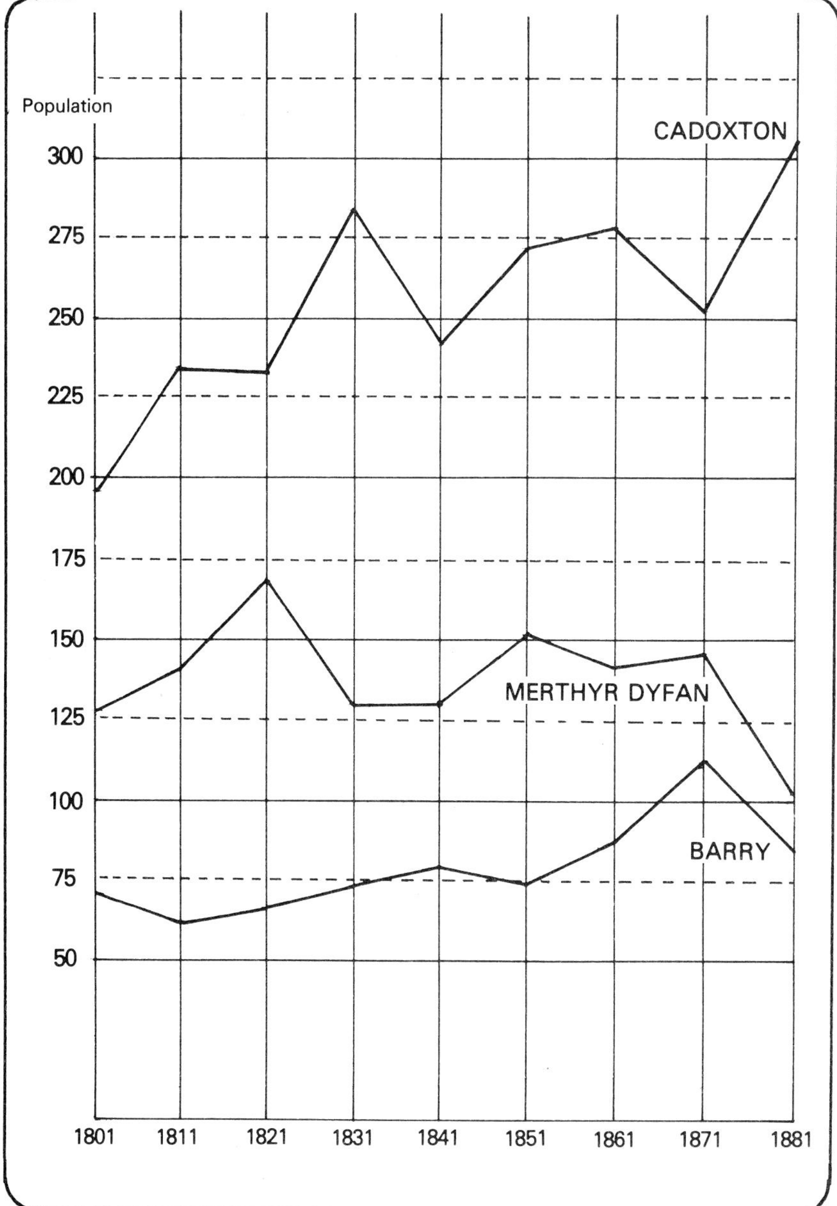

Fig. 59. Graph of local population in 19th century, from Census returns (figure for Merthyr Dyfan estimated). *M.G.*

this was managed jointly with her 34-acre Sweldon tenement in Cadoxton). Most of the farms in Merthyr Dyfan belonged to the Wenvoe estate. Farms in the parish were on average rather larger than elsewhere in the Vale at this date. In neighbouring St. Andrew's Major at the same date, the average was a more typical 61 acres, and only the 211-acre Biglis Farm could compare in size with either White Farm or Walters Farm. In addition, some smaller parcels of land were rented by farmers who did not live in the parish; the largest of these, 17 acres, was let to Jeremiah Davies by Jenner and Lee. Four other men rented parcels of less than ten acres. It is an easy matter to unravel the structure of the tenant farms in Merthyr Dyfan. The situation in Cadoxton was a good deal more complex; many farmers there rented land from more than one landlord and several might well also have owned land themselves. The following table attempts to describe the range of size of farms and the ownership of each tenement in the mid 19th century.

Table 15. Cadoxton farms in the 1840s and 1850s[a].

Tenant	Acreage	Name/location	Owner(s)
Thomas Thomas	120	Weston Farm	Jenner/Tho. Edwards & others
Eliz. Lowrie	88[b]	Old Mill	Jenner/Lee
Thomas Jenkins	84	Brooks Farm	Bassett/Lee/himself
Edward Greatrex	78	Court Land	Bassett/Lee/Treharne
Catherine Thomas	40	Witchill	herself
Rev. Gabriel Powell	38	Little Coldbrook (St. Andrew's)	Glebe/Jenner
Jeremiah Richards	34		Lee/Jenner
Ann Hopkins	34	Holton (M. Dyfan)[c]	Lee/Jenner
David Griffiths[d]	33		Lee/himself
Robert Spickett	30	Gibbonsdown	himself
Thomas Howell	28	Bowers	Miles Spickett
Thomas Spickett	26[e]	. . .	himself
Edward Williams	25	village	Lee/Jenner/Grace Roberts/Glebe
Will Stoddard	18	New Mill	Jenner
Thomas Harry	13	Wenvoe Arms	Glebe/Oddfellows/Jenner
Henry Kirby	10	Tŷ Verlon	Glebe/Britain

a Acreages based on the tithe apportionment

b 1861 census gives 221 acres

c Sweldon tenement; managed from Clap y Dwndwr, Holton

d Resident at the Three Bells in 1841, in 1851 at Pear Tree Cottage on Coldbrook Road, when he let the Three Bells to John Lowrie

e Land 'in hand' in the Tithe apportionment; in 1851 he farmed 40 acres and lived in Cadoxton village

This table is largely based on the tithe apportionment schedule, which also records that James Ball and Edward Jenkins were then lessees from the Wenvoe estate of an 88-acre moiety of Sheeping Moor, inter-commonable with St. Andrew's Major, and that there were 56 acres of common land in the parish, much of which was also on the Moors. It is this extensive area of grazing land which may explain the discrepancies between the figures for farm size derived from the tithe schedules and acreages given in the census enumerators' book: in 1861 William Lowrie's Old Mill Farm was said to have 221 acres, and William Stoddard of the New Mill claimed to farm 50 acres. It is quite possible, given the locations of these dwellings, that included in the larger acreages were extensive areas of rough grazing on the Moors. But whatever the difficulties associated with getting a precise idea of the size of farms, on balance Cadoxton farms were generally smaller than those in Merthyr Dyfan or Barry and, with an average area of approximately 34 acres, considerably smaller than was generally the case in the Vale by this date. The historic fragmentation of ownership in the parish, preventing the consolidation of holdings by a progressive gentleman landlord, must be the explanation for this difference between Cadoxton and

Fig. 60.
Plan of Highlight in 1767, copied from original in Glamorgan Record Office. There was little change in Highlight landscape after 1500. Little Brynhill Farm was probably established on former marginal land in 16th century.
H. J. Thomas.

its neighbours. A glance at Highlight completes this survey of the mid-19th century farms of the district. There the two farms in the extra-parochial district, Highlight (160 acres) and Little Brynhill (112 acres) were occupied in 1841 by Henry Richard and Thomas Morgan respectively.

Farming dominated the life of these rural communities, and the larger farmers ranked in status below the gentry and the clergy in the parish if any were resident. Most other folk were in some way dependent on the farmers for their livelihoods, whether as farm labourers or servants, or as providers of the services on which an agricultural community depended. In Barry, according to the 1851 census (which included the lodge in Cwmcidy) three households, as we have seen, were headed by farmers; six were headed by agricultural labourers working either on the tenant farms or directly employed by the Romilly estate, and the complement of thirteen household heads was made up by the two master mariners (one retired) who lived at Cold Knap, a gamekeeper and, living in Castle Cottage, Edward Thomas, described as a pilot and stone mason. Merthyr Dyfan had thirty households, as opposed to Barry's thirteen, and a total population of 130; twelve occupiers called themselves farmers and one, Edward Morgan of East Barry, stated that he was a 'land proprietor'.

The families of agricultural labourers made up the largest group in the population of Merthyr Dyfan; there were fourteen of these, fifteen if one includes in the same category Thomas Morgan of Church House, who described himself as a 'farm servant'. Thomas John, living at Stumphall, was a gamekeeper, presumably on the Wenvoe estate, while in Merthyr Dyfan lived Ann Jones, a farmer's widow. Cadoxton, the largest of the three villages, had 65 households in 1851 and a total population of 261. It was a community with a much wider range of occupations than Barry or Merthyr Dyfan and had craftsmen and tradesmen whose services must have been much sought after by Barry and Merthyr Dyfan folk. There were two thatchers, for example, Jacob Brook and William Herbert, two shoemakers, two carpenters, two blacksmiths, a butcher, a broom maker, a corker and a wheelwright. The parish had three public houses: the Wenvoe Arms, kept by Thomas Herbert; the King William IV, run by William Lewis; and the Three Bells, where John Lowrie was innkeeper. David Jenkins, aged 48, from Dinas Powys and Mary Jenkins, aged 54, born in Cadoxton, were carriers for the village, providing a rudimentary form of public transport and a delivery service for goods. These tradesmen accounted for twenty-one of the households in the parish. Sixteen of the remaining households were headed by farm labourers.

The effective leaders of the community were those who described themselves as farmers or 'proprietors of land'. This term is ambiguous for it seems to have carried rather more weight in people's minds than the simple 'farmer'. David Griffiths at Pear Tree Cottage said that he was a 'land proprietor of six acres', whereas he was more strictly a tenant farmer (renting land from the Lee family of the Mount, Dinas Powys) who, in addition, owned a few acres of freehold and a number of cottages in Cadoxton and Dinas Powys, including the Three Bells. The same description was adopted by two representatives of the Spickett family, who were freehold farmers; Miles Spickett, the 37-year-old proprietor of Bowers Farm, and Robert Spickett, twelve years his junior, of Gibbonsdown. Robert Jenkins of Golden Grove, 'proprietor of ten acres', was, on the other hand, not so much a farmer, more a small rentier who derived an important part of his income from the rents taken from the cottages and smallholdings his family had accumulated over the century since his great-grandfather, the 'extorter' William Jenkin, had arrived in Cadoxton in the 1740s. Indeed, it is unlikely that a man could have supported his family through the produce of a tenement smaller than 25 to 30 acres; and a number of the smaller farmers in Cadoxton must have had occupations other than farming that supplemented their incomes; probably they did this in the main by working part-time on the larger farms in the district. William Ellis described himself in the 1851 census return as a 'house carpenter, farmer and Greenwich pensioner' and, in so doing, he was perhaps being more honest about the reality of his status than some of his neighbours.

The Rector of Cadoxton who, in 1851, was the ailing Gabriel Powell,[55] lived just outside his parish at Little Coldbrook farm, and no Anglican clergyman was recorded in the Cadoxton census. Indeed, the only 'professional' person to be listed was a nonconformist preacher, John Williams, a native of Cadoxton, aged 63 in 1851. Although a National School had been established in the village in 1847, no schoolmaster was recorded on census night and it is probable that the school was supervised by Maria Greatrex, wife of the village butcher, who is listed on the census forms as a schoolmistress.

The 1851 census lists eight pauper households in Cadoxton. Perhaps surprisingly there was none in Barry or Merthyr Dyfan. William Miles, aged 66, described himself as a shoemaker and pauper—he may have been too infirm to make much of a living from his trade, with the result that he and his 42-year-old wife were partly dependent on the parish. The majority of the paupers, however, with the exception of Miles and 84-year-old Edward Harry, who was living with his aged wife Mary, were women, widows like Jane Brock, aged 73, who shared a house with her eleven-year-old granddaughter Mary, or Ann Llewelyn, 74, who had been born in Llancarfan and lived alone.

The largest households were those of the farmers, many of whom had domestic servants and farm labourers living alongside their families. One of the largest establishments in the district was that of Morgan Thomas, of Castle Farm in Barry, where he farmed 180 acres. Morgan was 49, his wife

47. At home with them they had three children; a 29-year-old son, Llewelyn, who must have been helping his father manage the farm; William, aged ten; and Ann Jane, aged six. Other children must have grown up and left home to work elsewhere. Sharing the house with the Thomases were two maid servants and three farm servants. One of the maids, Jane Edwards, aged 22, was Morgan's niece; the other was a 23-year-old Irish girl, Catherine Playne. Of the farm servants, John and Lewis Thomas were from Wenvoe, William Morgan from Llancarfan. The establishment at the Ostry was even larger. There were eleven folk living there in 1851, a widower, John Morgan and his ten children—seven sons and three daughters. With such a large family around him, Morgan perhaps had no need of servants, for his three eldest sons were of an age to help him on his farm, while his daughters looked after their domestic needs. It was usual to find one or two servants, however, on the larger farms. There were three at Cwm Barry in 1851, and they were to be found likewise in seven farming households in Merthyr Dyfan and in nine houses in Cadoxton. At Holton Farm, Jeremiah Richards had four servants. Both he and his wife Elizabeth were in their late seventies and it was probably their two unmarried sons, David (34) and Richard (31) who actually ran the farm. To assist on the farm were two living-in farm servants, eighteen-year-old John Thomas, and thirteen-year-old William Thomas, and there were also two girls, aged eighteen and eleven, to help keep house. As well as the two farm servants living in, Jeremiah employed four labourers on his 150-acre farm. In Cadoxton farms tended to be smaller

'ig. 61.
'iew of Cadoxton in
ıte 19th century.
'imon Prosser.

and, as a result, there were proportionately fewer servants living in their employers' households. There were seventeen living-in servants in thirty households in Merthyr Dyfan in 1851 but, in Cadoxton, only twelve in 65 households. However, it was not only farmers in Cadoxton who had resident servants, for they were to be found in the home of the butcher, Edward Greatrex; at the Three Bells; and in the household of a shoemaker, Philip Thomas. Otherwise, there were servants at Old Mill Farm; with Robert Spickett at Gibbonsdown; in William Stoddard's household at the New Mill; at Weston Farm, with Thomas Thomas; at Sea View, on Elizabeth Thomas's 35-acre farm; and with Sarah Lowrie, a farmer's wife, whose husband was absent from the parish when the census was taken. Weston Farm housed the largest number. Thomas Thomas, who was 33, and his wife Mary, one year his junior, had probably not been married very long, for they had only one child, ten-month-old Thomas. With no older children in the family to help manage house and farm it was necessary to employ labour and so the farmhouse also accommodated one maidservant, Ann John from Dinas Powys, and three farm servants: William Hughes and William Beagann, both Monmouthshire-born; and an Irish lad, Patrick Clerington.

Households that did not have living-in servants may well nonetheless have employed domestic help, for quite a number of younger folk still living in the parents' homes in Cadoxton were described as servants. Probably some worked not in Cadoxton, but in Merthyr Dyfan, Dinas Powys or Sully; others may have been out of work at the time of the census, but nonetheless gave 'servant' as their occupation. Catherine, the 38-year-old daughter of David Griffiths of Pear Tree cottage, one of the farmers of the parish, was a 'house servant'. Margery and Elizabeth Williams, 35 and 32 years old respectively, daughters of the preacher John Williams, were house servants, his son Isiah a farm labourer. Thomas Morris the pig drover had four adult children living with him, all unmarried. His two daughters worked as domestic servants, his sons as farm labourers.

A feature of 17th- and early 18th-century society in the Barry district was the permanency with which local families occupied the same houses, farms and cottages over several generations. By the middle of the 19th century families were much more mobile. In 1851, not one of the thirteen heads of household in Barry parish had actually been born in the parish. Nearest to Barry in their origins were an agricultural labourer, James John, and the pilot and stone-mason, Edward Thomas of Castle Cottage, both of whom were from Porthkerry. John Morgan of the Ostry and William Richards of Cwm Barry were Cadoxton-born. The remaining householders came from further afield. David Evans, who kept the Ship Inn in the old Storehouse, was from Llancarfan; Morgan Thomas of Castle Farm was from Pendoylan; and Thomas Hopkin, a farm labourer, from Llantwit Major. Of the two master mariners at Cold Knap cottage, William Parker was Monmouthshire-born, and Henry Thomas from Llanarth in Cardiganshire. Also from west Wales were James Lewis, a labourer from Laugharne, and John Williams, another farm worker, from Llandeilo. David Bailey, 33, farm labourer, was from Yeovil in Wiltshire.

In the larger parish of Merthyr Dyfan only six heads of household were natives. The majority had their origins elsewhere in the county, nine of the 30 householders having been born virtually on the doorstep, in Barry or Cadoxton, another twelve having come from parishes in the eastern Vale, within ten miles or so of Merthyr Dyfan. Only two had migrated from outside the county: Edward Morgan of East Barry, who was from Brecknock, and a labourer, Abraham Billet, from over the water in Somerset. There was a stronger tendency amongst Cadoxton heads of households to have been born in that parish; this was true in 23 out of 65 cases in 1851. But even here, folk native to the parish were in a decided minority. As in Merthyr Dyfan, a large proportion of outsiders had not travelled very far to settle in Cadoxton, but fourteen family heads had come a greater distance. Apart from the seven household heads who seemed to know only that they had been born in Glamorgan, Thomas Bevan, a 63-year-old thatcher, had come from Monmouthshire, while Edward Greatrex, a retired farmer, and father of the village butcher, was from Brecknockshire, and a farm labourer, John Williams, from Carmarthen. From across the Bristol Channel had come George Pain, a young labourer from Somerset, and the Cornish cork-cutter, Joseph Pears. William Stoddard, miller and farmer at the New Mill, was Scots by birth, and Edmund Flaherty, a labourer, from Ireland.

One must, therefore, not be misled by romantic notions of rural seclusion to imagine that the community in the mid 19th century was anything but highly mobile, even if, until mid-century at least, most movement was over a comparatively short distance. These migrants from near and far had taken the place of others who had quit the district. By this date farmers typically moved from place to place and from farm to farm at fairly frequent intervals. This was certainly true of local farming families and of farmers elsewhere in the Vale of Glamorgan. Farmers were no longer tied down by long leases to particular farms; short leases and tenancies at will enabled them to move from farm to farm according to their family circumstances. Often this might only mean that a man would take up a different holding on the same estate, but sometimes a longer distance might be travelled if a suitable tenancy became vacant. Morgan Thomas of Castle Farm, Barry, for example, had been born in Pendoylan; he had married a girl from Merthyr Dyfan, but it was in Pendoylan that his eldest son was born, about 1822. Thomas had arrived in Barry by 1840 and it was there that his two youngest children had their birth-place. Nearby, at Cwm Barry Farm, was

ig. 62.
almer's Cottage,
:wm Barry.
imon Prosser.

the family of William Richards. Richard was Cadoxton-born, had married a Barry girl, Sarah, and had four children. The two elder children, Richard, seven and Henry, six, had been born neither in Cadoxton nor Barry, but in Merthyr Dyfan. At Felonsway farm, in Merthyr Dyfan, in 1851, lived Robert John. He was 51 and had been born in Sully. His wife was three years younger, from St. Fagans. When they were first married, they had settled first in Llandaff, for it was there, in about 1828, that their daughter Mary was born, and their sons John and Edward. The family's move to Merthyr Dyfan took place in 1832 or 1833, between the births of Edward and Elizabeth, aged 19 and 18 respectively in 1851.

It was not only farmers who were on the move. If anything farmers were the most stable group in the population. Sons and daughters from all classes in the community had to move away to find work. Had it been normal for children to find work in their home parishes, the local population in the mid 19th century would have been much higher. Young men would leave to find work on a farm, to follow a trade in another village, or to try their luck in Cardiff or in the coalfield. Girls would quit the parish to go into service or to marry. The losses represented by these *émigrés* were partly made up by immigrants and by the 1850s, the eastern Vale was increasingly attractive to settlers from the west of England, west Wales, and Ireland. Overpopulation and agricultural depression had driven down agricultural wages in the West Country and in west Wales, stimulating distress that had found expression in rick-burning and in the Rebecca Riots. In Ireland the potato famine of the 1840s had set a nation on the move. While vast numbers of Irish emigrants sought a new life in the United States, others entered west Wales through the small ports of Cardigan and Pembroke and, finding little work there, drifted eastwards towards Glamorgan. Here wages were higher on the land, for the growth of the coal industry and its attendant docks and railways had pulled local folk away from the land, and farmers were forced to raise wages to attract labourers. In the Barry district all three parishes attracted such wanderers. Despite this influx of newcomers, however, the population of Cadoxton remained relatively stable, rising from 242 in 1841 to 282 twenty years later, falling again to 249 by 1871, but reaching 303 in 1881, the last census before industrialisation.

Merthyr Dyfan's population grew very little during the same period, from 128 to 145. Surprisingly, it was Barry, historically the smallest village of the three, that was to exhibit marked growth. This growth was due to the new building undertaken by the children of Sir Samuel Romilly, co-owners of the estate, after 1857. By the early 1870s Barry had twenty-two households, and St. Nicholas church was being rebuilt to accommodate an enlarged congregation.

Between 1857 and 1865 the Romillys seem to have been intent on remodelling Barry as an estate village; their building activity can be followed

g. 63.
rd Romilly's
lging house, Barry.
non Prosser.

in the time book of the Porthkerry estate,[56] which records payments to labourers employed on various agricultural and building tasks. A new cottage was put up in 1857, to be followed by a 'lodging house' for Sir John Romilly (*b.* 1802), son of Sir Samuel, afterwards Lord Romilly of Barry. This was built between 1857 and 1859 on the east side of the present St. Nicholas Road, just below its junction with Canon Street. Between 1859 and 1865 three coastguard cottages were built nearby, on the later site of All Saints' Church in Park Road. 1860 to 1862 saw new building going on apace. Barry's first shop was built in fashionable mock-Tudor style on the corner of St. Nicholas Road and Old Village Road in 1861—it is now an off licence. On the adjacent plot four labourers' cottages, modelled on the earlier Jordan's cottage, and given a deliberately quaint and rustic appearance with their thatched roofs and porches, were put up, and at the same time the estate commissioned the thatched Ship Inn, to replace the public house which had been kept in the 16th-century Storehouse nearby on the Harbour. To the north of the old village, in Cwm Barry, the Romillys built a cottage for their gamekeeper, George Palmer, and by 1865, Barry House, commissioned by Sir Samuel Romilly's sixth son, Col. Frederick, an intimate of the Prime Minister, John Russell, who is known to have spent his summer holidays there, stood opposite Lord John's lodging house on St. Nicholas Road. The last house to be built in 'old Barry', before the advent of the docks and the laying out of the new town, was Harbour Cottage, in Harbour Road, between 1871 and 1874.

As a result of this new building, by 1871 Barry's population was nearly 100, living in nineteen houses and cottages, with two unoccupied. As in 1851, few residents had actually been born in Barry. Catherine Green, who kept the village shop, was from Brecknock. Of the two coastguard boatmen who lived in the new cottages in Park Road, one, John Cashman, was from County Cork; his colleague, Isiah Parkman, had been born in Devonport. The birthplaces of his children show that he had lived in Ireland in the 1850s, moving by about 1864 to Lynmouth in north Devon, arriving in Barry subsequent to the birth of his youngest son George, who was two years of age at the time of the 1871 census. William Wilson, the Porthkerry estate's bailiff at Cold Knap farm, was a Scot; the Romillys' gamekeeper was from Northamptonshire. Alongside the village shop, Barry could now boast a boot and shoemaker, 37-year-old Evan Jenkin, from Cadoxton. The Ship was now kept by Edward Thomas, the former pilot who had lived at Castle Cottage, now in his 70s. While the Morgans still held the tenancy of the Ostry, Castle Farm was rented by Cadoxton-born John Morgan, Cwm Barry by a Sully man, Edmund John and his family.

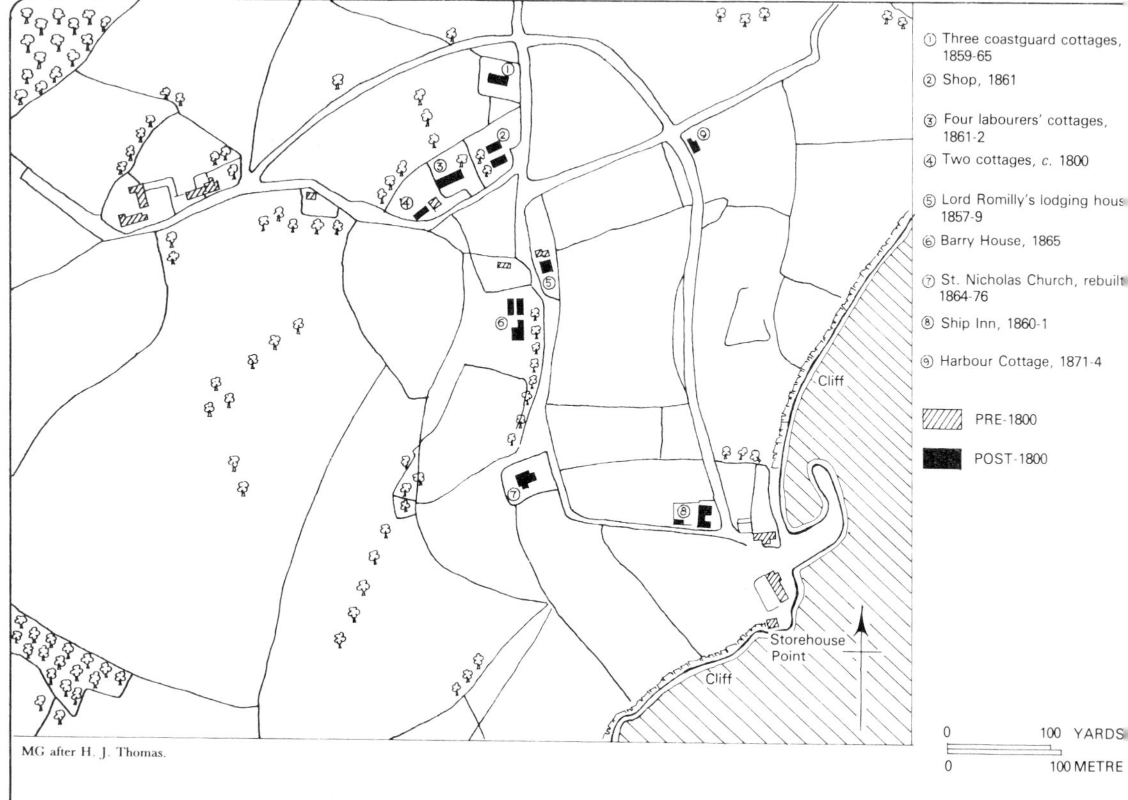

Fig. 64. Map of buildings in Barry before dock ar railway development

g. 65.
arry House.
mon Prosser.

Compared with events in Barry in the 1850s and 1860s, the major changes in Merthyr Dyfan and Cadoxton during these years can be briefly summarised. Chief amongst them was the continuing percolation of families and individual migrants from England and Ireland into the community, further diluting the ranks of those who could claim ancient ties with the district, and foreshadowing that much more massive migration that was to occur with the beginning of dock and railway construction in 1884. By 1871 there were four Irish families in Merthyr Dyfan, all headed by farm labourers; George Jones, who had taken over Buttrills Farm from the Wilde family, was a Middlesex man, and another West Country family had entered the parish, with John Murley. The birthplaces of his children illustrate how workers on the land would move from parish to parish in search of work. Murley, who was 48, had crossed the channel sometime before 1860, when he married a girl from Monknash; their first child, Mary, was born there in 1860 or 1861. Their second child, eight-year-old John, had been born after the family moved to Porthkerry. The next child, David, who was six in 1871, was born in Penmark parish, Margaret, three, in Porthkerry, and three-month-old Edward in Merthyr Dyfan. Two of the Irish families, the Kellys and the Driscols, had similarly moved more than once in recent years. Michael Kelly, 50 in 1871, had married his wife Joanna in Ireland, but by 1856, when their son Patrick (Patsy in the census) was born, they lived in Cardiff, moving to Sully the following year, where two more sons were born, and only subsequently to Merthyr Dyfan. Meanwhile, Merthyr Dyfan, like Barry, had acquired its first shop, a grocer's kept by Mary Matthews in Beggarswell cottage, not far from Cwm Barry Farm. The 1871 census also records that a new house was being built at the Buttrills.

Cadoxton in 1871 retained families like the Brocks, Jenkinses, Morgans, Griffithses, and Spicketts who had been resident there over several generations—one or two, like the Spicketts, since before 1750. However, families whose heads had been born in Cadoxton were very much in the minority—only 18 out of 67. Amongst the newcomers were names that will be familiar to many present-day Barrians, such as the Triggs—of Sussex origin—and a Somerset family, the Dunscombes. There were eleven English families in the village by 1871, four from Ireland, and two from west Wales. Robert Day, for example, was from Wells in Somerset, his wife from Beyford in the same county. He must have been one of those who had sought work for better wages in the Vale than he could find on the farms of his native county. Other migrants came for different reasons. Living with Daniel Bailey at Swiers cottage was one of Cadoxton's first policemen, 26-year-old John Allison from Magor in Monmouthshire. At Acrewell House lived the family of Joshua Barstow, the district highway surveyor, a Yorkshireman, while at Pleasant View had settled a Cardiff accountant, William Johnston Jones.

Fig. 66.
The Ship Inn, Barry
Simon Prosser.

g. 67.
hatched dwellings,
ld Village Road,
arry.
mon Prosser.

In 1871 the majority of the local population in Cadoxton, Barry, and Merthyr Dyfan, still worked on the land, or earned their living as craftsmen or tradesmen, but there is no doubt that by the 1870s, the Welshness of the community, which had been reasserted by the revival of the language in the district in the 18th century, was under assault. This was now a highly mobile population; better roads and the new railways—Cardiff was linked to London by Brunel's Great Western—had put Victorian people on the move and no longer need folk remain pinned, save in cases of dire necessity, to a corner of their native county. In 1891, the *South Wales Star*, from its offices in Vere Street, Cadoxton, wrote of the former village as a place of 'peaceful calm—a Sleepy Hollow, which a Rip van Winkle would not know in its metamorphosed state, when the only strangers were a few Cardiff folks who came to the garden of Wales for its fruit and flowers'.[57] The sentimental journalist should have known better than to indulge in such a romance. It was easy for a middle-class writer to make the mistake of thinking that a place of thatched and whitewashed cottages was a peaceful retreat from the busy world. But life on the land was always hard and unrewarding for the majority of people; many of the villagers in Barry, Merthyr Dyfan and Cadoxton had travelled a long and difficult road to find somewhere to earn their living. They were no more divorced from the unpleasant realities and harsh social values of Victorian Britain than a denizen of Merthyr Tydfil, Manchester or Glasgow. Even before industrialisation, the people of the Barry district had few real roots in the historic community; often they were as much strangers to the locality as the labourers and shopkeepers who flooded into the area in the 1880s.

A new era opened on 14th November, 1884, when a group of ship- and mine-owners trudged out to Castleland Point—near the later Docks Offices—to dig a small hole in the ground with the aid of a ceremonial spade, a wheelbarrow and a plentiful supply of planking to keep the autumn mud off their shoes. Modern Barry had begun.

1. Based on the summary statistics in *Census of Great Britain, 1851. Population tables* (1852), pp. 21-2.
2. Brian Ll. James, 'The Vale of Glamorgan, 1780-1850: a study in social history with special reference to the ownership and occupation of the land' (University of Wales (Cardiff) M.A. thesis, 1971), pp. 42, 48; Philip Jenkins, *The making of a ruling class* (Cambridge, 1983), pp. 38-41, 51.
3. *Ibid.*, p. 51.
4. GRO, D/DF vol. 50 (1749 rental).
5. GRO, Fonmon Deeds 714, 694.
6. GRO, unscheduled copy of court roll, Barry manor, 19 May 1719; D/DF vol. 50; Fonmon Deeds, 405 (1686), 707 (1750).
7. Joanna Martin, 'The landed estate in Glamorganshire *circa* 1660 to 1760' (University of Cambridge Ph.D. thesis, 1978), p. 56.
8. *Ibid.*, pp. 61-70, 72-3, 121-2; GRO, D/DF vol. 50; D/DF vol. 53 (1775-6); NLW, Coleman Deeds, DD 909; Cardiff Central Library MS. 4.1164 (1831); GRO, LTA/DP (Barry 1831); Private Act of Parliament, 4 George IV, c. 22 (1823).
9. B. E. Vyner and S. Wrathmell, 'The deserted village of Wrinstone, South Glamorgan', *Trans. Cardiff Naturalists Society*, XCVIII (1974-76), pp. 21-3.
10. NLW, Coleman Deeds, DD 909.
11. Patrick Medd, *Romilly* (1968), p. 247. Sir Samuel's son built Porthkerry House *c.* 1834: James, thesis, p. 58, n. 46.
12. H. J. Thomas, 'Cwmcidy—a lost farmstead', *Morgannwg*, XVII (1973), pp. 64-5; 'Cwmcidy', *ibid.*, XVIII (1974), pp. 77-9.
13. GRO, microfilm copies of census enumerators' books, 1841, 1851.
14. GRO, D/D Pl 1, map 23.
15. GRO, D/D We 1.
16. James, thesis, p. 44.
17. Brian Ll. James, 'Contributions towards a history of Wenvoe Castle', *Trans. Cardiff Naturalists' Society*, XCVIII (1974-76), p. 7; GRO, D/D Xqg (Wenvoe sale catalogue, 1769).
18. Historical Manuscripts Commission, *Report on the manuscripts of the Earl of Verulam* (1906), p. 255.
19. Brian Ll. James, 'Contributions towards a history of Wenvoe Castle', p. 7.
20. *Ibid.*, p. 11, citing Cardiff Central Library MS 4.877, the diary of William Thomas of Michaelston-super-Ely (hereafter cited as WTD), September 1774.
21. Brian Ll. James, 'Contributions towards a history of Wenvoe Castle', pp. 12-13.
22. GRO, D/D Xqg.
23. GRO, D/D We 2.
24. James, thesis, p. 44; Brian C. Luxton, 'Barry', in *South Glamorgan: a county history*, ed. Stewart Williams (Barry, 1975), pp. 143-4.
25. Som. RO, DD/PO 32/8, 17, 30, 34, 64, 71, 72, 81.
26. NLW, 4/308.
27. Som. RO, DD/PO 11; D/D Pot 134.
28. NLW, LL/PR: Wills of Miles Spickett, 18 October 1762 (d. 1761); Miles Spickett, 13 December 1781; Elizabeth Spickett, 19 September 1794 (d. 1783); James, thesis, p. 76.
29. GRO, LTA/DP *passim.*
30. NLW, Tithe plan and apportionment, Merthyr Dyfan.
31. NLW, Tithe plan and apportionment, Cadoxton-juxta-Barry.
32. NLW, LL/PR: Wills of Ann Griffiths (27 February 1828) and Robert Jenkins (23 June 1812).
33. GRO, D/D Pl. 1, map 23.
34. See notes 15 and 23 above.
35. WTD, 12 September 1767.
36. Calculation based on tithe apportionment schedules.
37. WTD, 11 September 1766.

38 NLW, LL/PR: Inventory of Arnold Hawkins of Barry, 1 October 1766.

39 WTD, 28 June 1767.

40 Frank Emery, 'The mechanics of innovation: clover cultivation in Wales before 1750', *Journal of Historical Geography*, II (1976), p. 44; Martin, thesis, pp. 103-4, 114-6.

41 *Cf.* the painting of Coldbrook Road made in 1899 by J. C. Fairbairn, formerly in the possession of this writer's parents, reproduced as plate 26 in Brian Luxton, *Old Barry in photographs*, vol. II (Barry, 1978).

42 Martin thesis, pp. 121-2.

43 GRO, D/D Xge 74/4/3.

44 See above, p. 151.

45 Brian Luxton, *A history of the old village church, Cadoxton-juxta-Barry* (Barry, 1980), pp. 39-40.

46 Ieuan Gwynedd Jones, *The Religious Census of 1851: a calendar of the returns relating to Wales*, I, *South Wales* (Cardiff, 1976), *sub* Glamorgan, Cadoxton-juxta-Barry.

47 Som. RO, DD/PO 32/77.

48 WTD, entries *passim,* 25 August 1762 to October 1766.

49 GRO, D/D Xqg.

50 Frances Wilmoth, 'Some documents relating to Barry Island', in *Annual Report of the Glamorgan Archivist 1981*, pp. 21-3.

51 R. H. Morris (ed.), *Parochialia*, etc. (1911), III, pp. 73-4.

52 WTD, March, 1765.

53 Wilmoth, *art. cit.*

54 The following account is based on the census enumerators' books for 1841, 1851, 1861 and 1871 for Barry, Merthyr Dyfan and Cadoxton, and on the tithe apportionments.

55 Mathew Griffiths, *Portrait of a parish* (Cardiff, 1980), p. 35.

56 GRO, D/DX im 1-4/1-30; additional information supplied by Howard J. Thomas.

57 Cited in Brian Luxton, 'Photographs of old Barry', in *Glamorgan Historian*, VII, ed. S. Williams (Cowbridge, 1971), pp. 149-50.

Plate XVI. Dock No. 1 at Barry in *c.* 1960, showing ships moored in tier, with part of 'Mothball Fleet'. *Welsh Industrial & Maritime*

CHAPTER VI

The Port and Railways of Barry

IORWERTH W. PROTHERO

arry Railway
ompany button.
mon Prosser.

THE choice of Barry as a site for docks was due to the existence just off the coast of an island, almost a mile in length and up to half a mile in breadth. Two headlands pointed seawards—Nell's (or Neal's) Point on the east and Friars (or Treharne's) Point on the west; between them lay Whitmore Bay, a huge expanse of sand. Between the Island and the mainland was the shallow Barry Sound, protected from the prevailing south-westerly winds by the Island itself and the configuration of the coast. The western end had served as the harbour and port of Barry for centuries, and considerable trade—coastwise, cross-channel and overseas—had been carried on. However, the Bristol Channel, in common with other long and tapering estuaries, was subject to a considerable range of tide, at Barry more than thirty feet (nine metres). Thus any dock in the vicinity of Barry would operate better if enclosed and fitted with gates.

The site chosen was in Barry Sound, where the natural hollow would reduce the amount of excavation needed, as well as the cost. The work was protected by dams, which were used as causeways for roads joining the Island to the mainland. The area eventually enclosed was occupied by two docks, an entrance basin, a deep-water lock (the Lady Windsor Lock), three graving docks, a partly-levelled area south of the New Dock, an eastern timber pond and a western feeder pond (the last-named was filled in after 1945 and is now used as a car-park). North of the dock area a system of rail approaches led to coal hoists (or 'tips') on the dockside for loading coal into the holds of ships. A passenger railway line served three town stations—Cadoxton, Barry Dock and Barry. It continued to the Island, where there were eventually two stations, the further situated at a pierhead inside the western breakwater. Much of the western end of the Sound was left open to the sea as a tidal harbour for small craft.

The mining and export of coal in South Wales

The South Wales coalfield extends from Blaenavon in Gwent to Milford Haven in Dyfed. It covers about 750 square miles in a long band, which is up to 16 miles wide. No pit was ever more than twenty-five miles from a port, and there were falling gradients to the sea, which made haulage by rail economical. Over twenty valleys each had at least one railway connected with at least three ports. Until the 1930s most colliery companies were small; for instance, in 1924 each company had an average of two pits. By the 1980s in South Wales the situation was transformed: in 1947 there were 214 pits, all privately owned; by 1984 there were only 28, all owned by the State, and some of these were expected to close before long.[1]

Two kinds of coal are mined in South Wales—anthracite and bituminous coal. Anthracite is mined mainly west of Glynneath. It is hard, and lends itself to slow combustion over a long period; it can heat houses, but needs a special stove to control the intake of oxygen. Bituminous coal is found in the eastern part of the coalfield and has many varieties, each with a special quality and use. Some coke well for iron working, some make good house coal, others produce gas successfully for lighting, heating and cooking. Welsh 'steam coals' were excellent for maintaining pressure in the boilers of marine steam engines, since they needed little attention and left little ash. Crack liners, warships and express railway trains used steam coals because of their smokeless quality. In the early days they were about 6*d.* a ton dearer than other bituminous coals, and ordinary ships would mix steam coal with cheaper varieties.

Until the middle of the 18th century most Welsh coal was mined in the anthracite areas, but when the Government forbade the felling of woods to make charcoal for smelting iron ore, the iron works turned to coal of the more combustible kind, which could be turned into coke as a substitute for charcoal. There were many places in the uplands of Gwent and Glamorgan where the necessary raw materials for producing iron were to be found: iron ore, coal, limestone and fireclay, together with running water to supply power. By 1820 every valley east of Rhondda had ironworks. Roads, tramroads and canals were constructed to move raw materials and finished products. The expansion of industry and commerce led to an enormous demand for steam-produced energy all over the world. The coal was cheap to mine and cheap to carry by sea; links were needed between the mines and the coast.

Canals had been first in the field. Already in 1794 the Glamorganshire Canal Company had opened a canal from Merthyr Tydfil to the mouth of the Taff at Cardiff, followed by a branch from Abercynon to Aberdare in 1812. Until the 1850s canal trade was considerable because dues were low and barges often conveyed goods both ways. But demand for coal exports was increasing, and greater capacity and speed were required of the hauliers. Railways developed apace and connected the pits to the ports.

Trade through Cardiff was growing, and the main landowner there, the second Marquess of Bute, decided to make a dock at the mouth of the Taff. Under Acts of 1830 and 1834 he built at his own expense the Bute West Dock or the 'Bute Ship Canal', which was opened in 1839. The port was served by the Taff Vale Railway, which reached Abercynon in 1840 and Merthyr in 1841. Coal shipments increased rapidly in the 1850s in response to foreign demand. More docks had to be made: Bute East Dock, Bute Tidal Harbour and Roath Basin. This work was put in hand by the Bute Trustees, because the second Marquess had died in 1848, when his heir was only one year old. Congestion at the port continued, and in 1874 the third Marquess obtained an Act to make yet another dock at Cardiff. However, he failed to proceed with the dock, and this led others to formulate a scheme for a dock at Barry in 1876 (which also did not materialise).

Just to the west of Cardiff at Penarth, where the Ely river came down to the sea, there was another possible site for a dock. The Penarth Harbour, Dock and Railway Company was formed, and opened Penarth Harbour in 1859, and the Dock in 1865, with a narrow-gauge connection to the Taff Vale line at Radyr, proceeding *via* Grangetown and Fairwater. This

late XVII.
.. end of Barry Island nd Barry Sound, from nainland before 1884, howing site of future ock.
. Beaudette Coll.

undertaking was worked by the Taff Vale Company under leases, though the Penarth Company kept its separate identity.

The 1865 scheme for a dock at Barry

In a letter to the *Cardiff and Merthyr Guardian* of 3rd August, 1861, John Thomas, a retired farmer of Barry Island, then residing at Barry, proposed a Glamorgan Coast Railroad starting at Pencoed, near Bridgend, and taking in Llansannor, Cowbridge, Aberthaw, Barry, and finally Cogan, which lay on the Penarth Dock/Grangetown line, then under construction. This was to be on the 'narrow' or 'standard' gauge for rolling stock with wheels 4 feet 8½ inches apart (there was also a 'broad' gauge of 7 feet, used by the Great Western and the Ely Valley Railway Companies). Thomas also advocated examining a site at Barry for a dock, which would develop imports of hay, grain and vegetables for the mining districts and exports of coal, iron manufactures and limestone.

Farmer Thomas was not the only person to think of Barry as a site for a dock. It occurred to certain railway promoters at the time. Tracing the idea requires a little background information on railway development. The engineer in charge of the Great Western tracks from Grange Court in Gloucestershire to Llantrisant Station was H. Voss; he was also Engineer to and Manager of the Ely Valley Railway Company. This Company had leased its lines to the Great Western. In 1863 the Great Western had absorbed the South Wales Railway Company, which had constructed the broad-gauge main line between Chepstow in Monmouthshire and Neyland in Pembrokeshire.

The Ogmore Valley Railway Company, incorporated in 1863 to make a narrow-gauge route to Porthcawl Dock, wished to increase its revenue by carrying coal destined for shipment at Cardiff and Penarth Docks. It projected a narrow-gauge line from Blackmill (Melin Ddu) at the end of the Ogmore Valley to the Ely Valley line at Gellirhaidd, a few miles north of Llantrisant Station, and proposed laying a third rail inside the existing broad-gauge track to take narrow-gauge wagons on to a junction with a line projected to join existing lines near Radyr, seven miles north-west of Cardiff. Thereupon Voss, wishing to divert this traffic over his lines, asked the Great Western Railway Company to lay a third rail inside the broad-gauge track between Gellirhaidd and Cardiff. But that Company refused to do so. Then Voss and J. Pyne suggested to Captain Jenner, of Wenvoe Castle near Barry, that he should consider making a dock at Barry, which would become the largest in its district, and connecting it by rail to Peterston on the main South Wales line a few miles east of Llantrisant Station. [2] Pyne was Land Agent to the Ely Valley Railway Company and to one of its Directors, Sir Ivor Guest, who owned the manor of Sully, near Barry, as well as a large estate in Dorset.

However, both Voss and the Great Western Company had second thoughts. Voss persuaded his own Ely Valley Company to deposit a Bill to make the narrow-gauge connection between Blackmill and Gellirhaidd and lay a third rail between Gellirhaidd and Llantrisant Station. He told the Court of Referees, a body appointed by the House of Commons to examine the engineering aspects of Railway Bills, that the Great Western Company positively intended to lay a third rail from Llantrisant Station to Cardiff. The Court of Referees rejected this Bill.

Jenner took up Voss's and Pyne's suggestion regarding a dock at Barry and a connection there, expecting that Parliament would eventually sanction some narrow-gauge connection between the Ogmore valley and Llantrisant Station. With Sir Ivor Guest, J. I. W. Fredericks (a landowner near Glynneath), J. Pyne, J. P. Treharne (a landowner north of Bridgend) and a Jenner brother, Captain Jenner obtained an Act in 1865 to make a narrow-gauge line from Peterston, on the main South Wales (broad-gauge) line eight miles west of Cardiff, through Wenvoe to terminate at the site a little east of the present Barry Dock Station. There was to be a short line off it to Warren Tump (a landmark since demolished) for the benefit of Guest, who wished to develop Sully for residences.

The Act empowered the Great Western Railway Company to work the proposed lines, that is, to provide staff and rolling stock, and if desired, to lay a third rail *outside* the Barry track to take broad-gauge rolling stock. There was provision also for a third rail to be laid *inside* the track of the main South Wales railway line between Newport and Llantrisant. It was left to a later Act to make Grangetown/Cardiff and Cogan/Cadoxton narrow-gauge lines; this would be necessary to allow passengers and coal to be brought to Barry from east Glamorgan and Monmouthshire. Traffic from the Rhondda, Aberdare and Merthyr valleys could leave the Taff Vale line at Radyr and reach Cogan over the narrow-gauge line of the Penarth Harbour, Dock and Railway Company *via* Fairwater, and thence over the main South Wales line at Ely and through Grangetown. Gauge ceased to be a problem only in 1872, when the Great Western converted its lines in South Wales to the narrow gauge, which became standard.

Jenner's schemes were completed by three Acts in 1866. The Barry Railway Alteration Act sanctioned diverting the 1865 line to obtain better gradients, and lengthening it to what is now the north-west corner of the Old Dock. The Barry Railway Extension Act authorised a narrow-gauge line off the Altered line at Cadoxton to join the Grangetown/Penarth Dock line at Cogan, which had opened on 10th June, 1865. The Grangetown/Cardiff connection was left out of this Act, because the Great Western included it in its own 1866 Act; the line was ready by May 1876. The Barry Company claimed that it intended bringing only visitors over its Cadoxton/Cogan line; Barry Island was very popular with Cardiff people in the 1860s. The above lines were planned by the Barry Company's engineers—H. Bolden and J. Tolmè.

The third Act of 1866 was the Barry Harbour Act, which authorised another company to make a 600-yard quay (preferred to an enclosed dock, because it would be cheaper), extending from where the Buttrills brook now enters the Old Dock to near the present north-west end of that dock. The channel of the Cadoxton River, which then entered the sea at Cold Knap, was to be deepened to allow large ships to reach the quay; a breakwater was to be made in the harbour (where the present one lies).

The 1866 Barry Harbour Act was promoted by Jenner, Fredericks, J. E. Powles, and S. E. Bolden; the last-named was Chairman of the Powell Duffryn Steam Coal Company and, like Guest, a Director of the Barry Railway Company. Other promoters were J. Balcombe, owner of lead mines near Aberystwyth, and J. P. Seddon, an architect. Seddon and his partner, J. Prichard, were the Llandaff Diocesan Architects; they had restored the Cathedral and various churches and built hotels, schools and schoolhouses. Seddon designed a hotel at Aberystwyth for Savin, the railway contractor, which was later to house the University College. Seddon was known as the leading 'Gothicist' of his day. He knew the Pre-Raphaelites and his life-long friend, D. G. Rossetti, poet and painter, died at Seddon's cottage at Birchington, Kent. Seddon obtained commissions for William Morris and Burne Jones to design stained-glass windows for Llandaff Cathedral, and for Rossetti to carve sedilia and paint the triptych 'The Seed of David' as a reredos there. He formed the Barry Building Company to buy Barry Island for the development of residences, but the plan was never realised, because none of Jenner's lines were ever laid.

The Ely and Vale of Neath Railway Bill, promoted by Ebenezer Lewis and David Davies, was connected with Jenner's schemes. It proposed narrow-gauge lines from their pits at Treherbert and Treorchy (due to open in 1866) to the Ely Valley Railway's broad-gauge line near Tonyrefail, and it sought power to lay a third rail inside that company's track to Llantrisant Station. The aim would be to reach a narrow-gauge port at Barry. However, the Bill was withdrawn in February 1866.

The Barry Railway Company offered its Ordinary Shares to the public in 1866, but the crash of Gurney, Overend and Co.—the Bankers' Bank—in May 1866 triggered a financial panic that lasted all the year. The Barry Company sold only £13,000 worth of the £160,000 of shares offered, and nearly all of that to Jenner. David Davies was saved from bankruptcy only because his own bank's deposits had been withdrawn a week before the crash.

The Barry Railway Company had made an agreement with Seddon's Company to construct a railway and a road across Barry Sound to the

Island. To forestall the objection of Francis Crawshay, owner of Barry Island, Jenner had bought the Island from him in November 1865.[3] On 31 May 1867 a Board of Trade Order (No. 580) was obtained to make a line $1\frac{1}{2}$ miles long off the Barry Railway Company's authorised Altered Peterston/Barry line, near the site of the present Cadoxton Station; it was to terminate where the present breakwater of the Old Harbour begins. The line was to be carried by a 150-yard wooden, stream-pile viaduct with seventeen permanent openings and one swing opening over the Cadoxton River. This river rises near Dinas Powys Castle and used to enter the sea at Cold Knap, but an Act of 1886 authorised its diversion to enter the sea where it does today—near the Bendrick rock.

ate XVIII.
. end of Barry
and, showing Friars
oint, from Old
illage Road on
ainland in *c.* 1897,
fore development of
omilly Park.
Beaudette Coll.

The only work done on Jenner's lines was to stake them out and fence them; offices were erected on Cadoxton Common. Although an Act was obtained in 1868 to extend the completion date of the lines to 1871 (the date for the Harbour was 1873), there was no life left in Jenner's schemes. In 1870 R. Price Williams and one of the Barry Company's engineers, J. Tolmè, met the Taff Vale Company's Board and proposed a scheme for a railway from Bridgend to Barry, but the Board refused to help. A railway and dock of some kind was certainly expected in the locality. This is clear from a petition of the Barry Parish churchwardens in 1872 to build a new and larger St. Nicholas church.[4]

It became clear to Jenner that no effective support for his scheme was forthcoming. The passing of the Bute Dock Act in 1874 must have been the last straw for him. An additional dock at Cardiff could cater for the increasing tonnages of coal requiring shipment. In August 1874 he petitioned to have the Barry Railway Company wound up, and this was achieved in November. Presumably the Barry Harbour Company was wound up at the same time.

Jenner's schemes failed because they did not attract support from the coal trade, which preferred to ship coal from Cardiff, where the colliery companies' and coal merchants' businesses were located. They also preferred that Lord Bute should spend his money on providing dock accommodation there. As a combination of commercial, property and recreational development, Jenner's schemes were truly impressive. Had support been forthcoming, Barry would have had narrow-gauge rail connections with most pits in east Glamorgan and Monmouthshire, Barry Island would have become a residential area and high-class seaside resort and there would have been easy access from Cardiff for both long- and short-stay visitors to the Island. This attractive prospect came to nothing.

The 1876 scheme for a dock at Barry

The Plymouth Estate Trustees (later the Windsor Estate Trustees) now enter the story. They administered huge estates in Shropshire and Glamorgan, particularly in the Merthyr, Aberdare and Rhymney Valleys and in Llandough-juxta-Penarth, Grangetown, Penarth, Lavernock and Sully. Robert Henry Clive, grandson of Clive of India, was also involved, since he had married the younger daughter of the fifth Earl of Plymouth. The Trustees decided to extend the Grangetown/Penarth Dock line from Cogan through Penarth to Barry Island, in order to develop their own coastal property, Sir Ivor Guest's at Sully and John Davies Treharne's at Barry Island, for residences. However, the huge cost of the last mile decided the Trustees to end the line below where Cadoxton Station now stands, and they called their Bill the Penarth, Sully and Cadoxton Railway Bill. Guest withdrew, because the Taff Vale Company, which was to work the line by supplying staff and rolling stock, offered too low a sum for doing so. Treharne also withdrew, no doubt because the line was now to end too far from Barry Island. He had bought the Island at an auction in July 1873 from the United Kingdom Insurance Company, Jenner's mortgagees.[5] He was a native of Pentre, Rhondda, and owned a coal mine; he was also a chemist at Cardiff.

The Trustees went on alone and obtained the renamed Penarth Extension Railway Act in 1876; they made the Cogan/Penarth Town line privately and opened it on 20 February 1878. The Taff Vale Railway Company worked it and ran passenger services into Cardiff over the Cogan/Grangetown line, which they had leased from the Penarth Harbour, Dock and Railway Company; from Grangetown, traffic used the Great Western Company's line, which had been completed by May 1876. The arrival of the railway at Penarth Town resulted in the development of Penarth by the Windsor Estate as a residential area and seaside resort.

Having decided to promote another railway to Barry Island, Treharne went on to develop the place. He made an iron jetty on Friars Point (taken down in the 1890s because it was unsafe) and enlarged Francis Crawshay's eccentric residence, known as the Marine Hotel, by adding a large dining room; he renamed it the Pier Hotel. It was later demolished by Lord Windsor. There was a regular service of brakes (wagonettes) between Cardiff and the Ship Hotel on the mainland, and Treharne provided a boat to ferry visitors to the Island when the tide was in. In the summer of 1876 over 12,000 visitors were brought to the Island in this way.

ate XIX.
arry Island as it ight have been: ustration of development envisaged in sale talogue of 1877.
lamorgan Record Office.

In August of the same year Treharne leased the surface of the Island to S. A. Tylke, a Cardiff insurance broker, on condition that he formed a company to develop the Island. The next month Tylke registered the Barry Island Company Limited. The lease reserved land for Treharne to make docks, roads, a tramroad and a railway station. The particulars accompanying the Notice of Sale of the Island on 11 October 1877 included a remarkable development plan for the Island, including houses, roads, places of worship, ten croquet lawns, a bowling green, archery butts, a lake, a music conservatory and a bandstand. Space was also allocated for a warehouse, a railway station and for docks.

In Cardiff pressure was being exerted on Lord Bute to proceed with the construction of the large Roath Dock, authorised by his 1874 Bute Dock Act. In reply to a request made by the Cardiff Chamber of Commerce in May 1876, Lord Bute replied in November, refusing to take action. He no doubt wished to delay any Barry Dock Bill and prevent it from being deposited in time for consideration by Parliament in 1877, as he did later in 1881.

There followed much activity. A deputation, which included Treharne and Riches, asked the Great Western Directors to support a scheme to make a dock at Barry, but the Board was non-committal. Then Treharne, Jenner and Lewis Williams deposited the plans of the 1866 Barry Railway Alteration Act to make a Peterston/Barry line. Williams owned a foundry in Cardiff and his wife was part-owner of East Barry Farm. Treharne and Jenner deposited plans of the works of the 1866 Barry Harbour Act. J. S. Gibbon, R. Basset, W. Bruce and R. Michell, the last a Great Western Company Director, deposited plans of an Ely and Rhondda Valley Junction Railway Bill to extend the Ely and Clydach line to Treherbert. With a back-shunt there, coal from the Rhondda Fawr pits would thus reach Barry *via* Tonyrefail, Llantrisant Station and Peterston. Gibbon was Chairman of the Ely Valley Railway Company and owned the Trecastle estate in the upper Ely Valley, as well as land at Cadoxton and St. Andrew's, near Dinas Powys. Gibbonsdown at Barry had been named after an ancestor of his.

Then Treharne, Gibbon and Tylke deposited the Penarth, Sully and Barry Railway Bill to extend the Cogan/Penarth Town line, when completed, to the Austry farm (earlier spelled 'Ostry'), which used to lie to the east of the Ship Hotel, Barry. By 18 November 1876 Forrest, the Windsor Estate Agent, heard that Brown and Adams, the Windsor Mineral Agents, had been asked to make a dock at Barry, and he wrote that he feared for the future of Penarth Docks, in which the Windsor family had a large interest. Treharne must have given Brown and Adams this commission.

However, by the end of November, Brown and Adams had asked H. M. Brunel, the younger son of the great Isambard Kingdom Brunel, to take over their commission to make the dock at Barry, as well as the Barry/Peterston line of the 1866 Barry Railway Alteration Act. The request had been conveyed by Adams, a friend of H. M. Brunel. Presumably Adams wished to avoid a charge of disloyalty to the Windsor Trustees, whose agent he was, for a dock at Barry would be a threat to the prosperity of Penarth Docks.

Brunel accepted Adams's invitation and within days planned an enclosed dock of 70 acres with 20 tips or staithes. With Treharne, J. O. Riches and Jenner, he held talks with the Great Western Board and some Rhondda coal-owners, including David Davies and Archibald Hood, with a view to financing all the schemes. The Board agreed to construct the Peterston/Barry line of the 1866 Act—but only after the money to make the dock had been found. Both the Great Western Directors and the coal-owners refused to take up any Deferred Shares in the Company which was to make the dock. Since no money could be found, all these schemes collapsed; but Barry was now known to offer a fine site for a dock. An editorial in the *South Wales Daily News* on 23 November 1876 lauded its advantages and prophesied that, were a dock to be made there, it would prove a formidable competitor to Cardiff. In the summer of 1882, when asked to report to the Freighters' Association at Cardiff on five possible sites for a dock outside Cardiff, unsurprisingly, it was Barry that Brunel recommended.

Treharne still wanted to develop Barry Island, and for this a rail connection with Cardiff was essential. In 1877, with Gibbon and Tylke, he obtained the Penarth, Sully and Barry Railway Act to extend the Cogan/Penarth line, then under construction, to a site at Barry opposite the Ship Hotel. The Taff Vale Company agreed to work it and to pay annually a sum based on a percentage of construction costs. But T. J. Evans, a Brecon banker, and part-owner of East Barry Farm, stood out for $\frac{1}{2}$% more. Then disasters struck: a depression overtook the iron and steel industry, a Welsh bank crashed and a mine in which Tylke was interested was flooded. Everyone lost heart and no shares were offered. The Penarth, Sully and Barry Railway Act was abandoned by Act in 1881.

Treharne decided to sell the freehold of Barry Island, but he failed to do so at an auction in October 1877. The Windsor Estate saw its chance to prevent a dock being made at Barry, and through Lady Mary Clive, mother of Lord Windsor, it bought Barry Island in January 1878,[6] and she conveyed it to her son when he came of age later the same year. He eventually became the first Earl of Plymouth of the second creation in December 1905.

Tylke now wanted to sell his lease of Barry Island, and offered it, together with Brunel's plans for a dock, to several parties, including David Davies. He succeeded in selling it in the summer of 1878 to the Windsor Estate, thus in effect giving that estate a vested interest in the future development of a dock at Barry. Had this not happened, Lord Windsor would probably have joined the fierce Bute and Taff Vale opposition to the next Bill to make a dock at Barry in 1884, and this too would have been rejected. It is to be noted that David Davies certainly knew of Barry's potential in 1876 and was acquainted with Brunel's plans. So a dock at Barry remained a dream until 1881, when colliery owners, mostly from the Rhondda Valleys, decided to put up the money to make one.

The 1884 Barry Dock and Railways Act

In spite of all the legal and parliamentary activity described above, and the efforts of landowners, entrepreneurs and contractors, the facilities available at Cardiff and Penarth for the export of coal in the early 1880s were still quite insufficient. New pits were coming into operation, especially in the Rhondda Valleys, and by 1880 coal from over two hundred pits was pouring down to Cardiff Docks. The depression in the iron industry forced iron companies which had their own mines to sell their coal as they took their blast furnaces out of operation. One important reason for the congestion at Cardiff Docks was the insufficiency of railway sidings; this resulted in coal wagons being stored on access lines, which were often blocked for hours. Ships had to wait longer than really necessary, and heavy demurrage charges were incurred. Wagons were mostly owned by the colliery companies and bore their own distinctive company names; if the return of empty wagons was held up, pits would often have to stop mining.

Note has already been taken of efforts made to persuade Lord Bute to increase the capacity at Cardiff Docks. In October 1880 a joint committee was set up by Cardiff Corporation and Cardiff Chamber of Commerce to hold talks with Lord Bute about selling or leasing his docks and about making another dock. In December a sub-committee of six was set up, including Archibald Hood, Rhondda Fawr coalowner, Rees Jones, Mayor of Cardiff, and J. O. Riches, President of the Cardiff Chamber of Commerce (Jones and Riches were fellow Directors of David Davies). Lord Bute indicated that he intended to retain possession of his docks and would make another one only if he could increase his revenue thereby and reduce his working costs. He had decided to make a smaller one than that provided for in his 1874 Act. Hood insisted on the larger dock and the charges authorised by the 1874 Act, and the talks broke down. In his report early in October 1881 to the Cardiff Chamber of Commerce, Riches said that if the colliery owners could not have facilities at Cardiff Docks on satisfactory terms, they would go elsewhere,[7] and he hinted that an important measure was in preparation, doubtless a Barry Dock Bill.

It is not certain who took the decision in 1881 to go ahead with a fresh scheme for a dock at Barry. David Davies of Llandinam usually receives the credit, but a statement made by Hood some years after indicated that Davies had at first been a little disinclined 'to join us',[8] fearing that intense opposition was to be expected; nevertheless he had later worked hard for the scheme and supplied a large amount of capital. It is possible to conclude that it was not Davies who originated the Barry Dock scheme in 1881, but that the credit belongs to Hood and probably Riches. These two had been prominent in every attempt after 1872 to have another dock made at or outside Cardiff.

ig. 68.
. *Farrow*
ter I. W. P.

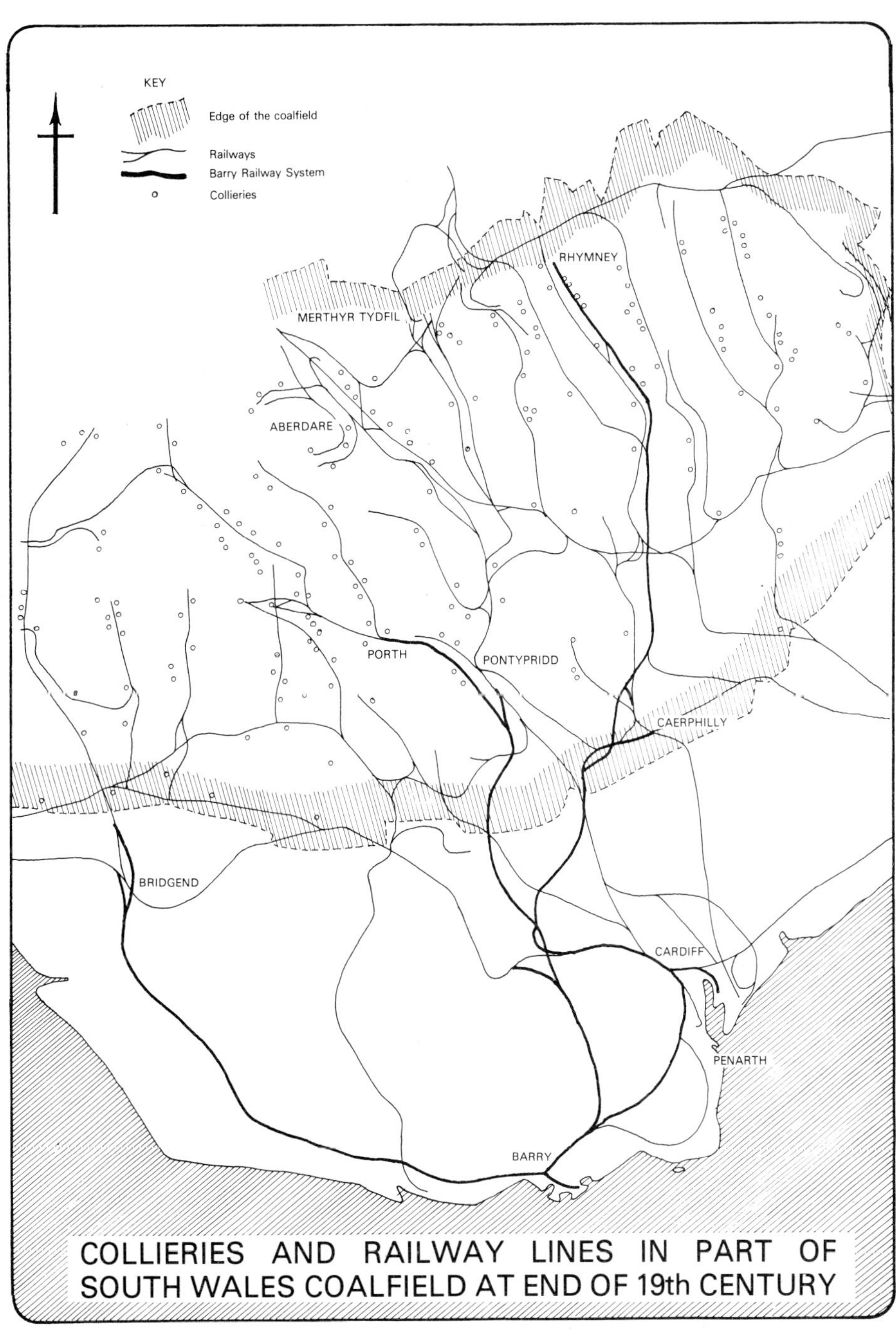

COLLIERIES AND RAILWAY LINES IN PART OF SOUTH WALES COALFIELD AT END OF 19th CENTURY

Various considerations influenced the Barry Dock promoters. A Roath Dock at Cardiff and a dock at Barry could together easily cope for many years with the huge increase expected in coal tonnages requiring shipment. A Barry company with its own rail connections could fix its own rates for hauling coal to Barry and undercut those to Cardiff. Rhondda coal-owners were paying over a penny a ton more than coal-owners in other valleys for having their coal hauled to Cardiff. New dock machinery, low dock charges and quick despatch of ships would persuade shipowners to use Barry. This was why the support of the Cardiff Shipowners Association was important for the success of Barry Dock, and much of the credit for enlisting this support must be given to T. R. Thompson, a Cardiff shipowner and one of the leading promoters of the Barry Dock scheme.

Another consideration was the revenue which would be earned from hauling coal from rail-heads north of Barry: there was Trehafod eighteen miles away, Treforest fifteen, and Peterston eight. The companies of David Davies, Archibald Hood and Lewis Davis were already sending coal to Cardiff and Penarth Docks by the Taff Vale Railway, for which they paid nearly £200,000 annually, of which at least half was profit for the railway company. If half this business could be diverted to a Barry concern, the £50,000 profit could be applied to paying the interest at 4% on the capital sum of £1¼ million to be borrowed, almost enough to make the dock and railway system at Barry.

The question 'why choose a site at Barry?' was answered by Hood in 1883 in the Lords Committee which considered the Barry Dock and Railways Bill: 'We were desirous of having a dock as near Cardiff as possible, but in a position in which we would not take any of Lord Bute's land'.[9] In fact, both Hood and Riches knew the worth of a site at Barry because in 1876 they had studied Brunel's plans and reports regarding a possible dock at Barry in preparation for talks designed to raise the capital. They must also have read an enthusiastic editorial in the *South Wales Daily News* on 23rd November that year on the advantages of a dock at Barry. A further point was that the sea had already done much of the work of excavation at Barry, while a site on Windsor land at Grangetown, for example, would require an enormous amount of excavation and embanking; moreover, in that location the Taff Vale Company would receive all the profits from hauling coal.

The Windsor Estate had in 1877 and 1880 tried to persuade the Taff Vale Company to make a dock on Windsor land on the estuary between Penarth and Grangetown, but the Company would agree only to support, not deposit, a Bill to extend the existing Penarth Dock. Such an Act was obtained in 1881 and the extension opened in 1884. The Taff Vale Company never made a dock, because it believed that it would then have to pay heavy damages for breaking a covenant in its agreement of December 1849 with the Bute Trustees to lease most of the eastern quay of Bute West

Dock to erect tips; that covenant bound it to do its best to ensure that goods carried over its lines for shipment should use a Bute dock. Another covenant bound it to make up to the Bute Trustees any lost revenue from goods shipped or unloaded at a Taff Vale dock instead of a Bute dock. It was thus inevitable that a Taff Vale dock would operate at a loss.

ate XX.
ortrait of The Right on. the Earl of ymouth, P.C., .B., M.A., J.P., .L. (formerly Lord Vindsor).
harter Souvenir.

It was a curious twist of fate that the purchase of Barry Island by the Windsor Estate in 1878, designed to prevent a dock from being made there, actually facilitated it in the end. Lord Windsor must have been disappointed when Lord Bute refused his offer of land at Grangetown for a new dock in 1881, and now that only Hood's group was interested in using Windsor land for docks, it was hard for Lord Windsor to avoid offering the use of the Island, even if the new project would be in competition with his interests at Penarth.

Hood's group now had the assurance of land for the dock, and they asked Brown and Adams to prepare plans. In the autumn of 1881 an impressive group of promoters assembled on the Island to perambulate it with Adams's plans. There were David Davies, his son Edward, J. O. Riches and W. Jenkins (all fellow Company Directors), R. Forrest and Adams himself (both Windsor Agents). A significant decision was made—to move the entrance to their proposed dock from the west of the Island to the east.

Plate XXI.
Portrait of Archibald Hood, J.P.
Glamorgan Record Office.

The essence of the situation now was an intense rivalry between the promoters of two separate schemes—Lord Bute planning an additional dock at Cardiff, and Hood and Davies planning a new enterprise at Barry. Each would have to be embodied in a Bill to be approved by Parliament, and it by no means followed that Parliament would approve two measures in quick succession for docks in the Cardiff area. The Barry Bill was delayed until the location of the Cardiff dock was known; this turned out to be east of the Roath basin and smaller than expected.[10]

The Rhymney Railway Company, almost wholly a Bute undertaking, then tried to forestall the Barry scheme by asking Lord Windsor for terms for leasing Barry Island and for his support of a Cardiff/Barry Island line proposed by the Rhymney Company.[11] This company did lodge a Bill to make railway lines, but not one to Barry Island, from which it may be concluded that Lord Windsor' support was not forthcoming.

Hood's group continued its efforts and was joined by T. R. Thompson, a Cardiff shipowner (after whom Thompson Street in Barry was later named). He had said that the Barry scheme was the greatest he had ever known, and told one Cardiff shipowner that he expected dividends of 15% and 20%. Thompson was a brilliant businessman and his judgement was sufficient to elicit support for the scheme from other Cardiff shipowners.

Lord Bute's Dock Bill came before Parliament in 1882 and, predictably, David Davies, Hood and Lewis Davis led a fierce opposition to it, claiming that the proposed dock would be too small to cure congestion at Cardiff and that the new charges were excessive. A particular bone of contention was an additional charge of a penny a ton, comprising up to ½*d.* a ton payable on coal, coke, culm and metal ores carried on the lines at Cardiff Docks, and up to ½*d.* a ton for shunting and other services provided by Lord Bute. From this penny charge originated the saying 'Barry was built for a penny'. But nevertheless, the Bute Dock Act became law and the Roath Dock was opened in 1887. The new penny-a-ton charge was authorised, but was later given up by Lord Bute. The Act also attempted to improve operating practices by directing the railway companies to haul loaded coal wagons direct to the tips or the sidings, instead of leaving them at fixed points for Bute locomotives to take over.

Meanwhile efforts were continuing on the Barry venture. Hood's group usually called the 'Freighters', asked for fresh reports on the site and sought agreements with various parties who would be affected. Customers were secured by an agreement with the companies of the leading Freighters to charge ½*d.* per ton per mile for hauling coal to Barry; the companies would send tonnages equal to those they would send to Cardiff and Penarth Docks combined. In November 1882 the promoters signed Heads of Agreement with local landowners: Lord Windsor, R. F. L. Jenner (Wenvoe Castle), the Romilly Estate and Lewis Williams and T. J. Evans (East Barry Farm). They were to receive £1 15*s.* 0*d.* per acre *per annum* as rent, and royalties of ½*d.* per ton on minerals and building materials shipped or landed there, as well as 5% of receipts from other traffic, including passengers. Provision was made for a station at Barry.

The Barry Dock and Railways Bill came before Parliament in 1883. It passed the Commons Committee but was rejected by the Lords. Naturally, the Bute Counsel denied that another dock was necessary, claiming that coal output and demand would soon stabilise and that the Barry scheme was a selfish one, designed to divert trade from others. In fairness to the Lords, it has to be recorded that there had been a plethora of Acts relating to South Wales: the Pontypridd, Caerphilly and Newport Railway Act (1878), the Penarth Dock Extension Act (1881), the Rhondda and Swansea Bay Railway and the Bute Dock Acts (1882), the Ogmore Dock and Railway Act (1883) and the Taff Vale Company's agreement with the Bute Trustees to make sidings at Crockerbton, Cardiff (1883). It was to be expected that their combined effect would alleviate congestion at Cardiff in some way or another.

The promoters of the Barry Bill were undaunted. Lord Windsor's Agent, Forrest, wrote to J. W. Barry, engineer to the promoters, saying that the sooner the Barry scheme were revived the better for 'all our friends'.[12] Forrest had learned from David Davies that the promoters of the Ogmore Dock and Railway Company were offering to extend their proposed line at Ewenny to Davies's Ocean Company pits at Treorchy and haul his coal to Ogmore for the same advantageous rate of ½*d.* per ton per mile. This would clearly pose a threat to the Barry scheme. Forrest realised that this might be the last chance to use Windsor land for a dock, and he seems to have dissuaded Davies from negotiating with the Ogmore Company, since its extension plan was never embodied in a bill.

The Ogmore Company then turned to the Great Western Railway Company for support, but without success. It looked as if the fortunes of the Ogmore Company would revive in 1888, when Colonel J. T. North, the 'Nitrate King', of Chile, became its Vice-Chairman, but North was persuaded to withdraw from the Ogmore scheme by Forster Brown, an engineer of the Barry Company, and support a scheme for a line from Barry to Bridgend and Coity instead. In December 1888 North's Navigation Syndicate deposited the Vale of Glamorgan Railway Bill, which became law the following year. The Ogmore Company had been outsmarted; it abandoned its undertaking in 1891.

But the above episode anticipates the Barry story. The Barry Dock and Railways Bill again came before Parliament in 1884 and again was fiercely opposed. But this time it was successfully passed, and received the Royal Assent on 14 August 1884. The Act authorised the construction of a dock at Barry with rail connections to the Great Western and Taff Vale systems. The Barry system was to comprise the following. The main line was to run *via* Cadoxton to join the Taff Vale main line at Treforest. At Tonteg Junction, a mile south of Treforest, a branch was to go *via* Pontypridd to the Taff Vale's Rhondda line at Trehafod, near Porth. At Drope, a mile north of Wenvoe, a branch was to go north-west to Peterston on the main South Wales line. At Tynycaeau, a mile further north, a branch was to curl south under the Barry main line to St. Fagans Station on the main South Wales line, to enable the Barry Company to operate a passenger service from its own Pontypridd station—the Graig—to Clarence Road, Cardiff (this service operated between 1897 and 1962). A branch was authorised from Creigiau to join the line of the Penarth Harbour, Dock and Railway Company, near Radyr, but it was never made.

The Barry Company had secured a very advantageous position for itself. Other companies would have to undertake the expensive work of collecting coal wagons from the pits and would leave them at junctions for hauling to Barry. They would also return the wagons to the pits of origin. In other words, the Barry Company would simply have to haul trains of wagons, already assembled, on uninterrupted runs to Barry, and return them empty to their respective junctions.

The 1884 Act also provided for the making of roads: a public road, later named Island Road, was to lead along the authorised dock to the Island; another would be made from the eastern end of the authorised dock to join a road from Weston Hill, Cadoxton; the Company was also to remake the Cadoxton/Biglis/Dinas Powys road as far as Eastbrook Cottage.

At last the stage was set for the ceremony which would proclaim to the whole world that Barry Dock and Railways were becoming a physical reality. On 14 November 1884 a select group of dignitaries and industrialists, some dressed in top hats and frock coats, solemnly assembled on Castleland Point, where Lord Windsor cut the first sod, followed by David Davies, who cut two more. Only three months had passed since the passing of the Act, and regardless of the approaching winter, work was beginning on the construction of great dams to contain and drain the area of the Sound so that work could go forward on the docks themselves, free of tidal interference. This was the beginning of the new Barry, the event commemorated in 1984, one hundred years to the day.

ate XXII. ommemorative edallion distributed y Barry Dock and ailways Company on pening of Barry ock in 1889. *ational Museum of Vales.*

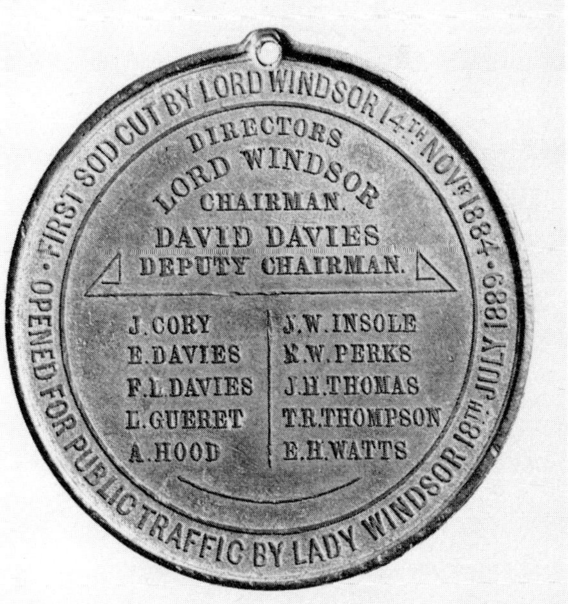

Plate XXIII.
Lord Windsor (later Earl of Plymouth) holds spade to cut first sod of Barry Dock on Castleland Point in 1884.
Glamorgan Record Office

The main engineering works of the Barry undertaking at this stage were the Old Dock, the Wenvoe and Tonteg tunnels, the viaduct over the Ely at St. George's and the viaduct over the main South Wales line near St. Fagans. The Engineer-in-charge was John Wolfe Barry (a happy coincidence of name); he was the Windsor Estate Engineer, and had already prepared the Penarth Town development plan in the 1870s. His partner was H. M. Brunel and his other colleagues were T. F. Brown, G. F. Adams (replaced on his death in 1884 by I. T. Rees) and J. W. Szlumper; the last-named was responsible for the Tonteg/Trehafod section of the lines, having been engineer on all David Davies's lines since 1861. Ultimately a total of 108 miles of track was laid. Contractors were involved on a large scale: T. W. Walker was responsible for the dock itself and for the lines to Saint-y-nyll, north of St. Fagans; he was contractor for the Penarth Dock Extension of 1884 and was about to finish making the Severn Tunnel. Lovat and Shaw made the lines from Saint-y-nyll to Treforest, and J. McKay & Son the section from Tonteg to Trehafod.

David Davies of Llandinam

It is worth pausing a moment to consider the role of David Davies. His name has tended to dominate accounts of the 1884 scheme, to the detriment of the reputations of others involved. Others before him had tried to make a dock at Barry—Jenner in 1866, and Treharne, Tylke and Riches in 1876; their efforts had at least made known the potential of Barry. Hood and Riches had made strenuous attempts from 1872 to obtain more dock accommodation. Lord Windsor's eventual support was important, both for its effect on other landowners and for reducing opposition to the 1884 Bill.

David Davies did not take the initiative in the decision of 1881 that led to the making of the first dock at Barry. The decision seems to have been due to Hood and Riches. Both were looking for lower haulage charges and were opposed to higher dock charges. They knew that in the existing situation the Taff Vale Railway Company was taking the cream of the profits from conveying coal between pit and port. They could see the logic of setting up another company in competition. They were, however, soon joined by Davies, and this might have been why Hood allowed talks between his sub-committee and the Bute Agents to break down in 1881.

Nor did Davies take the initiative, apparently, to redeposit the Barry Bill in 1883; this move seems to have been mainly due to Forrest. On the other hand, Davies gave impressive evidence in favour of the Barry Bills in 1883 and 1884. But had the issue depended on Davies alone, it is more likely that there would have been a dock at Ogmore instead. Yet in the long term the advantages of Barry were so patent that they were bound to lead to some group or another making a dock there.

late XXIV.
ortrait of David
avies of Llandinam.
lamorgan Record Office.

David Davies has gone down in Welsh history as something of a folk hero. He rose to fame from humble origins and founded a dynasty that has contributed richly to Welsh life in many spheres. He made one fortune as a railway contractor and another as a colliery owner. He was a brilliant businessman and leader, but a leader of equals. As Deputy-Chairman of the Barry Company, he guided it through its early years with his great experience, a particular advantage because the Chairman, Lord Windsor, was only 27 years of age when the Company began. Davies radiated confidence and infected all with his determination to make the Barry venture the great success that it turned out to be. His name was synonymous with Ocean Coal, and his wagons would be seen by the hundred in the docks to be. But his interests went beyond business: he was Member of Parliament for Cardigan Boroughs from 1874 to 1887.

His memorial in Barry is a statue, erected by the Barry Company in front of the Dock Offices, not far from where the first sod was cut in 1884.[13] There he is shown pondering over the plans for the Docks. His native village of Llandinam in old Montgomeryshire remembers him with a copy of the same statue, standing at the roadside not far from the youthful Severn on its circuitous course to the Bristol Channel. It is curious that the town of Barry has never commemorated him in any way.

Plate XXV. Dock No. 1 under construction. *I.W.P. Coll.*

ate XXVI.
ock No. 1 nearing
mpletion.
'elsh Industrial &
'aritime Museum.

The first dock at Barry

Barry Dock was to be the largest in the country—73 acres in extent. The area affected between the Island and the mainland was about 200 acres. The construction of the first dock (later to be known as the Old Dock) posed one special problem. Deep mud made it impossible to find a satisfactory foundation for the southern quay, and land on the Island had to be cut back to provide firm ground. It was a blessing in disguise, because the water area of the dock was thereby increased by almost half, and there was space to make a mole on the west quay, where more tips could be sited, leaving room for unloading imports on the south quay. A large space came into being at the eastern end of the dock, where ships could be turned, or moored while awaiting a vacant tip. Since ships would be already inside the dock, waiting in a queue or 'tier', time was saved in getting them through the lock. The enforced enlargement of the dock was probably the reason why it was not opened as intended in September 1888, but in July of the following year.

The sober ceremony of November 1884 was not to be compared with the exuberant spectacle which marked the official opening of the Docks on 18 July 1889. Over 2,000 distinguished guests were invited, and two special trains belonging to the Company were run *via* St. Fagans and Tynycaeau (to avoid any unpleasantness with the Taff Vale Company at Cogan). Ships were dressed overall and crowds of local people turned out to watch the proceedings. Lord Windsor, the Chairman of the Company, could not be present owing to a bereavement, and David Davies had to preside. Undoubtedly it was a day of satisfaction and glory for him; his own coal would soon be on its way from this new port to places all over the world. Unhappily, he did not have long to savour his triumph, for he died in 1890.

When the ceremonial ribbon had been cut, the first vessel sailed into the dock, the S.S. *Arno.* Six tips were ready for the opening, and soon six ships were being loaded with coal. One month later, 8,200 tons of coal were shipped in one day from the eight tips then completed. In the five months that remained of 1889, Barry exported 1.073 million tons and in the following full year 3.192 million tons. As Hood had expected, dividends of 10% were soon being paid on the Ordinary Shares, and in the 1890s, except during the strike year of 1898, they were never less than 9½%.

Colliery companies diverted coal from Cardiff and Penarth. In fact, Penarth's shipments were more than halved in 1890, and were exceeded by shipments from Barry. However, Barry did not overtake Cardiff Docks until 1901. But there was business for all, and those who had prophesied that demand for Welsh coal would continue to increase and allow all the docks to make a living were proved correct. A new dock was opened in Barry in 1898, and another in Cardiff, the Queen Alexandra, in 1907. In 1913 shipments of coal and coke from Barry reached 11.049 million tons, while the combined figure for Cardiff and Penarth was 14.135 million tons, only 3.115 million tons over their 1888 figures.[14]

Plate XXVII. Dock No. 1 ready fo[r] opening in 1889; 'Walker's Town' in centre distance. *Welsh Industrial & Maritime Museum.*

ate XXVIII.
reakwater under
nstruction at W.
ıtrance to Barry
ock, viewed from
ıckson's Bay at low
de.
'elsh Industrial & 'aritime Museum.

Dockside machinery

The most characteristic piece of machinery in Barry Docks for the first half-century of its existence was the tall coal hoist, also called a tip or a staithe. This was a framework of metal and wood designed to receive a loaded coal wagon, which would be raised up and tilted to discharge its contents into the hold of a ship by way of a chute. There were two kinds of tip: low-level and high-level. A low-level tip received a wagon on the quayside and hoisted it to the necessary height to reach the chute. On the Mole and on all the quays, except the northern one of the Old Dock, the tips were low-level. On the northern quay of the Old Dock and, later, the New Dock, they were high-level, the wagons being brought in at the required height on embankments, which were easily formed because the ground sloped upwards away from the dock. Such tips usually had two roads for full wagons and two for empty. The lines on the embankments sloped down towards the tips, almost to the weighbridges, because less engine power was needed to send full wagons down than to haul empty ones up.

The sides of the quays were vertical, except the northern ones on both docks; these were given a slope or batter, rather like the sea-shore, in order to save further excavation. The effect was to increase the water area and allow 'scarfing' of ships, that is, tucking one in between another and the quay to allow every tip to be used at the same time. The high-level tips were supported over the batter by staging.

Tremendous power was needed to work the tip appliances, the fifty-one cranes and the rams which moved the dock and lock gates, and it was obtained from water maintained at high pressure—'hydraulic' power. Electricity had not proved itself for such work by 1889. The hydraulic power-houses for the Old Dock were sited at the north-west end and near the entrance to the Lady Windsor Lock. That for the New Dock (it is still in existence) was sited near the south-eastern end of the dock.

The original plans for the two docks contained proposals for only a small number of tips—fifteen for the Old Dock and four for the New; these were increased to twenty-one and ten respectively from a desire to increase business and revenue; J. W. Barry had to persuade his Directors not to put tips even on the side of the channel connecting the two docks. Most of the tips were fixed in position, but some of them were moveable. By 1918 there were forty-one tipping appliances.

Plate XXIX.
A Sunderland collier negotiates Basin entrance on opening day, 1889.
Welsh Industrial & Maritime Museum.

Barry Docks acquired a good reputation for the quick turn-around of ships. This was due in the first place to the lavish provison of approach lines and storage sidings, but above all of it was due to the skill of three kinds of workers—the shunters, the tippers and the trimmers. The men in charge of the sidings, equipped with chalk and slates, had to ensure that every yard of storage capacity was filled. When the wagon reached the tip, the tippers took over, working usually in gangs of four, each with his own special task. One would get the wagon to the weighbridge, another would note its weight; the next would see it on to the cradle and the fourth would raise the cradle, cant it and pour the coal down a chute into the ship's hold. The wagon then ran back under gravity to another weighbridge for a second weighing, which would enable the amount of coal tipped to be recorded. Dock charges and the wages of tippers and trimmers were based on tonnage. Care had to be taken not to break the friable, large coal, since customers would not pay for small coal unless ordered. An anti-breaking device like a long box was introduced into the chute and gently lowered into the hold; a cone of coal was eventually built up which would itself check the impact of the incoming coal. The trimmers then shovelled the coal sideways until the hold was evenly filled and the load balanced. Unlike the shunters and the tippers, who were paid by the Railway Company, the trimmers were paid by the colliery companies. Once there were at Barry fifteen lodges where the trimmers ate and rested until called to perform their work.

ate XXX.
coal hoist in action, th empty truck turning to weigh-idge. Note coal dust water in eground.
elsh Industrial & aritime Museum.

Plate XXXI. 'Entrance to Barry Dock', painting by W. L. Wyllie, A.R.A., *c.* 1898. *Welsh Industrial & Maritime Museum.*

Railway working

The Barry Company also operated passenger services, and erected stations at Barry, Barry Dock, Cadoxton, Cogan, Wenvoe, Creigiau, Efail Isaf and Treforest. Later there were stations at Barry Island, Barry Pier and Pontypridd; a halt was made at Saint-y-nyll.

Each railway company kept looking for ways to increase its earnings by carrying more traffic; one way was to link with other companies. The Taff Vale Company decided to link with the Barry. A Cardiff, Penarth and Barry Junction Railway Act was obtained in 1885 to make to make a coastal line from Penarth to Biglis and give the proposed company running powers over the quarter-mile of Barry track into Cadoxton Station. It was promoted by Sir Ivor Guest, J. S. Gibbon and two Directors of the Taff Vale Company, which was to operate all the services. A Penarth to Lavernock service commenced at the beginning of 1887, but was extended to Biglis Halt only on 8 July 1889, because terms for use of Cadoxton Station and the track between had not been agreed. After an order from the Railway and Canal

Commission in January 1890, Taff Vale trains started running to Cadoxton Station on 22 May 1890. Only their excursion trains were allowed beyond that Station. That is why in later time passengers between Penarth and Barry always had to change at Cadoxton. The complexities of local railway working are illustrated by the direct service from Barry to Cardiff. The Barry Company began its passenger service as far as Cogan on 20 December 1888; those who wished to continue to Cardiff had to alight there and walk along a short path to Penarth Dock Station, where they would catch a Taff Vale train. When a passenger station was opened in 1893 at Riverside, Cardiff, Barry trains ran into it over the Taff Vale's line from Cogan to Grangetown and the Great Western's line from Grangetown to Riverside. The following year Barry trains ran further—to Clarence Road at Cardiff Docks.

Commercial competition between the local companies was intense, and each would constantly think of some new scheme to outsmart the other. In 1885 the Barry Company made an agreement with six large colliery companies to offer ton/mile rates for hauling coal wagons from the transfer junctions at about 20% below those of the Taff Vale Company. In return the companies would ship from Barry the same quantities of coal that they shipped from Cardiff and Penarth combined (this was similar to an earlier agreement of 1882).

The Taff Vale Company could not let this pass, and in 1888 reduced its own rates for carrying from 0.74*d.* per ton per mile to 0.55*d.* for full train loads. This was well below the Barry rate, and the Barry Company, greatly incensed, had to lower its rates further. Now the Taff Vale could afford to make this reduction because Lord Bute had agreed to give it a subsidy if it reduced its rates. In the event, trade improved and Lord Bute was not called upon to part with much money. It was the coalowners who benefited from this 'rates war'.

In 1888 also the Taff Vale Company supported a move by the Company making the coast line to extend their line from Sully past Hayes Point to where the Barry Company intended to build another dock. The Barry Company retaliated to this thrust by drafting a Further Powers Bill for running rights direct to pits served by the Taff Vale Company (Barry was always eager to secure running rights on anyone's line) to collect and return coal wagons. A compromise was reached between the two sides; the Hayes Branch Railway Bill was dropped on condition that the Barry Bill would ask only for contingent running powers, to be exercised only if the Taff Vale failed to deliver wagons at the junctions regularly and punctually. There was a Section 23 which allowed the Taff Vale to bring coal over the coastal line, but only for local use and not for shipment at Barry. There was also provision for the 'Hafod Bonus' a kind of subsidy payable by the Barry Company to assist the Taff Vale Company in meeting the great cost of collecting and returning wagons at the pits. The interpretation of this section was the subject of eight years of litigation and legislation. Such were the contents of Railway Acts.

In 1889 the Taff Vale Company saw an opportunity for making a pincer movement on the Barry Company by sponsoring the Cowbridge/Aberthaw Railway Act. This authorised a line southwards down the valley of the Thaw (or Ddawan) to the sea, terminating at Aberthaw. Six years later the Taff Vale absorbed this Company. The Taff Vale had good reason to be associated with this move, for the Barry Company was at that very time interested in an expansion to the west through a nominally independent Vale of Glamorgan Railway Company.

The Vale of Glamorgan Railway

Few areas of Wales offered a more prosperous and picturesque countryside than the Vale of Glamorgan—Bro Morgannwg. But the wall of limestone cliffs extending for many miles west of Barry offered few harbours, and certainly none capable of large-scale development like the site at Barry. The coalfield did not extend to these parts, so there were no mines, but it could be a zone of transit. North and north-east of Bridgend the coalowners of the Llynfi, Garw and Ogmore Valleys were looking for better outlets than that afforded by their natural access to the sea—the tiny port of Porthcawl. There was much talk of a port at Ogmore but this came to nothing. Aberthaw had a long history as a port, but it, too, was small.

An enterprising industrialist, Colonel J. T. North, the 'Nitrate King' (already mentioned), had bought up the liquidated Llynfi and Tondu Iron Company, through a syndicate which became North's Navigation Collieries (1889) Company. The Iron Company also owned coal pits, from which North wished to transport coal. He was persuaded by Forster Brown to leave the Ogmore Dock and Railway Company and make his own railway around Bridgend and along the coast to link with Barry Docks. Negotiations took place with the Barry Company and the conditions were embodied in the Vale of Glamorgan Railway Act, which was passed in 1889. However, the issue of shares in 1890 was a failure, and the project came to nothing.

Late in 1891 Hood suggested that the Barry Company should revive the Vale Company, and with the support of T. R. Thompson and Edward, son of David Davies, who had become the Barry Company's Managing Director, the Barry Railway Board was persuaded to agree (the Company had been renamed the Barry Railway Company in 1891). The Vale Company obtained an Act in 1892 extending the completion date of its authorised lines to 26 August 1896. The Barry Company in its 1893 Act to make the New Dock obtained a clause authorising it to guarantee an annual income to the Vale Company. A traffic of 750,000 tons of coal a year was assured over the new line. The shares were reissued and heavily oversubscribed. The guarantee of the prosperous Barry Company had made all the difference.

Construction of the Vale line started in August 1894. The engineers were J. W. Szlumper, his son Charles and his brother William. The contractors were J. Pethwick Bros. & Co. of Plymouth. The same engineers and contractors had been responsible for the line from Lydford to Devonport with its wonderful viaducts. Shillamill Viaduct, two miles south-west of Tavistock was a model for that at Porthkerry on the Vale line.

The Vale of Glamorgan Railway comprised 20¾ miles of double track and ran from Coity Junction (on the G.W.R.) through Southerndown Road, Llantwit Major, Gileston, Aberthaw and Rhoose to Barry. A spur south of Coity led to a bay at Bridgend Station. The line passed through limestone country, which posed peculiar engineering problems through the need for cuttings, embankments and tunnels. The most spectacular work was the viaduct in Porthkerry Park, about a mile west of Barry. It remains one of the great industrial monuments of the area. Made of stone, it has thirteen arched spans of 50 feet and three of 45 feet. With a maximum height of 110 feet, it dominates the little valley which leads down to the beach. Work on the viaduct was troubled with subsidence in 1896, but this was not disclosed to the Board of Trade Inspector, and he was induced to approve the

late XXXII.
orthkerry viaduct on
'ale of Glamorgan
ne.
. *Daly.*

structure.[15] The whole line was opened on 1 December 1897, but disaster quickly struck. On 10 January of the following year one of the huge piers slipped, and that part of the line had to be closed at once. A loop line of 2½ miles was made to the north, around Porthkerry Rectory, and used while the viaduct was being repaired; a special Act had to be obtained to authorise this loop in retrospect. The line was finally opened for goods trains on 8 January 1900, and for passenger trains on 9 April following. The set-back on the viaduct had been due to insufficient foundations, poor workmanship and unsuitable cement.

The main traffic over the Vale line was coal; about 9% of the shipments out of Barry came through the Vale. As a special inducement to customers the Barry Company made a reduction of 2*d.* per ton for coal carried over the Vale lines. There was traffic also in passengers, goods and animals; the stations were given goods yards, and Llantwit had animal pens. Barry, too, had pens. The design of the Barry Company's station at Wenvoe was adopted for all the Vale stations, which gave them a pleasing corporate identity—and revealed where the power lay. The Vale Company was

Plate XXXIII. Saddle-tank 0-6-0 locomotive 'Barry' on Porthkerry loop line in 1898. *B. J. Miller Coll.*

g. 69.
Farrow
ter S.R.B. in
, S. Barrie.

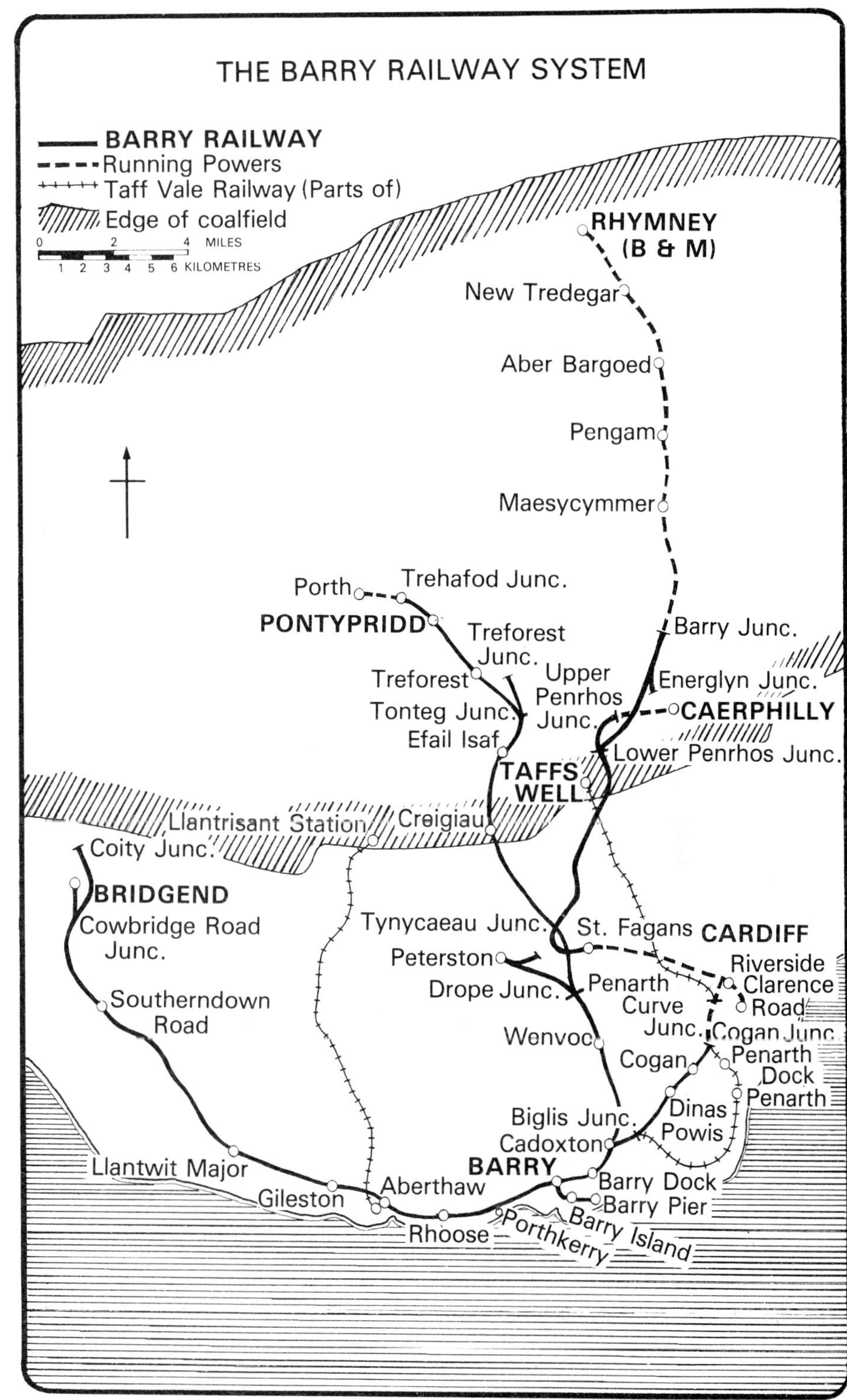

'worked' throughout by the Barry Company, but remained 'independent' until absorbed by the Great Western in 1922. Every year (except 1921) the Barry Company had to make up the sum it had guaranteed to the Vale Company out of the 60% of receipts to which it was entitled. The Vale Company's dividends remained at $4\frac{1}{16}$% every year from 1903.

Before returning to the Barry Railway, it is worth recounting the later history of the Vale of Glamorgan line. Additional halts were made at various times, including one at Llandow and another for the Royal Air Force at St. Athan. Curiously enough, no move was made to create a rail link with the international airport for Cardiff at Rhoose. The passenger service ceased between Barry and Bridgend on 15 June 1964, but the line is still used for diverted traffic of all kinds when the main South Wales line between Cardiff and Bridgend is closed for maintenance. The carriage of coal from pit to port has long ceased, but supplies of coal are delivered to the power station at Aberthaw and cement collected from the cement works there. Unusually, a new line was constructed in 1980 from the Vale line near Bridgend to the Ford Motor factory at Waterton, mainly to bring castings from Dagenham.[16]

The Barry Railway Company

In 1891 the Barry Dock and Railways Company changed its name to the Barry Railway Company, but this did not imply that it had given up working the docks. It had long intended to make a deep-water lock into the first dock, as well as a second dock entered through the first. The lock would be used instead of the basin, thus giving ships longer to leave dock, and saving water. A dock loses water through locking, evaporation and seepage. Sea water could be admitted when the dock gates were opened, provided that the tide was higher than the 29-foot level of the dock, and this only happened at the time of the equinoxes. The feeder on the west was also levelled up at the same time. For the rest of the year the level was, and is maintained by pumping water in from the sea.

The New Dock was authorised by an Act in 1893. It was to be 34 acres in extent, less than half the size of the first dock, which now became known as the Old Dock. The two docks would be interconnected by a channel; this would save the expense of giving the new dock its own entrance from the sea. A swing bridge would provide a crossing over the channel. The New Dock was opened without ceremony on 10 October 1898, the first vessel to enter being the S.S. *Solent.* There were ten high-level tips on the northern quay, and the southern and western quays were used to unload imports. Warren Tump was demolished in the making of the southern quay. Ships at first entered and left the Old Dock by way of the Basin, but with the completion of the Lady Windsor Lock early in 1898, that lock became the normal means of entry to the Docks. The lock is only 65 feet wide, compared with 80 feet for the Basin; large ships even today may have to use the Basin.

Visitors were now flocking to Barry Island to enjoy the seaside. The Barry Company planned to make a tramway from Harbour Road to Whitmore Bay, because the railway then terminated at Barry. This tramway, though authorised by the Act of 1893, was abandoned because of the huge number of trams that would have been needed to convey the large excursion parties which comprised the majority of visitors.

Clearly there was need to provide better access to the Island than the existing road across Dock property. In 1894 the Barry Company obtained an Act to make a railway from Barry Station to the Island over a new embankment. While this was being made the Company persuaded the Barry Local Board (forerunner of the Urban District Council) to petition the Board of Trade to sanction the making of a new road alongside the railway (the present road from the Ship Hotel). This was authorised and the road was ready in 1897. It was given to the Urban District Council in return for making private that part of the old Island Road that ran through Dock property. The Island station opened on 3 August 1896 in time to catch the main holiday traffic.

A station on Barry Island, only a hundred yards from the beach, was a tremendous incentive to the colliers and their families to leave the grim and smoky valley towns for a day out by the sea. Barry passenger trains started

ate XXXIV.
arry pier and
arbour entrance,
ith paddle steamers
Barry Railway
ompany's Red
unnel Fleet, in
1908.
Beaudette Coll.

running into the Taff Vale Station at Porth in March 1896, and there was the junction of lines into the two Rhondda Valleys. Hundreds of thousands of Valley folk were now offered a cheap, direct and short journey to a seaside paradise. In June 1897 the Barry Company began a passenger service, more useful to workmen and businessmen, from its Graig Station at Pontypridd to Clarence Road at Cardiff Docks; this meant exercising running powers over the Great Western line at St. Fagans. The Company still felt at a disadvantage in not having its own line between Cogan and Cardiff, where it had to rely on running powers given by its rival, the Taff Vale Railway, to use the coal transfer junctions at Llandough-juxta-Penarth and Penarth South Curve (at Grangetown), and to run a passenger service.

Pleasure cruises on the Bristol Channel

Once on the Glamorgan seashore, people felt the lure of the deep, whether or not they had essential business in great waters. The islands of the Channel and the sunny hills of the further side were a perpetual invitation to travel. The Barry Railway Company saw an opportunity for another enterprise—getting people into ships—after their success in getting coal into ships. The Barry Railway Act of 1896 authorised the continuation of the Barry Island extension line as far as the western breakwater, where a pier station was later made. This last stretch was opened in the summer of 1899 and passengers were embarked on pleasure cruisers by way of a pontoon floating in the sea. Barry was an excellent port for paddle steamers, because they drew much less than the constant 13 feet of water at Barry. It was thus possible to timetable sailings with railway services, and the porters on Riverside Station could boldly shout 'Barry Island and Boat Train!'. If steamers were late returning, special trains would be arranged.

Plate XXXV.
The paddle steamer *Barry* anchored off Clovelly, N. Devon, while passengers are ferried aboard, *c.* 1908.
B.C. Luxton Coll.

ate XXXVI.
ssengers embarked
Ilfracombe aboard
S. *Gwalia* on
August 1909.
C. *Luxton Coll.*

The company of P. & A. Campbell had already been operating cross-channel steamer services for goods and passengers since 1893, especially between Cardiff and Bristol. The Barry Railway Company had some difficulty in securing authorisation to run its own steamers, and when it did in 1904, it was excluded from the lucrative Bristol routes. It was not allowed to carry goods, and could only take passengers on regular services to ports within the Barry/Weston and Swansea/Ilfracombe limits (excursions however, could go anywhere). The services began in 1905, but unhappily they always lost money and were terminated in 1910. The Company then sold its steam cruisers *Devonia*, *Barry*, *Westonia* and *Gwalia*.

In 1910 and 1911 cruising services were operated out of Barry by the Bristol Channel Boats Company, but this venture did not survive. After 1921 there were no rivals to P. & A. Campbell, who operated their pleasure cruises in the Bristol Channel until 1970, except during the War. There was never really enough passenger traffic to keep all the cruising companies going, for profit was made only in July and August, and could be wiped out by a wet month. Before 1914 over 55,000 passengers booked through Barry Pier annually, about half going to Weston-super-Mare and a quarter to Ilfracombe. Since 1970 there have been occasional cruises out of Penarth; but the pontoon at Barry sank, making the embarking of large numbers impossible.[17] Other factors have been at work in the decline of passenger traffic in the Channel, particularly the extension of motor car ownership and the opening of the Severn Bridge.

Fig. 70.
Aerial panorama of Barry Island and Docks from S., drawn for Barry Railway Company in 1901.

The expansion of the Barry Company

The Company had ambitions to expand into Monmouthshire. In 1896 it succeeded at last in obtaining an Act to reach the Rhymney Railway Company's line direct and provide a shorter route for Rhymney coal to Barry. This line was to leave the Barry Company's main line at Tynycaeau North Junction, cross the Taff Valley over the Walnut Tree Viaduct (demolished in the early 1970s), and reach the Rhymney Company's line at Upper Penrhos Junction, a mile west of Caerphilly. It was to have powers to operate a passenger service into Caerphilly Station, but it never did so because of the expense of adapting Caerphilly Station (historians need to check Railway Acts with care, since their provisions did not always come to fruition). But the line to Upper Penrhos Junction did open for mineral traffic in August 1901; there was no regular passenger service, though excursion trains used the line.

The next step was to make a link with the Brecon and Merthyr Railway at Duffryn Isaf on the eastern side of the Rhymney Valley, starting from Lower Penrhos. This was great viaduct country, and the one at Pwll-y-pant, Llanbradach, was a particularly impressive structure. The line was authorised in 1898 by an Act which also gave the Barry Company running powers over the Brecon and Merthyr line to pits in the Rhymney Valley. This line opened early in 1905 for mineral traffic only, though it was also used by excursion trains to Barry Island. The Barry Company expended a great deal of money on the Parliamentary proceedings connected with their schemes for expansion in Monmouthshire, which were embodied in an

Act of 1907. The Company did not make these authorised lines, because its share of the coal carriage receipts would not have been enough to warrant the huge capital expenditure and still return a profit. At this time the Company had to look hard at its finances to maintain dividends.

The War of 1914-18

On the outbreak of war the Government took control of railway companies and docks. Trade was concentrated on Atlantic routes and safeguarded by the convoy system. In one sense Barry was well placed for this western orientation of activity, but in another it was bound to lose many foreign contacts and markets. Exports of coal were more than ever important to earn foreign currency for imports of food, raw materials and munitions. Because Germany had overrun the coal-producing areas of France early in the War, Britain, or more particularly South Wales, had to satisfy the fuel needs of France as well as those of the Allied Armies. Throughout the War Barry was a safe port of embarkation for thousands of troops.

Dock workers had to undertake extra duties to prevent sabotage, fires and explosions; they had to learn new routines and handle special equipment. Huge stores were set up containing timber for the pits and hay for use abroad; imported grain was stored in two large sheds. Thousands of naval and military transports were loaded with raw materials, equipment and munitions. The staff of the Barry Railway Company responded with alacrity to the call to arms; 757 joined the armed forces, but sadly, 59 failed to return.

The trade of the port up to 1922

The port of Barry came through the War with its prosperity relatively unimpaired, but it still depended mainly on the export of coal. Its import trade was never large. Other ports in the region—Bristol, Cardiff and Newport—had newer and larger docks with wider entrances. They had more and larger warehouses and transit sheds. More importantly, they had long-established trade connections abroad, and they were nearer that great area of population and industry, the Midlands.

It became clear that the coal trade was declining, but even as late as 1964 coal shipments from Barry accounted for half its total trade. Coal-related imports comprising pit props and mining timber were transported to the pits in coal wagons which had been emptied. Not all the coal loaded on to a ship was discharged at its destination; much of it was consumed on voyage to provide steam power to propel the ship and work its machinery—'the winch is the best man on a ship'. About 20% of the coal shipped at Barry was used directly for this purpose. On the other hand, even when coal was unloaded at the other end, it would often be stored in a dump eventually used to fill ships' bunkers. The immense quantity sent abroad may be realised from the fact that only 10% of coal shipments went to ports in the United Kingdom (which then included Ireland). The best markets were in France, the Mediterranean, the Black Sea, West Africa and South America. By 1895 Welsh coal had been driven out of markets east of Suez by coal from South Africa, India, Japan and Australia. But Welsh smokeless coal was still in great demand at stations of the Royal Navy all over the world. 'Coaling ship' was a compulsory and unpopular task, when Naval officers and ratings all became equally dirty.

Welsh coal undersold its rivals by its cheapness. There was cut-throat competition for orders among colliery companies and for cargoes among shipowners. Because pits were near the coast, the initial railway transport was cheap. Sea transport has always been relatively cheap, and there was competition there, too. It was said that Egyptian Railways paid less for their coal than did Kent Railways. Shipowners fixed their charges for carrying coal on the assumption that they would secure a second cargo for their profit at the destination.

Barry's import trade was always small and limited in variety. A timber business was started in 1886 by J. C. Meggitt of Wolverhampton under the name of Meggitt and Jones (later Meggitt and Price). Pit props and mining timber have already been mentioned. Small quantities of pig iron, wood, pulp, silver sand, zinc, and iron ore were recorded, and in 1905 and 1906 some gas coal. In the 1890s imports included gypsum, railway sleepers, flints and rice. Half the bricks used for the building of Barry came from Bridgwater, Somerset, and at first they were unloaded in the Old Harbour. Other imports were loam, sand, cement and slates; the sand came

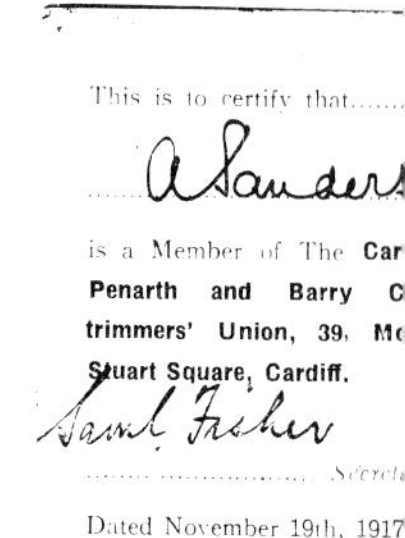
This is to certify that.......
A Sanders
is a Member of The Car
Penarth and Barry C
trimmers' Union, 39, Mo
Stuart Square, Cardiff.
Saml Fisher
Secreta
Dated November 19th, 1917
At CARDIFF

Fig. 71.
Coal-trimmers' Unio
membership card,
1917.
G. Beaudette Coll.

from close at hand, being dredged from the Channel.

From the beginning the Barry Company sought to attract firms to operate in the dock area, but with little success. In 1906 the company of J. Arthur Rank set up a mill to make flour and animal feedstuffs on the dockside. Its cathedral-like shape still stands, and the firm is now known as Rank-Hovis Ltd. It is not widely known that this firm would have gone to Cardiff, were it not for inducements offered by the Barry Company in the form of a lease of land for 250 years at a low rental, use of the Company's equipment at a low rate, a preferential carriage rate as if from Cardiff, and a loan of £40,000 to build the mill.

In 1910 and 1911 the Company arranged with Lord Ashby St. Ledger, son of Lord Wimborne (formerly Sir Ivor Guest), to make land at Sully available to firms from the Midlands to manufacture high-grade steel, rails, tubes and piping, but nothing came of the proposals. At the same time Brown, Lenox & Co., ships' chain and bridge cable manufacturers, contemplated moving their works from Pontypridd to Barry, but they decided to remain where they were.

The workforce and the installations

The Barry Railway Company succeeded in generating an intense *esprit de corps* among its employees. It expected a high standard of performance and devotion to duty, not to mention impeccable behaviour by those whose work brought them into contact with the public. To be a 'Company's Servant' was a privilege.

In 1920, almost on the eve of Amalgamation, the Company had a work-force of 3,169. It was overwhelmingly male; only 92 were women, and they were mainly cleaners. In the days of steam every engine driver needed a fireman, and it is not surprising that their numbers were almost equal: 170 drivers and 163 firemen. There were small numbers of wagon examiners, oil men and greasers, but a huge number of mechanics and artisans: 613. Even larger was the number of unskilled labourers: 890. There were train guards, ticket collectors and inspectors. The locomotives needed steam raisers, washers-out and coalmen. The movement of rolling stock required number-takers, yardsmen, shunters, couplers and brakesmen. On the 'permanent way' there had to be banksmen, platelayers, gangers and signalmen. The coal was loaded into the ships from the wagons by the tippers. But as well as coal and passengers there was a variety of goods to be moved by rail. All these activities ultimately depended on meticulous paperwork, requiring no less than 283 clerks. On the maritime side the Barry Company kept tugs, launches, a dredger, a firefloat and a floating crane. There was even a Dock Diver. The Company also had its own police.[18]

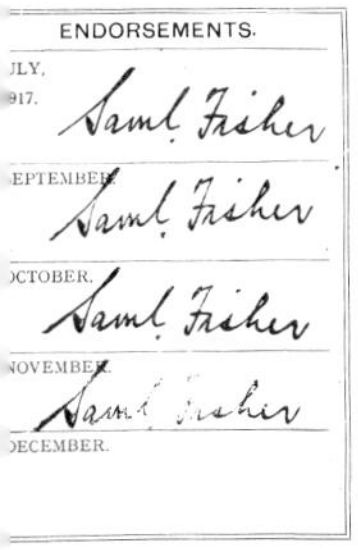

ig. 72.
oal-trimmers' Union
nployment card,
ith endorsements,
917.
. *Beaudette Coll.*

It must be remembered that many other workers, officials and organisations were vital to the working of the docks. There were offices for

H.M. Customs and Excise, the Port Health Authority, the Board of Trade and the Post Office. Ships entering dock had to take on board a pilot to guide them in, and the Barry Pilotage Authority had not only offices but a dormitory for its duty pilots. The colliery and shipping companies kept agents' offices on the docks, as did shipbrokers and insurance companies. There were fifteen trimmers' lodges for that numerous category of dock workers, the coal-trimmers, who were employed not by the Barry Company but by the coal companies.

There were many maritime stores and shops in Dock View Road and Thompson Street; some firms were attracted by the offer of rent-free accommodation to operate from within the docks. There were twelve shops and yards for repairing ships and three for wagons, not to mention numerous smaller workshops and offices. Banks arrived and coffee taverns appeared. The Missions to Seamen set up a hall, and the churches tried in various ways to take their message to the seamen and the dockers.

The capital assets of the Barry Railway Company in 1920 were enormous. Including the Vale of Glamorgan lines, there were 52 miles of running track and 108 single-track miles of sidings. There were well over 1,000 yards of viaducts and 2,500 yards of tunnels; these features demanded heavy expenditure both in construction and maintenance, and in this respect the Barry Company was less fortunate than the Taff Vale, which had only one tunnel, and that was later opened into a cutting. The Barry had 165 bridges to take the track across gaps and obstacles.

The system had seventeen stations, fifty-one signal boxes, two engine sheds, two carriage sheds, repair shops, smithies and foundries. The rolling stock ultimately comprised 148 steam locomotives, 194 carriages and brake vans, and 2,316 wagons and trucks.[19] To provide ready fuel for the locomotives there were coal stages or dumps at Barry, Trehafod, Treforest and Coity. The two docks had a total of 41 tips of various kinds, and

Plate XXXVII. Panorama of W. end of Barry Docks and town in *c.* 1907. Note extensive sidings and colliery companies' trucks. *H. Shirvington.*

numerous cranes. There were 47 mooring buoys, which were also used to warp or haul ships to and from tips and quays.

The rolling stock of the Barry Railway has been described and illustrated by D. S. Barrie in his book *The Barry Railway* (Oakwood Press, 1962). A few general points are worth emphasising here. The earliest priority was for mineral traffic, distances were relatively short and journeys had to be frequent to maintain the high volume of exports. In the case of passenger services, stops were frequent and distances between them usually short. These factors influenced the choice of rolling stock. Tank engines, that is, engines without a separate tender, were best for short-haul work involving much shunting. The final Barry design was an 0-6-4T, but the largest stock of any one model at the time of the Amalgamation was of the 0-6-2T. The vast bulk of the coal wagons belonged to the collieries and had to be returned regularly to their owners. From the 1880s ten-ton wagons were the rule; twenty-tonners came in during the First World War and later the thirty-tonner became normal. The Barry Company did have a certain number of freight trucks, as well as service vehicles for line maintenance. It also had to supply brake vans, one at the end of every goods train; most were fitted with vacuum pipes so that they could be used with passenger trains. The coaches were smartly painted in a reddish colour but were not luxurious inside, except for the first-class accommodation (those were the days of first, second and third class). None had steam heat or communication cords, nor were there corridors or toilets.

The end of the Barry Railway Company

Following the Railway Act of 1921, which embodied Government policy to reduce the number of small railways and amalgamate them into four main systems in England, Wales and Scotland, the Barry Company was amalgamated with the Great Western Railway on and from 1 January 1922. But the Barry Company's standing was such that it was given the

status of an associate rather than a subsidiary. It was a traumatic experience for the personnel, who now found themselves part of a huge undertaking covering a triangular piece of England and Wales delimited by Penzance, Fishguard, Aberystwyth, Shrewsbury, Birkenhead, Birmingham, London and Weymouth, answerable to a head office at Paddington. Their free tickets and privilege fares certainly took them a lot farther, but they found it hard to give the same loyalty to such a conglomerate.

But perhaps it was fortunate that the Barry Company came to an end when it did. It had enjoyed the golden age of the railway, and signs of decline were on the horizon. It was in a strong financial position: every £100 of Barry Ordinary Stock was exchanged for £220 Great Western Railway 5% Stock. The nominal dividends of the Barry Railway Company averaged over 8% between 1889 and 1922. The percentage actually received depended on the buying price of the Stock. Those who bought £100 of Stock in, say, 1885 at par, saw the market price increase by 1896 to £300, but a buyer at that price who received 10% on his investment was really getting only 3⅓%. The Barry Company's record was all the more creditable, because it had to shoulder disproportionately high maintenance costs for the kind of track which it had; it kept a lavish mileage of sidings to ensure speedy turn-round of loads, and latterly it found itself, as did other companies, having to make greater contributions to rates and taxes and to Government social insurance schemes. The Earl of Plymouth presided over the last

Plate XXXVIII. Barry Railway coal train, drawn by 0-6- tank locomotive No. 144.
Glamorgan Record Offi

late XXXIX.
arry Station in *c.*
908, with houses of
Harbour Road visible
eyond.
Velsh Industrial & Maritime Museum.

ordinary general meeting of the Barry Railway Company on 17 February 1922, and over the special meeting on 5 April to approve the terms of amalgamation.[20]

The town of Barry was founded on the Company's Docks. The Docks and the Railway gave employment to thousands of Barry's inhabitants, nearly all of whom had originated elsewhere. This cosmopolitan population had little class-consciousness. The immigrants came with many skills, and the first arrivals must have had more than their share of spirit, ability and courage in leaving their homes to seek a living in an unknown place. This was the human capital which made the community, and the social dividends can be seen in its subsequent history.

The Great Western period, 1922-47

In 1922 the Great Western Railway Company absorbed most of the railway companies of South Wales, together with their docks and other businesses. The following twenty-five years saw great changes in the economic and social scene generally and in Barry in particular. World trade and industry was still affected by the dislocation caused by the War of 1914-18. Coal shipments from Barry had experienced a modest decline from 11·049 million tons in 1913 to 9·807 million tons in 1922, but in 1930 a severe decline began. The Barry Company's near-monopoly of carrying passengers and merchandise in its area was soon to be threatened by the operations of new road-haulage and bus companies. It was a consolation that they could not compete in carrying coal.

Barry Docks failed to attract trade to make up for the decline in coal shipments for various reasons. It had no industrial base; it was not the nearest or most convenient port for manufacturing centres elsewhere; it was not on the main east-west axis of communication in South Wales; it had no good connection with the A48 Trunk Road until as late as 1982. Other ports were nearer the industrial Midlands. Both State and private investment in Wales went to the depressed areas or to large centres of manufacture and population, too far away to benefit Barry, which was never considered a 'depressed area'. The only factories that came to Barry were those set up during the 1939-45 War on Cadoxton Moors. Private investment in Wales went into the oil-refining, tin plate and iron and steel industries, drawing raw materials through other ports.

So new industrial development by-passed Barry, which had to remain dependent on the coal export trade. The U.S.A. seamen's strike in 1922 and the French occupation of the Ruhr Coalfield in Germany in 1923 helped the Welsh coal trade for a few years, and foreign demand picked up a little in the late Twenties, in spite of Britain's return to the Gold Standard with an overvalued pound. In 1929 coal shipments from Barry totalled 8·74 million

Plate XL. S.S. *Constantis* discharging pitwood No. 2 Dock in October 1947. *British Railways.*

'late XLI.
ank's Mills, with .S. *Anglian* dis-harging grain.
. *W. Hansen.*

tons, but by 1947 they had fallen catastrophically to 1·96 million.[21] There were various reasons. The world depression of the 1930s forced many countries to protect their own industries by imposing duties on imports or excluding them altogether. Welsh coal was thus made dearer. Most Welsh colliery companies were small and could not afford costly equipment such as power-loading systems, conveyor belts and coal-cutting machines. In addition, most pits were old, and adaptation of the old is more expensive than installation of the new. The coal nearest the surface had been mined long ago, and costs grew enormously the further a pit was sunk or extended. Some foreign pits were new, and hence mined coal near the surface. Many used the newest equipment and methods. Demand for Welsh coal dropped also because Britain's share of the world's carrying trade declined after the First World War, and partly because more ships turned to oil for fuel.

Foreign collieries were helped by the imposition of tariffs on Welsh coal. Poland paid the costs of transporting Polish coal to a port. The United Kingdom and the Scandinavian countries excluded Polish coal from their countries by bilateral agreement, but Poland then undercut Welsh coal in the Mediterranean. Italy, on the other hand, increased her hydro-electric output to reduce her imports of coal. Barry was in an economic backwater and stayed there.

Exports of tin plates remained small—6,281 tons in 1936. Cement exports from the Aberthaw and Rhoose works averaged 60,000 tons a year, except during the War and in 1947, and even reached 105,719 tons in 1936. Flour and grain exports, including offals for animal feedstuffs, increased to 53,828 tons in 1939, but fell to 9,718 in 1947.[22]

Fortunately during the Second World War, Barry was chosen to store petroleum and oil products, brought in by sea and mostly intended for re-export to the U.S. Armies in France. Cory Brothers & Co. with Government aid set up a tank farm on the Mole to store whale oil until sent elsewhere for manufacture into margarine, cooking fats, cosmetics and soap. This last development turned out well for the future, and in 1984 there were over a hundred tanks in use for storing oil derivatives on the south-western and western sides of the Old Dock, with a pipe-line to Cadoxton taking supplies for local use or further distribution by rail or road tanker. The Cory Company became in 1968 an associated company of the Powell Duffryn Oil Storage Company, which specialises in bulk storage and transport of oil and oil derivatives in this country and in the U.S.A.

The export of 'General Merchandise' averaged 10,000 tons a year during peacetime. During the last World War this increased to over 100,000 tons, because the term covered war materials and equipment also.

The largest classes of imports remained wood, grain and sand, except during the last War. Wood covered timber, deals, pitwood and mining timber. The sand was dredged from the Bristol Channel, and the salt in it had to be washed out before it could be used in building. Imports of this sand averaged over 30,000 tons a year during the War. Oil imports, negligible up to 1940, rose to 143,819 tons in 1943 but declined to 23,473 tons in 1947, reflecting the diminishing requirements of the U.S. Army. Total imports varied between 637,878 tons in 1926 and 280,209 tons in 1946.[23] The former figure was greatly inflated by coal imported during the General Strike.

In the Second World War, as in the first, Barry shipped large tonnages of coal and war materials to France. These ceased when France fell in the summer of 1940. Barry now became a great place of storage for food, strategic raw materials and war equipment, not only for domestic use but also for future military action against the enemy. A huge Supply Reserve Depot was set up on 130 acres of land south of Atlantic Mills on the New Dock. The War Department took over Rank's transit shed and reserved four shipping berths for supplying the Army. New electric cranes were brought in and another tug acquired. In 1942 the United States Army started using Barry to store goods and equipment for the use of its armies in the North African campaigns. It brought new handling equipment, such as gravity roller conveyors and iron spreaders, and hatch tents to give shelter from the rain; a fifty-ton crane with six-ton shackles was added and another transit shed made.

Imports greatly increased, and included new materials like steel spelter. Dumps of pitprops, coal, magnesite, steel rails and sawn wood were created. The timber ponds were used again after many years.

The danger of enemy attack had to be taken more seriously than in the previous war. Workers had to be ready for other emergencies, such as accidental explosions or fires. All this meant accepting training and carrying out duty watches, often for little or no pay. There was the added strain of operating the black-out regulations at night. Attacks did come. Between July 1940 and July 1941 there were seven air raids on on the port, five of them at night, but mercifully the damage and casualties were slight. Explosive, oil and incendiary bombs were dropped, and damage was caused to the Meggitt & Jones timber yard, Cadoxton Station yard, the Mole, the Lady Windsor Lock and both Dry Docks. Some railway track and wagons, pipelines and quays were also damaged. One person was killed and eighteen injured.

Preparations went ahead for the invasion of Europe, and Barry played an important part in these. Military vehicles were gathered together in Porthkerry Park, where trees offered concealment from aerial observation and attack. In June 1944 twenty-one ships left Barry for France, filled with troops, vehicles and equipment.

ate XLII.
S. *Elysia* discharging anadian flour and heat at Rank's Iills.
ritish Transport ommission.

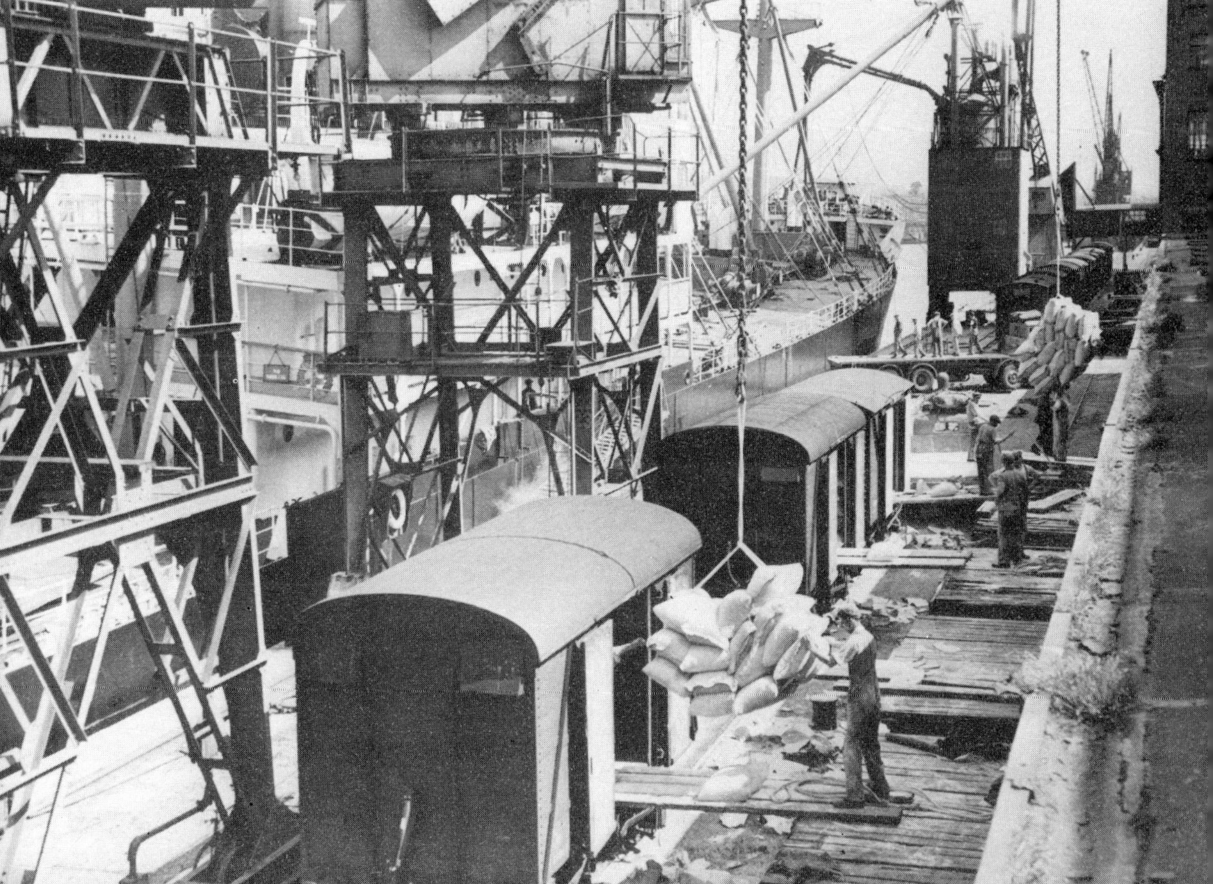

Returns for the 1939-45 War showed that the port of Barry dealt with 20,000 ships, exported 13½ million tons of coal and 4½ million tons of other goods.[24] As these exports were mostly used for warlike purposes, it was natural that when peace came in 1945, the port's trade should fall away. The diminution of coal exports from 5·57 million tons in 1938 to 1·57 million tons in 1945 led to the dismantling of the low-level tips; the number of tippers was reduced from 196 to 104, and coal-trimmers were transferred to duties connected with loading and unloading ships. Imports in 1947, however, were only 4,000 tons less than in 1938, owing to the pent-up need for pitwood and mining timber.

When the Great Western Railway's control of Barry docks and railways came to an end in 1947 as a result of nationalisation, a general decline in Barry's trade had set in. Even so, in percentage terms, the place of coal was impressive: it accounted for 80% of the trade of the port. But this kind of figure concealed an enormous decline in volume, and revealed nothing of the dismal prospects ahead.

It is surprising that the Great Western Company did not close any of its passenger services in South Wales, for many must have been losing money for years; it is not credible that the Llantrisant/Cowbridge/Aberthaw or the Penarth/Cadoxton service ever paid its way. The Company did demolish the viaducts at Penrheol and Llanbradach in 1937, but it retained the one at Walnut Tree until the early 1970s. Coal could still reach Barry from the

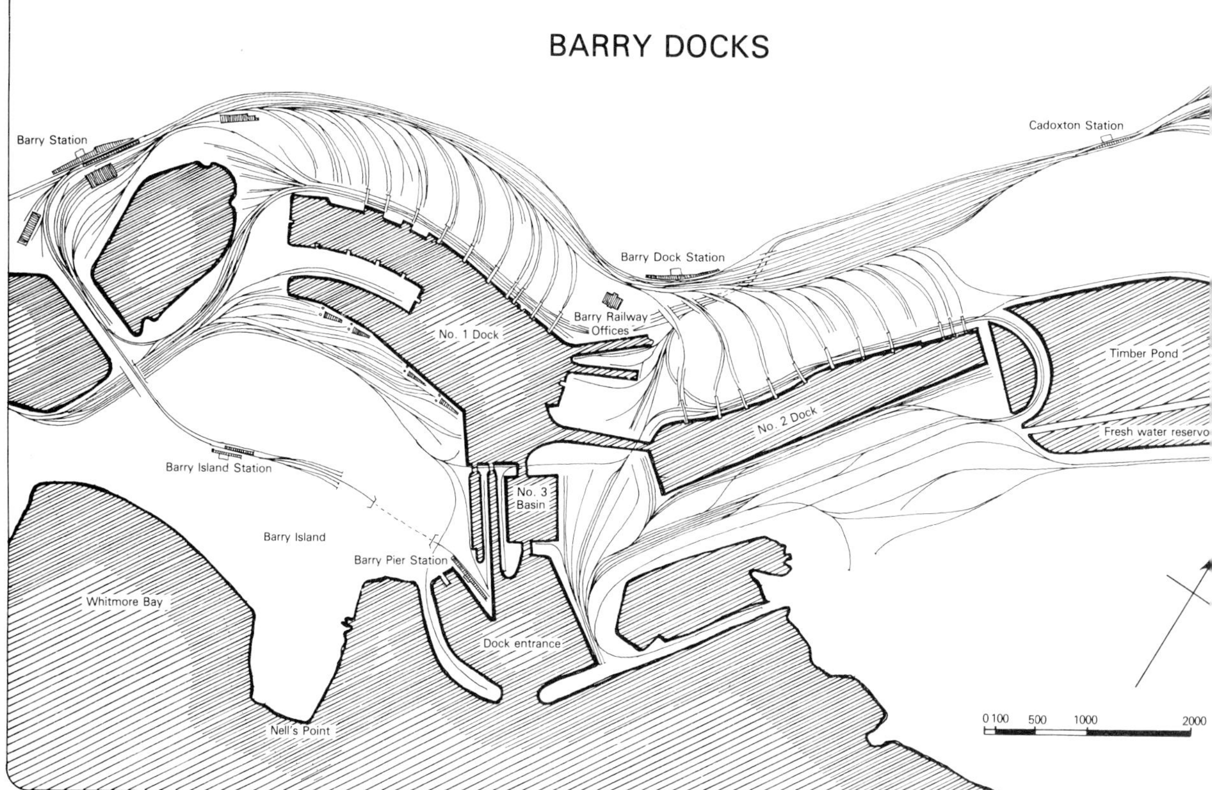

Fig. 73.
Plan of Barry Docks fully developed.
C. Farrow after G. W. R

Rhymney Valley pits *via* Radyr and Cogan, and it is curious that the Company did not send all the coal from the Merthyr, Aberdare and Rhondda Valleys by that route also. The rationalisation of the old Barry routes had to wait until the Beeching closures in the Sixties. Perhaps the Great Western was content with its 5% to 7½% dividends between the Wars. Perhaps it did not want to add to the misery of the Thirties. But when nationalisation came, it was clear that there were hundreds of miles of unneeded rail track and too many docks in South Wales for a trade that could only decline in volume as time went on. One major economy took place: there was no requirement for all the engine and carriage repair shops of the old railway companies, and so the work was concentrated at Caerphilly and Cardiff.

The period since nationalisation

A Labour government came to power in 1945 on policies of large-scale nationalisation, of founding a Welfare State and of achieving full employment. Its immediate task, however, was to return to civilian life millions of individuals who were serving in the armed forces or making war materials and equipment. This it effectively accomplished.

The railway companies were nationalised in 1947. They, their docks and other businesses were placed under the British Transport Commission. Control was exercised through the Railway Executive and the Docks and Inland Waterways Executive. This arrangement was replaced in 1962 by the British Railways Board and the British Docks Board operating under the Ministry of Transport. Waterways and certain other interests were reorganised under separate boards. A further reorganisation, affecting the Docks only, took place on 31 December 1982, when the British Transport Docks Board (so retitled in 1968) was renamed 'Associated British Ports'. In February 1983, in accordance with the Conservative government's policy of privatising national undertakings, that organisation became a subsidiary company of Associated British Ports Holdings PLC.

As far as Barry was concerned, two things had happened. Founded as an integrated undertaking, its docks and railways were now administered by two separate organisations. Secondly, they had been swallowed up in even larger bodies, where the seat of authority was even more remote. There was one consolation in this ferment of change. The Western Region of British Railways corresponded fairly closely with the old G.W.R., though the rationalisation of many main lines and stations led eventually to a rather different pattern of traffic.

Part of the full employment policy was to bring work to people in districts of low industrial activity. Government grants were made to private companies for capital construction. Trading Estates were set up or expanded, sites were cleared, services provided and cheap loans granted. Governments invested heavily in the coal, iron and steel industries. There

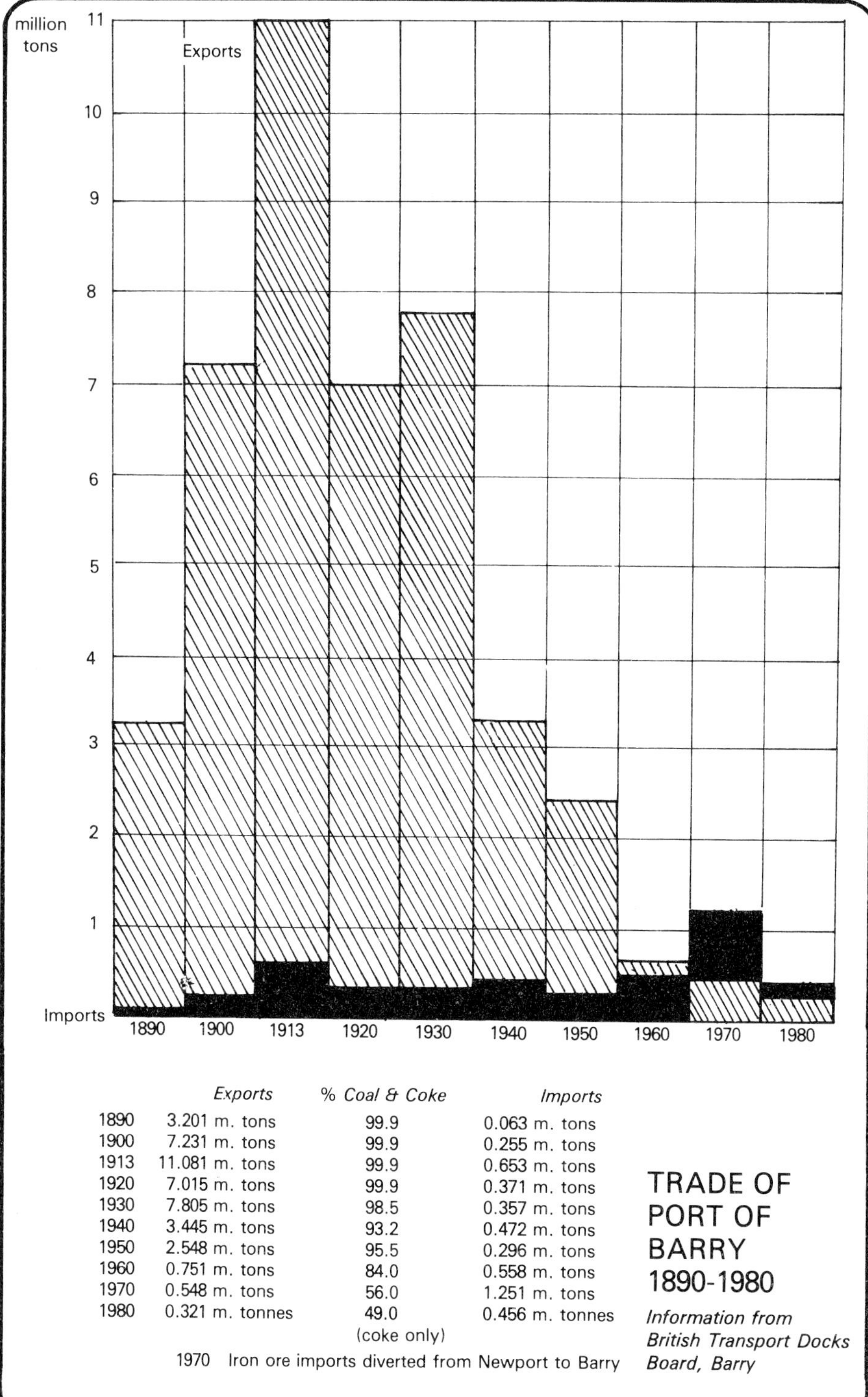

	Exports	*% Coal & Coke*	*Imports*
1890	3.201 m. tons	99.9	0.063 m. tons
1900	7.231 m. tons	99.9	0.255 m. tons
1913	11.081 m. tons	99.9	0.653 m. tons
1920	7.015 m. tons	99.9	0.371 m. tons
1930	7.805 m. tons	98.5	0.357 m. tons
1940	3.445 m. tons	93.2	0.472 m. tons
1950	2.548 m. tons	95.5	0.296 m. tons
1960	0.751 m. tons	84.0	0.558 m. tons
1970	0.548 m. tons	56.0	1.251 m. tons
1980	0.321 m. tonnes	49.0 (coke only)	0.456 m. tonnes

1970 Iron ore imports diverted from Newport to Barry

Fig. 74.

was much private investment in the oil, motor and steel industries. South Wales as a whole benefited greatly and reached a climax of prosperity, but unfortunately none of this investment came to Barry. Because it had hitherto depended on the railway for its exports and imports, its road connections with the rest of the country were woefully inadequate. Not until November 1981 was the Biglis/Pencoedtre link road opened to improve the connection with the A48 Trunk Road at Culverhouse Cross. The road connection of motorway standard to Capel Llanilltern on the M4, north-west of St. Fagans, is not due for completion until the end of 1984. The construction of both these roads has been assisted with grants from the European Economic Community. In an irony of fate the making of the latter road involved the demolition of the Barry Railway's viaducts over the river Ely and over the main South Wales line at St. George's.

In 1963 coal exports were concentrated through Swansea and Barry by Government policy. By this time coal from opencast workings was increasingly quarried. Even so, Barry's coal-exporting days were numbered, and shipments ceased in 1976. The last coal tip was taken down in November 1981, and this symbolised the end of an era. Coke and small quantities of duff continue to be shipped, and a bulk loading conveyor for coke was installed at the New Dock.

Since the War oil and iron ore have been brought to Britain in ships of increased carrying capacity, but not to Barry, because the eighty-foot width of the Basin gates prevents the entry of vessels of more than 22,500 tons dead weight. In any case, oil refineries are far away and Welsh steel works have nearer ports. The only liner trade that came to Barry was that of the Geest Line in 1957. It imported bananas from the West Indies and exported a variety of goods in return, accounting for about 30% of the trade of the port. The removal of Geest to Bristol in 1981 was a blow to Barry, but happily the firm returned in February 1984. At first this was a temporary arrangement, but present indications are that Geest will remain.[25] A liner firm needs a port with wide lock gates, large transit sheds and good road and rail connections, and Barry was deficient in some of these respects.

But within the limits of these over-riding constraints, successive Docks Managers have had considerable success in attracting new imports, and they have augmented and adapted accommodation and equipment to suit changing needs. Imports since 1947 have averaged 586,000 tons a year, compared with 385,000 tons a year during the Great Western period. Unfortunately, this modest increase has by no means made up for the massive loss of coal exports. Barry did not benefit from the closure of Penarth Harbour and Dock and of Cardiff West and East Docks; there was simply not enough trade in the Bristol Channel. It was small wonder that the Rochdale Committee, reporting on the Ports of Great Britain in 1962, recommended closing Barry Docks, to the consternation of the town.[26]

Plate XLIII.
S.S. *Geestland* at Barry Dock entrance, with tug Bargarth.
Simon Prosser.

Grain, pitwood and mining timber continued for some years to be imported in large quantities, but the cessation of coal shipments in 1976 meant that there were no empty wagons to take the pitwood to the mines. Coal is now shipped only out of Newport and Swansea in South Wales. However, coal has on occasions travelled in the opposite direction. During a local miners' strike or when coal was short, large tonnages were imported through Barry; the average was 42,000 tons a year from 1971 to 1975. Coal from the U.S.A. has often been cheaper than the home-produced variety, because it is mined cheaply from thick opencast seams by huge mechanical excavators, and then transported cheaply. Such imports are kept to a minimum by pressure from miners' and dockers' unions.

The successful establishment of a tank farm for oil products at the western end of the Old Dock has already been mentioned. Exports of fuel oil from this stock averaged over 90,000 tons a year from 1967 to 1981, when they fell steeply. Other imports included in the Trade Returns include building and road-making materials, non-ferrous ores, manufactured goods, wood pulp, scrap iron, wool and textile fibres, animal feeding stuffs, dairy produce, fish, fertilisers and cereals. Pumice is often brought in from the Greek island of Yali; it is used to give strength and thermal insulating qualities to breeze blocks. Chemical imports have been substantial. In 1971 and 1972 iron ore was unloaded at Barry for the steelworks at Llanwern, but this was a temporary measure while repairs were carried out at Newport Docks.

Until 1975 a motor vehicle ferry plied to Dublin and carried on some miscellaneous trade. In March 1983 the Welsh-Irish Ferries Company began a Cork/Barry service of three voyages a week, transporting long-distance lorries and a great variety of goods in either direction. To cover costs the Company needed a monthly income of £140,000, but its receipts were only £70,000. The Welsh Development Agency refused to guarantee a bank loan to pay the charter fee for the vessel in July 1983, and the Receiver was called in. The Norwegian-owned ferry, the *Ugland Trailer,* then sailed off to Belgium.

The most significant cargoes exported during recent years (representing quantities exceeding 10,000 tons in any one year) were: cement, processed food, vehicles, tin plate, iron and steel products, chemicals, fertiliser and sugar; scrap iron from a Sheffield firm and a local firm made a useful contribution to exports.

Not all the activities and enterprises going on in the dock area were sponsored by the railway or dock authorities, but all were affected by the changing fortunes of the port. The business of the Barry Graving Dock declined, and it has for some years been used for mooring private vessels. Outside the docks, the numerous moorings for small boats within the western breakwater bear witness to the growth in leisure sailing. Bailey's ship-repairing yard beside the Lady Windsor Lock struggled on until 1983, when it was closed.

On the railway the introduction of Diesel Multiple Units in 1958 for passenger services and then diesel locomotives for coal and goods trains led to the scrapping of steam locomotives and obsolete rolling stock. The first

'late XLIV.
)erelict locomotives
t Woodham's yard,
arry.
. *Daly.*

consequence was a considerable trade in scrap metal, but there followed a brisk sale of relics for restoration. A huge dump was created at Barry by David Woodham, containing both local items and many from far afield. The boom in Railway nostalgia, developing apace in the Seventies, resulted in the formation of railway preservation societies supported by the voluntary efforts of enthusiasts. These societies bought material from David Woodham; the Severn Valley Railway, for example, took seventeen locomotives.[27] The land occupied by Woodham is leased with Government aid, and has been made into a little industrial estate, where small firms operate.

The Natural Environmental Research Council (N.E.R.C.) now has its headquarters at Barry on the southern quay of the Old Dock, having been transferred from Plymouth in 1969 as an act of social policy. The Council was established in 1965 to supervise and develop research into every aspect of world environment, especially into the geology and geophysics of the sea floor and ocean circulation. Its vessels used to operate from Barry, where they were serviced, victualled and maintained. There were five ocean-going vessels and two coastal vessels. The Council has 1,000 feet of quay and 4½ acres of land, which provide space for offices, laboratories, stores and the headquarters (opened in 1972).[28]

Another welcome arrival for a permanent berth at Barry Dock was the minesweeper, H.M.S. *Waveney*, in 1984. This 900-ton vessel, the first of a new class, will be the sea tender of the South Wales Division of the Royal Naval Reserve, in succession to a series of different minesweepers which have discharged the same function over the years. This vessel is an operational unit in the forces of the United Kingdom and the North Atlantic Treaty Organisation. It is manned by members of a part-time voluntary force, drawn from the surrounding region. The headquarters of the Division, an establishment called H.M.S. *Cambria*, has been located at Sully in Ministry of Defence property since August 1980. It previously stood on the west side of the East Dock in Cardiff, and its sea tenders were based at Cardiff also, but with the redevelopment of the dock area there in the 1970s, it had to be moved.[29]

In February 1983 the management of Barry Docks was merged with that of Cardiff, but the Docks Superintendent and staff are still based at Barry. The staff and labour force then comprised 231 persons, including 80 registered dock workers. Work begins at 7.00 a.m. daily from Monday to Friday, but shifts and weekend overtime can be worked. There are nearly two miles of quayage for loading and unloading ships, eleven bulk and general cargo berths, nine petroleum berths, one bulk conveyor loading berth and two roll-on roll-off berths. There is still a considerable mileage of railway, and some track is surfaced to rail level to provide road access. The up-to-date equipment includes numerous cranes and fork-lift trucks, and the buildings include two transit sheds and two warehouses.[30]

The old Barry Railway system has almost disappeared, and what remains is in danger. There are still direct passenger services, using diesel units, from Barry Island to Treherbert and Merthyr Tydfil *via* Cardiff Central (the old 'General') and Pontypridd. There are connections at Cardiff Queen Street to Rhymney and Coryton. These services are mostly used by commuters and shoppers, and they have to be subsidised. Excursion trains still run from various parts to the Island in summer, but in much diminished numbers. Strenuous efforts are made to publicise rail travel and win back customers from the road. Timetables and station notices now appear in Welsh and English bilingually.

The passenger service between Barry and Bridgend ceased on 15 June 1964, and the Vale line is now used only for goods traffic and as a relief line for the main South Wales line from Cardiff to Bridgend. Goods, however, tend to be industrial raw materials rather than mixed merchandise for local distribution, and consequently all the goods yards on the line were closed in 1977. The tracks on the line between Cowbridge Road, Bridgend and Coity Junction have been taken up, as were those from Cowbridge to Aberthaw

Plate XLV. H.M.S. *Waveney*, minesweeper of S. Wales Division of Royal Naval Reserve. *Crown Copyright; by permission of Ministry of Defence.*

some time ago. Passenger services between Pontypridd, St. Fagans and Cardiff Clarence Road ceased on 10 September 1962, as did those between Cadoxton and Pontypridd (though goods trains used the latter line for more than a year after). The catalogue of closures continued with that of the Penarth/Cadoxton coast line on 6 May 1968. With incredible administrative folly the line was cut short at Penarth Town, instead of being allowed to continue to the end of the built-up area at Lower Penarth. The last boat train left Barry Pier on 11 October 1971, and the station closed a week later.

In terms of communication Barry is surviving the gradual demise of its railway system reasonably well, and roads are now beginning to improve in compensation. But the Docks pose a less tractable problem. In spite of a host of minor improvements in business, no effective substitute has been found for the coal trade, and the future looks dark. And yet it seems incredible that no constructive use can be found for this great capital asset. A large-scale project such as a marine development area for Severnside would be attractive, but is more likely to find favour east of Cardiff. The import of oil in supertankers has been pre-empted by Milford Haven with its superior deep-water access, but even there activity is declining. The effects of a Severn Barrage are problematical, and might leave Barry literally high and dry. Growth areas in British industry include electronics, computers, artificial fibres, furniture and footware, but none of these requires great space in which to operate, nor a great handling and sea-transport system for distributing its products. Industries that require bulky supplies, for instance, nuclear power, aircraft construction, motor manufacture and civil engineering equipment, have no particularly logical link with Barry and are already sufficiently catered for elsewhere. Undoubtedly there is scope for more service-based industry, but this does not require docks as such. It would be pleasant to end on an optimistic note, but unfortunately the future of the Docks, and to a great extent the future of Barry, will have to depend on some initiative yet to be formulated. A future historian may liken Barry Docks to the scaffolding raised to build the town and subsequently removed.

This article depends considerably on the author's personal knowledge and experience, to which references are not easily given. Many books and periodicals have been consulted, and a selection is listed to supplement the key references given in the text.

References

1 Figures of pits in operation in 1924: *Great Western Railway Guide*; in 1984: letter dated 13.8.1984 from Public Relations Officer, N.C.B., South Wales Area, Llanishen, Cardiff. This also stated that nine open-cast sites were being worked in November 1983.

2 *Law Journal Reports*, 1877, vol. 46, p. 206, *Law Reports*, Chancery 4, 1876, p. 315, *in re* Barry Railway Company, December 1876.

3 Jenner buys Barry Island: Barry Extension Railway Bill 1866. Lords Committee question to Jenner, no. 401. Indenture of sale and mortgage to United Kingdom Insurance Company, both dated 28.2.1867. GRO, Plymouth Estate Collection.

4 NLW MS LL/F/60; I am indebted to Mr. Howard J. Thomas for this reference.

5 Treharne buys Barry Island: Indenture of Sale dated 18.4.1874. GRO, Plymouth Estate Coll.

6 Windsor Estate buys Barry Island: Indenture of Sale dated 8.4.1878. GRO, Plymouth Estate Coll.

7 Cardiff Chamber of Commerce report: *Cardiff Times*, 15.10.1881.

8 *South Wales Daily News*, 16.8.1890.

9 House of Lords Committee, 1883, Question 6745.

10 *Cardiff Times*, 1.7.1882.

11 Letters dated 29.9.1881 and 15.10.1881 from Rhymney Railway Company. GRO, Plymouth Estate Coll.

12 Letter from R. Forrest to J. W. Barry dated 17.8.1883. GRO, Plymouth Estate Coll.

13 The statue of David Davies was unveiled on 3.3.1893.

14 Information on trade returns for Cardiff, Penarth and Barry Docks up to 1921 from notebook entitled 'Bute Docks, Cardiff, Statistics' compiled by C. S. Denniss, Manager of the Cardiff Railway Company; kept at Cardiff Dock Offices.

15 Report by Lt. Col. H. A. Yorke, R. E., dated 6.4.1898, on the failure of the viaduct and the subsidence of an embankment at Porthkerry on the Vale of Glamorgan Railway. PRO, Ministry of Transport Archives, sessional papers: House of Commons C.8910, 1898, vol. 81. In Appendices II and IV attention is drawn to serious discrepancies between sectional drawings of local strata and the situation already revealed by excavation.

16 British Rail Divisional Press Office, Cardiff, PR 575 'A new railway is built in South Wales'. September 1979, and PR 582 'A new railway opens', 15 January 1980.

17 For general treatment of subject: R. Wall, *The Bristol Channel Pleasure Steamers* (David & Charles, 1973).

18 Barry Railway personnel: PRO (Kew) Rail 23, piece 45.

19 Barry Railway rolling stock: H. N. Appleby, *Barry Docks: a description of the undertaking* (n.d.), p. 15, locomotives (148); coaching stock (194); goods and other wagons (2,316); p. 27, cranes in use on docks (65).

20 The end of the Barry Railway Company: R. J. Rimell, *A History of the Barry Railway Company* (Cardiff, 1923), pp. 102-3.

21 Coal shipment statistics 1889-1981: Cardiff Dock Manager's Office.

22 See ref. 21.

23 See ref. 21.

24 See ref. 21.

25 *Western Mail*, 16.8.1984, p. 11: report on negotiations between Geest Lines and officials of T.G.W.U. Subsequent news has confirmed the Company's intention to stay at Barry.

26 *Report of the Committee of Enquiry into the Ports of Great Britain* Cmd. 1824 (HMSO, 1962).

27 'Locomania', article in *The Guardian*, 5.2.1983, reporting interview with David Woodham.

28 NERC: souvenir publication on occasion of official opening of headquarters by Secretary of State for Wales on 16.9.1972. A local industrial dispute has since 1981 prevented the servicing and loading of NERC vessels at Barry.

[29] I am grateful to Commander Donald Moore, R.D., R.N.R. (retd.), for information about the R.N.R. at Barry.

[30] British Transport Docks Board, *Barry* (1980), current publicity brochure.

Principal published works consulted

D. Aldcroft, *British transport since 1914* (David & Charles, 1975).

G. C. Allen, *British industries and their organisation,* 4th ed. (Longmans, 1959).

S. W. Allen, *Reminiscences of Cardiff over fifty years* (Cardiff, 1918). Contains Tylke's account of Barry Island.

D. S. Barrie, *The Barry Railway* (Oakwood Press, 1962), and *The Taff Vale Railway* (Oakwood Press, repr. 1969).

D. Brock, *Small coal and smoke rings* (John Murray, 1983). The career of a Barry locomotive fireman.

N. Buxton, *The economic development of the coal industry* (Batsford, 1979).

M. Daunton, *Coal metropolis: Cardiff 1870-1914* (Univ. Leicester Press, 1977).

J. Davies, *Cardiff and the Marquesses of Bute* (Univ. Wales Press, 1981).

T. Ewbank, *The geography and history of Barry* (Cardiff, n.d.).

Glamorgan County History, vol. 5 (Cardiff, 1980).

Great Western ports, various editions, 1923-47.

T. I. Jeffreys Jones, *Acts of Parliament concerning Wales, 1714-1901* (Univ. Wales Press, repr. 1966).

C. M. Law, *British regional development since World War I* (David & Charles, 1980).

G. Manners, *South Wales in the sixties* (Pergamon Press, 1964).

B. Miller, *Rails to prosperity* (Regional Publications, Bristol, 1984). Photographs of the Barry Railway Company's steam locomotives and engineering works.

J. Page, *South Wales* (Forgotten Railways series, David & Charles, 1979).

S. Pollard, *The development of the British economy, 1914-1967* (E. Arnold, repr. 1973).

R. J. Rimell, *The history of the Barry Railway Company* (Cardiff, 1923).

R. Takel, *Industrial port development* (Scientechica (Publishers) Ltd. Bristol, 1974).

Ivor B. Thomas, *Top Sawyer* (London, 1938). Life of David Davies.

L. J. Williams and J. H. Morris, *The South Wales coal industry, 1841-1975* (Univ. Wales Press, 1958).

Articles and monographs

H. F. Adams, 'On the nature . . . of the coal seams in South Wales' (Institute of Mining, 1969).

J. Robinson, 'Barry Old Dock' in *Proc. Inst. of Civil Engineers,* 1890, and in *Proc. S. Wales Inst. of Engineers*, 1890.

South Wales Coal Annual, 1907 and 1917: articles on Barry Railway Company and North's Navigation Collieries Company.

D. A. Thomas, 'The growth of the trade in coal'. Address to Royal Statistical Society, 1903.

E. Picton Turberville, 'I saw them build a railway' (Vale of Glamorgan) in *Glamorgan County Magazine*, 1951.

Stewart Williams, *Glamorgan Historian,* vols. 7 and 11, for information on J. P. Seddon in articles on Llandaff.

Documents and records

Bristol University Library: for H. M. Brunel, copies of letters in Brunel Collection.

Cardiff Central Library: Arbitration—executors/T. A. Walker, Barry Dock and Railways Company, 1890; Bute Estate papers; printed evidence to Parliament on Dock and Railway Bills 1878-90.

Dock offices at Barry and Cardiff: printed evidence to Parliament on Dock and Railway Bills etc., 1879-1912.

Glamorgan Record Office, Cardiff: Wenvoe Estate papers; Plymouth Estate Collection; Randall Collection; records of North's Navigation Collieries (1889) Company Ltd.; Quarter Sessions deposited plans and Acts of Parliament.

Public Record Office, Kew: archives of railway companies; reports of Board of Trade Inspector on Vale of Glamorgan line, 1897, 1898, 1900.
National Library of Wales, Aberystwyth: Szlumper MSS 9242-3 for arbitration between J. Pethwick Bros., contractors, and Vale of Glamorgan Company.

Newspapers: Western Mail, South Wales Daily News, Cardiff Times.

Periodicals: The Engineer, Engineering, Illustrated London News.

Unpublished theses: L. N. A. Davies, 'The Barry Dock and Railways Company', M.A. (Wales), 1938. D. Lloyd, 'The coal export trade of the United Kingdom . . .' M.A. (Wales), 1932. Both at University Registry, Cardiff.

Acknowledgements

The author records his gratitude for help given by officials of the following institutions: the House of Lords Record Office, the Public Record Office at Kew and Chancery Lane, The Guildhall Library, London, the National Library of Wales, the Glamorgan Record Office, the Cardiff Central Library of the County of South Glamorgan, the British Transport Docks Board at Cardiff and Barry, and British Rail at Cardiff; also by the following individuals: Mr. G. Hallet, Cardiff, Dr. C. Donovan, Birmingham, Mr. David Roberts, Assistant Docks Engineer, Mr. H. J. Thomas, Mr. Malcolm Cook, Mr. A. Q. James, Shunting Inspector, Captain James Mason, Mrs. E. Poole, Weston-super-Mare (granddaughter of S. A. Tylke), Mr. Colin Chapman, Braunston, and Lady Gladwyn. Special thanks are given to successive Barry Docks Managers for access to the Managerial Library.

An Errand of Mercy

Since the Nursing Association was established in 18
over 5,000 Cases have been nursed
and over 150,000 visits paid.
Your practical sympathy in aid of this excellent institute
is earnestly invited.

CHAPTER VII

Ambition, Vice and Virtue: Social Life, 1884-1914

BRIAN C. LUXTON

)ate stone, Culley's
Iotel, Barry Dock.
imon Prosser.

THE coming of the railway and the building of the docks at Barry have been described in the last chapter. These remarkable developments had far-reaching consequences which transformed the villages of Barry, Cadoxton and Merthyr Dyfan into a complete, up-to-date town in the space of thirty years. A new community was created, very different from the old. In its early days there were scenes of squalor, vice and disorder, but ambition, hard work, discipline and high-mindedness eventually triumphed.

The *South Wales Daily News* declared in 1891: 'no port in the kingdom exhibits a more marvellously thriving record, or views the future with more confidence than this latest *protégé* of fortune'.[1] Barry abounded with ambitious projects, and was compared with the mushroom towns of the U.S.A. The members of the Barry and Cadoxton Local Board were described as 'the founding fathers'. Visitors were surprised and impressed, not least the Member of Parliament for the Rhondda, William Abraham (better known as 'Mabon') and Alfred Thomas, the Member for Cardiff, who came to see the dock in 1892. Another observer, General Booth, founder of the Salvation Army, recalled in 1894 that fifteen years previously there was nothing to be seen on the spot but a few rabbits and an occasional human being.[2] Barry had remained a rural backwater when nearby Cardiff was already transformed by the Industrial Revolution.

The source of Barry's new prosperity was the 'black diamond'—Welsh steam coal. This was exported to markets all over the world, and the heyday of the port was from 1889 to 1914. Coal exports began at 3,000,000 tons and rose to a world record of 11,000,000 in 1913. The town had to accept the consequences of this activity. The thunder of coal falling into the holds of ships echoed by day and night; clouds of coal dust rose continually, falling

Fig. 75.
Poster: Barry Nursing Association.
Gareth Howe Coll.

on residential areas. In the absence of wind, it settled on the surface of the docks so thickly that more than one unwary stranger mistook it for firm ground. No place in Wales developed more rapidly. The population grew from 500 in 1881 to 33,763 in 1911. Immigrants poured in from other parts of Wales, the West Country, Ireland, Scotland and elsewhere to take advantage of the boom. The present author's own antecedents—English Scottish and Irish—mirror the town's cosmopolitan nature. In public life, the first three chairmen of the Urban District Council were an Englishman, an Irishman and a Welshman. In 1896 only one third to a quarter of the population of 20,000 were Welsh.

The end of the old order

The local inhabitants and their traditions were overwhelmed by the 'foreigners'. Cadoxton's feast-day on the last Monday in July and other old customs such as the 'Mari Lwyd'[3] (celebrated on Christmas Eve) disappeared. The habit of whitewashing and bedecking graves with floral tributes on Palm (or Flowering) Sunday—*Sul y Blodau*—was still strongly observed in the 1890s but was less popular by 1914. Another local custom, 'chaining the bridegroom' waned. The newly-weds would find the Church exit blocked by friends who would request the wherewithal to drink the health of the bride and groom. The custom broke down with the influx of so many strangers unfamiliar with it. In April 1892 a newly-wed 'Happy Billy' was dragged roughly along the graveyard of the parish church at Cadoxton for failing to acknowledge the custom.[4]

The old villagers lost many of their privileges. By-laws prevented them keeping pigs and poultry in their gardens. A correspondent, 'Anti-Mutton', and others, in letters to the Press complained about sheep wandering the streets at night and eating garden produce. It was suggested that the 'horrid creatures' be butchered for mutton to be used in soup kitchens for the poor. Horses were seen to gambol wildly in Holton Road 'heedless of Sabbath-day decorum and public safety'. Many of the stray animals came from Cadoxton Common, and public attention was now focussed on the Common's future. The Common was being cut up by wagon wheels and encroached upon for housebuilding. Quoit players damaged the turf with their games. The Commoners were reluctant to relinquish their hereditary rights, but in 1896 a Barry Urban District Council Bill was passed in Parliament, and resulted in their being awarded compensation for loss of rights.[5]

Familiar landmarks were obliterated by street construction and important footpaths, such as that between Cadoxton and Sully, were lost. A thatched cottage on the brow of Cadoxton Common near the old parish pound had for more than a century withstood the ravages of time, but by April 1894 a considerable part of the roof had fallen in and the walls were collapsing through neglect.[6] The spot on which the cottage stood was one of the most picturesque in the neighbourhood. The beautiful scene was skilfully represented on canvas by J. Clark Fairbairn (*d.* 1913), who captured our heritage with this and other views of the district when yet unspoilt.

Rapid development resulted in the town's first conservation struggle. An attempt by the local authority to remove the Old Elm Tree—a meeting point for locals at the junction of Pencoedtre and Robins Lane—was vigorously opposed. The District Council bowed to pressure and built a retaining wall about the tree, but when it died in the summer of 1899, its removal symbolised the end of an era.[7]

The navvies arrive

The first of the new inhabitants were the navvies who excavated the docks, railways and other works. The work was forced at a rapid rate and caused about a hundred and fifty fatalities and five hundred serious injuries.[8] There were fewer casualties in the construction of the second dock. Although casualties were usually attributed to carelessness and negligence on the part of the workmen, most accidents were caused by falls of earth and rock, moving wagons or machinery.[9]

The navvies arrived in November 1884, and when the construction was at its height there were about three thousand employed day and night to complete the work. On the opening of the dock in 1889 a great number left to work elsewhere, although some remained to build the fast-growing town. Success led to the construction of the East Dock (renamed No. 2 Dock in 1896) between 1894 and 1898, when fully two thousand navvies were employed.[10] A further thousand or so were engaged in constructing the Lady Windsor Deep Lock, the Island and Pierhead railway and the Vale of Glamorgan Railway.[11]

Initially accommodation was insufficient and many slept in barns, stables and outhouses. Crudely-constructed wooden and iron huts were thrown up in Cadoxton and Barry.[12] Working conditions were grim at first, and little better when work began on Dock No. 2. The contractors neglected to provide shelter for the navvies on site where they could rest and have their meal breaks, and they were forced to find a cold stone, or wet plank, or simply to stamp about in the mud, eating 'cold tommy', with their backs turned to the sleet, wind or rain.

Navvies seldom complained, and were remembered a generation later by Thomas Ewbank as 'great lusty fellows, rough in manner, terrible fighters and as hard as nails. Yet beneath this rough exterior they were gentlemen at heart for they were always polite to women and generous to a fault. They lived well, would not wear anything shoddy and would never allow a mate to be in need'[13]. They loved dressing up for special occasions such as the annual Cadoxton Sports, held in the 1880s and 1890s. Spotless white trousers, red or purple plush waistcoats, brown velveteen coats with large buttons, red cotton neckerchiefs or brightly coloured scarfs were typical dress. The womenfolk were gaily dressed and wore plaid shawls and bonnets, decked with artificial flowers.

Building begins

Cadoxton, with High Street and its adjoining area in what was called 'East Barry' or 'Walker's Town', were the first districts to be built up. The construction of Holton Road and the adjoining streets in the early 1890s made Barry Dock into the new commercial centre in place of Cadoxton. In 1891 a local newspaper could rightly comment: 'The Barry Dock district is rapidly consolidating itself into a town, and we can see the day—not too far distant either—when Barry and Cadoxton will be merely handmaids to the central superstructure'.[14] The plan for the first house on the Island was passed in March 1892 and building proceeded rapidly in the spring of that year.[15] By December 1898 the town was losing its rough appearance; 'gaps in streets have not long to wait before being filled with substantial buildings, and some of the best architectural results of the time are in evidence . . . land has been laid out and houses built in all directions to meet the demands of those having work at the docks and in the neighbourhood. The country around is so pretty and healthy that the district is growing as a residential suburb'.[16]

Mud was a problem in the winter months. F. M. Harris, engineer and secretary to the Barry and Cadoxton Gas and Water Company, remembered the town in 1887 as being 'of the most dismal and dreary character, the whole of the area between Barry and Cadoxton being a

Plate XLVI. Culley's Hotel, Dock View Road, Barry Dock. Architect's drawing. *C.M.B.*

veritable wilderness of mud and discomfort with hardly a house to be seen excepting perhaps the Central Police Station'.[17] A postal employee later recalled that Thompson Street in 1891 was a muddy lake into which the tide flowed, and that he had to wade through it up to his waist. Eventually the lake was drained and Thompson Street was built. A stream flowed down what is now Tynewydd Road, and there was only one house there. Also there were woods from Newlands Street to the Central Police Station.[18]

In November 1888 the *Barry and Cadoxton Journal* commented on Cadoxton's roads: 'In the centre of Cadoxton itself the roads are veritable quagmires. At one point a small streamlet crosses the highway. In summer it is perhaps a purling, bubbling brook, but in winter, after such rain as has been recently experienced, it swells out into a mighty mud lake, two feet deep and over thirty feet wide. The unfortunate pedestrian is compelled to climb a clayey bank, plod through mortar-like mud, and after crossing the interposing Slough of Despond by means of a couple of planks, he is obliged to cling lovingly to a very wet and rough barked tree in order to avoid slipping down a muddy declivity, angled on either side to 40 degrees. Such on dark nights is the method of communication between one part of Cadoxton and the other'.[19]

In the winter of 1890 the mud on the streets in Cadoxton and Holton Road was more than ankle-deep, bringing trade to a standstill. Shopkeepers in Main Street, Cadoxton, where most trade was concentrated, complained to the Local Board that it was a common thing for people to be thrown from vehicles into the mud owing to the fearful condition of the roads.[20] The mud was nearly knee-deep in December. 'Of all places in the world', the *Cardiff Argus* declared, 'no place more closely resembled Bunyan's Slough of Despond than Cadoxton and Barry'. By November 1891 the condition of the roads was nearly as bad as in the previous year, and the mud was already several inches deep. Strangers in Holton Road preferred walking to Cadoxton Station rather than Barry Dock Station owing to ankle-deep mud in Thompson Street. When work began on the private improvements in Thompson Street and neighbouring streets in February 1892 the contractor experienced great difficulty in finding a solid foundation because of a great pool of mud. Kenilworth Road and surrounding streets were in a most miserable condition and an eyesore to the town. Strangers referred to Cadoxton in January 1894 as 'Mudoxton' or 'Slushoxton', but the *Barry Dock News* protested that the streets were decidedly cleaner and healthier than those of Cardiff.[21] One resident complaining of mud in Jewel and George Streets in December 1896 suggested that lifebelts should be placed at convenient distances along these streets for the safeguarding of life.

Early economic problems

The problem of mud could be overcome, but even in those days of booming prosperity the essential economic weakness of Barry was apparent to some. Its reliance on coal and its proximity to the economically more soundly-based Cardiff were pointers to the future. An observant newcomer wrote in July 1893:

> 'The Barry district . . . presents a very peculiar aspect in many respects. The unfinished streets, heaps of refuse, and large spaces of wasteland may be passed by as the usual adjuncts to a newly formed town . . . There are, however, several peculiarities . . . one . . . is the very large number of untenanted houses, more especially on the Cadoxton side. Under ordinary circumstances this would be an indication of decay, but . . . it is clear that the ordinary explanation does not hold good . . . The amplitude of work at the docks, the brisk business-like appearance of the inhabitants, the dividends of the Barry Company, the activity of building trades all testify to the healthy vigorous life of the young port. We must look a little below the surface for the cause of the half-deserted appearance of the district. The industries upon which Barry depends for its existence are very few. The export of coal, ship repairing, the management of the dock and railways and the building trades are practically the whole. There is no import trade worth speaking of, the small quantity of timber brought into port affording but little support to the inhabitants. For some reason or other a very large proportion of the coal-trimmers, engineers, boilermakers, and even men engaged in the building trades, reside in Cardiff and travel to Barry and their work in the morning and return to Cardiff at night'.[22]

The correspondent continued:

> 'Another deplorable custom of the Barry people . . . is that of rushing to Cardiff to spend the money which has been earned in the district . . . This custom must be put down to want of loyalty on the part of the inhabitants, which must, if Barry is to go to a position of power and importance, be eradicated and its place supplied by a strong local patriotism'.

In 1891 nearly a thousand workmen regularly employed in the Barry district returned every evening to their houses at Cardiff, Penarth and Cogan etc.[23] It was believed that extra housing would solve the problem. By 1893, however, many empty houses existed. Winter mud made the town unattractive. Wandering sheep and horses were a further unwelcome feature, while in November 1893 a visitor said Barry resembled Constantinople in the unusually large number of dogs infesting its streets to the annoyance of adults and the fright of children.

Naming the new town

A number of factors hindered development. From the beginning there was a jealous rivalry between Barry and Cadoxton. Cadoxton was mostly working-class, while the west end was referred to in June 1892 as 'swelldom'. It was the district which provided the professionals—merchants, lawyers, financiers, public officials, surveyors, clerks and the like—who were to be seen every morning alighting from the 9.40 train at Cadoxton station.[24] The relationship between the two places was likened to that between residential Penarth and work-a-day Cardiff. Residents could not even agree upon the town's name, which remained a matter of contention for some years. Rival claims were put forward. In 1890 it was suggested that Cadoxton be called 'Barry Dock Town'. The new name never became popular and by the beginning of 1891 was 'long forgotten as a dream'. Monsignor Williams, a Roman Catholic priest, suggested in May 1892 that Barry and Cadoxton be called 'Barry Town'. Others suggested 'Barryton' and the *Western Mail* commented : 'The present conglomeration of names is perfectly idiotic'. In 1894 the first meeting of the Urban District authority fixed its own name as 'the Barry Urban District Council'. An attempt to name it 'the Barry and Cadoxton Urban District Council' was defeated. A public enquiry was held in July 1895 to hear evidence for and against a U.D.C. proposal to unite the three parishes of Barry, Cadoxton and Merthyr Dyfan. J. A. Hughes, Clerk to the District Council, felt that it was very desirable that all the inhabitants of the town should feel that they belonged to the same town.[25] The area's fate was decided. It became 'Barry'. There remained many in Cadoxton who agreed with Thomas Jenkins, New House, that it was incorrect to name the town 'Barry'. In 1888 the *Barry and Cadoxton Journal* had predicted: 'we believe that the coming town will be called "Barry", not after East Barry nor after the Parish of Barry or Barry Island, but simply because the Dock is called the "Barry" Dock'.[26]

ˡate XLVII.
ˡock View Road,
arry Dock, *c.* 1905.
.ote trees planted by
ˡouncil.
ˡ.*C.L. Coll.*

Early development

Barry lacked a benefactor on the grand scale of Lord Bute in Cardiff or Lord Tredegar at Newport. Lord Windsor, the chairman of the Barry Company, which brought the town into being, was more a benefactor to Penarth than Barry, though he gave land on Nell's and Friars Points. In May 1895 a local merchant made a vigorous attack upon the Barry Company for failing in its civic duty and revealing the most utter unconcern and indifference to the town's development. He observed that with the exception of John Cory 'not a single member of the directorate or of the other principal shareholders . . . has contributed in any possible form whatever towards the growth and development of the town . . . The one supreme duty of the Barry Proprietors seems to be to make money to the utmost possible degree and to leave the town to struggle on for existence as best it may'.[27] The directors had made a negligible contribution to the erection of places of worship, to the Nursing Association, public reading rooms, and the establishment of an intermediate school.[28] They played an insignificant part in the social, intellectual and commercial development of the town.

The development of the town was left to speculators. Street layouts were determined by the boundaries of fields purchased by a particular company. This explains the sometimes puzzling and poorly-planned layout which is a headache to late 20th-century development. A grand design or centralised scheme was never considered and Barry grew irregularly, losing a golden opportunity to be a well planned town. This defect is apparent now that Barry is essentially a residential town. Speculation led to over-fast development, the use of cheap materials and the search for maximum profit. There was much shoddy workmanship, which even at the time was much criticised and regretted by those looking at the long-term position of the town. Black's *Guide to South Wales* described Barry as being in an unfinished state, with streets which were characteristic examples of the jerry-builders' style.[29] Speakers at the fortnightly meeting of the Barry Trades and Labour Council in May 1896 demanded the erection of suitable working-class dwellings because of the existing high rents and jerry-built houses. One delegate said that houses were literally swarming with cockroaches and other vermin, and owing to the defective material used in their construction they would literally fall, were they not sustained by somewhat better-built side houses. One builder was even charged with mixing the mortar and plaster with liquid sewage. Barry's streets were not all jerry-built. In September 1891 the 'really splendid class of houses that are in course of erection in Travis Street' were considered large and of pleasing appearance. The style and finish of houses in course of erection by E. J. Parfitt in Kingsland Crescent met with approval, and both streets when completed were to be amongst the best in the district.[30]

It was considered that the syndicates and companies which had exploited the town had built far too many houses. Rents fell, and in February 1892 there were 724 houses either unoccupied or only partially constructed. The trend was reversed, however, with the start of construction of Dock No. 2 in July 1894. Houses were once more sold at a premium. By November 1894 there was scarcely a dwelling house to be obtained in the town.

Speculators lost even greater amounts of money in hotel construction, and some thirteen hotels, magnificent buildings, to cost in aggregate £50,000, never obtained a licence.[31] The Cadoxton Hotel, Vere Street, with thirty rooms was built in 1886 at a cost of £4,500. It was refused a licence on the fourth application in October 1890 because there was no road in front of the main entrance. Its grand front porch still opens directly on to the railway embankment, because at the time of construction it was wrongly speculated that the main road would be there. Plans for the proposed £16,000 Imperial Hotel, Weston Hill, were hurriedly drawn up, to be placed before the Brewster Sessions in September 1897. They showed the drainage running

ate XLVIII.
arry Hotel, Broad
reet, Barry, 1983.
Daly.

uphill. This created much mirth, especially to the strong representation from the Temperance party, who were fighting the granting of licences. Needless to say, the hotel never obtained a licence and, like many others planned, was never built. Some were turned to other uses. The Osborne later became the Cadoxton Conservative Club, the Queen's Hotel in Weston Square became the South Wales Bible College; the Court for many years was a steam laundry, while Palmerstown Hotel and the New Dock Hotel, Cardiff Road, were converted into flats. The Barry Dock Hotel, Holton Road, became the Voluntary Hospital for the Destitute Sick and Dying. The Woodland Hotel, at the junction of Tynewydd Road and Woodland Road, became Council Offices; The Alexandra Hotel, at the junction of Newland Street and Woodland Road, was used by the Y.M.C.A. The Sea View Hotel, Dock View Road, became the Sea View Labour Club and Institute Ltd. Others, such as the Glebe in Arthur Street and Morlais Court in Morlais Street, have been demolished.

Local government and public health

To deal with the teething problems of the young town, a Local Government Board, with offices in Vere Street, was formed in 1888. But its powers proved insufficient to cope with the growth of the town, and the Barry Urban District Council was established in 1894. In January 1896 the Council Offices were moved from Vere Street to Nos. 158 and 160 Holton Road, but in 1908 they moved again to purpose-built public offices on King Square.[32] The Council's authority covered the parishes of Barry, Cadoxton, Merthyr Dyfan and Barry Island (the last-named having severed its centuries-long link with Sully parish); in 1896 they were constituted the civil parish of Barry.

When the first meeting of the Barry and Cadoxton Local Board was held on 12th July, 1888, the founding fathers of the new town were faced with a chaotic situation. The rapid increase in population had led to serious overcrowding of dwellings. A rough census, taken by the Medical Officer of Health in 1889, revealed an average of nearly nine persons to every house.[33] The demand for houses was so great that they were sold at high prices even before completion, and instances were known where houses were occupied even before the doors and windows were fitted. The houses at East Barry provided by T. A. Walker, the dock contractor, for his own workers were supplied with water and an adequate drainage system, but unfortunately the sanitary and water supplies for the greater part of the town were seriously at fault, which risked the grave possibility of an epidemic. Cadoxton in particular was honeycombed with imperfectly-constructed drains and cesspools which overflowed into the Cadoxton Brook at every shower; the stench during the summer months was not merely foul, but a serious health hazard. Matters were made worse in Cadoxton by an insufficient water supply. By 1888 the small leaky reservoir, constructed at Pencoedtre in

1870-3 to supply a population of three hundred, was totally insufficient for the six thousand inhabitants.[34] This shortage made it necessary to use the old village wells, but these were also subject to pollution. Apart from the shortage of living accommodation and of water and gas supplies, there was no provision for street lighting, and the roads were roughly laid.

The health hazard was the major concern. In April 1891 the sanitary condition of Holton was 'utterly horrifying and reprehensible'. The area was reeking with sanitary imperfections and sewage filth. In Castleland and Graving Dock Streets earth and stone barriers were constructed to prevent large pools and channels of dirty water from flooding the houses. In the back lanes of Evans Street and the adjoining area the liquid and other filth emanating from the scores of overflowing closet pans ran in 'a hideous stream' to Holton Road. In March 1891 a young man who lived in Evans Street died of typhus fever.[35] The approach of summer promised a worsening of the situation, so the Local Board took prompt and effective action. In April 1891 notices were served upon owners of property to remove the nuisances in private streets and back lanes. Failure to comply allowed the Board to deal with the defects and charge owners. By 1895 Dr. Williams, the Public Medical Officer for Glamorgan, stated that the sanitary condition

late XLIX.
'ater Inspectors of
arry Urban District
ouncil, 1904.
harles Nesbitt,
.J. Thomas Coll.

of Barry was satisfactory.[36] There had been much progress made to improve the health of the district during 1894 through the enforcement of by-laws for regulating seaman's boarding houses and the proper flushing of toilets. The Local Board tackled other problems with equal vigour. Soon after 1888 the housing situation was greatly improved by the erection of a large number of dwellings for dock workers. By 1890 the drainage was in a more satisfactory condition and by July 1891 it was completed with the opening of two outfall sewers—one at the Bendrick Rock and the other at the Old Harbour. Appalling nuisances caused by the outfall of sewage into Barry Harbour led to work on a new sewerage system, which was in operation by August 1894.[37]

Inadequate road surfacing and paving were dealt with by private improvements encouraged by the Local Board. By 1890 plans for paving and resurfacing the main streets of Cadoxton were under way to rid the area of its abominable mud. In October 1891 new roads from Cadoxton to the Central Police Station (*via* Weston Hill) and from Barry Road to the Central Police Station were opened and lit with gas-lamps.[38] By February 1891 the main streets and roads in the town were gradually assuming a tolerably satisfactory state. In November 1891 Barry Road had been 'transformed from a miserably narrow dingy lane into a fine, healthy, public thoroughfare'. However, mud remained a serious nuisance throughout the 1890s.

The Barry and Cadoxton Gas and Water Company, incorporated in September 1886, provided gas for street lighting and for domestic use and an abundant supply of fresh water. Gas was used for the first time in Barry in December 1889. In August 1890 the roads of Barry and Cadoxton were being dotted over with gas lamp pillars,[39] and in November a large number of public lamps were being lit for the first time in the Barry Dock district. The Barry and Cadoxton Waterworks at Biglis opened in October 1890, together with the high- and low-level reservoirs at Stumpy Hall and Pencoedtre.[40] The Local Board acquired both the Gas and Water undertakings in November 1894.[41] A new high-level reservoir at the Colcot, capable of supplying the town with an additional 10,000,000 gallons a month, was opened in April 1899.[42]

The Barry Dock and Railway Company's property was lit by electricity before the town. The Windsor Hotel, Holton Road, was the first building in the town, as distinct from dock property, to be lit by electricity. This was on Tuesday, 22 December 1896. It remained however something of a novelty, for it was not until December 1924 that the Council empowered the South Wales Electrical Distribution Co. Ltd., to lay cable for the town's supply.[43]

Two further improvements in public health were the provision of a public abattoir and the opening of the first refuse destructor in South Wales. The temporary slaughter house in Court Road was such a flimsy structure it was said that the first bull taken there would walk away with the building. However, when it opened in October 1892, G.M. Burnett, the butcher, killed the first oxen without mishap. A more permanent abattoir built between Court Road and Barry Road, was opened in December 1897.[44] On an adjoining site the refuse destructor, capable of burning 30 tons of refuse a day, opened in February 1901.[45]

Hospitals

Barry expanded its health and educational facilities to become one of the most socially-advanced towns in Wales. The growth of a busy seaport with the increased risk of accidents at the docks and the fear of infectious diseases reaching the town from abroad, led to a demand for hospital facilities, which was partly met by voluntary institutions and partly by the local authority. When work commenced on constructing the first dock, T. A. Walker kept a small hospital in High Street. It had a trained nurse as matron. It proved of great service and dealt with many accidents. Dr. George Neale was the surgeon to the men employed on the work.[46] It was closed in August 1889 and two rooms were taken in Princes Street, where persons injured at the dock could be treated. This primitive hospital was in charge of Dr. Gore.

The Barry and District Nursing Association, a voluntary institution, was formed in February 1891[47] to cope with the needs of the sick and poor. It was funded by the patronage of the local gentry and required £250 *per annum* to maintain its services. It charged a sliding scale according to means; Miss Allen, of Porthkerry Rectory, and Major General Lee, of the Mount, Dinas Powys, were the secretary and treasurer respectively. Dr. Neale, M.O.H., was chairman of the committee, while Sister Amy Evans in April 1891 became the first lady nurse (and later superintendent). The committee appealed for gifts of old linen and flannel for bandages to use amongst the poor cottagers. The Association provided trained, non-resident nurses to attend the sick poor at their own homes and also, at a cheap rate, untrained, respectable women as resident foster mothers when the mother of a household fell ill. On 1 June 1891 a home was opened at No. 36 Kingsland Crescent. By March 1896 there were four nursing sisters besides the superintendent, and their work extended over nine parishes with a population of 22,000.

The Local Board discussed the idea of establishing a cottage hospital supported from the rates as early as October 1891, but it was some years before the scheme took effect.[48] In January 1895 J. C. Meggitt purchased No. 34 Kingsland Crescent, the house adjoining the Nursing Association's Home. He handed it over for free use as a cottage hospital of six beds, to be worked by the Nursing Association for five years. The first patient was admitted in April 1895. Local medical men gave their services voluntarily, two being in attendance each month.

From the outset voluntary contributions proved inadequate and in December 1896 the Association requested the Urban District Council to undertake maintenance and control of the hospital. It was not until 1 March 1900, however, that the Council assumed control and management.[49] The increased volume of work made larger premises necessary, and in November 1908 the General Accident and Surgical Hospital in Wyndham Street received its first patient.[50] It contained twenty-seven beds, and performed operations recommended by the School Clinic as well as dealing with accidents. It was among the first three in the country to be municipally owned, controlled and supported. In addition, three specialised hospitals dealing with infectious diseases were established from the rates and were functioning by 1912. Barry and Cardiff Health Authorities combined in 1895 to erect a permanent Cholera, Plague and Yellow Fever Hospital of sixten beds on Flat Holm.[51] An agreement was made in 1905 between the Glamorgan County Council and the Barry Urban District Council to build a smallpox hospital of twelve beds off the Weycock Road, two-and-a-half miles outside the town centre.[52] A temporary, infectious diseases hospital, with three wards of three beds, was opened in a wooden building on the Barry Company's property in Dock Road on the eastern side of the timber pond near Mill Cottage in 1891. In 1894 the local authority was given three months' notice to remove the hospital, as the land was required for the construction of the new dock. The building was removed and re-erected at the Colcot. It was replaced by a public sanatorium of eighteen beds in 1898 for isolating cases of infectious disease, but it was not re-opened for its original purpose until late 1912. Two health institutions originated as voluntary, supported establishments. Miss Amy Evans, Lady Superintendent of the Accident Hospital resigned her post in a dispute over the imposition of levies and took over a hotel in Holton Road, which had failed to obtain a licence, in order to establish a 'Voluntary Hospital for the Destitute Sick and Dying'. It opened in April 1898 with room for nine or ten beds. The Royal Victoria Jubilee Nursing Home was built in Woodland Road with money raised by the townspeople to commemorate Queen Victoria's Diamond Jubilee. It became the new headquarters of the Barry Nursing Association when the Association moved from Kingsland Crescent in June 1899, and it was extended in 1904 to commemorate the Coronation of Edward VII.[53]

Schools and libraries

In compliance with the Elementary Education Act of 1870 the Cadoxton and Merthyr Dovan School Board was established in 1874, and the first Board School with accommodation for seventy-two children was opened on Cadoxton Common in 1879.[54] This school was enlarged in 1887, 1891 and 1895 to cater for the increase in pupil numbers. As the town expanded, other schools were erected—Hannah Street, Palmerstown Road, St. Helen's Roman Catholic School, High Street, Gladstone Road, Romilly Road, Clive Road, Barry Island and Holton Road—reputedly the largest school building in Wales at the time, with accommodation for over 2,000 pupils. By 1910 nine modern elementary schools with room for about 8,000 pupils had been erected.

The Barry authority was considered especially progressive in educational matters because of its buildings, equipment and staffing. It was among the first in the country to make provision for the teaching of backward and deaf children. A Special School was opened on 18 July 1904 with sixteen pupils and was held in the Fire Station. It was designed to give special help to those children who could not benefit from normal schooling. The authority was a pioneer in introducing kindergarten methods into the town's primary schools and in employing teachers fully trained for that work. Staff vacancies were filled only from applicants who were college-trained, and staffing was on a liberal scale so that there were no excessively large classes. Good facilities were early provided in each school for teaching cookery and laundry to the girls and manual work to the boys. Holton Road was the first school in Wales to teach metalwork. Work was not confined to metalcraft but included bookbinding, turnery and other craft occupations. The authority made good provision for further education and evening schools were commenced in 1886. In 1889 the School Board initiated a policy of providing better salaries and conditions to attract good teachers. It was very successful and helped greatly towards the high reputation Barry obtained in the educational world.[55]

Secondary education began with the opening of the County Intermediate School at the Buttrills in October 1896.[56] This was a result of the Welsh Intermediate Education Act of 1889, which attempted to fill the gap between the elementary schools and the newly-emerging university colleges in Wales with new schools, later known as 'secondary' for boys and girls of all classes. The County Council gave a grant of £2,000 towards the school on condition that £600 be provided in the district by means of voluntary subscription.[57] A further grant of £1,000 for scholarships in memory of David Davies of Llandinam was given by his son Edward; H. R. Norris became the first headmaster and was succeeded in 1899 by Major Edgar Jones, under whose headship the school was to achieve high acclaim. The school was co-educational until the autumn of 1913, when the girls moved to the Girls' Grammar School (now Bryn Hafren Lower School). In 1914, on a prominent site overlooking the town, the County Council established the Glamorgan Residential Training College for Women Students for the training of elementary teachers. By 1914, therefore, the foundations were adequately laid for the provision of both primary and secondary education in Barry.

Plate L.
A class outside T. A Walker's school in Queen Street, Barry in 1888.
R. F. Higgs.

The Barry and Cadoxton Local Board decided to adopt the Public Libraries Act, and in August 1891 free reading rooms opened at High Street, Holton Road and Main Street.[58] The lending library, situated next door to the public reading rooms in Holton Road, and containing several hundred volumes of carefully selected literature, was opened in November 1892 by Edwin F. Blackmore, secretary and librarian. The library and reading rooms were moved to more central and larger premises in the same road in the autumn of 1893. Blackmore wrote to Robert Forrest, Lord Windsor's representative, urging that relics discovered by John Storrie during his excavations on Barry Island be preserved as the nucleus of a town museum. Lord Windsor agreed, and in November 1895 arrangements were made for the reception of the relics in a room at the Public Library.[59] The generosity of Andrew Carnegie, an American multi-millionaire, led to the erection of the present town library at King Square in 1906 at a cost of £8,000.[60] New reading rooms were also opened at Cadoxton, Porthkerry and Barry Island.

Fire and police services

Barry's growth brought about an urgent need for fire and police services. In its early years the town failed to provide an adequate fire-fighting service. Its rapid development necessitated the erection of many temporary wooden structures which were a particular fire hazard. Buildings maintained barrels of water out of doors as a precaution against fire, but these were of little use in a serious outbreak. In August 1890 three sets of fire-extinguishing appliances, purchased by the Local Board, were supplied to each part of the town and were in care of the police. One set was at the Central Police Station, and a second was kept at the rear of the Royal Hotel. The third was probably housed in the High Street district. There was a public demand for the establishment of a Volunteer Fire Brigade in August 1891, but the police were reluctant to hand over the appliances. When in May 1892 a public meeting unanimously called for the establishment of a Voluntary Brigade, Chief Constable Wake said he did not think a Volunteer brigade was necessary. This sentiment was repeated in March 1895 by Superintendent Giddings who believed the police under his command were quite sufficient to act as a brigade and did not need the help of private citizens. However, in September 1896 the police experienced great difficulty in fighting a fire in Llewellyn Street, Cadoxton; being without a hand truck, they had to carry the hose to the scene of the fire.[61] As a result of mounting public pressure a Volunteer Fire Brigade was established in June 1899 with J. G. Walliker as captain. A centrally-situated Fire Station was opened in Court Road in 1901. The first engine was horse-drawn, but it was soon apparent that this single engine was insufficient and the Urban Council were urged to purchase a new motor fire-engine. The need was underlined by a fire that caused extensive damage at Meggitt and Jones Timber Yard in 1908, in which valuable buildings were destroyed. Superintendent Morris in a letter to the Council gave two reasons why more modern appliances were required. First, that with the present facilities, only one fire could be dealt with at a time, and secondly that any large conflagration necessitated the help of modern appliances from Penarth and Cardiff. Despite this warning it was not until May 1913, four years after a devastating fire at the old Theatre Royal and Hippodrome, that the town acquired its first motor fire-engine.[62]

The first policeman was housed in a small cottage in Main Street until the opening in 1886 of the County Police Station in Holton Road, built by T. A. Walker in what was then a country lane. The Barry Dock Police Court, built on an adjoining site, opened in January 1892.[63] In Cadoxton a branch station in Iddesleigh Street, which opened in 1890, was moved in December 1892 to a larger building adjoining, where the number of constables was increased from two to three. It was provided with two cells for the reception of 'prisoners of a desperate or notorious character'. In 1909 this station was replaced by a new one at the foot of Weston Hill, while a branch station at No. 44 High Street, which opened in the 1880s to serve the west end, was replaced in 1914 by a new station in Harbour Road.

Drink, disorder and crime

In the 1880s with the influx of nearly 5,000 men, whose accommodation was in huts characteristic of public works, there were many who indulged in night poaching, and on the outskirts of town it was not safe at night to be without a revolver for protection.[64] Every Saturday night, after 'closing time' doctors were called to attend cases of wounding as the result of drunken brawls, mainly of a family character. Police enquiries were daily arriving in the Barry and Cadoxton district from all parts of the U.K.; there was a feeling abroad that if a mischief-monger had made off, he could be found in Barry. Complaints were made of inadequate policing, especially at night, in the Barry Dock and Cadoxton districts. Vere Street was frequently

Plate LI.
Fire Station, Court Road, Barry.
B. Daly.

the scene of great disorder and obscenity. 'Last Saturday a fight took place between two navvies opposite the Mill Farm House and a woman was lying helplessly drunk on the pavement in Vere Street but there was no trace of the police'. In the late 1880s the Barry district was in charge of a couple of sergeants and three or four constables. As Barry grew, its status was raised to that of an inspectorate, and in July 1891 Edward Rees of Dowlais became the first police inspector in charge of the Barry district. In April 1894 the growing importance of the station led to the appointment of Superintendent Giddings as head of E Division of the County, with Barry Docks as headquarters. By November 1896 there were at Barry a superintendent in charge of the Division, an inspector, two sergeants, an acting sergeant and twenty-one constables of different grades.[65] Trouble continued at Cadoxton where 'as in no other part of the district, violent attacks upon the police are frequent'. In February 1891 it was reported that Cadoxton was becoming a notorious district for assaults on the police. It was served by only three constables and a sergeant, and only two officers were on duty at any one time. Trouble came at closing time on a Saturday night when one officer would be stationed at the top of Main Street and the other in Vere Street. Both would have more than their hands full; they were exposed to cowardly attacks and frequently received a mauling.

The 'demon drink' was a major cause of trouble. A particular nuisance were the shebeens, unlicensed premises where illicit drinking took place. Shebeens originated in Cadoxton, but by May 1892 the greatest number were found in the Barry Dock district.[66] One critic gave advice on how to run a shebeen: 'If you are a ganger, of say a body of navvies, rent a cottage . . . Inform your men that a drop of beer can be had at your new place of abode. Lay in a few casks of beer. Do not expend a large amount of money in furnishing the place. A rough wood form or two deal boxes turned up-ends with a plank placed across will make the usual seat for casual visitors. Cleanliness can easily be dispensed with. A few "blues" are far more necessary. By all means invest in a few gallons of fiery whiskey. The more it burns and tickles the throats of your thirsty customers the better name your "drinking shanty" will bear. It is almost compulsory that a fine buxom damsel should be engaged to wait upon the incoming lodgers. A lazy lout, with a red-tipped nose, to usher in your guests, or to chuck them out is another factor that must not be overlooked'.[67] Women such as the notorious Jane Meath alias 'Liverpool Jennie' were involved as much as men in running and frequenting the shebeens.

Shebeeners were liable to fines ranging upwards from £5 to the maximum of £100 or, in default, imprisonment with hard labour from fourteen days to a maximum of three months. The full penalty was first imposed in May 1894 on two occupants of Gueret Street, Barry Dock. Norah Collins had four previous convictions with fines of up to £50. Charles Hardy, who also had four previous convictions, went to prison for three months' hard labour. While Hardy was in Cardiff jail his wife carried on a shebeen. When the police raided the house it was filled with men and women, and outside a large crowd of men were involved in an *hôtel-de-marl* (an open-air drinking party). Police seized two four-and-a-half-gallon casks of beer and drinking utensils.[68] Law Officers involved in shebeen watching were nicknamed the 'flying squad'. They would watch houses for hours and would frequently be watched themselves by the shebeeners who could be violent and 'as sly as foxes'.

Another of those cases which added to the unenviable notoriety of Gueret Street happened when a policeman, passing an empty house at 3 a.m., heard sounds of revelry inside. He entered and saw about fifteen persons drinking from a four-and-a-half-gallon cask of beer. The lights were at once extinguished and the policeman was assaulted. Another constable arrived and he too was assaulted before three 'well known local loafers' were secured and taken against great odds to the Central Police Station.

Plate LII.
Ship stores on road into Docks, viewed from General Offices.
Glamorgan Record Office.

Thompson Street, which linked Barry Docks with the town centre, was as famous among seamen as Cardiff's Tiger Bay. Flanked by ship's chandlers and general provison stores, it attracted traders and residents from many parts of the world and was a great trouble spot. Cafés and restaurants, bars and barbers' shops, the Sailor's Rest, the Liberal and Coronation Clubs and mosque all gave it a unique character. Together with its side streets the area was notorious in the 1890s when it was compared with Merthyr's 'China' and Cardiff's Mary Ann Street. Anyone walking along the pavement from the corner of Holton Road through Thompson Street as far as Barry Dock Station at night would be accosted by at least a dozen prostitutes of the 'most ungainly, the filthiest and most abandoned type' that could be found in the 'foul vomitting dens of Babylonian Cardiff'. The problem was blamed on property owners in Gueret Street and other areas in Barry Dock who let houses to people of questionable repute, who at once converted them into 'the most unhallowed haunts of vice and degradation of every conceivable type'. Gueret Street (popularly pronounced 'Garret') was known as the 'Tiger Bay' of the Barry district.[69] The street had a most unenviable notoriety for immorality in all its forms. A resident complained of the desperate gangs of ruffians and other bad characters who had taken possession of houses in this neighbourhood:

> 'Rowdyism of some kind or another is daily, almost hourly, occurring . . . it is well known that brothels exist . . . under our very eyes without the slightest restraint . . . men cannot go out doors at night without being molested and solicited by immoral women living in several of these small streets. About five o'clock last Monday afternoon Gueret Street . . . was suddenly converted into a veritable hell. Every neighbour ran to the door; at least a dozen ruffians and their paramours were engaged in a most ferocious quarrel; several desperate fights took place and the atmosphere was completely darkened with the foul and debasing language which emanated from the filthy mouths of the gang of blackguards engaged in these disgusting proceedings. To state that in such immoral surroundings as these shebeens also run riot is quite unnecessary. This is the hideous state . . . in which we are obliged to live in these streets, the moral atmosphere of which has lately become a "Modern Babylon" '.[70]

In this area lived the 'crimps' who waylaid and robbed sailors, and a gang of rough-necks known as 'Liverpool corner-boys'. Colourful characters who appeared in Barry Dock Police Court included 'Liverpool Jennie', 'Black Annie', 'James Bond' and 'Lord Wellington'. Policemen would not venture alone into Gueret Street. The street's notoriety attracted the attention of Captain Lionel Lindsay the Chief Constable of Glamorgan, who was conducted on a visit of inspection through the area. Systematic police raids upon the brothels and shebeens of this miserable locality were only partly successful. Early in 1895 the drinking evil had been very effectively coped with, but the police found great difficulty in wiping out brothels in the face of a rigorous and united co-operation on the part of property owners.[71] However, the end was in sight for Gueret Street. In March 1895 three youths set fire to an untenanted house and the flames quickly spread. Thousands were attracted by the lurid rays which shot upwards from the fire. By 10 a.m. four houses were ablaze and the cries of the residents from the adjoining properties, as they fled for their lives, were appalling. The houses on either side of the fire were partially unroofed to stem the progress of the flames. By midnight the conflagration was under control. Difficulty was then experienced in shutting off the water at the stand pipe, and a jet of water shot twenty feet into the air, flooding the street. Police, fire and flood failed to wipe out the street's notoriety but the owner of two-thirds of the property suggested a remedy. He offered to rid the street of all its objectionable tenants, repair the houses and let them to respectable people. In March 1896 thirty-five houses 'all let to respectable working class people at a weekly rent of 5 shillings, 6 shillings and ten shillings' were offered for sale at £120 per house.[72] Finally, the District Council changed the name to Hirwaun Street and the notoriety of the street died with its name. Cadoxton, too, had some problem places, in particular Holmes Street and Courtenay Road, which 'has ever been a notorious neighbourhood for drunkenness and sin'. But none of these were anything as disreputable as Gueret Street. There were complaints that pedestrians on Weston Hill were constantly molested by prostitutes and beggars. Complaints were made, too, of the wild scenes which occurred in the old quarry leading from the Cwms to Court Road. On one occasion forty or more men and women were 'beastly drunk and free fights were indulged in'. It was probably the first time for open prostitution to be carried out in broad daylight on the sabbath and witnessed by the youth of both sexes.[73]

The port had hordes of 'crimps' who waylaid and robbed unsuspecting sailors they first befriended and made drunk. Barry was the first port sanitary authority to adopt the Board of Trade by-laws which combatted this problem by licensing and regulating seamen's boarding houses.[74] The Act was largely preventive of many sailor's grievances while ashore. By February 1895 the application of the by-laws had already driven out 'certain notorious persons who were crimps rather than boarding house keepers', first by refusing them a licence and then by prosecuting them for continuing to trade without a licence. In some cases unsuccessful applicants for licences left Barry for Cardiff, where similar regulations were not yet enforced. In Barry the combined efforts of the police and sanitary officers closed the disreputable boarding houses and crimping was to a large extent stamped out by 1895.

Bogus clubs, *hôtels-de-marl* and gambling were other problems for the police to deal with. Bogus clubs in Cadoxton and Barry Dock were described by a church leader as 'infernal haunts of debauchery and vice'. They were simply an excuse for drinking on Sundays and tended to demoralise society and the working classes in particular.[75] The police were determined that none but *bona fide* clubs should be tolerated. They usually raided them at midnight on a Saturday or a Sunday evening, took away the books for examination and carted off the drink. These clubs were located in all parts of the town, but their greatest concentration was in Holton Road. Among them were the Social Workmen's Club and Institute, the Independent Workmen's Club and Institute, the Marine Working-men's Club, the Tradesmen's Club and Institute, the Weston Hill Workmen's Club; the Mechanic's Club and Institute was kept by Enoch Morrison, a black man who was a well-known exponent of the noble art of boxing. The drink was usually confiscated by the Court which imposed fines of between £5 and £75 with costs, or in default between fourteen days' and two months' hard labour.

Drunkenness was a frequent sight and in December 1896 drunken women were conveyed in wheelbarrows to the Central Police Station. Open spaces were used to hold drinking parties. These were raided by the police who would confiscate the four-and-a-half or nine-gallon cask of beer and drinking utensils. On a Monday evening in July 1893 a crowd of men, women and children formed themselves into a ring on wasteland at the bottom of Bassett Street and the contents of a beer barrel were handed around indiscriminately. Many were soon drunk, and vulgar songs were sung with hideous accompaniment of minor instruments. When police arrrived, the disorderly crowd quickly dispersed. The police raided another *hôtel-de-marl* on wasteland near Travis Street on a Sunday evening in July 1894. They shouldered off a cask of beer, horsed and on tap, and dispersed a gang of about forty or fifty men. One September morning the same year a crowd of sailors and other of the 'lower class' congregated on wasteland near Forster Street, Cadoxton, where a nine-gallon beer cask was horsed on an adjoining wall. The company was liberally supplied with 'foaming brown'. Everything went merrily, with music and shouting galore, till rain set in and a shout of 'police' was raised. The 'marlers' suddenly shouldered the 'niner' to a neighbouring house, and the crowd dispersed from public gaze.

During the summer and autumn of 1898 a sort of *cwrw bach* was held on Sundays in a quarry at the upper end of Courtenay Road. In October a police raid discovered 'a scene of Bacchanalianism most indescribable. A crowd of men had drunk themselves helpless, free fights were indulged in, while others lay about utterly oblivious of their disgraceful surroundings'. The police arrested eight and dispersed the rest; one man totally drunk, with three casks of beer, was hauled off in a cart to the Police Station. The construction of Gladstone Road destroyed this site. Its correct name was Love's Quarry, but Cadoxton folk called this favourite haunt for a *hôtel-de-marl* the 'Khyber Pass'. Other stone quarries were also favoured by drinkers. One Sunday afternoon in March 1899 police raided the quarry in

Laura Street, Cadoxton Moors, where they found a gang of men engaged in card-playing and beer-drinking. Several men grew defiant and resisted the police, who made an arrest. As they were leaving with their prisoner they intercepted a cask of beer meant for the gang. These stories, and others like them, reveal the colourful nature of life in Barry during this period.

Gambling was closely connected with *hôtels-de-marl.* In March 1892 gamblers, who the previous summer had infested the moors with their evil practices, had taken up a more secluded abode in a little cave at Warren Tump, an ancient and familiar landmark destroyed in August 1894 during construction of Dock No. 2.[76] There, on Sundays, pitch-and-toss, drinking and gambling of every description took place. Crowds of roughs gathered every Sunday under Weston Bridge, Cadoxton, where they insulted pedestrians, indulged in pitch-and-toss and mouthed obscenities. The playing of pitch-and-toss on Sundays was still rife at Cadoxton in May 1895. One critic wrote 'I have never seen "pitch-and-toss" so persistently and extensively indulged in as at Cadoxton. My house overlooks the Moors and every fine Sunday . . . groups of men may be seen indulging in this illicit game . . . yesterday . . . I counted as many as fifty men and boys busily playing pitch-and-toss for several hours'.[77] The situation had not improved by May 1896, when gangs of navvies indulged in drinking and card-playing on Sundays. The police could not interfere because the Moors were private property belonging to the Barry Dock and Railway Company. A local J.P. who visited the spot one Sunday afternoon 'counted no less than six casks of beer, the contents of which were being drunk by groups of men who lay about on the grass. In one of these gangs was a woman, a creature who so far demeaned herself and her sex by drinking glass for glass with her mates'. The Barry District Free Church Council deplored 'the disgraceful scenes resulting from Sunday drinking and gambling' on Cadoxton Moors. A deputation met with the Barry Railway Company, and as a result the police made determined efforts to stamp out gambling. In February 1898 an inspector, two sergeants, and several constables of the Dock Police Force patrolled Cadoxton Moors. This policing effectively stopped the gambling.

Gambling spread to the town itself. The press reported: 'everyday in broad daylight on the pavement near the entrance to the Barry Company's property in Dock View Road . . . bookmakers—of both sexes—may be seen victimising the low-class crowds who habitually "loaf" about this spot. The same may be said of Holton Road and Thompson Street after dark'.[78] Working men were to be seen every day at the bottom of Station Street handing over their wages to 'disgraceful sharpers, bookmakers and respectable vagrants for the purpose of having a "bit" on horse races'. The problem had not diminished in October 1896, when street betting was becoming more audacious; 'a vice that was once confined to Dock View Road is now creeping stealthily into Holton Road'.

Places of entertainment

The young town sought its public entertainment in the theatre and later the cinema. Cadoxton was the first area developed and here in Kenilworth Road two temporary wooden structures served as the earliest theatres. The first, Mr. Alfred Orton's American Theatre of Varieties,[79] was operating by March 1888, but had closed before the Princess Theatre opened in September 1889. The Princess Theatre was an eyesore at the time of its removal in May 1891, when its place as the town's entertainment hall was taken by the Theatre Royal and Palace of Varieties in Iddesleigh Street. This building had seating for 2,500 and accommodation for fourteen musicians. Admission prices ranged from threepence to one shilling. To prevent the theatre becoming 'an evil utterly dangerous to the good tastes and morals' of the community it was not permitted to sell alcohol. The Rev. W. Tibbott, pastor of Bryn Seion Independent Chapel, considered it one of the numerous temptations of Satan, and warned the young townspeople 'to look on the red light, and beware of going to such a place'.[80] The theatre, sometimes referred to as the Iddesleigh Hall, was used for balls, bazaars and public meetings. It also staged wrestling matches. *Blue Beard*, the first grand Christmas pantomime performed in Barry was produced there in December 1896. N. W. Phillips, one of the proprietors, was involved in discussions to build an opera house. Sadly, nothing came of this. The Theatre Royal was defunct in 1910, when it was converted into a church dedicated to St. Aidan.

Little is known of the Theatre of Varieties which opened early in 1892 in Thompson Street, but the entertainment was said to be excellent. In the summer of 1894 the American Pavilion in Thompson Street was providing the theatre-going public with a change of programme every evening.[81] Victorian theatres were subjected to close public scrutiny. Complaints were made that the American Pavilion was the cause of disgraceful scenes in Travis Street late at night. The proprietor, A. Orton, protested that his theatre closed by 10.30 p.m. and did not open on Sundays. Despite many neighbours praising the theatre for providing harmless fun and frolics for the inhabitants of Barry Dock, Orton had the greatest difficulty in renewing his licence, and in May 1895 he took the Cadoxton Market Hall for theatrical purposes.

Solomon Barnett took a lease on the Public Hall, Thompson Street, where the Barry Dock Empire opened in June 1895. Barnett ran the theatre and the Theatre Royal, Cadoxton, to provide variety performances. It was renamed the Empire Music Hall by October 1896 and re-opened on Easter Monday 1897 under new management. Variety was the the predominant feature.

Two temporary structures, the Victoria Theatre in Holton Road and the Theatre Royal and Hippodrome, Broad Street, were built in 1906 and 1907 respectively. The latter accommodated 550 persons and provided the populace with a legitimate theatre as well as a hippodrome and palace of varieties. It was burnt down in 1909 and the present Theatre Royal, now a cinema, was built in 1910. This offered the 'principal London Companies in Musical Comedy, Drama, Variety and Animated Pictures'.[82]

Local drama and minstrel societies performed in these theatres. In February 1889 the Barry and Cadoxton Amateur Minstrels were at the Theatre Royal. The Cadoxton-Barry Histrionic Society, founded in January 1892, gave its first public performance in May. Its contemporary, the Barry Garrick Dramatic Society, offered Shakespearian and other literary productions. The proceeds of both societies went to charity, especially to the Cottage Hospital and the Nursing Association. Another society, the Barry Dock Amateur Dramatic Society, made its first public appearance in January 1893 at the Thompson Street Public Hall. In August 1899 a Dramatic and Operative Society was formed to produce *H.M.S. Pinafore.*[83]

Cinemas developed out of the music hall and theatres. Leon Vint who became a cinema proprietor before the Great War was a well known producer of music hall entertainment, which featured animated pictures in the 1890s. In January 1899 Vint's Grand Choir visited Romilly Hall. There were twenty lady artistes, including one who had the art of looking into the future; there were animated pictures, dioramic and panoramic pictures and various other novelties. The show ran for a week, when the hall was packed from floor to ceiling.[84]

Plate LIII. Walter Taylor & Sons, dealers in glass, china, haberdashery and paper, Holton Road, Barry, *c.* 1908. *Frank Taylor.*

It was in shows like this that the public first became familiar with 'living' pictures. In 1897 Messrs. Alexandra, Howe and Cushings Circus and Menagerie show included 'London's latest scientific craze, the Cinematographe'. In March 1899 a display of living pictures was produced nightly at the Romilly Hall 'by the latest perfected cinematograph coupled with the lecture on the Sudan conquest by Professor H. J. Blundell . . . illustrated by graphic limelight views'.[85] The heyday of the cinema was to be the inter-war years, but already before the Great War there were three Cinematograph Theatres. In December 1909 the first permanent cinema opened in Romilly Hall, showing 'Mr. Sidney Bacon's Animated Picture Entertainment'. The other two cinemas were Vint's Electric Palace, which began in the former Salvation Army Hall, Thompson Street, in February 1910 and the King's Hall, which opened in the following August on the site of the old Theatre Royal and Hippodrome as a Palace Theatre de Luxe, showing 'Animated Pictures and Bijou Vaudeville'.

Entertainment was provided by visiting circuses, menageries, waxworks and fairgrounds which were a link with the greater and more exciting new world developing in America, Africa and the East. In 1891, for instance, Barry was visited by Lane's varied amusements, Fosset's Circus, Wombwell's Menagerie, Mander's Royal Moving Waxwork, the grand American circus and hippodrome and Charles W. Poole's celebrated myriorama. Poole, who established his myriorama in 1837, visited Barry on a number of occasions. He tried to keep his tableaux topical, engaging a large staff of artistes to reproduce reliable sketches of important events as they occurred. For instance, on a visit to the Market Hall, Barry, one of the tableaux was labelled 'Darkest Africa', a living realisation of the famous march of Stanley through the Congo forest. An attractive feature of his show in June 1899 was a myriograph, a cinematograph which had, among other slides, the ever-interesting 'phantom ride'.[86]

In succeeding years Barry was visited by Bostock's Great Excelsior Menageries (1893); Bostock and Wombwell (1899); Messrs. Wm. Danter and Sons' fairground with steam roundabouts and galloping horses, which came in 1894 and subsequent years; Mr. Sedgwick's Menagerie—where the daring of the lion trainer was 'one of the finest displays of recklessness . . . ever seen'. When Messrs. Alexandra Howe and Cushing's circus and menagerie came in October 1898, their show had a hundred male and female performers from every land under the sun, a hundred and fifty horses and ponies, ten dens of wild beasts and a herd of performing elephants and camels. There were two circus rings and a central stage presenting as many as five performances at the same time.

The town was gripped by a severe bout of 'circus fever' in June 1894, when visited by Lord George Sanger's spectacular circus and exhibition which occupied the Gasworks Field in Holton Road. Sanger was one of the giants of circus history and his show cast a spell on the town. As the circus procession moved through the main streets, hundreds came out to see the spectacle. The largest gathering of people who had ever assembled at one place in the Barry district occupied the mammoth marquee for the opening performance. The climax was a realistic performance of the war in the Sudan. This military spectacle involved 250 horses, 500 people, batteries of elephants and camels and field artillery, all appearing in the tent at one time. This feature had been witnessed by Royalty on three occasions.[87]

Sanger made a further visit in 1899. The public procession held at noon on 6 June was a 'blaze of splendour nearly two miles long'. The leading feature was a naval and military spectacle entitled 'With Kitchener to Khartoum' depicting Great Britain's 'most recent glorious victories on the Nile'. Seven hundred men, horses, camels and elephants were in this grand pageant. When the climax was reached with the Battle of Omdurman and the annihilation of the Khalifa, involving the firing of muskets, women and children in hundreds made frantic strides for the exits, the whole thing being altogether too realistic for them.

Choirs and bands

Local *eisteddfodau* were popular on August Bank Holidays. Typical was one held in a marquee at the foot of Cadoxton Common in August 1890, when there were many entries in choral, solo, shorthand and other competitions.[88] These *eisteddfodau* gave opportunities for local musicians to demonstrate their talents and to compete against one another.

The earliest male voice choir, the Cadoxton Male Voice Party, was formed by Miss A. J. Lewis. It competed at the Cadoxton Eisteddfod in 1889. Irregular attendance led to its break-up in May 1892. During the rail strike in 1890 a Male Voice Party was formed among local railwaymen. In 1891 it had forty members and met at the Welsh Calvinistic Methodist Chapel, High Street, and the Presbyterian Hall. D. Farr, the choir's first conductor, had earned a reputation as conductor of the choir at Bethesda Welsh Congregational Chapel and was the first to introduce the performance of cantata into the district. This choir formed the nucleus of the Barry Male Voice Party, established in August 1892.[89] It practised at the Welsh Baptist Chapel, Holton Road, and competed successfully in local *eisteddfodau*. In 1896 Farr resigned and was succeeded as conductor by W. T. Llewellyn. Farr was then elected conductor of the newly-formed Barry District Glee Society, which had its headquarters at Bethesda Welsh Congregational Chapel. The choir went on a four-month tour in the summer of 1898 to the the south of England, raising relief funds for the Welsh coal strike. It had eighty-five regular members in September 1898. In March 1899 the two male voice choirs were united with the Barry Male Voice Party, joining the Barry District Glee Society, which continued to prosper under its conductor D. Farr. In July 1899 the choir won a magnificent victory in the Male Voice Contest at the Welsh National Eisteddfod at Cardiff. The test pieces were 'Hushed in Death' (Hiles), to be rendered unaccompanied, and 'Jesus of Nazareth', a charming new composition by Dr. Joseph Parry. The first prize was £75. This was the first visit of the Barry Glee Society to the National Eisteddfod. D. Farr, the conductor, was aged 35 and was composer of the song '*I godi'r hen Wlad yn ei hôl*'.

The present Barry Male Voice Choir began in 1902 with a handful of men who were associated with the Tynewydd Road Congregational Church. The choir had grown to 108 members in 1913, and between these years had collected nine first and eleven second prizes in choral competitions.[90] In 1913 the choir gave concerts to raise money for the dependents and survivors of the world's worst pit disaster at Senghenydd.

Bethesda Welsh Congregational Chapel provided another musician in J. P. Hicks who was conductor of the Barry Temperance Choir established in 1894. It competed at the National Temperance Festival held at the Crystal Palace, where it won first prize in class B in 1897. The choir comprised upwards of seventy 'zealous abstainers' and held its practices at Salem Welsh Baptist Chapel. In 1899 Hicks was replaced as conductor by W. T. Samuel, a well known composer and conductor at Cardiff, who was vice-president of the Tonic Sol-fa Association and a professor of the Tonic Sol-fa College, London. In December 1899 the choir, with 150 voices, performed Handel's *Messiah* before an enthusiastic audience at the Romilly Hall. A year later at the same venue the choir gave a grand performance of Mendelssohn's *Elijah*.

Among other early choirs was the Cadoxton Choral Union, whose Conductor was W. C. Howe. It met at the Shaftesbury Temperance Hotel in the early 1890s. The Barry Choral Society, a mixed voice choir, was formed in November 1895 with W. T. Llewellyn as conductor. Haydn's *Creation* was performed in February 1898 by a Barry United Choir conducted by D. Farr. Miss Beatrice Johnstone, R.A.M., in 1900 formed a Barry Ladies Choir to enter for the Ladies Choir Competition at the Barry Boxing-Day Eisteddfod. H. de Boer, a local violinist became conductor of the Barry String Band, formed in 1892. It was renamed the Barry District Orchestral Society early in 1894, and its charitable work included performing at concerts of the Cadoxton and Barry Histrionic Society in aid of the Nursing Association and the Cottage Hospital.[91]

Brass band music commenced in 1888 when the Cadoxton Brass Band, supported by voluntary subscriptions, was involved in festivities at the opening of the first dock.[92] It was founded by R. G. Morris, brother to the rector of Cadoxton, and had twelve or thirteen members. Thomas Buckler was the bandmaster and the band played at public occasions, such as the annual sports at the Witchill Athletic Grounds. In 1892 a public meeting discussed the reorganisation of the band. The band needed financial aid to enable it to secure a competent trainer and to recruit new members. It was hoped to secure the services of a first cornet player who would also conduct the band, for which he would receive a small remuneration. By March 1893 attempts to revive the band had failed and it passed into oblivion. In October 1891 plans were made for setting up a brass band at East Barry and an appeal was made for the purchase of instruments. As the Barry Railway Brass and Reed Band, it paraded the main streets in May 1892 for the first time. The conductor was A. Lewis of Cogan, and it practised in a room at East Barry House. There are references to the 'Barry Dock Town Brass Band', which in the summer of 1894 paraded the streets in aid of the Cilfynydd Colliery disaster. In 1896 the Barry Dock Town Band headed the procession at the Navvies' Union Sports at the Witchill Grounds. On summer evenings it played in front of the Marine Hotel, Barry Island. In October 1893 there is a reference to the Brass Band of the Victoria Lodge of the R.A.O.B., Barry Dock. Commonly known as the Barry Dock R.A.O.B. Brass Band, it played in the summer of 1895 at Barry Island. In July 1895 the band gave a grand concert at the Buffalo Institute, Thompson Street, for the benefit of the widow and family of the late bandmaster, J. Murston.

The majority of the bands formed during the 1890s were short-lived because of public failure to subscribe to them or the apathy of bandsmen.[93] By December 1896 the Barry Dock Town Band itself was defunct. Other bands included the Barry Dock Hibernian Drum and Fife band, formed by the Cadoxton branch of the Hibernian Friendly Society in October 1893, and the Cadoxton Wesleyan Brass Band, which held its opening practice in May 1896 under bandmaster T. Williams. Three bands were active in 1897. In April the Barry Dock Unionist Working Men's Club and Institute Band marched in aid of the Nursing Association, heading the annual horse-show parade. In June the band, together with its great rival, the Barry Dock R.A.O.B. Band, played in the procession of the third annual grand fete and athletic sports of the Barry District Friendly Societies. It was remarked in August 1897 that these two bands loved each other like 'Kilkenny cats'. A third band, the Wesleyan Brass and Reed Band, headed the parade of the Cadoxton Wesleyan School treat in June 1897. In September 1898 this band changed its name to the Barry District Brass Band. In December that year, as the Barry District Brass and Reed Band, it gave a successful concert at the English Wesleyan Chapel, Barry Dock. Its conductor was H. Palmer. In July 1898 the Unionist Brass Band secured the services of a new bandmaster J. A. Foxall, who came from Pontypridd. In 1899 this band and its rival the R.A.O.B. Military Band were still very active. In November that year J. Bryant of Cogan a well-known band conductor formed what was said to be a strong orchestral society for the Barry district. Bryant was the conductor of the R.A.O.B. Brass Band when it played at the R.A.O.B.

Institute, Vere Street, in February 1900. This band included in its instrumentation a quintet of saxophones, which could be said of no other South Wales band. Bryant, long associated with music in the town, was the first to introduce this beautiful instrument into South Wales. A Barry Town Brass Band which possessed a full set of instruments in August 1910, fused with the Penarth Band about 1913 to form the Barry Town Military Band.[94] This was a brass and reed band in dark-blue uniforms with silver braidings, under bandmaster John Bryant of Cogan.

In 1894 there were two Salvation Army Brass Bands. One of these, the Barry Dock Salvation Army Band, under its bandmaster J. F. Skinner was presented in April 1909 with a handsome and valuable set of new silver and brass instruments. In October 1913 the band led the funeral procession for the miners who died in the Senghenydd pit disaster.[95] Temperance bands were also active. In October 1895 a brass band was formed by the Order of Good Templars at Barry Dock. The Barry Temperance Band was formed about 1897 to play at the open-air services of the Princes Street Mission. In 1912 it was renamed the Barry Red Cross Silver Prize Band. In 1914 the Barry Town Military Band and the Barry Red Cross Band overcame their feeling of rivalry to play together at a Belgian refugee concert.

Athletics and sporting activities

Athletic events took place at the annual Whit-Monday sports held on Cadoxton Moors, 1888-90, and at the Witchill Athletic Grounds from 1891 onwards.[96] Prizes at the 1891 sports amounted to £120, and despite bad weather a crowd of three thousand attended. Athletic sports were popular on August Bank Holiday Mondays. In 1895, for instance, they were held at the Witchill Athletic Grounds in aid of the Navvies' Union. During the 1890s several attempts were made by sporting clubs to secure a recreation ground. Success came in 1896, when the Wenvoe Castle Estate gave fifteen acres at the Buttrills as a gift to Barry for recreational purposes. In June 1898 the Barry Dock Harriers was formed; the club started its first trial run from the Buttrills.

The ancient game of quoits was very popular. The Barry Quoit Club was formed in 1886 with its ground near East Barry House (which until recent years stood in Broad Street). In 1892 a quoit club was formed at Cadoxton. Little is known of this club, but the Barry team became prominent in the South Wales and Monmouthshire Union. In 1897 Barry was undefeated until the final, when it lost to Ton Pentre. It won the coveted trophy in 1899 with the largest margin of victory ever obtained. The club won the championship again the following year. It produced a champion of Wales in T. Greatrex (1898), who with S. J. Martin and J. Jones also represented Wales at an international level.

In 1895 it was rumoured that golf links were to be established on Cadoxton Moors, while a number of gentlemen were said to be forming a strong golf club. Land was being secured for links which it was hoped would equal those at Porthcawl, Penarth, Tenby or elsewhere in South Wales. This scheme did not come to fruition, and in January 1898 the Barry Golf Club established a nine-hole course at West Aberthaw. This site (where the Leys power station now stands) was about twenty minutes walk from Gileston Station on the Vale of Glamorgan Railway. Cheap return tickets were available to Gileston, and the Ocean House Hotel provided an excellent lunch. The captain was W. J. Darling and the membership was sixty-five. By April 1900 the Links at the Leys had been extended to eighteen holes and had become a really good sporting course.[97] The club had engaged a new professional, Chitty from Lewes, who was a groundsman, coach and first-class player. Barry was a young club doing its utmost to make headway, and was noted for its hospitality to visiting teams.

The Barry Lawn Tennis Club was in existence in the summer of 1891, for there are references in the press in November of that year to the club holding dances in the winter months. The second annual ball was held in February 1892 at the Barry Hotel. That month the club secured land near the Coastguard Station, Cold Knap, for two tennis courts. The formal opening of the club that season took place on Saturday, 7th May. On the same day a tennis court near Palmerstown opened for use by the Barry School Teachers' Association. It had about thirty members. A Cadoxton Lawn Tennis and Croquet Club opened in June 1906 at the Palmerstown Courts, situated at the top of Dobbins Lane where there were full-sized tennis courts and a first-class croquet lawn. The entrance fee was 10*s.* 6*d.* Major-General H. H. Lee, R.E., J.P., was president.

In August 1890 the first Grand Yachting Regatta was held on the Timber Pond (now the site of Dock No. 2) under the patronage of Lord Windsor and the directors of the Barry Dock and Railway Company.[98] At the second annual regatta in July 1891 there were thousands of spectators, and dock vessels were gaily bedecked with bunting. Events included a channel pilots' race and a coal-trimmers' shovel race with four men in a boat. A third annual regatta was held in August 1892. Owing to lack of funds a regatta was not held for some years after. In August 1896 it was revived under the patronage of the Barry Chamber of Trade and Improvement Society. In the channel-pilot race the first prize of £20 and silver cup was won by Frank Trott's *Marguerite.* The working class held their own regatta. In September 1893 a second annual Working Men's Regatta was held at Barry Harbour. The promenade facing the harbour was lined with hundreds of spectators, who watched with great interest. The Barry Dock R.A.O.B. Brass Band played at intervals between races and there were eleven events altogether.

The Barry Rowing Club was formed in February 1892, and the formal opening of the Boat House at Cold Knap took place in May.[99] Ladies were allowed to participate in the privileges of the boating club, if accompanied by a member, and they were supplied with a life-belt for use in emergencies. By March the following year the club possessed two gig fours (outriggers) with sliding seats; two four-oared gigs (in-rigged); two pair-oared and two double sculling boats. Annual regattas were held in Barry Harbour in July or August, and a brass band provided music. In 1899 the club gave a supper to Captain W. B. Whall in recognition of his constant efforts in the interests of the club and as its captain during the years 1893-98. Whall considered that athletics in general and rowing in particular were largely responsible for the position the Anglo-Saxon race enjoyed in world superiority, and he looked with confidence to the future for that supremacy to be upheld.

Other events which attracted a great deal of interest were horse-trotting matches, foot races, rabbit-coursing, pigeon-shooting and prize-fighting. Horse-trotting matches were held on Cardiff Road or the Port Road. The races nearly always involved horses or ponies of local tradesmen, who would put down £5, £10 or more a side on their horse. Typical was the one-mile trotting match for a purse of £40 which was raced on the Port Road in July 1890. It was run between B. Hoddinott's (Witchill Hotel) 'Visitor' and Evan Williams's (Victoria Hotel, Holton) 'Cymro Bach' in the presence of

late LIV.
n early automobile
: a hill-climbing
ntest organised by
outh Wales and
lonmouthshire Auto-
obile Club, Buttrills
ill, 1909.
'ardiff Central Library.

four hundred spectators. Both horses were ridden by their owners, and Cymro Bach showed the way, but was quickly overtaken by Hoddinott's mare, which won easily by 150 yards. The distance was covered in about three-and-a-half minutes.

Occasionally single foot races were run to settle a bet. In August 1898 Henry Frost of Cardiff and Abe Jenkins of Cadoxton ran a 125-yard race at Cadoxton Moors. Frost won the £5-a-side race by a couple of yards. In June 1893 a novel race was run by two residents of Barry Dock, Courtenay and Grist. The former had a wooden leg and was given a one-hundred-yard start in the race of 150 yards. He won quite easily and collected the prize—a nine-gallon cask of ale.

The Witchill Athletic Grounds were used for rabbit-coursing matches and pigeon-shooting. Typical was a pigeon-shooting handicap for £25 in November 1896 between two Cardiff men, who each killed eight out of nine birds, and so divided the prize.[100] Prizes were not always in money. A pigeon-shooting match held in a field near the William IV Hotel in November 1890 had as a prize a pig valued at £10. Fox terriers, greyhounds and whippets were used for rabbit-coursing. Stakes were usually £5 or £10 a match. On Saturday afternoon, 31 January 1891, a match was held at the Witchill for £5-a-side between Fred R. Stephens's dog 'Bess' (Cadoxton) and J. Morris's dog 'Face' (Cogan), the dog which picked up the first five rabbits out of nine to be declared the winner. The Cogan dog won easily.

Prize fights took place in secret in secluded spots or at an early hour. One of these fights was staged shortly after 5 a.m. in June 1891, when a crowd of about forty assembled in a field near Colcot Farm to witness a fight between William Harley, a fireman at Barry Dock, and Thomas Bumford, a plasterer, both living at Holton.[101] The amount at stake was £10, representing wages of £5-a-side. Bumford had one of his fists broken, and at the close of the eleventh round the sponge was thrown up in favour of Harley. In July 1893 it was rumoured that the boxing booth in Williams Field (a locality in the area of Holton Road) was to be removed to the vicinity of the goods station at Barry. This was the small boxing booth by means of which Enoch Morrison eked out a subsistence. Morrison, a black man, who hailed from Shrewsbury, was a familiar character in Barry sporting circles. In his earlier days he fought a number of game battles notably with 'Shoni Engineer', Sam Butcher and others. He died in March 1896.

A Homing Pigeon Fanciers' Society was formed in September 1894. Its headquarters were at the Bassett Arms Hotel and the first pigeon race was from Newcastle.[102] In October the following year a Barry District Fanciers' Association was established at Culley's Hotel. The Association had a strong and enthusiastic following and their first members' show was in January 1896 in a large hall connected with Culley's Barry Dock Hotel. There were over two hundred entries for poultry, pigeons, cage birds, rabbits and fancy mice. Later shows were held in the Cadoxton Market Hall. In one there were over 1,200 entries, and prize money of £300 was distributed in another.

During the Boer War rifle clubs were formed to enable men to become effective shots. In October 1900 a club was established at Barry.[103] This had the sanction of the War Office and was under the auspices of the National Rifle Association. Rifles were provided and the club rented a strip of land at the Romilly Hall, where a Morris tube miniature range opened in 1901. The club had about 200 members.

Cycling

Cycling became increasingly popular in the 1890s. Clubs were founded at Barry and Cadoxton and they organised runs in the spring and summer. The Cadoxton and District Cycling Club was in being by June 1891, with its club room at the Royal Hotel.[104] The club colour was grey, and its bugle bore the inscription 'C.C.C. 1891'. In April 1892 it was superseded by the Cadoxton Rovers Cycle Club, which had its clubroom at the Royal. The Cadoxton Cycling Club reformed in March 1894, when a good number of wheelers were present at the inaugural meeting at the Shaftesbury Hotel, Cadoxton. By September 1894 it was again defunct because of the members' indifference. A Cadoxton, Barry and District Cycle Club was established at Archer's Coffee Tavern, Main Street, in February 1896. The first outing on Good Friday 1896 left for Newport from the Royal Hotel, the club's headquarters.

Major-General Lee of the Mount, Dinas Powys, was a veteran cyclist who became a patron of cycling in the town and was president of the Barry Cycling Club. This began in March 1892 with 27 members, and there were 169 runs during the first season. Thomas Jones, the Demon Cyclist, was the captain and the club uniform was grey. Its headquarters was the Barry Hotel until 1895, when it moved to the more centrally-placed Bassett Arms Hotel. At its annual dinner in February 1895 Dr. P. J. O'Donnell, Chairman, spoke highly in support of cycling as recreation and pastime but condemned the habit of cyclists in bending forward while on the machine. In May 1896 the Barry Cycling Club invited the Cadoxton Club to join them in the first Barry May Show procession, successfully held at the Witchill Athletic Grounds. W. Thomas, the Hayes, Sully, one of the most popular and successful breeders of stock in the country, was president. He was the driving force which led to the creation of the Barry District May Show Society. Competitors were confined to the area of the Council's jurisdiction, but all classes of horses used in the town were eligible for exhibition.

Cycling became fashionable for ladies, and in June 1894 it was thought the best and most decent cycling dress for women included knickerbockers rather than skirts. Some clubs were snobbish and exclusive. In 1897 the new Romilly Cycle Club was only open to members of the Barry Lawn Tennis

Club. Other clubs included the Barry Dock Mechanics' Cycle Club, formed in 1898, and the Unionist Athletic Cycling Club. The sport's popularity led in 1899 to a regular series of Cycling Notes appearing in the *Barry Dock News*.[105] Annual Cycle Carnivals raised money for institutions such as the Voluntary Hospital for the Destitute Sick and Dying and the Army and Navy Veterans' Home.

Football and cricket

Rugby was probably first played by teams made of navvies and other workers engaged on the construction of Dock No. 1. The first team was formed at Cadoxton in 1887 with T. Howard Morgan of Vere Street as its captain. It played on a ground at Palmerstown.[106] The Club A.G.M. in the summer of 1889, held in the Picnic Hall (a building forming part of the Wenvoe Arms, Vere Street), decided that in future the headquarters would be at the Witchill Hotel. T. H. Morgan was re-elected Captain for the third year. Negotiations with Jenkin Brock for a field to play on proved successful, and in February 1890 the team described as the Cadoxton and Barry first XV played at Brock's field. Spectators were requested to keep outside the boundary line and not, as so frequently happened, encroach upon the pitch. In September 1890 the club's headquarters remained at the Witchill Hotel. Its colours were navy-blue and amber. The club dissolved a year later and its equipment was given to a newly-formed Barry and Cadoxton District United Football Club. W. M. Douglas, an ex-Cadoxton Club committee member, was the leading promoter of the new team which he hoped would rival those of Cardiff, Newport, Swansea and Penarth. The new club was ill-fated from the start. W. M. Douglas chaired a meeting which was attended by T. H. Morgan, ex-Captain of the Cadoxton Club, and W. Murphy, ex-Captain of the Barry Club. Murphy and his colleagues were not prepared to amalgamate with Cadoxton and would not play at the Witchill Grounds. They claimed that if the Barry Club did amalgamate, another club would immediately form at Barry. Although the new club was established by a meeting in August 1891 at the Victoria Hotel, it was only in name a United District Club, for the Barry team preserved its separate identity. This failure was tragic for the future hopes of a town team aspiring to the first-class game. The new club played on the Witchill Athletic Grounds, the only enclosed field in the neighbourhood with a gate; the large changing-room in the Witchill Hotel contained two baths and opened directly on to the field. The club colours were navy-blue with yellow sash. The chairman W. M. 'Billy' Douglas, a former captain of Cardiff who won Welsh caps while playing for Cardiff in 1886/87, was closely connected with the growth of rugby in Barry until the years after the Great War. The club was handicapped by low 'gates' and the same team did not play together twice during the season. Consequently in their first season the team only won five of the fifteen matches and by September 1892 most of the players had joined two new clubs, the Cadoxton Stars, who played in a field near the Murch, Coldbrook, and the Cadoxton Rovers, who played on the Quarry Field near the Witchill Hotel. Lack of facilities led to the club being liquidated in 1893. Its place as the leading Cadoxton team was taken by the Cadoxton United Football Club whose headquarters were the Wenvoe Arms.

In the autumn of 1890 there were two rugby teams at the west end, the Barry Rovers and Barry. The latter had its changing rooms at the Barry Hotel but the Barry Rovers appear to have been the premier side. Its playing field was at the Buttrills. The club colours were navy-blue with white sash. In 1891 amalgamation between the Barry Rovers and Barry team broke down because of what a Rovers player described as the 'arrogant attitude of the Barry team'. During 1891/92 season the club was simply referred to as the Barry Football Club and appears to have dropped 'Rovers' from its name. Its headquarters was the Barry Hotel. In July 1893 the colours remained the same but in a different form. It was decided to affiliate with the Cardiff and District Rugby Union. The 1893/94 season was a poor one because of the apathy shown by visiting teams in keeping fixtures. The club also lost its ground at the Buttrills which was taken for the site of the intermediate school. By September 1894 it had secured a new field near Holton Farm and the headquarters was the Victoria Hotel. The Cadoxton United R.F.C. complained that the Barry Club, which could not keep its players together and win matches, was continually poaching members from local clubs. Despite the complaint, Barry was received into membership of the South Wales and Monmouthshire Rugby Football Union in September 1895. During the 1895/96 season the club continued to play on the Holton Field, while their headquarters was the Clarence Temperance Hotel, Holton Road.

In the 1896/97 season the club played on a new ground at the Buttrills (Jubilee) Field. The first XV played some of the most popular rising clubs in the county, including the invincible Llwynypia, Bridgend and Pontypridd, winning 11, losing 12 and drawing 5 matches. The club prospered fairly well until the 1898/99 season, which was a disaster. Two basic reasons were the low gates and the 'poaching fiend'. Many of its best players, including the captain Alf Jenkins, transferred to Penarth or Cardiff. In January 1899, despite victories over Pontypridd and Treherbert, the club was bottom of the South Wales League. In September 1899 the club, which at one time showed much promise, was defunct. There remained several junior teams such as the Barry Dock Crusaders, which played in the Cardiff and District League. In September 1906 the Barry R.F.C. was reformed by a meeting held at Dunraven Hall, Vere Street, Cadoxton. The Rev. J. S. Longdon, rector of Cadoxton, was in the chair. Longdon, an Oxford rugby blue, played centre three-quarters for Swansea, Neath, Aberavon and London Welsh and was also one of the best cricket bowlers in Glamorgan. The problem of acquiring a suitable ground was a major hindrance to development. In 1907 the club was unsuccessful in obtaining permission from the Council to enclose the ground at the Buttrills, but within a few years it again disbanded. In August 1912 a reformed Barry R.F.C. under the presidency of W.M. Douglas decided to change the name of the club to Barry Town R.F.C. In their latter years they wore cherry-and-white hooped jerseys, and were popularly known as the Barry Parade R.F.C. They played at Romilly Park, and their headquarters was the Ship Hotel. This club wound up in 1922.

By the late 1890s the Association game supplanted rugby as the leading winter sport. In 1890 requests were made for the formation of a town soccer team but it was not until August 1892 that a meeting of enthusiasts held at Rosser's Coffee Tavern, Holton Road, decided to form a club.[107] The following week a list of rules was adopted for the Barry District Association F.C. at the new club room of the Victoria Hotel. Twenty-six people were enrolled as members, with H. Roberts as captain. They played at the Witchill Athletic Grounds and the colours were blue and white vertical stripes. In 1894 the club decided to affiliate with the South Wales and Monmouthshire Association and to compete for the senior and junior challenge cups. In 1896 it reached the final of the cup tie, but owing to appeals by the opponents it had to play Brecon three times. The final match resulting in a draw it was decided that the cup should be held jointly six months each. In 1897 the club joined the South Wales Football League but continued to play in the South Wales and Monmouthshire Association. By December 1897, 'Socker was the favourite pastime of the youth of Barry'. A meeting in 1898 at the Unionist Temperance Hotel, Holton Road resulted in the formation of the Barry Dock Unionist Athletic A.F.C., which took the place of the former Barry District team. A Scot, Dr. J. Livingstone, 'practically the founder of Association Football in the district', was elected president, with J. Sheldon as captain. The senior team included the pick of the old Barry District cup winners and it played on a field between Tynewydd and the Cemetery, Merthyr Dyfan. The club colours were chocolate and brown. It became one of the leading teams in the principality. The 1898/99 season was the first in which the Barry team entered for the Welsh cup. It was defeated in the fourth round by Wrexham but had some recompense when it beat Rhayader in April 1899, to win the coveted trophy of the South Wales and Monmouthshire Football Association Challenge Cup. The press considered that 'Socker' was rapidly taking the place of rugby in the Barry District, and in May 1899 the club secured the Jubilee Field, at the Buttrills. In the 1899/1900 season it was a semi-finalist in the South Wales and Monmouthshire Challenge Cup, which it won in the succeeding year, 1901. Impetus was given to the soccer code in 1913, when the town team acquired a permanent home at Jenner Park, and in March 1914 it joined the Southern League.[108]

Cricket was the first organised game in the town; teams were composed of the engineering staff who worked on the construction of the first dock. This was in 1885 and 1886, when the Barry Dock Cricket Club had an excellent eleven, but from various causes the club declined, many of the best players leaving for Buenos Aires. The game developed at Cadoxton where Dr. P. J. O'Donnell, an Irishman, was a founder and captain of the Cadoxton Cricket Club in 1887. In 1890 the club played at the Witchill Athletic Grounds. During 1891 the club ground was in a field adjoining the Cadoxton market. A Barry and Cadoxton District Cricket Club was formed in January 1891 to represent the district, as distinct from the two local teams at Cadoxton and Barry. The club played on the Witchill Athletic Grounds and its colours were Oxford dark blue. Although the Cadoxton Cricket Club amalgamated with the Barry and Cadoxton District Cricket Club in November 1891 to form a first-class team, the 1892 season was not a success. Difficulties arose because the population was so migratory that it was difficult to know who were the good players. Petty jealousies between the different districts also made it more difficult to establish a good representative team. Cricket was still flourishing at Cadoxton in 1905/06 when a Cadoxton Cricket Club with Dr. E. J. H. Budge as captain played at the Witchill Athletic Grounds.

The Barry Dock Cricket Club which played in the late 1880s became the Barry Cricket Club in 1890. It played at Buttrills Field with T. Higman as captain. In 1892 an amalgamation with the rugby club proved to be a mistake because the football had 'completely ruined' the Buttrills Ground pitch. The club continued to play at the Buttrills during 1893. In the 1894 season the club had a first, second and Wednesday eleven. Every year bats were presented for the best batting and bowling averages. In 1895 the club affiliated with the Cardiff and District League. It retained the Holton Field for play but the following year it played on the Buttrills Ground adjoining Holton Road. By May 1897 cricket was to all appearances non-existent in the town and one enthusiast asked 'Where, oh where, are the knights of the willow?'. Despite the collapse of the cricket club, teams representing Barry and Cadoxton played in July 1897 on Cadoxton Moors, where Barry won by eight runs. In 1898 a meeting of 'votaries of the willow' at the Bristol Temperance Hotel, Vere Street, resolved to form a cricket club. A deputation met R. Evans, general manager of the Barry Railway Company, seeking consent to form a pitch on Cadoxton Moors. Many prominent cricketers promised their support but no more was heard of this scheme. The present Barry Cricket Club was formed by a meeting in the Church Hall, St. Nicholas Road, in January 1899. The Rev. H. H. Stewart, rector of Barry, 'a wielder of the willow of considerable repute', was the first captain. The team played at Porthkerry Park before moving in 1904 to its present site at the Island where a pavilion was opened in May 1908.[109]

Cultural activities

Intellectual pursuits had their votaries. A Barry District Chess Club, formed in March 1896, met weekly at the Shaftesbury Temperance Hotel and matches were played against teams from Penarth and elsewhere. In November of the following year the Barry District Chess Club met on Wednesday evenings at the Windsor Hotel Barry Dock, but in September 1898 the club resumed playing at the Shaftesbury Assembly Room Cadoxton. This was short-lived, for in December they were back at the Windsor. In 1900 a West Barry Chess Club, with Captain H. Murrell as president, met on Thursday evenings, while a Barry Draughts Club was holding meetings at the Witchill Hotel, Cadoxton. A Barry Debating Society met in 1898 on alternate Monday evenings at the Universal Restaurant, Barry. The objects were to provide for the interchange of thought and opinion on matters relating to current affairs and other topics.[110] Subjects of discussion included: 'Does sport monopolise too much of our spare time?', 'China', 'Party Government' and 'Is Britain Destined to be Predominant in the Future Civilisation of the World?'. In the winter of 1899/1900 a Barry Literary and Social Society with about eighty members met on Tuesday evenings at the Church Hall, Barry. Among addresses delivered were 'Bird Islands of Pembrokeshire', 'Ghosts' and 'A Dip into Rudyard Kipling'.

The seaside resort

Barry's natural advantages as a seaside resort had long been recognised. In 1804 the Rev. J. Evans described the island as an 'unmolested retreat', and feared that its isolation would prevent development.[111] The construction of docks linked the island to the mainland, and in August 1891 a visitor wrote 'already the sands are studded with bathing machines and Barry bids fair to be a favourite seaside resort'. Boat trips across the channel were popular from an early date. In June 1888 the *Barry and Cadoxton Journal* advertised an afternoon excursion from Barry Island to Watchet by the new steamer, *Earl of Dunraven*. In 1890/91 Messrs. Edwards, Robertson and Co., of the Bristol Channel Passenger Services Ltd., ran excursions from Barry Dock entrance to Watchet by the steamers *Earl of Jersey* or *Earl of Bute*, wind, weather and circumstances permitting.[112] In succeeding years this company ran trips from the old pier on Friars Point to Weston and elsewhere in the channel. By the summer of 1892 visitors disembarked at Barry railway station and crossed to the island over a paved footway which ran along the embankment and over the bridge. In this, its first full season as a holiday resort, the island had over 100,000 visitors. Local Board by-laws in 1894 caused great resentment. Bathing was strictly prohibited between 8.00 a.m. and a certain hour in the evening every day, except with the use of bathing machines. The machine operators increased their charges, and in response to complaints the Local Board marked off a portion of Whitmore Bay where the public could bathe at any time of the day with proper bathing dress. That summer the Local Board appointed the first Inspector of Bathing and Pleasure Boats.

Despite the construction of the Causeway Road in 1894, the island was not easily accessible until the Barry Railway was extended to the island on August Bank Holiday Monday, 1896, when on that first day between 30,000 and 40,000 visited the place. The Railway was further extended when the Pier branch line was brought into use in June 1899.[113] This terminated alongside the passenger pontoon used by pleasure paddle steamers belonging to P. & A. Campbell and the Red Funnel Fleet of the Barry Railway.

Visitors complained about the lack of facilities. In 1895 the place was in the hands of a monopoly and there was an absence of much needed refreshment stalls around Whitmore Bay. The following year visitors had to return to the town for refreshments; only one comparatively puny refreshment room catered for public needs. The facilities were lamentably deficient and matters were little improved in 1900. One tripper commented: 'There are no shelters . . . no attraction of any sort . . . There is not a public convenience . . . not to mention such a necessity as a ladies lavatory'.

Plate LV. Donkey riders, Whitmore Bay, 1910; note number plates on donkeys' foreheads. *B.C.L. Coll.*

In 1894 Lord Windsor and family occupied Friars Point House (formerly the old Marine Hotel) as a summer residence. Determined to make Barry Island an attractive seaside resort, he began by having the green in front of Friars Point House laid out for gardens on the same lines as Penarth gardens. In 1897 the Windsor Estate constructed a wide embankment above the whole of the foreshore at Whitmore Bay with the view to conversion into a public promenade. Work began in the summer of 1903 and the Promenade and Pleasure Gardens opened on May Day 1905.[114] This was known as the 'Half-penny Promenade' owing to the turnstiles at either end which required a half-penny tariff for entry. Below it a low wall surmounted by iron railings separated the dunes from the beach. The promenade was made more attractive by two bridges built over tunnels giving access to the sand.

The Half-penny Promenade overlooked the stalls and side-shows which were allowed on the beach until the construction of the sea wall and present promenade in 1923. The Barry Urban authority offered spaces to let each year for the erection of stalls, roundabouts and swings. Thousands were delighted by beach entertainments such as that provided in the summer of 1902 and following seasons by Jimmy Shields, the one-legged comedian and his troupe of pierrots. 'Boat-shops' were used before stalls were permitted on the beach, and their sails acted as sun awnings. They sailed up the beach on the spring tides and remained there through the summer, selling fruit, sweets and mineral waters. In late September the boats would either go fishing or be moored in the Old Harbour. A Council by-law banned their use as shops after the 31 August 1909.[115] Beach donkeys with licence numbers on their foreheads were popular. In June 1897 the District Council ordered that boys in attendance upon the donkeys had to wear blue jerseys, blue trousers and blue caps with distinguishing badge. The saddle of each donkey also had to be provided with a white cover. The Switchback Railway from the Cardiff Exhibition was erected in February 1897 at the west end of Paget Road, but was replaced as the chief attraction by the Figure 8, built in 1912 on the site of the present fairground.

Further improvements were made in June 1905, when two terraces of stone bathing cubicles, one at the east end for men and one at the west end for ladies were opened, and in July the Council took over management of the beach.[116] In 1909 Lord Windsor made a handsome gift of the Whitmore Bay Grounds to Barry by conveying to the Urban District Council, with the approval of the Board of Trade, the whole of the land between high watermark and Friars Road and the adjoining foreshore. This gave the local authority control over the whole range of delightful sands of Whitmore Bay. Within two years plans were approved by the Council for the construction of an extended permanent promenade along the line of the sea-front, together with the erection of a large shelter and the laying out of public pleasure gardens. Provision was made in a Parliamentary Bill in 1913 to obtain the necessary statutory powers to proceed with the work, but the First World War delayed development until 1922.[117]

The growing resort was dubbed the 'New Brighton' and the 'Princess of Welsh watering places'. This development did not meet with everyone's approval. One visitor wrote:

> 'The new railway will change the whole character of Barry Island. Already the hand of civilisation has been placed upon it. The modern speculative builder is steadily advancing, the old roads leading to the Sandy Beach have been made prim, and stand-offish iron railings are being erected to restrict the free passage of the visitor. There is still left intact a bit of the native heath, a perfect treasure to the naturalist in all seasons. Spring, summer and autumn, it is rich with vegetable and insect life. If you feel too lazy to botanise, chase butterflies and moths, or to hunt for insects, you may throw yourself down upon the spongy turf, and lazily watch the craft passing to and fro in the Barry Roads, or loll and read your book. The natural beauties of that little heath will always remain a pleasant memory with me; but it is doomed'.[118]

'late LVI.
'rowd around boat
hop, Whitmore Bay,
7 June 1907.
.C.L. Coll.

Places of worship

In 1884 religious needs were catered for by the three parish churches, dedicated to St. Nicholas (Barry), St. Dyfan and St. Teilo (Merthyr Dyfan), St. Cadoc and St. Illtyd (Cadoxton), together with four nonconformist chapels at Cadoxton, the largest of the villages. These were the thatched roof Philadelphia Welsh Baptist (1813), Bethel Welsh Wesleyan Chapel and Sion Welsh Calvinistic Methodist Chapel, both founded in 1815, and Cadoxton English Wesleyan Chapel, opened in 1862. The dramatic influx of people necessitated a spate of church building. The Established Church built daughter churches in the Gothic style, St. Paul's (1893), St. Mary's (1905) and All Saints' (1908). In the interim use was made of mission buildings. A Church of England Mission which opened in 1891 in a large room in Thompson Street was replaced in 1892, when the present Parish Hall, adjoining St. Mary's, Holton Road, was opened for services. An iron building in Iddesleigh Street, which was erected in 1865 and used as an engineer's office, a stable and a grocer's shop consecutively, was converted into the Church Mission Room at the Cwms in 1887. In 1906 the bankrupt Theatre Royal and Palace of Varieties, Main Street, which had stood empty for many years was licensed for Divine Service. Much of the work of the 'tin church', as the people called the Mission Room, was immediately transferred to this newly-acquired building, which was converted into a church and hall dedicated to St. Aidan in 1910.

Fig. 76.
St. Nicholas Church, Barry.
Simon Prosser.

ate LVII.
'ount Pleasant
nglish Baptist
hapel, Cadoxton,
pened 3 March 1889.
C.L. Coll.

The Rev. Gomer Price conducted week-night services in Welsh in 1889 at the Mission Room, Iddesleigh Street, but these were discontinued on his departure that year. A few months later a Welsh class was formed at the Mission Room, and after a few weeks Sunday services in Welsh were started. The congregation worshipped in the club room of the Royal Hotel before moving in 1892 to the proposed Barry Dock Hotel opposite the Central Police Station. In 1896 they moved to St. John's Welsh Church, an iron building on the corner of Court Road and Wyndham Street. This served as the Welsh Church for the Anglicans of the town until its closure in 1951. At Merthyr Dyfan the 'iron room', which until recent years adjoined St. Paul's, was opened as a mission church in 1886. In Barry the Parish Hall, St. Nicholas Road, opened in September 1892. Increasing numbers led to the opening of a new mission church off Romilly Road in 1897. St. Baruch's, a new mission church under the jurisdiction of the rector of Sully, opened in Clive Road, Barry Island, in November that year.

Barry was rich in the diversity of its nonconformist chapels. The various sects began with meetings in private houses, above stables and shops, or in temporary wooden or corrugated-iron buildings. There was often a delay of some years between the commencement of a cause and the erection of a permanent chapel. In June 1892, for instance, three Welsh causes were worshipping in the proposed Dock Hotel opposite the Central Police Station—The Calvinistic Methodists, Wesleyan Methodists and the Welsh Anglicans.[119] By October 1898 there were about thirty places of worship in the town, including nine buildings connected with the Church of England, one with the Roman Catholics, and the remainder belonging to the various leading nonconformist bodies. These buildings were provided at an aggregate outlay of about £60,000, mainly by subscriptions from the hard-earned wages of the working classes.

Philadelphia was the 'mother' of the Baptist chapels in Barry. From there two Welsh causes were formed. In 1890 the pastor, the Rev. G. Llechidon Williams, left with about 25 members to start the Welsh Baptist Church at Barry Dock. They originally met in a loft over a stable in Thompson Street, but in 1891 moved to a temporary chapel in Beryl Road. There Salem Chapel was erected on an adjoining site in 1898. The congregation which remained at Philadelphia moved to a new chapel, Calfaria, Court Road, which opened in 1897. The influx of English speakers necessitated the erection of English Baptist chapels. The members of Mount Pleasant met in 1886 in a room at Cadoxton Board School before their chapel opened in 1889. The English Baptist Church, Barry Dock, began early in 1890, when members held weekly prayer meetings in different cottages. They used unfinished shops in Holton Road and a loft over a stable before acquiring a temporary wooden hut in Holton Road in 1892. This was replaced in 1898 by the present chapel. The English Baptist cause at the west end commenced in 1890, when a small number met weekly in a large room attached to Wallace's Sea View Coffee Tavern, Broad Street. In 1891 they formed themselves into a church. Lack of space led them to move in 1892 to the late Market Hall, but it proved too large. Land was taken at the corner of Harbour Road and a corrugated iron structure was opened in 1893. It was replaced in 1903 by the present church. Meanwhile, the iron old building was re-erected on Weston Hill, where it opened as Weston Hill Baptist Chapel in 1902. It replaced a mission for the Baptist Forward Movement which had started in 1900 in a room at the top of Weston Hill. Two more Baptist Forward Movement chapels, one at Cadoxton Moors and the other at Barry Island opened in 1898 and 1899 respectively.

A Wesleyan Methodist society worshipped in a large room at the proposed Barry Dock Hotel, Holton Road, from 1890, before erecting a hall on the corner of Holton Road and Llantwit Street in 1892. When this proved too small, a large chapel, Crossway, was built in 1911. The Bible Christians, an offshoot of the original Wesleyan Methodists, came to Barry in 1890, when the Rev. Jabez Honey preached for two Sundays in the open air near Barry Dock Central Police Station. Meetings were then held in a large room at a new hotel in Holton Road. In 1891 they worshipped in a large tent on a site near the chapel in course of erection in Court Road. This chapel opened in September that year. The Methodist Free Church, another branch of the original Wesleyans, commenced worshipping in a building in Spencer Street, Barry Dock, in 1897. A larger, new school chapel was opened in

Buttrills Road in 1898. In 1905 they joined with the Bible Christians to form the United Methodist Church. The Porthkerry Road Methodists worshipped at East Barry House and then in a thatched cottage in Old Village Road. In 1887 they purchased land in Porthkerry Road where they met in a hall until 1898, when the present church was dedicated. A Primitive Methodist Chapel and Schoolroom in Pyke Street opened in 1897, and in 1901 the Methodist Church was erected on Barry Island.

Welsh Calvinistic Methodism began in 1815 at Sion Chapel, Hatch Hill, Cadoxton and spread to Penuel, High Street (erected 1893 on the site of a temporary structure). New Jerusalem was erected in Tynewydd Road in 1899, and Seion in Pontypridd Street in 1891. The English Calvinistic Methodists (or Presbyterian Church of Wales) at Cadoxton took on a separate identity in the spring of 1886, when seven members left Sion. They met initially at the Picnic Hall, but later built the Presbyterian Hall in Melrose Street, before erecting Bethel Court Road (1891). In 1895 a new Presbyterian Chapel (English Calvinistic Methodist) opened in Trinity Street. The congregation had worshipped in an adjoining schoolroom for the past seven years. Their cause had begun in the autumn of 1888 when Divine Service was held for the first time in the Old Board School, Queen Street. A Presbyterian 'Forward Movement' cause was founded on Barry Island in 1904.[120] In April 1903 the large, Forward Movement Dinam Hall was opened in Barry Dock.

Plate LVIII. Holton Road, Barry Dock, looking towards King Square and Council Offices, *c.* 1912. *B.C.L. Coll.*

The Welsh Congregational cause began in 1886. They met in the Wesleyan Chapel, Cadoxton and for a time the Wesleyans and Congregationalists worshipped together, and each found a preacher for alternate Sundays. In 1887 they quit the Wesleyan Chapel and for the next eighteen months used the old schoolroom at the National School, Cadoxton. A site was taken up on which a schoolroom was built. It opened in October 1887, and a year later the Rev. W. Tibbott was inducted there as a minister of Bryn Seion, Court Road.[121] In 1889 a number of Welsh Congregationalists resident in Barry who were members of the church at Cadoxton decided to start a cause in their part of the town. They rented a wooden shed from T. A. Walker, the contractor. In 1890 a new schoolroom was opened, but when the Public Hall in High Street, built originally by T. A. Walker as a mission hall, was offered for sale, it was purchased and opened in 1892 as Bethesda Chapel. To meet the needs of Welsh Congregationalists in Barry Dock, Tabernacle was built. The cause began in January 1890, when members of the Penarth Church decided to establish a chapel in Holton Road for members who had moved to that district. Services commenced in April 1890 in an iron building, replaced in 1894 by the present church. The eloquent preacher, the Rev. Ben Evans, pastor of Tabernacle 1899-1918, was the father of Dan Evans, founder of the Barry Department Store in 1907, and a grandfather to Gwynfor Evans, president of Plaid Cymru and that party's first Member of Parliament.

The English Congregationial cause began in the town in 1889, when a meeting at Seacroft, Park Road, the home of J. C. Meggitt, decided to erect a church. A school-chapel on the site of the existing church at Windsor Road opened in 1890. It flourished until 1899 when the school building was placed further back to make way for a large church. The new school building opened in 1900 and the church in 1904. A Congregational Church in Tynewydd Road opened in 1894 when the iron building, first used by the Welsh Congregationalists of Tabernacle, was purchased. It was replaced by a new building, opened in 1901. Meanwhile, the iron structure was removed to Weston Hill for the newly-formed Cadoxton Congregationalists, eighteen members leaving Tynewydd Road Church to join the Cadoxton cause. This church opened in 1900.

The influx of Irish working-class families increased the Roman Catholic community. In 1886 mass was celebrated in the home of Dr. P. J. O'Donnell, Yara Yara, Barry Road. O'Donnell sponsored the movement to obtain at first a regular system of priestly visits from Cardiff, and later in 1889, the installation of Fr. Hyland as resident priest. St. Mary's Roman Catholic Mission Church met at the Picnic Hall of the Wenvoe Arms Hotel, Cadoxton, free of charge in the years 1887 to 1892, thanks to the proprietor, Henry Chappell. Each Sunday an altar was erected on the magistrate's rostrum, since the same room was used during the week as the local court. It was necessary to carry the altar furniture to and from Fr. Hyland's house in Lower Guthrie Street. Sunday School and evening services were also held in this mission church. By 1892 the Catholics had purchased an acre at the junction of Court Road and Wyndham Street, and on this a school-chapel was built. It was dedicated in 1892 and served as a school on weekdays and a church on Sundays. In 1898 an infants' school and presbytery were built. By 1907 the church of St. Helen had arisen on the same site.[122]

Youth organisations

The influence of institutional religion has much diminished in the 20th century. Some of the churches are derelict or put to secular use, and in a few instances are demolished. For many they were the centre of their local community. In them people acquired their ideas of morality, self-discipline and respect, and their spiritual, social and cultural lives found expression. Members' needs were catered for from cradle to grave. In 1892, for example, Windsor Road Congregational Church held Sunday afternoon Bible classes for young men, and there was a separate class for young women. They had a Sunday school and choir and a successful Band of Hope. During the winter months a guild for devotional and recreational meeting was held weekly and the vestry was converted into a reading and recreation room, newspapers, periodicals, chess, draughts and so on being provided; in the summer there was a cricket club. Youth and other organisations established by or connected with churches carried the influence of Christian teaching to a wider circle of the population.

The Boys' Brigade was established in 1883 by a Sunday School teacher, William Smith of Glasgow. It aimed to teach children between the ages of twelve and eighteen 'obedience, discipline, manliness, punctuality, neatness and general good behaviour'. The original local Brigade was the First Cadoxton-Barry Company, formed in January 1892. It was attached to Bethel Calvinistic Methodist Chapel, Court Road. Meetings or parades were held twice weekly in the schoolroom, and Wallace Davies was the captain. This company does not seem to have survived long.

Its rival and off-shoot, the Church Lads' Brigade, was conducted on Church of England principles, but otherwise there was little difference, for both organisations made provision for the physical, moral and intellectual welfare of the boys. In August 1894 a company of the Church Lads' Brigade was formed in Barry Parish. A Cadoxton Company was established the same month. The contingent was drawn from the four churches at Cadoxton and was under the command of Wallace W. Davies, sergeant instructor. They held their inaugural meeting in September 1894, at the Public Hall, Vere Street. In 1895 the three companies of the Church Lads' Brigade at St. Cadoc's, St. Nicholas and St. Paul's were formed into a battalion.

To counter this Anglican movement members of the nonconformist churches met at Mount Pleasant English Baptist Chapel, Cadoxton, in 1894 and decided to form a Boys' Brigade. By 1895 local companies of the Boys' Brigade were in existence. In 1897 a new drill hall in Park Crescent was opened. Fitted with all the necessary apparatus for a first-class gym, it was claimed to be the first institution of its kind ever established for the Boys' Brigade. There was a Bible class, gymnastics, drill and military drill.[123]

The Boy Scouts took their name from the army scouts of the Boer War. The most successful of all youth movements, they were founded by Sir Robert (later Lord) Baden Powell in 1907 to train boys in woodcraft and nature study and to direct character and habits. In Barry the movement soon became very popular. The first patrol of the Barry Scouts, the Woodpeckers, was formed in 1908 and was closely followed by a patrol at Cadoxton, which met in the former Sion Chapel, Hatch Hill. In July 1909 four patrols—Peewits, Otters, Wolves and Panthers—numbering about thirty-two boys, were formed at Cadoxton. J. Chambers, the old village blacksmith, who lived at Yew Tree Cottage, was the Scoutmaster. There were two organised patrols in the west end. The Scouting movement appealed to a young go-ahead town like Barry, and in October 1910 Colonel J. A. Hughes stated there were three hundred Boy Scouts in the town. The First Barry Troup grew out of the original Woodpecker patrol and had their headquarters at the Wesleyan Chapel, Porthkerry Road. King George V presented the King's Banner to the best scout troop in the country. The First Barry King's Troop had the distinction of winning the banner in 1911 and

Plate LIX. Juvenile Tent of St. David's Lodge of Independent Order of Good Templars, established at Cadoxton in 1888. *H. Shirvington, B.C.L. Coll.*

the two succeeding years. This coveted Challenge Banner, competed for by all the Scouts in the United Kingdom on only four occasions, was won in the fourth year, 1914-15, by another Barry Troop, the Fourth Barry (St. Paul's) B.P. Scouts. This remarkable achievement reflected the high standard of scouting in the district.[124]

The Band of Hope, a religious organisation catering for children, instilled principles of temperance and promoted its objectives by moral social and legislative action. In 1893 the Rev. J. H. Evans, curate of the Welsh Anglican Church, Barry Dock, formed two branches for the Church children of Cadoxton parish. One met in the Mission Room, Iddesleigh Street, and the other in the Welsh Mission Room at Holton Road. Other denominations formed their own Bands of Hope and the movement was especially popular at the turn of the century.

The chief object of the Young Men's Christian Association was to encourage young men, irrespective of denomination, to lead a full Christian life. The inaugural meeting of the Barry branch was held at the Public Hall, East Barry, in 1890 and was attended by members from various churches and chapels.[125] In November 1890 two rooms were taken in Broad Street, and during the winter Bible, essay and debating classes were conducted. Open-air meetings were held every Sunday during the summer months and the Association Rooms were moved from Barry Dock Road to High Street. In 1907 the Association through the munificence of John Cory acquired an unlicensed hotel in Woodland Road which remained the headquarters until recent years.

Campaigns against drinking and immorality

Churches were closely involved with the National Vigilance Association and the Cadoxton and Barry Temperance Crusade Council. Both organisations attacked the evil of drinking, shebeening and immorality. The National Vigilance Association was formed in 1880 to expose the traffic in innocent English girls to the continent for a life of prostitution. The Barry and Cadoxton branches were formed in July 1891 to deal with the large amount of vice prevalent in the district.[126] George Pike, Secretary of the Cardiff District, urged that those identified with vigilance work 'should be ladies and gentlemen who themselves lived pure and holy lives'. Canon Allen was elected President with the Rev. J. Honey as secretary. Public attendance at a meeting in November 1891 at the Bible Christian chapel, Court Road, was so small as to be 'almost a reflection upon the moral character of the community'. Honey spoke of the deplorable immorality in Barry and said married women sent their nine- or twelve-year-old daughters out to the streets to procure 'by means of their shame' the money to pay for drink. The Rev. L. Ton Evans said immorality was due to the deplorable sin of drunkenness, so painfully prevalent, and he strongly condemned placing young children in the theatre for exhibition purposes.

In 1893 an official enquiry was held at the Police Court, Barry Dock, into shebeening and immorality in the town. County Alderman J. C. Meggitt, a member of the Joint Police Committee presided. Those present included Lionel Lindsay, chief constable; the Rev. J. Honey, the Rev. Christmas Lewis and Mr. G. Pyke represented the Ministers' Fraternal Association, the Temperance Council and the National Vigilance Association respectively. The proceedings were conducted in private, but as a result the police became increasingly vigilant in suppressing illicit drinking. The middle-class character of the National Vigilance Association is reflected in press reports of speeches being delivered to 'ladies and others' in private residences. The Association was energetic in influencing local government and education to adopt its views. In 1894, for example, it decided to bring a copy of the Birmingham code of moral lessons for use in elementary schools to the notice of the School Board.[127] The same year the Association sought the co-operation of the Temperance Council and the Ministers' Fraternal in preventing men of doubtful character being elected members of the Urban District Council. Deputations were appointed to meet candidates to elicit their views on temperance. In 1895 the Vigilance Association praised the success of the Barry police in stamping out shebeening and immorality. They also offered legal assistance to the police in prosecuting property owners who let houses in the lower quarters of the town for immoral purposes. At the A.G.M. in 1896 it was resolved to recognise 'the good services done by the police during the past year in their efforts to suppress drunkenness, illicit drinking and street annoyance'. Electors in the forthcoming District Council election were urged to vote for candidates prepared to 'promote the moral welfare of the people'. It recognised with gratitude the improvement in the tone of the Press and in public opinion in relation to moral lessons, and it trusted that the Press would continue to deal plainly and gravely with the social evils which imperilled the well-being and progress of the community.

Temperance organisations abounded and there was certainly a need for them. In 1891 illicit drinking had become a raging evil and at least a dozen cases of helpless drunkenness were witnessed in different parts of the town on Sunday, 15 February. There is insufficient space to examine all the Temperance movements in Barry and only the main organisation, the Barry Temperance Council is detailed. In 1892, J. C. Meggitt presided over a public meeting to consider the best ways to suppress shebeening. The Rev. L. Ton Evans blamed shebeening on the large numbers of wholesale licences granted to tradespeople. Two years previously only thirteen wholesale licences existed but now the number had almost trebled. It was decided to urge the Joint Police Committee and J.P.s stringently to enforce existing laws. Law-abiding citizens were urged to assist the police by volunteering information and evidence. J. R. Llewellyn, editor of the *Barry Dock News*, promised the full assistance of the local press in stamping out the evil.

Plate LX.
Barry Dock Dairy,
Kingsland Crescent,
with proprietor,
Samuel Lewis (right),
president of Barry
Temperance Ironsides
in 1889.
Bryn Lennox.

This meeting was held during a Temperance Crusade when notices were served upon wholesale beer dealers, warning them their sale of beer infringed the terms of their lease. The first meeting of the Cadoxton and Barry Welsh Temperance Association in 1892 decided to boycott wholesale dealers who would not cease their connection with the drink traffic. Many temperance supporters vigorously enforced this policy. In June 1892 a Barry Temperance Council was formed with two delegates from each place of worship and temperance organisation.[128] This Council exercised a supervising influence over the kindred organisations in the locality. Meetings were held at the Bible Christian chapel, Court Road.

In June 1892 the magistrates were active in the suppression of shebeening and had imposed fines of between £10 and £20 on two shebeeners. A public meeting called for the Temperance Council deprecated the amount of drunkenness, poverty and crime due to the availability of alcoholic drinks. It urged the licensing justices not to grant any new applications brought before the Brewster Sessions. Year after year the Temperance party were to make their presence felt at these Sessions where they vigorously opposed the granting of new licences. The Rev. Jabez Honey claimed in May 1893 there remained a large number of shebeens but no prosecutions had been made lately. He blamed the magistrates for dismissing cases which in Cardiff would have been convicted. There were more houses in the district than required and agents were careless about the letting of these to tenants who used them for immoral purposes. A great deal of soliciting occurred in the streets and a portion of the Victoria Hotel was frequented by prostitutes. The Barry District National Vigilance Association was keeping a watch on certain houses and information obtained was to be passed to the police. In July that year a great Temperance Demonstration included a procession through the district followed by a mass meeting in the open air. The Temperance Council in 1894 congratulated the police for the energetic way they prosecuted shebeeners,[129] but regretted that the police were not receiving backing from the magistrates. By January 1895 shebeening was greatly diminished and its heyday was over, but bogus working men's clubs increased instead. The Temperance Council in 1896 organised a monster petition amongst householders at Barry Dock, where most of the clubs existed. Upwards of a thousand householders signed the petition which was presented to owners of property, demanding the closure of clubs or the adoption of measures for their strict regulation. The Temperance Council suggested that the police should keep a register of drunken persons seen to emerge from public houses and lay this information before the magistrates when applications were made for licence renewals. They further urged the police to stop drunken men from entering public houses and to warn publicans against admitting such people on their premises. However, by January 1897 it was clear the Council was running out of enthusiasm. The apathy of delegates in attending meetings was seriously affecting the effectiveness of the Council. Work was further hampered by lack of funds, and ministers of religion had entirely abandoned them. It was claimed that for every convert to a religious cause in the district there were nine drunkards. A month later the Temperance Council was declared defunct.

The Temperance movement continued to play its part in town affairs. In August 1897 E. Tennyson Smith, founder of the Temperance Ironsides, delivered a series of addresses to crowded gatherings during a ten-day mission. The mission ended with a 'Trial of the Notorious Criminal, Alcohol' at the Romilly Hall, which was filled with an enthusiastic audience composed mainly of adherents of the Temperance cause. On a visit in July 1898 he was billed as the 'Prince of Temperance Advocates and Hero of Prohibition Victories'.[130] Others came, too. The local Free Church Council and Temperance Societies continued to organise campaigns to pursuade public opinion to oppose new licences for hotels. The success of their campaign is evidenced by the great number of hotels which failed to obtain a licence.

Welfare services

Churches tried to provide help today given by the services of the Welfare State. Severe winter weather led to the suspension of outdoor work and a great number of labourers were unemployed. In December 1890 the severe weather resulted in scores of Cadoxton labouring-class families being thrown out of work to suffer cold and hunger.[131] In response to a circular issued by the Rector, Ebenezer Morris, a meeting of tradespeople was held at the Wenvoe Arms Hotel on 30 December 1890. A committee, which included nonconformist ministers and doctors, established a soup kitchen. The soup was made in a boiler at the Old Wenvoe Arms belonging to Mrs. Matthews. Meals were served at the Picnic Hall, the mission room, Iddesleigh Street, and the Long Room at the Shaftesbury Temperance Hotel. On New Year's Day 1891 tickets were issued and in the afternoon the first distribution of soup, comprising about eighty gallons, took place at the Picnic Hall. On 16 January the severe weather continued and much hunger and distress was evident. Hundreds of men employed by the building industry and the Local Board were laid off without pay. Poverty and hardship spread. The bitterly cold weather reached its crisis on Saturday night, 18 January, when ten degrees of frost were recorded. Mean temperature during the frosty weather was from 26° to 30° fahrenheit. Following the 18th January there was a gradual rise in temperature and the worst of the severe weather was over. The soup kitchen was closed on Saturday, 31 January. Upwards of £80 worth of soup and bread had been distributed during the previous six weeks. Soup kitchens and relief work for the poor were provided in the winters of 1894/95 and 1895/96. The colliers' strike in the South Wales Coalfield, which lasted for over five months in the spring and summer of 1898, had a devastating effect, and in Barry hundreds of dockworkers and railwaymen were laid off for over four months. A soup kitchen was established to cater for the needs of workers and their families.[132]

Missions to the poor

The Navvy Mission Society was formed in 1870 by a young clergyman who ministered to the navvies at Lindley Wood in the upper reaches of Wharfedale, where they were constructing reservoirs for Leeds Corporation. Lay ministers working under the supervision of a neighbouring clergyman conducted the services. J. Pearce, an experienced evangelist, came to Barry in 1892. Encouraged and assisted by Canon Allen, Pearce did excellent work amongst the navvies. The mission began on Sunday evening, 21 August 1892, in a wooden building near Brook's Farm. It was opened in September as a reading room from 7 p.m. to 9.30 p.m., and at noon when the men through bad weather or other causes were unable to work. Sir John Jackson the contractor of the deep-water lock subscribed £50 towards the missionaries' salary, while Price and Wills, contractors of the new dock, subscribed £25. At least once a month one of the local clergy conducted holy communion at the mission room. In 1894 Pearce left and was replaced by Walter S. Symes. The mission ran a Sunday school, Band of Hope and Bible class. As the mission grew the building was extended and a small classroom was erected. A visitor one Sunday evening in 1896 was 'agreeably surprised to find the structure well-filled with a devout congregation of navvies and their families. The service—a suitable abridgement of that from the Book of Common Prayer—was heartily rendered, both by the minister and his flock, and the singing, although perhaps not particularly refined or artistic, was of a distinctly sincere and effective character, Sankey's hymns being sung with an earnestness bordering upon enthusiasm'.[133] A new and larger mission room, with seating for 400 worshippers, was opened at the foot of Weston Hill in 1896. That September a reading, recreation, and smoke room was opened in Quarella Street. It was a gift of George Garnett, a well known friend of the navvies. The premises, previously used by the Salvation Army had a refreshment room where food, temperance drinks and tobacco were available. Cadoxton was the busiest of all the navvy mission stations during 1897/98 as a result of the New Dock works. W. Symes was assisted by Miss Jane Greenwood and about twenty-eight navvies who formed themselves into a body of teachers to deal with the very large Sunday school which by April 1898 numbered over four hundred. By November 1899 hundreds of navvies and their families had left the town owing to the completion of the New Dock. In April 1900 Walter Symes formed a new branch of the Society at Cardiff but retained oversight of the Cadoxton mission, which continued to prosper. The lease ran out on the Weston Hill site so the mission room was dismantled and reassembled in Harvey Street, where it opened on Sunday, 19 May 1901.

No religious movement in Barry in these years worked with greater energy or met with greater success than the Salvation Army. In 1889 Captain Hirst was appointed First Officer in command of the movement in the Barry District. The first contingent was established at Cadoxton where in the mission hall, Quarella Street, daily meetings were held. In the summer months the contingent accompanied by a band and a banner held open-air meetings on Cadoxton Common. Sometimes drunken louts disturbed the meetings but the army continued to prosper and in August 1892 its membership was increasing. Their enthusiasm caused them trouble. In July 1893 complaints were made against them for singing and playing loudly as they marched through Holton Road on Sunday mornings, disturbing church services. As the town developed, a new meeting place was established in Holton Road, and the Cadoxton Mission Hall was removed to more convenient premises in Main Street. The infant branch soon outgrew the parent contingent and in 1895 a site was secured in Thompson Street for the erection of permanent barracks which opened in 1896. The Salvation Army was forced to relinquish their hall in Thompson Street and for two or three years meetings were held in temporary premises in the same road. In October 1912 they opened in their present hall in Holton Road which had formerly been used as a skating rink.[134] The new premises provided seating accommodation for upwards of a thousand people.

The British and Foreign Sailors Institute (or Bethel) Barry Dock, was opened in November 1891, with Captain Edward Sharples, the missionary in charge.[135] The building, near the Dock Offices, consisted of a large reading and worshipping room, and a large coffee room with kitchen. Upstairs were eight bed- and sitting-rooms for distressed or ship-wrecked seamen. Bethel freely distributed copies of the scriptures and parcels of literature. It provided free meals, paid for lodgings for destitute seamen, sheltered them overnight and also paid the fares of the sick to hospital in Cardiff. During hard weather in the winter scores of destitute sailors found shelter and sustenance at the mission. Captain Sharples believed that the best form of Christianity was the feeding of the body as well as the soul.

The Order of St. Paul, an Anglican Monastic Order founded in India in 1884 to help sailors, came to Barry in 1894, when the Rev. Charles Walker, better known as Fr. Austin, a zealous and energetic priest arrived at Barry Dock from Calcutta to organise a mission amongst the seamen.[136] He organised the mission in a seven-room cottage, known as the Home Priory, Station Street. One of its rooms was fitted out as a chapel, while others catered for the well-being and comfort of merchant seamen. Well-wishers supplied the home with gifts of furniture, books on social questions of the day and newspapers. Within a few years the Priory moved to Broad Street, where accommodation was provided for sailors who were given religious instruction, recreation and the advantages of home, including free meals. The Order gave its sympathy and help, arranged for medical attention where needed, and acquired copies of lost discharge papers from the Board of Trade. It guarded and tended the graves of dead seamen. On the piece of land adjoining the Priory the Order built an iron church—the Seamen's Priory chapel—which opened in April 1898. It was claimed in April 1900 that a larger number of destitute seamen were housed and fed at the Barry Priory than at the Order's London Priory. By February 1900 seven thousand sailors had passed through the Priory in the previous four years. It closed in 1912 when the Order withdrew from Barry.

In about 1885 T. A. Walker established the Barry Gospel Mission.[137] At the turn of the century this mission held regular open-air meetings. A new hall situated at the junction of Porthkerry Road and Island Road was opened in October 1899. By this date the population of Barry was very mixed. The turbulent, expanding working-class population attracted the endeavours of many evangelists. Among them was the indefatigable Gerald R. Coultas, who came from London in 1895. He established his Gospel Mission, strictly unsectarian, in a tent in Thompson Street. For several months services were conducted every evening. That winter a building was used in the same street, but a rapidly-growing population made it necessary to open the Gospel Hall, Merthyr Street, in March 1896. It was a wooden structure, roofed with corrugated iron. In May 1896 Coultas held services in a tent lit by gas, erected in a field opposite the Gas Works in Holton Road.

ate LXI.
roclamation of
cession of King
eorge V, King Square,
May 1910, in
esence of 20,000
ople.
C.L. Coll.

The mission's work continued throughout the late 1890s with an indoor service at the Gospel Hall in the winter and in the Gospel tent in summer. The mission work embraced Bible meetings for young men, special meetings and a clothing club for the women, and Sunday school and Band of Hope for the children. It effected much moral and spiritual good amongst the poorer townspeople. The energetic efforts of Coultas resulted in the opening of an iron building as a Presbyterian Forward Movement Hall in Friars Road, Barry Island, in 1900. A Forward Movement Hall on the site of the temporary Gospel Mission Hall in Merthyr Street, named Dinam Hall, was erected in 1903.

Friendly Societies

Before the Welfare state working people banded together in Friendly Societies to pay for education, health and funeral costs. The earliest in the Barry district was the Cadoxton Loyal Glamorgan Garden of Wales Lodge of the Independent Order of Oddfellows M.U., which was established in 1838.[138] Their lodge room was at the King William IV Hotel. The society held its procession and feast day on the last Monday in July every year. Typical were the festivities held in 1891, when they met at the lodge room shortly before noon. About thirty members dressed in the quaint but attractive regalia of the Order and headed by the Cadoxton Brass Band formed a procession. They proceeded to the parish church, where the Rev. E. Morris preached an appropriate special sermon. Afterwards they paraded through several streets, returning to the lodge room about two o'clock for dinner. Although the lodge only numbered about fifty-six members, it was one of the wealthiest branches of the Order in the country. It was very conservative and did not encourage new members, for which it was severely criticised. Dr. O'Donnell, the lodge surgeon, had urged the admission of younger and more energetic members but the lodge ignored the advice. Newcomers to the town joined a proliferation of new Friendly Societies. Among these societies were the Monmouthshire District of the Ancient Order of Druids (founded 1890, headquarters Victoria Hotel), the Royal Cadoxton Lodge of the Ancient Benefit Friendly Society (1889, Royal Hotel) the Loyal Barry Dock Lodge of the Grand United Order of Oddfellows No. 3047 (founded 1889), The Cadoxton Court of Forresters (*c.* 1890, Witchill Hotel), the Cadoxton Branch of the Royal Hearts of Oak Yearly Dividing Benefit Society (1890, King William IV Hotel), the Hope of Barry Lodge of the Sons of Temperance Benefit Society (1889, Davies Refreshment Rooms), the Loyal Victoria Lodge R.A.O.B. (1890, Victoria Hotel), the Cadoxton Barry Hibernian Benefit Society (1890, Witchill Hotel), the Loyal Lord Windsor Lodge of Oddfellows of Barry (1892) and the Prince of Wales Lodge of the Order of Buffaloes (1891). The Cardiff and County Conservative Working-men's Superannuation and Benefit Society founded a branch at the Presbyterian Hall, Cadoxton, in 1891, which made provision not only for sickness and death but also for old age. The Independent Order of Good Templars (Rechabites) established a lodge in the Reading Room, Courtenay Road, Cadoxton, on 1 March 1888. The Independent Order of Rechabites Salford United Friendly Society established a branch in Barry in 1890 which met at the Bible Christian Chapel, Court Road. To avoid social and moral contamination they would not meet in a public house. In November 1891 complaints were made that the inordinate multiplicity of Friendly Societies in the Barry and Cadoxton district might become a nuisance. There was already a glut of lodges, especially at Cadoxton. A Federation of Friendly Societies in the town was formed in November 1897.[139]

Conclusion

This has been a review of Barry's first thirty years as a new town, based for the most part on reports in local newspapers. Then, as now, the more sensational stories reached the columns and humdrum virtue often passed unnoticed. One constant factor was the continued growth of the town, and no one could see an end to its expansion. In 1897 *The Manchester Guardian* considered that Barry was threatening to outgrow Cardiff,[140] while two years later the *Bristol Times* regarded it as the most dangerous rival of Bristol.[141] Barry's emergence from obscurity was so rapid that many outsiders had no idea of its location. In 1897 a Middlesex firm wrote to a Barry company: 'We shall be pleased to quote if you would kindly let us know where Barry is; we cannot find it either in the conveyance directory, the timetable or the very detailed map we possess. If it is not in England, we cannot quote to advantage, as these are inland works, but if it is anywhere in the Midland counties, we can quote favourably'.[142]

By 1914 Barry was a place of nearly two hundred streets, mostly well paved and well lit; it had good gas and water supplies and was provided with modern hospitals, schools, a library and all the facilities of early 20th-century town life. It was filled with a sense of destiny and with hope for the future. Its ambitions knew no bounds. There were plans for a third dock, a transatlantic passenger service, an iron and steel works and a zinc works. On a cultural and academic level some inhabitants dreamed of an opera house and even a university. These grand dreams were to be shattered by that terrible experience—the First Great War. In its aftermath Barry was no longer the greatest of coal-exporting ports, and had to struggle to find a new role in a different world.

References

The author of this chapter has relied mainly on local newspapers for his sources, and the number of references, if all were given, would be far in excess of what is normally expected in a book of this character. Only the more significant and representative items have been included below, but a fully detailed list can be obtained on request from the author or the editor. Abbreviations are used for the four publications most commonly quoted.

B.D.N. = *Barry Dock News*

B. & Dist. N. = *Barry & District News*

B. & C. J. = *Barry and Cadoxton Journal*

W. Mail = *Western Mail*

1 Quoted in *B.D.N.*, 29th May, 1891.
2 *B.D.N.*, 30th March, 1894.
3 Thomas Ewbank, *The geography and history of Barry* (Cardiff, 1921), p. 25 ff.
4 *B.D.N.*, 15th April, 1892.
5 *B.D.N.*, 26th February & 5th March, 1897.
6 *B.D.N.*, 27th April, 1894.
7 *B.D.N.*, 19th May & 16th June, 1899.
8 *B.D.N.*, 13th March, 1891: 'Barry—past and present', paper read to Y.M.C.A. by E. A. Thomas.
9 *W. Mail,* 10th June, 1887: report of tragedy occasioned by landslip.
10 *B.D.N.*, 14th February & 21st August, 1896.
11 *B.D.N.*, 12th February, 1897.
12 Ewbank, *op. cit.*, p. 51.
13 *Ibid.*, p. 51.
14 *B.D.N.*, 15th May, 1891.
15 *B.D.N.*, 11th March, 1892.
16 *B.D.N.*, 16th December, 1898.
17 *B.D.N.*, 31st October, 1890.
18 *B. & Dist. N.*, 1st November, 1929.
19 *B. & C. J.*, 24th November, 1888.
20 *B.D.N.*, 14th November, 1890.
21 *B.D.N.*, 19th January, 1894.
22 *B.D.N.*, 28th July, 1893.
23 *B.D.N.*, 8th May, 1891.
24 *B.D.N.*, 19th February, 1892.
25 *B.D.N.*, 26th July, 1895.
26 *B. & C. J.*, 14th April, 1888.
27 *B.D.N.*, 3rd May, 1895.
28 *B.D.N.*, 11th March, 1892: directors of Barry Co. refuse to contribute towards Cottage Hospital.
29 Black's *Guide to South Wales and Monmouthshire* (9th ed., 1896).
30 *B.D.N.*, 4th September, 1891.
31 *B.D.N.*, 13th January, 1911: Mrs. Grundy's jottings.
32 *B.D.N.*, 24th April, 1908.
33 First Annual Report of the Medical Officer of Health (1889).
34 Ewbank, *op. cit.*, p. 79.
35 *B.D.N.*, 3rd April, 1891.
36 *B.D.N.*, 25th January, 1895.
37 *B.D.N.*, 3rd & 11th August, 1893.
38 *B.D.N.*, 2nd October, 1891.
39 *B.D.N.*, 29th August, 1890.
40 *B.D.N.*, 24th October, 1890.
41 *B.D.N.*, 16th November, 1894.
42 *B.D.N.*, 14th April, 1899.
43 *B.D.N.*, 26th December, 1924.
44 *B.D.N.*, 17th December, 1897.
45 *B.D.N.*, 1st March, 1901.
46 *B. & C. J.*, 29th December, 1888 & 19th July, 1889.
47 *B.D.N.*, 27th February, 1891.
48 *B.D.N.*, 9th October, 1891.
49 *B.D.N.*, 12th January & 16th February, 1900.
50 *B.D.N.*, 27th November & 18th December, 1908.
51 *B.D.N.*, 15th May, 1896; see also 23rd September, 1898 for cholera hospital.
52 *B.D.N.*, 11th August, 1905; see also 20th March, 1908 for smallpox hospital.
53 Ewbank, *op. cit.*, p. 82.
54 *Ibid.*, p. 46.
55 *Barry Education Week Guide* (July, 1923): valuable articles on education in Barry.
56 *B.D.N.*, 9th October, 1896.
57 *B.D.N.*, 2nd February, 1894: editorial.
58 *B.D.N.*, 6th February & 7th August, 1891.

59 *B.D.N.,* 1st November, 1895.
60 *B.D.N.,* 6th March, 1906.
61 *B.D.N.,* 18th September, 1896.
62 *B.D.N.,* 30th May & 4th July, 1913.
63 *B.D.N.,* 15th January, 1892; see also 18th September, 1891 for building.
64 *B. & Dist. N.,* 23rd August, 1929.
65 *B.D.N.,* 27th November, 1896.
66 *B.D.N.,* 13th May, 1892: Mrs. Grundy's jottings.
67 *B.D.N.,* 18th March, 1892: Mrs. Grundy's jottings.
68 *B.D.N.,* 6th July, 1894.
69 *B.D.N.,* 28th April, 1893.
70 *B.D.N.,* 6th January, 1893.
71 *B.D.N.,* 8th March, 1895.
72 *B.D.N.,* 20th March, 1896.
73 *B.D.N.,* 22nd July, 1898.
74 *B.D.N.,* 9th February, 1894: editorial & 24th August, 1894.
75 *B.D.N.,* 19th February, 1892.
76 *B.D.N.,* 11th March, 1892 & 24th August, 1894.
77 *B.D.N.,* 10th May, 1895.
78 *B.D.N.,* 4th May, 1894.
70 *B. & C. J.,* 24th March, 1888.
80 *South Wales Star,* 22nd May, 1891.
81 *B.D.N.,* 3rd August, 1894.
82 *Official Guide to Barry District and the Vale of Glamorgan* (1911).
83 *B.D.N.,* 4th August, 1899.
84 *B.D.N.,* 20th & 27th January, 1899.
85 *B.D.N.,* 17th March, 1899.
86 *B.D.N.,* 2nd June, 1899.
87 *B.D.N.,* 1st & 8th June, 1894.
88 *B.D.N.,* 8th August, 1890.
89 *B.D.N.,* 23rd July, 1897.
90 Barry Male Voice Choir 75th Anniversary Concert, *Souvenir Programme.*
91 *B.D.N.,* 26th January, 1894.
92 Ewbank, *op. cit.,* p. 96.
93 *B.D.N.,* 29th December, 1899.
94 *B.D.N.,* 5th August, 1910.
95 *B.D.N.,* 24th October, 1913.
96 *B.D.N.,* 17th April, 1891.
97 *B.D.N.,* 13th April, 1900.
98 *B.D.N.,* 1st August, 1890.
99 *B.D.N.,* 19th February & 13th May, 1892.
100 *B.D.N.,* 13th November, 1896.
101 *B.D.N.,* 12th June, 1891.
102 *B.D.N.,* 14th September, 1894.
103 *B.D.N.,* 2nd November, 1900.
104 *B.D.N.,* 19th June, 1891.
105 *B.D.N.,* 22nd September, 1899.
106 *B.D.N.,* 6th June, 1890.
107 *B.D.N.,* 12th August, 1892.
108 *B.D.N.,* 15th November, 1912.
109 *B.D.N.,* 8th May, 1908: Mrs. Grundy's jottings.
110 *B.D.N.,* 11th November, 1898.
111 The Rev. John Evans, *A Tour in South Wales* (1804).
112 *B.D.N.,* 15th August, 1890 & 19th June, 1891.
113 D. S. Barrie, *The Barry Railway* (Oakwood Press, 1962), p. 175.
114 *B.D.N.,* 19th May, 1905.
115 *Barry Herald,* 27th August, 1909.
116 Borough of Barry, *Charter Souvenir* (1939).
117 *W. Mail,* 28th April, 1926.
118 *B.D.N.,* 12th October, 1894.
119 *B.D.N.,* 3rd June, 1892.
120 *A brief history of the churches of Barry and the Vale,* printed on the occasion of the Barry and Vale Royal National Eisteddfod of Wales (August 1968).
121 John Williams (ed.), *A history of Congregationalism in Cardiff and district* (Cardiff, 1920), p. 125.
122 *B.D.N.,* 3rd May, 1907.
123 *B.D.N.,* 10th September, 1897.
124 Information kindly contributed by Mr. Ron Croome.
125 *B.D.N.,* 13th November, 1891.
126 *B.D.N.,* 17th July, 1891.
127 *B.D.N.,* 12th January, 1894.
128 *B.D.N.,* 17th June, 1892: editorial.
129 *B.D.N.,* 2nd March, 1894.
130 *B.D.N.,* 12th February, 1897.
131 *B.D.N.,* 2nd January, 1891.
132 *B.D.N.,* 23rd September, 1898.
133 *B.D.N.,* 14th February, 1896.
134 *B.D.N.,* 2nd August & 11th October, 1912.
135 *B.D.N.,* 29th May, 1896.
136 *B.D.N.,* 27th July, 1894.
137 *B.D.N.,* 13th October, 1899.
138 *South Wales Star,* 31st July, 1891 & *B.D.N.,* 18th April, 1902.
139 *B.D.N.,* 26th November, 1897.
140 *B.D.N.,* 19th November, 1897.
141 *B.D.N.,* 10th November, 1899.
142 *B.D.N.,* 15th October, 1897: Mrs. Grundy's jottings.

CHAPTER VIII

The Building of Barry

RICHARD W. THOMAS

Architectural detail from Nos. 69-72 High Street, Barry. *B. Daly.*

IN 1884 the navvies of T. A. Walker started construction work on No. 1 Dock. Their very presence created a need for housing, and the first stage in the building of modern Barry was the immediate provision of temporary accommodation and basic amenities for hundreds of workers and their families close to the access points into the dock area; these were the tunnels under the new railway line at Island Road, Dock View Road and the foot of Weston Hill. This was the start of the process which transformed the scattered villages and farms of Barry, Merthyr Dyfan and Cadoxton into a new town.

Other workers, tradesmen and professional people began to arrive with the intention of settling down as long-term inhabitants. This led to the second stage of development, when large numbers of permanent houses were built, followed by shops, offices, schools and places of worship, not to mention hotels and places of amusement. The town gave shape to its corporate identity by means of civic offices, municipal library and reading rooms. At the beginning of the first World War Barry was a thriving community of 38,000 people, well provided with essential services, roads parks and amenities. This second stage was thus a period of both pioneering and consolidation.

The period between the Wars may be regarded as the third stage, by no means as ebullient as the previous. The fortunes of the Docks had declined. There was a falling-off in coal exports and little growth in other trade to compensate. The situation was aggravated by a world-wide recession. However, an upsurge in government spending and local-authority housebuilding had some effects on the appearance of the town, and there was a significant development on the west side of the town, which owed much to private enterprise inspired by an architectural philosophy—the Barry Garden Surburb. The residents probably did not realise how novel and pioneering the venture was at the time. Efforts by the local authority to emulate this example were by no means as successful.

Plate LXII. Air view of Barry from S., *c.* 1975. *Copyright West Air Photography.*

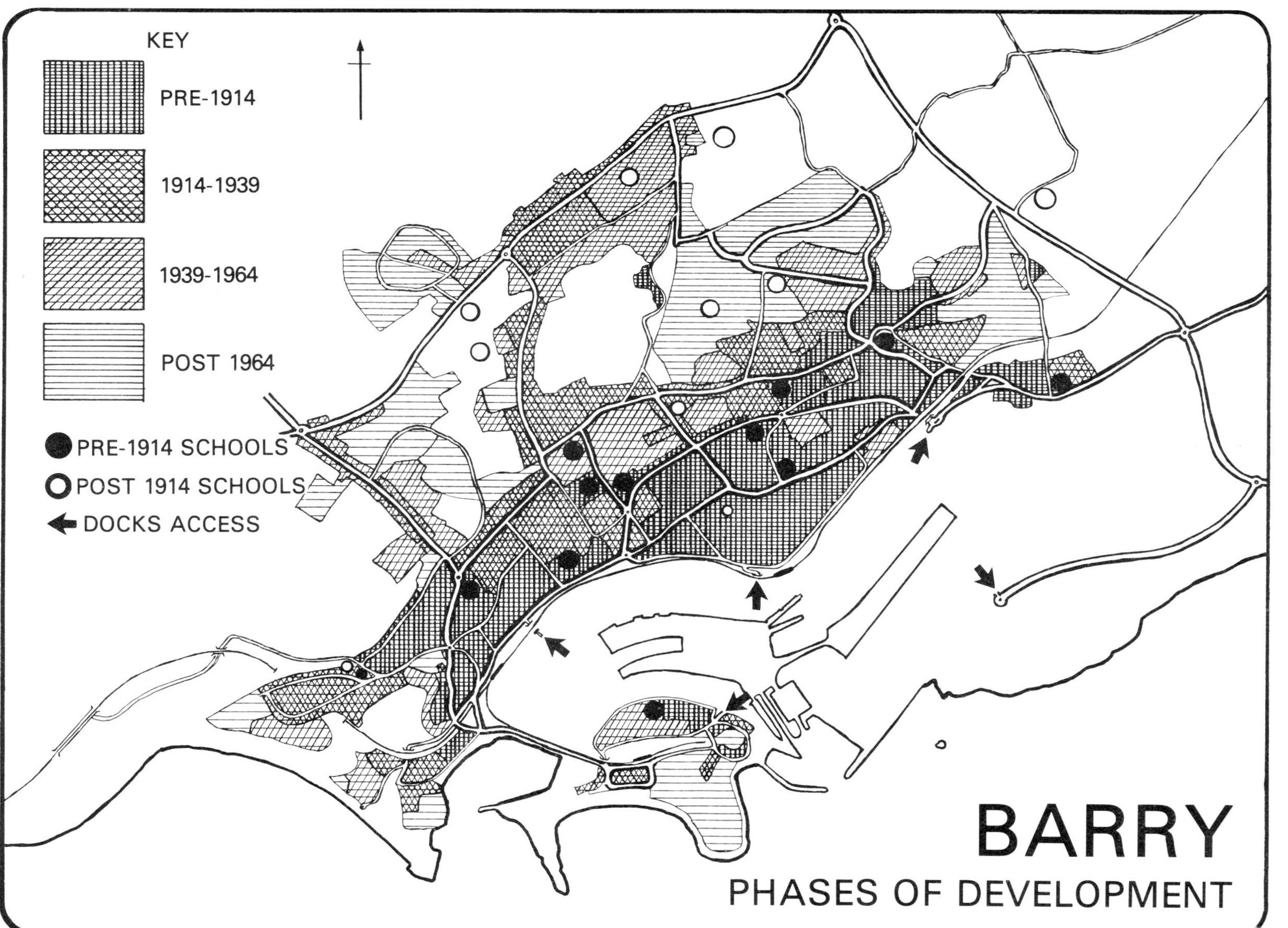
KEY
PRE-1914
1914-1939
1939-1964
POST 1964
PRE-1914 SCHOOLS
POST 1914 SCHOOLS
DOCKS ACCESS
BARRY
PHASES OF DEVELOPMENT

The second World War, as in so many other fields, created a pause in development, and its end marked a turning point, which could be said to begin a fourth stage in the growth of the town. This reflected the economic and physical growth of the country as a whole. Barry was fortunate in one respect: in spite of occasional air raids, the fabric of the town had survived almost unscathed, and the housing stock was predominantly Victorian and Edwardian. Expansion took place on the periphery for a significant reason: Barry was becoming a dormitory town, mainly for Cardiff, but also for industrial centres in the Vale of Glamorgan, and workers commuted increasingly by road. Within the town the development of chemical industries on Cadoxton Moors and the growth of the seasonal holiday business on Barry Island and the Knap provided some economic support to counteract the decline of the Docks.

A fifth stage may be detected in the late 1970s and early 1980s, but this related not so much to building development but to the construction of an improved road network, a recognition that sea and rail communications were no longer able to sustain a town whose original function—the export of coal—had disappeared. The challenge now was to create fast road links with the growing motorway system of the country as a whole and overcome the risk of isolation.

Housing the residents, 1884-1914

The first stage centred around the problems of quickly providing housing for thousands of migrant labourers and craftsmen who came to work on the construction of the new dock, as well as on the railway which was to forge the links between Barry and the mining valleys. The line of the new railway made a sinuous curve, forming the northern boundary of the dock development area, and freeing all the space to the landward side for housing and commercial development. There were, however, some major constraints, particularly the fragmented ownership of large areas of land; indeed, the major landowners, the Jenner family of Wenvoe, were reluctant to sell parts of the Wenvoe Estate for development; secondly, the topography of the area between Barry Village in the west and Cadoxton in the east was hilly, and there were few level areas in the steep-sided bowl bounded by the ridge to the north; thirdly, the construction of the new railway meant the formation of a deep cutting through rock near Castleland Point and of high embankments to the east and west. As a result, the only means of access to the Dock was *via* tunnels under the railway tracks at Weston Hill, Dock View Road and Island Road.

A temporary timber 'town' was built on Dock Road (renamed 'Broad Street' in 1899) by T. A. Walker to house some of his workers. At the same time land around this area and at Cadoxton was rapidly being acquired for housing development by individual builders or, more usually, by syndicates of local investors, co-ordinated usually by solicitors who dealt with the often

Fig. 77.
Map of Barry, showing phases of development.
R. W. T.

voluminous paperwork and procured finance for the builders. Houses would be constructed to the designs of the architects and surveyors who formed part of the syndicate. Syndicates acquired parcels of land field by field from the landowners, designed road layouts and rudimentary house dispositions, laid the vital roads and sewers to enhance the land value, and then leased blocks of house plots to builders to construct the terraced housing which still characterises the older parts of Barry. Through these syndicates huge numbers of houses were financed and rapidly built between 1884 and the late 1890s. The layout of Barry's streets from the initial developments at High Street and Cadoxton reflected the importance of the east-west link formed by the roadway past Holton Fach and down into Cadoxton. On either side of what became Holton Road, the syndicates bought fields and constructed new roads to connect with those already adjoining their development. Thus the street plan of Barry grew organically outwards from the original pathways and cart tracks, field by field, until some physical or economic boundary was reached. The temporary limits to development formed by field boundaries can still be seen in the road layouts of certain areas of the town, such as the irregularities of Lower Pyke Street and Jewel Street in an otherwise regular pattern of roads, or in the manner that Crossways Street forms a curved boundary to the houses to the South.

The sydicates' street plans were submitted to the Urban District Surveyor to check their compliance with the local adaptation of the Model By-laws issued nationally in 1877 under Section 157 of the 1875 Public Health Act. That Act was introduced to improve the desperate conditions then prevalent in the major industrial cities. Owing to its late start, Barry had none of the cramped, insanitary 'back-to-back' houses or tenement blocks that were accepted as the norm for workers' housing prior to 1875. Instead, thanks to the local by-laws, the roads throughout post-1884 Barry were at least 36 feet wide, and allowed daylight into the houses on either side; each house had to have at least 150 square feet of open area belonging exclusively to that house, usually located at the back and opening on to a back lane, which was used by coal delivery men and the scavengers who collected domestic refuse.

These 'by-law' housing layouts in many towns and cities often resulted in serried rows of terraced houses, bleak and treeless, monotonously rigid in appearance. Fortunately, Barry was built on a naturally hilly site and few streets are either level or straight. As a result the terraced rows snake around corners, drape themselves over contours and thus offer fascinating roofscapes and interesting views.

The houses themselves add considerably to this variety by their size and appearance. Those in Cadoxton and at the eastern end of Barry Road tend to be smaller and less ornamented than the more generous homes built towards the western end of the town for the higher-paid railway workers who settled near High Street to be close to the Railway Company's workshops.

This variety of house-type demonstrated the flexibility of the syndicate system in responding to the varying demands of different income levels and aspirations and also the ability of the terraced house to provide a wide range of accommodation in superficially similar buildings. The Barry Estate Company, for example, was a High Street syndicate which included the well-known Cardiff shipowner John Cory amongst its directors and the local solicitor J. A. Hughes as its secretary;[1] it leased plots on its estate for a variety of house types. Towards the eastern end of High Street, in Queen Street and in Princess Street the houses are simple, undecorated, stone-faced, terrace cottages, whilst in York Place and Windsor Road there are spacious three- and four-storey houses for the better-off. The larger volume of space was used to provide additional rooms of similar size rather than fewer, larger rooms. In this way, because of the housing shortage, rooms could be sub-let to mitigate the rental burden. Wealthier families, on the other hand, would use the additional rooms for one or two domestic servants living in. The size and character of the houses would be clearly defined by the ground rent, by the covenants contained in the lease and by the architects' plans. Different qualities of houses would be segregated, since people of different social classes preferred to live out of sight of each other; there were thus clear visual distinctions between streets of houses of different values.

Several house plans are shown to illustrate the range of accomodation that was available in Barry. That in turn was fairly typical of the new housing available throughout the country, following the introduction of the Model By-laws in 1877. Plan 1 shows a double-fronted, four-room house, with a 22-foot frontage and about 620 square feet of floor area. It was designed by

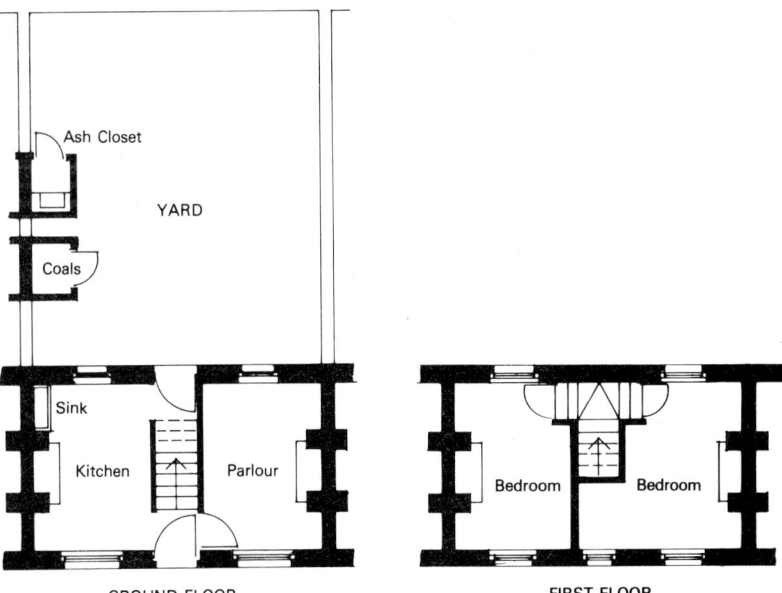

Fig. 78.
Plan of No. 129 Harvey Street, Cadoxton, 1891 (Plan 1).
R. W. T.

the Cardiff office of architects Bruton and Williams, to be built for Mr. L. Walters in Harvey Street, Cadoxton, in 1891. This four-room house was unusual owing to its broad street-frontage; moreover, it lacked the rear annexe that characterised most by-law terraced housing, suggesting that the house was designed for owner-occupation rather than as an investment. Each room had a grate and chimney for open, coal fires. The by-law requirements were observed, which gave a minimum headroom of eight feet and a window area equal to at least 20% of the floor area of the room, half of which had to be openable. All this ensured reasonably comfortable and healthy living conditions for the occupants. The most noticeable shortcoming to modern eyes was the absence of any internal toilet provision. There was an outhouse containing an ash closet, located in the rear yard, from which waste could be collected by scavengers. Waste water from the sink ran to an underground drain and was taken to a sewer running through the rear yards of adjoining terraced houses.

Plan 2 shows a larger house, also in Harvey Street, designed in 1891 for Miss Sarah Lewis by the Barry office of Bruton and Williams. This house had a 17-foot frontage and the addition of a two-storey, rear annexe provided a floor area of 960 square feet and sufficient rooms for a family of five or six. Once again there was no provision for a water closet, but there was a much-improved scullery, complete with washing copper, together with a larder and a linen cupboard on the first-floor landing.

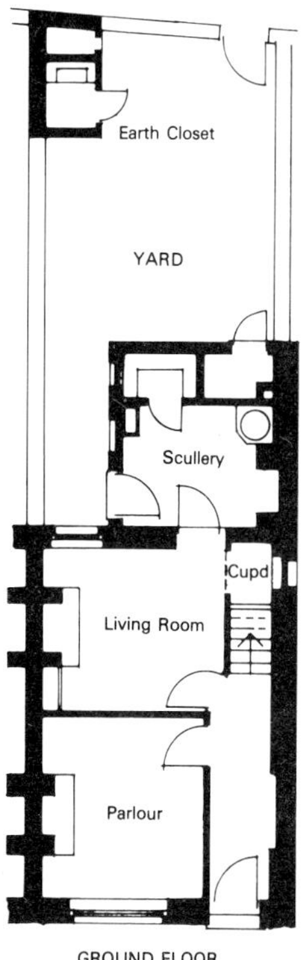

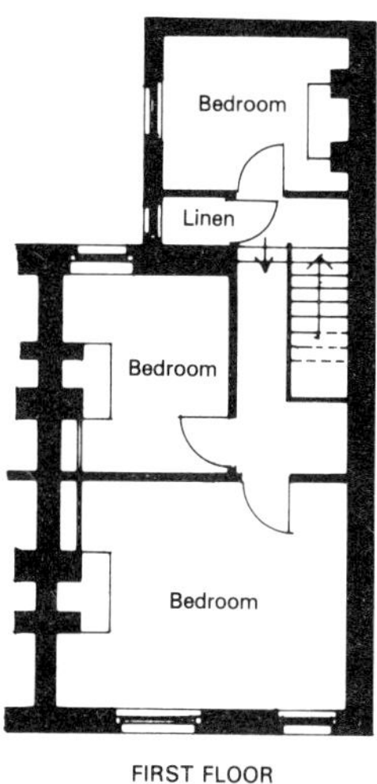

Fig. 79.
Plan of house in Harvey Street, Cadoxton, for Miss Sarah Lewis. 1891 (Plan 2).
R. W. T.

Plan 3 shows a much larger and more expensive house, one of a terrace built in 1899 in Windsor Road, opposite the Barry Hotel. This was on land leased by the Barry Estate syndicate, which sought to maximise the return on its ground rents by close control over the quality of the properties constructed. Thus, this house, which was built two years before the preceding examples, had two water closets, one externally at ground-floor level and another at the end of an extended rear annexe. It also had a bathroom next to the toilet, five bedrooms and a boxroom. The area of the house was 1,650 square feet, almost double the area of the previous example; with its separate scullery, breakfast room, dining room and parlour, it suggests a totally different lifestyle on the part of its occupants from that experienced by those living in Harvey Street. Resident domestic servants would be commonly employed by the middle-class occupants of houses such as these, so that there was abundant labour to light, replenish and clear up the seven coal fires in living rooms and bedrooms, to attend to the gas mantles and to maintain the house in general. Few three-story houses were built at this time, partly because of the restricted financial opportunities open to builders, but partly also because of structural limitations imposed by the load-bearing capacity of the economical brick wall,

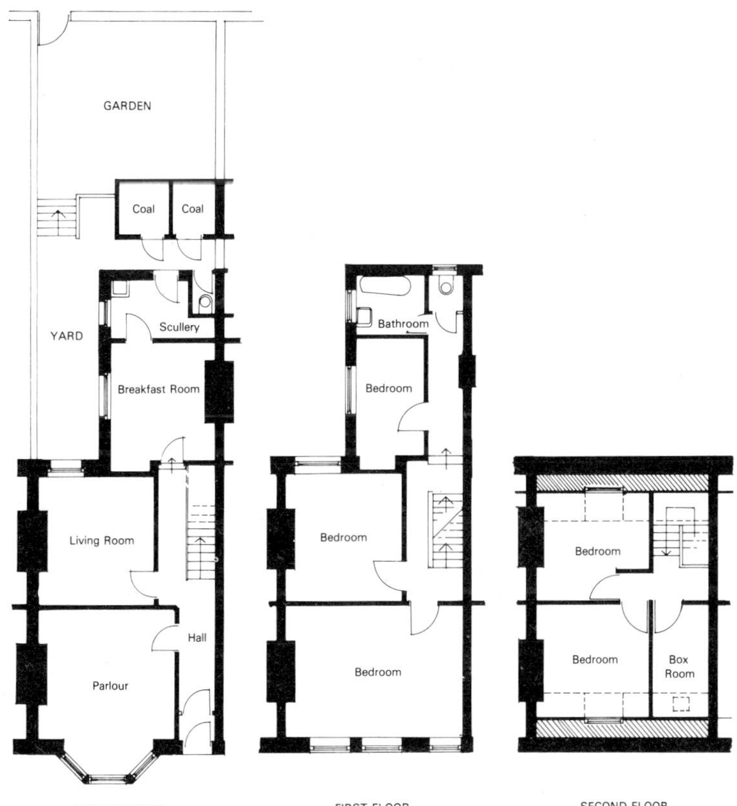

Fig. 80.
Plan of No. 4 Windsor Road, Barry, built by W. B. Shepherd, 1889 (Plan 3).
R. W. T.

which was nine inches thick. In consequence; most of the three-storey houses in Barry involved the formation of attic rooms within their roof construction. This created a profusion of decorative dormers and gables, which add great character to the roofscape of the town.

Housing community services and cultural activities, 1884-1914

The juveniie population of Barry soon outgrew the school provided by Walker in Queen Street, and the present High Street School had to be opened in 1888. Prior to this the only other school in the area was the Board School at Cadoxton, opened in 1879 for 57 pupils, following the Elementary Education Act of 1870. An extension was started in 1885 and opened in 1887 for 241 pupils, but even this proved inadequate, and a further extension was opened in 1891 to house, in total, 240 boys and 240 girls, the old part being converted to hold 203 infants.

By this time the child population was growing enormously and a new Board school was built in Holton Road to serve the community in this area. Designed by architects of standing, Seward and Thomas,[2] the brick- and terracotta-faced building opened in 1892 and is typical of the then-current approach to school design. Large, high windows let in maximum daylight whilst the lofty, well-ventilated classrooms were arranged in two floors symmetrically around a central hall, allowing similar but segregated facilities for both girls and boys. The elevations followed the 'Queen Anne' style adopted by E. R. Robson, first architect of the London School Board

Plate LXIII. Cadoxton School, opened in 1879, extended in 1887 and 1891.
B. Daly.

ıte LXIV.
ılton Road School,
rry, opened in
92.
W. T.

and author of the influential *School Architecture*, published in 1874. This style allowed greater freedom in planning than the semi-ecclesiastical Gothic style which characterised earlier schools and which was exemplified in the design of the original Cadoxton School.

The growth in the population and physical size of Barry is clear from the succession of schools that were built to serve the new generations of children. Romilly School was opened in 1894 to ease the pressure on High Street School, and was extended in 1898 and 1906. The older children were accommodated in a new Intermediate School at the junction of Buttrills Hill and Barry Road, designed by W. H. Dashwood Caple and opened in 1896. Construction also started at the opposite end of Barry in 1899 to the designs of Jones, Richards and Budgen, on a site abutting Hannah Street and Barry Road. There was initial opposition to this site and the *Barry Dock News* carried an article on 14 January 1898 criticising the choice of the site as being '. . . far removed from the town and in a direction where there is not the remotest likelihood of an extension of the town . . . alongside a proposed destructor, at the rear of the slaughter house and close by a public urinal'. Further east, Palmerston School opened in 1899, the same year that Barry Island School was built. Designed by G. A. Birkenhead, the latter was completed in five months and included a novel form of combined heating and ventilation in which a 5hp gas engine forced air through a matting screen saturated with water to filter out the vast amounts of dust emanating from the nearby coal hoists on the south side of the Docks. The cleaned air was then heated and forced through ducts feeding inlets in each room and allowed to escape through low-level outlets to the open air. The mechanism for this relatively advanced system was supplied by Musgrove & Co. of Belfast and it enabled the children to study in a clean atmosphere free from clouds of coal dust emanating from the nearby dock.[3]

School building continued until the start of the first World War. Gladstone Road Schools opened in 1906. The growing numbers of older children were accommodated by the building of a separate Girls' County School in 1913. A Training College for elementary school teachers was built nearby in 1914. Both the latter establishments occupied commanding positions on Buttrills Hill.

Commerce and trade concentrated initially in three areas: High Street and Broad Street in the west, Main Street and Vere Street in Cadoxton and an extended strip along Holton Road. By 1890 speculative blocks of shops with dwellings on two upper floors were being built along Holton Road, which was rapidly becoming the focus of the new town. The names of these early speculators can still be seen on the plaques high above the western end of Holton Road; 'Lewis Place', 'Sydenham Buildings', 'Herberts' Buildings', 'Thomas's Buildings' and the more modestly named 'Central' and 'Holton' Buildings. These commercial developments were unremarkable in their construction and character, with the exception of Nos. 69-72 High Street, designed in an Italianate *palazzo* manner by W. E. Knapman; they formed the junction with Market Street, so named after the Market, designed in 1890 by Haberson & Fawckner[4] but later converted into the Romilly Cinema.

Plate LXV. Architectural detail from Nos. 69-72 High Street, Barry, *c.* 1889 *B. Daly.*

The most important building in Barry, both for its commerce within and appearance without was the General Offices of the Barry Railway Company. Built on a plateau close to Castleland Point and overlooking the Docks, the building was an imposing landmark, unequalled by any subsequent building in Barry. It was designed in 1897 by Arthur E. Bell and is a formally competent design, using the then-current neo-Baroque style

ıte LXVI.
:neral Offices of
ırry Railway
ɔmpany, with statue
David Davies in
ɔnt.
W.T.

g. 81.
an: Barry Railway
ɔmpany New
ffices, as first
oposed, without
wer.
thur E. Bell.

that adorned town halls and civic offices all over Britain. As originally designed, it lacked the central clock-tower but this was added during construction and it thus falls into line with other neo-Baroque buildings using the tower as, perhaps, a symbolic substitution of merchant power in place of the spires of declining church authority. The plan is a simple rectangle. Typical of the lingering Victorian preoccupation with fresh air and health, the marble and brass-equipped toilets and washrooms are located in a virtually free-standing, well-ventilated block at the rear, bereft of any of the decorative features that adorn the main bulk of the building.

Plate LXVII. Holton Road, lookir towards King Squar with Council Offices and Public Library. *B. Daly.*

The linear flow of Holton Road underwent a diversion at its junction with Tynewydd Road, adjacent to what was Maes-y-cwm Quarry. This important central site was vacant when it was decided to erect a Town Hall and library, to be the subject of an architectural competition held in 1903. The successful architects, C. E. Hutchinson and E. Harding Payne of London, designed a façade that provided an imposing backdrop to the open square formed in front of it. This square is slightly elevated and south-facing and affords an excellent view to the south-west along Holton Road, whilst punctuating the otherwise monotonous run of three-storey buildings fronting on to Holton Road. The building was constructed in two parts; first the Library, built with the aid of the Carnegie Fund and, secondly, the first

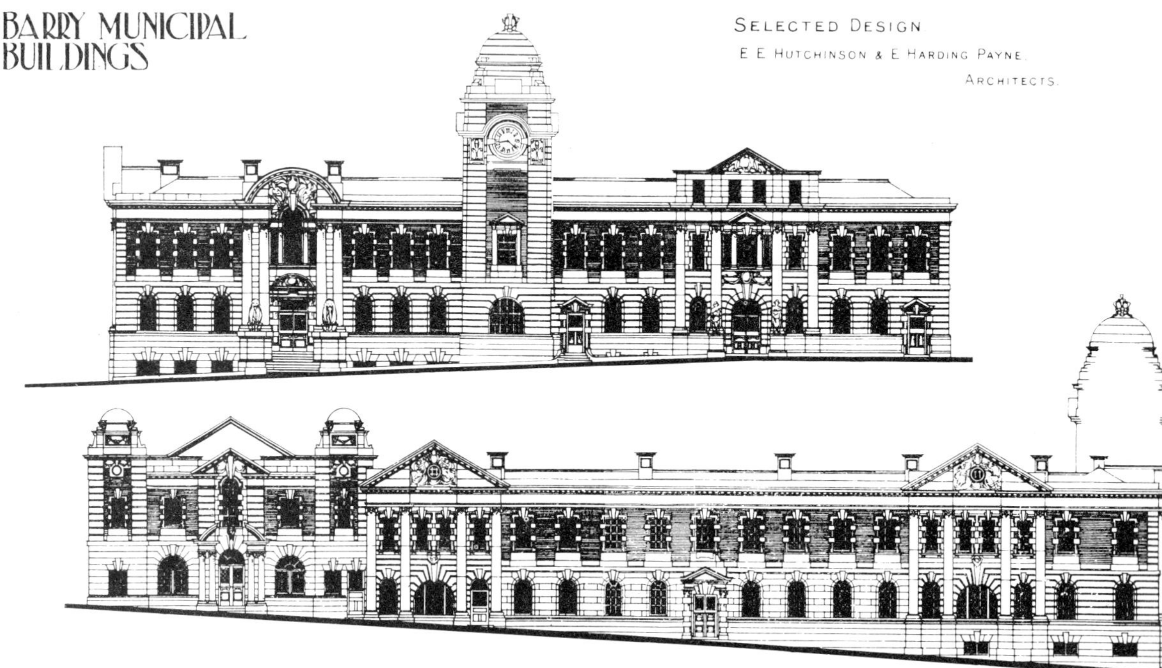

Fig. 82. Elevations of Barry Municipal Buildings

DAN EVANS

phase of the Town Hall, linked to the Library by a centrally-located clock tower. The design was again neo-Baroque, with stone-faced ground-floor rustication, window mouldings and cornices and red brick infill. The main elevation was dominated by the clock tower, but the wings on either side were not symmetrical in every detail. The plain, pilastered entrance to the Library, lacked the lightness and inventiveness of the semi-circular headed aedicule or portico forming the entrance to the Town Hall. The later phase of the Town Hall was never built and the rear elevation remains an unfinished eyesore. The remainder of the quarry was formed into Central Park, a small intimate open space that has never reached its full potential as a public meeting-place, despite its ideal location.

The growing town required a full range of services for its citizens and Barry, starting with a clean slate, could take advantage of all the latest innovations when building new facilities on green-field sites. The abbatoir in Court Road was opened in 1897; it was designed to handle an annual throughput of 18,500 animals per year, sufficient for a population of 37,000. Nearby, a refuse destructor with two furnaces capable of handling 30 tons of refuse per day was completed in 1901 and in addition provided electric power to the nearby Hannah Street School.[5]

These buildings were all designed in the Borough Surveyor's Office under the direction of the Borough Surveyor, J. C. Pardoe, A.M.I.C.E. He was also responsible for the design of the many small hospitals with which Barry was quickly provided to cope with the demands arising from the hazards of the intensive dock operations and of the contagious diseases brought to the town by visiting seamen. The earliest efforts to cope with infectious diseases involved the construction of a cholera, plague and yellow-fever hospital on the island of Flat Holm, the costs of construction and operation being shared with the nearby seaport of Cardiff. The need for an isolation hospital to deal with the more common infectious diseases was met by the provision of an 18-bed hospital at the Colcot, followed later by a smallpox hospital near Weycock Cross, well to the north of the town. The first public hospital in Barry was the Nursing Home in Woodlands Road, built to commemorate Queen Victoria's Diamond Jubilee, designed by George Thomas, and extended in 1904 to commemorate the coronation of Edward VII.

The more general medical needs of the inhabitants were met either by a voluntary hospital in Kingsland Crescent or by recourse to Cardiff Royal Infirmary, until the construction of the General Accident and Surgical Hospital in 1907. Designed by J. C. Pardoe and built with smooth, red brick and stone dressing, this hospital was an unremarkable architectural work, but was ideally situated in Wyndham Street; the wards were provided with south-facing verandahs overlooking the newly-formed Central Park.

The spiritual needs of the inhabitants of Barry were fulfilled by a large number of newly-constructed churches and chapels. Some were hasty, temporary constructions of wood and corrugated iron, such as the Bethel English Baptist Church built in 1893 on the corner of Harbour Road and Park Road and later replaced by permanent stone chapels. Others, such as the Priory of St. John, built in Broad Street, remained in use for many years before being converted to a billiard hall and, later, a restaurant. This prefabricated chapel was typical of hundreds erected at this time. A virtually original chapel of the same kind is now the Moose Hall, still standing at the junction of Court Road and Wyndham Street, whilst a simpler version was built at the junction of Romilly Road and Park Crescent, now used as a Girl Guides centre.

During the 19th century the Welsh nonconformist chapel had become an essential part of the cultural and social life of the Welsh valleys as well as being a religious focus. Barry, having been built at the end of the 19th century, has no truly 'classical' Welsh chapels, since that style had fallen into disfavour by the mid 1870s.[6] Two large chapels which still remain unchanged followed the traditional plan, but differed in elevational treatment. The Welsh Congregational Chapel in Holton Road, designed in 1893 by Seward and Thomas, had a stuccoed façade with pilasters and surface ornamentation, and plain elevations to the sides and rear.

The English Baptist Chapel in Holton Road, completed in 1898, used the traditional plan, which gave an impressive, spacious, two-storey interior. The balcony continued around all four sides of the chapel and the space was dominated by an impressive organ, whose pipes almost covered the south wall. The chapel was designed by John Morgan of Blaenavon and the rather coarse façade of blue Pontypridd Pennant stone and Bathstone dressings was described at the time as 'Italian Rennaissance'. The remainder of the building, holding nine class-rooms and a large basement hall, is devoid of any overt architectural style. Although lacking the generous proportions of this chapel, the Welsh chapel in Beryl Road, completed in 1892, had a higher standard of finish and an elegantly moulded and decorated ceiling dominating an intimately-scaled interior.

The use of the traditional cubical form of the Welsh chapel had declined in most areas by the 1880s and was replaced by a much freer adoption of the symbolic plans and eclectic elevations used in Anglican and Catholic churches.

This development away from the regular plan towards a freer use of Anglican cruciform floor-plans and 'Gothic' elevational treatment is well shown in Barry by two examples that illustrate first, the inventive integration of a 'chapel' balcony and cruciform plan and, secondly, the predominance of social facilities in the form of schoolrooms, halls, *etc.* over the space allocated for worship.

The New English Presbyterian Church, now known as Holy Trinity Presbyterian Church, was built at the junction of High Street and Trinity Street in 1894. Designed by T. G. Williams of Liverpool, it featured a typically Anglican cruciform plan at the level of the traditionally nonconformist balcony. The two transepts were merged into a widened 'nave' at ground-floor level, with rostrum and organ situated in the vestigial chancel, and the congregation seated in a semi-circular array of pews focussed on the rostrum. This inventive plan was complemented by a highly articulated Gothic exterior with a tower, pinnacle, gables and prominent windows. The already small site is further congested by the schoolroom at the rear of the church.

The provision of additional facilities is most evident at Windsor Road Congregational Church. This church, designed by W. Knapman in 1904, is an example of maximum use obtained from a difficult site. Bounded by steeply-rising Windsor and Porthkerry Roads, a plateau was excavated, on

Plate LXVIII. English Baptist Church, Holton Road, Barry Dock, completed in 1898. *B. Daly.*

which a substantial church was erected. This was then surrounded by two large school-rooms, many smaller rooms, kitchens, toilets and a large hall complete with stage. The church itself is devoid of any references to the style of the traditional Welsh chapel, and apart from the lack of a chancel would be indistinguishable from an Anglican church of the period.

An unusual and inventive exception to the tendency away from traditional forms of chapels is Dinam Hall, built in 1903 at the junction of Merthyr Street and Belvedere Crescent, for the Presbyterian Forward Movement. This inventive solution was designed by George Thomas, F.S.I., formerly a partner in the Cardiff practice of Seward & Thomas, architects for Cardiff's Central Library and the Coal Exchange. The awkward, steeply-sloping, triangular site resulted in the adoption of an unusual plan for the traditional balconied chapel, entered via a grand staircase beneath a crenellated, circular tower. The chapel itself was in the form of a triangle with seats at balcony level at the 'base' and 'apex' of the triangle, linked by a narrow access balcony on each side. The columns penetrated upwards through the large, semi-basement hall, through the chapel above, supporting the balcony, and continued upwards to support a rectangular clerestory with a stained-glass window running the full length of each side.

The last Anglican church to be built in Barry was All Saints' in Park Road. Constructed in two stages in 1908 and 1915, it was designed by E. M. Bruce Vaughan of Cardiff in the sparse, simple style favoured by Pugin and the Ecclesiological Society.[7] The latter, in numerous pamphlets published after 1841, advocated emphasising the importance of the altar by various means:

late LXIX. ▲
xterior of Dinam
all, Merthyr Street,
arry Dock, built in
903.
. *Daly.*

late LXX. ►
nterior of Dinam
all.
. *Daly.*

the differentiation of nave and chancel by a chancel arch, the graduation of ornament internally and the use of different roof heights externally. The attached porch and vestry with separate roof are elements which, together with the tower, formed strong, asymmetric façades. The use of simple, rough stonework externally, plain undecorated interiors and open timber roof shows All Saints' to be a church which, possibly for reasons of economy, reverted back to a style of the 1840s. The need for economy in design probably resulted in the omission of the spire, shown as a continuation of the tower on Bruce Vaughan's original drawings, which would, if constructed, have further enhanced All Saints' as an outstanding landmark in the surrounding town.

Plate LXXI.
All Saints' Church, Park Road, Barry; nave, 1908; chancel and tower, 1915.
B. Daly.

Fig. 83.
Original design for All Saints' Church by E. M. Bruce Vaughan, including tower with spire.

Building between the Wars

The coming of the First World War checked the meteoric rise of Barry's coal trade and, following the peak year of 1913, trade through the Docks fell steadily as steam coal was replaced by oil as the major energy source in ships and factories. As a consequence of this decline, the development of the town came to a virtual standstill during and immediately after the War; there was no commercial development of significance and little housebuilding activity.

The period between the two Wars was one of great social change throughout the country and this was reflected in the actual houses built during the period and the manner in which they were created. Barry, with so little building activity during this period, offers clear examples of three distinct types of housing development, the Garden Suburb, the Council development at Buttrills, Central Estate and Witchill and suburban ribbon-development, such as Colcot Road, by private enterprise.

The first example, the Garden Suburb, came into being as a consequence of the formation of the Welsh Town Planning and Housing Trust Ltd. in 1914 to purchase land in bulk and to provide the initial roads and drainage.[8]

The Barry Garden Suburb Ltd. was registered as a Public Utilities Company and thus under the 1909 Housing and Town Planning Act was permitted considerable latitude in the observance of current building by-laws. The architect for the scheme was T. Alwyn Lloyd, who had worked with Raymond Unwin on the design of Hampstead Garden Suburb. Unwin and Parker had been pioneers in the realisation of Ebenezer Howard's dream of a 'garden city' which would combine 'all the advantages of the most energetic and active town life with all the beauty and delight of the country'.[9] The garden cities that were built at Letchworth (1905) and Welwyn (1920) were true attempts at creating a city that would provide an opportunity 'to secure healthier surroundings and more regular employment . . . in short, to raise the standard of health and comfort of all true workers of whatever grade'.[10]

The Garden Suburb at Hampstead was, however, an adaptation of the garden city objective of providing good, cheap, healthy accommodation for working people by purchasing land in bulk and renting it to members of the society set up to manage the scheme. Alwyn Lloyd worked closely with Unwin on the designs for Hampstead Garden Suburb, and when the Barry Garden Suburb Ltd. was formed, Unwin became the consultant architect. Through this close link with one of the foremost exponents of the utopian philosophy, the Barry Garden Suburb possessed many features that were fundamental concepts in the design of Hampstead Garden Suburb:

1 Persons of all classes and standards should be accommodated.
2 Cottages and houses should be limited to eight to an acre.
3 Roads should be 40 feet wide and houses 50 feet apart, gardens occupying the spaces between.
4 Plot divisions should not be walls, but hedges, wire fences or trellis.
5 Every road should be lined with trees, making a colour scheme with the hedges.
6 Woods and gardens should be free to all tenants.
7 Houses should be so planned that none should spoil each other's outlook or beauty.

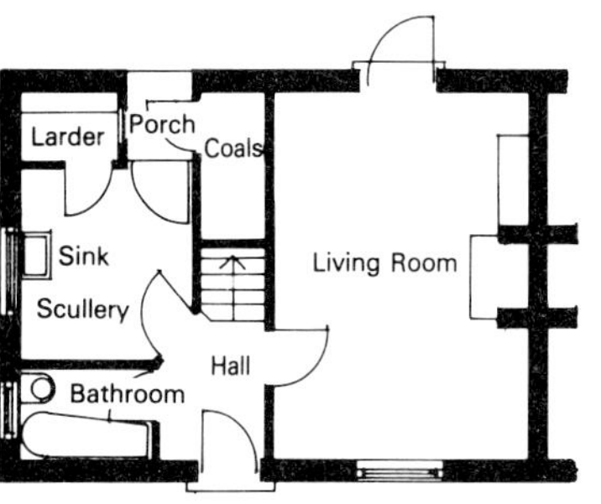

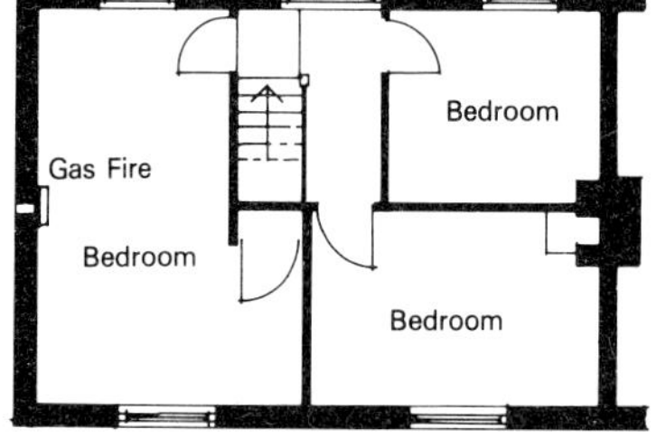

Fig. 84.
Barry Garden Suburb plan of House Type 1A for 5 persons, designed by T. Alwyn Lloyd.
R. W. T.

The striking difference between the Suburb and the previous by-law housing in Barry resulted from the ability of the architect to depart from the constraints of the building by-laws which in themselves had transformed the style of housing in the large industrial towns and cities since 1877. The styles of houses are shown in the illustrations, and mark the changing appearance of the houses throughout the development of the Suburb from 1914 until its completion in the late 1930s. The houses themselves were relatively small, varying between 800 and 950 square feet and were of both parlour and non-parlour type. They were well provided with a relatively spacious scullery and convenient access to a cool larder and coal store. The bathrooms were placed downstairs to minimise plumbing costs and to allow maximum space on the first floor for the three bedrooms. Although the aim was to provide housing for all classes of people, the manner in which this actually came about was not quite as planned. The first development of 52 houses was let by 1917, but the second block of 52 was sold, owing to competition from the low rents then being offered by the Council. As a result of the surplus of cheap accommodation, the Barry Garden Suburb Ltd. entered into an agreement in 1923 with the Great Western Railway Company to erect 108 houses for its employees. By the time these were completed, the Depression was making it difficult for the directors to be sure of enough tenants for any further rented property and so the remainder of the Suburb was built for sale.

The influence of Parker and Unwin reached far beyond the small numbers of garden villages designed by them. During the first World War, the govenment was acutely aware of the problems they would face upon the return of thousands of young soldiers, eager to set foot in the better world promised by the politicians after the 'war to end all wars'. The reality that faced them was different. As a result of the Land Values Duties Act of 1910, housebuilding had declined nationally until, by the outbreak of war in 1914, new construction barely kept up with the demolition of old slums. During the War the 1915 Rent and Mortgage Act froze rents and mortgages at 1915 levels, driving investors away from the private housing market and resulting in a desperate housing shortage, so that many old and decaying properties became the only homes available to those with lower incomes and dependent on rented accommodation.

In 1919 the Garden Cities and Town Planning Association presented a memorandum to Dr. Christopher Addison, President of the Local Government Board, stressing the futility of building around large towns, where land was expensive, and extolling the virtues of the garden city ideals. The 1919 Housing and Town Planning Act and the Housing (Additional Powers) Act were intended to stimulate the provision of housing, in the first instance by making it mandatory for local authorities to survey the need for housing in their area and to carry out plans to provide it and, secondly, by providing a subsidy of £150 for the builder of any house for sale or rent.

To ensure that houses of good standard were built, the government issued a *Housing Manual*, giving advice and instructions to local authorities as to the terms on which government grants would be available. This *Manual* adopted all the broad principles of an earlier document, a Report published in 1918 from a committee chaired by Sir John Tudor Walters, set up to consider questions of the building of dwellings for the working classes.[11] The committee included Raymond Unwin, and, not surprisingly, the Report recommendations were strongly influenced by the ideals of the Garden City Movement. The adoption of twelve houses to the acre (eight in rural areas), meant that large gardens would allow the houses to receive plenty of light and air and offer a pleasant environment in which families could live and grow.

To overcome the monotony of by-law streets, roads should be gently curved, with houses set back with at least 70 feet between opposing elevations, along a varied building line, retaining existing hedges and trees wherever possible. Short *culs-de-sac* and drives with quite narrow carriageways would help both to reduce road costs and to offset the higher land cost brought about by the reduced density of development. The areas of these houses should be 885 square feet for three-bedroomed, non-parlour types and 1,055 square feet for parlour types.

The influence of this Report and the *Housing Manual* which brought its recommendations into force can be seen in Barry in four local authority housing estates constructed in the 1920s and 1930s: the Central, Buttrills, Witchill and Colcot Estates. The foremost example of the garden city ideals is Central Estate where a geometric road layout is centred around the large open space of Alexandra Park, with radiating roads linking into the existing road pattern around it. A variety of house-designs were incorporated, including some two-storey blocks, each containing four flats. The use of white rendering on the houses resulted in a visual effect similar to that achieved in the Barry Garden Suburb but, perhaps due to the absence of equally caring owner-occupiers, the Central Estate never matured into the leafy suburb intended by its designer, R. R. Hinchsliff, Borough Architect and Surveyor, as had been achieved in the Garden Suburb.

The use of geometric road plans continued in the Buttrills and Witchill Estates, subject to the constraints of adjoining property, as the town expanded its boundaries outwards from the pre-war core of by-law streets. A radical departure from this was the creation of the Colcot Estate on flat land to the north of the town. The surroundings offered freedom of arrangement but the road layout was comparatively regular; only the symmetrically-bifurcated central road made any concession to the need to reduce the monotony of straight streets.

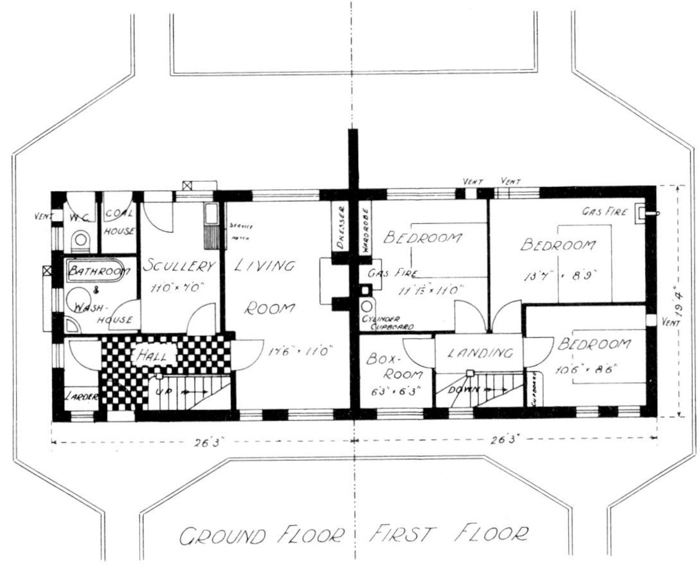

g. 85.
entral Housing
tate, Barry: plan of
n-parlour, three-
droomed house,
30-35.
R. Hinchsliff.

Whilst private investors had largely lost interest in building property for rent, after the first World War private housebuilding continued at a reduced level, catering for the growing numbers of professional and middle-class people drawn to work in the slowly-maturing business community of the town. Two factors were of major importance in the design of houses during this period. First, there was the reduced size of families, since the average number of children per family had fallen from 3·5 in 1901 to 2·2 in 1931; the average professional and middle-class families were significantly smaller than those of the manual worker. This reduction, together with an increase in the total number of households due to earlier marriages and greater life-expectancy, led to a growing demand for smaller houses.

The second factor was the scarcity of domestic servants following the War. At the height of Victorian prosperity even modest households often employed domestic staff who lived on the premises; houses were designed to accommodate them in small attic bedrooms and in extensive scullery and kitchen areas. The newly affluent, with their smaller families, did not require help in managing the household. There was a growing use of gas fires in place of dusty coal fires and improvements in kitchen equipment such as cookers and refrigerators, made possible by the introduction of electricity to Barry in 1928 by the South Wales Electrical Distribution Company. As a result, houses built for sale to the aspiring middle class during the 1920s and 1930s were generally compact, with two or three bedrooms and an efficient kitchen, placing the emphasis generally on lightness, cleanliness and convenience.

Barry did not generate as great a demand for these new houses as did larger towns and cities such as nearby Cardiff, so no large suburbs developed but, instead, some of these newer houses sprang up alongside the main roads leading out of the town, Pontypridd Road, Colcot Road, Port Road, Barry Road and Pencoedtre Road. They showed considerable variation from the norm, owing to the extended period over which they were built. The immediately post-war houses were mainly substantial red-brick villas, such as the southern end of Colcot Road or smaller, terraced houses, as on Barry Road or Jenner Road. As the ribbon of housing grew along the roads, bungalows gained preference and can still be seen on all the main roads, especially Pontypridd Road.

In 1935, following the 1932 Town Planning Act, a plan for the development of the town was produced by the U.D.C. Engineer E. R. Hinchsliffe showing the uses proposed for land within the town boundary. No great change was foreseen, only the continued slow growth of the town, but the most striking feature of the plan was a grid of major roads traversing the town in east-west and north-south directions. These are still reflected in the present-day road network, with the exception of a missing link from the bend in Colcot Road adjacent to the Sports Centre, eastwards past Merthyr Dyfan and across to Pencoedtre Lane via Treharne Road.

Whilst there are no outstanding examples of architectural merit in the houses constructed in Barry during this period, there is one group of houses that illustrate the development of popular taste in house styles to be found throughout suburban Britain. The row of houses built on the east side of Romilly Park Road between its junction with The Grove and the crossroads with St. Nicholas Road and Park Avenue was built during the inter-war period. Starting at No. 1, nearest to the Grove, they are typical of the Edwardian gentleman's villa, built of bricks, some with rendered walls, bay windows and large gables. As one travels towards the railway line, the style is simplified into more angular forms, and is transformed into full-blown 'stockbrokers' Tudor', to use Osbert Lancaster's satirical epithet. These house sport all the popular 'vernacular' details such as leaded windows, dormer windows in the hipped and gabled tiled roof, and white-rendered walls articulated by pseudo half-timbering. As one nears the crossroads, the effects of the *avant-garde* Modern Movement in architecture become apparent. The strictly functional view of a house as 'a machine for living in' propounded by Le Corbusier in his architecturally influential *Vers Une Architecture*, published in 1923, had little influence on the internal planning of most houses. But the visual effects of Le Corbusier's use of concrete for walls, floors and flat roofs, and his large windows, made possible by the use of this material, were copied by developers and builders to add impact to otherwise ordinary houses. The last three houses in Romilly Park Road show the use of curved, rendered brickwork, windows bridging the corners and, in the case of 'Beach Park', balcony railings to echo the image of ocean liners, used by Le Corbusier as an example of functional design.

Modernist influences can also be seen in its furthest extremes in Barry. First, as a decorative feature to distinguish otherwise unremarkable semi-detached houses built on a small estate at Cwm Barry, the curved, metal-framed windows are used to join the stepped part of the front elevation to the main part of the house.

The second example was a genuine attempt to relate the functional aspects of the building to its form. Sully Hospital was built to accommodate patients suffering from tuberculosis and other bronchial disorders, for which sunshine and fresh air were recognised as major components in the curative treatment. The plan was laid out to afford sea views and sunshine in each ward, which themselves varied in size, unlike the regular 'Nightingale' wards of more traditional hospitals which were still being built, as at nearby Llandough Hospital.

Plate LXXII. Sully Hospital, designed by A. R. Pite in reinforced concrete, 1934. *R.W.T.*

In complete contrast to the relative modernity of this hospital, the design for the Memorial Hall in Gladstone Road by Major E. R. Hinchsliffe was carried out in a stark, stripped, classical style, reminiscent of Sir Edwin Lutyen's memorials erected in the war cemeteries of northern France and Belgium. The building was completed in 1932 with the help of funds raised by public appeal, despite some opposition from those who, in the words of Dudley Howe, '. . . did not want a hall in which to dance on the graves of dead soldiers'. The hall was built by Vickery Bros. using a patent reconstructed 'Portland stone facing' and brickwork for the bulk of the upper walls. It seated 932 persons and was constructed with an orchestra pit and organ chamber, for a cost of £23,000. The subsequent economical and simple design results in a building that still is, in the words of the *Barry Dock News*, '. . . in its noble spaciousness, its purity of line and lack of ostentation . . . worthy of those in whose honour it was raised'.

There were later additions: the Annexe, designed by Alex Gordon and Partners in 1966,[12] and the changing rooms on the north side, designed by the Borough Engineer's Department, are remarkable only for the uncompromising manner in which their stark elevations ignore both the scale and proportions of the main Hall.

Plate LXXIII. Barry War Memorial Hall as originally buil[t] in 1932, with cenotaph on right. *R. W. T. Coll.*

Developments since 1945

The port of Barry played an important role in the Second World War. Both docks and town attracted aerial attacks, but they escaped with very little damage, and no large-scale reconstruction was required as in other South Wales ports such as Swansea. The most significant building development following the end of the war was in the area to the east of the Docks, known as Biglis Moors, for the manufacture of chemicals. This industry grew steadily until by the 1980s two plant operators, British Petroleum Ltd. and the Dow Chemicals Company Ltd., had become the largest employers in the area. The growth in these industries was, however, counterbalanced by a decline in the trade through the Docks; coal exports had virtually ceased by the 1960s, their place being only partly taken by imports of gas, oil and West Indian bananas.

One consequence of the lack of job opportunities was a steady emigration, but this was balanced by a natural local increase in population until the late 1970s, when the release of more land for housing led to an immigration of Cardiff commuters unable to find suitable housing in Cardiff and the eastern Vale of Glamorgan. Population figures for Barry are given below:

Table 16. Population figures for Barry, 1921-81.

Year	*Population*	*Source*
1921	39,000	National Census
1961	42,100	,, ,, ,,
1971	41,600	,, ,, ,,
1976	42,400	County Council Estimate
1977	44,100	,, ,, ,,
1981	44,826	National Census

With few significant changes in the number or fortunes of its population, Barry underwent no major change in its appearance; development was concentrated mainly on housing and ancillary educational, social and welfare facilities, designed to cope first with a post-war 'bulge' in the birth-rate, and then with a population which grew but slowly.

National Housing priorities immediately after the War were to replace those dwellings destroyed during the conflict with new houses that were '. . . suitable for younger families, who by reason of war conditions, had been unable to obtain a separate home of their own; the needs of these families with their varying numbers would, it was thought, be most appropriately met by the parallel provision of two-bedroom, temporary houses and three-bedroom, permanent houses'.[13]

The 1949 *Housing Manual* increased the typical superficial area of a three-bedroomed house to 900-950 square feet, as opposed to the 800-900 square feet recommended in 1944 (similar to the areas laid down in the 1919 Manual). These improved standards were curtailed in 1951 as the incoming government realised that the national demand for houses was not being met by the resources available, and it introduced pressures for continued economy which have been maintained by central government to the present time; in consequence, local-authority housing has frequently failed to create high environmental standards. The major areas of local-authority building in the early years after the War were in the infill site north of Gladstone Road, between Buttrills Road and Tynewydd Road; to the north-west of the old village of Cadoxton, centred around Treharne Road; on the south side of Weston Hill; and to the east of the earlier development at Colcot. These areas are uniformly depressing in appearance because the higher densities demanded by economy resulted in small gardens, terraced blocks of houses and blocks of flats. There was little of the 'garden city' feeling that pervaded the best of the local-authority housing built in Barry between the Wars.

The importance of tourism to Barry as a whole rather than just to Barry Island was acknowledged by the commissioning of Geoffrey Jellicoe to prepare a landscape design for the foreshore of Barry. The report was presented in 1956 and showed considerable redevelopment of the fairground and Nell's Point, linked by a narrow-gauge railway to Porthkerry, *via* a wall forming a boating lake in the old harbour and a tunnel blasted through the projecting Bull Cliff overlooking Pebble Beach. A large model was produced and displayed on Barry Island for many years, whilst the Report and its recommendations passed into obscurity.

There was comparatively little private housebuilding in Barry between 1945 and 1960 owing to lack of suitable land and its high cost when available. In 1961 the Parker Morris Report recommended detailed, new and improved standards for all houses, in keeping with the rising tide of national prosperity.[14] The recommendations of the report became mandatory for local authorities in 1969; there were improved space standards, generous provision for power points, adequate storage areas and room layouts designed for their function rather than their tradition. Differences between local-authority houses and those provided by the private sector became less obvious. The adoption of the Report's general principles by house-builders followed slowly, as public expectations rose. As a consequence of this convergence towards improved common standards, private housing came to resemble that of the local authority in the late 1950s and early 1960s, and there was a widespread adoption of symbolic additions to identify privately-owned property, for example, non-functional shutters, ornate porches and lamps. After 1969, however, local authority housing in Barry reflected a national concern felt amongst those involved in providing houses about the adverse social implications of very large estates, especially in redevelopments to house people of similar age groups and class. The reaction to this problem was to provide large but mixed estates, containing accommodation ranging from single-bedroom flats, through a range of house sizes and ending with old peoples' bungalows.

The first phase of the Gibbonsdown Estate, designed by Alex Robinson & Peter Francis aimed to provide just such a mixture of flats, houses and bungalows, served by a peripheral road feeding short *culs-de-sac*; this was a 'Radburn' layout plan.[15] The loss of traditional street patterns in this layout is unfortunately not matched by any gain in environmental quality, and results in small, poorly-screened gardens with ill-defined boundaries between public and private spaces and a low standard of landscape provision and maintenance.

Later stages of this development followed more traditional lines, with flats for pensioners and a hybrid scheme of houses and flats fronting on to short *culs-de-sac* in the phases designed in the early 1970s by Andrews, Gay & Partners. This scheme was designed for district heating, using gas-fired boilers in a centrally-located boiler-house to feed heating mains which distributed hot water to some 350 dwellings. The system was found difficult to run equitably and so was abandoned in 1981 in favour of individual, gas heating-units for each dwelling.

Most special flats for old-age pensioners were provided by the local authority, but the provision of general rented housing was split between the local authority and housing associations, set up to provide purpose-built dwellings at cost rent with the aid of government finance, such as that east of Thompson Street and at Palmerston Road. The Coldbrook Estate was built for private sales by Wimpey Ltd. on redundant marshalling yards east of Cadoxton Station, according to their normal design policy of grouping detached and semi-detached houses in short *culs-de-sac*. The long waiting-list for rented accommodation combined with a slump in private-house sales led to a deal being struck in 1977 between developer and the local authority, to be followed later by a similar arrangement to complete the Gibbonsdown Estate development in the early 1980s.

With the return to power of the Conservative government in 1979, local authority housing slowed to a standstill as a result of restrictions on spending. This the government intended to be partly offset by the sale of tenanted properties to their occupiers, thus making funds available for constructing dwellings for special categories, such as the elderly. The combination of rising building costs and stringent central government financial constraints meant that the funds realised from sales was barely sufficient to cover repairs to the less attractive properties that remained unsold, which were thus the continuing responsibility of the authority. The visual result of this policy was the individualising of ex-council houses by their proud new owners; they were embelished with new windows, porches and even reconstructed-stone cladding to the exterior elevations. Whilst the 1920-30 estates are not of conservation-area quality, their uniformity of materials and proportions are worthy of retention and enhancement by landscaping.

Private house-building made little impact on Barry until the 1960s, when private estates were developed at Merthyr Dyfan and Gibbonsdown Farm, using simple curvilinear road layouts with *culs-de-sac* to serve straightforward bungalows and houses. Small infill areas provided most of the new sites until a large area of land at Highlight Farm, north of Port Road West, was made available in the mid 1970s. This land, although outside the previously planned boundaries of urban development, was developed by Wimpey Ltd. Large numbers of unimaginative, standard-design dwellings were provided, catering exclusively for the younger, upwardly-mobile commuter families who were able to survive without shopping provision nearby or public transport to reach central Barry.

After this development, land on either side of Pontypridd Road became available in 1978. Bounded on the northern side by Colcot Road and on the southern by Claude Road, the Cwm Talwg area was intended to provide opportunities for smaller builders to compete against national companies by obtaining small parcels of land within a larger area delimited by the local authority, and provided with an internal road network connected to the existing roads. Apart from a small number of 'self-build' bungalows, the resulting development was a dismal failure, with narrow, congested roads serving a motley collection of houses and bungalows, each builder trying to attract purchasers by some striking feature or other.

In March, 1964, the Glamorgan County Planning Department indicated to the local authority that, in view of the pressing demands being made upon the authority, some form of development plan should be prepared to show at least the circulation, zoning and town centre indications for the future, so that a degree of comprehensive planning co-ordination could be achieved. H. A. Halpern and partners were commissioned by the Borough Council to prepare such a plan and report, bearing in mind the County Council's advice that a population of some 70,000 to 75,000 could be anticipated by 1984, with a probable eventual maximum of 100,000.

Apart from the construction of a dual carriageway 'box' to divert holiday and industrial traffic around the town, the most striking aspect of the resort was the proposal for a traffic-free Holton Road by means of a sunken 'spine road' serving up to 6,000 car-parking spaces for workers in the new shops, office blocks and civic centre, all to be linked by a pedestrians-only podium, beneath which the service roads would run.

Faced with the huge scale of this scheme the local authority did nothing, and there was a paralysis of commercial development in Barry. The secondary shopping streets of High Street and Main Street declined as the major national retail companies occupied premises in Holton Road. As old buildings deteriorated, property developers took advantage of the opportunity to redevelop the area immediately to the east of King Square. The greater opportunity offered by the large, open square was missed, and the unimaginative façades of the new shops turned away from the square and faced traffic-choked Holton Road, condemning the square to a lifeless future.

At the same time, the sweeping headland of Nell's Point, offering prime views up an down the channel was leased to Butlins for the erection of a massive holiday camp, with disastrous visual results and little financial benefit to the town.

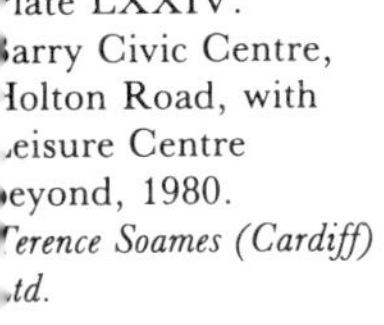

Plate LXXIV. Barry Civic Centre, Holton Road, with Leisure Centre beyond, 1980. *Terence Soames (Cardiff) Ltd.*

The only other commercial development of significance was the construction of a parade of shops, with flats above, on the south side of Broad Street. This has never drawn great numbers of shoppers owing to the flow of traffic passing, but the mass does help to enclose the street visually and provide a brightly-lit promenade in what has become Barry's major restaurant area, bringing life to Broad Street and High Street until the early hours.

Barry was well provided with schools until the children of the post war 'bulge' reached school age. Extensions were built on to most Barry schools, gaining time to construct large new schools for most of the secondary school age group. Barry retained single-sex schools when the changeover to the comprehensive system took place, and the large, boys' school on Port Road West was joined by an even larger Bryn Hafren girls' school on Port Road East in 1973.

The most recent development has been the construction of a new Civic Centre and adjoining Leisure Centre on the site of the old Gasworks. The buildings, designed by David Preece & Associates are based on a steel and concrete system that has proved popular with many of the new District Councils in South Wales, and it enables the architect to attach an appropriate cladding material. Whilst the brickwork chosen for Barry Civic Centre is similar to that in wide use throughout the town, the lack of small-scale detail makes the building gross and over-powering, dwarfing the sunken area which forms an apologetic approach to the building. In the Leisure Centre the opportunity to create a 'fun' pool with the irregular shapes, shelving 'beaches' and wave machines, popular in other resorts, was not taken up, and instead a barely adequate rectangular pool was constructed, resulting in a Centre that hardly meets residents' expectations, much less attracting visitors and holidaymakers.

The old Town Hall now lies empty, its future uncertain. Much of Holton Road's prosperity has been drained away by competition from nearby towns and the shop-keepers that remain have been hard-hit by the national decline in trade. As a result, many shops that have served the inhabitants of Barry for the past century lie empty, their structures decaying from neglect. The town's former major employer, BP Chemicals, has reduced its staff to a sixth of its original size and started to demolish the chemical plant that once stood for Barry's future prospects. The town that sprung up around the new dock in 1884 must in 1984 expect a future very different from its past, and this will change its visual identity for better or for worse. The older dwellings were, in general, sturdily built, and with interior modernisation could last for a long time. In spite of demolitions, replacements and additions, the architectural character of much of the town still recalls its days of greatness. It is to be hoped that new development will be sensitive to this inheritance.

References

1 J. Arthur Hughes was a well-known local solicitor who was appointed Clerk to the first Barry and Cadoxton Local Board on 12th July, 1888 and became its Chairman in 1902. He was also the author of *Mate's Illustrated Barry and Barry Dock*, one of a national series of town guide books, published in 1904.

2 The architectural practice of Edwin Seward and George Thomas had developed from the well-established Cardiff practice of James, Seward and Thomas, designers of many well-known Cardiff buildings, such as the Royal Infirmary, the Coal Exchange in Mount Stuart Square, Queen Street Arcade, and Central Library in the Hayes. Seward and Thomas were the Managing Directors of the Barry Dock Town Syndicate and designed houses in Brook Street, Pyke Street and Quarella Street. They also were the architects for the Welsh Congregational Chapel in Holton Road and the Bassett Hotel.

3 This system unintentionally provided a sophisticated air-conditioning mechanism, because heating cold, winter air reduced its relative humidity, but passing it through saturated matting restored the humidity to a level appropriate to its raised temperature. The architectural historian Reyner Banham argues in the *The Architecture of the Well-tempered Environment* (London: Architectural Press, 1969), that the 1903 Royal Victoria Hospital in Belfast was the first major building to be deliberately air-conditioned for human comfort, using a similar system, although within a building plan laid out to maximise the efficiency of the duct system.

4 W. G. Habershon and J. F. Fawckner also designed the Park Hotel and Roath Park Presbyterian Chapel in Cardiff.

5 The electricity was generated by a horizontal, single-cylinder, steam engine which is now preserved in the Welsh Industrial and Maritime Museum, Bute Street, Cardiff.

6 Capel y Tabernacl in the Hayes, Cardiff, designed in 1865 by J. Hartland, has a facade of some originality and restraint.

7 Augustus Welby Pugin (1812-1852) assisted Sir Charles Barry in the design of the Houses of Parliament and was a key figure in spreading enthusiasm for a revival of Gothic architecture.

8 The Trust also developed land at Rhiwbina, on the northern boundary of Cardiff, and built a large estate with community facilities, on a larger scale than that at Barry.

9 Ebenezer Howard, *Garden Cities of Tomorrow* (Faber, 1946), p. 45.

10 *Ibid.*, p. 51.

11 *Report of a Committee on Questions of Building Construction in connection with the provision of dwellings for the working classes* (H.M.S.O., 1918).

12 Alex Gordon joined the Cardiff practice of T. Alwyn Lloyd, architect of the Garden Suburb, and the practice later became known as Alex Gordon & Partners. Alex Gordon was elected President of the Royal Institute of British Architects in 1973.

13 *Housing Manual* (H.M.S.O., 1949).

14 *Homes for Today and Tomorrow* (H.M.S.O., 1961).

15 The separation of through traffic from pedestrians was based on the principles put forward by Clarence Stein and known by the name of its first application at Radburn, New Jersey, U.S.A., in 1928.

CHAPTER IX

The Town that had come of Age: Barry 1918-1939

PETER STEAD

orough of Barry
:oat of Arms, granted
ı 1939.
Reproduced by ermission; from Charter Souvenir.

IN the period after 1918 the citizens of Barry went about their business quietly. They were aware that the great years of drama and growth were over but they continued to take pride in an earlier chapter of history in which a few obscure coastal villages had been transformed into a world-famous seaport. Barry people lived with the knowledge that the most important and interesting thing about their town was the way in which it had been created and they were proud to have been pioneers, or the sons and daughters of pioneers. As the children of Barry were taught what had become almost a legend, there was an inevitable nostalgia for that Late Victorian and Edwardian period with its economic prosperity and social mobility. Yet, transcending this, was the personal pride of Barry people in the way in which entrepreneurs, engineers, tradespeople and working men and women had responded to opportunities in such a way as to create a spectacularly successful docks and a busy yet attractive town.

Victorian civilisation and prosperity had rested on coal, and the growth of the South Wales Coalfield was one of the great success stories of the whole Victorian economy. In a period of just over half-a-century, pits were sunk, winding gear constructed, railways built and millions of tons of coal transported to the coast. Around the pits and up and down what were to become the notorious valleys the mining villages and towns developed. At the coast the seaports mushroomed. Fortunes were made and a new society was created. Barry was as much a part of this great Victorian economic drama of coal as were Tredegar, Tonypandy and Tiger Bay. Yet its citizens were never to think of it in quite that way. It was not just that Barry was geographically removed from that coalfield on which it was 'parasitic', but rather that Barry's whole history was distinctive. Barry had come late, and it had come as a result of one specific commercial gamble. It was

Plate LXXV.
Major Edgar Jones, O.B.E., M.A., Headmaster of Barry Boys' County School.
Gwyneth Vaughan Jones Coll. Reproduction by N.L.W.

entrepreneurial *bravura* which had created the town. Barry people were aware of that but also of the gamble they themselves or their parents had taken in throwing in their lot with a new venture and a new town. Coal had created a new South Wales, the coal trade had created Barry, and yet from the outset the inhabitants were more aware of how they themselves had created and shaped a new community. Certainly we need to see Barry as a symbol of the Age of Coal, but to most of its citizens its growth was a kind of Late Victorian romance. To come from Barry was to be enchanted by that tale and to know that you were from South Wales but not entirely of it. [1]

The Victorians were men of action and they had created Barry. The Romance of Barry was to be recalled and embroidered in a later and more troublesome period. However different Barry might feel itself to be, its fortunes were tied to coal and the great days of the South Wales Coalfield were over. In Gwyn Thomas's later judgement that 'the town in its modern form blew into being as one of the last bursts of the volcanic energy that brought Britain through the last century and up to the first World War', the key word, of course, is 'last'. [2] Even before 1914 some of the shrewder South Walians and Barrians knew that the good days were over although the Coalfield as a whole went on behaving as if it had not heard of the difficulties being experienced by the wider British economy. After 1918 few doubted that a harsher dispensation had arrived. There were to be no more sudden breakthroughs, no more quick fortunes, no more dramatic elevations to the gentry. The age of *bravura* and of mushroom growth had given way to one in which resources would have to be carefully harnessed, investment shrewdly planned, options carefully studied and competitors rigorously assessed. Pride in the Romance of Barry could not be allowed to interfere with the fight to improve amenities and facilities in a less promising age. The social momentum and civic pride that had come hard on the heels of commercial success had now to be maintained in an age in which industrial viability would be problematic.

The Late Victorian and Edwardian periods had seen the emergence of busy docks and then of a proud little town. The story of Barry since 1918 shows how that town has sought in the face of difficulty to keep its docks busy, while at the same time developing a more diversified commercial pattern as a base for its identity. A Late Victorian port has survived into the 20th century defying suburban blandness, refusing to be an anomaly, rejecting redundancy and channelling all energies into maintaining a distinctive community capable of rewarding its citizens for their labour and fulfilling their wider social and cultural ambitions.

The news that the Great War was over reached Barry on a Monday morning and immediately 'the townspeople with one accord "downed tools" and gave themselves over to heartfelt thanksgiving'. Soon there was bunting on every house and crowds braved the November rain to fill the streets. The 4th Battalion of the Lancashire Fusiliers left their camp at the Buttrills and marched in parade through the town, as did detachments of police and the Scouts. There were torchlight processions until well into the night, as there were to be throughout the week. Four days after the news had arrived crowds of wounded soldiers, Scouts and other organisations carried lights and flags to King Square where 'an effigy of the Hun War-Lord, the ex-Kaiser was set on fire and reduced to ashes amid a scene of great excitement and enthusiasm, the only regret felt being that the Arch-Demoniac himself was not present to submit to the fiery ordeal'. The week ended on Sunday when bands led processions to a memorial service at St. Mary's and there was a united service of prayer at the Theatre Royal.

The War was over but Barry had not finished with the Kaiser yet. Soldiers and prisoners of war returned to the town with further stories of 'the innate brutality of the Hun' and of 'German barbarism', and at a Peace Day celebration in July 1919, a huge crowd of anything up to 20,000 gathered at the Square on another wet day to hear the Chairman of the Council, Howell Williams, report that 15,000 Barrians had enlisted and that 700 had died on sea or land. He made clear his personal disagreement with those who said that the Hun was now being too harshly treated. To drive home the lesson a local businessman and magistrate, J. C. Meggitt presented 7,000 local school children with *The History of the War.* Perhaps it was not surprising that just a few days after Peace Day a group of local Scouts pulled an effigy of the Kaiser up Holton Road and arraigned it in King Square in front of a large, taunting crowd. The Great War had affected Barry very deeply and, although passions were to cool, the memory of sacrifice lingered and in later years the moving Armistice Day services at the Cenotaph and the construction of a Memorial Hall remained as powerful expressions of how much the town had suffered.

Memories of the War were to loom large in Barry in part because of the sacrifices that had been made but also because of the pride that had been generated by the town's involvement in the War itself. The fighting had occasioned a tremendous outburst of patriotism in which each section of the nation was eager to fulfil its responsibilities, and so the War allowed the young town of Barry to prove itself and to express itself as never before by contributing its all to the war effort. In a sense the War had marked Barry's coming of age.[3] Much of the patriotic zeal that had characterized Barry's War could be explained by the prosperity of the Docks where the labour force had been given four and a quarter years of 'hard and constant work'. The Barry Railway Company had contributed over a quarter of its work-force to the armed forces and lost 52 men in the fighting, but those that had remained cleared 'an immense volume of work' and had filled about 10,000 military transport vessels with vital materials. As the dockers worked, so the rest of the town responded. There had been plenty of volunteers for the forces from Barry, and the town was happy to entertain the artillery, the engineers, the infantry and the American navy who had made Barry their first port of call as they entered the War. The Barry Fort on Nell's Point controlled a vital and busy section of the Bristol Channel. The hospitals of Barry had taken many of the wounded, and numerous Belgian refugees had been housed. Over 3,000 citizens had worked on allotments and many had contributed to War Savings collections and responded to War Charity appeals.[4] The workers of Barry Railway Company had perhaps been mindful of all this when they had refused to join in the strike of their South Wales colleagues. Barry had done its bit in the War and it was not surprising that there were those who wished to prolong this new communal zeal which had developed under the cloak of patriotism into the post-war world. For months and years to come there were military parades and military bands to boost the purchase of War Bonds and speed up contributions to various appeals.

There were many matters to be settled in post-war Barry but one of the most important was settled very quickly and at a time when passions were still running high. Having won the War, Lloyd George wanted to win the Peace, and so in November 1918 he sought an electoral mandate for his Coalition Government. Supporters of the Coalition could never have been in doubt that the new parliamentary constituency of Barry and Llandaff would return a supporter of Lloyd George, but for some time there was confusion as to the political identity of the Coalition candidate. For almost two years Major William Cope of Southerndown had been the official Conservative candidate, but the new constituency had been carved out of the old South Glamorgan seat which had been won in 1906 and subsequently held by the Lib-Lab miners' leader William Brace.[5] Not without justification the Liberals assumed that in this new seat the mantle of Brace would fall on them, and they had adopted Sir Evan Jones as their candidate. Jones had later withdrawn his name, but as the War was ending the Liberals chose William Graham, J.P., a prominent Barry industrialist and public figure, to replace him. So there were two Coalition candidates in Barry and no indication as to which would receive Lloyd George's endorsement—the famous 'coupon'. In fact it seemed as if the Coalition leaders were prepared to see a party fight in Barry, but at this point Major Cope pulled out all the stops and banged the patriotic drum. He explained that military duties had kept him away from the area but that 'Mr. Graham on the other hand had never donned khaki'. He outlined his objections to Mr. Asquith and the Liberals, said that he would be in favour of 'hanging the Kaiser' and of keeping 'Britain British' by sending home prisoners and by kicking out enemy aliens. He explained that he was an Imperialist, a Protectionist, and an opponent of Irish Home Rule and this issue occasioned one of his favourite jokes: that Home Rule would come 'when the people of Ireland are ripe for it, but when they will be ripe for it heaven only knows'.

Mr. Graham could not take this kind of barrage and withdrew on medical grounds leaving Major Cope as the only Coalition candidate. Conservative, Unionist and Coalition voters gave Major Cope a clear majority over Captain Russell Jones the Labour Candidate who none the less polled over 6,000 votes and pledged that Labour's day would come.[6] Over 1,500 people voted for the Independent candidate, Dr. Charles Sixsmith, an Irishman, a lover of the turf and one of Barry's greatest characters who could find no fault with Cope other than that 'he was a Tory'. But clearly Cope had been returned on more than Tory votes, and throughout he had been anxious to make his appeal on personal grounds. After his election he stressed that 'he represented in Parliament, not a section of a community, not even a party, but the vast majority of the electorate'. Major Cope had responded to the highly unusual political circumstances and the war atmosphere of 1918 by forging a political identity that seemed old fashioned in its transcendence of party but which was perhaps well suited to the character of the Barry Division.

The 'Kaiser' had been burned, Major Cope had been elected and Barry now had to come to terms with peace and normality. The town was a seaport and that brought prosperity but it also brought problems of various kinds. As a new town in the years before 1914, Barry had made efforts to develop institutions and amenities and to take its place as a settled and mature Edwardian community. It enjoyed a great deal of success in this respect and had come a long way, but it remained a seaport with a waterfront and so it was difficult for it to become just another respectable little town. The Docks brought business but they also brought in sailors, foreigners and those elements which made the town, to use the word popular at the time, 'cosmopolitan'.

The Docks were a tough area. In most weeks there were serious and even fatal accidents in or around ships and cranes, the local press was full of court cases involving sailors and labourers, and increasingly after the coming of peace there were incidents relating to foreign seamen and immigrant workers. A mass meeting of seamen protested against the owners of a steamship whose crew was made up largely of Lascars at a time when hundreds of local sailors were unemployed owing to the post-war decline of trade. There were accusations that coloured seamen were only given jobs if they made cash payments to union officials. Tension was rising and perhaps some kind of incident was inevitable. On the 11th of June, 1919, a thirty-year-old dock labourer, Frederick Longman of Beverley Street, Cadoxton, was way-laid near his home by two negroes and stabbed. Longman who had served in the artillery for four and a half years and who had fought in Palestine, Egypt and France died straightaway. Crowds gathered immediately and made for the streets in which the negro sailors lived; there were angry scenes and cries of revenge, but a strong body of police were able to prevent any serious escalation of unrest. Later that night though one of the negroes was reported to have hit John Goldsworthy of Robin's Lane in the eye with a knife. Extra police were drafted into Barry and officers talked openly of 'The Coloured Trouble'. The old soldier Longman was given a military funeral at Merthyr Dyfan, several people were held on rioting charges and a negro sailor Charles Jackson was accused of inflicting grievous bodily harm on Goldsworthy. The most serious charge was against Charles Emmanuel, a marine fireman from the French West Indies who was accused of Longman's wilful murder. At the Coroner's hearing it was conceded that Emmanuel was probably 'irritated by some remark' and in the magistrates court evidence was given that Longman had hit Emmanuel and asked 'What are you doing in this street?'. At the Glamorgan Assizes the charge was changed to manslaughter and the accused was sentenced to five years penal servitude.[7]

In September of that same year two seamen were charged with the murder of a Chilean seaman Jose Martinez. The incident had occurred in Travis Street but had developed out of a quarrel in Thompson Street between British and coloured sailors. The prosecuting counsel, J. A. Hughes, commented on 'the strong feeling amongst some people against foreigners' and speculated whether it was 'as a result of the war, or whether a feeling of nationality, or whether owing to the American sailors, of whom there were a number in port'. Undoubtedly the War had intensified the peoples' feeling of Britishness, and in Barry the victory celebrations and the election had given evidence of that, but it was almost certainly the prospect of unemployment which had led to scuffles and incidents on the streets. In 1919 Barry, like several other ports, certainly experienced a wave of prejudice against coloured seamen, who were of course by far the most obviously alien in the community; but in no real sense can we talk of race riots in the town. In essence these were the kind of incidents that frequently occurred in all ports and it was only the heightened excitement and rhetoric of 1919, when feelings were running high against not only coloured but all foreigners, that threatened to make the situation look ugly. In 1921 a newspaper headline announced that 'Jap shoots Jap at Barry Docks' but by that time people knew that it was drink rather than racial tension which occasioned what appeared to be violent and exotic incidents in and around the Docks.

There were many people who feared that Barry would be disrupted by a far more serious force than racial tension. Quite fundamental to the whole future of the town was the mood and temper of the labour force. 'Labour' as one local politician had it, was 'the burning question of the day'. The trade unions had grown greatly in size and were certainly going to be far more militant after the War. The Railwaymen were by far the most powerful and best organised group in Barry and any display of militancy by their unions was bound to disrupt not only the local economy but the whole life of the town. The railwaymen were to have their strikes in the post-war years and troops were brought in to protect vital stores but perhaps a more serious problem were those sailors, labourers and returning soldiers who could not find jobs. Unemployment was a problem in Barry from the moment war ended. The great fear was that militancy and unemployment would somehow combine to bring revolution. The clue to these fears was in the language of public life and in the frequency with which speakers referred to the Bolsheviks. Any unruly citizens were immediately referred to as 'Bolshevists' and there were constant references to the 'dangers of Bolshevism' as illustrated by 'the adventurers of the Red Guard' in Russia. General Booth of the Salvation Army told an audience at the Theatre Royal that the Bolshevist movement in Russia was 'a manifestation of conflict against Jesus Christ' and several radical candidates for the Council stressed their support of democratic movements 'but not Bolshevism'. These were anxious times.

In fact, the town was too busy for revolution or even for any sustained labour unrest. This was a port which had to offer both its visitors and its natives a full range of diversions. The local hotels proudly boasted of their fine ales, of their billiard tables 'with Burroughs and Watts latest improved cushions' and of their 'assembly rooms'. All the latest Hollywood films were shown at the Romilly, the Theatre Royal, the King's Hall and the Cadoxton Palace whilst at Leon Vint's Palace there were 'Twice Nightly' revues with matinees on Saturday. At Jenner Park the Linnets were competing in the Welsh League. Soon after the War they had been forced to sell Tich Evans to Swansea for £100 but they still hoped that their core of professional players would help gain them re-admission to the First Division of the Southern League and even possibly to the Third Division of the Football League itself.[8] Barry was a town of sportspeople; there were bowlers, cricketers, rugby and baseball players and there was a keen interest in boxing with first-class bouts often being staged at several venues around the town, including the Stadium in Thompson Street. There was culture too, and in particular there was choral music, an activity for which Barry was long to maintain a national reputation. The Barry Choral Society gave concerts at the Dinam Hall, and the Barry Male Voice Choir's concerts at the Y.M.C.A. and elsewhere were the highlights of the cultural calendar. In August 1919 the Allington Charsley Opera Company with over a hundred artistes and full orchestra came to the Theatre Royal to perform *Il Trovatore, Rigoletto, Lohengrin, Faust* and a few other lighter works. Regular patrons were assured that the Opera Company had agreed to the current film serial *Stingalee* being shown before their own performances. Meanwhile many groups throughout the town were busily preparing for the Royal National Eisteddfod of Wales which was due to be held in Barry in 1920. A huge crowd attended the Proclamation Ceremony in June 1919 and the local press detected 'a deep interest—notwithstanding the fact that the proceedings were conducted in Welsh'. To this day the Gorsedd Stones stand on the slope overlooking Romilly Park.

Barry offered a variety of entertainments and for many years its citizens were to persist in the old Edwardian habit of living full lives with a constant round of social, religious, sporting and cultural activities. For a significant number of local people there was also the constant round of public and political affairs. Barry was a town of almost 40,000 inhabitants and, like many towns of that size, it had been given a wide-range of powers and encouraged to assume responsibility for its own affairs. There was the Urban District Council which had come into being in 1895 and whose work was now done largely through a range of key committees, whilst the War had seen the growth of many other semi-official committees which were often dominated by the same people. This local framework had brought into being a set of leaders, who by their very nature had to assume and articulate a concern for the community. The Barry of 1918 and 1919 was a bustling town with a hectic range of diversions and a number of frightening tensions, but in the midst of all this frenetic activity it was the local leaders who had to take a long-term view and decide as to precisely where Barry was going in the post-war world. They could see perhaps that racial tension would subside and that there was little genuine fear of a Bolshevik take-over, but that nonetheless Barry faced serious problems.

Plate LXXVI. Gorsedd Stones above Romilly Park, Barry. *B. Daly.*

At the outset Barry had to fight for its very identity. Eight miles away was the ambitious city of Cardiff, which in the years immediately prior to the War had flourished as the metropolis of South Wales. As the War ended so Cardiff was prompted to suggest a local government fusion with Barry, the town which had, of course, come into being by cocking a snook at Cardiff. The merger scheme came to the Barry Council from its own Parliamentary Committee and it occasioned sharp disagreement at Council meetings and subsequent public meetings. There were many obvious advantages to fusion in particular with regard to local services and amenities but Barry, as we shall see, was immensely proud of its record especially with regard to services such as gas and water and according to one councillor 'a glass of Barry water was worth a gallon of Cardiff water'. The whole issue generated a good deal of emotion and there was talk of 'the Birthright of Barry' being 'worth more than a Mess of Potage', and references to the 'nefarious designs' of Cardiff. The *Barry Dock News* nicely resorted to the language of the day as it spoke of Cardiff's determination to keep ahead of Swansea, of its long-standing designs on Penarth and of how, when all was said and done, 'the little nations are wide awake and will not allow themselves to be entrapped by a cry of "Greater Cardiff" '. This kind of emotion probably counted for more than the prominent businessman J. C. Meggitt's cogent and prescient arguments that the Docks would certainly be merged one day, that education powers could almost certainly be retained and that in the meantime Barry needed improved lighting and power, would benefit from the Cardiff tram system, and above all urgently needed soft water so as to attract industry. In a plebiscite 5,957 citizens voted against the merger, 3,309 voted for, and just over 4,000 did not vote at all. The majority of local leaders and councillors probably shared Dudley Howe's view that Cardiff was a prodigal authority, whilst Barry's finances were on a much sounder footing and so were delighted with this result. Their feeling was that Barry was 'an enterprising and progressive township' and that merger would have reduced it to being 'an insignificant parochial nonentity'. The winning argument was put best by Councillor Mrs. Lewis, who maintained that Barry 'as a town that had just commenced to walk, was far in advance of what Cardiff ever tried to be'.[9]

Barry was to remain politically autonomous, but, as J. C. Meggitt had suggested during the fusion crisis, there was the possibly more serious question of Barry's commercial future. The whole identity and prosperity of Barry had been bound up with the fortunes of the Barry Railway Company and the town had always basked in the reflected glories of the Company's success. It had openly boasted of dividends that had been paid, of the statistics of coal transported and exported (in the peak years the Docks had received 80 to 90 coal trains a day) and of the Company's passenger services, coal wagons and, above all, coal-tips. The first thing that any Barry person would tell you was that the Docks formed the only port in the Bristol Channel which vessels could enter or leave at any time or state of the tide. Emotionally, and to a large extent economically, Barry had been a Company town, but the War had changed things greatly. Certainly there had been continued prosperity as the war economy had to be maintained, but those years of crisis also served to drive home a new bureaucratic and managerial logic. The Government took over the railways of the country in 1914, and whilst guaranteeing profits to the companies, they had really taken a decisive step along the path of organising a national rail network. There were so many railway problems to sort out, not the least being the militancy of the unions, that in 1919 the Government decided on two more years of railway control. It was obvious now that there could be no return to the Edwardian pattern, and the Railway Act of 1921, whilst returning the railways to private ownership, regrouped the companies into four great regions. The 1921 Act was a triumph for the Great Western Railway Company which consolidated its empire and preserved much of its identity. A later historian once claimed that 'the G.W.R. seemed to exist by Divine Right', but in fact in 1921 many new problems had to be faced.[10] Almost by accident the G.W.R. now found itself the owner of one of the two largest docks groups in the country. It had taken over the ports of South Wales at a time when the coal trade, on which those ports were almost wholly dependent, was bound to decline, and when there were almost certainly to be major industrial disputes involving the miners and the railwaymen, and possibly the dockers as well. Whatever the managerial and business logic of regrouping, there must have been few senior G.W.R. officials who relished the thought of what was likely to happen in South Wales. By the same token there were not many people in Barry who warmed to the idea of the town passing into the hands of the G.W.R.

The Barry Company itself was justifiably indignant. They had been paying a dividend of 10 per cent before the War, this had dropped to 9½ per cent during the War itself but was back up at 10 in the years after 1919 at a time when the G.W.R. were only paying 7¼ per cent. There were great difficulties in 1919, but by the time of regrouping the directors were sure that recovery was well under way. At the sixty-sixth and final annual meeting of the Company, the Earl of Plymouth, Chairman of the Company and a shareholder and director since the very beginning in 1884, boasted of the overall record and 'wound' things up defiantly:

> 'The Barry Railway Company was authorised by Parliament in the face of strenuous opposition and its development was made in the same spirit, but notwithstanding this, the Company's progress has been one of uninterrupted success from its commencement, and your Directors have every confidence that if it were possible for the Company to have remained as an independent undertaking they might have anticipated a period of still greater prosperity.'[11]

Something at least was to be salvaged in 1921. The original plans had designated the Barry Railway Company as a subsidiary company but there had been so many howls of protest from the Board and from its influential friends in Parliament that the Grand Committee conceded and elevated the Company, along with the Cardiff Railway Company, to the status of Constituent Company so it would now have a Director on the G.W.R. Board, and in the short-term was able to secure better terms. This victory, taken with the fact that so many of the Barry Docks senior officials would be staying on to work with the G.W.R., re-assured many people and allowed them to argue that the whole arrangement made good business sense. In general the town was not convinced.[12]

Already Barry was experiencing distress unlike anything experienced before the coming of Peace. The depression that had hit the Docks at the end of the War had gone away but it had left a pool of unemployment in its wake. By the winter of 1920-21 there were well over 2,000 unemployed and largely unskilled men in Barry and the Council was having to organise relief road work and make appeals on behalf of a Town Fund. The railway strike of April 1921 added to the misery and soon it was apparent that Barry was facing a major crisis. The Barry Relief Committee reported that there were 500 distressed seamen in Barry and that whilst 257 of these were receiving unemployment pay, there were others in 'dire need of sustenance'. It was decided to step up assistance to the Missions to Seamen who were now giving daily meals at the Mission and at the Sailors' Rest, and in addition the Committee itself was to open a kitchen at St. Mary's Hall. There were soon hundreds of takers at these and other kitchens: the Salvation Army reported that they were providing 2,300 meals a week at Barry and 2,000 at Cadoxton, and that many of these were given to needy mothers and children who were not in direct receipt of relief.

This was the unpromising context in which the G.W.R. took over Barry. The *Barry Dock News* praised Major Cope's valiant battle in Parliament to secure better terms but it was firmly of the view that 'the proposed concessions and guarantees on the part of the G.W.R. are not worth the paper they are written upon'. The local fears were that, in what was bound to be difficult times, Barry would lose out to the other G.W.R. ports and that, in any case, the simple fact that there was no longer any genuine competition could only be to Barry's detriment. It was thought in particular that the railway side of the Barry undertaking would suffer as routes were rationalised, through-workings introduced and repair depots merged, but there were also the longer-term fears that much-needed improvements at the Docks would not be undertaken. In the short term things did get better as trade picked up after the national rail strike, but it was now realised that Barry would have to maintain a constant pressure and fight, not only to obtain new trade and jobs, but just to hang on to the old. Of course, the

G.W.R. was to modernise and to do what it could for Barry, but after 1922 the people of the town always really suspected that the Docks were being under-used and not given the fullest opportunity to fulfil their potential. Barry had lost its economic autonomy and that had created a new anxiety that was never to be far beneath the surface of local politics.

It took the great French historian Elie Halévy to remind the British that in the 19th century their country had been made up essentially of localities that were self-governing communes. By the 1920s power had shifted decisively to Whitehall, but the local government framework had ensured that, whatever the reality, the counties and towns still tended to think of themselves as being essentially self-governing communities. Whatever fears and anxieties there were about the future of Barry it was in the meetings of the Urban District Council that they were most fully expressed. The history of modern Barry is best told by looking at the affairs of the Council and at the way in which the Council Chamber has seen debates and battles in which a group of men and women who thought of themselves very much as the town's leaders gave vent to their fears and expressed their hopes. Barry has remained a small town and its public affairs have been conducted by a remarkably small number of men and women, some of whom found it difficult to be anything but parochial; but in their debates and transactions we are provided with a microcosm of the 20th-century British experience. There have been councillors who have wanted to spend and those who have wanted to retrench; there have been some with grandiose notions of expansion and others who were just happy for Barry to consolidate; there were those who opposed any intervention, whilst others sought to make the Council into one of the sharpest cutting-edges of the Welfare State. The Council debates are the key to modern Barry.

The Barry Urban District Council had been created in 1894, and by 1921 it was responsible for the affairs of some 39,000 people and had a rateable value of over £280,000. Its twenty-one councillors were returned from seven wards, and once elected they served on a number of powerful committees which controlled many aspects of local life. The key committee was the Finance Committee, which determined the district rates and which used the six-monthly rate adjustment to comment on the whole state of the local economy by reviewing the health of the Docks, the level of unemployment and the general prospects for local shopkeepers and traders. There were to be many worries in the 1920s but there was a general feeling that Barry was a well-run town and that its finances were on a sound basis. To a large extent this stability was dependent on gas, for the Chairman of the Gas and Water Committee, who controlled one of the largest, cheapest and most efficient gas undertakings in South Wales, was often able to announce that substantial profits would once again enable the Finance Committee to avoid rate increases. There were other important committees such as the Housing

Committee, the Hospital Committee, which was responsible for several local hospitals, the Health Committee, the Public Works Committee and an Education Committee on which the whole Council served and which was responsible for a local system of schools of which the whole town was proud. There were also committees for Public Works, Parks and Licensing, Allotments, Public Libraries, Child Welfare, Electricity Supply, the War Memorial, the Cold Knap Development and, of course, a Parliamentary Committee. At every point the people of Barry found their affairs coming within the jurisdiction of their elected representatives. The Council Committees met regularly and their proceedings were widely reported. The result was that local government matters in the small, compact and geographically well-defined town of Barry were always to have a great immediacy and often a great urgency.[13]

The years before 1914 had seen Barry develop as four distinct sub-towns —Cadoxton, Barry Dock, Barry and Barry Island—each adjacent to a docks-entrance and a railway station and each with its own business and shopping districts.[14] The residential areas were at first huddled around the docks-entrances, but as the town developed, so terraces and villas crept up the slopes above each sub-town to form that great fan-shape or amphitheatre

'late LXXVII. Queen Street, Barry, showing terraced houses on slope; outline of All Saints' Church in centre distance. *R. W. Thomas.*

of houses that has remained the characteristic form of modern Barry and which is best seen by looking back from the sea. There were large houses and workers' terraces in each part of the town, but already the western slopes were becoming slightly more fashionable as they were closer to unspoilt beaches and rural scenery and cliff-walks, and also, as in most British towns, they were up-wind of domestic and industrial smoke. Barry had emerged as a community of terraced streets for dockers, sailors and above all railwaymen, but already captains, pilots, managers, teachers and tradespeople were creating more fashionable streets and more exclusive suburbs. Now with the coming of Peace this young town, which had really had very little time to settle as an organic community, was thrust into two lively debates about its general image and its whole shape and function as a town.

Edwardian Barry was famous the world over as a coal-exporting port, but nearer home it had developed a subsidiary reputation as a seaside resort. The Barry Railway Company had come into existence to bring coal to the coast but it also gave the growing population of Cardiff and the valleys of Monmouthshire and East Glamorgan direct access to Barry's impressive Whitmore Bay. Visitors came in even greater numbers after the completion of the rail extensions to Barry Island in 1896 and to the Pier in 1899. Seaside resorts had been the boom towns of the late Victorian and Edwardian period as cheap rail tickets helped to create a new craze for holidays, but more especially for excursions. Each resort had its own particular charms or sought to publicise and even create its own gimmicks, but in general, a uniform pattern of expectations and attractions developed.[15] Visitors came for the sea and perhaps even more for the sea air, but these were never enough to sustain interest through a long day and so people had to be fed, refreshed, distracted, amused, entertained and, of course, encouraged to come again. All over the country resorts and railway companies were competing for custom. As in so many things Barry was inevitably a late-starter, but the die was soon cast, for with its decision to take over the management of the beach in 1905 and then the surrounding land in 1909, the Barry Council had really decided that the town was going to offer serious competition as a resort. The War had held up several proposals, but in 1919 the way was clear for the town to carry on with the development of its attractions and in particular to decide on what kind of resort it really wanted to be.

The Twenties were to be the vital decade for Barry's identity as a resort. Each year saw the development of new facilities and attractions and as the resort's popularity grew it assumed a very distinct personality and one which was to remain largely unchanged in later decades. At the Island the sea wall, promenade and arcade were completed, the two headlands were acquired and 1924 saw the opening of Collins' Fairground in time to become one of the most famous fairgrounds in the country, not least because of its

Plate LXXVIII. Lake and bungalows, Cold Knap, Barry in *c.* 1930. *Mary Lennox Coll.*

notorious 'Figure 8' railway. At the same time the Council acquired the beautiful pebble beach at Cold Knap from the Romilly estate and developed there a swimming lido and marine boating lake. Described in this way the growth of Barry's popularity and the development of its fame, and one may even say notoriety, as a resort all sounds straightforward, logical and ineluctable. In fact, the story was more complicated and controversial and at every stage there was considerable anxiety as to whether the right choices had been made and whether the town was maintaining the right image and developing in the proper way. Throughout the story we can identify 'boosters' who believed that Barry had the potential to become one of the country's finest resorts, but also opponents who thought of any resort development as a threat to Barry's inherent charms. It is not going too far to say that the community of Barry has always been a little uneasy about its status as a resort.

Perhaps the greatest irony about Barry's emergence as a resort was that its new attractions developed as a direct result of the slump in the coal trade and the consequent unemployment at the Docks. In this post-war period unemployment in Barry was running at about 10 per cent of those insured and in bad years like 1920 it could climb to 20 per cent. At every stage of its plans for developing the resort, and indeed for all its improvement plans, the Council turned to the Government and requested assistance from the Ministry of Health and the Unemployment Grant Committee. The result was direct financial help and a stipulation that only registered unemployed men could be used to work on the building of the sea wall at the Island and on the development of the front and later the Knap. These schemes brought much needed relief to small groups of workmen but they also helped concentrate the minds of Barry's leaders on the issue of the town's future. As the coal crisis deepened and trade again declined it seemed to several people that Barry would do better to concentrate on its future as a resort than to rely on the recovery of the Docks. When, rather belatedly for some, a Barry Development Committee was set up in 1925, Dan Evans, the President of the Chamber of Trade, commented that he was 'much more hopeful of the future of Barry with regard to its possibilities as a seaside resort than he was in connection with its industrial future'. It was in 1926, at the very time when the whole future of the coal trade seemed in doubt, that one councillor was to suggest that the town should change its name to Barry-on-Sea. The sad fact was then that whereas the great resorts of the country had been sustained by late Victorian and Edwardian affluence, both the personality and role of Barry Island had to be determined at a time of growing hardship and distress both in the town itself and in the South Wales hinterland. Barry Island was never really to shrug off the imprint left by the hard times of the inter-war years.

With the War over, the crowds came back to Barry Island: there were 70,000 there on the Whitsun Bank Holiday in 1919 but soon the normal Bank Holiday figure was back up to 100,000 and it was now not much below that on most summer weekends. The picture was a familiar one, a crowded beach with every inch of sand taken, a cricket match in progress, paddle steamers and pleasure boats in the channel and a silver band playing on Friars Point. One new feature was the road congestion, for those years just after the War saw the rise of the charabanc; the G.W.R. had now a formidable rival. Dozens of charabancs now poured into Barry on weekends

Plate LXXIX. Whitmore Bay, Barry Island, with charabancs, in *c.* 1930. *Charter Souvenir.*

and the locals soon became accustomed to the cries of 'It's the sea, it's the sea' as the vehicles rounded corners on the slopes above the town. The charabancs clinched Barry's role as the playground of the Valleys, and every weekend and during holiday periods the Island was taken over by people who came, in the words of the local press, from 'the hill-districts'.

Protests were inevitable. The 'juggernaut charabancs' were the last straw for Mr. Austin Beynon who wrote to the local press to tell of how he had bought a large house on the Island in 1899 at a time when 'it seemed one of the fairest spots on earth'. Who, he wondered, would want to buy his house now, surrounded as it was with vast crowds, refreshment houses, broken paths, roundabouts, beach shanties, silver bands and monkey booths. Mr. Beynon could only register disgust 'at the way in which the Island has been exploited by the Council in the vain hope that one day Barry will rank among the chief watering places in the land'. There was an immediate response to this letter and someone describing himself as 'An Anonymous Bandsman' met Mr. Beynon's points one by one and then concluded with this peroration:

> 'You say that twenty-three years ago you built a big house at great trouble and expense. You thought Barry Island was at that time the fairest on earth, and that nobody will buy today amid such conditions, but I should like to remind you that there are many ex-servicemen, myself included, and others who are forced to live in filthy, unhealthy conditions, packed in houses like sardines in a box. I don't think Mr. Beynon would have much trouble in selling if he had the pluck to offer at a reasonable price. But that's the way. What you should have done twenty three years ago is to have bought the whole of the Island and fenced it in just for yourself.'

There have always been and there always will be disputes over private and public access to beauty-spots but in this minor squabble we are given a clear reminder of how Barry developed very much as a democratic resort. The Council was making a fun-spot available for the masses, and the masses came and made Barry Island their own. In so doing they were to annoy not only individual residents like Mr. Beynon but also quite powerful local pressure groups. In his letter Mr. Beynon had been particularly concerned with the desecration and obliteration of the Sabbath at Barry Island and his specific grievance against the bands was their playing of 'secular ragtimes—during service time'. His complaint came at a time when there was growing unease amongst the churches and chapels of Barry about the whole question of the extent to which the Island should be allowed to function unchecked as a resort on the Lord's Day.

Barry was very much a Christian town. It had come into being at a time not only of general Christian belief but also of religious revivals. People came to Barry as Christians and there they found a Railway Company and a local business and trading *élite* eager to sustain Christian values and discipline. Barry was a railway town and railwaymen the country over were known for the regularity of their habits and the orderliness of their lives, and perhaps in cosmopolitan Barry these characteristics were more assiduously developed by way of contrast with the disorders of the waterfront. The image that Barry had chosen for itself was that of a town of hard-working and good-living artisans, and the churches and chapels of the town played a decisive role in sustaining that image. The people of Barry lived their social round and conducted their public affairs within a Christian idiom, and local leaders, whether they were managerial, shopocracy or artisan, were invariably described as officers or deacons of various places of worship. There was a flourishing and important Catholic church and several imposing Anglican churches, but in general the mood of the town was Nonconformist. Several of the chapels belonged to Welsh denominations,

Fig. 86.
Programme of Barry Cymmrodorion Society, 1929-30.
Gareth Howe Coll.

SWYDDOGION Y GYMDEITHAS.

Llywydd—Parch. W. R. JONES (Gwenith Gwyn).
Is-Lywydd—Miss KATE JONES.
Cyn-Lywydd—Mr. E. J. RICHARDS, B.A.
Pencerdd—Mr. D. J. MARTIN.
Trysorydd—Mr. GRIFFITH R. JONES.
Archwilwyr—Mri. J. JENKINS a T. W. LEWIS.
Ysgrifennydd Adran y Plant—
Mr. H. M. DAVIES, B.A.
Ysgrifennydd yr Urdd—Mr. GWYNALLT EVANS, B.A.
Ysgrifennydd Cyffredinol—Miss HULDAH BASSETT, B.A., "Afallon," Colcot, Barri.

AELODAU'R PWYLLGOR.

I Ymneillduo yn 1930:
Mrs. Champion, Miss P. Owen, Mri D. M. Humphreys, Edwin Lewis, J. Petty, D. Rees, J. M. Williams.

I Ymneillduo yn 1931:
Misses Elen Evans, M.A., Cassie Davies, M.A., Myfanwy Thomas, B.A., Aeronwen Evans, Mr. Ashton, Parchn. G. H. Havard, M.A., B.D., T. B. Matthews.

I Ymneillduo yn 1932:
Mrs. Hutton, Mrs. Joslin, Miss Lal Williams. Mrs. Morgan (Park Avenue), Mr. Edgar Rees, Mr. Glyn Rees, Mr. Williams (Court Road).

ENW'R AELOD:

Barry and District News

"FY IAITH, FY NGWLAD, FY NGHENEDL."
CYMDEITHAS CYMRODORION Y BARRI.
(Sefydlwyd Gwyl Ddewi, 1906).

RHAGLEN

Y Pedwerydd Tymor ar Hugain.

1929 — 1930.

PRIS Y RHAGLEN - - 2s.

☞ Rhaid dangos y Rhaglen hon wrth y drws ar eich mynediad i'r darlithiau.

and the members of these combined with local teachers, members of the Cymmrodorion and the staff and students of the local training College to ensure an element of Welshness in local life. Far more people, however, belonged to the chapels of the English denominations and it was the English

Baptists, but perhaps even more the Methodists and Congregationalists, who were to be the decisive influence in setting the tone of modern Barry. That influence was usually discreet, but on occasions it emerged as a specific lobby, and the new popularity of the Island on the Sabbath was a development to which it had to respond.

Matters came to a head in 1922 when the Council's Parks Committee agreed not to oppose plans for regular Sunday bus services to the Island. The result was that the next full Council Meeting was invaded by a large deputation of local religious leaders and during heated altercations there was fierce heckling of those councillors like J. T. Maslin of the Island who welcomed the new services. The intensive lobbying succeeded, for the Council decided to oppose the Sunday licence, but it was a hollow victory as the bus proprietors, behaving in the words of one councillor like 'a little Soviet', just went on running their buses, and as they were backed by the Ministry of Transport, the Council had to bow to the inevitable. This developed into a general pattern. The Barry Free Church Council, the Temperance Council and the Sunday School Union came together to support the local option for prohibition, to oppose the Sunday opening of cinemas and above all to clamp down on the Sunday operating of pleasure boats from Barry. There were some minor victories but not as far as the Island was concerned, for there the masses were voting with their feet, and business could only respond to and government only accept this new life-style. One Barry 'Churchman' was realistic enough to read the message of his times and he reminded the Free Church Council that 'Barry is to a certain extent a cosmopolitan town'. What was described as the 'hurly-burly' of the Island had to be accepted even on Sundays, but of course a moral and spiritual resistance could still be upheld. Reports that men and youths were bathing 'under vulgar conditions', that men were undressing on the rocks near the ladies' bathing houses and then wearing 'drawers only suitable for children', combined with the all too frequent accounts of drunken and riotous behaviour by trippers from Aberdare and such places to convince local people that, in the summer at least, Barry Island had passed into the hands of the Devil.

In the press accounts of court cases arising out of incidents at the Island the word 'trippers' was always used and it soon came to be the Barry way of expressing disapproval of those outsiders who came in to enjoy the attractions of the town. There was felt to be a sharp contrast between the sturdy artisan virtues of the locals and the lumpen-proletariat carousals of the 'trippers'. To some it underlined the point that it had been a mistake to develop Barry at all, whilst to others it proved that Barry was being developed in the wrong way. In 1925 a local newsagent reported that he had hoped to bring a national conference to Barry but soon realised that the town lacked hotel accommodation and a conference centre. It appeared to him that 'apparently so far Barry has gone all out for what one may term the one-day tripper' and so had operated with 'only one eye open'. As the decade progressed so many others came to think that the Council had been too parochial and short-sighted in their plans for Barry, and that somehow the town may have been cheated out of its proper destiny. In 1928 Councillor Llewellyn, in trying to halt the proposed development of Barry, remarked how 'there were hundreds of thousands of day trippers coming to the town who left nothing behind save a huge litter of broken bottles, paper bags and fag-ends'. His dream was of a residential resort that would bring profit to more than just a few Island traders and licensed franchises, but his regret on what had happened to Barry could only be in part a criticism of the Council for it was far more a comment on an era in South Wales history. Barry Island developed at a time when local resources were limited and the recreational demands of the South Wales working class were pretty singular. To have expected style and fashion at Barry Island would have been to expect those things at New York's Coney Island. Most Barry people realised that they had lost the Island and contented themselves with the quieter charms of the Knap and of Porthkerry Park which the Council had acquired in 1926. The boast 'of course, we never go to the Island' became one of the badges of Barry respectability.

The future of the Island was a favourite subject for debate in the Barry of

Plate LXXX. Marine Lake, Pebble Beach, Swimming Pool, and Watchtower Bay in *c.* 1976. *West Air Photography.*

the Twenties but it did not take up as much time as the issue of housing. Pre-war Barry had been almost entirely built by private builders and they had responded to the town's boom by providing a glut of houses. At a time when, in any case, local authorities had been extremely cautious of taking advantage of the legislation which allowed the provision of municipal housing, there had been little need for the Barry Council to take any great initiative, and the only exciting variation from private housing in the town had been the Garden Suburb public utility scheme of the War years. In general Barry had congratulated itself on its whole approach to housing and planning and, in particular, on the way it had avoided many of the worst features of Victorian working-class housing. This smugness was to survive the War, and in 1919 a local Labour Party election address commented that 'We in Barry, feeling the superiority of a new-grown town, thanked God there are no slums here' and then almost apologetically inquired 'but are we sure that there are no one-room dwellers in Barry?'. The fact was that there were many one-room dwellers in the town, for the War had brought about a very new set of circumstances. There had been very little building in the War, and the private builders seemed to be no longer interested in major developments. In 1920 the Chairman of the Council gave it as his view that 75 per cent of local discontent was related to housing difficulties; since 1913 the population had grown from 33,000 to 39,000 and yet 'only two or three houses were built', and that he had not the remotest idea where the 39,000 inhabitants slept at night—often there were four families in one house.

Housing was now a national issue, and to allow 'homes fit for heroes' to be built the Government changed the regulations and the basis for state support and encouraged local authorities to tackle local shortages. The Welsh Town Planning and Housing Trust and the Garden Suburb Company were quick off the mark and suggested further extensions to their schemes in the west of the town. But the Council could see that a new era had opened up, and that circumstances were forcing it to become a major housing agency. There was a new feeling of public spirit. Reconstruction was in the air, and in Barry the Council's scheme for 500 new houses on the recently acquired Witchill Estate became the symbol of this new chapter in local government history. Prospectuses were prepared and at special Council meetings and public meetings the full details of Government loans and of Government refunds and losses incurred by bond schemes were explained. As the public were urged to respond so the necessity of the Witchill development became increasingly more apparent. There were 638 applications for houses at the Witchill, many of them from ex-servicemen, precisely the group that the Government were most eager to help. There was no doubt now that there was a major overcrowding problem and the Council admitted that a thousand houses were needed and it outlined plans for the provision of 830 of those.

Lloyd George's Government had given the green light to local authorities and in the words of the local press Barry's response had 'not been timid'.[16] By the end of 1924 over £¼m. had been spent on housing, and throughout the 1920s building continued on two great council estates and the Council also assisted the extension of the Garden Suburb. As Barry pushed out into the surrounding fields so some of the worst overcrowding was overcome, but build and borrow as the Council did, the general problem did not go away. The Council was not dealing with a once-for-all problem, but rather embarking on what would become one of their most permanent controversial concerns. In 1926 with 525 houses built and over £350,000 spent, the Council still conceded that there were as many as 1,500 families still requiring homes. As the decade closed there was growing speculation that Council house rents were too high for many families, who consequently preferred to stay in overcrowded accommodation in the older parts of the town. Considerable publicity was also given to those families crowded together in the old army 'hutments' at the Butrills; the conditions there were scandalous and prompted the Council into yet further developments.

Plate LXXXI. Barry Urban District Council housing of mid 1920s. *R. W. Thomas Coll.*

In 1925 a local press cartoon by J. C. Walker had a Barry man listening to the wireless as a broadcaster spoke of the 'Marine Lake, Promenade, Electricity, Soft Water, Hospital Extensions' all this being described as the Barry Council's programme for that year; the man's response was to draw heavily on his pipe and thoughtfully stroke his chin. Faced with a housing shortage, with serious unemployment and the need to improve local services and amenities the Barry Council had markedly stepped up their expenditure and embarked on a whole series of ventures. It was doing this at a time of crisis in the coal trade and of uncertainty at the Docks, but there was confidence that the profit from gas and the huge rate payment by the G.W.R. would help maintain a stable financial base; the local boast was still that rates at 11*s*. 10*d*. per head were lower than in Cardiff. As electricity was brought to the town and plans made to improve the water supply the feeling was that local councillors were involved in 'a great business of handling a gigantic undertaking' and that 'municipal management' had become altogether a more serious and challenging effort. As the local press reminded citizens at the time of elections in 1926 these important issues 'must not be anybody's job'—the need was for men of experience and training.

Barry passed into the era of modern local government in the hands of a small group of well-known leaders whose careers had been spent in local management and business. They were men whose own lives had been caught up with the whole development of the town and they saw their task as one in which new difficulties had to be overcome as the image of Barry as a progressive and yet thoroughly business-like community was maintained. Councillors like David Boon, Charles Griffiths, Ben Carpenter, Dr. P. T. O'Donnell and Dudley Howe were determined to modernise and improve Barry, and yet their plans seemed to be threatened by the new economic difficulties of the post-war world. One of their main concerns was to maintain pressure on the G.W.R. to ensure that the Barry Docks were not passed over as that Company sought to overcome the coal crisis and at the same time modernise its rail and dock facilities throughout South Wales. Their fears were at their worst in the great coal crisis of 1925 and 1926, and at that time Barry's leaders were constantly seeking reassurances from the G.W.R. with regard to their intentions for Barry. Sir Felix Pole, the General Manager of the G.W.R., came to Barry in December 1925 to open officially the third section of the Garden Suburb housing scheme and he emphasised that the Company's wish was 'not only to see Barry regain its pre-war status but to see a universal revival as well'. At the same time he assured the Council that no coal would be diverted from Barry to other South Wales ports and that no railway repair work would be closed down.

Fig. 87. Menu card from civic dinner of Barry Urban District Council, given in 1925. *Gareth Howe Coll.*

: : List of Chairmen : :
OF THE
Barry Urban District Council.

Dec., 1894 to Apl. '96	J. C. MEGGITT, J P.
1896—1897	P. J. O'DONNELL, J.P.
1897—1898	WM. THOMAS.
1898—1899	ED. TREHARNE, J.P.
1899—1900	J. H. JOSE, J.P.
1900—1901	WM. PATERSON.
1901—1902	J. L. DAVIES.
1902—1903	J. A. HUGHES.
1903—1904	J. A. MANATON.
1904—1905	J. C. MEGGITT, J.P.
1905—1906	J. A. MANATON.
1906—1907	JAMES JONES.
1907—1908	W. J. WILLIAMS, J.P.
1908—1909	W. J. WILLIAMS, J.P.
1909—1910	D. LLOYD.
1910—1911	W. R. LEE, J.P.
1911—1912	J. WILLIAMS.
1912—1913	P. J. O'DONNELL, J.P.
1913—1914	THOS. DAVIES, J.P.
1914—1915	S. R. JONES.
1915—1916	J. MARSHALL.
1916—1917	C. B. GRIFFITHS.
1917—1918	J. E. LEVERS.
1918—1919	G. WAREHAM.
1919—1920	W. FOWLER.
1920—1921	H. WILLIAMS.
1921—1922	D. E. S. BROWNE.
1922—1923	E. WALTON.
1923—1924	P. J. O'DONNELL, J.P.

Barry Urban District Council.

Dinner

GIVEN BY
The Chairman:
Mr. Dudley T. Howe, J.P.,
AT THE
Gladstone Road Girls' School
(Central Hall),
ON
Thursday, 22nd January, 1925,
at 7 p.m.

E. J. LLEWELLIN, PRINTER, CADOXTON, BARRY.

Sir Felix was back in Barry in early 1926 as chief guest at the Chamber of Trade dinner and his entire speech was devoted to stressing the G.W.R.'s commitment to Barry. He was aware that 'all sorts of things are said in South Wales' such as 'that the G.W.R. has canvassed against Barry', but this, he claimed, was 'absolutely untrue'. He assured his audience that 'our duty is to hold the balance evenly between the various ports—I want you to regard the G.W.R. as part and parcel of the Community of Barry'. He admitted that trade had declined sharply at the Docks and that a better station was urgently needed at Barry Dock, but reminded his audience that the G.W.R. paid £73,374 in rates and a weekly wage-bill in Barry of £10,000. He showed that he understood the uniqueness of Barry, telling them that 'you are the beings almost of a railway company' and promised them that as long as David Davies's grandson Colonel Davies was a director of the Company 'you need have no fear as to the welfare of Barry'. These were strong and emotional promises, but during that evening Sir Felix was to hear Councillor Dudley Howe talk of the 'unprecedented depression' at Barry and of the need for new factories and new continental shipping links. 'Today' he said in a phrase that summed up so much of the concern of his fellow councillors, 'Barry was the adopted child of the G.W.R.'. Councillors were planning a progressive Barry just as its economic *raison d'être* was being undermined and its trading prospects becoming more remotely controlled.

Sir Felix had been a guest of the Chamber of Trade. This organisation, which had been set up in 1922 to represent four hundred local traders, was now working closely with the Council to fight to improve Barry. They both co-operated in 1925 to set up the Barry Development Committee, and it was really at the meetings of these three organisations that the development of the town was being planned. The dominant voice in the Chamber of Trade was the local businessman Dan Evans, and on the Council the key men were Dudley Howe, a director of a local company, and Ben Carpenter, who was Deputy Docks Manager. In the 1920s they were the 'boosters' of Barry, determined to rescue the Docks, to fight off the challenge of Cardiff, both in terms of local government control and as a shopping centre, and to prove that the Urban District Council could offer financially sound and yet greatly improved services. They went on boosting and planning through coal crisis after coal crisis, and inevitably they were to come under attack. Council meetings were never anything other than stormy, and amongst what was really a very small group of men there were several personality clashes. The possibilities for tension and disagreement were enormous, for quite apart from trying to attract trade and protect jobs, from developing the Island and building new homes, the Council, as we have seen, was running local gas, electricity and water services, as well as health and hospital provision and a large school system. For the most part these councillors, Liberal or 'Independent' in politics, were to carry the majority of votes with them throughout the 1920s, and although there was a notorious election in 1928, when several well-established local leaders were defeated by Ratepayers candidates protesting against levels of expenditure and increased rates, these men were undoubtedly regarded by most as the natural leaders of the town. It was their Barry, as they had seemed to be the spokesmen of the best interests of the town and the shapers of a natural consensus.

The Ratepayers were to have their moments of glory at the end of the decade, but throughout this period the official opposition to the 'boosters' came from the steadily developing Labour Party. From the very moment

'ig. 88. :lection address of)udley Howe in Jrban District ;ouncil election of 928. *;areth Howe Coll.*

Barry Urban District Council Election, 1928.

To the Electors of the Cadoxton Ward.

LADIES AND GENTLEMEN,

On Monday, April 2nd, you will be called upon to elect a member of the Barry Urban District Council for the Cadoxton Ward, and I beg, once again, to offer myself as a candidate. For the last 15 years I have been your member, during which time I have striven to study your best interests, and, apart from the 4 years I served with His Majesty's Forces I think I can claim to have represented you faithfully and well.

Upon all occasions it has been my aim to represent the community as a whole, and not any particular section.

My activities in industry, education and public matters in general are well-known to many of you and my efforts in the direction of attracting new industries to our town, will, I believe, commend themselves to your consideration and confidence. A few months ago I was a member of a small deputation waiting upon Sir Felix J. C. Pole, General Manager of the Great Western Railway Company, impressing upon him our needs for industrial developments, and at his suggestion a Committee, consisting of two G.W.R. representatives, the Chairman of the Barry Urban District Council and myself, was appointed to investigate the possibilities of Barry from a G.W.R. point of view. That Committee has been at work for a few months and has, I can state with a degree of confidence, succeeded in arranging for the transfer of works to Barry that have hitherto been established on other parts of the G.W.R. system.

In addition to the foregoing I am actively engaged in co-operation with a few prominent townsmen in negotiations, which we hope will mean a fresh industry for Cadoxton Moors. These negotiations are at present in a position which might be jeopardised by publicity and I must consequently refrain from giving any further details.

Our present difficulties may be attributed to two causes. First, the burden of rates, and second, the absence of industry, other than shipment of coal. There is hope, as already indicated, that Barry will recover some of its former prosperity, but although your Urban District Councillors attempt by economy to reduce our rates, it must be borne in mind that the Cardiff Board of Guardians, and the Glamorgan County Council, should also be urged to reduce very considerably the demand they make upon us before we can make any substantial reduction.

I am making an effort personally to wait upon all electors before the election, but as this may be impossible, I am arranging to address two Public Meetings—one at Cadoxton Schools on Wednesday, March 28th, and one at Palmerston Schools on Friday, March 30th, both Meetings to commence at 7.30 p.m. At these Meetings questions will be welcomed.

Respectfully I beg to solicit your vote and interest, and remain,

Ladies and Gentlemen,

Yours faithfully,

DUDLEY HOWE.

Printed and Published by E. J. & I. J. LLEWELLIN, Cadoxton-Barry.

that War ended the managers, businessmen and shopkeepers who ran Barry knew that they were going to be engaged in a struggle to preserve their consensus against the rising claims of the Labour movement. As we have seen there was much talk of 'Bolshevism' in 1919 and 1920, and railway strikes and the general unrest seemed superficially at least to suggest that society itself was under threat. But revolution was never the issue. What was at stake, both nationally and locally, was the extent to which an existing structure of government and pattern of values were going to change to accommodate an increasingly well-organised Labour movement. The Unions were poised to fight for better wages and conditions and the Labour Party to broaden the whole area of political debate. At one level the 'boosters' were trying to implement their vision of Barry as a dynamic and progressive town whilst at another they were fighting to head off what they thought of as the sectional and irresponsible appeal of working-class politics.

Miners' leaders like William Brace, who had been the M.P. for South Glamorgan from 1906 to 1918, had contrived to sustain Lib-Labism as the official creed of the South Wales working class, but long before 1914 the sharper and firmer ideas of working-class independence and working-class power had become a reality in most towns and Barry was no exception.[17] There had been a strong Independent Labour Party branch active in adult education and propaganda and successful in electing local councillors. But even more, there had been an impressive degree of unionization. When the Amalgamated Society of Rail Servants had its A.G.M. at Barry in 1910 the General Secretary commented on the 'strong trade union sentiment' in the town and estimated that there were a greater number of Trade Unionists in all trades proportionate to the number of men employed, than any other town in the country. This local union strength was dominated by the A.S.R.S. and by 1914 that union had three branches in Barry with a combined membership of over 1,700.[18]

Edwardian Barry was a company town, and railway companies were notorious for their attempts to dominate their labour force. The Barry Railway Company was no exception and used economic and moral pressures to mould a town of model Victorian working men, regular in their habits and conscientious both at work and on their allotments. But Barry was also a new town, and that made all the difference. In a cosmopolitan town created late in the history of industrial society there was a tendency to accept new and contemporary ideas. This was not going to be a company town in which Victorian masters disciplined a proletarian work-force, for there were far too many professional people in the town eager to drink deep of the progressive gospel of the era. Adult education, social reform and municipal socialism had been in the air in Edwardian Barry and had been part of the town's image from the very beginning. In a sense this unique Barry spirit sanctioned Lib-Labism of a progressive and dynamic sort and

Barry Educational Society,
1925-1926.
(Inaugurated February 19th, 1901.)

PRESIDENT:
J. LOWDON, Esq., J.P.

VICE-PRESIDENTS:

Miss E. P. Hughes, M.A., LL.D.	Dudley T. Howe, Esq., *Chairman General Committee.*
Miss M. E. Meredith.	Col. J. A. Hughes, C.B.
Miss Esther Morgan, B.A.	Rev. D. H. Williams, M.A.
Miss Ellen Evans, M.A.	Major Edgar Jones, M.A.
Miss J. S. Fleming, LL.A.	Dr. P. W. Kent.
Miss Litchfield.	

COMMITTEE:

Mrs. Beatrice Lewis.	John Jones, Esq.
Mrs. J. R. Llewellyn.	T. Eddolls, Esq.
Miss H. Rowland.	Rev. R. H. Lomas, M.A.
Miss Llewellyn.	W. G. Rees, Esq., B.A.
Miss Ella Smith.	G. B. Davies, Esq.
Miss J. H. Thomas.	J. J. Joslin, Esq.

HON TREASURER:
Miss Edith Thomas, Jenner Park Girls' Schools.

HON. SECRETARY:
Mr. W. Humphreys, 85, Tynewydd Rd., Barry Docks.

Name Mr. Dudley T. Howe
This Card to be produced at Lectures.

Barry Dock News.

Syllabus of Lectures.

1925.
Friday, Feb. 13—At Wesley Hall, Holton Road
"The Child of To-day and Long Ago."
Lecturer:
Dr. STANLEY WATKINS, M.A.,
University College, Exeter.

*Friday, March 13—At Unity Hall, Barry.
"Sunlight and Childhood."
Lecturer:
Dr. C. W. SALEEBY, LONDON.

* *Illustrated by Lantern Slides.*

LECTURES TO COMMENCE AT 7.30 P.M.

Fig. 89. Membership card and syllabus of lectures of Barry Educational Society 1925-26. *Gareth Howe Coll.*

also sanctioned a responsible form of trade unionism. When the Amalgamated Society of Railway Servants (A.S.R.S.) were at Barry in 1910, J. E. Williams, their General Secretary, could talk of the fact that there were already Labour councillors, guardians and magistrates in Barry and at the same time refer to the fact that the town was 'in the van of progress so far as its municipal enterprise is concerned'. The two things were clearly related, for the special circumstances of Barry's growth had allowed the town to slip into Edwardian Progressivism far more surely than any other town in South Wales. Indeed one could argue that Edwardian Progressivism was long to be the distinctive hallmark of Barry and that much of the town's pride and optimism and certainly its strong belief in education can only be understood in that light. Nevertheless it would be a mistake to assume that Barry's Labour Movement, sanctioned as it was by local reformers, was in any way lacking in determination and militancy. The local branches of the A.S.R.S. went on expanding not because of the peculiarities of local politics but because they had fought first for a Conciliation Board, then they had challenged that Board to improve wages and conditions and then they had stood four-square with their national union in the great unrest of 1912. Barry's railwaymen were not well-behaved Lib-Labers, rather they were hardened and utterly professional trade unionists.

The War had greatly strengthened the trade union movement and paved the way for a major post-war confrontation. As the industrial challenge loomed so many former Lib-Labs and Progressives found themselves increasingly out of sympathy with this more aggressive working class. In the years after 1918 there were many local Labour Parties and many Trades Councils who found themselves standing alone against a formidable middle-class phalanx. This was never entirely to be the position in Barry, for there a decisive and distinct section of the old Edwardian Progressivism firmly took its stand with Labour, and was even to survive moments of doubt and criticism during the great industrial unrest of 1921 and 1926. The local Labour Movement continued to be sanctioned by an older and wider tradition, and there was never to be a stark choice between middle-class respectability and working-class militancy. In the General Election of 1918 Captain Russell Jones's 6,607 Labour votes did not come entirely from the working-class, and in the County Council elections of 1919, though unsuccessful, a Baptist minister the Reverend Howard Ingli James tried to give expression to a viewpoint that was not 'Bolshevist or even Socialist' but was concerned to 'uplift and better the condition of all the people who are unfairly and unjustly treated, and to make life a brighter and gladder thing for everybody'. An element of Fabian and Christian Socialism went on enriching the local Labour Party and allowed a Cardiff barrister, J. A. Lovet Fraser, to pick up over 9,000 votes in the General Election of 1922 and to beat the prominent businessman J. C. Meggitt, who had tried to revive the old Progressive cause, into third place. At the time of this election there were complaints that the vast majority of Barry's ministers were anti-Labour, but in fact the Reverend R. H. Lomas had become a member of the Party and spoke of the local Labour leaders as 'men and women of intelligence, character and idealism and faith' with whom he would find it an honour to work. There was a Liberal revival in the Election of 1923, and the Labour candidate Tom Worrall, a Barry welder, was badly beaten into third place. In 1924 when the tide was running for Labour again, a new candidate, Ellis Lloyd, mounted an intensive and wide-ranging campaign, which took him into second place with over eleven thousand votes and well ahead of the Liberals. Major Cope contrived to hold the seat for the Conservatives but only because the Progressive and working-class vote was divided between the Labour and Liberal parties.

The parliamentary Labour candidates made a broad appeal, but the bulk of their votes came from a trade union movement which was still engaged in a massive struggle. By 1919 the National Union of Railwaymen had over 2,000 members in Barry, organised in five branches, and these, together with the members of the Dockers' Union and the Coal Trimmers, formed a sure local basis for the national struggles in the 1920s. The Docks were brought to a standstill in October 1919 and again in April 1921, when the Barry Railway Strike Committee voted to express their regret that the national leaders of the N.U.R. had let down the miners, their partners in the Triple Alliance. In 1926 the two thousand Barry N.U.R. members were able to organize an effective local manifestation of the General Strike. After the nine dramatic days were over, the town was able to congratulate itself on the 'philosophical calm' that had prevailed, for the strikers had behaved with 'exemplary good taste' and 'not a single case of lawlessness occurred'. The *Barry Dock News* was sure that 'one thing at any rate will be said of us by the historian of the future and that is that in troublesome times we did not lose our heads nor our reputation for fortitude and courage.' There was much praise for Councillor Dudley Howe, the local Emergency Officer, for Councillor Charles Griffiths, the Food Officer, and for the many volunteers who had come to their help, but this emergency administration was by no means in control of the town. It was reported that a local tradesman had sent his van to Barry Station to collect flour only to be told that he would first have to collect a permit from the Unity Hall headquarters of the Central Strike Committee. The buses went on running and a shift at Rank's Mill ignored their Union's instructions, but Jim Gerry, the Secretary of the Central Committee, assured Howe that he himself spoke for the vast majority of the local population and reported that three out of every four men were on strike. There were strong complaints against the Council's decision to let Howe use the Council Offices to recruit volunteers, but at the railwaymen's Unity Hall, which had been opened in 1923 by Jimmy Thomas of the N.U.R., the Central Committee had a very useful and well-placed headquarters, and they were also to use the Romilly Cinema for their well-attended mass meetings. In Barry many things helped to take the tension out of the situation, huge crowds flocked to the beaches, there were nightly concerts and lots of jokes and amusing incidents as bicycles, old cars and varied carts and wagons were pressed into service, but there was no disguising an impressive display of working-class solidarity. David Watts Morgan, the Rhondda miners' leader, came to the Theatre Royal to tell the workmen of Barry that the miners had been 'strengthened by your magnificent response'.[19]

It was at times of industrial unrest, or perhaps during general elections, that the Labour movement received most publicity, but the strong local union structure provided a whole range of services for its members and the day-to-day administration of union branches, of industrial relations and of benevolent funds, was carried out by branch officials who were developing skills and experience that were greatly strengthening the local Labour Party. The railwaymen in particular gave Labour its backbone in Barry. There had long been Labour representatives on the Urban Council, but in 1919 Josiah Finch, railwayman, Methodist Sunday School Teacher and secretary of the Constituency Labour Party, won the first County Council seat for Labour in Barry by defeating John Lowden, a prominent Barry Liberal. Finch was succeeded as Constituency secretary by E. C. Gough, a railway clerk who was himself elected to the local Council in 1920 in an election in which Labour gained five of the seven seats fought. There was now a real Labour presence on the Council, and although in a permanent minority, and always likely to lose their seats, they kept up a fight for more and cheaper municipal housing and especially for a far more dynamic response to local unemployment. They saw the relief work that the Council had been providing at the Island, at Cold Knap and on the road works at Port Road as only a 'toying with the problem' and as undermining the trade union movement. At every step the actions and policies of Dudley Howe and the boosters were assessed and debated by the four or five Labour councillors and by the Joint Trades Council. At the time of the General Strike Labour Councillors E. C. Gough, Mrs. Beatrice Lewis, the first woman on the Barry Council and the wife of a coal-trimmer, W. Beck and Fred Cook provided full assistance to the Central Strike Committee, and left nobody in any doubt that they saw themselves as the elected representatives of a local Labour force.

In the years after the General Strike the whole future of Barry as a port remained the main concern of local councillors. In December 1928 Sir Felix Pole came to Barry to meet the officers of the Development Committee and once again to give evidence of his company's concern for the town. He agreed with them that Barry Dock station was far from adequate (amongst other complaints he conceded that 'passengers had to use the same approach as sailors of all nationalities') but at that time there was no money available for any improvements. He did promise that Barry Island station would be improved, but then rather ominously added that 'they had been too prone to regard Barry as a coal shipment port', for 'in Barry Island they had wonderful possibilities of a great seaside resort that would advantage Cardiff as well as Barry'. In fact Sir Felix's news was that the G.W.R. were to close three coal tips at the Docks. Things were now bad at Barry and there were weeks in late 1928 and early 1929 when there were almost three thousand workmen unemployed. At a meeting called in February 1929 in order to set up a Distress Committee the Reverend Dynvant Williams spoke of 'very acute' distress in the Cadoxton area and of how 'street after street, home after home were without clothes and fuel and the cupboards were empty' and a Mr. Whittock reported that there were 'families at Barry Island really down and out who do not know where to turn' quite apart from the 'scores of families that we know nothing at all about.'

There was a minor shipping boom in early 1929 and unemployment dropped by about a thousand but the theme of local distress was to dominate the 1929 General Election in Barry. Two prominent Labour councillors had been defeated in the March local elections, but the Tories knew that Labour would pose a serious threat in the June General Election, especially as the Liberals were certain to use the sudden accession of wealth from the Lloyd George Funds to mount a more serious campaign than in 1924. The *Barry Dock News* spoke of how 'Barry, committed as it is to extensive developments and dependent on the revival of industry, can have no doubt as to its choice', good municipal government at Barry and the recovery of the docks, necessitating the re-election of Sir William Cope and of a Conservative Government. The last edition of the paper before the Election carried a front page blank except for an indication that a vote for Cope was 'The Road to Prosperity' and inside a rather frenetic news story spoke of 'great new industries at Barry and Ely'. In what was described as the Conservatives' 'bold effort to relieve unemployment' a new chocolate factory employing a thousand would be developed at Ely and several hundred jobs would be created at a new factory at the Docks at Barry. The source for this news was Cope himself and as far as the Barry development was concerned it was made clear that there would be no go-ahead if the Conservatives were defeated.

Such reporting was sure evidence that the Labour candidate was feared. It was quite easy to depict Labour as the party of the General Strike, of industrial chaos and of wild nationalisation schemes, but it was more difficult to do down a responsible, respected, educated and distinguished-looking candidate like Ellis Lloyd who had been nursing the constituency assidously since his defeat in 1924.[20] The *Barry Dock News* warning was that 'Mr. Ellis Lloyd is an outstanding case of a pink person tied to a very red standard'. It argued that 'Mr. Lloyd's Socialism has the same deceiving quality as that of Mr. Ramsay MacDonald, and Mr. Philip Snowden, but the electorate must ask themselves whether in the face of the extreme majority in the Socialist ranks such a policy would prevail in the undesirable event of a Socialist government'. It went on to warn 'fugitive voters' of the danger of voting for a candidate who had yet to define his position and who was therefore 'rather silently tied to the nebulous fanaticism' of the Party responsible for 'the treacherous blow of 1926'. The warnings were in vain, for the distress was real in Barry and the Labour movement knew that they had a good candidate. Ellis Lloyd won Barry for Labour in an election in which the party gained over 130 seats and came back to power to form a second government. The Barry Tories regretted the defeat of a man who had given 'ten-and-a-half years of faithful service', placed the blame fully on the twelve thousand or so who had voted Liberal and waited fearfully for the rule of a party that 'promises heaven on earth and therefore in terms of practical administration nothing'. For the Labour movement in Barry, Ellis Lloyd's victory was a tremendous boost and a new confidence became apparent in all its activities. The local elections of 1930 were more keenly contested than ever before and it was reported that Labour was fighting every ward and making 'extraordinary efforts to gain success'. Most Labour candidates were defeated but Leonard Finch captured the Castleland Ward and Stan Awbery was only defeated by Charles Griffiths in the Court Ward after two recounts. What Ellis Lloyd had shown the local Labour Party was that Labour need not be just a section, a minority within Barry society, that Labour could move out from its trade union base to become the voice of local consensus. Labour was only to hold the Barry seat for two years, but an example had been given, and in the Thirties the minority group of Labour councillors were inspired by the knowledge that victory was possible.

The Barry of 1930 offered scenes of 'Victorian poverty' and the large pool of unemployed men posed a constant challenge to local politicians, but the town was not standing still, and whatever the long-term economic prospects, everything was done to ensure that improvement went on. Barry had to remain a modern town, it could not afford to become a historical curiosity. With so many improvements completed at the Island and Cold Knap there was more and more talk of Barry as 'The Blackpool of Wales' and more and more thought had to be given to the devising of entertainments to ensure that the visitors kept on coming. The Chamber of Trade were always keen on a summer Carnival with a procession, bands, fancy dress and the crowning of a carnival queen and this soon became a fairly regular feature of the Barry calendar. So successful was the 1932 Carnival that the profits came to well over £400 and it was decided that these should be used to fund illuminations. In September 1933 the Barry sea front was lit up for the first time and the whole Island was 'bathed in the glow of a myriad coloured lights with the sea as an ever changing background'. Now that Barry had its September lights and therefore a longer season, one local writer found it 'gratifying to think no longer will the amusement caterers fold up their tents like the Arabs and silently steal away at the end of August'. The Island remained the big attraction but the resort went on trying to improve its status. One of the most important events in the Barry of the inter-war years was the opening of the War Memorial Hall in November 1932. Political and economic difficulties had held up the unveiling of a Cenotaph and the opening of the Memorial Hall, and, given the significant role that Barrians had played in the Great War, these delays had occasioned a great deal of local criticism. Barry now had its Memorial Hall and this distinguished and distinctive building was to be a cause of much controversy, but at its opening at least there was a general understanding that the resort of Barry had gained a new amenity. The auditorium could hold 1,372 people. There was a large stage, an orchestra pit and four dressing rooms. The town now had a good theatre and concert hall and an ideal conference centre which it was hoped would attract national organisations.

Barry was to be proud of what Lord Davies, the main sponsor of the new building, referred to as 'the austere beauty' of the Memorial Hall, but it was never to be loved in quite the same way as another of the town's institutions. Bindles dance hall at Cold Knap had opened in 1928 and by the end of the 1920s it had secured a reputation as one of the best-designed and most modern dance halls in South Wales. Coaches were to bring dancers to Barry from Cardiff and the Valleys but this was one amenity that the people of Barry were to claim very much as their own, especially in the winter months, and the list of local associations and organisations holding annual balls at Bindles grew longer and longer. In February 1929 local government officers and their wives had a ball in which they had officially welcomed the 'Paul Jones' to Barry, and that dance it was reported had 'placed everyone on happy terms with each other'. Since then 'the foxtrots were soon going with a swing', the Melodists 'surpassed themselves' and the 'coloured lights for which Bindles is noted commenced to flash in upon the company, red, green, blue, rose and fell as if to the rhythm of the music'. The most popular dance of the evening was the Valeta waltz, and the dancers 'clamoured for

Plate LXXXII. Memorial Hall, Barry, south elevation, soon after construction. *R. W. Thomas Coll.*

Fig. 90. Advertisement for Bindles dance hall in *Barry & District News*, 26 October 1934. *Gareth Howe Coll.*

several encores and got them'. On this occasion the beneficiary was to be the National Benevolent and Orphan Fund, but for many years to come national and local charities were to benefit from dances held at Bindles. In these dances local organisations and groups of employees established an *esprit-de-corps* and identity that fed back into the personality of the town, and at the same time the men and women of Barry, dressed in their dinner jackets and long dresses and dancing to the latest American music, were asserting that they belonged to a town capable of offering first-class, stylish and thoroughly contemporary entertainment. It was at Bindles that Barry people felt most like fully-fledged citizens of the 20th century.[21]

In June 1929 an advertisement pointed out that at the Palace Theatre, Josephine Earl and Dick Henderson could be 'seen and heard' in a film called 'For Men Only'. The Palace had become 'Barry's Talking Theatre' and only the second cinema in Wales to instal a sound system. A local reporter visited 'the Talkies' with some scepticism but remained to be impressed, although admitting that 'the house has to be in absolute quietness in order that the words can be heard distinctly'. Soon, as the advertisements suggested, 'everybody was talking of the Talkies' and the cinema began to play a larger part in most people's lives. There were constant rows on the Council as to whether charities should be allowed to organise Sunday film shows, and Councillor Farr had no doubt that if this right was to be conceded 'they would be slowly moving towards Sodom'. Others were more concerned by the dominant hold that Hollywood had established over film-goers, and in 1930 the people of Barry were to hear of one minister's concern as to what the American film magnates were offering. In films he found 'untrue, grotesque, ridiculous views of life and human nature spiced with the nasty sweepings of silly and salacious minds' and yet 'any old stuff the Yanks like to boost for us we swallow without a murmur'. The coming of sound to places like Barry made matters worse. According to the Reverend Mr. Selley, the magnates had cried 'Eureka' and his sad reflection was that 'Guess now they'll kinda eat outer yer hand'. As the 1930s went on, there were to be many ministers who would reflect on the loss of their flocks to the appeal of Hollywood. When the next American

Fig. 91. Advertised programme of Royal Cinema for week beginning 29 October 1934.
Gareth Howe Coll.

invasion of Barry came the soldiers were to find a town long accustomed to American idioms and very much enchanted by American music.

Dance-hall and cinema proprietors ensured that Barry remained abreast if not ahead of the times but they could hardly be said to be developing their properties on a wave of local prosperity, rather were they offering diversions from a prevailing depression. In 1932 Councillor Maslin, an out-spoken and very prominent local leader, gave it as his opinion that 'the growth of the town had far outgrown itself since the Great War' and the evidence for that was that 'hundreds of people were unable to earn a living'. Throughout the 1920s Barry had suffered as the coal industry had suffered, but now there was a national depression and the growing problems of the Docks were very apparent. Keen observers of the shipping trade noticed how British ships were lying idle and that only foreign ships were keeping dockers busy. It was also noticed that as ships got larger so the capacity of Barry Docks was getting smaller. There were again complaints that Barry was not being able to compete fully as other docks were favoured, but the G.W.R. countered with the argument that given the decline in trade they would have been justified in closing even more of the coal hoists at the Docks. There were those who were prepared to blame the workmen for Barry's decline, and both shipowners and the G.W.R. agreed that restrictive practices by the fifteen hundred coal-trimmers, especially with regard to the night shift, had made Barry less competitive in terms of bunkering than for example the ports of the North-East.

But whatever the national, regional and local reasons for the collapse in trade, Barry now had a major unemployment problem and this was a major challenge for local institutions and agencies. After 1930 the situation was deteriorating month by month and the nadir came in 1933 when there were over 4,000 men and women unemployed in Barry. This represented over 40 per cent of the labour force at a time when the population of the town was 38,330. Government policy was to pay unemployment benefit at subsistence levels to the unemployed and then to leave the more general question of dealing with unemployment to various local and charitable organisations. Coping with unemployment became the last great task of voluntary agencies and in taking on this task they were playing a vital role in changing attitudes towards the whole question of organising social and welfare services. In Barry the lead came from ministers like the Reverend Austen Davies, the Reverend H. G. Fiddick and the Reverend R. H. Lomas, who was Secretary of the Churches Movement to Help The Unemployed. Huge audiences packed into meetings organised by these ministers and there was soon a whole range of local activities organised for the unemployed and pressure for an unemployed centre to be opened. The first activities to be organised were sing-songs and discussions on current events such as the war in China, and out of these developed literary classes in which the unemployed were taught how to appreciate good books and also gym classes. Mr. Lomas was soon talking of these classes developing into a 'University of the Unemployed' but his first aim was always to use whatever centres emerged to provide some kind of work. By April 1933 there was a workshop centre at the Subway Road under the management of Dick Hughes, with benches provided by local firms, including Vickery and Rendell, and soon a hundred men were repairing boots, doing woodwork and helping to build their own clubroom. About 170 men, mostly young and married, were members of the centre, and they were reported to have already organised a cricket team and two soccer teams, one of which competed in a local league.

The voluntary agencies in Barry as elsewhere were only touching the surface of the problem and were in truth only helping to sustain the morale and self-respect of a minority of the unemployed. In general the unemployed either left Barry to look for work in the new boom areas around London or Birmingham, or just waited for the upswing in trade to come. Such a wait was a long one, for new jobs became available very slowly. In May 1934 the Barry Employment Exchange indicated that unemployment stood at only 87

Plate LXXXIII. H.M.S. *York*, led by tug *Windsor*, arriving at Barry Docks in June 1933.
M.I. Washburn Coll.

less than a year before, but that nonetheless over 600 jobs had been filled since the disastrous Christmas period. Since January there had been 150 new jobs for seamen, 40 for coal-trimmers and railwaymen and 100 at the cement works. In addition almost 100 of the women and girls registered as unemployed had found seasonal work at the Island. The unemployed total however still stood at the daunting figure of 3,500, and even that did not fully convey the amount of distress at Barry, for, as a number of reporters pointed out, the town had the additional problem of low wages. In the years since 1929 the coal-trimmers had experienced a sharp fall in wages, and with half-a-dozen or so coal tips closed, the coal-tippers found it expedient to accept a lower minimum in order to keep Barry competitive. Inevitably local traders felt the draught from this very noticeable decline in living standards and there were references to the sixty or so empty shops in the town's main shopping centres. There was hardship too amongst traders and landladies and landlords, who were dependent on visitors to the town. A report spoke of how 'the lack of spending power in the South Wales coalfield' had greatly reduced the income from seaside activities and yet local business people still had to pay their over-heads and rents. The result was that many small seaside traders and boarding house keepers were 'on the margin of poverty'. Almost inevitably the Depression was confirming that Barry would be a resort for trippers and not for holiday-makers and national conferences. Barry Island was not going to provide much help in allowing a town to escape from the Great Depression.

As with other periods in history, the Depression is best approached in terms of the lives of the individual men and women who lived through it, but inevitably at the time far more attention was paid to the fate of the town itself. The stagnation at the Docks and the slump in living standards was threatening to undermine the whole municipal structure of Barry. It was one thing to boost and improve a town with a flourishing local economy at a time when there was much patriotic talk of Reconstruction, but it was quite another to sustain optimism and pride when step by step the local economy seemed to be disintegrating. As problems increased there were inevitably those who wondered whether the town could survive as any kind of entity. In 1930 a dinner was held to mark the passing of the local Board of Guardians, and as for customs purposes Barry had already been merged with Cardiff, a very prominent local journalist and politician, J. R. Llewellyn, wondered whether the time had come for a more general merger with the nearby city. At the same dinner a Cardiff businessman, J. Llewellyn Morgan, confessed that 'Barry had had its chance and had not taken advantage of it'. Not surprisingly, J. R. Llewellyn's own paper now suggested that 'the balance of argument' would seem to be in favour of a merger, for 'single comparatively small towns like small businesses find it increasingly difficult to stand up to modern competition'.[22]

The Barry Council had pressed on with improvement, building new houses and modernising local services. Its greatest achievement in these years had been the guaranteeing of the water supply. Since 1890 the town had depended on water from wells at Biglis Moors but not only had this water been very hard water, but it had become increasingly difficult to pipe it to some of the new housing on the heights above the town. There were even stories of housewives collecting rain water in bottles for their weekly washing. For years the Council had tried to get Government help to improve the water supply but it was only in 1930 that Councillor Charles Griffiths, Chairman of the Gas, Water and Electricity Committee, was able to conclude a deal that allowed Barry to purchase water from the Taff Fechan Water Board. Now Barry was to have abundant soft water from a new concrete retainer near St. Lythan's. The scheme had cost £165,000 and it ensured not only good water for the town but also for the G.W.R., who had been party to the scheme and who saw it as making Barry more attractive for industrialists. This provision of better water had long been an ambition of Councillors like Charles Griffiths and in a way its completion marked the final step in Barry's municipalisation, but it came at a time when few other such bold ventures could be envisaged.

As we have seen Barry's local government structure was responsible for gas, electricity, water, hospitals, schools, parks and recreational activities and much else besides, and all these things had to be financed from the rates. As the Depression tightened so the pressure on the rates increased and so the finances of local government became more and more a matter of public debate and it was during this debate that many began to wonder whether Barry could survive. Throughout these years the Barry Ratepayers held meetings to condemn what they thought to be the extravagance of the Council, and in 1930 they achieved a good deal of publicity for their claim that the town was faced with 'an immense indebtedness'. The Chairman of the Ratepayers, Mr. A. E. Baker, estimated the debt to be £846,859 10*s*. 9*d*. which worked out at £21 14*s*. 0*d*. per head and meant that interest payments alone accounted for a 3/- in the pound rate. In the spring of 1931 a rate increase of 9*d*. was announced, making the total rate charge 8*s*. 9*d*. in the pound for the next half year, and not long after what were described as 'drastic cuts' were made in the salaries of local officials. It was said that the Council and its officials 'were in a state of warfare'. At the next half-yearly meeting of the Finance Committee the recommendation was that there should be another 6*d*. rate increase, but in the end the Council decided on a rate of 9*s*. in the pound for the half-year, the equivalent of 18*s*. 0*d*. in the pound for the whole year. It was at this meeting of the Finance Committee that Councillor Tom Davies, a Ratepayers' representative from the Park Ward, summed up the fears of many local business people with respect to the prospects of the town:

'I am sure that it is already a ruined town. This summer I know of a large number of people who have left Barry hoping that they can live cheaper in Cardiff where the rates are 12*s.* 1*d.* in the pound. Barry is a quietly declining town and I dread to think of the future.'

Barry was having a bad Depression. Many of the coal tips were idle and many shopkeepers had boarded up their premises, but the financial crisis affecting the Council was the product of a much wider set of circumstances. The local coal trade was suffering, but the Depression was a national phenomenon and its tentacles stretched into Barry from a number of directions. Barry's slump was of course directly related to the far more catastrophic slump in the South Wales Valleys, for less coal was being mined and fewer trippers were coming in on the excursion trains, but the links were more complicated than that. Barry, like most of the coal-mining valleys, was part of the County of Glamorgan and it was that authority that had to carry the brunt of the social consequences of mass unemployment in South Wales.[23] As the Barry town rates increased so local councillors became more and more eager to point out that it was the County Council who were very largely to blame. In 1931, for example, when the Barry half-yearly rate was fixed at 8*s.* 9*d.* in the pound, it was explained that the 9*d.* increase was mainly due to an increased demand of £18,676 from the County Council, and that working on the basis of a yearly rate, the County Council would receive 9*s.* 1½*d.* as compared to the Urban Council's 8*s.* 4*d.*, 'which showed that the County contribution was more than the whole of the local expenditure.' This whole question of the County precept now became a major issue in Barry politics. In 1931 the town was represented on the County Council by three Independent members, but they found themselves on an authority which had been Labour controlled since 1925. It was not difficult then for the increased expenditure of the County Council and the new demands imposed on Barry's ratepayers by the precept to be attributed to Socialist extravagance. Labour councillors like Fred Cook and Len Finch did their best to argue that the County were faced with quite staggering problems in areas like the Rhondda and that public assistance alone accounted for over half of the increase in the precept. In general, though, the critics of the County seemed to have the more powerful case.

Prejudices against the County developed apace and criticisms of the Socialist majority punctuated every debate on local finance. The threat of the County was a considerable factor in influencing those who felt that Barry would be better off if it threw in its lot with the City of Cardiff. In 1931 Councillor Dr. Owens wanted a strong protest sent from the Barry Council to the County Council and a meeting was arranged for the members of the Finance Committee to meet the local County Councillors. Later that year the Council agreed to a resolution moved by Councillor Beck that property should be assessed uniformly for rating purposes throughout the County.

CELEBRITIES OF PENARTH AND BARRY—By MATT

Fig. 92.
Cartoons of local celebrities by Matt, 1930.
Sunday Graphic.
Gareth Howe Coll.

His argument was that in Barry, which had just been transferred into Glamorgan for public assistance purposes, houses that could be rented at 7*s.* 6*d.* a week were assessed at £12 whilst Rhondda houses which could be rented at the same rate were assessed at £9 so that 'Barry Ratepayers are called upon to make a much larger contribution to the rates of the County than the ratepayers in many other districts in the County'. There was criticism too of the way in which the 'Socialists', as they were always termed, conducted the Council, and in particular of the way in which, on gaining control in 1925, they had immediately taken all the aldermanic seats so as to guarantee their hold on committees. There were several councillors in Barry who thought that the County was actually hindering economic recovery, for the rates were far too high for prospective industrialists and the authority was contributing substantially to what Councillor Dr. Owens described as South Wales's reputation for being 'a Little Russia'. In the run-up to the County Council elections in 1934 somebody writing as 'Watch Dog' drew the attention of Barry electors to the fact that the County Rate, which stood at 6*s.* 2*d.* when the Socialists took over, now stood at 14*s.* 9½*d.* His argument was that since 1931 Glamorgan was one of only eight out of 61 counties to increase their rates, and that whilst a Government grant of £60,000 in 1933 should have led to a 6*d.* reduction, the relief given was only 1*d.* But what clinched 'Watch Dog's' case that Socialists were 'spendthrifts'

Plate LXXXIV. Election handbill issued by Dorothy M. Rees, Labour candidate.
Gareth Howe Coll.

County Council Election.

BARRY DOCKS DIVISION.

DOROTHY M. REES

THE

Labour Candidate

For 3 years Mrs. Dorothy M. Rees has been the elected representative for Barry Docks on the Glamorgan County Council.

The Barry Labour Party asks you for a RENEWAL OF CONFIDENCE in the service that she is rendering to every section of the community.

POLLING DAY—MARCH 1st—ST. DAVID'S DAY, 8 a.m. to 8 p.m.

Pleidlais o Ymddiriedaeth ar Ddydd Gwyl Dewi

and 'extravagant' was that in the past year members' expenses had totalled over £5,000 and that whilst 27 Councillors, 25 of whom were Socialists, had personally claimed over £50, all three of Barry's Independents had claimed under £50.

In fact Labour was to pick up a County Council seat in Barry Dock in 1934 with the election of Mrs. Dorothy Rees, and as she was immediately made an Alderman, there was a by-election in which another Labour man, William East, was successful, thereby giving Barry two Labour representatives on the County Council. Meanwhile the criticisms of the County became even sharper. 'Old Barrian' wrote of how 'the introduction of Socialist politics into the affairs of the County has set up a political tyranny' and Councillor Maslin argued that 'if there had been less Socialism in this part of Glamorgan, and had the Socialists done one iota as much for trade and industry as they have to embarrass it, Glamorgan would not be in the position it is to-day'. To Maslin 'the Socialists are the people who are trying to gull the poor chap at the street corner, telling him he can have anything he wants when they know they can't fulfill it'. In 1936 ex-Councillor Ernest Williams told the Chamber of Trade that Glamorgan's Public Assistance Committee was far 'too lavish' and it was that knowledge that prevented English counties from giving any help. His experience was that 'any talk of economy at its meetings was like a voice talking in the wilderness'.[24]

Barry felt that it was under constant pressure from a desperate County but there were several other developments which had intensified the crisis over rates. In 1935 the Council sent a delegation to the Minister of Health to press for additional assistance to the town. The Council's evidence referred to the 36 per cent fall in the volume of trade at the port since 1929, to a decline in the Rateable Value from £311,137 to £211,161 in the same period, to the dwindling population and to an unemployment rate of 44 per cent. The Council could point to savings of over £12,000 in these years and to the postponement of sewerage, house-building and seaside schemes, but the situation was still serious. The crisis, it was explained, had been brought about not only by the depression in coal and the claims of the County but by a whole series of Government measures which had undermined the Council's finances. The Local Government Act of 1929 had been a disaster for Barry as it involved an immediate loss by de-rating of rateable value amounting to over £82,000. A year later had come the Railways (Valuation for Rating) Act which specified that the G.W.R. was to be assessed as a whole so the rates it paid at Barry would be adjusted in the light of its national investment pattern. This was to lead to the Barry Council losing another £14,561 of rateable value at a time when the G.W.R. was paying about 12 per cent of the town's total rates. In addition, the Gas Undertakings Act of 1929 restricted the application of gas profits to the rates, whilst the National Economy Act of 1931 had severely reduced the level of educational grants to the Council.[25]

Barry had suffered many blows but it was now hoped that the Government would begin to help the town by reducing the rates of interest on the money borrowed to finance unemployment relief schemes, by continuing various other grants and loans and perhaps, above all, by including the town in the schedule of Special Areas.[26] It was now becoming very apparent that new industries were needed to help reduce the level of local unemployment and yet there was very little indication that businessmen were interested in the area. Barry's case was very well put in the 1937 *Industrial Survey of South Wales,* which stressed that there were 'very large areas of land at the dockside and adjoining the docks, which are available for industrial undertakings', but which then had to add that whilst 'this is one of the most remarkable sites in South Wales' it was 'not within the Special Area' as defined in 1934. The survey went on to argue that it had been a 'serious error to exclude the coastal districts' as 'the numbers of unemployed in Newport, Cardiff, Barry and Penarth are almost as large as those in the Rhondda'.[27] In 1935 four thousand of Barry's insured work force of ten thousand were unemployed and the local Council could see little prospect of new employers being attracted to the available sites in the town.

These were difficult days for men and women who had gone into local government and who found themselves battling to cut expenditure and to save money, whilst at the same time having to offer some relief to the unemployed, to improve housing and to maintain educational standards. Barry councillors found themselves agreeing to build more Council houses at Buttrills and elsewhere so as to reduce the waiting list of 930 names at the very time they were being denounced by the Ratepayers and by a number of Public Economy Associations. On every front there were social initiatives the Council should take, and yet the demands were for 'commonsense', for 'capable and reliable administrators' and for a 'curtailing of local expenditure'. Articles in the local press argued that 'the more businessmen we have on the Council the better' and that the need was for 'not politicians' but 'sensible persons'. In fact the town was still in the hands of Independents who tended to be from a business or managerial background and who were, in a favourite phrase of the time, 'heavy ratepayers'. The great financial squeeze of the early and mid thirties became very much the personal problem of Councillor Dudley Howe, the Chairman of the Finance Committee, and he was backed up by E. L. Pritchard, the Council's Financial Controller and by other Independent Councillors like Charles Griffiths, D. J. Boon and W. T. Ace, and by Dan Evans, who joined the Council in 1932. As these leaders of the town, some of whom were Conservative, some Liberal and some genuinely Independent, tackled the immense problems of those years and tried to counter the logic of the

Ratepayers, so they had to face up to what they saw as the danger of a Labour take-over in Barry itself. The deepening of the Depression was changing the nature of local government and making social issues the main subject of debate. The feeling of the Independents was that the state of the country had encouraged Labour to emphasise national policies and issues at elections and so make it more difficult for Independents to stress their own personal qualities and their individual hopes for the town of Barry. In 1933 Charles Griffiths warned the local Conservatives of the danger of Socialist predominance on the Council and argued that 'the effort to fight Socialism is needed more at the present moment than at any other time'. In the subsequent elections the local press spoke in very revealing terms of how 'from the commencement the Socialist candidates fought their battles on purely political grounds'. In 1934 a report of a Council Meeting at which the rates had been adjusted spoke of how 'during the debate, politics were brought in by the Socialist Section'. The Socialists were obviously bringing far more urgency into local government elections and were displaying a new confidence and sense of purpose. In 1934 Councillor Holbrook warned the Barry Conservatives that there were urgent lessons to be learned from the Socialists, who 'always used local contests as stepping stones to success in parliamentary elections' and who did not just create an organisation a few weeks before an election, but rather 'as soon as one election was over began preparing for the next'.

The 1931 General Election was a disaster for the Labour Party nationally, and Barry was just one of the many seats Labour lost, as Ramsay MacDonald's recently installed National Government won a landslide victory. What was vital at Barry was the absence of a Liberal candidate. A week before the election the highly respected elder-statesman and local businessman, J. C. Meggitt, who described himself as a lifelong Liberal who had voted Liberal in the last twelve elections in the division, came out as a National Government supporter for he felt it was 'putting Nation before Party'. He warned electors to beware of the Socialist programme recently agreed to at Scarborough as 'its application would ruin any country in the world'. This is a useful indication of how Barry's Liberals were thinking, for Ellis Lloyd, the Labour candidate, was to poll almost exactly the same number of votes which had given him victory in 1928 and yet now he was defeated by a huge majority of almost 12,000 votes. In Barry, as in many other areas, the 1931 Election really killed off that Late Victorian Progressive Liberalism that had characterized many business, professional and chapel-going families. In a new age of political polarization there were to be many Barry families who thought that the Conservative-Labour battle did less than justice to the political identity of a town that had sprung up in the Progressive age. For many years a phrase that would be heard was that 'Barry was really a Liberal town'. In fact the division now, and for the next nine years, belonged to Patrick Munro who had been described at his adoption meeting in 1930 as 'a certain winner'. He had returned to this country after twenty-two years in the Sudan, he had 'a charming wife', he 'spoke well', he was 'tall and athletic' and, leaving nothing to chance, he could even claim to have played rugby thirteen times for Scotland.

The defeat of Labour's much-loved Ellis Lloyd was to be a bitter blow for the Barry Party, but in some ways the very formation of the National Government had provided a new challenge to local Labour Parties. Although Labour was badly defeated in the October 1931 Election, one senses that what had happened at Westminster had put new fire into Labour's belly and given a new edge to their rhetoric. In his campaign Ellis Lloyd had spoken of how he was now experiencing 'a feeling of new freedom', for he could see that the financial crisis had not been of Labour's making but rather had been a crisis of Capitalism itself, 'only Russia was on its feet', whilst in Britain 'the new Government was a Tory Government with Tory policies with regard to unemployment'. At the same time Councillor Len Finch had described the new Government 'as the beginning of a dictatorship'. This 'dictatorship' now gave Labour politicians a specific target against which they could direct their fire, and the early years of the National Government saw battles to protect local government spending on housing and education and to oppose the Means Test. Out of these battles came a new confidence and status. In 1934, as we have seen, Barry was to find itself with two representatives on the County Council, Alderman Dorothy Rees and Councillor William East, and furthermore there was now a Socialist Chairman of the Urban District Council. For the Labour Party the local elections in Barry could often be a question of swings and roundabouts with seats gained and lost, but slowly the number of Labour councillors was creeping up to challenge that of the Independents and by 1933 the count was twelve to nine. Obviously Labour's position now entitled them to provide at least an occasional Chairman of the Council, and in 1934 a definite turning-point was reached in this respect. Writing as 'Vigilant' a local journalist noted that previous 'Labour' or 'working-men's' Chairmen of the Council like W. R. Lee, Howell Williams and W. Beck had not 'fought under the Socialist banner' and were therefore not strictly Party men. By contrast the new Chairman, for whom Dudley Howe had given way, was Fred Cook 'the first dyed-in-the-wool Socialist Chairman', who was 'definitely an out-and-outer with nothing of the apologetic, pink, progressivist about him'. According to 'Vigilant', Fred Cook differed from his colleagues inasmuch as he lacked 'Stan Awbery's lively sense of humour and Len Finch's deep-rooted idealism', and he was 'rather inclined to be influenced by personal prejudices', but what he did have was 'the faculty of being able to hack his way to an object by virtue of sheer single-mindedness of purpose'. This kind of mischievous article was the stock-in-trade of the local press, but 'Vigilant's' conclusion that henceforth 'meetings will not be dull' confirmed that things were changing on the Council and that Labour were very much a force to be reckoned with. As it happened Fred Cook was to die before his year of office was over, but by that time he was acknowledged to be 'one of the best leaders the town had ever had', and he had impressed all sides by his 'uncanny grip' and impartiality. His career had summed up so many of the strands that were feeding into the Barry Labour Party, for he was a Somerset man who had been a miner for many years at Pontypridd before a leg injury had forced him to come to Barry as an insurance agent. He had been on the Barry Council since 1926 and had combined his outspoken Socialism with an active membership of the Holton Road Baptist Church.

In the General Election of 1935 Patrick Munro asked the Barry electors to consider whether they wanted 'a continuance of steady Government under proved men from all Parties' or whether they wanted 'to try another experiment in Socialism' by those who in 1931, had 'refused to face the crisis' and had 'run from their responsibilities'. Munro was re-elected with a greatly reduced majority and Ellis Lloyd came very close to regaining the seat. In the same year Labour made another gain on the Council by defeating Dudley Howe, the man who had so long dominated local politics, and then with one more gain in 1936 they had brought their total to within one of the Independents. As their opponents were now all too well aware, Labour needed just one more gain for control, as there were now ten Labour councillors out of a total of 21, and for the first time there were two women on the Council, Dorothy Rees and Mary Holland, both representing Labour. The new Chairman was also a Labour man, Ernest Cawley of Cadoxton, who, like Fred Cook, had first been elected in 1926. The tradition in Barry was that during his year of office the Council Chairman became a J.P., and during Cawley's installation Charles Griffiths could not resist asking whether he (Cawley) would continue his custom of sitting down during the playing of the National Anthem, to which Cawley replied that he would stand but that in other respects 'he would not be an orthodox Chairman'. A few days later Councillor Maslin returned from a meeting of the Hospital Committee at which the chairmanship had been given to H. B. Adams, a Labour man, and declared that this 'had been the most disappointing period in his life'. He warned the local Conservatives that 'loyalty' and 'strong and sustained activity' were needed 'to combat the imminent peril of Socialist domination' and that 'if the Socialists obtained one more seat, they (the Independents) might just as well stay home as to attend Council meetings'. This was a tantalising period for Labour as they waited for that one gain that would give them control, but they were to be frustrated, for Dudley Howe was re-elected at a by-election in the Holton Ward in May 1936; there was to be no change in 1937, and in 1938 a seat was lost in Cadoxton. Labour remained in a minority on the Barry Urban District Council, albeit now as a minority with a good deal of confidence and experience. The local Labour movement had a well-established group of widely respected leaders, and outside the Council Chamber there were lively and well-attended debates at the Barry Trades Council and at the Barry branch of the Left Book Club. The backbone of the movement was of course still provided by the N.U.R. who in 1939 had six Barry branches with 1,354 members, of whom over 800 were paying the political levy.

The Independents just about managed to hang on to political control in pre-War Barry and it was under their guidance that the town slowly clambered out of the Depression and out of its own financial crisis. It was a long, hard process and the town alternated between moods of hope and of deep gloom. Penarth Docks had been closed and there were often rumours that the G.W.R. was going to repeat this operation in Barry. One rumour had it that the G.W.R. was going to concentrate all its trade on only two ports in South Wales. As coal tips were dismantled and shipping transferred to Cardiff, the worst fears were seeming to be confirmed but, at the same time, the Company assured Patrick Munro that they were spending money on new cranes and dock-gates and that they were optimistic for the future of the Docks. Meanwhile unemployment remained a major problem, as was evinced by the fact that the Churches and Unemployment Movement was still having to provide training at workshops and entertainment in the form of concerts and plays. In 1933 some 3,859 insured persons were unemployed in the Barry area and in September 1938 the figure was still as high as 2,148. Concern was now concentrating on the lack of opportunities for young people in Barry, and in 1936 Ernest Williams told the Chamber of Commerce that in recent years the local school population had gone down by a thousand as the 'best citizens had left the town for their children's sake'. Dudley Howe was the Chairman of the Barry Juvenile Advisory Committee which struggled to find local jobs for boys and girls or arranged to have them transferred to jobs elsewhere, especially, as far as girls were concerned, in domestic service, but he was forced in 1937 to tell the Minister of Labour that 'acute depression continues to prevail in the Committee's area'. The population of Barry which had been as high as 39,260 in 1929 had fallen to 38,000 by 1938, and by 1939 a school system which could accommodate over 9,000 was in actual fact only having to cope with 5,608 children.

As always in these years it was during discussions on local finance that the Jeremiahs became most eloquent. Albert Baker, the President of the Ratepayers, remained the leading critic of the Council and especially of the housing that the Council had gone on building. His main argument was that council houses were built at a cost of £349 and yet rented out at 12*s.* 9*d.* a week, so that not even the capital cost was recovered, and each tenant was being subsidised to the extent of several shillings a week. The other leading critic was Ernest Williams, who referred to 'the mania for building houses' as well as demanding further educational cuts. Plans for nursery education were held up but after two very close votes there was still no decision as to whether Palmerston School would be closed, although this would have saved £1,000 a year. 'This', said Williams, 'stuck in his gizzard'. The critics were also outspoken on the subject of what the Council had invested in Barry as a resort. The locally produced guidebooks now referred to Barry as 'the prince' or 'the gem' of Welsh seaside resorts but the town really had failed miserably in its attempt to become a holiday resort. Millions came to Barry, but only as trippers, and they contributed very little to the wealth of the town. In 1937 the Finance Committee was told that all the Council's services at the Island and the Knap had brought in a profit for the summer of only £2,572. This was little to show for all the efforts that had been made and the Ratepayers demanded a rethink on Barry as a resort.[28]

In 1936 the rates were 19*s.* 10*d.* in the pound, and Edgar Pritchard, the Financial Controller, was again blaming the county precept, the loss of government grants and further rate refunds to the G.W.R., yet his assurance was that 'with the exception of the economy that would accrue from the closing of a school, the expenditure of the Council is now at a minimum'. It was perhaps this strict economy that the Council had insisted on that now helped the town to round the corner into recovery. In 1937 Pritchard reported that economies of £12,000 had been made since 1929/30, and quite apart from helping the rates these had been vital in winning over the various Ministries. In the early 1930s Barry had often been criticised by Whitehall for extravagance, but now the evidence was that new legislation would prevent Barry losing grants that were due to be withdrawn. For the first time Pritchard was able to express hope as the Ministries made sympathetic noises, and he went out of his way to praise the way in which Councillors Howe and Boon had laboured over four years to reduce expenditure, whilst at Westminster Patrick Munro had kept up a full round of lobbying.[29] The rates were down to 18*s.* 0*d.* in the pound in 1937, but were to be up at a level of 19*s.* 0*d.* again in 1938, when increased wages, but even more the county precept, were held to be responsible. Howe reported that in ten years the county precept had grown from 38 per cent to 55 per cent of the local rate and yet 'there was a profit on every service provided to the town by the County Council'. The problem was still public assistance which everyone in Barry felt should be a national charge, but in the meantime Barry, 'the plum of the county', was getting very little for value. The old complaints were still being made and there was, as ever, a running battle with Socialist Glamorgan, but the worst was clearly over. More traffic was handled on the Docks in 1937 than in any year since 1931, and sure evidence that new jobs were being created in the district was given in 1938, when Pritchard reported that there had been a great decrease in the amount owed in rates arrears.

There was a general feeling that Barry had pulled through the crisis. The background to those difficult days was perhaps best summed up by John Ireland, the Chairman of the Council, when in 1936 he told a meeting that Barry was a comparatively young town which had been 'started in days of prosperity' and 'whilst its early administrators had visions they did not foresee that bad times were to come, with the result that they had left loads which the present Barry Council finds it hard to bear'. Those loads had been borne but was the Urban District Council strong enough to keep up that performance? That was the question which in 1938 led local councillors to the conclusion that Barry needed to enhance its status by becoming incorporated as a Borough. This move had been considered in 1906 and 1927, but now as the fiftieth anniversary of the Docks approached, it was felt that the time was ripe for a new petition under the 1933 Act. In the last fifteen years some sixty new boroughs had been created, and Barry councillors were anxious to add Barry to that list. Barry, it was argued, had a larger population than Neath, was roughly of the same size as Llanelly and Port Talbot, and was considerably larger than the ancient but adjacent Borough of Cowbridge whose Mayors had long enjoyed precedence over Barry's elected leaders.

As the Incorporation bandwagon got under way there were soon dissenting voices. On the Council itself Mrs. Dorothy Rees was to have initial doubts and wondered whether 'they might be pursuing the shadow and not the substance of local government'. She asked whether enhanced status would of itself 'make administration more efficient or improve education and health services' and she reminded her colleagues that even mighty Cardiff with all its powers was still pressing for Distressed Area status. At a meeting of the Chamber of Commerce misgivings were aired especially with regard to the likely increase in the cost of bureaucracy, and a communication from Weston was discussed which referred to the cost of 'fur cloaks, silver mace and other trimmings' that would have to be purchased. As the Council's own campaign for Incorporation got under way and Councillors were sent to address local organisations, so formal opposition developed in various quarters. Councillor R. G. Cook emerged as the leading critic on the Council, arguing amongst other things that the Council Chamber was too small for additional council members, whilst in the Park Ward an Independent candidate, Creighton Griffiths, stood for election very much on an Anti-Incorporation platform. Mr. Griffiths was not elected, but his manifesto was a very good statement of the opposition's case. He argued that prospective investors and businessmen were never really influenced by status, and that the only advantage of incorporation was that money could be borrowed at a lower rate of interest, but the very point he wished to make was that things had already gone too far in that direction and 'that scourge needs no further encouragement'. The debate was kept alive, and as the date of the public hearing approached, the worrying news was that the Trades Council and N.U.R. branches were organising a petition against Incorporation. There was a certain amount of last-minute panic, but in the end there were only 1,688 names on the petition, and most people accepted the spirit of Councillor Awbery's estimate that 99 per cent of the town was in favour. In the event the Council's own Petition as presented 'To the King's Excellent Majesty in Council' was able to cite the support of a long list of local organisations including the Chamber of Commerce, the Rotary Club, local Conservative and Labour clubs and a number of trade union branches.[30]

In the Petition the Council's case was magnificently dressed up in formal language which referred amongst other things to the fact that 'Barry is a place of great antiquity', but in truth the arguments deployed were very simple ones. Barry was proud of its record and boasted of the way in which the Urban District Council had not only provided the normal services of local government, including housing, but had also operated gas, water and electricity undertakings, an elementary schools system, a maternity and child welfare service, and had also been the only U.D.C. in the country to maintain an Accident Hospital. The Council confessed that it had experienced severe financial difficulties during the Depression but now felt

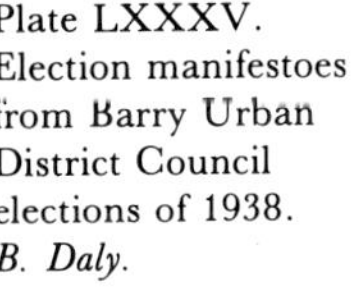

Plate LXXXV. Election manifestoes from Barry Urban District Council elections of 1938. *B. Daly.*

quite able to justify its record. Notwithstanding the economies made, the rates were high but that was largely due to the loss of rateable value and to the assistance policy that the nation as a whole had adopted, and in any case it was now felt that a low rate in the pound was 'no longer an index of good government'. The Financial Controller was able to report that 'in spite of all the difficulties the Council have managed to keep intact the working capital (cash) balance of £29,500 on the General Rate Fund and on no occasion during the last five years has there been a deficiency on the General Rate Fund'. There was no doubt that the crisis had been met, and Pritchard's summing up was that 'the financial position of the Council is thoroughly sound and all commitments that have been entered into are well within the capacity of the town to bear'. The Council's record could stand up to any investigation for 'throughout the past few years the Council have manifested a desire to conduct their financial affairs in a progressive, businesslike and efficient manner'.

Incorporation would be in part a reward for having weathered the storm, but the Council were also trying to enhance Barry's status so as to ensure that things would never be so difficult again. For all the grandiose references to Barry's antiquity and all the emphasis on the 'soundness' of Barry's finances the Petition for Incorporation was very much motivated by the desire to explore another means whereby Barry could be pulled out of its stagnation. As Councillors prepared their case they heard from other areas about the advantages of borough status. From the Town Clerk of Southgate came the news that just after Incorporation they had made an issue of stock and 'found that the terms of issue were at least one-quarter per cent more favourable than would have been the case had we not attained to Borough status' and that had meant a saving of 'at least the equivalent of a halfpenny rate for a period of thirty years'. Manifestly there were concrete advantages to be gained which would bring relief in precisely the form Barry most needed. Furthermore it was felt that the Docks and resort of Barry could only benefit from more publicity and that new industry might be brought in, if only the name of the town could be made better known, whilst at the same time it was felt that the request for Incorporation would not in any way affect Barry's application to be certified under the Special Areas Act. Inevitably there was a great deal of boosting during the weeks when the Petition was being drawn up, but perhaps the most realistic note was struck by the concluding sentences of a document circulated by the Clerk's Department during the campaign, for, when all was said and done, the essential argument was 'Barry has been badly hit by industrial depression' so 'why not become a Borough and see whether we cannot improve our fortunes?'[31]

In truth the town was in search of a massive psychological boost and that boost was to come in August 1939, appropriately just after the Docks had celebrated its fiftieth anniversary, when it was announced that the King had approved the Charter that bestowed on Barry the status of a Municipal Borough. Extensive and elaborate preparations were made and although the country was now at war again, an impressive ceremony was held at the Memorial Hall on Wednesday, 20 September, when the King's representative, Lord Portal, a Director of the G.W.R., presented the new Charter to the Earl of Plymouth, the last Chairman of the Company which had shaped the town, and who had been chosen to serve as the Charter Mayor. The many distinguished guests were entertained by a massed choir of one thousand local children and were witnesses of a dignified and picturesque ceremony involving Barry's new sterling silver gilt mace as well as the new colourful robes and chains of office. Speeches were made by Lord Portal, the Earl of Plymouth, by Mr. J. C. Meggitt, the Deputy Charter Mayor, who had been a member of the first local Board in Barry and who had served as first Chairman of the U.D.C. in 1894, and also by Councillor C. B. Griffiths, who was carrying out one of his last functions as the last Chairman of the U.D.C. The whole day was a marvellous celebration of Barry's dramatic past and of its more recent administrative triumphs. In his address Lord Portal asked his audience 'to look back and see who is responsible for the state of efficiency in Barry' and he thought it 'only fair to pay tribute to the work of your Urban District Council' for 'they have worked very hard for the success of Barry and today it is their crowning achievement that the Charter is going to be given'.

Plate LXXXVI. Incorporation Day: Dan Evans, Mace-bearer and Dudley Howe. *Western Mail; Gareth Howe Coll.*

The new Borough Council was to have the first meeting in November 1939, and councillors gathered 'resplendent in their robes of purple' before a public audience of over five hundred and under the chairmanship of the Earl of Plymouth. At this meeting decisions were taken that summed up so much of Barry's inter-war history. The twenty-one councillors, representing seven wards, were joined by the Borough's seven new Aldermen, all of whom were local politicians of long experience. The Aldermen were Charles Griffiths, J. T. Maslin, W. T. Ace, D. J. Boon, Ernest Cawley, W. H. Butcher and Stan Awbery, and an interesting reflection of the state of the town's politics was that the last three men on that list were Labour representatives. It was agreed that the Borough's first Mayor and Deputy Mayor would be Dudley Howe and Dan Evans, the two champion boosters of the 1930s, the two men who had dominated the efforts of the Council and of the Chamber of Commerce to shrug off recession and to develop confidence. Above all, the new status of Barry must be seen as a personal triumph for Dudley Howe for who the Chairmanship of the Incorporation Committee had come as the latest chapter in a long record of service to the town that he so much loved. Dudley Howe was the son of Christopher Howe who had been the first assistant overseer for the parish of Barry, and since 1910 he had been a Director of Meggitt and Jones, the well-known timber importers of Barry, Cardiff, Gloucester and Aberystwyth. He had been first elected to the Barry U.D.C. in 1913, and then, after being commissioned in France in the Great War, he returned to involve himself in nearly all the most important of the town's affairs in the 1920s and 1930s. His greatest achievements were to be the organisation of the Memorial Hall fund and the subsequent completion of that fine building, the stabilisation of the town's finances in the Depression and finally the campaign for the Charter itself. He was the most important man in Barry in the Thirties, but he should be seen more as a representative figure. He was a booster because his family's history and his own business interests were so closely bound up with the whole story and success of the port and of the town; he was a Liberal in politics and yet never strictly a party man for the town's interests always came first, and he was a regular member of Bethel Presbyterian Church, Cadoxton, at a time when the chapels did so much to determine the tone of public life in Barry. In these years Dudley Howe served on an astonishing range of committees, but perhaps we should highlight his interest in education as something which again illustrates how representative a Barrian he was.

Plate LXXXVII. The Borough's sterling silver gilt mace, after style used in House of Commons. *Charter Souvenir.*

The Barry Council, as we have seen, was responsible through its Education Committee for running an elementary school system, and for many years Dudley Howe was to be Chairman of that Committee. In Barry there were eight provided elementary schools and one Roman Catholic school with a combined capacity for over eight thousand pupils, although by the late 1930s there were only some 5,694 children in these schools. The

Board of Education had allowed the town an establishment of 206 teachers, eighteen of whom were graduates, and nearly all of whom were certificated. Barry was immensely proud of its school system and this was reflected in the Charter application. The Secretary of the Barry Education Committee, E. G. Habakkuk, commented on how 'Barry, being a town of comparatively recent growth, was particularly fortunate in its early days in having School Boards and, later, Education Committees composed of men and women with vision, with the result that the town has always been regarded as one of the leading Education Authorities in England and Wales'. Late Victorian and Edwardian Progressivism had been much in evidence in the young Barry and though much of that idealism was to be crushed by the harsh realities of the inter-war years, it survived in local educational circles and was to be most clearly seen in the enthusiasm, seriousness and high standards that local leaders like Dudley Howe always brought to the deliberations of the Education Committee. As difficulties increased in the 1930s constant references were made to the pioneers like Dr. Lloyd Edwards, John Lowdon and Dr. P. T. O'Donnell, who had always insisted on the best for Barry's schoolchildren. The town had certain advantages: it was an attractive place to live in, and the Training College brought into the locality able prospective teachers from all over Wales, many of whom did their best to stay on in the town. So as long as good salaries were paid, Barry could always ensure that it was employing well-qualified teachers and head teachers.

The ever-present fear in the inter-war years was that financial hardship would endanger standards, and in common with so many other depressed areas, Barry had to admit failure with regard to non-grammar secondary education. The Hadow Report of 1925 had advocated that all students should go to a new grade of school at the age of eleven, but Barry's plans for the adaptation of four schools as Non-Selective Senior Schools had been held up by educational 'cuts', and the War came before the Education Committee could make any real progress in this area. Failure in this respect, however, was never allowed to interfere with the considerable pride that the town took in its two Secondary Schools. These schools came under the jurisdiction of the County Council, but the Board of Governors consisted in part of U.D.C. representatives, and for many years Dudley Howe was to be Chairman of the Governors and E. G. Habakkuk acted as their clerk. This system of control allowed local educational idealism to influence secondary education in the town just as it had more fully shaped elementary provision. When the plans for Intermediate Education in Glamorgan had been announced in 1894, there had been no provision for a school at Barry as it was thought that the school at Penarth would suffice. The town fought for its school and was successful, and perhaps this initial struggle was to ensure that after 1896 the County School, or the County Schools as they became when the Girls' School opened in 1913, had a special place in the affections of the town.[32] What is certain is that from the outset the young progressive town of Barry saw its Intermediate School as an adornment, as a prestige symbol and as an institution which, if properly supported, could only bring fame to the town. The Edwardian years saw the town developing close and perhaps even unique links with its school; in particular the Barry Education Authority pioneered a bursary system, as well as supplementing scholarships awarded by the Governors with its own system of 'District Council Scholarships'. The whole town developed a keen interest in the list of ninety boys and ninety girls who had gained admission to the County Schools, as they were generally called, and competition for scholarships and bursaries was keen. Perhaps nothing sums up the close interest that the town took in education so much as the decision in 1925 of the local grocers, Williams Stores, to offer four scholarships of £4 each for four years to the top two boys and girls in the Scholarship examinations. Those wishing to register were asked to fill in a coupon and were reminded that the firm was 'Famous for the Quality of its Bacon'.

The undoubted success of the Boys' and then of the Girls' School at Barry was a reflection of the local pride and determination to be progressive that the town's history had engendered, but it was also a reflection of the impact of one man. Edgar Jones was born at Llanrhaeadr-ym-Mochnant, Montgomeryshire, in 1868, educated at the Northern Institute at Liverpool and then at the University College of Wales, Aberystwyth, where he obtained his B.A. and an M.A. before becoming a headmaster at Llandeilo. He came to Barry as the second headmaster of the County School in 1899 and he was to remain in that position until 1934. During those 35 years, Major Edgar Jones (he served with the Royal Engineers in Cardiff during the War) became one of the most respected and influential educationalists in Wales and although he served on many committees his fame always really rested on his school at Barry, which he developed into the model Welsh grammar school. He was sometimes referred to as the Thomas Arnold of Wales, and, like that other great headmaster, he valued not only educational success but also dignity and personality. Stan Awbery was to say of him that 'he moulded the lives and character of more men in Barry than anyone else', that 'he taught by example' and 'was much more than a schoolmaster', he was a friend to whom they could go, and did go, for help and guidance even years after they had left the school.[33]

The name of Edgar Jones became almost synonymous with Barry itself, but it was to be a particularly tragic event that most forcibly brought home the place he had won in the affections of the town. In 1935, just a year after his retirement Edgar Jones heard the news that his thirty-year-old son, Gareth, had been murdered by the Chinese bandits whose captive he had been for some months. The family's shock and sense of loss was shared by the whole town, and especially by all those who had any connection with the school. Gareth Jones had been regarded as one of the most brilliant pupils to pass through the Barry School, and after university he had developed into one of the country's most famous war correspondents, and it was his very ability and flair which had taken him into the Asian battlefields. At the Memorial Service held at the Memorial Hall the Reverend Gwilym Davies stressed that above all he had been 'a Barry Boy' with a 'pride in Barry'. It is not difficult to see that the tremendous emotional shock that the school and town experienced when it heard of Gareth Jones's death was an indication of the extent to which he was seen as the classic product of the educational system that both Barry and Major Edgar Jones himself had wanted to develop.[34] Barry was a small town that would always need a certain number of local leaders, teachers and professional men, but the majority of successful Barrians would inevitably have to leave the town and follow up their triumphs at school with triumphs in the wider world. The bitter-sweet irony of developing good schools is that a town's best sons and daughters are sent away, and those left behind have to be content with a reflected glory and with the knowledge that throughout the world men and women retained a pride in their home town and gratitude for the start it had given them. Perhaps no town the size of Barry has been so proud of what its County school achieved, and almost certainly few small towns can rival its record of success in producing distinguished men and women. When Major Edgar Jones retired in 1934, Dudley Howe spoke of the 'lustre he had shed upon the town of his adoption'. By that time the local press was continuously recording the successes of his old students and this pattern was to continue under his successors at the Boys' School and at the adjacent Girls' School, where, very appropriately, his daughter, Miss Gwyneth Vaughan Jones, was later to be a distinguished head very much in her father's mould.[35] However else one judges the town of Barry in the 20th century one should recognise that it was the successful dream of teachers like Edgar Jones and of politicians like Dudley Howe that whatever the state of the local economy the town would continue to send whole cohorts of academics, scholars, authors, doctors, musicians, diplomats, soldiers, explorers and sportsmen into a wider world. Barrians were never left unaware that educational success was the passport into the national mainstream and into all the highways and byways of Empire. Education was always the clearest expression of Barry's innate Progressivism and its surest and most persistent guarantee against parochialism and anonymity.

It has often been suggested that the adults of the 1920s and 1930s were a generation that consciously lived between two wars.[36] Barry's Cenotaph had been unveiled by the Earl of Plymouth in a moving ceremony on Armistice Day 1930, and that Memorial Hall which meant so much to the town was opened two years later. Two years after this, in August 1934, the

Barry Council joined with Patrick Munro in an effort to get some of the Woolwich Arsenal, part of which was to be moved away from London, to come to Barry. Ten councillors supported this action and only four others voted with Ernest Cawley, who had argued that if an arsenal was established at Barry, the first place enemy aircraft would make for in the event of war being declared was Barry. In June 1935 the local press reported that over a recent weekend Barry had been subject to a mock bombardment, in which the town had been bombed by 'a big R.A.F. machine' and attacked from the sea by 'enemy ships'. The operation was supposed to be secret, but in fact it had been watched by thousands who had known about it for weeks and many of whom would presumably have shared the *Barry Dock News*'s conclusion that 'whatever the efficiency of the territorial units at Barry', manoeuvres showed that defences were 'hopelessly out of date' and 'useless against air attack'. The onus, it was felt, was clearly upon the War Office. The citizens of Barry feared war and above all feared an aerial war. In July 1938 the steamer *Marconi* put into Barry and its shrapnel marks gave evidence of the bombing it had experienced at Valencia where its crew had seen 'huge bombers', allegedly manned by German and Italian airmen, and commented on how 'screaming aerial bombs produce a state of terrorism'. Armistice Day 1938 was felt, even at the time, to be one of the most moving to date, and in Barry it was reported that on a grey day the crowds stood in silence, and then suddenly 'the great silence was over, the most significant silence ever'.

Whatever the fears, the Government and the War Office were responding, and to some extent the country was to be ready for war when it came. In some ways war preparations contributed to economic recovery, and the development of a huge R.A.F. station at St. Athan after 1936 gave not only tangible evidence of the country's readiness to fight, but also a totally new diversion to the local economy by creating many construction and service jobs.[37] As far as the readiness of Barry itself was concerned, there were always to be doubts about how efficient various schemes were, and all too frequently apathy was the main response to appeals for people to enlist as Air Raid Precaution volunteers, but, at least by the time war came, committees were in existence, government booklets in hand and there was a loyal core of A.R.P. volunteers, of firemen, of ambulance drivers and of messengers; there were even plentiful supplies of gas masks and sand bags. The people of Barry had perhaps been psychologically prepared for war for some years, and the knowledge that the Docks would once again be crucial helped to lubricate the wheels of bureaucracy as, during late 1938 and 1939, war became almost a certainty. Barry had struggled out of the Depression and become a Municipal Borough just in time for a war in which, once again, great losses were to be incurred, and yet a war in which much local pride was to be regained.

Table 17.
Parliamentary Elections affecting Barry.

Llandaff and Barry			
1918	Major William Cope (Con.)	Maj.	7,700
1922	Major William Cope (Con.)	Maj.	3,598
1923	Major William Cope (Con.)	Maj.	837
1924	Major William Cope (Con.)	Maj.	4,192
1929	C. Ellis Lloyd (Lab.)	Maj.	2,968
1931	Patrick Munro (Con.)	Maj.	11,853
1935	Patrick Munro (Con.)	Maj.	1,422
1940	C. H. Lakin (Con.) (By-Election)	Maj.	5,655
1945	Lyn Ungoed-Thomas (Lab.)	Maj.	6,598
Barry			
1950	Mrs. Dorothy Rees (Lab.)	Maj.	1,025
1951	Raymond Gower (Con.)	Maj.	1,649
1955	Raymond Gower (Con.)	Maj.	7,363
1959	Raymond Gower (Con.)	Maj.	9,523
1964	Raymond Gower (Con.)	Maj.	4,266
1966	Raymond Gower (Con.)	Maj.	1,394
1970	Raymond Gower (Con.)	Maj.	8,671
Feb. 1974	Sir Raymond Gower (Con.)	Maj.	5,547
Oct. 1974	Sir Raymond Gower (Con.)	Maj.	2,903
1979	Sir Raymond Gower (Con.)	Maj.	8,792
Vale of Glamorgan			
1983	Sir Raymond Gower (Con.)	Maj.	10,393

Plate LXXXVIII.
Sir Raymond Gower, M.P.
Peter Wilson Photography.

References

1 Generations of Barry children and their teachers took their local history and their myths from Thomas Ewbank's, *The Geography and History of Barry* (Cardiff, 1921).

2 Gwyn Thomas, Foreword to *Old Barry in Photographs* (1977). Much of what I have written here has been inspired by this volume and its sequel, *Old Barry in Photographs,* Vol. II (1978), both published by Stewart Williams of Barry. The photographs sustain a marvellous sense of the town, as do Brian Luxton's full and excellent commentaries.

3 For the First World War and British Society, see Arthur Marwick, *The Deluge* (1965). In a forthcoming Ph.D. thesis Antony M. O'Brien shows how the War encouraged several groups in Aberdare and then the town as a whole to seek a fuller recognition.

4 Letter from J. A. Hughes, 'How Has Barry Done?'; *Barry Dock News* (*B.D.N.*), 15th November, 1918.

5 Only 16,769 of the Constituency's 34,452 electors lived in the Urban District of Barry (Ewbank, p. 99). The Constituency formed a rural semi-circle around Cardiff and included Llandaff, Whitchurch and Ely. These areas of Cardiff ceased to be part of the Constituency in 1950, when the name of the Constituency was changed to Barry.

6 See Parliamentary Election Results. Table 17.

7 Neil Evans discusses events at Barry in the context of other disturbances at Newport and Cardiff in 'The South Wales Race Riots of 1919' in *Llafur,* The Journal of the Society for the Study of Welsh Labour History, Vol. 3, No. 1, Spring 1980. At the time much was made of Longman's military record and rather less of his twenty previous convictions.

8 For the growth of soccer in South Wales see Peter Corrigan, *100 Years of Welsh Soccer* (Cardiff, 1976).

9 Cardiff had been a city since 1905 but in local government terms it was a County Borough. In 1921 its population was 219,580 as compared with Barry's 38,945.

10 Herbert Williams, *Railways in Wales* (Swansea, 1981).

11 R. J. Rimell, *History of the Barry Railway Company, 1884-1921* (1923).

12 The coming of the G.W.R. is best described in D. S. M. Barrie, *A Regional History of the Railways of Great Britain,* Vol. XII, *South Wales* (1980). See also O. S. Nock, *History of the G.W.R.,* Vol. III, *1923-1947* (1967) and the G.W.R.'s own *The Docks of the G.W.R.* (1924).

13 During the Second World War there were to be rows over the exclusion of the press from the Council Chamber but mercifully there were full and lively reports in the inter-war years.

14 John A. Giggs, 'Barry, An Urban and Social Geography', Ph.D. thesis (University of Wales, 1967).

15 For a lively account see Kenneth Lindley, *Seaside and Seacoast* (1975).

16 The best introduction to the housing revolution of this century is provided by John Burnett, *A Social History of Housing, 1815-1970* (1978).

17 I discuss William Brace's politics in 'The Language of Edwardian Politics' in David Smith (ed.), *A People and a Proletariat* (1980).

18 *Annual Report and Proceedings of the A.S.R.S.*

19 For labour struggles in Barry, Harold Finch, *Memoirs of a Bedwellty M.P.,* (Risca, 1972) and also Philip J. Leng, *The Welsh Dockers* (Ormskirk, 1981).

20 Ellis Lloyd, a native of Newport, was a journalist and novelist who had been called to the Bar at Gray's Inn in 1926.

21 Bindles closed in 1982 and was used subsequently by a television company.

22 *B.D.N.,* 4th April, 1930.

23 The 1929 Local Government Act had abolished the 635 Boards of Guardians and transferred their powers to the Counties and County Boroughs.

24 The problems facing the County Council are best summarised in Dorothy Rees, *Reminiscences of the Glamorgan County Council* (Cardiff, 1974). Ivor Jenkins, the Director of Social Services, recalls joining the County Council Staff at the very moment when the County's Public Assistance Committee was set up and when the County was giving relief to 35,784 unemployed people every week. He explains that for the year ended 31st March 1931 'the Glamorgan rate for public assistance purposes was more than the total county rate of Surrey and Middlesex'.

25 Full Reports of Barry Council Deputations to Sir James Milne, General Manager of G.W.R., and to the Minister of Health, *B.D.N.,* 11th January, 1935. The dock and railway rate liability expressed as a percentage of the total for Barry fell from 75% in 1912 to 11% in 1930. Government grants were intended to offset this loss but D. A. Dalwood has calculated that in Barry there was an increased rate burden on the general body of ratepayers of about 3%. See D. A. Dalwood, 'Impact Studies and the Planning Process—A Case Study of the Impact of the Port Transport Industry Upon Barry', M.Sc. thesis. (University of Wales, 1972), pp. 81-83.

26 The Cardiff-Barry area was excluded from the Special Areas (Development and Improvement) Act of 1934, the most spectacular product of which in South Wales was the Treforest Trading Estate. K. O. Morgan, *Rebirth of a Nation, Wales 1880-1980* (1981), pp. 225-227.

27 *Second Industrial Survey of South Wales,* Part II, *Facilities* (1937), p. 327. This point is also discussed in H. A. Marquand, *South Wales Needs A Plan* (1936).

28 In the Thirties there was a long-standing row over whether the Council should municipalise the various facilities at the Island and Cold Knap which were given out on contract to M. W. Shanley. This matter was only resolved in 1937 and the many angry debates indicated the widely-held belief that Barry was not obtaining sufficient financial benefit from its seaside attractions. Letters to the press demanded that trippers should be taxed.

29 Pritchard himself was playing an active role presenting Barry's case on a Losing Areas Committee, for the town was a 'classic example of a losing area' as far as block grants were concerned. *B.D.N.,* 19th May, 1937.

30 'Petition of The Urban District Council of Barry for the Grant of a Charter', incorporating the Urban District of Barry as a Municipal Borough, 1938.

31 Private Document, 'Points in Favour of Incorporation', Clerk's Department, 1938 (in possession of Mr. Gareth Howe), p. 7. For full statement of Barry's case see *Incorporation Inquiry,* 23rd November, 1938.

32 *Barry Education Week Guide* (Cardiff, 1923), p. 25, *et seq.*

33 Stan Awbery, *Let Us Talk of Barry* (Barry, 1954), p. 88.

34 See Glyn Daniel's Foreword to *Old Barry in Photographs,* Vol. II. There are several unanswered questions about the death of Gareth Jones and there could well be clues in his diary which is now in private hands.

35 On 19th May, 1939, it was reported that two beautiful leather-bound books had been printed which showed that the Barry Schools 'had turned out some of the most brilliant men and women in their various spheres of life'. The *Barry Dock News* listed many of the names from the books. On 5th June, 1942, the same paper printed a photograph of the County School's Rugby team of 1910-11 and then showed how many of those boys had gone on to have distinguished war records and then brilliant careers.

36 Samuel Hynes, *The Auden Generation* (1976), p. 40.

37 The R.A.F. station at St. Athan came into operation in 1936. The background story of rearmament is told in Basil Collier, *The Defence of the Kingdom* (1957).

Plate LXXXIX. The Charter Mayor (The Right Honourable The Earl of Plymouth, P.C.). *Charter Souvenir.*

CHAPTER X

Barry Since 1939: War-Time Prosperity and Post-War Uncertainty

PETER STEAD

232

Utility mark.
Simon Prosser.

THE paradox of all wars is that they occasion tragedy and yet encourage progress. The tragedy and suffering are experienced by individuals and their families, whereas progress is more evident amongst wider social groups. The two great World Wars of the 20th century claimed a heavy toll in terms of human life from the small South Wales town of Barry, and yet the wars really formed exciting and creative chapters in what was otherwise a comparatively unremarkable modern history. Quite apart from claiming lives, the First World War effectively brought to an end Barry's commercial autonomy, but it did also allow a young town to boast proudly of its contribution to the defence of the kingdom and indeed of the Empire. The Second World War brought a further loss of life and a further diminution of Barry's commercial identity, but, more than anything else, the war against Hitler gave the people of Barry important jobs to do. Once again the Docks, the town and all its inhabitants became busy. The new war ended a period of introspection and uncertainty and, in effect, Barry was pulled out of a torpor as its citizens found themselves either directed to all corners of the globe or playing host to strangers for whom the town was now of vital importance. The economy, public affairs and perhaps, above all, social life moved up a gear and if there were still some parochial tensions, they were thrown into relief by wider horizons, new values and a more national perspective. This was to be classically 'the People's War' because it was they who fought it and organised it, but their war, too, because out of the novel experience of being both busy and important, people acquired greater expectations and a new confidence. Between the Wars Barry had suffered commercial decline and its population had been entrapped in the politics of failure, but now a war took them out of that rut and made them, as never before, full citizens of a democratic nation.[1]

We will never know what would have happened if the Germans had really fully committed themselves to an invasion, or even to a total aerial bombardment, of Britain. The threat of invasion was there for several years but it never came, and the country as a whole was never to experience a sustained bombing campaign. Preparations were made in Barry and district. Barrage balloons were put in place to deter low level attacks from the air. A dummy fort was constructed on Cold Knap Point to distract the enemy's attention from the real fort on the Island. Many people in Barry committed themselves to various activities on the home front. An Information Bureau was established in Holton Road and soon local groups and clubs were eagerly knitting 'comforts' for the troops or organising collections of various sorts, whilst many individuals were digging for victory in gardens and on allotments. The Earl of Plymouth and the Mayor, Dudley Howe, soon launched an appeal to help pay for a new Toc H Centre which would offer social and leisure facilities for troops, and successful financial appeals were soon to be a continuing feature of the town in the early years of the war. Barrians gave generously to the Spitfire Fund and later helped to buy 'eight more bombers to batter the Nazis'. Conscription, of course, had been introduced and many young people had already left the town to serve in the armed forces. Meanwhile in the town itself there were appeals for A.R.P. volunteers, for auxiliary firemen and then for Local Defence Volunteers. Many responded to these appeals and there was in particular a rush to the Drill Hall to join the L.D.V., who were soon to be re-named the Home Guard. There were at least five hundred initial volunteers for this new organisation in Barry and within six months a local paper was openly boasting of how the town's Home Guard now formed a 'highly-organised, well-armed and well-trained' body of over nine hundred men. They became a familiar sight, and their commander, Lt. Col. Shirley Beavan, the manager of the Graving Docks, became one of the most prominent men in the town. Road blocks were built to control the approaches to the town and manned by the Home Guard.

In Barry, as in the country as a whole, the period of the 'Phoney War' saw lots of frenetic bureaucratic activity and it was perhaps miraculous that so much was achieved. At the same time it was becoming apparent that not enough had been done to satisfy everybody. When Britain had gone to war in 1914, people had celebrated. In 1939 and 1940 criticism was more in evidence than celebration, criticism not of the decision to fight but rather of the tardy response to the demands of war. It was really remarkable how quickly a section of opinion changed from being uninterested in matters of defence to a frantic concern that everything should be done properly. In November 1939 the *Barry Dock News* referred to the extensive criticism there had been by Barrians of the local A.R.P. arrangements, but after checking for itself the paper was able to reassure readers of 'the excellence of the Barry section'. Things were to get even better after mock air-raids over the town later that month, but further exercises in May 1940 revealed urgent needs for volunteers to organise first-aid parties and for vehicles to transport those injured in any attacks. The Regional Commissioner for Civil Defence, Colonel G. T. Bruce, appealed for cars to be made available, explaining that police permits would be given, free petrol issued and W.V.S. drivers brought into action. Slowly the full-scale bureaucratic complexity of Home Defence was becoming apparent to the citizens of Barry but the response was still far from satisfactory. The situation during the 'Phoney War' was that for every enthusiast who could see what needed to be done there were several others who remained complacent. At a meeting of the Barry Education Committee in May 1940 there was a debate on whether children should start school a year or so earlier. Some councillors thought this too dangerous at a time of war but the Deputy Mayor, Dan Evans, re-assured members that he 'considered an air-raid to be a remote possibility'.

The pattern was for renewed activity as real action got nearer, but at every stage criticism was to continue. As the German bombing of southern England began, so the Barry Council took their campaign to the people. In June over 10,000 handbills were put out inviting citizens to a Memorial Hall meeting to 'hear what should be done in an Air Raid'. The response was disappointing, and the Memorial Hall was only half-full to hear A.R.P. officers warn that war was 'bound to come to this country' and to suggest that A.R.P. work itself was 'an excellent antidote to fear'. The Chairman of the Barry A.R.P. reported that he was still short of a thousand volunteers and that he still needed more firemen and first-aid workers.[2] The local press took all this to be evidence of 'serious deficiencies in Barry', yet as war became more real the average family was probably far more concerned about the provision of air-raid shelters than they were about the voluntary services. Somebody was always suggesting that there were not enough shelters in various parts of the town, and there was real concern in Cadoxton where the rock was too hard for Anderson shelters and where, according to Councillor Griffiths, the sirens could not be heard when there was an east wind. The people of the Island complained, as they were to do on so many occasions, that they had not been given enough attention, especially considering their exposed position. All this culminated in a petition of some 3,000 signatures being drawn up by the Barry Co-operative and Labour Parties, who claimed to be speaking on behalf of two-thirds of the town. They protested strongly against the poor materials used in the construction of shelters, the lack of sanitary facilities, the vulnerability of shelters against gas and the inadequacy of particular types of shelter, especially the Anderson shelter, which tended to flood in wet weather.[3]

Twelve Counties in England were Bombed this morning

Are you NOW interested in Air Raid Precautions?

THE MAYOR

has been requested to convene a Meeting of Townspeople to hear what should be done in an Air Raid.

THIS MEETING

will be held in the

BARRY MEMORIAL HALL

— ON —

THURSDAY NEXT, JUNE 13th

at 7 p.m.

COME AND HEAR WHAT YOU SHOULD DO TO PROTECT THE LIVES OF YOUR FAMILIES AND YOUR OWN HOMES.

Mayor's Parlour,
7th June, 1940.

DUDLEY HOWE,
Mayor.

[illegible], PRINTERS, CADOXTON, BARRY.

Fig. 93. Handbill to arouse interest in Air Raid Precautions. *Gareth Howe Coll.*

Barry was probably no better or worse off than any other part of the country but as the war got closer the sense of vulnerability remained. The first raids over Barry in July 1940 were minor affairs but the news from elsewhere was not good. A Barry couple, Mr. and Mrs. Reg Rendell, were killed in London in October 1940, when the house they were staying in was bombed, and three more Barry people were killed during the first 'blitz' on Cardiff in January 1941. A lead article in the *Barry Dock News* spoke of how the ordeal of Cardiff 'has brought a new value and meaning to the almost despised letters A.R.P.' and reported that although there was a 'sharp division of opinion in the town over the state of Barry's preparations' the Barry Committee were still complaining of a 'serious shortage of volunteers'. The complaints went on and there were criticisms of the A.R.P. being 'ill-informed' and 'confused by the dark of night' right up until the summer of 1941, when there was a number of more serious raids on the town. In the event the debate was largely academic for Barry was to be spared the fate of Swansea, and even of Cardiff, and can count itself lucky that it received so little attention from the Luftwaffe.[4]

The question of whether Barry was ready can never be answered, but, in a sense, all the criticisms of the A.R.P. and of the shelters were far more interesting as a reflection of a new mood than as comment on defences as such. Historians have noted how attitudes towards the Government and towards 'the authorities' as a whole changed rapidly in 1939 and 1940. There was a general feeling that 'Hitler should have been rumbled earlier' and this broadened out into a wider impatience with delays, half-hearted measures, incompetence and selfishness in all walks of life and at all levels. In Barry the readiness with which the local press not only discussed but almost encouraged criticisms of local Civil Defence matters and the constant reporting of complaints about shelters were firm evidence of a new and more open politics. At times the wrangle over A.R.P. arrangements and shelters sounded carping and parochial, but these issues were just a tip of a much more significant iceberg. One feature of 'the new politics' was the wide variety of groups and individuals who were prepared now to participate in open criticism of the authorities and of the public arrangements they had made, but from the outset the Labour Movement was bound to be the main benefactor of the new disgruntlement. In May, 1940, a dinner was held at the Sea View Labour Club at which it was reported that five shillings a month was being sent to club members in the forces, but at the same dinner Tom Knight fiercely attacked Sir John Simon's recent Budget and in particular his taxing of beer and tobacco. He warned that 'when the war was over and the Labour Party once more in power, they would remember'. A week later a local paper announced in a banner headline 'Council Accepts Principle of Collective Bargaining'. The Barry Council had accepted the system of war bonuses for local government employees recommended by the

Joint Staff Advisory Committee, but even this was not really going far enough for some councillors. Councillor R. G. Cook pointed out that it had taken them fifty years to establish collective bargaining and that the Council staff were 'seething with discontent'.

Throughout the town Labour's confidence was growing as the status of the working man was being transformed. The War was not many days old when new cargoes for France started leaving Barry, and it was soon apparent that a new era was beginning for those who worked in and around the Docks. Unemployment was already being whittled away as the Railway Executive Committee of the Ministry of Transport took over the nation's railways. After considerable initial confusion the ports of the Bristol Channel were brought under the jurisdiction of a Regional Port Director with his own Port Labour Superintendent. As the nation's economy and labour force were subjected to unprecedented government control and regulations, so the whole context in which trade-unionism operated in towns like Barry was transformed. The great symbolic breakthrough for Barry and for all ports came with the National Dock Labour Scheme of September 1941. All dock work was to be regarded as essential work and dockers had to be willing to take any suitable work, or even to travel to other docks where work was waiting, but in exchange there would be guaranteed work, a week's paid holiday a year and a much improved wage structure. The Dock Labour Scheme received a great deal of publicity, but perhaps of even more significance for Barry families were the new serving conditions for merchant seamen. The Merchant Navy was also covered by an essential work order and the seamen were now given not only continuous employment rather than having to be engaged from trip to trip, but also entitlement to leave, war bonuses and, after April 1941, the same rights of compensation as applied to the Royal Navy.[5]

The importance and the dignity of labour were being recognised as never before, and just as the Labour Party's national leaders moved into positions of importance in the Government, so at the local level Labour councillors began to appear less as the leaders of a section and more as the natural spokesmen of the town. At the outbreak of war Councillors Howe, Boon and Evans were still the key men in Barry, and indeed they were all to be responsible for vital war work, but they now had to concede much of the limelight to their old opponents. Dudley Howe was succeeded as Mayor by Alderman William Butcher, who had come to Barry as a baby, gone to sea at the age of fifteen, become interested in Socialism during the 1911 strike, started work as a coal-trimmer in 1913 and had then picked up an education in the classes of the National Council of Labour Colleges and the Workers' Educational Association. A year later Alderman Butcher gave way to yet another Labour Mayor. It was now the turn of Councillor Stan Awbery who was well on his way to becoming one of the most respected and best-known leaders produced by the Barry Labour Movement. He had started out as a dock worker in his native Swansea and was already a District Secretary of the Transport and General Workers' Union when he came to Barry in 1926. Throughout the Thirties he combined his union with his responsibilities as a deacon of Holton Road Baptist Church and he still had time to contest the Clitheroe Constituency, albeit unsuccessfully, in both 1931 and 1935. Now during his period as first citizen of Barry he remained the prospective parliamentary candidate for the Bristol Central constituency.[6] Within a year the Barry Council had chosen first a coal-trimmer and then a dockers' official to serve as Mayor. Whatever else the War would bring, by 1941 it was difficult to avoid the conclusion that Barry's Labour Movement, which had fought so many battles over a period of half a century, had already turned a significant corner.

These were better days too for at least some of Barry's ethnic communities. This was not the case for the small Italian community which had been forcibly interned during 1940. Although the war necessitated the registration of all aliens, care was taken to avoid any return to the excessive racism of the First World War. From the early days of the Second World War foreign nationals became familiar figures in Britain, and it was realised that not only more recent refugees but all the so-called aliens from allied and occupied

Plate XC. War Savings Week: the Mayor buys a National Savings Certificate (Mrs. Dudley Howe in centre). *Barry & District News; Gareth Howe Coll.*

countries could contribute decisively to the war effort. In a sense the war helped to break down many of the racist and nationalist assumptions of the British people, and there was often a new respect for certain European nationalities. In Barry there was a new awareness of the quite sizeable Greek community, as under the leadership of Mrs. Angelinakis of Newland Street it began to collect on behalf of Greek soldiers who had put up 'a wonderful display against a formidable foe'. In 1943 Greek Independence Day was celebrated at an impressive ceremony at King Square attended by civic leaders, and Mr. Baizos, the Greek consul in Barry, spoke of the town's close ties with Greece, especially with its Merchant Navy. Far more attention was also being paid to Barry's coloured community and in particular to its newly formed Coloured Society. In 1943 the Society was entertaining and passing on gifts to coloured seamen who visited Barry and also holding parties at the Colonial Club in Thompson Street for the children of its own members. The Society's President, Mr. Abby Farrah, reported that a cricket team had been formed and would soon be looking for local fixtures. Once again the War had brought about the kind of breakthrough which should perhaps have happened many years earlier. Barry had always been cosmopolitan but it was only during the Second World War that there was official and more general recognition of how many sub-cultures there were feeding into the everyday life of Barry. In this respect, as in so many others, old attitudes suddenly seemed very unworthy and inadequate.[7]

At home the War was creating a new politics, but meanwhile other Barrians were experiencing the sharp realities of action. In June 1940 the flags were out in Merthyr Street to welcome home Herbert Partridge, who had been seriously injured on H.M.S. *Punjabi* at the Battle of Narvik, whilst Evans Street gave a warm welcome to Stanley German who had been on the Dunkirk beach for thirty hours and had only been saved by the sand covering thrown over him by a previous bomb. For an increasing number of families the news was not so good. The first headline 'Barry Soldier Reported Missing' also came in June 1940; the report told of how nothing had been heard of Arthur Hodges of Morel Street, who, having gone to sea as a mess-boy before serving in the army on the North-West Frontier, had more recently joined the Royal Tank Regiment. In the last letter to be received by his father he had written that 'Jerry is certainly taking everything in his stride and the sooner we stop him the better'. At the same time there was news that Percy Baker of Morgan Street was presumed missing or had been taken prisoner. Baker, who had been a merchant seaman before the War, had now been serving on H.M.S. *Glorious* and was one of four brothers, all of whom were in the Royal Navy. Barry men fought in all the major actions of the War. The relatives of Thomas Mitchell of Graving Dock Street heard that he had been killed at Dunkirk. Several Barry men went down with the *Prince of Wales* and *Repulse* but there were also some survivors of that disaster. In 1943 the town heard that

Clarence Welfoot of Abingdon Street, Cadoxton, who had been in the navy for ten years and who had been awarded the D.S.M. after the Russian convoys, had now been killed on submarine duty. For long the news was mainly bad news. Only in 1943 could a lighter note be introduced as messages started to come in from Barry men serving with the Allied troops. These messages clearly indicated a general feeling that the worst of the War was over. In 1943 thirteen Barry men describing themselves as the 'Thirteen Desert Mice' sent news from North Africa that they were receiving the *Barry Dock News* every week. Later that year Staff Sgt. G. F. Davies who had once worked as a journalist in his native Barry reported that the town was far more famous than he had thought, for Egyptian waiters and shopkeepers in Tripoli had all seemed to have been to Barry and walked on its beaches at some time or other. The War took Barry people to wherever there was action. As victory came, so the *Barry Dock News* reported that 80 per cent of the copies it printed were going overseas to India, North Africa, Italy, Palestine, Burma and to 'everywhere a Barry boy is serving'. Not all had served in distant theatres of war. Several had gone no further than Bletchley, Bucks., where they took part in secret intelligence work, which helped to speed the end of the War.

Inevitably Barry's greatest contribution to the War came at sea. Many press reports concerned local men serving in the Royal Navy, and the brief description of their careers showed that they had gone to sea at an early age, and in many cases had years of experience in the Merchant Navy. As war approached, the Royal Navy had caught the imagination of Barry's youth as was suggested by the later boast of Mr. and Mrs. Whyman of Burlington Street that all six of their sons were currently serving in the senior service. Meanwhile other Barry men stayed on in the Merchant Navy, and it was undoubtedly in this respect that the town's record in the Second World War is worthy of remembrance. The Docks were Barry's *raison d'être* and from the earliest days of the town Barry families were to have connections with the sea. In times of peace it was the dockers, coal-trimmers and railwaymen who received most publicity, and little was said of the many men who regarded Barry as their home but who earned their living as officers, engineers, or just as seamen on ocean-going merchant vessels. The Second World War was to highlight Barry's role as the home of merchant sailors, and it did so because their efforts were so vital in the whole war effort. One of the strangest features of the Second World War was that, whilst the role of pilots in the Battle of Britain and efforts of the Eighth Army were soon to be known about by every schoolchild, relatively little attention was ever given to the Battle of the Atlantic. Churchill was to concede that the loss of this battle had been his greatest fear. The Merchant Navy were to become the great unsung heroes of the War, and yet there were many families in Barry who knew how dangerous and costly the battle to keep Britain provisioned had really been.[8]

The danger to shipping could actually be seen by the people of Barry, as throughout the war damaged ships limped into port, whilst other regular visitors departed never to return.[9] In a sense the town was ready for the bad news that was soon to come in a constant stream. In July 1940 concern was expressed after the torpedoeing of a British ship, for whilst a Mr. Galton of Queen Street, Barry was saved from a raft, there was no news of Charles Williams of Station Street or William Piper, the ship's cook, of Travis Street. Galton described how the ship, on which all three Barry men had been serving, had gone down in three minutes and how subsequently the German submarine had been clearly visible. A Mr. Feismeiir of Hirwaun Street had been on the S.S. *Brookwood* when it was torpedoed 100 miles from land, but he had survived after being in an open boat for five days, and nineteen-year-old Ron Seagrim of Lee Road, Cadoxton was to survive although torpedoed twice in three months, on the second occasion having been in the water for three hours. There were many miraculous escapes, but much tragedy, too, and Barry men who survived sinkings often had to report the probable death of their Barry colleagues. By the summer of 1941 the *Barry Dock News* was talking openly of the 'Nazi toll of Barry seamen', and in 1943, under the headline 'Bad News Comes Again to Barry', the paper told of how a further six Barry men were missing and of how wives 'received cold, business-like letters stating that the ship in which their kinsfolk were serving had become a casualty and that news of the crew was awaited'. One of the most remarkable stories was that of Vivian Fowler of Morel Street who had survived twenty-six days in an open boat after his ship had been torpedoed a thousand miles from land. The U-boat commander had spoken to Mr. Fowler and his 36 fellow survivors (one of whom was a Mr. Owen of Evelyn Street) and then given them loaves made of potatoes and maize, which were not eaten 'in case there was something wrong with them', the men choosing rather to depend on their supplies of Horlicks and chocolate tablets. Their voyage was remarkable, as they were shelled again by Germans before their final rescue.

The contribution that Barry was making to the Battle of the Atlantic and to similar battles in Russian and Asian waters could no longer be ignored. The town was suffering the same shortages as elsewhere: citizens were told not to waste bread, that potatoes should be used instead of flour and that dried milk and eggs should be used more extensively, but in Barry people were aware of the realities of the sea war and of the struggle to keep the country fed. A lead article in the local press asked the people of Barry to 'consider the Merchant Navy', for there were 'no headlines of triumph' and 'no peal of bells' when its ships come safely into port, and yet 'all but ½ per cent of our convoys come safely into port'. The next step was national recognition, and *Reynolds News,* the national Sunday newspaper, carried a tribute to Barry under the headline 'The Port That Craves Adventure'.

Barry, it was claimed, had 'lost more Merchant Seamen in the war than any other seaport of comparable size in Britain' and there were 'few streets in the town and dock area which have not lost men at sea as a result of enemy action'. The article claimed that there were probably Barry men serving in most Merchant Navy convoys throughout the world and that 'heavy losses of life and incredible hardships suffered by Barry men had not dismayed the youth of the port', for they were 'still entering the Merchant Navy as soon as they are old enough and can be absorbed by the service'.[10]

In 1944 a new Merchant Navy club was opened and it almost seemed as if Barry had come of age as a sea-faring town. As it happens the *dénouement* of this story was not totally glorious, for at the end of the War Merchant Seamen were excluded from Barry's Welcome Home Fund, which had been sponsored by the Mayor. The *Barry Dock News* which had regularly saluted the contribution of the Merchant Marine was stunned by this exclusion, and so reminded Britains of their 'Debt of Honour'. The paper had often spoken of how 'Barry has probably lost more of her boys in proportion to her size than any other town in the country' and it now calculated that the town had lost 'five hundred out of the 3,500 to 4,000 who had registered'. This story was taken up by *The Seaman*, the journal of the National Union of Seamen, which reported that the vast majority of the town were in favour of Merchant Seamen being made eligible to receive support from the fund.[11]

The Second World War had become a massive exercise in social mobility. Thousands of men and women left Barry to serve in the forces or to take up jobs in other parts of the country, but then, as the War progressed, many thousands of outsiders began to move into or through Barry. The town was always full of men in uniform; soldiers and sailors, as well as airmen from St. Athan, were frequently entertained by local organisations and in family homes. The most dramatic visitors were the Americans, who were to make a significant impact in the later years of the War not only on Barry's economy, but on its social life as well. The Docks had become busier during the Lease-lend period but after their entry into the War the American authorities decided to use Barry as one of their main cargo ports and storage depots, influenced in part by the relative safety of the area from aerial attack. Porthkerry Park became a huge vehicle park. The Americans' use of Barry stepped up as D-Day approached, and eventually some 21 vessels transported over 15,000 tons of military equipment, including 1,269 vehicles as well as 4,000 U.S.A. troops, from the Docks to the beaches of Normandy. Thereafter there was a steady flow of American equipment and personnel through the town until some months after the War.

Americans entered into the social life of Barry with great gusto. In August 1943 a Barry Army Day was held at the Island cricket ground and members of the British forces, the Home Guard, the A.T.S. and Cadet Units, together with members of the U.S. forces competed in various athletic events. Lt. D. P. Richards of the Home Guard and one of Barry's best-known athletes, won the mile 'in magnificent style', and a Sgt. Hughes won the 'bomb-throwing' competition! But one of the most thrilling events of the afternoon was an inter-Allied and Services relay race which developed into a struggle between Britain and America. Britain led in the 440 and 220 yards sprints, 'but in the half-mile an American runner made up the leeway and won the event for his country amid the cheers of a large crowd'. American soldiers exercised a strange fascination on young ladies and also, of course, on children. In 1944 the local press commented on the 'pernicious and fast-growing habit of small boys and girls stopping any American soldier or sailor they may see to demand gum or, worse, money'. The Americans, it was thought, were too soft-hearted, and although sweet-rationing was 'none too liberal', the paper appealed to the Americans 'to harden their hearts and not give anything'. American generosity was channelled instead in other directions, and early in 1944 some 250 children from Cadoxton and Jenner Park schools were entertained by the U.S. Transport Unit as the first stage in an exercise in which it was hoped that all 5,000 children in the town could

Plate XCI.
Floating steel-section roadway, installed across timber pond at E. end of No. 2 Dock, for movement of military vehicles to transport ships prior to D-Day, 6 June 1944.
L. W. Hansen; I. W. Prothero Coll.

be catered for. The children were taken to the camps in trucks and there they listened to a dance band, watched Popeye films and were given chocolate and chewing gum. The G.I.s were popular at dances because they had more money in their pockets and they could also be relied on to throw the best parties. V.J. Day was celebrated quietly in Barry, but the Americans let off fireworks and crackers, held a dance on the Square where they chaired a police sergeant and drove around the town in trucks and jeeps. The Yanks, as they were always called, had posed a special problem for the Barry police for their great supply depot, which had the cryptic title of G.40, became the source of a flourishing black market, and the local magistrates' court was kept busy dealing with theft cases. By the end of the War the C.I.D. had fairly successfully clamped down on this black market, but nevertheless 'thousands upon thousands of stuff had been written off', including in December 1945 '400 pairs of nurses stockings'!

In the summer of 1944 the American and Canadian servicemen in Barry were joined by another group of outsiders. London was now being attacked by flying bombs, and once again families were being evacuated to safer parts of the country. In the early months of the War, when the first great evacuation had taken place, Barry had not been regarded as particularly safe and in fact many local families had actually applied through the Education Committee Secretary, E. G. Habakkuk, to have their children sent abroad, and some children were actually sent to South Africa. Now Barry was thought to be safe for 400 'refugees' from London and they were accommodated at first in chapels while arrangements were made for them to be distributed to local homes. In fact, the response to appeals for accommodation was disappointing, for, as the local press pointed out, Barry was already seriously overcrowded with 500 'unofficial' evacuees and hundreds of key industrial workers already billeted in many homes. In the end compulsory billeting was needed to find homes for these Londoners. Barry was indeed a strange and busy place in these years. In August 1944 a cartoon depicted a typical Barry Street scene with Yankee soldiers, both black and white, passing jeeps and evacuees carrying 'From London' labels; a pipe-smoking train driver emerges on his way to work, 'Gee, Bud', says one of the Yanks, 'one of those local guys'. The cartoon was entitled 'B-Day: The Invasion of Barry'.[12]

The early years of the War had sanctioned a new freedom to criticize and had suggested that a new politics was in the making. The emergence of this new politics was to be characterised in Barry by a perplexing mix of parochial impatience on the one hand and of sterling idealism on the other. Much of the impatience developed out of an appreciation that the town was not moving quickly enough to cope with the new social demands of war. Certainly lots of entertainment was laid on for the people forced to spend the War in Barry; the Old Vic Company with its stars Dame Sybil Thorndyke

Certificate of Service

BARRY'S "WELCOME HOME" FUND COMMITTEE.

We, the Mayor Aldermen and Burgesses of the Borough of Barry

hereby present to Arthur John Griffith Sanders
being a resident of the said Borough, this Certificate in
recognition of the Loyal and Gallant Services rendered by him
to his Country during the Second World War 1939~1945
and in sincere appreciation of his devotion
to duty in the cause of Justice and Peace.

Mary Holland Mayor

and Lewis Casson came to the Memorial Hall to perform *Macbeth*, and there was in general a full programme of film matinees, concerts by choirs and bands, community singing, sporting events and boxing tournaments. But the council absolutely refused to allow the cinemas to open on Sunday, which struck many people as both a disservice to men in uniform and as an act of hypocrisy, as throughout the summer months the Barry Island fairground (with its merry-go-rounds and Figure 8) was in full swing for seven days a week. There was a good deal of discontent about the pattern of entertainment in the town and matters came to a head in 1943 during a bitter debate over the use of the Memorial Hall. Part of the Hall was being used as an emergency hospital, but the main auditorium was used for concerts on Sundays and for twice-nightly shows on week nights. In February 1943 Alan Martin, the producer, who was organising the variety shows, announced that he could not afford the increased rent demanded by the Council, so he was closing down. This caused much local resentment, especially as some people thought that perhaps 'the real reason' for the increased rent demand was that Councillors objected to 'the class of entertainment' or 'at least to some of the material'. Feelings were all the more bitter, as it was felt that Mr. Martin had been the first person to use what the local press referred to as 'Barry's white elephant' for a genuinely popular purpose. The Council were reminded that they had not spent anything to put up the building, but had rather relied on the generosity of Lord Davies, that the Hall had never attracted the expected national conferences, and that it was perhaps too idealistic to think of it becoming a Welsh cultural centre after the War. The Memorial Hall now became the subject of an angry debate which was resolved with tragic irony on Whit Monday 1943, when the building was destroyed by an accidental fire. The fifteen hospital patients were evacuated and no lives were lost, but the disaster led to fierce criticisms of the fire-watching services and the state of the fire-hydrants. But the Council's critics could only be struck by the humour of the whole situation. One letter to the local press told of how Barry's 'white-elephant had become a black-elephant' and reminded readers that if Mr. Martin had remained, the fire would not have happened. Mr. Martin's last show, by the way, had been called 'The Sky's The Limit' and, said the correspondent, for the Memorial Hall 'now it is!'. There were demands for an enquiry but nobody commented on the fact that only a few years earlier, *Macbeth*, always regarded by actors as 'the unlucky play', had been performed in the Memorial Hall by the Old Vic Company!

Fig. 94.
Certificate of Service during Second World War, signed by Mayor of Barry.
A. J. G. Sanders. Borough Coat of Arms reproduced by permission.

Discontent over the Council's handling of Sunday cinema and the Memorial Hall merged into more serious issues. The complexion of local politics was bound to change as men and women of all parties, including the Communist, came together to organise a local 'Help for Russia Fund' week. Strange bedfellows were coming together to man war-time committees and to cement a new political consensus in the face of those other individuals and groups who remained critical of the British war effort. In the midst of this re-alignment the sudden death occurred in May 1942 of Patrick Munro, the 59-year-old M.P. for Barry and Llandaff. There followed a fascinating and important by-election. The hope of the Conservative Party and of their Labour partners in the Government was that the electoral truce would be respected and that there would be no contest. This was also the view of the local Communist Party who urged that all the main parties should meet together to select a National Candidate. Arthur Horner of the South Wales Miners' Federation came to urge Barry's Communists to support both the National Government and Winston Churchill, and to press the case for an immediate Second Front in Europe to take the strain off Russia. The Labour Party leaders urged the Barry Labour Party to respect the truce, and in the end the local Party deferred to this advice but at the same time they made it clear that they would really have liked a contest, for they called on the National Executive of the Labour Party 'to terminate the truce' which served 'no useful purpose in this War'.

Fully aware of their responsibilities, the Conservatives chose an ideal candidate: 48-year old Cyril Lakin, a Barry boy who had been educated at Cadoxton, the County School and then at Oxford. He had been commissioned in the First World War, called to the Bar, and had eventually become Assistant and Literary Editor of *The Sunday Times* and a frequent broadcaster. In his adoption speech he explained that he 'stood for the vigorous prosecuting of the war, and for full aid for Russia both in munitions and by the opening of new allied fronts'. The local Conservative Chairman, Mr. Arthur Meggitt, expressed his admiration for the way the Labour Party had overcome their urge to fight, but nevertheless Cyril Lakin was forced into a contest by two independent candidates. An Australian solicitor and former member of the Labour Party, Ronald Mackay, stood as an Independent Socialist, pledging support for Churchill but demanding an immediate General Election to get rid of what he described as 'the worst Government since Lord North' and one 'which would surely lose the Empire'. 'I am going to bust the election truce', said Mackay, and he went on to argue for the nationalisation of key industries, for a proper statement of peace aims, for a Federal Europe, an Atlantic Charter and a world economic plan. At the very last minute the nomination of a Mr. Malcolm Paton was received, and this heavily-bearded Herefordshire farmer announced that he would be standing as a Welsh Independent in favour of Churchill, but demanding self-government for Wales and a reform of the coal industry.

The by-election result was known on June 19th, 1942. Mr. Paton received only 975 votes, and Cyril Lakin, with 19,408 votes, had a 5,655 majority over Ronald Mackay. Barry did not provide one of those shock by-election defeats that Churchill's Government was to experience at this stage of the War, but nevertheless the election fits into the national pattern. Mackay was not a lunatic-fringe candidate but the representative of a national body of opinion who were critical of how the War was being fought and who thought that the House of Commons was unrepresentative. In the by-election he was able to cite the support of such national figures as J. B. Priestley and Vernon Bartlett.[13] It it not easy to use the Barry result as a comment on how the war was being fought, for Mackay's impressive 13,753 votes presumably came in the main from hard-core Labour voters, but it is interesting to note that in the reporting of the by-election and in its immediate aftermath a great deal of publicity was given to the demand for a Second Front. In early 1943 Leonard Finch of the Barry Communist Party sent an open letter to Lakin with a number of points including a demand for action against the 'Fascist Revival in Britain' but in particular stressing again the need for the Allies to follow up Stalin's magnificent progress with some kind of initiative in the West.

The Second Front was perhaps the great issue of 1942, but by these early months of 1943 it had been eclipsed by an issue which was far more likely to develop into a popular cause. Sir William Beveridge's Report, which advocated a plan of National Insurance, but which also recommended in the strongest possible terms that a full Welfare State be established, was published on December 1st, 1942. Beveridge was a great publicist and he was determined to sell his proposals to the nation, and he found a public all too willing after three years of gloom to take up his ideas. All the various discontents had been given a cause and here was the best guarantee that this war would not be wasted, for a land 'fit for heroes' was now in sight.[14] The Beveridge Report caught the imagination of a nation and provided a golden opportunity for local Labour Parties to begin to construct a politics on their terms. The *Barry Dock News* reacted to Beveridge in a wise and balanced fashion. It joked that any M.P.s not enthusiastic about the Report would probably not want to seek re-election, it warned against Utopian dreams, suggested that for some people jobs would be a higher priority than social security, but in general hoped that the proposals would become law without much alteration. In fact, Conservative ministers were to be luke-warm in their response to Beveridge, and in their open letter the Barry Communists forced Lakin to declare his position. His response was an expression of 'whole-hearted support' and he made public his disappointment with the Government's response, which he described as being 80 per cent in favour of the proposals. He promised to prod ministers and to keep up his demand for a Minister of Social Security, but he appealed for groups 'not to bring about disunity over this', for if it became a party issue then we would be 'playing Hitler's game'.

Lakin was to be kept under constant pressure on the Beveridge proposals. Letters from the Trades Council and a local branch of the A.E.U. prompted the Council's Finance Committee under Dudley Howe to express their support of the Report. In March 1943 Lakin received a petition of 302 signatures (most of whom were railwaymen) which criticised the Government's tardy response. In an accompanying letter to Lakin a Mr. Charles Thomas repeated the call for a Second Front, but then went on to demand further efforts from the M.P. on the Social Security issue, before ending with the point that 'we never thought that the Government would surrender to the Insurance Companies without firing a shot'. Lakin came to Barry to tell a Co-operative Hall audience that the Government had accepted 16 of the 23 main points in principle and as yet only one had been rejected; he stressed that Beveridge was 'not a political party question' and that 'making it one will only wreck it'. It is clear from the local debate that support for the new proposals came from a wide cross-section of opinion but there was a vital difference between those who, like Lakin, were generally in favour of Beveridge and those in the local Labour Movement who wanted the whole Report implemented without compromise. War-time conditions sanctioned a much fuller reporting of left-wing meetings and so it is possible for us to sense the new confidence that was undoubtedly inspiring Socialists whether they belonged to the Labour or Communist Parties. Many people were talking about the post-war world, the Barry Rotary Club for example drew up their own Education Report in which they advocated that all education should be centralised and taken away from local authorities, but it was Labour that was now making all the running, and in so doing making all moderate positions look like fudging. The winds were filling Labour's sails and already they could sense that they had won the debate. The Unity Hall became the headquarters of the new politics, and in a way it eclipsed the Council Chamber as the sounding-board of future plans. At the Unity Hall, Labourites, Communists and Trade Unionists spoke confidently of the future that was theirs. At a May Day Rally in 1943 local members of the Labour Party and Trades Council heard strong criticisms of Churchill from a Mr. Weston of the T.U.C. and from David Grenfell, M.P., who had actually been in the Government until the previous year. Grenfell said of Beveridge that it was 'a perfection of all the Socialists have been trying to do since 1898', he reminded them that Churchill was 'a Tory', and so he gave his audience the vital advice 'don't let them get away with it'.

Labour was alive and well in Barry and very much looking forward to a new political dispensation. It was largely national issues and influences that had inspired this revival in their fortunes, but as the War was being won, so in Barry Labour began to benefit from a mounting hostility to incumbent local councillors and it was this which gave the final edge to the new politics. Tension was inspired by the fact that there were no local elections during the War and so councillors elected between 1936 and 1938 were forced to serve for the duration. Those who did stand down or die were replaced by co-opted members of the appropriate party. The War, as we have seen, occasioned many changes in values and attitudes, and had almost encouraged people to have their say. Just as it was inevitable that many people came to see that a House of Commons elected in 1935 was unrepresentative, so it was equally inevitable that they would begin to question the mandate and legitimacy of what was now seen as a left-over Council. It was really the issues of Sunday-opening and the Memorial Hall which started the local bandwagon of criticism and, we may even say, abuse. In November 1943 the Council appealed to local citizens to throw open their doors to the Allied Forces at Christmas-time, but the *Barry Dock News* immediately jumped down their throats by denouncing their hypocrisy, for local people had always entertained service personnel, whilst the Council still denied them entertainment. The paper went on with relish to talk of a body of men who far too long had 'been cribb'd, cabin'd and confin'd' and who in some cases 'have outlived their constructive usefulness'. This superbly written lead article spoke of how the War had created a new spirit which would not 'tolerate the imposition of the will of a few on the legitimate desires, aspirations and hopes of all those who have risked their lives to sunder once and for all the shackles of Whitehall or King Square'. A month later the Council eventually voted 13-12 in favour of Sunday film-showings after a battle led by Councillor Arthur Jones in which there had been petitions and counter-petitions, but the *Barry Dock News* took the opportunity to remark that 'by comparison Nero was a mere novice, he fiddled while Rome burned, the Barry Council fiddled while the whole world was burning'.

The local press took great delight in drawing attention to how councillors were 'showing distinct signs of nervousness' and in suggesting that their instability and peevishness could be explained, for they were 'like sleepers suddenly awakened from a deep and prolonged sleep', and similarly their being rattled could be accounted for by the fact that 'the Day of Judgement is at hand'. The discontent was being fuelled by many local issues, of which the shortage of houses was probably the most important, but there were other things, such as the failure of the Council to buy Jenner Park and so ensure the future of professional soccer in the town, there were constant criticisms of the inadequacy of local fire-hydrants, there were regular references to red tape and there were even some accusations of local employers dismissing employees who had been to the cinema on Sundays. Issues may have been important but, of course, the main trouble was that a small group of important councillors had just been around for too long. History had forced them to stay in power in what were really very different times. Inevitably attention focused on Councillors Dudley Howe and Dan Evans who had seemed to run Barry for as long as most people could remember. A cartoon in March 1944 depicted 'Dudley and Dan', and in so doing confirmed their symbolic status as the twin representatives of the old order, of what was now seen as the establishment in Barry. After years of service they now had the misfortune to become the scapegoats of the local manifestation of the new national mood of impatience. Dan Evans probably had to take even more criticism than Dudley Howe, and towards the end of the War much of it was personal criticism. Evans had been born in Carmarthenshire and had come to Barry as a young man in 1899, when his father became the minister at Tabernacle Welsh Congregationalist Chapel. In 1902 he had become the manager of a new ironmonger's shop in Holton Road, but in 1905 he bought the shop and began to develop what was to become Barry's most famous business, and what was, in effect, a high-class departmental store. The Dan Evans Company was always to boast of the very personal service it offered the people of Barry, of the high quality of its staff and of the superannuation scheme run for that staff. But Dan Evans himself was equally proud of his Welsh cultural heritage and of his membership and staunch support of Tabernacle Chapel.[15] In the Depression he had been the main inspiration of the Barry Chamber of Commerce and the Development Committee, and nobody had fought harder to boost Barry as a viable commercial entity, but now the whole rhetoric of politics was against his style. In 1944 he followed his doctor's advice and turned down the opportunity to become the Mayor of Barry. The *Barry Dock News* once again urged 'the Old Gang Must Go'; a whole era in the history of the town was coming to an end.

Historians have long debated whether the British people voted for Socialism in the General Election of 1945. Their considered conclusion is that those who voted Labour voted not for a doctrine but for a new deal that would give them more jobs, better social protection and health services and perhaps, above all, would give them homes of their own.[16] Certainly in Barry the need for more houses, and especially council houses, was the main talking point from 1943 onwards. A local Brains Trust was held at the Y.M.C.A. in March 1943, and the panel were immediately asked whether the town would get more council houses, to which Mrs. Spivey replied that 'Barry should become more suburban minded'. In August a merchant sailor informed the press that for all the fanfares that his profession had received in the War, his family, which included three children, had been waiting ten years for a council house. Throughout 1944 the Council wrangled over what measures could be taken to cope with the housing shortage and over what particular schemes should be adopted. It was apparent now that, whatever the long term policies and the extent of government aid, there would have to be emergency measures to provide temporary homes at the end of the War, and plans for the construction of factory-made bungalows and 'prefabs' were approved. As hostilities ended in 1945, the Council were faced with 1,600 applications for new houses, many of them from ex-servicemen. The post-war years would necessarily see the Borough of Barry becoming greatly concerned with housing policy and housing finance.

There was considerable pride in Barry's war record and it was thought very appropriate that the King and Queen and Princess Elizabeth should come to Barry for a brief visit in March 1944. The Royal party toured the Docks, visited a W.R.N.S. hostel and in general made a great impact. This was the first visit of a monarch to Barry, and King George looked splendid in his admiral's uniform; the local feeling was that they were 'more natural than our own selves' and that Princess Elizabeth was 'a typical English girl'. On V.E. Day buildings were decorated, street parties were given and prisoners-of-war were welcomed home. There was dancing at the Square and effigies of Hitler suffered various fates throughout the town. People were well aware of what Barry had contributed to the War in terms of personnel and there was open praise for the way in which the Docks had risen to the challenge and had shown in particular that it could be used for general cargo and was not totally dependent on coal. But there was no smugness and complacency in 1945, and eyes were very firmly on the future. A cartoon was headed 'I SAW A CITY—AN IDEAL OUR BARRY BOYS ARE FIGHTING FOR' and separate pictures depicted Houses for All (a detached bungalow), No Customers at the Labour Exchange (the staff were shown playing cards), Brilliant Street Lighting (papers could be read at night), a Fair Share of beef, fruit, butter, eggs and wine, An Adequate Water Supply for Fire Fighting and finally a Mayor formally inviting the Press into the Council Chamber. Later in the year the news that the Bartax Car Hire firm were organising an essay competition with cash prizes in which County School children were invited to give their ideas on how Barry could be improved inspired our local cartoonist to suggest that the footbridge at the Docks be re-opened so that Barry Islanders could have access to the town, that Porthkerry Park be defended as an undeveloped area with the dodgems kept out, and that T.N.T. be used to clear derelict shops and houses on Dock View Road.[17] It was obviously a time when people felt inspired to cast off chains, to break down restrictions, and to demand new freedoms. The time had come to demand a better tomorrow.

In 1918 Major William Cope had won the Barry and Llandaff Division with 13,307 votes in an election in which fewer than 22,000 people had voted. In 1945 the same constituency was won for Labour by Major Lynn Ungoed-Thomas who received the huge total of 33,706 votes in an election in which over 70,000 people voted. Mass politics had come to Barry with a vengeance. Local Labour supporters were in a militant mood and many ex-servicemen and merchant sailors were demanding better homes; the local Labour Party had ensured victory by picking a man who could beat Cyril Lakin by appealing to as many potential Labour voters as possible. Major Ungoed-Thomas was a Haileybury and Oxford-trained barrister who had nursed the constituency for some years and who now campaigned in his Royal Artillery uniform. With such a candidate Labour could afford to ignore the press warnings that spoke of the danger of the country being 'dictated to by a bunch of nonentities' and of how 'Octopus-like' State Control would reach out its tentacles. The *Barry Dock News* had probably sensed the local mood before polling day for it asked readers to 'think well before you turn this freedom-loving country into a State-controlled machine' and reminded them that if they wished 'to give Labour a run for their money—without endangering National security—then what better opportunity than the local elections in November next'. Those elections duly came and the majority of Barry citizens voted Labour for a second time. The November results were sensational as Labour captured control of the Borough by sweeping the polls and winning 18 out of 21 seats. Dudley Howe and D. J. Boon were amongst the defeated and in fact only two Independents remained on the Council. A local paper thought it 'only natural' that of the 18 Labour Councillors 9 or 10 'had to do with the Docks or railway'. The Aldermanic elections took place and Labour conceded one to the Independents; the subsequent by-elections were held and Labour consolidated its position so that now it had 25 out of 28 places on the Council. The new Mayor was Mrs. Mary Holland, a Catholic and the first woman ever to serve as Barry's first citizen. In fact there were now six women councillors which perhaps indicated as much as anything how the nature of political priorities had changed. Barry was ready to enter the Age of the Welfare State.

In December 1945 the *Barry Dock News* detected a feeling of 'anti-climax' in the town and spoke of how Barry, like any other place, 'struggles on, a little bit war-weary and depressed, but accepting the situation with stoicism'. That sense of anti-climax was to pervade the whole post-war period. The Welfare State was set up and rapidly eroded much of the Victorian poverty that had lingered on in many parts of Britain and abolished the many indignities and anxieties that had blighted the inter-war years. There was now a National Health Service which brought into being a far more comprehensive range of services and especially a fully integrated hospital system. There was a far more effective system of secondary education; there was National Insurance; there were homes and above all there were plenty of jobs. Many of these things were soon taken for granted, but in any case, the benefits that they brought were often disguised by the shortages and the enforced austerities that were to be the hallmarks of Labour's period in office between 1945 and 1951. Those who had suffered in the Thirties gave grateful thanks, whilst others, many of them young, complained of delays, waiting-lists and restrictions. In early 1944 at a time when the Barry Council was setting up its post-war Reconstruction Committee, a correspondent had written to the local press to tell of how many people who could 'remember the absolute want and poverty which stalked the streets of Barry not so very many years ago' were hoping that there would be no return to that situation. In particular he argued that the time had come to put Barry's 'dilapidated houses in order'; bathrooms needed to be supplied to many homes and the time had come for electricity to be used to light both homes and the streets. We are reminded that Barry needed the Welfare State, and the period after 1945 brought striking and dramatic improvements. Poverty and want were driven from the town and symbolically electric lighting came to abolish much of the Victorian gloom in old houses and streets. Nevertheless, dissatisfaction and impatience remained very much in evidence.

Housing had been the main local issue in 1945 and it was to remain the most emotive and contentious issue right through until the 1950s and possibly well beyond. The whole town focused its attention on the performance of the Barry Borough Council as a housing authority, and there were constant rows about shortages of building materials and other delays. The statistics of housebuilding dominated political debate and began to assume an almost mystical significance. Between 1919 and 1944 the Barry Council had built 1,170 houses, but now the situation was as serious as it ever had been. The post-war programme began with the provision of 42 houses and 100 'prefabs' in 1946, and then continued with 96 houses in 1947, 90 houses in 1948, and so on. The Council was well aware that the vast housing estates it had built in the Depression had lacked many amenities, had failed to develop as communities and tended to form a rather featureless

Plate XCII. 'Cornish' pre-fabricated concrete dwellings, O'Donnell Road, Barry. *R. W. Thomas.*

environment. There was now a conscious attempt to plan housing, and greater care was taken.[18] Estates were somewhat smaller, amenities such as playing fields and shops were provided and housing types were mixed. In general private builders were putting up houses on the west and north peripheries of the town, while many council houses were built within existing housing areas on old allotments and on land previously thought to be too steep. There were still large areas of unrelieved new council housing at the Colcot and around Cadoxton, but in other areas of the town there was a new blend of council and private housing. Barry was becoming more of a patchwork quilt in housing terms. There were many satisfied families, for by 1951 a total of 530 houses of one sort or another had been provided, but the general problem remained. On the Port Road and at the Buttrills there were many families living in disgusting and unhealthy conditions in old army huts, who wondered when their turn was going to come. In 1951 one resident of the Crow Hill Camp described the awful conditions in which he was living, and reflected on the fact that the Council could pay for a Festival of Britain clock at the Island. Meanwhile many other young couples went on living in rented rooms or stayed on in overcrowded family homes. In early 1951 there were 1,800 on the housing waiting list, but before the end of the year the figure had reached 2,000. The Council, first under Labour and then, after 1949, under the Independents, was kept under constant pressure to acquire yet more land and to plan even larger schemes. All over Barry building was going on and the scramble to secure a family home went on.[19]

Austerity took the edge off the Welfare State, but in Barry the post-war sense of disappointment could also be related to a general realisation of the diminution of the town's role in the modern world.[20] Barry had successfully achieved borough status, but at a time when the balance of power was passing away from municipal authorities. The War had seen the state avariciously claiming power and this tendency continued in the post-war world. At every step the Barry Borough Council came up against the harsh realities of the national economic situation and of Treasury control. Even at a more local level there was a perceptible diminution of local power as the Glamorgan County Council became more influential. Power had tended to drift away from the town and towards County Hall throughout the Thirties but the loss of municipal autonomy was more keenly felt in the post-war world. The vital loss came in terms of education, for Barry failed in its bid to become an 'excepted district' under the 1944 Butler Education Act, and so the whole Barry school system now became the responsibility of the County Council. The demise of the Barry Education Committee caused a good deal of resentment and there were fears that the high standards for which the town had been famous would be swamped by a new mediocrity. Several people saw this transfer of power as marking the end of that Progressive identity which had been the hallmark of the town since the Edwardian period. Before the War the town council had seemed to control so many activities and there were so many interests for councillors to pursue. Now the schools, like the hospitals, had been taken into other hands. A few years later Barry's gas undertaking became part of the new national system, and another distinctive local institution disappeared; for years the town had boasted of what was one of the most efficient and profitable gas systems in the country. The Council's powers were being whittled away, and increasingly people tended to think of the Borough as just being responsible for housing and for the parks. The County Council now seemed an altogether more prestigious body, although the paradox was that people took far less interest in its affairs. County Hall was less than ten miles away, yet it seemed remote, and most county council elections were characterized by apathy. Barry now had six representatives on the County Council, and in the immediate post-war years they were all Labour representatives. But in 1949 the Independents were to sweep the deck by capturing the three seats up for election. Even the victorious candidates, however, confessed that there had been little interest in the elections, a fact which one of the victors, Dr. P. D. Richards found strange as, in his view, the County now played as big a part in local affairs, if not more so than the Borough'.

By the end of the War both the major political parties had accepted that full employment had to be maintained at all costs.[21] For Barry this meant that there was to be no return to the tragic conditions of the 1930s. There was a good deal of speculation as to where the new jobs might be created. At first the R.A.F. station at St. Athan figured prominently in local speculation. There was talk of the aerodrome becoming 'Britain's principal. . . Trans-Atlantic Air Service Terminal', and at one point the local press suggested that the decision on this would 'inevitably make or mar the future prosperity of Barry'. Delegations went from the town to the Ministry of Civil Aviation; the case was that possibly the whole future prosperity of South Wales would depend on the development of St. Athan as an international airport. In December 1945 the *Barry Dock News* referred to the possibility of St. Athan becoming 'the Clapham Junction of the world' and also urged that Barry should be developed as a major sea-plane base. The paper's only fear was that Cardiff would be the real beneficiary of all these new ventures, and that once again there would be a threat to Barry's independence. Nothing came of these speculations, but interest in St. Athan waned, as suddenly there was news about new jobs in Barry itself. In what was really a bolt-from-the-blue, the international company, Distillers Limited, announced that in conjunction with associated companies they would be constructing a complex of three operations concerned with the manufacture of plastics and chemicals on a 200-acre site just to the east of the Docks. Soon there were construction jobs, and then perhaps as many as

1,500 permanent jobs in a plant which looked like something out of science fiction and which was destined to change the industrial face of Barry. In a dramatic fashion the town was being shown the future and being invited to step into a new scientific and technological world. It was a new world, too, in terms of employment conditions with complicated shift systems and new side-benefits, such as sports facilities and social clubs.

The arrival of Distillers did much to sustain an optimism about employment prospects, but it could not dispel anxieties about the future of the Docks. As we have seen, the War had forced Barry to become a more versatile port; the provision of extra tracks, of new hydraulic cranes and dockside equipment and the setting-up of oil installations had all improved Barry's claim that it had the potential to become a general cargo port. It was obvious that there could be no return to the great coal-exporting days, if only because most coal was now badly needed for home industries. General cargo was the obvious solution but the management at Barry Docks was well aware of the many disadvantages hampering the port as it competed for custom. Like other South Wales ports, Barry never previously had to compete for general cargo, and so was coming late to a situation in which other ports had established preferential rates and long-standing commercial ties. There was fierce competition, too, from the East Coast ports, which

Plate XCIII.
S.S. *Pine Hill* loading war material for Korea in September 1950.
L. W. Hansen; I. W. Prothero Coll.

had been effectively out of use in the war-years but which were now rapidly forging new links, especially with Europe. The importing of oil was the most encouraging sign, but in general there seemed little chance of fully employing the labour force at the Docks. Things were made more frustrating by the new administrative arrangements. The G.W.R. had done its best in difficult days in the Depression, but it had never been accepted emotionally by the people of Barry. The railway companies were under Government control until the end of the War, whereupon there followed a period of uncertainty until nationalisation became a reality on 1st January, 1948. At a time of great economic difficulty the various regions of British Railways were now faced with the enormous task of repairing, re-equipping and modernising the railway system. In rail terms Barry was now just part of the Western Region, whilst the Docks became one of the five ports administered by the South Wales Docks division of the British Transport Commission's Docks and Inland Waterways Executive. Whatever the merits or demerits of nationalisation, the plain fact was that Barry Docks had become one small facility in a very big system. Whatever claims were made for Barry would have to be processed through a vast and remote bureaucratic structure. The Docks now belonged to the people, but control over them had passed into anonymous hands.

Some people had talked of the possibility of a New Jerusalem in 1945, but the reality was to be a world in which things were better but far from perfect. The great social benefits were obvious but so were the economic constraints and the remoteness of the new bureaucracies. Not surprisingly it was a period of political uncertainty. Labour had virtually eliminated the other political parties from the Council Chamber in 1945, and yet in 1949, the Independents, who were now mainly, but not exclusively, Conservatives, were back in control. It took Labour two years to regain the Council, and then they managed to hang on for thirteen years. The same uncertainty was apparent in Parliamentary elections. During 1949 Ungoed-Thomas made the strange decision not to seek re-election in Barry as presumably he thought he could find a safer seat. In the event he was to be defeated at Carmarthen in the 1950 Election, although he went on to win Leicester North-East in 1951, and, as Sir Lynn Ungoed-Thomas, to serve briefly as Solicitor-General. Meanwhile the Barry Labour Party had to find a new candidate to defend the seat, and the person eventually chosen was Alderman Dorothy Rees. As Labour had taken over in Barry in 1945, certain people had seemed to symbolize the new politics. One such person was Stan Awbery, then the M.P. for Bristol Central, and another was Mrs. Dorothy Rees, who, with her great interests in educational welfare, seemed almost to be the local spokesman of the Welfare State. Mrs. Rees had been born in Barry in 1898, the daughter of a dock-worker; she won a scholarship from Holton Road School to the County School and then trained as a teacher at the Barry Training College. Her first teaching jobs took her away from Barry, but then she returned and immediately threw herself into the local political struggle. She was elected to the County Council in 1934, some two years before she joined the Urban District Council, and her perspective was always to be county-wide rather than narrowly municipal. In a sense, her career symbolized the way in which decision-making was moving away from Barry's small Council Chamber, and pointed to the need for the town to go outside itself in the fight for better schools and for better services. In the War Mrs. Rees worked as full-time liaison officer with the Ministry of Food before becoming a full-time Labour organiser for the local party in 1945.

Boundary changes had removed Llandaff from the Barry constituency and so it was a smaller electorate that went to the poll in the General Election of February 1950. The Liberal candidate, Alun Emlyn Jones, fought a good campaign and polled 6,180 votes, which helped Mrs. Rees to defeat the Conservative candidate, Meurig Evans, by the narrow majority of 1,325. In the campaign Meurig Evans, a banker and journalist, had talked of 'the failure of the Socialists to deliver the goods in the form of food, houses and a rising standard of living for all', and these failures he attributed to their having put 'theory before practice and party before country'. Mrs. Rees saw full employment as the main issue and explained the victory over mass unemployment in terms of 'a positive policy and careful planning'; the need now was to 'increase productivity, raise exports, to increase efficiency and to keep purchasing power and productivity marching together'. Labour's majority in the House had been reduced to six and so Mrs. Rees was kept busy both in the division lobby and as Private Parliamentary Secretary to Dr. Edith Summerskill, the Minister of National Insurance, although she did become involved with one or two bitter local quarrels. Mr. Atlee's majority faded away, and so within twenty months there had to be another General Election. The Barry Conservatives now had a new candidate in the 33-year-old Cardiff solicitor Raymond Gower, who had made a good impression when he fought Ogmore in 1950 and who had used the 18 months in which he had been prospective candidate to hold 153 meetings and to visit 7,000 homes. The General Election of October 1951 was keenly contested and the young children of the town could be heard singing either 'Vote Vote Vote for Dorothy Rees' or 'Vote Vote Vote for Raymond Gower'. There was an increased turn-out compared with 1950, and both Labour and Conservative increased their total vote. What was decisive was the absence of a Liberal candidate, and it was this which allowed Raymond Gower to make Barry one of the 24 seats gained throughout the county by the victorious Conservative Party of Winston Churchill. Mr. Gower's majority was only 1,649 and not surprisingly the Labour Party were furious at the way in which prominent local Liberals had worked for the Conservative candidate. Dorothy Rees resumed her distinguished service on the County Council, but in terms of Parliamentary representation the era of Raymond Gower had begun.[22]

Barry had developed virtually overnight from a few small villages into a fully-fledged town, but perhaps the most remarkable feature of its modern history was that Barry was to remain just a small town. It crystalized into a town of 40,000 people. Professor Brinley Thomas has reminded us that 'the major influences which have shaped the growth of the Welsh economy have been international', and Barry must be seen as having been created by international forces in the late 19th century, and then as being stunted by a new set of circumstances in the 20th. In the period after 1918 Barry was more at the mercy of domestic economic considerations, and although there was a decline in population of almost 5,000 between 1926 and 1939, post-war developments and the slightly increased birth-rate were to confirm Barry as a town of 40,000 people. Essentially, modern Barry has remained singularly unchanged in its general dimensions. In the late Forties and early Fifties Barry could have been selected as the quintessential small British town. There was a small class of prosperous business people and managers who, together with professional families, formed some kind of local gentry. Similarly, the town had its genuine working-class leaders, men like Jim Gerry, a train-driver, who for fifty years had been the inspiration behind the N.U.R., the Trades Council, and Co-operative and Socialist adult education in the town, or like Charlie Clemo, who recalled angry strikes at Rank's Mill and was now the secretary of a Transport and General Workers' Branch that had become a cornerstone of the local Labour Movement.[23] Yet in a sense the class divide was not the most marked feature of local life. The main social distinction was probably between unskilled labourers and those working-men who prided themselves on traditional artisan values. The tone of the town was determined by the way in which railwaymen, coal-trimmers and other workmen came together with clerks, teachers, shopkeepers and shopworkers to maintain older standards of respectability. Even in those post-war years it still seemed as if the personality of Barry was being determined by that social alliance which had been forged in churches and chapels. It was this, taken together with the not unrelated general lack of public-houses, which led visitors from the Valleys to think of the town as being 'posh' or *petit-bourgeois*. Certainly the town had distinct values and these rested in the main on the way in which organised Christianity, housing patterns and similar incomes had brought together the train-driver and the local government clerk.

Welsh visitors to Barry were never quite sure where the town stood in class terms but they were also foxed by the town's cultural identity. There were several Welsh chapels in Barry and an active Welsh-language cultural life. Many of the teachers in the early days were Welsh-speaking, but in general the town seemed to differ greatly from the rest of South Wales and to be in some undefinable way English. The truth was that Barry was English, or at least as much English as it was Welsh. There had been a massive migration of people into Barry from the West Country and also of people from the Valleys of South Wales whose families had earlier come from English counties. Barry had come too late to be dominated by that classic Welsh Nonconformity which moulded most of South Wales, and it often seemed to have more in common in its social patterns and values with West Country communities such as Bristol and Swindon. The majority of Barry people became very proud of being Welsh, and Welsh rugby and soccer teams as well as Welsh boxers received enthusiastic support from the town, but many families knew that they were Welsh by adoption; obituaries in the local press gave constant examples of careers which, like that of Jim Gerry, had begun in Somerset or Gloucestershire. In 1964 one writer was to say of Barry that 'it is not a particularly Welsh town—nor is it English' for 'the intermingling of peoples from many different places have given it a character of its own'.[24] The most obvious evidence of that character was the distinctive Barry accent, which, like the very similar but less attractive Cardiff and Newport accents, owed more to the West Country and possible Ireland than it did to Wales. Barry people were proud of being Welsh but they knew that their town had its own history and its own identity and that therefore they were just different.

In social terms education remained the decisive factor in shaping the careers of Barry children. These were the classic years of the '11 Plus' and Barry's eight junior schools competed as keenly in the scholarship examinations for places at the boys' and girls' grammar schools as they did at the annual sports day. Barry's housing pattern meant that all the junior schools reflected the general social unit of the local population; they were all to achieve successful results in the scholarship examinations. There was no hierarchy of schools, although there was an occasional ribbing of Romilly's pretensions to be the school for the more socially-ambitious west end of the town. Romilly Junior School did have an excellent record, but one which was somewhat affected by two developments in the early 1950s. In 1952 pupils from the Park Ward area were transferred to Barry Island School, a step to which many parents objected and the result was a famous 'strike' of school-children which lasted for a term and which led to unofficial classes being held in Luen's Café at Cold Knap. Then the opening of the Welsh school, Ysgol St. Ffransis, in 1953 took many more students away from Romilly. Success or failure in the scholarship was vital, for there was little chance of a subsequent transfer from the new secondary modern schools to what were always referred to in Barry as the 'County Schools'.

County School students were conscious of being a local *élite.* From all over the town they came in their green or black blazers to the two schools which stood on either side of the Training College in what was really an amazing educational complex on the upper slopes between Buttrills Road and College Road. There were many different types of pupils at the County Schools and there were those who left at any age between 15 and 18 for

Plate XCIV. Barry College of Education, accommodation blocks. *B. Daly.*

clerical or commercial jobs, but both schools were unashamedly academic in their values. Like many grammar schools the staff rooms were richly blessed with characters and nick-names; anecdotes and jokes abounded, but both schools, and especially the Boys' School, lived with an exciting confidence in their academic excellence and with the constant challenge that the distinction that had already been achieved could be rivalled or surpassed. 'We have produced', Gwyn Thomas once said, 'the odd genius and the odd clown', but to go to the schools and to take them seriously was to enter into a world as mythic as that created by any leading public school. The legends concerned the greatness of Edgar Jones, the academic ability of the staff and the glorious trail that had been blazed by old boys and girls. The *Honoris Causa* boards were there for all to see, but the talk, too, was of Sir Charles Woolley's distinguished diplomatic career, of Barnett Janner's Parliamentary fame, of how Dr. Dixie was one of the world's greatest geologists, of Leslie Illingworth the cartoonist, of Grace William's rising stature as a composer, of Bryan Hopkin's brilliance as an economist and of how a clutch of young scholars Glyn Daniel, Keith Thomas, Hrothgar Habakkuk and David Joslin were threatening to take over the disciplines of History and Archaeology at Oxford and Cambridge. There was a litany of famous names, and not the least of them was Ronnie Boon, who had played for Wales and who had dropped a vital goal in that legendary 1933 win at Twickenham.[25] The message for young pupils was clear and it was neatly summed up by one of the best known masters at the Boys' School, for Gwyn Thomas was fond of the phrase 'go thou and do likewise'.

Barry pupils did well because the whole ethics of the town sanctioned academic success. Parents and teaching staff conspired to maintain standards and to cherish talent. In education the Edwardian legacy lived on, but the general size and identity of the town played a part. With only one boys' school and one girls' school for the whole town, the schools could become very much the cutting edge of the community's ambitions and quest for fame, whilst at the same time the cosmopolitan mix of the local population contributed richly to every-day life in the schools. Glyn Daniel has described the excitement experienced by boys from the Vale of Glamorgan as they travelled into the busy town and to the crowded school.[26] In fact, village boys and girls came face to face with pupils from deepest Cadoxton and Barry Docks, the children of professional people met the children of coal-trimmers, children from Welsh-speaking homes became more aware of their Welsh identity, morning assembly was held in Welsh once a week (and perhaps it is no accident that Plaid Cymru's Gwynfor Evans was a product of the school), but these Welsh boys and girls delighted in the friendship of classmates with strange Irish, Greek and sometimes even stranger English surnames. The excellence of education in Barry rested on ineluctable standards but also on a delight in personality and individuality which allowed pupils to discover their own essential genius. The schools did not impose a regime but were content to act as catalysts. So strong were the foundations and so sure the traditions that they were to survive the coming of comprehensivisation and the eventual transfer of both schools to fields outside the town. The quality of education remained, and further outstanding successes were to be achieved, but many older Barrians felt that the move of the Boys' School in 1959 was the end of an era. As the young poet T. Maroulis of VI Arts had it,

> 'Farewell you lump of Victorian grace
> We leave you for an age of space.'[27]

In 1953 *The Barrian,* the magazine of the Boys' Grammar School printed a symposium on the past, present and future of the town in which Philip Gabriel maintained that 'it would be near the truth to say that Barry's entertainments are the cinema in the winter and all pertaining to the sea in the summer'.[28] The immediate post-war years had been the classic period of cinema-going and it was possible for enthusiasts to see anything up to twenty different films a week. Cyclists rushed to get the newsreels from one cinema to another, there were frequently long queues, and each cinema had its own adherents: 'The Rom' always had good films, the Theatre Royal had surely been built to accommodate the whole population of Barry, and 'the Tiv' just had that extra bit of style not to mention an exotic aroma and warmth that made a visit there a real treat. Some complained that films did not come to Barry soon enough whilst others regretted the almost total absence of theatre and concerts, a situation that continued until the Memorial Hall reopened in 1957. There was dancing, of course, at Bindles and the Savoy, but nothing really challenged the supremacy of the movies. Sport remained a great passion, and in the summer it often seemed as if most of the town were playing bowls. In winter small crowds would gather to watch either Barry or the Grammar School play rugby but most rugby followers were more concerned to get into Cardiff to see the world's greatest club rugby team, especially as two local men Haydn Morris and Geoff Beckingham were prominent members of that side. But Barry was essentially a soccer town and that meant support on alternate Saturdays for Cardiff City and for Barry Town. 'The Linnets' had survived many crises, especially at the end of the War, but the town had been scandalised at the thought of there being no professional soccer at Jenner Park, and on several occasions local businessmen had to step in to rescue the team. League football had never come to Barry, but in the early Fifties Barry Town, whilst playing in the Southern League, often played football of Football League standard. The team was superbly managed by an old Barry player Bill Jones, it blended old league players like Stan Richards and Charlie Dyke with rising stars like Derek Tapscott and it played in front of large and enthusiastic crowds especially on those occasions when the opponents were the classy but dreaded rivals from Merthyr. The finest hour for Barry Town and their fans came in 1955, when the team beat Chester in a replay at Ninian Park to win the Welsh Cup.

In the summer, as we have heard, Barry turned its attention to the sea. Quite simply Barry people loved the whole aspect of their town. They spent hours looking out from the slopes of the town at shipping in the channel and looking through binoculars or telescopes to see if there were signs of life in a Somerset that that on clear days could seem just a mile or two away. There were many great walkers in the town, and these well-tanned hardy folk could be seen making their way through the streets and through Romilly Park towards Cold Knap or through woods and along cliffs towards the magnificent unspoilt freedom of the park and beach at Porthkerry. In winter months the whole town belonged to the walkers but in the summer it was invariably towards the Knap and Porthkerry that local people were drawn. In these years Barry made great efforts to become a holiday centre and guidebooks boosted the resort in more fulsome language than ever. A 1951 guide to what was described as 'the Premier Welsh Seaside Resort for Health and Pleasure' spoke of the town as offering 'an endless round of amusements' and reminded potential holiday-makers that 'Glamorganshire has been the supreme desire of all men for nearly a thousand years from the days when the Normans coveted it for its military importance to the present when its coast resorts are the most popular in Wales'. A 1954 guide explained that the town was 'ringed with first-class golf links and is noted as the golfing cradle of international star Dai Rees'; it then went on to describe the joys of looking out from Barry towards the West Country, for 'at times the chequered pattern of fields glows clear in unnatural storm-light—at others a soft fine-weather haze gives only fleeting and mysterious glimpses'. The ad-men worked hard and families did come to stay in the many Barry homes that were prepared for at least part of the year to give 'bed, breakfast and evening meal'. But Barry was never really cut out to be a holiday resort, and it remained a mecca for day-trippers. Barry Island had become famous, and in the summer months local people were quite prepared to leave it to the invading hordes.[29]

Plate XCV.
Cover of Barry Guide, 1972.
Barry Borough Council. R. W. Thomas Coll.

For people who grew up in the Valleys of South Wales during their classic phase, a day-trip to Barry Island was one of the great ritual highlights of the year. Trips were always eagerly anticipated, especially when they came in the form of chapel or club outings, when people of all ages and sizes were packed into buses and trains, and when the old people often seemed as excited as the young. Writing in 1943 the poet Idris Davies summed up what trippers of an earlier period had expected to find at Barry:

> 'Let's go to Barry Island, Maggie Fach,
> And give all the kids one day by the sea,
> And sherbert and buns and paper hats,
> And a rattling ride on the Figure Eight;
> We'll have tea on the sands, and rides on the donkeys,'

He went on to remind us of the psychological role that Barry could play:

> 'Leave the washing alone for today, Maggie Fach,
> And put on your best and come out to the sun
> And down to the holiday sea.
> We'll carry the sandwiches in a big brown bag
> And leave our troubles behind for a day.'[30]

What Barry people saw were crowded trains with exuberant children, all but falling out of the windows as they waved and screamed, and endless convoys of buses which came in throughout the morning and which always seemed to have difficulty in getting up the steep climb out of the town in the evening. Local boys became experts on all the bus-fleets of South Wales and the West Midlands, and the different liveries could be identified from miles away. Many bus proprietors were dependent on the appeal of Barry but perhaps nothing was quite as awesome as processions of twenty or thirty red double-deckers belonging to Rhondda Transport as they arrived from a presumably deserted valley. At the Island itself what Barry people saw were visitors who were prepared to spend hours on a crowded beach, who consumed meals, snacks, toffee-apples and candy-floss as if they had not eaten for days, and who more than anything were just prepared to spend money to enjoy themselves. It was not the Barry style, but perhaps there was a slight envy of people who could so unashamedly revel in pleasure.[31] The locals did not have to go to the Island to know that people were enjoying themselves, for from the famous fairground came the screams and cries of

Barry

visitors who were determined to sample every experience that the day out could offer. Above it stood the massive structure of the Scenic Railway, the symbol, it has been suggested, of all that Barry Island represented in those years. A ride on the scenic railway was a pretty frightening experience, but it is the sounds that one remembers best, and there can be no finer evocation of Barry Island in its heyday than David Baker's speculation as to whether he had heard the wind or 'the last despairing cry of little girls hurtling backwards into oblivion'.[32]

The trippers were always thought of as coming from the Valleys or the Birmingham area, but perhaps the majority of them were just from nearby Cardiff. In a sense Barry was an isolated town, a pocket of urban development within the rural Vale, some miles to the south of main east-west lines of communication and really quite distant from the Valley towns. But Barry was very near to Cardiff and the town had always lived within its shadow. In the period before the Second World War there had always been a fear of Cardiff's aggrandisement, but Barry enjoyed sufficient political and commercial autonomy to be able to turn its back on its larger neighbour. It was generally appreciated that Barry people would do some of their shopping in Cardiff, but this was offset by the money that trippers spent in the summer and by the small but vital number of jobs available in Cardiff during the Depression. It was only really in the 1950s that the symbiotic relationship of the town and the city became more fully apparent. Now more than ever Barry was becoming 'Cardiff's summer playground' whilst throughout the year Barry people commuted by top-road or lower-road bus or by train to jobs in the shops and offices of a Cardiff that was becoming far more of a regional centre. The really dramatic development of Cardiff as a capital city still lay ahead but by the Fifties it was contributing decisively in the form of wages and salaries to Barry's total income. Figures suggest that about a fifth of Barry's labour force earned their living outside the Borough, and whilst some of those jobs would have been to the west of the town at the two cement works, at R.A.F. St. Athan and at the new Leys Power Station, the vast majority would have been in Cardiff.[33] People were also increasingly going into Cardiff for entertainment: for sport, for theatre and concerts, for films or for the annual pantomime and circus. Barry was still a town in its own right, for it was geographically well-defined; its Council had wide powers and its prominent citizens were determined to ensure a full civic life and social round, but for a minority Barry had already become a suburb and there were fears that these commuters were pointing to the future. Cardiff was ensuring the prosperity of Barry, but already perhaps beginning to undermine what had been its commercial and communal quiddity.

The 1950s were to form one of the most crucial decades in the history of modern British society, for it was a time of full employment and of rising incomes for many families. It was the 'Age of Affluence', of mass consumption, with even working-class families acquiring cars, televisions, washing machines and refrigerators, and a time when at last many people were escaping from the social and economic constraints associated with Victorian or Depression notions of class. Barry was to have its full share of 'affluence' and that controversial phrase that people 'had never had it so good' could quite aptly be applied to the town. This was partly the result of national wage patterns and the changing nature of the labour force as the number of clerical and service jobs increased but it was also a reflection of Barry's success in attracting new jobs. These were the years of what some people called the second, and others the third Industrial Revolution, for spectacular growth was coming now in new industries and new processes, and different parts of the country were competing to attract this new wealth. By any standards Barry was doing well. The miraculous arrival of Distillers had taken Barry into a new technological age and into the age of the multinational corporations, but developments did not stop there. In 1951 Midland Silicones, which in common with a part of the Distillers operation was jointly owned by the Dow Corning Corporation of Michigan, decided to manufacture silicone products in the United Kingdom; at Barry they decided to build a fully automated plant that would employ 600 people and would therefore be 'the largest factory of its type in Europe'. The area to the

Plate XCVI.
Air view of industrial area at Sully in 1976.
A. BP Chemicals.
B. Dow Chemicals.
C. Sully Hospital.
D. Wincanton Transport.
E. Dow Corning.
Photograph: Mike Woodward, per Terence Soames (Cardiff) Ltd. By permission of BP Chemicals.

east of the Docks seemed destined to become one of the most dramatic growth points within the whole South Wales economy. Nearby there were other smaller but encouraging developments such as the Sidroy Mills and Collis Engineering which were creating jobs for both men and women. What Barry had to do now was to build on those initial successes by attracting further investment. Competition was fierce, for all over the country local authorities were issuing prospectuses in which they listed their unrivalled attractions and facilities. Barry joined in this scramble for the new industries and publicized its own not inconsiderable advantages. In 1963 the Council put out a press advertisement in which Barry was shown to meet all the requirements of any managing director on the look out for a new site. The town could offer land for development on long leases and at reasonable rents, all the usual gas, water and electricity services, good road and rail access, a small civilian airport at Rhoose, deep-water dock facilities, vacant factory units at the Tŷ Verlon Estate, and, of course, all the excellent educational and leisure amenities of the town. In addition the Council, which now controlled over 3,000 council houses, was in a position to offer homes to key workers coming into the locality.[34]

Fig. 95.
The Barry Graving Dock.
From pamphlet: The Port of Barry (1955).

As the national and local economies boomed in the Fifties and early Sixties, what gave particular pleasure was the involvement of the Docks in this new prosperity. The Docks had gone through a sticky period just after the War but things had started to go well as Britain's international trade picked up in 1949. Raymond Gower was to describe this as a period in which 'successive mayors, aldermen, councillors, industrialists, trade unionists, dock managers and officials have pondered, worked, consulted, negotiated and used every conceivable means of building up the import and export of general cargoes'. Slowly at first, but then more dramatically, these efforts paid off. Ironically the new industries which had seemed to symbolise Barry's new prosperity had little use for the Docks, but other developments were under way. Above all it was the new oil-terminals which seemed to indicate the way in which Barry should develop, but there were also further extensions at Rank's Mills, and a 1959 decision that brought Geest to the port. All this even prompted the British Transport Docks Board to step up its investment. All seemed to be going well, but then in 1962 came the great trauma of the Rochdale Report. There was to be very little disagreement with the Report's general conclusion that there was 'excessive obsolescent capacity in Britain's 300 or so ports', but Barry was stunned by a recommendation that there should be a gradual transfer of trade from Barry to Cardiff 'with a view to the eventual closure of the former'. The Report conceded that 'considerable sums of money had been invested in Barry in recent years', but insisted that in South Wales port activities had to be rationalised and concentrated so that excessive capacity could be reduced. The closure of Barry seemed the most obvious step 'as no real hardship need be involved'. It was not thought necessary to recommend the closure of any other British port.[35]

From the outset there was anger in Barry for Lord Rochdale and his Committee had made only a brief visit to the Docks and they seemed to have ignored their profitability and to be totally unaware of their advantages and their role in the community generally. The town had to fight back, and soon people were commenting on the magnificent spirit of unity as political parties, unions and management came together in an attempt to head-off the closure. The Council prepared an impressive case stressing the speed with which ships could be handled at Barry, and in all making thirty quite telling points.[36] The Mayor, Bert King, presented this Report to the Minister of Transport in January 1963 and at the same time asked for specific assurances. There was no immediate response from the Minister but meanwhile the Docks were replying to Rochdale in the most effective way. The 600 or so dockers at Barry were kept pretty busy as trade continued to expand, and what was especially pleasing was that, once more, significant amounts of coal were being exported. In 1963 Raymond Gower could report that 'there have been days recently when the activity in Barry Docks in the opinion of some old residents has been reminiscent at least of the great days of the port'.[37] It was generally appreciated that Barry Docks had their limitations, for the narrowness of the locks and the shallowness of the docks severely limited the size of the ships that could be accommodated but in the 1960s all the evidence suggested that the Docks could remain busy and profitable and extremely useful to a number of regular users. Even hard-headed businessmen could see that Barry was a viable port, but there were other local boosters who argued that just a little more imaginative investment by the Docks Board could turn Barry once again into a port of major significance.

The Docks were playing their part in Barry's general economic recovery, but the Rochdale Report deepened anxiety about their long-term prospects that had really always existed since the War. The Docks were busy, but there was not sufficient evidence that the Docks Board regarded them as one of their priority ports. This made the Council all the keener to attract other industries, and there was a fairly general appreciation that the town's commercial future could not depend on the Docks and on dock-side activity. Much had been achieved, but Barry's confidence had been badly shaken. There remained a constant fear that Cardiff Docks would always be given priority, but now one other proposed development came to symbolise all the fears about Barry's future. The 1965 news that the Port of Bristol Authority was to develop a new docks at Portbury shook Barry people almost as much as had the Rochdale Report. A letter to the local press expressed the widely-held local belief that politicians in London had given up the state-owned South Wales ports and that Portbury was the 'death-knell' of Barry. There were many signs now that the consumer-boom of the Macmillan era was over and that a whole range of economic problems was going to make new jobs harder to find. Affluence remained, but it was now accompanied by all sorts of anxieties; Portbury was a huge black cloud on the horizon, suggesting not only that the Docks might go, but that all local industrial development would become more difficult.

The post-war years had seen austerity give way to affluence, and the Conservative Party had moved into a position of electoral dominance as they

Plate XCVII.
S.S. *Patrician* loading general cargo for Mediterranean ports at No. 2 Dock in July 1956.
British Railways; I. W. Prothero Coll.

became associated with that change. Raymond Gower had won Barry narrowly in 1951 but more convincingly in 1955 and 1959. In 1964 the national trend was moving perceptibly in Labour's favour as Harold Wilson mounted a sustained critique of Tory economics and seemed to be speaking on behalf of a whole generation of frustrated graduates, technicians and white-collar workers. Labour still had a firm hold on the Barry Council and it was thought that this could be used as a powerful base from which to capture the Parliamentary constituency in the 1964 General Election. Labour had chosen an excellent candidate in David Marquand, who was a distinguished scholar and journalist and the son of Hilary Marquand, who had earlier been so prominent in the affairs of South Wales. Marquand identified housing as the key local issue and argued that Labour would build more houses and so bring prices down and help to reduce Barry's waiting-list of 2,000. For his part, Raymond Gower rejected Labour's accusation of 'thirteen wasted years' and spoke of 'remarkable achievements' not the least of which was the revolution in home-ownership. In the country Harold Wilson edged home, but there was great disappointment for Labour in Barry, where a 9 per cent swing to Labour was not enough, and Raymond Gower was able to defeat Marquand by over 4,000 votes. In part this was a reflection of the local boundaries which ensured a good Conservative turn-out in the villages of the Vale, but it was also a reflection of Raymond Gower's personal popularity, for he had emerged as an M.P. with a model record in constituency matters. He had been very much identified with the opposition to Rochdale and the fight to bring new jobs to Barry but he had also displayed considerable energy and ingenuity in making himself known to individual constituents and in taking up their personal problems.

Harold Wilson's majority was a small one and he needed another General Election to consolidate his position. The Labour Party was confident that with an all-out effort they could take Barry in 1966, although there was considerable disappointment that David Marquand, who had spoken of how just 'one more heave' was needed, had gone off to a safer seat. The new Labour candidate was a Welsh barrister Jeffrey Thomas, and he took up the fight against the Conservatives with great vigour, stressing the threat of Portbury and questioning whether Raymond Gower's commitment to Barry Docks was firm enough. Much was made of Harold Wilson's leadership, and housing was again a great issue as Labour stressed the virtues of the Rent Act, of leasehold reform and of its home-ownership plan. It was confidently predicted 'many hundreds of people in this Constituency have decided to vote Labour for the first time' in the forthcoming election. Many outside observers thought that the Gower era was about to end, but the count revealed that, although there had been a 2.8 per cent swing to Labour, Thomas had been beaten by just 1,394 votes. Raymond Gower was now the only Conservative M.P. in South Wales, and the local press had no doubt that it was 'a personal vote' that had sent Mr. Gower, as he was always referred to locally, back to Westminster. It had become fashionable for psephologists to deny that the personality of the candidate made any difference in general elections, but the 1966 result in Barry had clearly shown that it was very difficult to beat a candidate who had through his own efforts made his name so well known throughout the constituency. After the count Mr. Gower acknowledged that there had been a large Labour vote in the town of Barry itself and promised that he 'would bear it in mind during this next period of service'. This narrow victory helped to confirm in Raymond Gower's mind what he had always suspected, that to hold Barry one had to be something more than a party politician. He was well on his way to becoming the best kind of old-fashioned independent member of parliament and he was able to retain his seat in the following four elections before the demise of the Barry constituency led to his becoming the first member for the new Vale of Glamorgan seat. He was knighted in 1974 for political services, and at that time reference was made to his two periods of duty as a Parliamentary Private Secretary, but his services had always been to the constituency rather than to the Party. In elections opponents found that he was almost above party-political issues and as a new Toryism developed in the aftermath of Edward Heath's defeat and removal, Sir

Plate XCVIII. The last locomotive to be repaired at Barry Locomotive Works, 1959.
B. J. Miller Coll.

Raymond seemed more than ever to represent an older tradition of political service and almost to be a symbol of Barry's own independence from the rest of South Wales.

Barry's history and geographical location had always seemed to put the town in a somewhat anachronistic position in relation to the rest of South Wales. The area seemed dominated by powerful corporations such as Cardiff and Swansea or by the proud and mighty County of Glamorgan whose political base was centred very much in the mining valleys. Barry shared many of South Wales's general problems, but seemed to be standing a little apart from the wider political and commercial struggles. Barry's independence was made manifest above all in the work of its Borough Council, which was faced with the task of meeting local housing needs and at the same time fighting to keep the Docks alive and to bring in new industry. Local politicians could come together to defend local interests, but there were some sharp differences of opinion between the parties over local issues. The long period of Labour dominance did not help matters and Conservative and Independent councillors often objected to the way in which the aldermanic system was used to consolidate Labour's statistical majority, and there were frequent references to 'the ruling Labour faction'. The biggest row was to come in 1965 over a proposed Parliamentary Bill in which the Barry Corporation sought to extend its powers in respect of planning, finance and health matters, and in particular sought powers to redevelop the town centre. The Bill followed a report which had been commissioned jointly by the Council and by Ravenseft, a London development company; amongst other recommendations there was a suggestion that the small Central Park should be sold to make room for an extended central business district. The notion was that a re-developed town centre would become the main shopping area for the Vale of Glamorgan as a whole and for a bigger Barry whose population could go up to 70,000. Great things seemed to be planned but there were immediate suspicions, and soon the Council were facing opposition from all quarters. Some people were afraid that the Council was seeking excessive powers, others objected to the loss of Central Park, a much-used patch of greenery which had been referred to as the town centre's 'vital lung' and nearly everyone criticised the great secrecy with which matters were being handled. After a feverish and acrimonious debate a referendum was held which turned out to be something of a fiasco but nevertheless on a 25 per cent poll there was basically a 10 to 1 vote against the Bill.

The best known man in Barry now was H. W. Durman, an ex-Labour councillor and former Mayor of the town, who emerged as the outspoken chairman of a Vigilante Association. Some years earlier the rather independent Durman had been expelled by the Labour group, but following the referendum he turned on his former Labour colleagues and demanded their mass resignations. For months he sustained a blistering attack on local Labour leaders, causing a good deal of anguish to men like Brinley Williams, Jack Trezise, Terry Price and Fred Cook who had fought for years to develop Barry and who could see that some bold planning was needed if the town was to break out of what had become a rather restricting and unexciting mould. It had really become for Barry a question of now or never and as Councillor Fred Cook pointed out at the time of the referendum 'unless the town did re-develop it was bound to be absorbed by a greater authority'. Whatever the virtues or faults of the Barry Corporation Bill there were many people who could see that it was time for the Council to be streamlined, for in all kinds of ways it was falling behind. The Development Committee had become cumbersome, factories were not being attracted to the industrial estate, far too few houses were being built, some sort of renewal was urgently needed in the town centre, and far more planning of leisure facilities and open spaces was called for. In 1964 the Council had agreed to let Billy Butlin build a holiday camp on Nell's Point, Barry Island. The argument had been that this would create jobs and bring in additional visitors, but many saw this step not only as a confession that the Island was alien territory belonging more to visitors than to locals, but also as an indication that the Council did not have the resources or the flair to develop the area on their own terms.

Plate XCIX. Air view of Barry Island, showing Friars Point (nearer) and Nell's Point with Butlin's Holiday Centre (beyond). *Terence Soames.*

In a way the whole logic of events was moving away from small municipalities like Barry. The fight for jobs, the need to build roads, to maintain rail services and the challenge of investing in the airport at Rhoose could only go on in the context of a wider regional economy. Barry had shared in the national prosperity in the good years, but it had really only managed to stand still as a town in its own right. Daily it was becoming more dependent on Cardiff for jobs, and clearly its whole economic future lay in the context of a south-east Wales or even Bristol Channel economy. The opening of the Severn Bridge in 1966 and the development of what became after 1965 the County of Glamorgan's airport were amongst the factors forcing Barry to think in wider terms. In so many respects the town was having to come to terms with economies of scale and the need for the integration of services over a wider area. The town had always been proud of its hospitals, and in the old days had often boasted that it had one of the few hospitals in the country run by a town council. Over the years there had been many rows about the Barry Hospital and there had sometimes been tension between the municipal hospital and the neighbouring Amy Evans Hospital, but at least local people had felt that facilities were near at hand. Now as Cardiff was developed as a regional hospital centre there were plans to close Barry's hospitals. This time the Council, the Vigilantes and many other groups came together in what was to develop into a passionate and emotional campaign. There were massive and angry demonstrations and women's groups chanted 'We'll be underneath before we reach the Heath'. The logic of a modern age was crowding in on Barry and in so many ways the partially successful fight to save local hospitals can be seen very much as a brave effort by a town that was not going to go down without a fight.

The British do not rush into local government reform. In the 1960s the county still had a system that had basically been set up in 1888 and 1894. But now the need for change was widely accepted, and as the decade progressed many proposals and counter-proposals were put forward by political parties, academics, government commissions and councils themselves.[38] Major reform had to come, and the demise of Barry as a municipality was more or less inevitable. The Labour Party had thought that the new era of local government would be shaped in terms of its own priorities, but in the event it was to be the Conservatives who regained power at the vital moment and who were therefore able to devise a new system. When the Government announced their plans in 1971, there was immediately a hostile response from many different parts of the country and from nowhere more than South Wales. The new system allowed for a division of powers between counties and new district authorities, and as far as Glamorgan was concerned, the Secretary of State for Wales's initial thinking had been that the old county should be divided into two new counties, one in the East and one in the West. Cardiff's political leaders

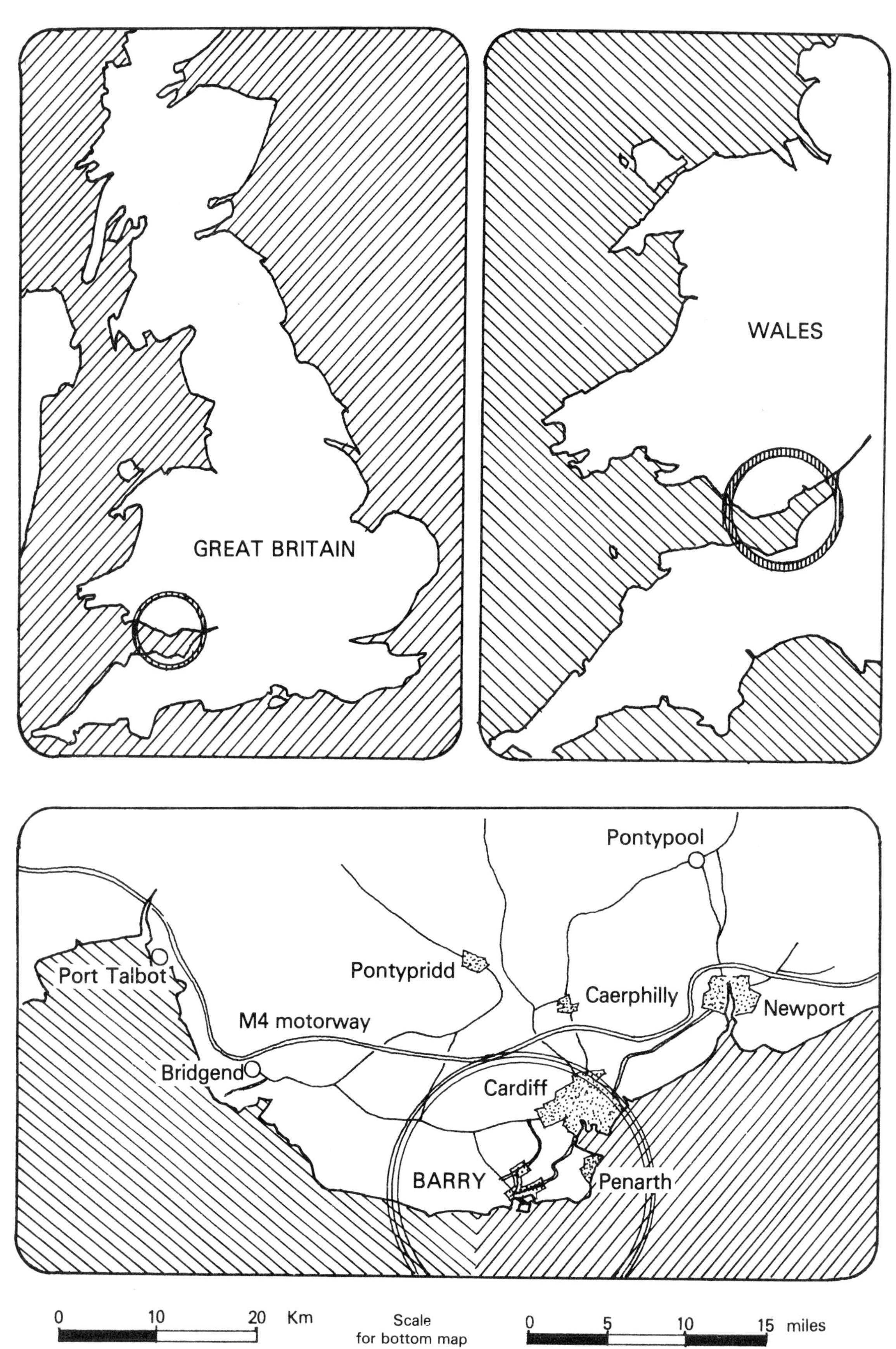
GREAT BRITAIN
WALES
Pontypool
Port Talbot
Pontypridd
Caerphilly
Newport
M4 motorway
Bridgend
Cardiff
BARRY
Penarth
0
10
20
Km
Scale
for bottom map
0
5
10
15
miles

◀ Fig. 96.
Series of maps to show location of Barry.
Simon Prosser.

were horrified by this suggestion that the city should lose its identity and be merged into a county that, like the old Glamorgan, would be controlled from the Valleys. Furious lobbying began on Cardiff's behalf with the main arguments being that the new county of East Glamorgan would be far too large and that Cardiff itself would lose any effective status that it had as a capital city. Edward Heath's government was impressed with these arguments and it was announced that the old Glamorgan would now be divided into three new counties. It was now the turn of the Labour leaders of the old Glamorgan to object for what they feared was that the proposed Mid Glamorgan County would have no obvious focal-point and would inevitably, as a county consisting almost exclusively of the old mining valleys, emerge as the poor relation of South Wales, whilst at the same time the richer county of South Glamorgan would be simply Cardiff writ-large and would no doubt be dominated by the Tories. To the Welsh Labour Party this looked like good old-fashioned gerrymandering, and the Glamorgan County Council immediately inaugurated a campaign to oppose what was seen as a successful coup by the Conservatives of Cardiff. The campaign passed into the hands of a 'Two Not Three' Committee led by County Council employees Norman Draper and Doug Nicholls. Their supporters, who included many active members of N.A.L.G.O., the N.U.M. and other unions, were soon achieving a good deal of publicity as they fought with great spirit to keep Cardiff in its place. This was a fascinating struggle as it seemed to symbolize so many of the tensions and forces that had characterized the modern history of South Wales. The County of Glamorgan was a dynamic and progressive authority that had been shaped in its modern manifestation by the values of the mining valleys and of an industrial proletariat, whilst the City of Cardiff which had developed first as the capital of a coalfield was now making a bid for a new role as the centre of a more varied economy and for a new status as the political capital of Wales as a whole.

In retrospect it was inevitable and wholly proper that Cardiff should have won. The new county of Mid Glamorgan was a nonsense and clearly in that respect alternative proposals should have been considered but there was an obvious logic about the new county of South Glamorgan which would take in Cardiff itself, Barry, Penarth and much of the Vale of Glamorgan. The 'Two Not Three' campaign had received considerable support from the people of Barry but there had been others who saw the logic of the new system. Since its earliest days Barry had lived with the fear of a Cardiff take-over and in a sense that take-over had now been successfully completed. But this was a very different dispensation, for many Barry people now depended on Cardiff for jobs and for vital services and there were so many ventures that could only be embarked on jointly. In any case, Barry would have nine representatives on the new County authority which would be responsible for education, social services and planning. The new District authority of the Vale of Glamorgan would have considerable powers in respect of housing, planning, health and development, and although Barry was now brought together in this authority with Penarth, of which it had always been suspicious, and a rural area of a very different political complexion, the town was to have 21 out of 36 seats on the Council and would therefore be in a position to dominate it. And finally there was still to be a Barry Community or Town Council which was rejected by some as a token institution with no real power, but which was soon to be valued by others as an extremely useful structure for defending and improving the quality of local life.[39]

Plate C.
Vale of Glamorgan Civic Offices, Barry.
B. Daly.

The new local government system was far from perfect and it was to take several years before it was understood by the majority of electors, but in time political leaders came to see not only the extent to which the new structure corresponded to economic realities but also the extent to which it coincided with the patterns within which most people lived their lives. Public transportation had pointed the way but it was really the motor-car which had clinched the meaningfulness of South Glamorgan. The story is one in which Barry surrendered much of its political and institutional identity, and yet the realists saw that this was perhaps less important than efficiency, and, even more, less relevant than the need for Barry to integrate itself more fully into the general development of the Cardiff region. Barry could afford to become a suburb if there were to be far more jobs in the Cardiff area generally. The Welsh capital was developing in a spectacular fashion and Barry's adjacency to those new jobs in local government administration, in broadcasting and in services and retailing generally had become the town's greatest advantage.

Future British historians will see the 1980s as a curious period in which prosperity existed alongside economic difficulty and exciting growth alongside stagnation. Perhaps these historians will alight on Barry as a useful and representative microcosm. The development of an international airport, the provision of a fine leisure centre, the construction just outside the town of huge television studios and the long overdue improvement of the road network will all be seen as confirmation of Barry's place in the modern suburban world, and yet the town will offer evidence of very different trends. Reference will be made to the closure of a College and to how buildings that had seen so much achieved under the auspices of the Training College and the Polytechnic of Wales were allowed to stand vacant for so long. Barry's modern petro-chemical plants will be pointed to as examples of how industrial modernisation predicted a much smaller labour force.[40] Barry will also be used to show how unemployment once more became a serious issue, and in particular of how few opportunities there were for young people, such as those leaving the two comprehensive schools or the College of Further Education.[41] There, as elsewhere, the shrinking of the industrial base will be held responsible for the disappearance of apprenticeships and the drying up of all sorts of skilled labour. As always, education would have remained the escape route out of Barry, but even that route will seem a less sure one for an increasing number of students. As far as housing is concerned, Barry will be cited as a classic example of an area with an ageing housing stock and with far too many council houses with structural defects. Above all, future historians will wonder whether Britain had chosen the right economic options. Whatever form economic recovery will have taken in the 1980s there will be those who will reflect on whether more money should have been invested in smaller industrial enterprises. The story of Barry Docks will be told and of how they remained profitable at a time of only limited expenditure on improvements and new equipment, but nevertheless those Docks will have faded into relative oblivion because there was no public or private agency with the resources to develop them and the imagination to use them as the base from which to expand a local economy.

There is undoubtedly something a little unsatisfactory and even sad about the story of modern Barry. In a way almost anything that happened after 1918 was likely to be an anti-climax, but the collapse of the South Wales coal trade and the rationalisation of railway and dock control effectively ended any possibility of major development at Barry Docks. The Docks were the reason for Barry's very existence and yet for sixty years local people were to live with the knowledge that what was an efficient and profitable port was not really being allowed to maximize its opportunities. The town had to develop alternative strategies, and for a long period that was a difficult and painful process. In the end local prosperity was ensured by the arrival of Distillers and Midland Silicones and by the growth of Cardiff as a regional capital. But even then the town was really only standing still rather than experiencing dynamic growth. The 1980s indeed saw a decline in the fortunes of B.P. Chemicals at Cadoxton. Many became frustrated by the apparent inability of Barry to break out from its Edwardian shell and there was often bitter criticism of the Independents who controlled the town before 1945 and of the Labour leaders who have tended to control it since.

In 1945 the *Barry Dock News* asked its readers to look back over the past decade and to ask themselves whether the town had 'progressed as much as it should have done'. 'Do you think', asked the paper, 'that Barry had missed the bus on more occasions than it should have done?'. This was precisely the point most frequently made by critics: the town, in responding to the new opportunities of the 20th century, had not made sufficient use of its own advantages. Perhaps with respect to Barry Island this indictment had point, for surely we can conceive of a more imaginative development of the Island as a whole and in particular of the Old Harbour, of Nell's Point and Jackson's Bay. But Barry, as we have seen, had to develop as a resort at a time of depression when there was great pressure on the local rates. In terms of industry Barry, like the whole of South Wales, has found it difficult to diversify and to go on attracting jobs. There has been strong competition, and the town was forced to settle for reasonably full employment rather than for a further industrial revolution. It has been a difficult century, and perhaps both the critics and the romantics have underestimated how well Barry has done in overcoming its isolation and in keeping its people in work, and thereby allowing them to taste the fruits of affluence. Perhaps the most surprising aspect of Barry's recent history is that not more Cardiff people have made it their home. That city's most spectacular suburban developments have been to its north-east and then in the Vale itself. But things are changing now as South Glamorgan as a whole is merging into a Greater Cardiff and as the road access to Cardiff is greatly improved. Urban renewal has already changed the look of old Barry, and at the periphery the fields of the Vale are being eaten away. Barry is being invited to join a suburban world and obvious benefits will accrue, but meanwhile all the Preservation Society's efforts will be needed to defend some of the old architectural clues to the town's proud past as well as some of its rural charms.

The failure of Barry to develop in commercial terms is only one side of the story, for what the people of the town have always known is that Barry, more than anything else, is just a very pleasant place in which to live. In part this is a question of social activity, for Barry has always been a busy community in which people have belonged to churches and chapels and to whole hosts of cultural sporting and recreational organisations. One of the last Mayors of the Barry Borough Council, Councillor Jack Trezise, commented at the end of his year in office on how much he had enjoyed his two hundred engagements. The leaders of Barry have presided over a full calendar of local events in which all citizens who enjoy good fellowship have been invited to participate. It is an energetic town and it is not difficult to see its excellent record in education as a reflection of this local emphasis on participation and fulfilment. To come from Barry is to come from a town that has given its native sons and daughters a tremendous curiosity, an easy and quite classless social style, a love of conversation and perhaps most usefully a considerable degree of personal confidence.

Perhaps Barry is a pleasant town because it has been the right size. It is certainly a pleasant town because of its superb location. It can only be counted as a tremendous privilege to belong to a small town of quite densely packed terraced houses that yet offered spectacular views of the busy Bristol Channel, that in summer months invited its inhabitants to spend their time on unrivalled beaches and at all times offered direct access to some beautiful countryside. In the last analysis all disappointments and local tensions have counted for little against the pleasure and pride that people have taken in just being able to live in Barry.[41]

Plate CI.
View down Tynewydd Road, looking towards old Council Offices.
B. Daly.

References

1 The impact of the Second World War on British society is best discussed in Angus Calder, *The People's War* (1969), and Richard M. Titmus, *Problems of Social Policy* (1950).

2 *B.D.N.*, 21st June, 1940. The handbill issued by the Mayor on 7th June, 1940 was headed 'Twelve Counties in England were Bombed this morning, Are you *Now* interested in Air Raid Precautions?'.

3 *B.D.N.*, 13th December, 1940.

4 Only one person died in Barry as a result of bombing.

5 War-time arrangements are summed up in the Ministry of Information's *Home Front Handbook* (1943) and *Manpower* (1944); also by W. K. Hancock and M. Gowing, *The British War Economy* (1949).

6 Stan Awbery was to be M.P. for Bristol Central after 1945, but he remained a resident of Barry and was for years the town's foremost local historian.

7 *B.D.N.*, 27th July, 1943. The Colonial Office was impressed by Barry's coloured community and found the Thompson Street-Travis Street area less depressing than Cardiff's Tiger Bay. PRO, Colonial Office Papers 876/28. I am grateful to Neil Evans for this reference.

8 In 1946 it was estimated that 30,248 Merchant Seamen had been killed in the War and another 4,654 were still missing: *Strength and Casualties of the Armed Forces and Auxiliary Services 1939-1945* (Cmd. 6832, 1946). The story is told in C.B.A. Behrens, *Merchant Shipping and the Demands of War* (1955) and J. Costello and T. Hughes, *The Battle of the Atlantic* (1977). The full drama of the Atlantic convoys is brilliantly evoked in Martin Middlebrook, *Convoy*, the story of convoys SC.122 and HX.229 (1976); his full list of casualties includes four Barry names.

9 How the war would have affected Barry people is described in the official histories, especialy *British Coaster 1939-1945* (Central Office of Information, 1947) and in Franask Mason, *Battle Over Britain* (1969).

10 *B.D.N.*, 2nd July, 1943.

11 *The Seaman*, January/February 1946.

12 For the American invasion of Britain see Charles B. MacDonald, *The Mighty Endeavour* (New York, 1969) which tells how 'at every turn airfields and little cities of half-moon shaped Nissen huts pimpled what had before been the world's most orderly countryside'. Also Norman Longmate, *The G.I.'s, the Americans in Britain 1942-45* (1975) and Leslie Thomas's novel *The Magic Army* (1981).

13 Coalition Conservative candidates were to be defeated in by-elections held during 1942 at Grantham, Rugby and Wallasey. See Calder, *op. cit.*, p. 334, and *The Times House of Commons 1945*, p. 134.

14 The best introductions to the Beveridge Report are Arthur Marwick, *Britain in the Century of Total War* (1968) and John Stevenson, *Social Conditions in Britain between the Wars* (1977).

15 History of Dan Evans Limited in *The South Wales Spectator*, Vol. 7, No. 51, June, 1964.

16 Paul Addison, *The Road to 1945* (1977).

17 *B.D.N.*, 26th October, 1945. This was one of a whole series of very effective anti-Council cartoons.

18 John A. Giggs, *op. cit.*, p. 80. For the continuing problems of council estates in Barry see John A. Giggs, 'Socially Disorganised Areas in Barry: a Multivariate Analysis' in H. Carter and W. K. D. Davies, *Urban Essays* (1970).

19 For a general discussion of post-war housing see Arthur Marwick, *British Society since 1945* (1982).

20 For Austerity see Arthur Marwick, *op. cit.*, and Roger Eatwell, *The 1945-1951 Labour Governments* (1979).

21 The 1944 White Paper on Employment Policy and the subsequent commitment to a 'high and stable level of employment' was by far the most important shift in social policy to take place during the War. See Addison, *op. cit.*, p. 245 *et seq.*

22 Dorothy Rees was Chairman of the Glamorgan County Council 1964-65. She discusses her career in *Reminiscences of the Glamorgan County Council* (Cardiff, 1974).

23 Roger Goodwin interviewed Charlie Clemo for the *B.D.N.* 2nd January, 1964. In the issue of 9th January he spoke to Evan Evans of the coal-trimmers.

[24] *The South Wales Spectator*, Vol. 7, No. 51, June, 1964.

[25] See an interview with Ronnie Boon in *The Times*, 2nd February, 1983.

[26] Glyn Daniel, Foreword to *Old Barry in Photographs*, Vol. II. See also his novel *Welcome Death* (1954).

[27] *The Barrian* (1959), p. 40.

[28] *Ibid.,* (1953), p. 25. In this symposium Wynne Jones pointed out that whilst 'drama, music and sport have played their part in Barry's education—one aspect has been sadly neglected—the technical-minded have always had few facilities'.

[29] Annual guidebooks were printed with a variety of titles and messages. The 1934 guidebook gave 'Hints on Sunbathing' and warned 'continuous exposure to sunlight might be harmful'. The 1961 edition returned to the idea of Barry-by-the-Sea.

[30] Islwyn Jenkins, *Collected Poems of Idris Davies* (Llandysul, 1972), p. 103. The poem has been reproduced on a poster and postcard illustrated by Susan Shields and published by the Welsh Arts Council and Gwasg Gomer.

[31] Barry's sensitivity to the image of the Island was reflected in the angry response to Gwyn Thomas's television description of the resort as 'The Kingdom of the Chip', *Barry Herald*, 13th June, 1957. In these years Thomas was Barry's best known personality. He discussed Barry in *A Welsh Eye* (1964).

[32] *The Barrian* (1974), p. 16. The Scenic Railway which replaced the Figure 8 in 1939 had lasted for 35 years. For the story of Barry Island and of Collins's Pleasure Park see Brian C. Luxton, 'Barry', in Stewart Williams (ed.), *South Glamorgan: a County History*, (Barry, 1975) and his section on Barry Island in *Old Barry in Photographs*, Vol. II.

[33] D. A. Dalwood, (Impact Studies and the Planning Process—A case study of the Impact of the Port Transport Industry upon Barry), M.Sc. thesis (University of Wales, 1972), p. 98.

[34] 'The Barry Story', *Western Mail Review*, 23rd October, 1963.

[35] Ministry of Transport, *Report of the Committee of Inquiry into the Major Ports of Great Britain*, September, 1962, Cmd. 1824. For the Docks in this period see the *Annual Reports of the British Transport Docks Board*, and *The Welsh Ports* (Welsh Council, 1973); also Graham Hallett and Peter Randall, *Maritime Industry and Port Development in South Wales* (1970) and Peter J. Randall, *The History and Development of the Port of Barry.* For the economic context see J. Hamish Richards, 'Transport', in Brinley Thomas (ed.), *The Welsh Economy—Studies in Expansion* (Cardiff, 1962).

[36] Submission by Barry Corporation to Ministry of Transport, January, 1963.

[37] *Western Mail Review*, 23rd October, 1963.

[38] The story of local government reform is told in Frank Stacey, *British Government 1966-1975, Years of Reform* (1975).

[39] The population of the new county of South Glamorgan was 391,600. In 1971 the population of Barry was 41,578.

[40] British Petroleum laid off 600 men in 1982 and the plant was moving towards a position in which it would only be employing about half the number of men it had employed in the Seventies. In 1983 13·6 per cent of the labour force was unemployed in what was now officially termed 'The Cardiff Travel-To-Work Area'.

[41] For these two subjective but hopefully impartial essays I have relied heavily on the files of the *Barry and District News* (formerly the *Barry Dock News*) and the old *Barry Herald,* for, like most Barry people, I have long been an avid reader of the local press. I owe specific thanks to Miss Sylvia Davies of the Barry Public Library, to the staff of the Cardiff Central Library and to Mr. Gareth Howe and Mrs. Eva Trezise, who both allowed me full access to private material in their own hands. Above all, I have to thank those many friends and also the members of my family with whom I have over many years talked and argued at length about Barry.

INDEX

A

B

C

D

E

F

G

H

I

J

K

L

M

N

O

P

T

U

V

W

Y

NOTES

NOTES

WENVOE C
Watercress Beds
Goldsland Brook
Wenvoe Castle
Front Lawn
Great Hamston
Old Wallace
New Wallace
Bears Wood
Northcliff
Northcliff Cottage
Golf Course
Nant Brynhill
Lidmore
Mill
Coed Garw
Great Brynhill
Pencoed Farm
Reservoirs
Little Brynhill Farm
Lidmore Wood
Church (remains of)
Golf Course
Merthyr Dyfan
Sutton
Suddon Mawr
Sutton Wood
Highlight
Colcot
Cold Brook
Cross
Piggery
Zoological Garden
Coed Mawr
Ffynnon yr Hofel
Coed yr Ychen
Hospital
Recn Gd
College
Middleton Plantation
Walters Farm
Middleton Wood
Welford Wood
New Farm
Green Farm
BARRY C
BARRY
College
Welford
Cwm-cidy Farm
Allot Gdns
PORTHKERRY C (Det)
Model Farm
Cwm Cidi
Mill Wood
Scrap Metal Yard
Works
West Ridge
Barry Brook
Cwm Barr
Oil Storage Terminal
Docks
Porthkerry Park
Westward Corner
Tumulus
Romilly Park
Viaduct
Bull Cliff
Porthkerry House
Bullcliff Rocks
Porthkerry (Porthceri)
Storehouse Point
Barry Harbour
The Knap
Barry Island
Chapel (rems of)
Jackson's Bay
The Bulwarks Fort
Pebble Beach
Little Island
Whitmore Bay
Holiday C
Watch House Bay
Cumuli
Coastguard
Nell's Point
Flagstaff
Cold Knap Point
Friars Point